Miscellanea Genealogica Et Heraldica

MISCELLANEA

GENEALOGICA ET HERALDICA

VOLUME III

GRANT OF ARMS TO JOHN HARINGTON OF KELSTON, 1568.

*TO ALL and Singuler as well nobles and gentlemen as others to whome these presentes shall come be seene, heard, read or understande Sir Gilbert Dethick Knight alias Garter principall Kinge of Armes, Robert Cooke Esquire alias Clarencieulx Kinge of Armes of the South partes and William Floure Esquire alias Norroy Kinge of Armes of the North Partes of Englande sendith greetinge in our Lorde God everlastenge For asmuch as aunciently from the beginninge the Gallaunt and Virtuouse actes of excellent personnes have been commendid to the worlde and posteryte with sondrey monumentes and remembrances of their goode deseartes, Amongst the which the chiefest and most usuall hath ben the bearinge of signes in shildes called Armes beinge none other thinge then demonstracions and tokens of prowesse and valoir, diversely destributed accordinge to the qualytes and deseartes of the personnes meritinge the same. To the entent that such as by their Vertues do shew foorth to the advauncement of the common weale the shyne of their goode lyfe and conversation in daily practyse of things worthy and commendable, beinge the very true and perfect tokens of a right noble disposition, may therefore receyve due honor in their lyves and also deryve and contynew the same successively in their posteryte for ever And Whereas John Harington of Kelston in the Countie of Somersett sonne of Alexander Harington descended of a younger brother of the Haringtons of Brierley in the Countie of Yorke, by right (as one abstract from such a Stock and descended of such Auncestors) ought to be in the nomber of the bearers of those tokens of honor: and yet not knowinge in what maner he ought to beare his Armes, the tyme beinge now so longe since his Auncesters first descended from out of the sayd house of Brierley: hath required us the said Kinges of Armes to assigne unto him his Armes and Creast with such difference of bearinge as may not be prejudiciall or offensive to any of his blood or name. In Consideration whereof

* The initial letter in the original contains the figure of Garter King in his tabard.

and for a perpetuall declaration of the Worthynesse of the sayde John Harington, and at his instant request We the Kinges of Armes aforesayde by power and authoryte to be committed by letters patentes under the greate Seale of England have assigned unto the said John Harington his Armes and Creast to be boren in maner followinge That is to say, the fielde Sable a frett humette argent, a bordure checque of the second and first Upon the haulme on a torce argent and sable a lyon's hedde golde langet guelues with a coller checque argent and sable mantelid guelues doubled argent as more plainly appeerith depicted in this margent. Which Armes and Creast and every part and parcell thereof We the sayd Kinges of Armes do by these presents assigne unto the sayd John Harington and his posteryte for ever to be by him in such maner boren and shewed at all tymes and for ever heerafter at his liberty and pleasure without the impediment lett or interruption of eny parson or parsons In Witnesse whereof we the sayd Garter, Clarenceulx, and Norroy Kinges of Armes have signed these presentes with our handes and sett thereunto our severall seales of Arms xij[th] day of ffebruary in the yere of our Lord God a thousande fyve hundred sixty-eight

---

A MEMOIR OR NOTICE OF JOHN HARINGTON, ESQ,

The Founder of the Branch of the Haringtons of Kelston in Somerset

The gentleman in whose favour this grant of arms was made in 1568 and who is described in it as of Kelston, co Somerset, was not we think at that date generally resident at Kelston, but in London Kelston which had pertained to Shaftesbury Abbey up to the time of the Dissolution of the Religious Houses, was without a mansion suitable for a resident owner, so until this defect could be remedied, Harington, though owner of the manor, did not reside on it, but in his town house, near the Bishop's Palace at Lambeth The branch of the family to which he belonged had been sadly impoverished by the attainder, as well of Sir Robert Harington as of Sir James Harington of Brierley, after the fall of the House of York, and victory of Hen VII at Bosworth (1485) The subject of this notice was probably born in Stepney, in which district there is some evidence that persons of the name had wharfage property, and to which neighbourhood the sons of Thomas Harington, Rector of Kelston, returned after the decease of their father London was in those days, it would seem, as now, the field or scene of enterprise in which families of broken fortune sought to repair their losses And one of the first points which strikes us as worthy of remark in noting the history of John Harington of Stepney is the singular recovery he achieved of something like the old family position but in a totally different sphere from that of his northern ancestors Taking into consideration the fall of Sir James Harington from the pinnacle of fortune after Towton (where Hen VI fell into his hands) to the depth of distress and ruin at Bosworth, after which battle Hen VII wreaked his vengeance on the adherents of Richard, how is it that a descendant of Sir James should be found in favour with Hen VIII, and afterwards a trusted servant of his daughter Queen Elizabeth? Through what influence did this change of feeling of the same Royal family towards the Yorkist Haringtons come to pass? There seems no evidence that the Rutland branch of Haringtons with Lord Harington of Exton at their head—now most flourishing when the northern Haringtons were most depressed in condition—did anything to help them regain their lost lands from Lord Monteagle, or to restore the fortune of their broken relatives in any other way The ultimate union of the Roses may, it is true, to some extent have softened the asperity of the early days of Hen VII, and thus the Haringtons, with their old name and known fidelity to whatever King they professed to serve, have moved back again to Court and courtly favour But, after all, we cannot but think that the incident in John Harington's career to which we are about to allude, in his alliance with Hen VIII's natural daughter, gave the chief impulse to his fortune This would probably have been more obvious had his first marriage taken place during the lifetime of King Hen VIII But although this marriage did not so take place, it may have been already pre-arranged and known as a coming event before the King's death Ethelred or Awdrey Malte the natural daughter of Henry whom Harington married, was a special favourite with her Royal parent, who placed her for protection and education with a wealthy citizen and merchant tailor of London, named John Malte or Mawlte This man, in return for acting confidentially in these private matters, received from the King a valuable reward in the shape of a grant dated 38th Hen VIII (1546) of church lands, being part of the spoils of Bath Priory and Shaftesbury Abbey We must not allude, I suppose, to the irony which is patent in this act of reformation, but simply go on and add that these confiscated lands were to remain to the use of Malte himself for his life, then to pass to the use of his adopted daughter Ethelred and her heirs, if she had any, and if not, to revert to the heirs of Malte These points in the Memoir will be assured by documents bearing upon them given in brief Malte, the reputed father of Ethelred, did not long survive the King indeed he died a few months after He died rich, and bequeathed to Ethelred by Will (over and above the

Stran

ı of Kirkby Fleetham, co. Y

vas buried there 23 August, 1657

Thomas Strangwayes, bapt. Fleetham, and buried there

ıug. 1612, at Kirkby Fleetham aforesaid. le, and was living 1669.

Richard Strangwayes buried there 8 May, 1(

ed 30 Nov. 1671, at Kirkby o Edward Webster of the , and was buried 1673.

Catterick, co. York, 597, at Kirkby the Archdeaconry = Margaret, living 1697.

Edward Strangways, of Langthorne a Myres, co. York. Will dated 25 Marc 30 May, 1701, by Mary, his widow an the Archdeaconry Court of Richmon

aye, spinster, Francis Living 1728.

Anne, bapt 1663, at Ki Fleetham. ried to Rich Sadler.

Ann, bapt. 1 Jan. 1687, at Catterick. Living 1697.

Dinah, bapt. at Hornby. Married firstl and 2ndly . . .

yes of Gray's , and of Bar- he parish of 3rd son. , at Kirkby d 16 March, M.I. = Elizabeth Ann Holt of Readi Holt, only bro Holt, Knt.), by Knyvett of Br city of Norwic 12 May, 1764, a

Nicholas Carter of Burneston aforesaid, afterwards of Knaresborough. Bapt. 13 May, 1701. Buried 1 Jan. 1766, at Knaresborough, æt. 65. Will dated 23 Oct. 1765, proved at York and again, 16 Sept. 1766, in London. (332 Tyndall.) = Alicia, died 24 Dec. 1766, æt. 56.

George Carter, bapt 31 March, 1703.

John Carter, bapt. 22 Oct. 1707. Living 1765.

Mary, bapt. 15 Aug. 1736 at Babworth. Living 1787.

Christophe Snape Hal parish of W 25 July, 1 25 Jan. 177 aforesaid.

Oak Villa, but only t. at Well Aug. 1828, Sept. 1828. = Louisa, only surviving child, and heir to her brother John. Born 7 Aug. 1750. Died 15 and bur. 23 Nov. 1840, æt. 90, at Well aforesaid. 3rd wife. = Catharine, dau'r of Tho of Spennithorne, co. Y 28 April, 1756. Died 24 March, 1781, æt. 25, a said. 2nd wife.

and for a perpetuall declaration of the Worthynesse of the sayde John Harington, and at his instant request We the Kinges of Armes aforesayde by power and authoryte to be committed by letters patentes under the greate Seale of England have assigned unto the said John Harington his Armes and Creast to be boren in maner followinge That is to say, the fielde Sable a frett hunnette argent, a bordure checque of the second and first Upon the haulme on a torce argent and sable a lyon's hedde golde langet guelues with a coller checque argent and sable mantelid guelues doubled argent as more plainly appeerith depicted in this margent. Which Armes and Creast and every part and parcell thereof We the sayd Kinges of Armes do by these presents assigne unto the sayd John Harington and his posteryte for ever to be by him in such maner boren and shewed at all tymes and for ever hereafter at his liberty and pleasure without the impediment lett or interruption of eny parson or parsons In Witnesse whereof we the sayd Garter, Clarencieulx, and Norroy Kinges of Armes have signed these presentes with our handes and sett thereunto our severall seales of Arms xij[th] day of ffebruary in the yere of our Lord God a thousande fyve hundred sixty-eight.

A MEMOIR OR NOTICE OF JOHN HARINGTON, ESQ,

The Founder of the Branch of the Haringtons of Kelston in Somerset

The gentleman in whose favour this grant of arms was made in 1568. and who is described in it as of Kelston, co Somerset, was not we think at that date generally resident at Kelston, but in London Kelston, which had pertained to Shaftesbury Abbey up to the time of the Dissolution of the Religious Houses, was without a mansion suitable for a resident owner, so until this defect could be remedied, Harington, though owner of the manor, did not reside on it, but in his town house, near the Bishop's Palace at Lambeth The branch of the family to which he belonged had been sadly impoverished by the attainder, as well of Sir Robert Harington as of Sir James Harington of Brierley, after the fall of the House of York, and victory of Hen VII at Bosworth (1485) The subject of this notice was probably born in Stepney, in which district there is some evidence that persons of the name had wharfage property and to which neighbourhood the sons of Thomas Harington, Rector of Kelston, returned after the decease of their father London was in those days, it would seem, as now, the field or scene of enterprise in which families of broken fortune sought to repair their losses And one of the first points which strikes us as worthy of remark in noting the history of John Harington of Stepney is the singular recovery he achieved of something like the old family position, but in a totally different sphere from that of his northern ancestors Taking into consideration the fall of Sir James Harington from the pinnacle of fortune after Towton (where Hen VI fell into his hands) to the depth of distress and ruin at Bosworth, after which battle Hen VII wreaked his vengeance on the adherents of Richard how is it that a descendant of Sir James should be found in favour with Hen VIII and afterwards a trusted servant of his daughter Queen Elizabeth? Through what influence did this change of feeling of the same Royal family towards the Yorkist Haringtons come to pass? There seems no evidence that the Rutland branch of Haringtons, with Lord Harington of Exton at their head—now most flourishing when the northern Haringtons were most depressed in condition—did anything to help them regain their lost lands from Lord Monteagle, or to restore the fortune of their broken relatives in any other way The ultimate union of the Roses may, it is true, to some extent have softened the asperity of the early days of Hen VII and thus the Haringtons, with their old name and known fidelity to whatever King they professed to serve, have moved back again to Court and courtly favour But, after all, we cannot but think that the incident in John Harington's career to which we are about to allude, in his alliance with Hen VIII's natural daughter, gave the chief impulse to his fortune This would probably have been more obvious had his first marriage taken place during the lifetime of King Hen VIII But although this marriage did not so take place, it may have been already pre-arranged and known as a coming event before the King's death Ethelred or Awdrey Malte, the natural daughter of Henry, whom Harington married, was a special favourite with her Royal parent, who placed her for protection and education with a wealthy citizen and merchant tailor of London, named John Malte or Mawlte This man, in return for acting confidentially in these private matters, received from the King a valuable reward in the shape of a grant dated 38th Hen VIII (1546) of church lands, being part of the spoils of Bath Priory and Shaftesbury Abbey We must not allude, I suppose to the irony which is patent in this act of reformation, but simply go on and add that these confiscated lands were to remain to the use of Malte himself for his life, then to pass to the use of his adopted daughter Ethelred and her heirs, if she had any, and if not, to revert to the heirs of Malte These points in the Memoir will be assured by documents bearing upon them, given in brief Malte, the reputed father of Ethelred, did not long survive the King, indeed he died a few months after He died rich, and bequeathed to Ethelred by Will (over and above the

Strangwayes and Morton Pedigree.

Manors of Kelston, Easton, and St Catherine, all near Bath, which, as shewn above, would now fall to her fortune by the King's provision for her) another manor in Somerset, situate near Glastonbury,—the Manor of Andersey, otherwise Nyland, and now included in the parish of Rodney Stoke The will of Malte is dated Sept 10, 1546, and was proved June 7th, 1547, and in the year following we would place as probable the marriage of John Harington and Ethelred Malte in London or its suburbs The wealthy endowment of his wife would be of prime importance to a man like Harington,—a man of fallen fortune but of lofty aspirations —a man of decided talent and taste, who could write good sonnets, and (being more or less a friend of the famous composer Tallis) could write a Sanctus too, though, be it confessed, the only music of this kind handed down to us is the extraordinary Black Sanctus to Satan * He was a man, too, of historic name and family, and now in his present fortune he could fill a place at Court in any capacity in which he might be called upon to serve the Queen

But let us pursue his domestic career The union with Ethelred, if happy, was of short duration The issue of the marriage was an only child, a daughter Hester or Esther, whose birth about 1549 was probably the cause of her mother's early death Where she was born or baptized is at present unknown She survived her mother some years, and is spoken of in a deed affecting the Harington property 10th Elizabeth (1568) This is all that we can glean about her history she would seem to have died unmarried, and thus ultimately, all her mother's endowments passed to her father, and then from him to his heirs by a second wife During the minority of his daughter Hester, certainly before 1554, and probably about 1550 (as *vide* the 'Nugæ' and Harington's sonnets to "sweet Isabella Markham") John Harington married Isabella, daughter of Sir John Markham, Lieutenant of the Tower of London She was a Lady-in-Waiting on the Princess Elizabeth, and both husband and wife suffered imprisonment in the reign of Queen Mary for their fidelity to Elizabeth

The date of his death was 1st July 24th Eliz, at his house in Lambeth His place of burial (as stated in the 'Mis Gen et Her,' New Series, Vol II, p 361) was in the Church of St Gregory by St Paul's, London There is an Inquisition post mortem of his property extant at Wells Diocesan Court under date 18th March, 25th Eliz, the details of which will be given, his son John (afterwards Sir John) being then twenty-one years and upwards

There seems only to remark further, in concluding this memoir, that the Monumental Inscriptions, Registers, and other data of this branch of the Haringtons, descending from John of Stepney, commence from 1582 in Somerset, all evidences previous to this must be looked for in London and its precincts

---

EXTRACT FROM THE WILL OF JOHN MALTE, CITIZEN AND MERCHANT TAILOR OF LONDON (A confidant of King Henry VIII)

Will dated Sept 10, 1546 (Alen 39)

"William Horner son of my daughter Horner shall have the Manors of Greenhall, Bramfield, and Ewell, Herts, and in default of issue *Anthony Skutt*, son of my daughter Bridget Skutt, shall have the parsonage of Wholstone, etc etc Mary the wife of Richard Egleston, and Elizabeth wife of Bradyssley, my first wife's daughters, £20 each To Joane Dyngley, otherwise Joane Dobson, £20 £5 to the *foundling child*, that was laid at my gate To Awdrey Malte, MY BASTARD DAUGHTER,† begotten on the body of Joane Dingley now wife of one Dobson, *the Manor of Andersey otherwise Nyland in Somerset*, etc To my sister Margaret Fuller 20 marks per an'm," etc etc

[Proved June 7th, 1547]

GALWAY, EARL OF.—The arms borne by Henry de Massue de Ruvigny, the worthy son of a noble sire, were—Quarterly. 1st, arg a fess gu, in chief three martlets sa on a canton or, a battle-axe of the 3rd, 2nd, gu a chaplet of laurel or, a chief cheque arg and az, 3rd, arg. three mallets gu On his advancement to the Earldom in 1697, he was granted for supporters "two savages, crowned and girt with laurel, each holding in his hand a club, and on the same arm a shield with the arms of Ireland, all ppr." At his death, æt. 72, 3 Sept. 1720, Lady Russell, at the age of 84, succeeded to his property Although deprived by Act of Parliament of the Portarlington estate, the leases he had granted to some of the Huguenot exiles for lives, renewable for ever, were not interfered with, but still continue in force. See Smiles' 'Huguenots,' (1870) p. 216-7

New Univ Club. HY. WAGNER.

* *Vide* Nugæ Antiquæ of Harington —'The Monk's Hymn to Saunte Satan, Chaunted daily in their Cells till goodlie Kynge Henry Spoyled their Singing' (1546) "O tu qui dans oracula," etc The music of this hymn is described as peculiarly learned and *Tallis*-like'—a point which I presume will remain a "moot" one among musicians

† The King was alive when Malte wrote this, and no doubt required it of him in return for the grants of land

STAYNINGS FAMILY.*

Will of Charles Staynings 1693.

In the name of God Amen. I Charles Staynings of Holnycote in the County of Somersett Esqre being of perfect mind and memory (I blesse my God for the same) and not knowing the certaine time of my departure I doe make and appoint this my last Will and Testament revoking and annulling all former Wills and Testaments by me heretofore made Impr's I committ my body to the dust to be decently buried by my Executor hereafter named in my Great Grandfather's Grave next my wife as my Trustees and Executor shall direct and my Soule I give to the Great God that gave him. Item. I give and bequeath unto Robert Siderfin of Croydon in the County of Somersett Esqre and Richard Troyte of Streame in the same County Clerke and to the survivor of them and to the Executor and Administrator of such survivor All my messuages lands tenem^{ts} mills and hereditam^{ts} with the appurten'nces lyeing within the severall p'ishes villages or tythings of Nether Stowey and Over Stowey in the aforesaid County of Som'sett To have and to hold the aforesaid messuages lands tenements mills and hereditaments whatsoever with the appurten'nces unto the aforesaid Robert Siderfin and Richard Troyte their executors and assigns and to the Executor and Admin^{r} of the survivor of them for and during the whole terme and time of ninety nine years fully to be complete and ended If Lewis Staynings my brother and Grace Oram of Sellworthy in the County of Somersett Widdow they or either of them shall soe long happen to live nevertheless to be only lyable to the trusts and for the uses hereafter mens'oned (that is to say) to lease out the said pr'mises att an yearly rent and to pay the sume of Eighty Pounds in manner and forme following (that is to say) forty pounds p'te of the said Eighty Pounds, I doe appointe the said Robert Siderfin and Richard Troyte and the survivor of them and the Executor and Admin^{r} of such survivor to pay annually unto my brother Lewis Staynings by quarterly paym^{ts} during his naturall life and twenty pounds other p'te of the said Eighty Pounds, I doe appointe the said Robert Siderfin and Richard Troyte and the survivor of them and the Executor of such survivor to pay annually to Mrs Grace Oram before named during her naturall life and twenty pounds residue of the said Eighty Pounds I doe appoint the said Robert Siderfin and Richard Troyte and the survivor of them and the Executor of such survivor to pay annually unto my nephew Joseph Braford of the Citty of London during the naturall lives of my brother Lewis Staynings and Grace Oram and the survivor of them and likewise to pay all rates taxes and other outgoings as shall become justly due and payable out of the aforesaid pr'm'sses during the said trust And it is my Will and pleasure that the said Robert Siderfin and Richard Troyte and the survivor of them and the Executor and Admin^{r} of such survivor doe annually account to my Executor hereafter named for all such sume and sumes of money as they shall receive and take out of the aforesaid messuages lands tenements mills hereditam^{ts} over and above the said sume of Eighty Pounds or the annuityes paid which said overplus I doe give and bequeath unto my said Executor. Item I doe give and bequeath unto my brother Lewis Staynings the house he now lives in called the West House being parte of my Mansion House in the p'ish of Sellworthy aforesaid for the terme of his naturall life and after his decease I give and devise the said house unto my nephew William Martin of the City and County of Exeter Esqr his heirs and assigns for ever Item I give and devise unto my said nephew William Martin and his heirs All that my Mansion House Messuages Lands Tenem^{ts} Barton Farme Mill and hereditam^{ts} whatsoever with their and every of their appurten'nces lyeing and being within the severall p'ishes tythings hamletts and villages of Sellworthy and Succombe in the County of Somersett. To have and to hold the said Mansion House and all and singular the said messuages lands

* Communicated by Michael Williams, Esq., F.S.A.

tenements barton farme mill and hereditam[ts] whatsoever with their and every of their appurten'nces unto the said William Martin his heirs and assigns for ever. Item, I give and devise unto my said nephew William Martin and his heirs my Mannor of Hollincote with all the Royaltys and priveledges belonging to the same and all and singular my messuages lands tenements and hereditaments whatsoever with their and every of their appurten'nces lyeing and being in the severall p'shes tythings hamletts and villages of Sellworthy, Succombe, Winsford, Exford, Porlocke and Dulverton in the aforesaid County of Somersett. To have and to hold the aforesaid mannor messuages lands tenements and hereditam[ts] whatsoever with their and every of their appurten'nces unto the said William Martin his heirs and assignes for ever. Item, I give and devise unto the aforenamed Robert Siderfin and Richard Troyte and their heires and to the heir Executor and Admin[r] of the survivor of them All my Mannor Messuages Mills Lands Temen[ts] and Hereditaments whatsoever with their and every of their appurten'nces lyeing and being in the severall p'ishes villages tythings and hamletts of Nether Stowey and Over Stowey in the said County of Somersett upon this further trust (that is to say) after the death of my brother Lewis Staynings and Grace Oram and the survivor of them to and for the use of my nephew Joseph Braford for the terme of ninety nine years if he shall soe long happen to live. And after his decease or expiration of the said terme then in trust for such child and children as shall lawfully be begotten by the body of the said Joseph Braford such child or children liveing to the age of one and twenty yeares then to such child or children and the heirs of their body lawfully begotten and for default of issue lawfully begotten by the said Joseph Braford or for default of issue liveing to the age of one and twenty yeares or for default of issue by such child or children as shall be lawfully begotten by the said Joseph Braford then I give and demise unto my said nephew William Martin and his heire All my said Mannor Mills Messuages Lands Tenem[ts] and hereditam[ts] whatsoever with their and every of their appurten'nces lyeing and being in the aforesaid p'ishes tythings hamletts and villages of Nether Stowey and Over Stowey To have and to hold all the said Mannor Mills Messuages Lands tenements and hereditam[ts] whatsoever with their and every of their appurten'nces unto the said William Martin his heirs and assigns for ever. And I hereby will and authorize the said Robert Siderfin and Richard Troyte and the survivor of them and the Executor and Admin[r] of such survivor to allow and pay them and himself for such care cost and trouble as they or either of them shall reasonably deserve or be at in manageing the said trusts. Item. I give and bequeath unto the aforenamed Grace Oram now living with me the sume of One hundred pounds to be paid within one yeare after my decease. Item. I give and bequeath unto my trustees Robert Siderfin and Richard Troyte the sum of Tenn Pounds each to be paid within three months after my decease. Item. I give unto my servant Edward Stoate the sum of Twenty Pounds. Item. I give unto Joane Mitchell, Widdow, one other of my servants the sume of Five Pounds. Item. I give unto every other of my servants as shall be liveing with me at the time of my death the sum of forty shillings each. Item. I give to the poore of Sellworthy Twenty Pounds to be put in Stocke and the use thereof to be distributed yearly and to the poore of Succombe Five Pounds to be put into Stocke and the use thereof to be distributed yearly, and to the poore of Dulverton five pounds to be put into stocke and the interest yearly to be distributed and fifty shillings to the poore of Winsford and fifty shillings more to the poore of Exford to be distributed at my death. Item. I give and devise unto my nephew William Martin and his heirs All my Mannors Messuages Lands Tenan[ts] and Hereditam[ts] whatsoever (not by me already devised within the County of Som'sett and elsewhere). To have and to hold the said Mannors Messuages Lands Tenan[ts] and hereditam[ts] with their appurten'nces unto the said William Martin his heirs and assigns for ever. Item. After my legacies paid and funerall expenses borne I give and bequeath all the rest of my goods and chattles whatsoever unto my aforenamed nephew William Martin whom I doe constitute appoint and make my whole and sole Executor of this my last Will and Testament In Witness whereof I the said Charles Staynings have published and declared this my last Will and Testament this fourteenth day of February Annoq D'ni 1693 and in the sixth yeare of the Raigne of King William and Queen Mary CHA STAYNINGS.

Signed sealed published and declared by Charles Staynings Esqre to be his last Will and Testament in the presence of us—John Galard Rect^r de Sellworthy—Elias Falvey Rect^r de Oare—Edward Stoate—Will Siderfin.

[Proved at Taunton the 4th day of February 1700 on the Oath of William Martyn the Executor]

NOTES

Extract from the Will of "William Martyn of Netherex in ye County of Devon, Esquire," date, 28 Dec 1661

"Item I give unto my daughter Susanna Martyn, ye summe of five hundred pounds to be payd unto her by my executor hereafter mentioned, when she attains to the age of twenty and one and shall further leave her to be better provided for at ye good pleasure of her dear Aunt, my sister Stennings"

From the Will, dated 29th Dec 1663, of Dame Elizabeth Martyn of Oxton in "the County of Devon Widow late Wife and Relict of Sr Nicholas Martyn of the same, Knight"

"To my cozin Thomas Gorges of Heavytree in ye countye aforesaid Esqre I give one hundred pounds of currant money of England, under the Trust and use followinge, that is to say to buy with the said one hundred pounds two jewells with what convenience may be and then to deliver or cause to be delivered, unto my daughter Susanna Staynings for her use during her life, and after her death, to her eldest son or daughter and in case she dyes without any issue, then the sayd jewells to be delivered unto my Grandchild Nicholas Martyn of Heavytree afores^d Esqr"

Marriage License at Exeter.
June 1705

"26 L^a mi inter Wm Martyn de Oxton in com Devon, Ar et Susannam Martyn, filiam Wm Martyn de Holnicot in Com Somerset, Ar"

SELWORTHY REGISTERS

1685	May 21	Susanna Staynings was buried
1700	December 12	Charles Staynings was buried

MONUMENTAL INSCRIPTIONS

Here lyeth ye body of Phillip Steynings ye sonne of Charles Steynings of Holneycott, Esq who died ye 12th daye of Avgvst in ye yeare of ovr Lord God 1631 and of his age ye 6th moneth

---

Here lyeth the body of Anthony Steynings ye sonne of Charles Steynings of Holneycott Esq who died ye 10th daye of May in ye yeare of our Lord God 1635 and of his age ye 4th yeare

---

An epitaph made in memory of that worthy gentlewoman Mrs Margarett Steynings widdow who died ye x^th day of March in ye yeare of our Lord God 1631 and of her age ye 70th &c &c

---

Here lyeth the body of Cicell Staynings sometyme the wyfe of Charles Staynings of Holneycott Esqvire by whom she had seaven sonnes and sixe davghters She departed this lyfe in the fayth of Christ the xxi^th daye of Jvne in the yeare of ovr Lord God 1646 and in the 47th yeare of her age

---

Philip Stenynges Esquier married unto Alice ffrie daughter of William ffris of Membrie Esquier by whome he had nyne sonnes and five daughters departed this life the five tenthe daie of January in ye yere of our lord god a thousand five hundred fourescore and nyne

---

Sacred to the memory of Charles Staynings Esq of Holnicote in this p'ish, the last of y^t ancient family and of Susanna his wife daughter to Sr Nicholas Martyn late of Oxton in ye County of Devon K^t She departed this life the 8th of May 1685, he the 1th of Decemb^r 1700 aged 78 haveing made and order'd the following verses to be written on his monument —

Here lyes Charles Staynings by his wife
Who lov'd him as she did her life,
As hee did her, their loves increas'd
Till that sad day his wife deceas'd,
To whom her husband now is gone
Both liv'd togeather thirty yeares and one

This was erected by William Martyn Esqr his heir and sole executor in testimony of his profound respect and gratitude Anno 1701

TIBI NON DIESSE
H. Strangways

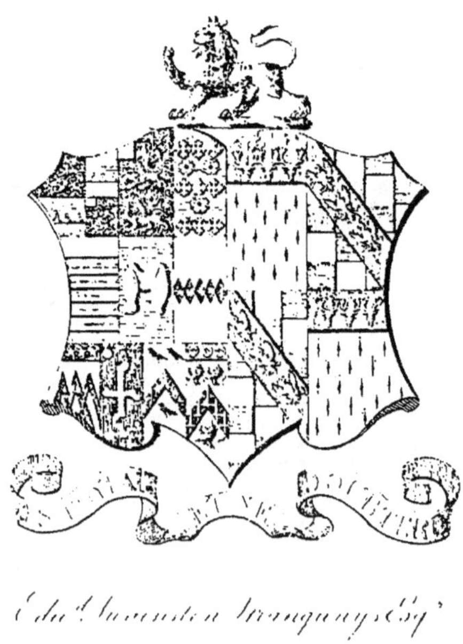

A

William Morton.=Elizabeth Myers.

George Morton of London, Solicitor, b. 27 July, 1778. Died in the Charter House, aged 83.=. . . .

Ada, married George Hutchinson of Gainford.

Major Harcourt Lancelot, a Peninsular veteran, born 27 October, 1785. Died 4 June 1854, aged 68. Buried at Masham.=Martha, da. of Lieut.-General Andrew Gammell. Died 8 Feb. 1871, aged 80. Bur. at Masham.

Elizabeth, born Sunday 16 Jan. 1780. Married . . . . Hickson of Guisborough co. York, and ob. s. p.

Mary, born 6 Jan. 1782.=Charles Picksley of Sheffield, merchant. Marr. at Masham 23 April, 1810.

Ann, born 3 Nov. 1783. Died 28 Feb. 1864, aged 80.=Samuel Russell of Blyth, co. Notts, Surgeon, born at Knaresbro' 1784. Died 30 Apr. 1855, aged 71. Marr. at Masham 17 Dec. 1807.

Martha, born 13 Jan. 1788. Died unmarried. Buried at Masham.

Charles Harcourt, died young.

William Morton, married Susan Mehetabel, da. of Thomas Darling of Connecticut, U.S.

Henry George died young.

Edwin John of Wakefield, Solicitor. Died Nov. 1867, s. p.=Hannah, da. of William Starkie of Wakefield, Surgeon.=William Wood, M.D., of Wakefield. 2nd husb.

Frederick Richard.=Emma, da. of . . . . Hope.

Mary Ann, died 25 Aug. 1813, aged 13 months. Bur. at Masham.

Martha Elizabeth, died in 1858. Married Henry William Ward of London.

Louisa, marr. William Smith of Sheffield, Solicitor.

Mary, mar. James Rigby of Doncaster, Surgeon.

William Cook Russell of Doncaster, Surgeon. Born Aug. 12, 1812.=1. Martha, da. of Cornelius Clark of Whitby. Died 16 April 1850. Bur. at Balby.=2. Betsy Eleanor, da. of Samuel Cooper of Worsbro.

1. Sarah, da. of Wm Warris of Sheffield. Ob. 1854, æt. 51.=Samuel Russell of Blyth, b. 13 Dec. 1815. Ob. 9 Aug.=2. Sophia Rebecca da. of . . . Wells.

Henry, a medical student. b. 4 Feb. 1813. Died May 3, 1833.

(By 1st wife:) Maria, ob. 30 Oct. 1874, unmarried. Bur. at Balby. — Cornelia.

(By 2nd wife:) Florence Mary. — Amy. — Gertrude.

1. Samuel Younge, ob. unmar. 1856, æt. 14.

2. William Warris.

Mary Elizabeth.=Benjamin Weston Wells of Kentish Town, London.

Sarah Alathea.=John Charles Coupe of Doncaster.

Richard of Bawtry, an Engineer, born 5 Nov. 1817; accidentally killed 3 Dec. 1864.=Sophia Elizabeth, da. of Jonathan B. Sheardown of Doncaster.

Edgar Richard Brown. — Ada.

Lancelot Russell of London, Solicitor. Born May 19, 1819. Married at Croydon 25 Feb. 1865.=Anne, 2nd da. of Edward Hancock of Thornton Heath, Croydon.

Percy Lancelot, born 11 Feb. 1872. — Rhoda May, born 20 Feb. 1866.

George, Student at King's College, London. Born 3 Jan. 1823. Died 5 Jan. 1844 unmar. at Blyth.

Martha Ann, born 26 Feb. 1822. Died at Blyth unmar. in 1873, aged 54.

B

Rev. Richard Morton, bapt. at Babworth, Nottinghamshire, 17 June, 1744. Matriculated at Balliol Coll. Oxford, Dec. 16, 1763; B.A. 1767; M.A. 1770. Vicar of East Retford, Rector of Kirton, Notts, and Vicar of Beighton, co. Derby. Ob. 20 April, 1821, aged 76; bur. in East Retford Church. = Judith, da. of William Mason of Eaton, Notts. Born 28 Dec. 1750. Died 18 Feb. 1840, aged 90, buried in East Retford Church.

Children:

- 1. Judith Morton, bapt. 26 July, 1778. Marr. 30 Oct. 1822. Died 14 Nov. 1862, bur. at Carlton in Lindrick, co. Notts. = Harry Nevill of Hackney, Merchant. Born 4 Feb. 1777. Died 18 June, 1846, bur. at Carlton.
- 2. Rev. George Morton, bapt. 20 July, 1779. M.A. of Jesus Coll. Cambridge, Curate of Sturton, Notts. Died unm. 9 Dec. 1818, bur. in East Retford Church.
- 3. Jane, bapt. 21 Feb. 1781. Died 3 Aug. 1782, bur. at East Retford.
- 4. Jane, bapt. 27 Aug. 1782. Died 22 Nov. 1783, bur. at East Retford.
- 5. Mary, bapt. 17 Sept. 1784. Marr. 16 Feb. 1806. Died 27 Aug. 1816, buried in East Retford Church. = Richard Thomas Sharpe, Solicitor, of Worksop, co. Notts.
- 6. William, bapt. 26 July, 1786. Died 1 Nov. 1786, bur. at East Retford.
- 7. Catherine, bapt. 25 July, 1787. Died 16 Aug. 1787.
- 8. Ann, bapt. 13 Jan. 1789. Died 18 March, 1793, buried at East Retford.
- 9. Eliza, bapt. 30 Oct. 1790. Marr. 22 Oct. 1828. Died 28 June, 1876, bur. at Bridlington, Yorkshire. = Michael Wynne Thorold, gent., of Harworth, co. Notts, son of Rev. Michael Thorold, Vicar of Heydor, co. Lincoln. Born 21 March, 1803. Died 6 May, 1872, bur. at Bridlington, Yorkshire.

Children of Mary Morton and Richard Thomas Sharpe:

- 1. Richard Thomas Sharpe, born 9 Mar. 1808. Died abroad.
- 2. Henry Tierney, born 6 Sept. 1809. Died abroad.
- 3. Sarah Eliza, born 1811. Buried 14 Oct. 1823, aged 12, at East Retford.
- 4. James Sibury, born 12 Aug. 1812. Died 20 Dec. 1873, aged 61, bur. in Highgate Cemetery.
- 5. Rev. William Robert, born 21 July, 1816. [M.A. 1842.] Marr. 1 Dec. 1846. Late Fellow St. Catharine's Coll. Camb. Vicar of St. Chad's, Haggerston, London. = Charlotte, 3rd da. of Joseph Clarke of Ashby-de-la-Launde, co. Lincoln. Born Dec. 29, 1822.

Children of Rev. William Robert Sharpe and Charlotte:

- Rev. William Robert Sharpe, born 30 Aug. 1850. M.A. 1877 Keble Coll. Oxon. Curate of Harpsden, Oxfordshire.
- 2. John Ambrose Morton, born 4 March, 1852.
- 3. Mary Charlotte Agnes, born 11 July, 1854.
- 4. Beatrice Sarah, born 5 June, 1857.
- 5. Cyril Herbert, born 14 Ap. 1860.

Children of Eliza Morton and Michael Wynne Thorold:

- 1. Michael Richard Thorold of Sutton Bridge, co. Lincoln. Born 25 Sept. 1830. Marr. 21 Dec. 1853. = Anne, eldest da. of Edward Gillbee, of Western Bank, Sheffield.
- 2. Edmund, of Bath, M.A., late Fellow of Mag. Coll. Oxford. Born Sept. 8, 1832. Marr. 2 Aug. 1859, Louisa, 2nd da. of Edward Gillbee. She died 16 Mar. 1876, buried at Bath.
- 3. Rev. William, born 15 Sept. 1833. St. Bees' Coll. Vicar of Weeton, co. Lanc. 1865. Married Fanny, da. of George Nelson of Grafton House, Leeds, 24 April, 1862.
- 4. Eliza Mary, born 23 July, 1835.
- 5. George Henry, born 12 Aug. 1838. Bur. at Carlton in Lindrick, co. Notts, 11 Feb. 1839.

Children of Michael Richard Thorold and Anne:

- Michael Edward Thorold, born 17 Oct. 1855. B.A. Caius Coll. Cambridge.
- 2. Mary Catherine, born 11 Jan. 1858.
- 3. Richard Gillbee, born 24 Dec. 1859.
- 4. Ethel Anne Louisa, born 9 June, 1861.
- 5. Margaret Rose, born 11 March, 1863.
- 6. Mabel, born 9 Jan. 1866. Died 11 Nov. 1875, bur. at Sutton Bridge, co. Lincoln.

GENEALOGICAL NOTES OF THE FAMILY OF ROBERTS OF WILLESDEN, MIDDLESEX, PREFIXED TO A VELLUM MS. IN THE BODLEIAN LIBRARY, CONTAINING TREATISES BY ADAM THE CARTHUSIAN, R. ROLLE, AND WALTER HILTON.*

EDMOND ROBERTS, ANN. D. 1553.

1548 —Memorandum, that I was maryed vnto Francis Wells apon Candellmas daye at Roystone, beyng the 11[d] daye of Febrare in the III[d] yere of the rayne of our soveraigne lord Kyng Edward the VIth.

Ser Robert Tyrwytt and Ser Robert Chester and my lady Francis Leydon wer godfathers and godmother to Frances Roberts, who was crystened at Roystone, a° 1550.

My lady Mestres Katheryne Chester and Mestres Gryssell Sadler and Master John Armyster, Master of the Temple and lord of Nesdon, wer godmothers and godfather vnto Katheryne Roberts, who was crystenyd at Wyllesdon, a° 1552.

Mystres Alles Reskymer and Mestres Mary Egerton and M. Jesper Umpton godmothers and godfather to Marye Roberts, beyng borne apon our Ladyes eve

M[res] Clarensyous and my lady Broke godmothers and M[r] Lofe godfather, and was crystenyd at Wyllesden Churche

The names of the childeryne of Edmond Roberts of Wyllesden, esquyer, and the daye and yere of ther byrth —

Frances Roberts was borne the viii day of Februare, beyng Shrove Sondaye, in the afternone, bytwen vi and vii of the cloke in the afternone, and in the vth yere of the rayne of Kyng Edward the vi[th], and a° Dni M D.L. 1550.

Katheryne Roberts was borne the last daye of June betwen v. and vi. of the cloke in the mornyng, beyng Thursdaye, in the vi[th] yere of the rayne of our Soverayne Lord Kyng Edward the vi[th] and in a° D'ni 1552

Marie Roberts was borne apon our Ladis Eve in the mornyng, betwen v. and vi of the cloke beyng Thursdaye, and the vii[th] daye of Desember, in the ferst yere of the raygne of our soverenge lady quene Marye and a° Dni 1553

Marie Roberts the yongar was borne the xth daye of Februarie, beyng Sondaye, betwen iiij and v of the cloke in the mornyng, in fyrst and second yere of the rayen of our soveregn lorde and lady the kyng and quene Phillip and Marie, A° Dni 1554 †

1558.—Thomas Roberts was borne at Neasdon the xxx[th] daye of July, at v. of the cloke in the afternone, beyng Frydaye in a° Dni. 1558, and cristenyd the laste daye of August, and M[r] T. Gresham and M[r] Jno Newdegat godfathers, and M[res] Brydeman godmother. I praye God make hyme hys servantt.

Elyzabethe Roberts was borne at Nesdon the xii[th] day of June at x of the cloke at nyght, beynge Wensdaye, a° Dni 1560, and was crystenyd the xvi. of June, and M[res] Hyde and M[res] Browe wer godmothers, and M[r] Armygell Wade godfather.

1560 —And the xx[th] daye of July Francys my wyffe departyd thys worlld, whoes solle God pardon, who was dawghter and eyre unto Rychard Wells of Ware, esquyer, and lefte iiij chillderyne alyve, whome Jhu' send grace to lyve in thys worlld to hys pleasor, and she was buryd in Wyllesdon churche the xxv[th] of July, beyng sent James daye, 1560. God have mersy on her solle, I beseche Jhu' Amen.

1563 —Memorandum, that I was maryed vnto faythe my wyfe the viij[th] daye of Junein the vth yere of quene Elyzabeth, and A° Dni 1563 at Wyllesden, w[ch] was the mondaye after trynyte Sondaye wth faythe ys dawgtr and here of John Patynson of london gentellman and one of the que' ma[ts] Customh' of london. and the sayde faythe was at hallowtyde after xviij yeres of ayge as doth apere in the Churche at St Stevens in Collman Street

Thomas Roberts was borne att nesdon the xviij daye of Januare A° 1565

* Rawlinson C 894

† This paragraph and the next are struck out in the MS

beynge ffrydaye, bytwen viij and ix of the cloke in the mornynge and was crystened at Wyllesden churche the 22 of Jan, hys godfathers Mr George brydemane and Mr Wyll'm pynchbeke and Mrs Allys payne godmother. I pray god make hym hys seruante Amen

Edmond Roberts was borne att nesdon the xxj of July 1570 beyeng frydaye betwene v or vj of the cloke in the after none and was crystenyd at Wyllesdon churche the 27 of Julye, hys godfathers Mr Aser bovelvtely (?)* Mr gregorye Champanty and Mrs pynchbeke godmother God make hyme his seruante Amen

1574.—Mary Roberts was borne att nesdon the 29 daye of June bytwen one and towe of the cloke in the mornyng beyng mondaye A° 1574, and was crystenyd the fyrste daye of Julye and my lady Harbard and Mres Wynkefelld wer godmothers and Mr Edward Ellryngton godfather

Memorandum I Fraunces Roberts tooke to wiffe Mari barne the dafter of John Barne esquier, and was maried at wollwiche the xxth of Nouember beinge Sonndaye Anno Domini 1575 laus deo. Amen

here followethe the names of the chyldren of ffraunces Roberts the eldest sonne of Edm'nd Roberts and ffraunces welles his wiffe

1576.—Jhesus.—Mem. that barne Roberts was borne att nesdon the fyrste daye of September beyng Satterday betwen on and ij of the cloke in the afternone and was crystenyd in Wyllesdon churche the iiijth daye of September A° 1576 and my ladye Jugdde was godmother and Edmond Roberts and John barne godfathers and allsoo graundfathers to the chyllde god make hym hys seruante and well to prosper in thys worllde and in the worllde to come. Amen

Jhesus.—Edward Roberts was borne at neasdon the thyrd daye of September beyng wensdaye betwene the oures of too and thre in the afternowen yn the yeare of oure lord god 1578 and was Chrystened in wilsden Churche, Mr Edward Elryngton Mr George Brydeman godfathers, and Mrs Barne his grandmother godmother. I praye god to blesse and make him his seruante. Amen.

Jhesus.—George Roberts was borne at neasden and died within ye monethe, being christened

Jesus.—ffrauncis Roberts was borne at neasden the second daye of September 1581 on sonday mornyng betwene tenne and eleuen of the clocke in the mornyng and was chrystened in the parler, Mr Paramore godfather and Mrs Jane Barne her grandmother and Mrs Elizabeth Altam her aunte godmothers I pray god blesse her and make her his seruant. Amen

Jesu.—George Roberts was borne at Welsden the 6 of Julij in the yeare of our lord god 1583, in the afternowne betwene 8 or 9 of the clocke on a friday. Sir Edward herbert Mr George Barne barne (*sic*) godfathers, my lady Gerrarde, the Mr of the roles his wiffe, beinge godmother. the lord blese him and make him his seruant Amen

Jesu.—John Roberts was borne at Nesden the x of December in the yeare of our lord god 1584 about eyght of the clock in the in (*sic*) fore noune beyng thursday Mr Edward Altam Mr Emanuell Wolley godfathers, Mrs Alese hoddesden godmother. the lord blese him and make him his seruant Amen

Jesu.—Mary Roberts was borne at Wilsden and died wthin the moneth, the lade Rivers and Mrs Altam godmothers Mr Christofer hodsden godfather. she died within the moneth and was buried, 1587, in mi chappell

Jesu.—Jane Roberts was borne at Wilsden the six daye of may beying sonday betwene one and too of the clocke in the mornyng, Mrs paine and her grandmother barne her godmothers, Mr Edward Altham godfather Jesu make her his seruant. Anno Domini 1588 Amen

Jesu.—Elizabeth Roberts was borne at Saint Jones streete Robert Roberts was borne in Saint Johnes Streete the vj of februari 1591 being satersday betwene the howeres of one and too in the mornyng and was there Chrystened, Mr Robert

* This name is unintelligible

Wrathe Mr Rychard paine godfathers, Mrs Bowes his godmother the wiffe of Mr William Bowes Jesus Christ be mercifull vnto him and make him his seruant. Amen.

Mari Roberts was borne at Wilsden the xiiij^th^ of december 1592 being thursdaye betweene the howers of vj and vij in the morning and was chrystened there, Mrs Mari Altham M^rs^ francklin her godmothers, Mr Thomas Roberts her godfather. Jesu Christe be mercifull vnto her and make her his seruant Amen this Mari died w^thin^ the monethe at marke halle and there lieth buried

Anne Roberts was borne at Willsden.

William Roberts was borne at Wilsden the xvij^th^ of Juli 1596 being Satersdaie betwene the houres of fore and fiue in the morning, and was Christened in Wilsden Churche, Mr William Bowes Mr Giles Howland godfathers, Mrs Mari Altham godmother Jesu Christ be mercifull vnto him and make him his servante Amen

Jesu —1597 —Jeames Roberts was borne at Wilsden the xxiij of october 1597 being Sondaye betwene the howeres of vj and vij and was christened in neasden parler, Mr William Gerrard Mr Jeames Altham his Godfathers, Mrs Carr his Goodmother. Christe Jesu blese him and make him his servant Amen.

Jesu —Memorandum, That ffrauncis Roberts was maried vnto Mr Richard ffranklin of Cannons the second daye of nouember 1598 I prai god blese them and send them his grace that thei maie see there childerens childern to the glori of god and his kingdome

Anno Domini 1600.

Memorandum that John ffrancklin the sonne of Richard francklin and fraunces his wiffe was borne at Neasden in Wilsden the 22 of aprill being twesdaye about six of the clock in the morning and was christened in Wilsden churche, Mr John Barne great grandfather M^rs^ ffrauncis Robert grandfather his godfathers the ladi Judd the great great grandmother his godmother. Christ Jesu blesse him and make him his servant Amen.

1600 —Mari Roberts was borne at neasden the xviij daye of december being thursdaie betwene the houres of xj and twellue at nyght and was christened in the parler Mr Richard francklin Godfather Mrs Mari Altham the wiffe of Mr Jeames Altham esquier and Mrs Barnsdale her godmothers. God blesse her and make her his servante Amen

Thomas Roberts the sonne of ffrances Roberts and Mary his wyfe was borne att Nesden in the parishe of Wilsden the last daye of Junne in the yeare of o^r^ Lord 1606, being the tenth sonne of the sayd ffrances and Mary. god make him his servante

Eleanour Aty was borne in Sheer-lane in London between 9 and 10 in the morning on a Saterday being 4 June 1608. Was buried ye 22 of November, 1678

The Age of the children of Sr William and the Lady Eleanor Roberts —

Edmund ye first sonne was borne 23 July 1625 dyed Lent following
William ye 2^d^ sonne was borne the 9th of June 1628. dyed 13th of same moneth.
Mary ye First daughter borne 14 Septemb 1629.
John ye 3^d^ sonne borne 10 May 1631 dyed Aug following.
Anne ye 2^d^ daughter borne 12 September 1632
Jane ye 3^d^ daughter borne 30 March 1634
Frances ye 4th daughter borne 8 March 1634 dyed July 1646.
William ye 4th sonne borne 22 April 1637 dyed march follow'g.
William ye 5th sonne borne 21 June 1638 dyed 14° March 1687–8
Elizabeth ye 5th daughter borne 19 Septem 1639. dyed 25 Octob follow'g
Eleanor ye 6th daughter borne 6 Aug 1641.
Edward the 6th sonne borne 28 Novemb 1642 dyed 2 Jan. 1662.
Thomas *alias* Naseby ye 7th son born 27 June 1645.
Francis ye 8th sonne borne 26 Novemb 1646.
Richard ye 9th sonne borne 2 Aprill 1648

The Age of the children of Sr William and lady Sarah Roberts who were married 8 April 1658 —

William Roberts son of William Roberts was borne horâ quartâ pomeridianâ 17 Jan 1658.

Ellinor Roberts daughter of Sr Wm Roberts Bar^t was borne 21 Dec. 1670 betweene the houres of 2 and 3 in ye morning and christened the same day the Lady Ellinor Roberts and Mrs Jane Gibbs and Mr Francis Roberts were her wittnesses. She dyed the 26 day of February following.

The Age of the children of Mr Barne and Mrs Anne Roberts —

Anne Roberts was borne 14 Aug 1602

Barne and William Roberts were borne 21 Apr. 1604. Barn died 1 Feb 1617. William died 19 Sept 1662.

Francis Roberts was borne 27 July 1605.

Richard Roberts was borne 15 Aug 1606

Mary Roberts was borne 11 Jun 1609.

Elizabeth Roberts was borne 2 July 1611

The Age of the children of Mr John and Mrs Anne Nelthorp who were married 15 Mar. 1652 —

William their eldest sonne was borne at Wilsden 10 Jan 1654. since dead and buryed at Harrow.

John their 2^d sonne was born at Wilsden 12 Sept. 1655 since dead and buryed at Wilsden.

Eleanor their eldest daughter born at Wilsden 2 Nov 1656.

John their 3^d sonne was born at Wilsden 2 Mar. 1657 since dead and buryed at Wilsden

Edward their 4th sonne born at Westminster 19 Mar 1659

Elizabeth their 2^d daughter born at Westminster 23 Octob 1662.

John their 5th sonne born at Wilsden 18 Aug. 1666.

Jane their 3^d daughter borne at Wilsden 3 Febr 1668. since died 19 Septemb. 1669.

Mary their 4th daughter born at Wilsden 27 Octob. 1672.

The Age of the children of Mr Samuel and Mrs Jane Gibbs they were married 11 Febr. 1650.

William their eldest sonn Born at Wilsden 19 Apr 1652 Buried at Wilsden.

Eleanor their eldest daughter born at Wilsden 20 Octob. 1653.

Samuel their 2^d sonn born at Clerkenwell 24 Aug 1655

Anne their 2^d daughter born at Wilsden 24 Octob 1657.

James their 3^d sonne born at Wilsden 24 Nov. 1659.

William their 4th sonne born at Clerkenwell 27 Aug. 1661. Dead 1662 and Buryed at Clerkenwell.

Edward their 5th son born at Petty Franc Westm^r Mar 1662. Buried at Clerkenwell.

William their 6th son born at Wilsden 2 Aug. 1666.

The Age of the children of Mr Luke and Mrs Eleanor Cordewell. They were married 17 Nov. 1664.

[Mr Cordwell died at London 7 Septemb. 1670]

Eleanor their eldest daughter born at Wilsden 11 Sept 1665.

Anne their 2^d daughter was born at Wilsden 18 Mar. 1666.

Mary their 3^d daughter born at Higham in Kent 29 Jan 1668

Jane their 4th daughter born at Wilsden 9 Febr 1670

The Age of the children of Mr Thomas and Mrs Mary Harrison —

Thomas Harrison son of Tho Harrison Esq was Baptized June y^e 6th 1650.

Margaret their second daughter borne at Wilsden 17 Febr. 1654.

GRANT OF CREST TO RALPH LAWSON OF BURGH, CO. YORK, 1592.*

To all and singuler aswell Nobles and Gentiles as others to whom these presents shall come Edmond Knyght esquire alias Norroy principall Herault and Kynge of Armes of the Este Weste and Southe partes of this Realme of England from the Ryuerr of Trente northwards sendeth greetinge in our Lord God everlastinge. Wheras auncientl from the begininge the valiaunt and worthy Actes of Vertuous persons haue byne comended to the worlde and posteritie with sundrye monuments and remembraunces of their good desertes Emongest which the cheefest and most vsuall hath byne the bearinge of signes and tokens in Sheildes called Armes beinge evidendent Demonstracons and testimonies of vertue and Prowes distributed accordinge to the quallities and deserts of the persons meritinge the same, the which as yt was euidentlie deuised to stirre vpe and enflame the hartes of men to the imitacon of vertue Soe hathe the same byne contynued from tyme to tyme to th' entente that they who haue done comendable seruice to their Prince or . . . . . ethere in warr or peace should not onlye themselues receiue dewe honour for the same in their lieff tyme but . . . . also mighte be contynuwed and remembred vnto their posteritie for ever. Emongest which number Raphe Lawson of Burghe in the countye of Yorke esquire beinge one of the bearers of these auncient Armes and not knowinge of any Creast or Cognizance belonginge to the same as to many auncient armes their belongeth non hath required me the said Norroy King of Armes to assign and sett fourth to him and his posteritie such a Creast or Cognizance as he and they may lawfullye vse and bear without prejudice or offence of any person or persons. In consideracon heirof, his request beinge reasonable I . . . . . . and have by these presents geven and graunted vnto the said Raphe Lawson and to his posteritie for . . . . . cognizance as followeth vidz vppon the heaulme on a Chappeau gould turned vpe ermyne a Marlett sable as the same more plainlie appeareth depicted in the margent which said Armes and Creaste or . . . . . Norroy Kinge of Armes by power and

* Copied from the original Grant in the possession of Sir John Lawson, Bart.

auctboritie to me comitted by l'res patents vnder the great seall of England doe by these presents Ratefie confyrme geue graunte and delyuer vnto the said Raphe Lawson and his Posteritie for ever And hee and they the same to vse beare and shewefourth with due Differences to whom the same shall appertayne at all tymes and in all places hereafter accordinge to the auncient Lawes of Armes with owte lett . . empedement or interruption of any person or persons. In witenesse wherof I the said Norroy Kinge of Armes haue herevnto subscribed these presents and also putt to the Seall of myne Office. Dated at London the second daye of January in the yeare of our Lord God one thowsand fyue hundereth nynetie and twoe And in the thyrtie and foure yeare of the Reigne of our most soueraigne Ladye Elizabeth by the grace of God Queene of England France and Ireland Defender of the Faith, etc.

EDMOND KNYGHT *alias*
Norrey Roy d'armes

Recorded in the Heralds' Office London and examined therewith this 25 day of July, 1774, by me
RALPH BIGLAND,
Norroy King of Arms

FLETCHER WILLS.*

From the Lichfield Registry.

1548. April 6 Will of Thom's fletcher "body to be buryed in the churche yard of Aston upon trent" To the six children of Rychard Plasten To Ales my doughter To Richard Plasten, and to Cristofer his son—residue "to John my son and my wyfe whom I make my executors." Thom's sateswell and robert hall overseers. Proved 1550 in Bishop's Registry. Inventory, Sm' vii[li] v[s] x[d].

1551. 5 Edw VI. April 6 Will of Thomas Flecher of ffotherley of the paryshe of Shenston—to be buried in churchyarde of Shenston. To Rowland eldest sonne, to John son, and to ffraunces son, xl[s] of goods each. To my brethren's children To M'get Wall To Thomas Gryndey. To Emott Coxe Rest unto M'gett my wiffe whom I appoint executrix with my sonne Rowland Mast[r] Rowland Rydgeley, overseer Proved 1551 in Bishop's Registry Inventory praysyde by Robert Gresbrooke and others xxx June 5 Edw VI. S'ma to[lis] xv[li] iiij[s]

1587 October 12. Administration of the effects of Thom's fflecher of Chesterfield, granted by the Bishop's Registry. The Inventory, taken 18 Dec 1587, and exhibited 22 Jan 1587, alone is preserved Summa totalis Ciiij[li] xxvij[s] x[d]

1586. 28 Eliz. August 14. Will of Thomas Fletcher of Darbie in the Countye of Darbie Miller. Body to be buried in All Saints Church in Darbie Bequeaths legacies to the children of brother Richard Fletcher, brother William Fletcher the children of Thomas Norman deceased, the children of William Eginto' of Howbruck, the children of Robert Doringto', sister Grace dwelling in London, the children of Thomas Shepherd deceased, my Aunt ffletchar, my Aunt Cicilie, her daughter, my godchildren, Nicholas Harwood, the children of Thomas Bagaley, the children of Alexander Dawson, poor, at my buryal, Thom's Ball, Raphe Pilsley, William Roy, Thomas Bramley, Cicilie ffoye, Als Dawson, J Hales Halam, Margaret Hudson, residue to Ann ffletchar his daughter, whom he appoints sole executrix. Overseers, brothers Richard and William and brother-in-law Antony Blodworthe. If daughter Ann dies before marriage, overseers to have 30*l*, rest amongst his sister's children. Inventory taken 7 June 1587 Will proved in Bishop's Registry

30 Eliz, June 10. Will of Thomas Flecher of the Hamsh in the paryshe of Staveley in the County of Derby husbandman. To Wife An Flecher. Elizabeth

* Communicated by W. G Dimock Fletcher, Esq, B A

Holland, and two of her children. Arthur Fletcher, Grace Fletcher, Jane Fletcher, and Mary Fletcher, my children. Ether Walshe Ann Fletcher and Arthur Fletcher, Executors. Edward Kay, sup'visor Inventory taken 30 Oct. 1590 by George Flecher and others Apud Chesterfield 12 Dec 1590. Proved in Bishop's Registry

1725 12 George, Nov 4. Will of Mary ffletcher of Cannock, co. Stafford, widow and relict of Thomas ffletcher late of Cannock deceased Cordwayner To daughter Ann ffletcher, son Thomas ffletcher, son William ffletcher, daughter Jane ffletcher, daughter ffrances, daughter Mary Wootten Son Thomas ffletcher and daughter ffrances ffletcher executor and executrix Will executed in the presence of Daniel Knight, John Fletcher, and Thomas Smith. Inventory appraised 2 Dec. 1725 by Thomas Gaunt and Daniel Knight Will proved 11 February 1725, in the Court of the Dean and Chapter of Lichfield by Thomas Fletcher and Frances Fletcher.

1691 September 25. Administration of the effects of Thomas Fletcher, late of the parish of Cannock deceased, was granted by the Court of the Dean and Chapter of Lichfield to Thomas Fletcher of Cannock, Ellen his widow having renounced. Inventory taken 23 Sept. 1691 by William Averill of Cannock and Richard Whitehouse.

1714. July 14. Will of Thomas Fletcher of Cannock, co Stafford To my two daughters Catherine and Elizabeth Fletcher, £100 each, all my freehold lands in Great Wirley in the parish of Cannock to be charged with the payment. Personal estate to wife Catherine for life, remainder to son Thomas Wife Catherine, sole executrix. Witnesses: Isabel Alport, Elizabeth Hide, Ann Hide. Proved at Lichfield in Court of Dean and Chapter 13 July 1718 by Catherine ffletcher Inventory taken 28 March 1718 by Walter Byrch and Humphrey Short.

173½ Jan. 4 Will of Catherine ffletcher of Great Wirley, widow and relict of Thomas Fletcher late of Wirley, co Stafford. To daughter Catherine Hodgetts, my father-in-law Thomas Richards, my daughter Elizabeth Fletcher; my daughter Ann Fletcher Residue to my son Thomas Fletcher. Executor, son Thomas Fletcher. Witnesses Elizabeth Keen, Elizabeth Haddock, John Walker Proved in the Court of the Dean and Chapter of Lichfield 23 February 1731 by Thomas Fletcher.

There are about 200 Fletcher Wills and Administrations dated prior to the year 1700 at Lichfield.

REA, MARSTON, AND COPE FAMILIES.

ENTRIES ON A FLY-LEAF OF A BOOK OF COMMON PRAYER. Folio. Cambridge. 1754.*

Mary Rea, born March the 14th a quarter past 3 o'clock in the morning 1739. Married December 26th 1763 to Thomas Marston.

Margaret Rea Marston born October 30th 1764 at half past 5 in the morning, married the 22 of $\frac{\text{October}}{8}$ 1791 at Kensington Church at 10 o'clock in the morning to John Jenkins died Dec[br] 26th 1808

Elizabeth *Rae* Marston born December 6th 1774 half-past six in the morning and Christened at St Martin's Church January 1st 1775 Died Dec. 18, 1849

Emma Marston Jenkins born August 30th 1795 died 21st Dec. 1831 daughter of John and Margaret Jenkins.

Matilda Marston Jenkins born August 17, 1797 daughter of John and Margaret Jenkins married Charles Cope at St Pancras Church May 31st, 1828.

Arthur, son of Charles and Matilda Cope born March 22nd 1829

Emma, daughter of Charles and Matilda Cope born August 13th 1830.

Francis, son of Charles and Matilda Cope born 12 October 1832

Kate, daughter of Charles and Matilda Cope born March 11th 1836 died 9th Nov[r] 1836.

* Communicated by R Hovenden, Esq

EXTRACTS FROM THE REGISTERS OF BURIALS IN THE PARISH OF CHELTENHAM, GLOUCESTERSHIRE.*

[These extracts, arranged chronologically, are illustrative of names and dates in the "Monumental Inscriptions in the Parish Church, Cheltenham, Gloucestershire" which have been published in the last volume. In a few cases, as may be perceived, there are slight discrepancies between the Inscriptions and the Registers; and (not to refer to those persons who were buried elsewhere) the names of some which appear in the former, are not to be found in the latter. This, and the fact that there is not any register forthcoming for a period of nearly twenty-three years (from July 15, 1653, to June 4, 1676), will account for the non-appearance of some names and dates in the following list. With the exception of this break, the registers of baptisms, marriages, and burials are continuous from November, 1558, to the present time; the books are sixty-three in number, and are in good condition.]

$161\frac{7}{8}$	February 23.	Edmund Wallwyn [Walweyne], Gentleman.
1620	August 2.	Mrs Anne Higgs
1632.	April 9.	Henry Lane, of Sandford [Cheltenham].
1643	August 9	Jane, ye wife of John English, Dr in Div.
1644.	September 22.	John Lygon, of Arle [Cheltenham], Esqr.
1646.	September 30.	Margery, ye wife of Walter Lane
1647.	November 26	John English, Dr in Divinity, ye Rector here.
		[The date of Dr. English's death is not given on the monument, though he left a space for it. For sundry particulars of him, see 'Notes and Queries,' 5th S., viii. 67, 179, 359, 395.]
$164\frac{8}{9}$.	January 27.	Barnaby [Bernard] Higgs, Gent.
1676.	December 31.	Henry Sturmy, Mercer [General Dealer]
1678.	May 5.	Katherine Lady Dormer.
		[Daughter of John Lygon, Esq., of Arle Court, Cheltenham, and wife of Sir Fleetwood Dormer, of Arle Court, who emigrated to Virginia. But he appears to have returned, for in one of the Cheltenham registers there is this entry:—"Dyed here ye 27th (August, 1696) Sir Fleetwood Dormer, Kt." He was third son of Sir Fleetwood Dormer, of Lee Grange and Purston, whose grandson was created a baronet in 1661. See Burke's 'Extinct and Dormant Baronetcies,' p. 162, London, 1844.]
——	December 17.	Judith Jones, daughter to Mr Robert Jones.
$167\frac{8}{9}$.	March 21	Thomas Higges, of Sandford
1679.	September 8.	Sarah, daugh. to Mr William Roberts.
——	September 27	Thomas, son to Mr William Roberts.
1680.	November 20.	Mr William Prynn.
		[Not to be confounded with his namesake. See 'Notes and Queries,' 5th S., viii. 207, 279, 517.]
1682.	August 26.	Walter Cox, of Alstone.
——	September 26.	Mr Richard Wood, son to Mr Rowland Wood, of Brookrup [Brookthorpe, Gloucestershire].
1683.	September 24	Mary Buckle, Widdow, aged near 95.
1684.	December 22.	John Buckle, of ye Lane
$168\frac{4}{5}$.	January 2.	Mrs Mary Pates, Widdow.
——	January 17.	Mrs Anne Gregory, of ye Mill.
1686.	November 24.	Mr Richard Banaster [Bannister].
1688.	April 12.	Mrs Sarah Cox, of Alstone
——	April 13.	Mr John Pates, of Alston.
——	July 8.	Mr Thomas Watters.

* Communicated by the Rev. BEAVER H. BLACKER, M.A., Cheltenham.

1689.	August 30.	Mr John Buckle, of Woodmacott [Woodmancote, Bishop's Cleeve, Gloucestershire].
169$\frac{0}{1}$	January 20	Mrs Joyce Banister, Widow.
1691.	December 5.	Anne, wife of Edward Mitchel, Gent
169$\frac{1}{2}$.	February 16.	John, son of Thom Packer, of Arle, Gent.
1692	July 25.	Walter Ireland, Gent
169$\frac{2}{3}$.	January 23.	Mary, wife of Joseph Ludlow, Gent.
1694	April 22.	George, son of Thomas Packer, of Arle.
——	May 6.	Alice Gynes, Wid.
——	December 24.	Sarah Howlet.
169$\frac{4}{5}$.	January 26.	Elizabeth, wife of William Sloper.
1695.	July 22.	Mary, wife of Edward Mitchell, Gent.
——	October 1.	Joseph, son of Thomas Packer, of Arle.
169$\frac{5}{6}$.	March 28.	John, son of Henry St Leger, Mercer.
1696.	July 29	John, son of James Etheridge.
——	November 27.	Mary, wife of Richard Bannister.
1697.	April 12.	Lodwick, son of Thomas Packer, of Arle.
——	August 23.	Mrs Ann Pryn, Widow.
1698.	August 20.	Edward, son of Edward Mitchell, Gent.
1699.	April 7.	Mary fframe [Freame], of Norledge [? Northleach, Gloucestershire], Widdow.
——	May 14.	Anne Carnell [Carnoll], Widdow.
——	May 19.	Lodowick, son of Thomas Packer, Gent.
——	October 4.	Joseph Arkell.
1700.	August 14.	John, son of James Beckett, of Alston.
——	November 15.	Mary Whyttorn [Whithorne]
170$\frac{1}{2}$.	January 5.	Roberd Roggers, Gent. [Revd Robert Rogers], Master of the free Scoole. [Master of the Cheltenham Grammar School, and described on the Manor Rolls as "a good man and excellent scholar."]
1702.	July 29.	ffrances Pates, Widdow, of Alston.
——	October 9.	ffrancis Owen [illegible] of Norledge [? Northleach] [Master of the Cheltenham Grammar School.]
170$\frac{2}{3}$.	January 17.	Cox, son of Will. Roberts, Gent.
1703.	August 7.	Sarah, wife of Thomas Ashmead.
1704.	March 12.	Ann Hind.
——	July 28.	Shusan, daug. of Tho. Packer, Gent
——	December 29.	Edmund Cotten [Cotton].

(To be continued.)

THE MONUMENTAL INSCRIPTIONS OF THE FAMILY OF HARINGTON, CO. SOMERSET,

AS WELL OF THE DAUGHTERS AS OF THE SONS OF THE HOUSE, WHICH MAY BE FOUND IN THE CATHEDRAL OF BRISTOL, THE ABBEY OF BATH, AND IN SEVERAL OTHER PARISH CHURCHES NEAR THOSE CITIES.*

M I. in Bristol Cathedral on an oval tablet encircled by a wreath, set up near the Choristers' room in the South Aisle

In remembrance of Rowland Searchfield S T P Bishop of this See, who departed this life Oct 11th Ano Domi 1622 Also of *Edward Chetwynd*† *S T P Deane of*

* Communicated by the Rev FRANCIS J. POYNTON, M A , Rector of Kelston

† The marriage of Dr Chetwynd with Helena Harington, eldest dau of Sir John Harington, Knight, of Kelston, took place at Kelston 26th Oct. 1620. The Dean was of the family of

this Cathedral Church, who departed this life May 13th *An^{o} D^{i}* 1639, *and Helena his wife deceased Nov^{r}* 7th *An^{o} Dom^{i}* 1628 Also of . . . . . . The remains of all these persons were interred* near the Com^{n} Table of this Cathedral Church

---

M I. at Kelston cut in hard grey stone; formerly on the Chancel floor, and now set up in the Churchyard wall (1877).

In memory of
Sir John Harington K^{nt} 1612
John Esqr - - 1654
John Esqr - - 1700
Henry Esqr - - 1769
In line descended from Johannes Baron
de Harington in Cumberland created
first Lord of that house 1324 by K Edward II.
Also of Mary, wife of Henry and daughter of
Richard Backwell Esqr 1731
. . . Lady Mary, wife of Sir John Harington
daughter of Sir Geo Rogers 1634
. . . Helena wife of John Esqr daughter of
Benjamin Gostlett Esqr 1713
. . . Gostlett Esqr son of John (Harington) Esqr
1706.

Mural Tablet inserted in the churchyard wall, Kelston.—

Hic jacet Maria
uxor Johannis Harington Armiger
Filia Petri Specot de Thornbury
in comitate Devon Armig'
Quæ obiit 24th Aug^{to} A^{o} Dom^{i}
1660 †

Monument in the church of Kelston, surmounted by a shield of Arms Quarterly, Harington and Specot of Devon. Harington 1 and 4, Specot 2 and 3.

Here lyeth the Body of
John Harington
Son of John Harington Esq
and Mary his wife daughter
and coheir of Peter Specot of
Thornbury in Devon
who died the 20th day
of Feby 1674 ‡

(*To be continued.*)

Chetwynd of Ingestre, co Stafford, came to the Deanery from Sutton Colefield Rectory, co Warwick, was also Vicar of Banwell co Somerset His son John who edited Sir Jno Harington's 'Treatise on the State of the Church,' was born at Banwell, and was subsequently Vicar of the Temple Church, Bristol

* From this it is evident that the tablet with these names is a mere record of other stones or monuments which have been displaced, and are no longer extant Fragments of the Arms from off the originals are inserted in the wall near the tablet —F J P

† The above memorial is specially valuable, as no record of this interment occurs in the Registers, owing to an hiatus at this period for 20 years —F J P.

‡ This gentleman (who was the heir presumptive) died vitâ patris, his father surviving him by four years died in 1700 —F J P

s of

Pedigree of the Longs of Semington.

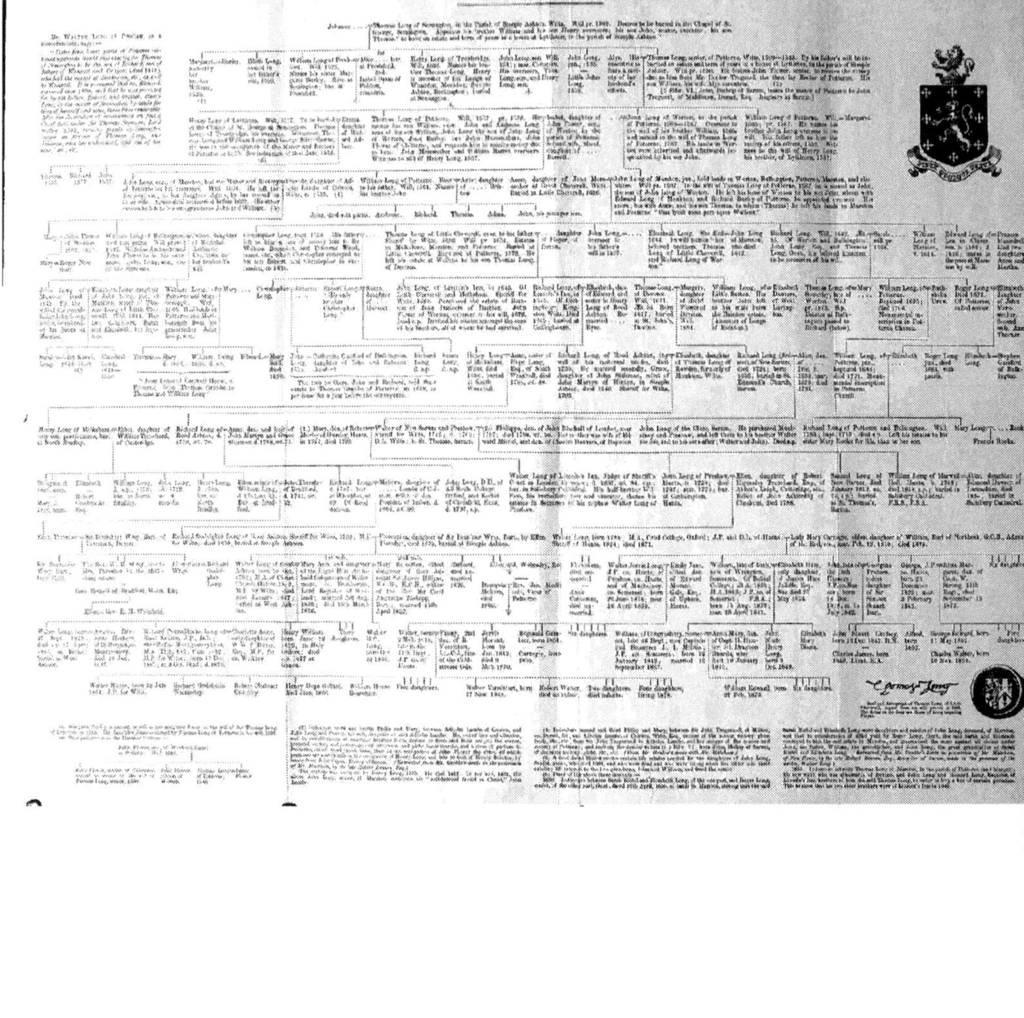

Gresham Wills.

(*Continued from* Vol III., p. 13.)

ANNE GRESHAM, 1697.*

In the name of God Amen The seaventh day of May in the yeare of our Lord one thousand six hundred ninety and seaven I Anne Gresham of the parish of St Nicholas in Guildford in the County of Surrey widow being in good health of body and sound memory and understanding (God's holy name be praised) yet considering the frailty and the uncertainty of Humane life and nature doe take this opportunity to make and ordaine this my last Will and Testament in manner and forme following ffirst I com'end my soule into the hands of my dearest Lord and Saviour Jesus Christ humbly beseeching him to wash it tho'ly in his most pretious blood from all the defilements it hath contracted in this world My body I would have buried at Haslemore decently as neare the body of my deare Husband which is there interred as may be according to the discretion of my Nephew Thomas Molyneux of Losely in the County aforesaid Esqr Whom I doe hereby make my sole Executor of this my last Will and Testament Next in humble acknowledgm^t and thankfulness to Almighty God for his mercies and goodness towards me and in dutifull observance of the desire and request of my late deare Husband I give and bequeath unto the Master and Governors of Christ's Hospitall within the City of London for the time being the sum'e of Two hundred pounds of good English money to be paid within two yeares after my decease and then by them with the consent and approbac'on of my said Executor to be imployed in such acts of mercy and charity as they and he together shall thinke fitt Provided nevertheless that if the Master and Governors of the said Hospitall for the time being shall after my decease have take or claime any legacie or guifte of any part of my late Husband's personall estate by vertue or force of any words or bequest contained in his last Will and Testament Then in such case my will intent and meaneing is not to give them any thing and that this legacie and guift of Two Hundred pounds to them as aforesaid shall be absolutely void and null to all intents and purposes anything herein to the contrary notwithstanding and I doe will that my said Executor shall have the said two hundred pounds Item I give unto my Nephew Mr John Gooff and to his two sisters M^rs ffrances Jorandon and Mrs Judith Ward the sum'e of Ten pounds apeice to be paid within one yeare after my decease Item I give to my said Nephew Gooff my Tankard Caudle cup and cover and six spoons of silver and my lynnen The remainder of my Lynnen I will to be divided betweene his said two sisters equally Item I give to my cozen More Molyneux the sum'e of One hundred pounds of good English money to be imployed by my Executor (his ffather) in paying and dischargeing the like sum'e of the Debts of Sr William More, Baronet deceased yett lying on Losely estate Which said Estate will descend or come to the said More after his ffather's decease Item I give to the foure younger children of my said Executor Thomas Molyneux the sum'e of one hundred pounds of like money to be divided among 'em in manner following that is to say To Margrit Elizabeth and Nathaniel the sum'e of Twenty pounds a piece And to Ann the sume of fforty pounds if they severally shall attaine and accomplish the age of twenty one yeares or be marryed which shall first happen And in case any of 'em doe dye before the said age and before then marryage Then I will that the dividend and share of every of them so deceaseing shall be equally divided betweene the survivors and survivor of them share and share alike But in case they all happen to dye under twenty one yeares of age and before their marryage and that my said Executor then happen alsoe to be dead In such I will that my said cozen More Molyneux their elder brother shall have the said Hundred pounds given to his said

* Widow of James Gresham of Haslemere, whose will occurs in Vol II, p 465

brother and sisters as aforesaid Item I give to the Maid who shall happen to live with me (a yearely servant) at the time of my decease all my weareinge apparell All the rest and residue of my goods money rents bonds securityes whatsoever for money and personall estate whatsoever the legacies herein and hereby given together with all such debts as I shall owe at my death being truly paid and satisfied my funerall expences discharged and five pounds to the poore of the parish where I shall happen to dye and five pounds to the poore of the parish where I shall be buryed (if distinct parishes) distributed by my Executor I give and bequeath to my said Executor Thomas Molyneux And I doe hereby revoke annull and make void all former and other Wills and Testaments Guifts Legacies and Executors at any time heretofore made given will'd or ordained by me And I do make and ordaine these presents to be my last Will and Testament and none other or otherwise In witness whereof I have subscribed my name and sett my seale the day and yeare above written unto each of these two sheets wherein my true and only last Will and Testament is contained.

*

These two sheets were signed sealed published and declared by the said Anne Gresham as and for her last Will and Testament the day of the date hereof in the presence of us—Hugh Eaton—Thomas West—Thomas Badslad Memorandum—The witnesses hereunto did sett their hands hereunto in my presence the seaventh day of May one thousand six hundred ninety seaven—Anne Gresham.

[Proved at London 20 June, 1700, by Thos. Molyneux, Esq., the Ex'or.]

ELIZABETH GRESHAM, 1718.†

In the Name of God Amen I Elizabeth Gresham of the parish of St Ann within the Liberty of Westminster in the County of Middlesex Spinster being in good health of body and of perfect memory and understanding (God be praised for the same) doe make and ordain this my last Will and Testament in Writeing in manner and forme following ffirst and principally I commend my soule into the hands of Almighty God with hope of Eternall salvation in and through the merrite and intercession of my Lord and Saviour Jesus Christ And my body I committ to the Earth to be privately buryed by my Executors hereinafter named without pomp or shew in the Country and not in London or Westmr or within seaven miles thereof and to be attended with a Herse and two Mourning Coaches only And as for such worldly Estate as it hath pleased God to bless me with I will that the same shall goe and be disposed of as follows (vizt) I give and bequeath unto the Right honourable the Countess of Stamford the sume of ffive hundred pounds Item unto my Cousin John Lee of Adlington in the County of Chester Esq. I give the sume of Two hundred pounds And if the said John Lee shall happen to dye before me

* From the original will in the P.C.C. The quarterings on the seal are—1. Az. on a cross arg. five martlets. [MORE.] 2. Arg. four lozenges conjoined in pale, each lying fesseways sa. [DANIELL.] 3. Barry of six or and vert a bend gu. [POYNINGS.] 4. Per pale az. and gu. a fess dancetté counterchanged. [*Query* whether these are the arms of Fitzpaine differenced. Burke says that Poynings quarter Fitzpaine, and gives the arms Per pale az. and gu. a fess counterchanged. Here the fess is dancetté. The coat was in any case brought in by Poynings.] The will is throughout in her own handwriting; the signature and seal occur three times, and it is endorsed "My Will."

† She was the only child of Sir Edward Gresham, Bart., and Dame Martha his wife, whose administration will be found in Vol. II., p. 52.

Then my will and meaning is that his said legacy of Two hundred pounds shall goe and be divided in equall proportions betweene such Children of the said John Lee as att the time of my decease shall be liveing both sonns and daughters And unto Elizabeth Lee and ffrances Lee the two daughters of my said Cousin John Lee I give the sume of One hundred pounds a piece and in case either of them the said Elizabeth Lee and Lucy ffrances Lee shall happen to dye before me Then my will and meaning is that the legacy of her so dying shall goe and belong to and be payable and paid unto the survivor of them the said Elizabeth and Lucy ffrances Lee Item I give and bequeath unto my cousin Henry Colchester Citizen and Drugster of London the sume of Two hundred pounds And if the said Henry Colchester shall happen to dye before me Then my will and meaning is that his said Legacy of Two hundred pounds shall goe and be divided betweene such Children of the said Henry Colchester as shall be liveing att the time of my decease both sonns and daughters in equall proportions share and share alike And unto my Cousin Mary Colchester his daughter my God daughter I give the sume of Twenty pounds And in case of her death before me Then my will and meaning is that the said Legacy of Twenty pounds shall goe and be divided betweene such other Children of the said Henry Colchester both sonns and daughters as shall be liveing at the time of my decease in such shares and proportions as my said cousin Henry Colchester (if he shall be then liveing) shall by any writeing under his hand and seale attested by two or more Credible witnesses or by his last Will and Testament attested as aforesaid direct or appoint Butt in case of his death before me or for want of such direction or appointment then to be divided betweene them in equall proportions share and share alike Item to my Cousin Jane Grant the wife of John Grant Doctor in Divinity I give the sume of One hundred pounds and in case she shall happen to dye before me then I give the said sume of One hundred pounds to John the son and Jane and Hester the two daughters of the said Doctor John Grant and Jane his wife equally to be divided betweene them share and share alike if they shall be all liveing at the time of my decease butt in case of the death of any one of them the said John Jane and Hester the sonn and daughters before me then my will is that the said sume of One hundred pounds shall goe and be divided in equall proportions betweene such of them the said John the sonn and Jane and Hester the daughters as att the time of my decease shall be surviveing And in case of the death of any two of them the said John Jane and Hester the sonn and daughters before me then my will is that all the said sume of One hundred pounds shall be payable and paid to such of them the said John Jane and Hester the sonn and daughters as shall then happen to be the only survivor Item I give and bequeath unto the said John Grant Jane Grant and Hester Grant the son and daughters the sume of ffifty pounds a peice and my will and meaning is that in case of the death of any one of them the said John Jane and Hester the sonn and daughters before me the legacy of him or her soe dying shall goe and be divided in equall proportions betweene such of them the said John Jane and Hester the son and daughters as at the time of my decease shall be surviveing And in case of the death of any two of them the said John Jane and Hester the son and daughters before me then my will and meaning is that the severall Legacies of ffifty pounds a peice shall all of them be payable and paid to such of them the said John Jane and Hester the son and daughters as shall then happen to be the only survivor Item I give and bequeath unto my Cousin Henrietta Howard dresser to the Princess of Wales the sume of ffifty pounds Item I give and bequeath unto my Cousin Mary Pyrke of little or middle Deane in the County of Glouc[r] widow the sume of Twenty pounds and unto my Cousin Thomas Pyrke of little Deane in the said County of Glouc[r] Esq[r] I give the sume of Tenn pounds and unto his daughter my God daughter I give the sume of Tenn pounds Item I give and bequeath unto Dorothy Hobart the daughter of S[r] Henry Hobart late of Blickling in the County of Norfolke Barronett and of his wife both lately deceased the sume of ffifty pounds and to Jane Walters the wife of Walters of the City of Bristoll the sume of ffifty pounds Item I give and bequeath unto Ann the wife of Rauffe ffreke of Hanington in the County of Wilts Gent. and unto Jane Colchester and Elizabeth Colchester the three daughters of my Cousin Maynard Colchester late of Mitchell Deane in the said County of Gloucester Esqr deceased the sume of Twenty pounds a peice And in case the said Ann ffreke shall happen to dye before me then my will and meaning is that her said legacy of Twenty pounds shall goe and be divided betweene such Children of the said Ann ffreke as att the time of my decease shall be liveing both sonns and daughters in equall proportions share and share alike And likewise in case either of them the said Jane Colchester and Elizabeth Colchester shall happen to dye in my life time then my will and meaning is that the legacy of her so dying shall goe and belong to and be payable and paid unto such of them the said Jane and Elizabeth as at the time of my decease shall be surviveing Item I give and bequeath unto Hester Lowndes of the parish of St James within the Liberty of Westminster widow the sume of Two hundred pounds And in case of her death before me I give and bequeath her said Legacy of Two hundred pounds unto Hester Smith the wife of Sebastian Smith of the said parish of St James's Westminster Esqr and daughter of the said Hester Lowndes if she shall be liveing at the time of my decease Item I give and bequeath unto the said Hester Smith the wife of the said Sebastian Smith the sume of Two hundred pounds and unto Elizabeth Basnett of Ealing in the said County of Middlesex widow I give the sume of ffifty pounds And in case of her the said Elizabeth Basnett's death before me I give her said Legacy of ffifty pounds unto Ann Basnett and Elizabeth Basnett the two daughters of the said Elizabeth Basnett widow equally to be divided betweene them share and share alike if they shall be both liveing at the time of my decease but in case of the death of either of them the said Ann and Elizabeth Basnett the daughters before me then my will and meaning is that the said Legacy of ffifty pounds shall all of it goe and be payable and paid unto such of them the said Ann and Elizabeth Basnett the daughters as at the time of my decease shall be surviveing Item I give and bequeath unto the said Ann Basnett daughter of the said Elizabeth Basnett widow the sume of Eight hundred pounds And in case of her death before me I give the said legacy of Eight hundred pounds unto the said Elizabeth Basnett her sister if she shall be liveing at the time of my decease Item I give and bequeath unto the said Elizabeth Basnett the daughter of the said Elizabeth Basnett widow the sume of ffifty pounds And in case of her death before me I give the said Legacy of ffifty pounds unto the said Ann Basnett her sister if she shall be liveing att the time of my decease Item I give and bequeath unto Ann ffeilding the wife of George ffeilding of Windsor in the County of Berks Esqr the sume of ffifty pounds if she shall be living att the time of my decease and unto Elizabeth Wright of the said parish of St Ann's Westminster widow I give the sume of Twenty pounds if she shall be liveing at the time of my decease Item I give and bequeath unto Ann Dawes of the said parish of St Ann's Westminster widow the sume of Twenty pounds if she shall be liveing at the time of my decease And unto Jane Dawes her daughter I likewise give the sume of Twenty pounds if she shall be then living Item I give and bequeath unto Jane Barrell the daughter of Edmund Barrell of Sutton at Hone in the County of Kent Clerke my silver Tea Kettle and Lamp Item I give and bequeath unto Margarett Harris the wife of Thomas Harris of the parish of St Andrews Holbourne London Gent. the sume of One hundred pounds And in case of her death before me I give her said Legacy of One hundred pounds unto Jane Harris and Margarett Harris two daughters of the said Thomas Harris and Margaret his wife equally to be divided betweene them share and share alike if they shall be livinge at the time of my decease Butt in case of the death of either of them the said Jane and Margaret Harris the daughters before me Then my will and meaning is that the said Legacy of One hundred pounds shall all of it goe and be payable and paid unto such other of them the said Jane and Margarett Harris the daughters as at the time of my decease shall be surviveing Item I give and bequeath unto the said Jane Harris and Margarett Harris the daughters the sume of ffifty pounds a peice And in case of the death of either of them the said Jane and Margarett Harris the daughters before me then my will and meaning is that the Legacy of her so dying shall goe and belong to and be payable and paid unto such of them the said Jane and Margarett Harris as at the time of my decease shall be surviveing Item I give and bequeath unto Sarah Bonwick of Darking in the County of Surrey widow the sume of Twenty pounds And in case of her death before me I give her said legacy of Twenty pounds unto Mary Bonwick her daughter if she shall be surviveing at the time of my decease Item I give and bequeath unto the said Mary Bonwick the daughter of the said Sarah Bonwick the sume of Eight hundred pounds my Gold Watch and all my wearing apparell both lynnen and Woollen Item I give and bequeath unto Tindall of the parish of S[t] Paul Covent Garden in the County of Middlesex Apothecary the sume of Twelve pounds and unto John Anderson of Oxstead in the County of Surrey Grocer I alsoe give the sume of ffifteene pounds And likewise unto John Dawling of Westerham in the County of Kent Grocer I give the sume of Thirty pounds Item I give and bequeath unto George Dibble of Limpsfeild in the said County of Surrey Coachman the sume of ffifty pounds And unto Margaret Gilbert the wife of Richard Gilbert of Limpsfeild aforesaid Smith I give the sume of Twenty pounds Item I give and bequeath unto Hester Mills the wife of Marmaduke Mills of Limpsfeild aforesaid Smith the sume of Twenty pounds and in case of her death before me I give her said Legacy of Twenty pounds unto my God daughter Elizabeth Mills their daughter And I likewise give unto the said Elizabeth Mills my God daughter the sume of Twenty pounds Item I give and bequeath unto Robert Steele Edward Steele and Deborah Steele the sonns and daughter of Ralph Steele late of Titsey in the said County of Surrey Clerke deceased to each of them the sume of Twenty pounds for or towards a stock to inable them to sett upp in and carry on the trade or buisness to which they shall respectively happen to be educated or brought upp or as they shall otherwise thinke fitt to follow or imploy themselves in for gaining a livelyhood And my will and meaning is that their respective legacies of Twenty pounds a peice shall be paid to them the said Robert Edward and Deborah Steele respectively when and so soone as they shall have attained their respective ages of one and twenty yeares And my will and meaning is in case any one of them the said Robert Edward and Deborah Steele shall happen to dye before me or before he or she shall have attained his or her said age of one and twenty yeares that the legacy of him or her so dying shall goe and be paid in equall proportions share and share alike betweene such of them the said Robert Edward and Deborah Steele as shall be then livieng and be payable and paid to such survivors at his and her respective age and ages of one and twenty yeares And in case of the death of any two of them the said Robert Edward and Deborah Steele before me or before he or she shall have attained his or her said age of one and twenty yeares then my will and meaning is that the said legacies of Twenty pounds a piece shall all of them be payable and paid to such only survivor of them the said Robert Edward and Deborah Steele at his or her age of one and twenty yeares Item I give and bequeath to the said Deborah Steele the further sume of ffifty pounds Item I give and bequeath unto William Holloway the sonn of William Holloway of and of Susanna his wife the sume of Twenty pounds for or towards setting him up in the Trade of a shoemaker which he was putt an Apprentice to or for or towards setting him upp in such other Trade as he shall thinke fitt to follow or imploy himselfe in for the obteining a livelyhood the said Legacy of Twenty pounds to be paid him within one month next after he shall have attained his age of one and twenty yeares if the terme of his Apprenticeshipp shall be then expired and if nott within one month next after the expiration thereof And unto Phillip Holloway the younger son of the said William and Susanna Holloway I give the sume of Twenty pounds towards putting him forth an Apprentice to some Trade or imployment to be paid by my Executors hereinafter named to the person to whom he shall be bound an Apprentice whose receipt shall be a sufficient dischairge to my said Executors And I likewise give unto Elizabeth ffrost the daughter of the said Susanna Holloway by a former husband the sume of twenty pounds to be paid her when and so soone as she shall have attained the age of one and twenty yeares

Item to such person as shall happen to live with me as my ffootman at the time of my decease I give the sume of Tenn pounds All the rest and residue of my moneys goods plate houshold stuffe and personall Estate whatsoever and wheresoever after my debtes legacies and ffunerall expences shall be paid and satisfyed I give and bequeath the same unto my said Cousin John Lee and Cousin Henry Colchester equally to be divided betweene them share and share alike To their owne use and uses And I doe hereby constitute and appoint my said Cousin John Lee and Cousin Henry Colchester Executors of this my last Will and Testament And my will and desire is that my debts and ffunerall charges be paid and satisfyed by my said Executors as soone as conveniently they may after my decease and that such legacies for which I have nott herein before appointed any time for payment be paid within Twelve Calendar months next after my decease And in Case any Legatee or Legatees named in this my will shall not have attained to his her or their age or ages of one and twenty yeares at the time or times of his her or their legacy or legacies are hereby directed or appointed to be paid Then my will and mind is that my said Executors shall pay the Legacy and Legacies of such Legatee and Legatees as shall not then have attained his her or their said age or Ages of One and twenty yeares unto the father And in case of his death unto the mother and in case of the death both of father and mother unto the Guardian or Guardians of such Legatee and Legatees not haveing attained his her or their said age or ages of one and twenty yeares or to the person or persons acting as such Guardian or Guardians whose receipt and receipts shall be from time to time a sufficient discharge and discharges unto my said Executors their Executors and Administrators And lastly I do hereby revoke annull and make void all former and other Will and Wills whatsoever by me at any time heretofore made And do declare this to be my last Will and Testament conteined in Eight sheetes of paper In witness whereof I have to the first seaven sheetes of paper wherein this my Will is conteined subscribed my name and to this last sheete thereof sett my hand and seale this One and Twentyeth day of June in the ffourth yeare of the reigne of our Soveraigne Lord George by the grace of God of Greate Brittaine ffrance and Ireland King Defender of the faith &c. Annoq' D'ni 1718.

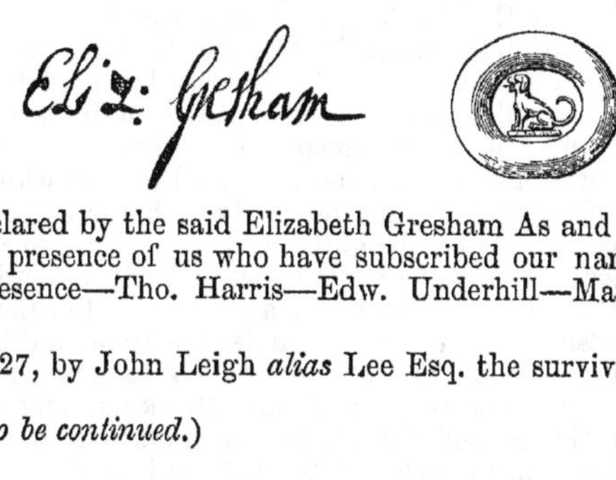

*

Signed sealed published and declared by the said Elizabeth Gresham As and for her last Will and Testament in the presence of us who have subscribed our names as witnesses thereunto in her presence—Tho. Harris—Edw. Underhill—Marke Greene.

[Proved at London March 8, 1727, by John Leigh *alias* Lee Esq. the surviving Ex'or.]

(*To be continued.*)

WARCUP FAMILY.—I should be thankful for information on the following matter: Elizabeth, dau. of Thos. Warcup of Easton Field, Ebor., is said to have married Anthony Lucas of Fenton, Linc. circa 1608, or earlier. What was the exact date of her marriage, and had she any children? The Fenton Register mentions Anne as the wife of Anthony Lucas and mother of his children, so possibly Elizabeth Warcup may have been his first wife, and Anne .... his second.—C. H. LUCAS.

* From the original will in the P.C.C. The seal bears a talbot seiant.

GRANT OF ARMS TO ISAAC HAWKINS BROWNE OF BADGER, CO. SALOP, 1779.*

To All and Singuler to whom these Presents shall come Thomas Browne Esquire Garter Principal King of Arms and Ralph Bigland Esquire Clarenceux King of Arms of the South East and West parts of England from the River Trente southward send greeting. Whereas Isaac Hawkins Browne of Badger in the County of Salop Esquire only child of Isaac Hawkins Browne of Lincoln's Inn in the County of Middlesex Esquire deceased member of Parliament for Wenlock hath represented unto the Right Honorable Thomas Earl of Effingham Deputy with the Royal approbation to the most Noble Charles Duke of Norfolk Earl Marshall and Hereditary Marshall of England that he is desirous of having the Armorial Ensigns borne by his Family confirmed to him with some variation to distinguish his Branch from others of the name and requested his Lordship's Warrant for our exemplifying and confirming the same quarterly with the Arms of Hawkins in memory of his grandmother Anne daughter and at length sole heir of Isaac Hawkins Esq. Barrister at Law to be borne by the descendants of his grandfather William Browne Clerk Prebendary of Lichfield according to the Law of Arms. And forasmuch as his Lordship did by Warrant under his Hand and Seal bearing date the 11th day of May instant authorize and direct Us to grant exemplify and confirm the said Armorial Ensigns of Browne and Hawkins accordingly know ye therefore that we the said Garter and Clarenceux in pursuance of the consent of the said Earl of Effingham and by virtue of the Letters Patent of our several offices to each of us respectively granted under the great Seal of Great Britain do by these presents grant exemplify and confirm to the said Isaac Hawkins Browne the Arms following Quarterly first and fourth Ermine on a Fess counter embattled Sable three escallops Erminois for Browne, Second and third Or on a chevron between three cinquefoils Azure as many Escallops of the field on a Chief per Pale Gules and Sable a Griffin passant Ermine for Hawkins and for Crest on a Mural Coronet a Stork's head erased ermine charged with an Escallop Azure as the same are in margin hereof more plainly depicted to be borne and used for ever hereafter by him the said Isaac Hawkins Browne Esquire and by the Descendants of his Grandfather William

* Communicated by Reginald Stewart Boddington, Esq.

Browne aforesaid with due and proper differences according to the Laws of Arms without the Let or Interruption of any person or persons whatsoever. In witness whereof we the said Garter and Clarenceux Kings of Arms have to these presents subscribed our Names and affixed the Seals of our several offices this 14 day of May in the 19th Year of the Reign of our Sovereign Lord George the third by the Grace of God King of Great Britain France and Ireland Defender of the Faith, etc. and in the year of our Lord 1779.

GENEALOGICAL MEMORANDA RELATING TO THE BROWNE AND HAWKINS FAMILIES.*

William Browne of Etwall, co. Derby.= Will dated 21 July, 1624. Possessed leasehold property at Etwall and freehold at Boylestone.

1. John Browne=.... of Etwall. Purchased estates in Burnaston in Parish of Etwall, Hilton, and Egginton. | .... Survived her son. Lived at Etwall.

2. William Browne.=.... By his father's will took freehold estate in Boylestone. Purchased property at Thurvaston.

1. Elizabeth. — 2. Ellen. 3. Margaret. — 4. Ann.

.... Browne.=....

William Browne of Thurvaston, co. Derby, Aug. 1725.

William Browne, had property=.... dau'r of .... and at Burnaston, and bought property in co. Stafford. After his marriage lived at Uttoxeter. Buried 6 August, 1674, at Uttoxeter. M.I. | .... dau'r of .... and widow of .... Jefferye (by whom she had a dau'r who married ... Webb). Had a good jointure & a house at Woodford, near Uttoxeter, co. Stafford. Died 1715, aged 75.

Daughters, one of whom survived her brother William Browne. She lived at Etwall, and got possession of family papers, plate, and linen.

William Browne, M.A. of Trin. Coll. Cam., and Fellow of that College for seven years. Property at Burnaston, co. Derby, and purchased Fauld in parish of Hanbury, co. Stafford. Incumbent of Burton-on-Trent, Vicar of Wing, and Rector of Grove, co. Bucks. Prebendary of Gaia Major, Diocese of Lichfield. Buried 12 January, 1746, at Wing, co. Bucks. =Ann, 2nd dau'r and coheiress of Isaac Hawkins. Married 31 January, 1705, at Burton-on-Trent. Buried 2 November, 1739, at Burton-on-Trent.

A

* Communicated by Reginald Stewart Boddington, Esq.

A

1. Isaac Hawkins Browne, born 21 Jan. 1706, at Burton-on-Trent, & bapt. there 27 Jan. 1706. M.A. Trin. Coll. Cam., having been previously at Lichfield & Westminster Schools. Barrister-at-Law of Lincoln's Inn. M.P. for Wenlock. F.R.S. In 1754 published his Latin poem "De Animi Immortalitate," and wrote English poems. Died 26 February, 1760, in Great Russell St., Bloomsbury, intestate. M.I. in Chapel of Trin. Coll. Cam. = Jane, daughter and co-heiress of Venerable Archdeacon David Trimnell, Archdeacon of Leicester, Precentor of Lincoln, etc. See 'Westminster Abbey Registers,' published by Harl. Soc. p. 42, etc. Marr. 10 Feb. 1744. Died 6 October, 1783, aged 66. M.I. at Badger, co. Salop.

2. Philip Hawkins Browne, bapt. 18 July, 1708, at Burton-on-Trent, and there buried Dec. 18, 1710.

3. Anne, bapt. 24 Sept. 1710, at Burton-on-Trent. Marr. Settlement dated 22 October, 1742. Died 22 April, 1788, and buried at Burton-on-Trent, where is M.I. = Edward Cheney, Attorney, of Monyash, co. Derby, etc. Bur. 22 June, 1773, at Monyash. See Burke's 'Landed Gentry,' Cheney of Badger Hall, co. Salop.

Henrietta, eldest daughter of Hon. Edward Hay, Governor of Barbadoes (by his first wife Mary, dau'r of Peter Flower), 4th son of George Henry, 7th Earl of Kinnoull. Born 20 August, 1753. Married 11 May, 1788. Died 11 April, 1802, s. p. Buried at Badger, where is M.I. Her sister Mary marr. 7 Oct. 1771, Right Rev. Lewis Bagot, D.C.L., successively Bishop of Bristol, Norwich, and St. Asaph. Brother of 1st Lord Bagot. = Isaac Hawkins Browne, born 7 Dec. 1745. Educated at Westminster and Hertford Coll. Oxford. F.R.S., D.C.L. Barrister-at-Law of Inner Temple. M.P. for Bridgnorth for 30 years. High Sheriff for co. Salop, 1783. Sold Fauld, in Hanbury, in 1785. Purchased Badger Hall, co. Salop. Died 30 May, 1818. Buried at Badger. Monument there by Sir Francis Chantrey. Devised his estates, subject to his wife's life interest, to the descendants of his Aunt Anne, who married Edward Cheney. = Elizabeth, 2nd surviving dau. of Thomas Boddington of Clapton, co. Middlesex. See Vol. II., pages 188 and 244. Born 9 Feb. 1769. Died 10 Oct. 1839. Buried at Badger. M.I. there. s.p.

Robert Hawkins of Newport. co. Salop =

William Hawkins of Newport, co. Salop. =

William Hawkins of Newport, co. Salop. Died 29 Aug. 1735, aged 51. Buried at Newport. = Catharine, dau'r of John Gisborne of Derby.

A

A

1. William Hawkins, Barrister-at-Law.

2. Isaac Hawkins, Attorney, of Burton-on-Trent. Died 8 Feb. 1800, aged 91. Buried at Burton-on-Trent. Appointed as his executors, Isaac Hawkins Browne and Rev. Thomas Gisborne. = Anne, dau'r of Rev. James Gisborne, Rector of Staveley, co. Derby, and Prebendary of Durham. (See Burke's 'Landed Gentry,' Gisborne of Yoxall Lodge, co. Stafford, etc.)

3. Philip Hawkins of St. Ives, co. Hunts.

1. Mary. = Richard Muckleston of London.

2. Jane. = John Holland of Shrewsbury, Draper.

3. Catherine. = Joseph Muckleston of (?) Shrewsbury, Brother of above Richard Muckleston.

.... Hawkins of Muxton, in parish of Lilleshall, co. Salop, a family possession of long time. = ... dau'r of .... Hawkins. Died ... 1717, very aged.

Isaac Hawkins, Barrister-at-Law, of Burton-on-Trent. Buried 28 March, 1713, at Burton-on-Trent. = Elizabeth, dau'r of Daniel Watson of Burton-on-Trent, an active Parliamentarian, M.P. for Lichfield. Barrister-at-Law, of Gray's Inn. J.P. for co. Stafford. Son of Henry Watson, tanner, of Burton-on-Trent, by Anne his wife.

Rebecca. Died 25 Jan. 1756, at Newport, co. Salop, s.p. = Richard Walthall of Malin's Lee, co. Salop. High Sheriff, co. Chester, 1715. See Ormerod's 'Cheshire,' vol. iii. Died 7 June, 1729.

Anne. = William Browne, Clerk in Holy Orders.

See Browne Ped.

Elizabeth. ? died unmarried.

Robert Alionby Slaney of Hatton Grange, co. Salop, etc., married 7 February, 1812, Elizabeth, only child of William Hawkins Muccleston, M.D., and sole heiress of her uncle Joseph Muccleston of Walford, Sheriff for co. Salop, 1788. See Burke's 'Landed Gentry.'

See Thornton of Brockhall, co. Northants, for marriages with family of Trimnell. Burke's 'Landed Gentry' and Baker's 'History of Co. Northants.' I ask for additions to these pedigree notes of families of Browne and Hawkins. Isaac Hawkins Browne believed his ancestors to be of the same family as that of Shredicote in parish of Bradley, co. Stafford, but this has not been proved.

BROWNE PEDIGREE.

From the Visitation of Co. Derby, by Sir William Dugdale, 1662, in the College of Arms.

Thomas Browne of Shre*dd*icote in the parish of Bradley in com. Stafford. Ob. Anno 1633. = Apo*ll*ina, dau'r to George Southwike of London, Merchant, widow of William Fairfax of London, goldsmith.

A

A

1. Thomas. Died unmarried.

2. George Browne of Shre*d*icote, cœlebs. Ob. 1652.

3. William, Barrister of Gray's Inn, aged 57, 1662.

4. Edmund Browne of Hungry Bentley, in com. Derby, æt. 51 A° 1662. = Dorothy, 2nd dau'r of Sir Edward Vernon of Sudbury, in com. Derby, Knt.

5. Edward Browne of Waldley, in com. Derby.

1. Mary. = Carew Stury of Rossal, in com. Salop. (See Harl. MS. 1396, 'Visit. of Salop, 1623.')

2. Apo*l*ina. Died unmarried.

1. Thomas. Living 1662.	4. Rupert. Living 1662.	7. Charles. Living 1662.	10. Mark. Living 1662.	Edward. Died young.
2. Edmund. Living 1662.	5. George. Living 1662.	8. Walter. Living 1662.		Benjamin. Died young.
3. William. Living 1662.	6. John. Living 1662.	9. Philip. Living 1662.		Richard. Died young.

1. Mary. 2. Apo*l*ina. 3. Dorothy. 4. Margaret. 5. Elizabeth.

(See Glover's 'History of Co. Derby' for continuation of this pedigree.)

ADMINISTRATIONS, GRESHAM FAMILY.

(*Continued from* Vol. II., p. 24.)

1572. 24 Jan. Commission to Margaret Gresham, the relict, and to Thomas Gresham, son of Paul Gresham of Tekingcote, co. Rutland, gent., deceased, to administer goods, etc.

1574. 18 Nov. Commission to William Crofte, next of kin of Paul Gresham, late of Tekingcote, co. Rutland, deceased, to administer, inasmuch as no goods had as yet come to hand.

1585–6. Jan. 21 day. Commission to John Partridge, of the parish of St. Thomas the Apostle in the City of London, one of the creditors of John Gresham, late while he lived of the parish of St. Helen in the City of London, deceased, to administer.

*

*

* From deed of 6 Dec. 8 Eliz., relating to Sanderstead, among Col. Wigsell's deeds.

1634–5. The last day of March. Commission to Francis Sholdham and Mary his wife, Anne Willson, and Edward Rust, next of kin to the Lady Anne Gresham, widow,* late of the Precincts of Christ Church in the City of Norwich, to administer.

1768. 13 May. Administration of Richard Gresham, formerly Lieutenant of Foot under the command of Col. Batterot, but at Inverness in North Britain, and Lieutenant on half pay, a widower, deceased, granted to Beatrice Edwards, widow, the cousin german, next of kin, and curatrix or guardian of William Gresham, a minor, the natural and lawful son and only child of the said deceased.

1785. 10 Sep. Administration of Charles Gresham, formerly of Christ Church, Newgate, London, late of Bengal, a bachelor, granted to Susanna Halliday, wife of Robert Halliday, the sister and next heir of the deceased.

1794. 2 June. Administration of Edward Gresham, late of Limpsfield, deceased, a bachelor, granted to Sir John Gresham, Bart., the nephew and only next of kin of the said deceased. Sub £20.

TITSEY LINE.

1564. 17 June. Commission to William Gresham, natural and lawful father of James Gresham† of Tittesey, deceased, to administer the goods of the said James during the minority of Thomas Gresham and William Gresham, brothers of the said deceased.

1576. 21 May. Commission to William Gresham, the father, and Thomas Gresham, the brother, and Mary Gresham the sister of James Gresham, late of Tytsey, co. Surrey, to administer.

1576–7. 2 Jan. Commission to Elizabeth Gresham, natural and lawful daughter of the lady Catherine Gresham,‡ widow, late of the parish of St. Michael Basinghawe to administer.

1676. 25 April. Letters of administration to John Warner, principal creditor of Thomas Gresham,§ late of y^e fleete prison in the parish of St. Bride's, London, Esqre, to administer all and singular the goods chattels and debts.

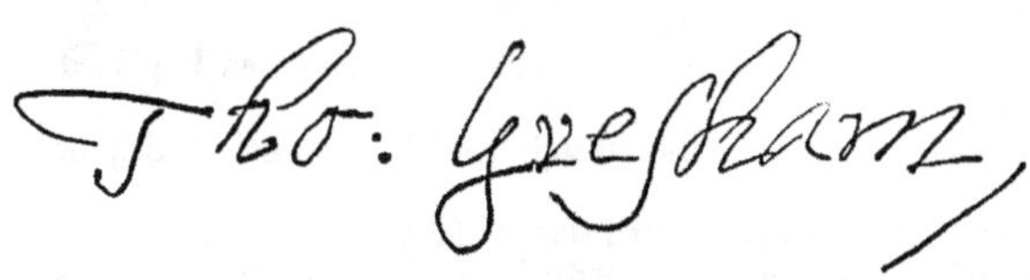

1751. 26 February. Administration of the goods, chattels, and credits of Sir Charles Gresham,|| Baronet, late belonging to the East India Ship the Mumford in parts beyond the seas, a batchelor, deceased, was granted to Dame Ann Gresham, widow, the natural and lawful mother and next of kin of the said deceased.

* She was widow of Sir Richard Gresham, Kt., whose will occurs at page 284.

† He was eldest son of William Gresham, Esq., whose will occurs at p. 18.

‡ She was widow and second wife of Sir John Gresham of Titsey, Kt., whose will occurs at p. 12.

§ He was eldest son of Sir Edward Gresham, Kt., by Mary Clerke, his first wife, and was disinherited by his father. The seal and signature are from a deed of 28 Aug. 1649, relating to Tatsfield, among the Titsey muniments.

|| He was the fifth Baronet, and eldest son of Sir Marmaduke Gresham, whose will occurs at p. 89. He died under age, and was succeeded by Sir John Gresham, the sixth and last Baronet.

Examples of Armorial Book-Plates.

RIDGWAY.*

This book-plate has been used by three, if not four, generations. It was probably first engraved for JOHN RIDGWAY, of Ollerton, co. Chester, and of Audenshaw, co. Lanc. gent. [sixth in descent, of the same Christian name, from John R. of Ollerton, yeoman, living 1612], who died 9 Feb. 1802, leaving by his wife, *Elizabeth Priestner*, who died 11 Dec. 1810, four sons: 1. *John*. 2. *Thomas*. 3. *Joseph R.* of Duddon, co. Chester, an officer in the army who fought in the Peninsula, o.s.p. 1831. 4. *Samuel R.*, an officer in the Army, and Lieut. 2nd Royal Lancashire Militia, o.s.p.

The eldest son, JOHN RIDGWAY, of Ollerton, Audenshaw, and Manchester, Esq. was born 30 January, and bapt. at St. Anne's Church, Manchester, 9 March, 1769. Appointed Captain 2nd Royal Lancashire Militia 28 June, 1803. Sold the Ollerton property. Died at Dunkirk, s.p. (having been twice married) 25 March, 1833.

The second son, THOMAS RIDGWAY, of Liverpool, merchant, died at Duddon, co. Chester, where he had an estate, 27 April, 1827, having had, by his wife, *Mary Waine*, of Stapleford, co. Chester, 3 sons and 3 daughters; the eldest son

JOHN WITHENSHAW RIDGWAY, of Manchester, Esq.,† was born 28 May, 1803, and died 25 January, 1851. He married at Warrington, 13 Feb. 1834, *Dinah*, daughter of *John Clare*, of Warrington, merchant, Captain Loyal Warrington Volunteers, and Local Militia, and left issue with a daughter, Mary Elizabeth, who died unmarried 1868, a son

JOHN CLARE RIDGWAY, of Sankey and Warrington, merchant, born 23 April, 1840; married at Eccleston, 14 June, 1871, *Annie Maria*, daughter of the late *John Houghton*, of Barrowfield, in Eccleston, co. Lanc., gent., by whom he has issue a son, *John Herbert Ridgway*, born 1875, and a daughter *Mary Frances R.*, born 1877.

EXTRACTS FROM THE PARISH REGISTERS OF STAPLEFORD, NOTTINGHAMSHIRE.‡

(1) Thomas the sonne of Laurence Broadbent and Mary his wife was buried the seaventh day of July, 1656.

.... widdow of Edward Dodson late Minister of this Church was buried the nyne and twentieth day of March, 1657.

Laurence the sonne of Laurence Broadbent and Mary his wife was baptized the seaventh day of July, 1657.

(2) Anne, the widdow of Gervase Teverey, Esqr was buried the twentieth day of August, 1657.

Laurence Broadbent was buried the eleaventh day of November, 1657.

Robart Leigh, minister of this towne of Stapleford, in Nottinghamshire, was buried the 25 day of .... 1659.

(3) Richard Jaques sonne of Richard Jaques and Mary his wife was baptized the four and twentyeth day of July, 1660.

Hannah, a child that was nursed and kept at ye towne's charge, was buried the 29 of Aprill, 1663.

Joseph Wright, Buttler at ye Hall, was buried the eight day of May, 1663.

(4) Mr Andrew Palmes was buried the sixteenth day of ffebruary, Anno Dm. 1663–4.

* Communicated by J. PAUL RYLANDS, Esq., F.S.A.

† Had the "W" engraved upon the book-plate. The editor has in his collection impressions of the plate before and after this alteration, the one without the "W" is printed in green ink.

‡ Communicated by Captain A. E. LAWSON LOWE.

(5) William Palmes, sonne of William Palmes, Esqr and the Lady Marie his wife was baptized the nineteenth day of Aprill, 1664.

The said William Palmes was buried the sixth day of May, 1664.

Margaret ye Daughter of Will. Palmes, Esqr and Dame Mary his Wife was Bapt. ye 30 of March, 1665.

(6) George Jackson, of this towne, and Sarah Stanfeild, of Radfourd, was married the nynth day of September, Anno d'ni 1667.

Arnold the son of Arthur Warren, Gen. and Anne his wife, was baptized October the seaventh, 1678.

(7) Arthur, the son of Arthur Warren, Esqr and Anne his wife, was baptised Novem. ye 15th, born ye 14th of ye same month, 1681.

Charles, the son of Mr Arthur Warren, Esqr and Anne his wife was baptised June ye 8th, 1683.

Charles, the son of Mr Arthur Warren, Esqr and buried June ye 24th, 1683.

(8) Ann ye daughter of Arthur Warren, Esqr was baptised November ye 27th, 1684.

(9) James ye son of Arthur Warren, Esqr was baptised July ye 22nd, 1686.

(10) John the son of Arthur Warren, Esqr and Ann his wife was Baptised July ye 20th, 1690.

John Rivel, Junior, who was kiled axordentily in the steeple of Stapleford Church March the 28, and was buried March the 31, 1692.

Baldwin the son of Arthur Warren, Esqr and Ann his wife was baptised March the fifteenth, 1693.

(11) Arthur Warren, Esq., was buried November the 29th, 1697.

(12) Old lady Anne Warren was buried August the 21 day, Anno domini 1703.

(13) Arthur Warren son of Borlace Warren, Esqr and Anne his Wife was baptised May ye 24, 1704.

(14) Arnold, son of Borlace Warren, Esqr, and Anne his wife was baptised September ye 2nd, 1705.

Old Mrs Jackson was buried August ye 21, 1706.

Young Mrs Jackson was buried October ye 2, 1706.

(15) Charles, son of Borlace Warren, Esqr, and Anne his wife, was baptised August ye 9th day, 1707.

Katherine, daughter of Borlace Warren, Esqr, and Anne his wife was baptised June ye 20, 1711.

Katherine Warren was buried ffebruary ye 12, 1712.

(16) Frances, ye daughter of burlas Warin Esq. and Ann his wife was baptized *Gannewаre* (sic) ye 17th, 1713–4.

(17) Ladie Ann Cullin was buried Septembar ye 18, 1714.

Dorothy, daughter of Borlace Warren, Esqr, and Anne his wife was baptised January ye 7th, 1714.

Dorothy Warren was Buried January ye 10th, 1714.

(18) Elizabeth ye Daughter of Borlace Warrin, Esq. and Ann his wif. was baptis. December 18th, 1715.

(19) Mary, Daughter of Borlase Warren, Esqr, and Anne his wife was baptis^d April 5th, 1717.

George Jackson was buried January ye 24, 1716.

Mr Arthur Warren buried October ye 19, 1727.

(20) Charles Cockayne, Lord Viscount Cullen, of Rushton, in Northamptonshire, and Mrs Anne Warren were married April 18th, 1732.

Anne ye Daughter of Charles Cockayne, Lord Viscount Cullen of Rushton, in Northamptonshire, and Lady Anne his Wife was Baptised February ye 21st, 1732–3.

Anne ye Daughter of Charles Cockayne, Lord Viscount Cullen of Rushton, in Northamptonshire, and Lady Anne his Wife was Buried May ye 10th day, 1733.

(21) Mrs Warren the Wife of the late Borlace Warren, Esquire, Buried Ap^l the 3rd, 1752.

(22) John Borlace Warrin, Esq[r], and Bridget Rossell married at Risley, Novem[r] y[e] 14th, 1752

(23) John Borlace Warren, son of John Borlace Warren, Esq[r], and Brigit his wife, was baptised October the 5th, 1753

(24) Franciss, Daughter of Jhon Burlice Warrin and Brigit his wife was Babtised November 17, 1755.

(25) Arnol the Son of John Borlace Warrin, Esq[r], and Brigit his wife was Babtised Jencary 27, 1759.

(26) Benjamin Price Withers, Esq[r], and Ann Warrin *alias* Fox was married November y[e] 9th, 1758.

(27) Edward Tutin and Catherine Rossill was married April 19th, 1763.

(28) John Borlace Warrin, Esq[r], was Buried August the 10, 1763.

(29) Arnol Warrin Esq[r] was Buried August 20th, 1767.

(30) M[r] Arthor Warrin Buried November 11th, 1770

(31) The Rev[d] M[r] James Warren was Buried Dec. 23rd, 1773.

(35) Mary Warren Buried August 22nd, 1783

(32) Frances Maria, Daughter of Sir John Borlace Warren, Bar[t], and Dame Caroline, his Wife, was Baptised May the 9th, 1784.

(35) Frances Warren Buried July 31st, 1784.

Caroline Diana, Daughter of Sir J[no] Borlace Warren, Baronet, and Dame Caroline, his Wife, born 24th and baptised August 27th, 1786.

Caroline Diana Warren Buried August 30th, 1786.

(33) William Henry, son of Sir John Borlace Warren, Bart., and Dame Caroline his Wife, was baptised the 14th day of February, 1788

(34) Diana Martha Clavering, Daughter of Sir John Borlase Warren and Dame Caroline, his wife, born February 17th, and baptised the 23rd, 1790.

(35) Elizabeth Warren was Buried March 21st, 1794.

(36) George Charles Sedley, Esquire, and Frances Maria Warren married August the 25th, 1802

(37) Arnold Warren, Esq[re], buried August the 29th, 1829.

NOTES

(1) In the time of Queen Elizabeth a considerable estate in the parish of Stapleford was held by John Brodbent, who obtained a grant of arms from William Camden, Clarencieux, in 1601 He had, however, no male issue, and his only daughter and heiress was married to one Gervase Jackson (Thoroton's 'Antiq of Notts,' p 212)

(2) An inscription upon a monument in the south aisle (in which part of the church she is presumably interred) refers to this lady as "ex veteri prosapia Ashbyorum de Quenby in agro Leicestrensi oriunda." She was daughter of George Ashby, Esquire, and widow of Gervase Teverey, Esquire, a Justice of the Peace for the county of Nottingham, whose ancestor John Teverey, of Long Eaton in Derbyshire, had acquired an estate in this parish, about the time of King Richard the Second, by marriage with the heiress of the Stapleford family This Gervase Teverey died August the 31st, 1639, and was buried with his ancestors in the south aisle of Stapleford Church beneath a large monument adorned with the effigies of himself and his lady, now in a sadly mutilated condition By his above-named wife he had an only son, John, who died an infant, and three daughters namely Mary, married to Sir Brian Palmes, of Ashwell, in the county of Rutland, and of Lindley, in the county of York, Elizabeth, who died unmarried in her father's lifetime, and Anne, married to Ralph Huband, of Ipsley in the county of Warwick, Esquire, and died March the 23rd, 1672, in her 59th year. The earlier portions of the registers of this parish have been lost, and the above is the only entry relative to the Teverey family that remains

(3) A family named Jaques, *alias* Gamboul, residing at Toton in the adjoining parish of Attenborough, possessed some interest in Stapleford Richard, one of the younger sons of George Jaques, *alias* Gamboul, of Toton, gentleman, and Sarah his wife, was baptised at Attenborough March the 30th, 1627, and is probably identical with the above

(4) This Andrew Palmes is usually described as of Sherborne, in Hampshire. He was a younger brother of Sir Guy Palmes, of Ashwell and Linley, and was uncle of Sir Brian Palmes, who married the coheiress of Gervase Teverey, Esq. as above noted By Elizabeth, his wife he had seven sons and three daughters, of whom Thomas, William, and John were all killed fighting for their King at the battle of Worcester, Edward, another son, settled in New England, where he married and had issue, whilst Brian, who appears to have been the youngest son, was an apothecary at Melton Mowbray, in Leicestershire, and was living at that place in 1681, being then married and having three sons and a daughter. This Andrew Palmes appears to have been

in his seventy-first year at the time of his decease, and was presumably interred in the Teverey vault (Nichols' 'Hist and Antiq of Leicestershire,' vol ii, p 295)

(5) William Palmes Esquire (the father) was the third and youngest son of Sir Brian Palmes of Ashwell and Lindley by Mary his wife, eldest daughter and coheiress of Gervase Teverey Esq "The Lady Mary," his wife, was a daughter and coheiress of William, sixth Lord Euers, of Wilton in the county of Durham This William Palmes had succeeded to the Stapleford estates upon the decease of his elder brother, Francis, but in 1668 he obtained a special Act of Parliament, under which he disposed of his Nottinghamshire estates and settled in Yorkshire

(6) George Jackson was the son of George Jackson of Stapleford, gentleman, sometime Chief Constable for the southern division of the Broxtow Hundred, and was grandson of Gervase Jackson, who married Mary, sole daughter and heiress of John Brodbent as already mentioned The registers contain many entries relative to the family of Jackson, which became extinct in the main line upon the decease of John Jackson of Stapleford gentleman, in 1853

(7) See his burial in 1727

(8) Married to Charles, fourth Viscount Cullen See her burial in 1714

(9) He was the fifth son of Arthur Warren, Esquire, and resided at Little Marlow, in Buckinghamshire, where he died in 1774 His remains were interred in the south aisle of the parish church of Little Marlow, and the following inscription was placed above his grave —

> "Under this stone are deposited the remains of James Warren, Esq, the last and only surviving son of Arthur Warren Esq, of Stapleford, in the County of Nottingham, by Anne his Wife, Daughter of Sir John Borlase, Bart, who departed this life March ye 29th, 1774, ætatis 89"

(10) He died unmarried February the 3rd, 1733, and was buried at Little Marlow

(11) Arthur Warren, Esquire, purchased Stapleford Hall and a portion of the estate from William Palmes, Esquire, about the year 1670, and settled at Stapleford According to Playfair ('Family Antiquities,' vol vii p 138, Ap) Ormerod ('Hist and Antiq of Cheshire vol iii p 343), and other authorities this Arthur Warren was descended from William Warren of Caunton in the county of Nottingham,—a younger son of Sir Lawrence Warren of Poynton, in the county of Chester There are, however reasonable grounds for disputing this assertion Arthur Warren of Stapleford was the grandson of Sir Arnold Waring, of Thorpe Arnold in the county of Leicester who was knighted March the 4th 1632 He was son of William Waring, buried at Thorpe Arnold in 1592, son of another William Waring, buried there in 1583 who was nephew of William Waring, merchant of the staple of Calais, whose inq post mort is mentioned by Thoroton In his will, which is sealed with a merchant's mark, he states that he was born at Tanworth in Warwickshire, and mentions his cousin William Waring, of Berry Hall in the parish of Solihull in the county of Warwick The Warings of Tanworth bore—Azure, a chevron between three lions passant or,—a coat widely differing from that borne by the Warrens of Poynton, and there is no reason to suppose that there was any connection between the two families There is no record of any arms in the Stapleford family until those of Poynton were used to a release, dated 1676, by the above-named Arthur Warren The arms used at the funeral of this Arthur in 1697 were—Checquy or and azure within a bordure sable and over all a canton gules charged with a lion rampant azure No arms were, however, recognized to the family until 1802, when they were established to Sir John Borlase Warren, Bart, and to the descendants of his father ('Herald and Genealogist,' vol vii p 208) This Arthur Warren, who was a Captain in the Nottinghamshire Militia, and also executed the office of High Sheriff for the county, was buried in a small vault at the east end of the nave above which the following inscription yet remains

> "Here
> Lies the Body of
> Arthur Warren, Esqr,
> who departed this Life 2nd
> November, A Domini 1697"

(12) Only daughter and heiress of Sir John Borlase, of Little Marlow in the county of Buckingham, Bart, who died in August, 1688, having survived his only son, John, who had died without issue (Lipscombe's 'Hist and Antiq of the County of Buckingham' vol i p 310, vol iii p 607) She married Arthur Warren, Esquire, in 1676, and had issue seven sons and one daughter Her remains were interred in the same vault with those of her husband.

(13) See his burial in 1770

(14) See his burial in 1767

(15) He was educated at Emmanuel College, Cambridge, and graduated as B A in 1729 and M A in 1734 He was presented to the rectory of Ludgershall, in Buckinghamshire, by his father, Borlase Warren, Esquire, and was inducted into that benefice May the 9th, 1747 He died unmarried in the following year

(16) See her burial in 1784

(17) Only daughter of Arthur Warren, Esquire, by Anne his wife, and married Charles, fourth Viscount Cullen, by whom she had, with other issue, a son who succeeded to his father's title and estates

(18) See her burial in 1794

(19) See her burial in 1783.

(20) Charles fifth Viscount Cullen was the son and successor of Charles, fourth Viscount Cullen, whose wife was the only daughter of Arthur Warren, Esquire (as above mentioned) His

wife, who was thus his first cousin, was the eldest daughter of Borlase Warren, Esquire, and Anne his wife Her baptism is not recorded in the Stapleford registers, and has not been found.

(21) She was the only daughter of Sir John Harpur, of Calke Abbey in the county of Derby, Baronet, by Anne his wife, second daughter of William, Lord Willoughby of Parham, and was married to Borlase Warren, Esq, in 1702, and had issue five sons and six daughters Her husband, who died in 1747, was buried at Little Marlow

(22) John Borlase Warren, Esquire, was the eldest son and heir of Borlase Warren, Esquire, by Anne his wife. His baptism has not been found Bridget Rossell was the youngest daughter and coheiress of Gervase Rossell, Esquire (the last male heir of the ancient family of Rossell, of Radcliffe-upon-Trent), by Frances his wife, daughter of William Green, of Thundercliffe Grange in the county of York, Esquire Gervase Rossell dissipated the greater portion of his estates, and after his decease his widow kept a boarding house at Wirksworth in Derbyshire Mrs Warren survived her husband (see his burial in 1763), and afterwards married the Reverend Graham Chapell, LL B She died May the 1st, 1785, and was buried in the chancel at Orston, in Nottinghamshire

(23) John Borlase Warren, elder son of John Borlase Warren, Esquire, and Bridget, his wife, succeeded to his father's estates in 1763. In 1774, a few months after attaining his majority, he was elected M P for Great Marlow, and was created a Baronet May the 20th, 1775 He was subsequently elected for Nottingham. and became a member of the Privy Council, and was likewise Groom of the Bedchamber to H R H the Duke of Clarence His eminent services as a naval officer are well known He attained the rank of Admiral of the Red, and was rewarded for his valour with the Grand Cross of the Bath and with other orders of knighthood He was married December the 13th, 1780, to Caroline, third daughter of General Sir John Clavering, by the Lady Diana his wife daughter of John, first Earl de la Warr, and by her he had two sons, both of whom died in the lifetime of their parents, and three daughters Admiral Sir John Borlase Warren died at Greenwich Hospital February the 27th, 1822 and his remains were interred at Stretton Audley, in Oxfordshire Lady Warren survived her husband for some years, and died at Stapleford Hall December the 21st, 1839, in the seventy-ninth year of her age

(24) Only daughter of John Borlase Warren, Esq, and Bridget his wife She married Augustus Parkyns, Esquire, by whom she had several children, and dying June the 21st, 1821, was buried in the south aisle of St Peter's Church, Derby, where there is a mural tablet to her memory

(25) See his burial in 1829

(26) Benjamin Price Withers, of Westbury in the county of Buckingham, Esquire, by his will, dated in 1771, recites several deeds between himself, the said Benjamin Price Withers, and Anne his wife John Borlase Warren, Esquire, the Honourable Borlase Cockayne, Arnold Warren, Esquire, and the Reverend James Warren, under which the manor or royalty of Westbury was settled upon his descendants for ever (Lipscombe's 'Hist and Antiq of the County of Buckingham,' vol iii p 142)

(27) Edward Tutin was an apothecary residing in Bridlesmith Gate, in the town of Nottingham Catherine Rossell, who was baptised at Wirksworth April the 9th, 1725, was one of the daughters and coheiresses of Gervase Rossell, Esquire, and sister of Bridget, the wife of John Borlase Warren, Esquire The issue of this marriage was an only daughter

(28) Eldest son and heir of Borlase Warren, Esquire, upon whose decease. in 1747, he succeeded to the Stapleford estates He was for some years a Justice of the Peace for the county of Nottingham, and was High Sheriff in 1751 His remains were interred in a vault at the east end of the south aisle in Stapleford Church

(29) Third son of Borlase Warren, Esquire, and Anne, his wife He died unmarried

(30) Second son of Borlase Warren, Esquire, and Anne his wife Also died unmarried.

(31) Youngest son of Borlase Warren, Esquire, and Anne his wife He was educated at Emmanuel College, Cambridge, and took his degree as LL B in 1738, and was Rector of Stretton Audley, in Oxfordshire In 1748 upon the decease of his elder brother, Charles, he was presented to the Rectory of Ludgershall, in Buckinghamshire He died a bachelor

(32) See her marriage in 1802

(33) Second son and fourth child of Sir John Borlase Warren, Bart., and Dame Caroline his wife He died young

(34) Third daughter and youngest child of Sir John Borlase Warren, Bart, and Dame Caroline his wife She also died in the lifetime of her parents

(35) These three ladies, the unmarried daughters of Borlase Warren, Esquire, and Anne his wife, are buried in a vault at the north-east end of the nave near to where the pulpit now stands A large oval tablet, inscribed to their memory, is placed on the north wall of the nave above the vault

(36) George Charles Sedley, Esquire, was the eldest son of Henry, third Lord Vernon,—then the Hon Henry Sedley—who had assumed the name and arms of Sedley in 1779, upon his marriage with Elizabeth Rebecca Anne Sedley, heiress of Sir Charles Sedley, of Nuthall Temple in the county of Nottingham, Bart In 1813, upon his father's accession to the title, he assumed the family names of Venables-Vernon, and succeeded as fourth Lord Vernon in 1829 He died November the 18th, 1835 Frances Maria his wife, was the eldest daughter and eventually sole heiress of Sir John Borlase Warren, Baronet In 1826 she assumed the name of Warren, and after her decease (which occurred on the 17th of September, 1837) her only son, George John, fifth Lord Vernon, assumed for himself (but not for his issue) the name and arms of Warren only, —both of them so doing in compliance with the will of Elizabeth Harriott, Lady Bulkley, the sole

daughter and heiress of Sir George Warren, of Poynton, in the county of Chester, the last male heirof his line. The presumed relationship between the families, already referred to, was thus recognized. The present Lord Vernon does not bear the name of Warren, but his younger brother, having succeeded to the estates of his great-grandfather in Nottinghamshire and Oxfordshire, took, in compliance with his will, the names of Borlase-Warren before those of Venables-Vernon, by royal license dated June the 4th, 1856. (Burke's 'Peerage and Baronetage;' 'Herald and Genealogist,' vol. vii. p. 208.)

(37) Younger son of John Borlase Warren, Esquire, and Bridget his wife, and the last surviving male representative of his family. He died a bachelor, and was buried in the vault at the east end of the south aisle in Stapleford Church.

TANNER.—I should be much obliged to any correspondent who would give me information concerning the early part of the Tanner pedigree. It appears that the three brothers, Anthony, William, and Laurence Tanner, married three sisters (query whether daughters of a John Fuller, who left More House to Will'm Tanner?). In Berry's 'Sussex Genealogies' the Fuller pedigree is given, but I cannot find a John Fuller mentioned with three daughters, one being Sarah. More House was left (see Horsfield's 'Sussex,' p. 227) to a Mr. John Fuller by Frances, the sole heiress of John Middleton, Esq., of More House. She married Robert Day, Esq., and died s.p. in 1764.

Exeter Coll., Oxford. CHARLES NEVE.

. . . . Tanner.=

- 1. Anthony Tanner Gent. of . . . . co. Sussex. = ... d'r of . . . . Fuller.
  - Will'm Tanner of Wivelsfield co. Sussex Esq. = Ann d'r of . . . . Field.
- 2. Will'm Tanner of . . . . co. Sussex. = ... d'r of . . . . Fuller of . . . .
  - 2. Anthony ob. s.p.
  - Will'm Tanner of More House in Wivelsfield Esq. ob. 1831. = Sarah d'r of . . . . Hampshar of . . . .
    - Richard Tanner of More House Esq. ob. unmar.
    - Will'm Tanner of Patcham co. Sussex Esq. = Philadelphia da. of . . . . Scrace.
      - Left issue three daughters and coheirs, now living.
    - John ob. s.p.
    - Four dau'rs, all of whom married.
  - Jane Tanner ob. unmar.
- Laurence Tanner of . . . . co. Sussex. = Sarah d'r of . . . . Fuller of . . . .

CRABB.—Charles Trelawney of Coldrinnick, St. Germain's, Cornwall, died without issue in 1764; the name and estate were then inherited by his cousin Henry Darell, who also died without issue; then by *Darell Crabb,* the son of his cousin Frances, the wife of *John Crabb* of Plymouth, Esq., who also dying without issue in 1795, the name and estate then passed to the grandson of another cousin, Anne, ancestor of the present possessor.

I am very desirous to find out the arms and descent of the above *John Crabb;* probably he came of the family of that name at Castlewich, near Callington. (Harl. Pub., Cornwall Visit., 1620.)

Alice Crabbe, in 1682, married Saml. Cory, of Holsworthy, Devon, Esq. Was she of the same family or related to *William Crabbe* Mayor of Bristol in 1676?

Any information will be thankfully received.

J. C. C.

EXEMPLIFICATION OF A CREST BY WILLIAM CAMDEN CLARENCEUX TO GEORGE HYDE OF SOUTH DENCHWORTH, NOVEMBER 22, 1600.

To all and singular to whom theis presents shall come to be sene read or heard William Camden Esquire *alias* Clarenceux Principall Herald and King of Armes of the East West and South partes of England from the river of Trent Southward sendeth due comendac'ons in Our Lord god everlasting. Forasmuche as it evidently and plainely appeareth by divers and sundry auncient evidence dated the fieft yeare of King Edward the third That the Ancestors of George Hyde of South Denchworth in the county of Berks Esquier have heretofore in thier seales vsed for their devise or Cognizaunce a Lance or Horseman's Staff with a flagge or Cornet thereat &c And being required by the said George Hyde Esquire to ratefie and confirme vnto him the said devise emprese or Cognizance have at his request ratefied and confirmed and by theis presentes doe ratefie and confirme vnto the said George Hyde Esquier and to his Posteritie that is to say On a Wreath Argent and Gules a Lance or Horseman's staffe silver with a flagge or Cornett gules fringed argent as more plainly appeareth depicted in the margent which creast or Cognizaunce, I the said Clarencieulx King of Armes by power and authoritie vnto my office attributed and annexed doe by theis presentes confirme and warrant to the said George Hyde Esquier and to his posteritie with their due differences and he or they the same to vse beare or shew forth at his or their libertie and pleasure for evermore without any Contradiccion or Controllment of any person or persons whatsoever In witnes whereof I the King of Armes aforesaid have hereunto sett my hand and seale of Office Dated the Twoe and Twentieth day of November in the Three and Fortith yeare of the raigne of our Soveraigne Lady Elyzabeth by the grace of God Quene of England Fraunce and Ireland defender of the Fayth, &c. 1600.

WILL'M CAMDEN Clarenceux
Kinge of Armes.

[*The same Confirmation occurs in Gough MS. Berks,* 16 *f* 72*b*, *being copied from the Ashmole MS in an abridged form. A copy of the same occurs in Ashmole MS.* 858, *p* 208.]

EXTRACTS FROM THE REGISTERS OF BURIALS IN THE PARISH OF CHELTENHAM, GLOUCESTERSHIRE.*

(*Continued from p.* 33.)

$170\frac{4}{5}$.	January 13.	Gyles Harvey
1705.	April 16	Mary, wife of Richard Hyett.
——	September 18.	Mrs Mary Johnson, Widdow.
1706	December 14.	William Roberts, Gent
$170\frac{6}{7}$	March 24.	Thomas Ashmead.
1707.	June 20	Martha, daughter of Henry St Leger.
——	June 21	George, son of James Smalpeece, Gent.
——	December 21.	John, son of Richard Hyett, Gent.
1708	May 19.	John Howlett
——	November 19.	Thomas Packer, Gent.
1709	November 28.	Thomas, son of Francis Gregory, of Alstone.
$170\frac{9}{10}$.	January 31.	Thomas, son of James Smallpeice.

* Communicated by the Rev. BEAVER H. BLACKER, M A. Cheltenham

1710.	April 10.	Mrs Ann Ashmead, Widd.
——	May 31.	Edward Bartom [Barkman], son of James Smalpeece.
——	July 3.	James, son of James Beckett.
1711.	July 19	George Sturmy, Gent.
——	December 30	Katherine, wife of Toby Sturmy.
$171\frac{1}{2}$	February 27	Mrs Mary Geenes [Gynes].
1713.	May 4	Richard Beckett, Mercer.
——	September 5.	Edeth, wife of Robert Cox.
1715.	May 4.	Mrs Elizabeth Isles [Iles], Widow
——	May 14.	William Roberts, of Allstone, Gent.
——	June 4	Mrs Alice Sturmy
——	November 27	William Sloper, Gent.
$171\frac{5}{6}$.	January 15.	Mary Buck, Gen
1716.	December 19.	Jane, wife of Richard Comb, of Allston.
1717.	April 29	Bridget Petty
——	August 12.	John, son of Will Buckle, Esqr
1718.	July 14.	James Beckett.
——	October 19.	Mr Capel Buckle.
1719	April 29.	Sarah Roberts, of Alston.
——	August 21.	Mr James Wood
——	December 30	Pates, son of James Beckett, of Allston.
$17\frac{19}{20}$	January 16.	Richard Combe
1720	April 1.	Joseph Ludlow, Gentleman.
——	August 19	Ann Watters, Widow
——	September 2.	Lodwick Packer, Gent
$172\frac{0}{1}$	March 24	Frances Arkell, Widd^{w}.
1721	June 6	Robt Owen.
1723.	April 23.	Mrs Hester Sturmy
——	August 30.	Hannah Wood, Widdow
1725.	June 7.	Henry St Leger, Senr
——	November 17.	William, son of Charles Mount, Gent
1727.	September 12.	Mrs Elizabeth ffrench [French].
——	September 25	Edward Michell, Gent.
1728.	April 16.	Arabela Michell, Widow.
——	April 24.	Charles, son of Charles Mount, Gent
——	April 25	Mrs Elinor Inion [Onion]
——	August 4	Sarah Beket [Beckett], Widdow
——	August 25	John Bukle [Buckle], of Cleve [Bishop's Cleeve]
1729	September 14	Hester Stephens [? Ireland].
1730.	October 10	John Michell, Gent
——	December 19.	Joseph Nichols, Gent
1733.	November 29.	Ann, daug of Mr Longford
$173\frac{3}{4}$	January 23	Elizabeth, wife of John Longford.
1734.	April 12.	John, son of John Longford
——	May 30.	Jane, the daug^{r} of Mr Longford.
——	October 22.	Eliza [Elizabeth], wife of Mr Gabril Curle [Gabriel Curll].
1737	June 7.	Henry, son of Henry Savage
1738	August 11.	Henry, son of Henry Skillicorn
1740.	May 9	M^{rs} [Mary] Ann Hartlebury.
——	May 29	Edmund Meyrick, Minister.
		[Incumbent of Cheltenham, 1734–40, having succeeded the Rev George Stokes]
1741.	June 19	Anne, wife of Thomas Benfield.
——	October 25	Thos Sergeant [Sargeaunt]
1742	April 4	[Elizabeth] Sergeant [Sargeaunt], Wid^{o}.
1743.	August 28.	Mr Richard Andrews.

$174\frac{5}{6}$. February 14. Will. Wood.
[No mention in the register of any other William Wood about this time.]
$174\frac{6}{7}$. January 12. Mary Acremon [Akerman].
1747. April 14. Mrs Gallaway.
—— August 8. [W. S.] William, son of Henry Savage.
$17\frac{49}{50}$. January 10. Cath. Packer.
—— February 25. Edward Packer, Gent.
1751. November 1. Elizth Stokes.
$175\frac{1}{2}$. January 13. Elizth, wife of Jno Ailway.
1752. April 6. Wm Cook.
—— November 15. Elizabeth, daughter of Charles Hetheway.
1754. November 15. William Wood.
1756. March 20. Mrs Katherine Packer, Widow.
1758. April 22. Elizabeth Mathews.
1759. March 8. Mr Robert Cox, Senr.
1760. December 30. The Revd Mr Stephen Cull.
1763. January 29. Mrs Applgate [Applegarth], Widow.
—— March 26. Mrs Mary Packer.
—— October 18. Mr Henry Skillicorn.
[Full particulars of Captain Henry Skillicorne may be found in p. 413 of last volume.]
1764. March 23. Mrs Elizabeth Packer.
1765. January 8. Mrs Wood, Widow.
—— February 3. Mrs Sarah Chester.
—— February 27. Mr William Slopier [Sloper].
1766. June 10. Mr Thomas Benfield.
—— June 25. Jno Benfield.

(To be continued.)

TANNER, p. 52.—The following may be of interest to Mr. Neve. Any Hamshar and Farncombe notes would be welcomed by

HENRY WAGNER.

New University Club.

Henry Webb of Moulscombe, near Lewes. (See Ped. in Berry's 'Sussex Peds.' p. 101.) Ob^{t} 1628. = Mary, d. of (?) . . . Harris.

Richard Webb* of Moulscomb (only son). Buried in the Quakers' Cemetery at Rottingdean, 30th day of 8th Mo. 1672. Ob. æt. 54. = Ann, d. of (?) . . . living 1684.
A

Margaret. = John Austen of E. Grinstead. Will dated 1 June, 1676.

Jane ob. 1693. = John Wood of Wivelsfield, yeoman. Will da. 24 Nov. 1671. Pr. 7 Feb. following.

Jane Wood D. 1718. = Thomas Jenner of Chailey B. 1639. D. 1714.
Philip Jenner, m. Sarah Hamshar, as below.

Ann Wood. = Thos. Wade.

* The births of his six children, all born at "Mouscomb," are entered in the Rottingdean "Register of Children born before their Parents were convinced of the truth." His grandfather, John Webb, of "Mouscom," by his Will dated 23 Apr. 1555, left to y^{e} mother Church of Chichester ii^{d}, and to ye High Altar of "Peckham" (Patcham) xii^{d} for 3 Masses at his burial and 4 dirges. The father of the latter, by Will dated 1550, left to Richard Farncombe iii^{s} iiii^{d} and to Ellenore "Ferncome" xii^{d}.

A

1689. William Hamshar of Preston. D. 5 May, 1738, æt. 83. Second husband to Marg[t] Bradford. = Elizabeth Webb. B. 23rd of 9th Mo. 1651. D. 18 Oct. 1694. 1st wife. = 1673. John Farncombe of Patcham. D. 1675. 1st husband.

John, only son, D. 1700, unm[d].

Richard Hamshar of E. Preston. Will pr. 1698. = Mary, d. of ?... D. 2 June, 1698, æt. 44.

Sarah, d. & coheir. = Philip Jenner of Chailey. B. 1686. D. 1787.

Elizabeth, d. & coheir. D. 18 Oct. 1752, æt. 62. = John Michell (Attorney) of Lewes. D. 12 Nov. 1735, æt. 53.

John Webb of Falmer (a Quaker). B. 7th of 12th Mo. 1642. D. 18 July, 1698. Bur[d] Preston. = Margaret, d. of John Bradford. D. 23 Jan. 1731, æt. 73. Bur. Preston. Second wife to W[m] Hamshar.

John. — Anne. — Elizabeth. — Margaret. All 4 mar.

Richard Webb. B. 20 Apr. 1693. D. 14 Apr. 1748. Bur[d] Preston. = Ann, d. of . . . Hains of Chichester. D. 9 Mar. 1770, æt. 73. Bur[d] Preston.

Mary marr. license dat. 1706. B. 18 Dec. 1749, æt. 62. = Henry Scrase, of Withdean. Will pr. 3 Nov. 1728.

Elizabeth. B. 1 Jan. 1690. M. at Falmer 1711. = Thos. Ade.

William Hamshar of Patcham, Yeoman. D. 6 Sept. 1739. Bur[d] Preston. Will pr. 5 Jan. 1739-40. = Martha, d. of John Bradford, of Falmer. Marr. settlement da. 13 Sep. 1718. D. 13 Mar. 1758, æt. 66.

Susannah. D. 8 Dec. 1805, æt. 77. = 1758. Richard Scrase of Withdean. B. 1714. Bapt. 1730. D. 2 Nov. 1790. = 1746. Anna Kemp.

Philadelphia, d. of Charles Scrase, and Philadelphia Bradford. Buried at Preston, 6 Feb. 1809, æt. 87. (She was, according to Mr. Lower, first coz. to the above Henry Scrase). = John Hamshar, of Standean. D. 27 Apr. 1788, æt. 68. Will da. 24 Apr. Pr. 14 June, at Lewes.

John. — William. — Edward. Katherine. — Isabella. — Sarah. all 6 married.

Harry Scrase Farncombe. = Philadelphia Hamshar. Bapt. 8 Apr. 1752.

Sarah Hamshar. Bapt. 14 Dec. 1759. = William Tanner, of More House, Wivelsfield. D. 1831.

Thomas Scrase, of Patcham. D. 18 Sept. 1855, æt. 83. = Philadelphia Farncombe. D. 1 Apr. 1811, æt. 35.

Philadelphia Scrase only dau. = William Tanner, of Patcham. D. 23 Apr. 1870, æt. 78.

3 dau'rs.

Philadelphia Tanner. = George Farncombe, nephew to the above H. S. F.

VAVASOUR FAMILY, Vol. I.—In the Registers of All Saints', Evesham, is the following entry:—"1674(5) March 23 Samuel y[e] son of Simon Vavasour of Peterburrough was baptized." To what branch of the family can I affix Simon?

JUSTIN SIMPSON.

Stamford.

The following entries were incorrectly printed at p. 22, Vol. III.:—

STAYNINGS FAMILY.—*Burials at Selworthy, Somerset.*

" 1685. M[d] Susanna Staynings was buried the 21st May.
" 1696. M[r] Lewis Steynings was buryed ye 7th of Janny (9$\frac{5}{6}$.)
" 1700. M[r] Charles Staynings was buried ye 12th of Decemb[r]."

He [illegible]

| A

1689. ╤ William Hamshar ╤ Elizabeth Webb.

LONG OF WRAXALL, DRAYCOTE, &c., CO. WILTS.

... evidence from

... were in any way indebted to them for any part of their

states, and as to the name of the family, that may be pronounced to be a joke of neighbour Bonham's"

EXTRACTS FROM CHURCH REGISTERS RELATING TO THE FAMILY OF SHELMERDINE.*

NORTHENDEN.

Baptisms.

1564	June 17.	A child of Humfrey Shelm^{r}dyne called James.
1564	October 20.	A child of Edward Shelm^{r}dyne called William.
1568.	June 12.	Robert son of Edward Shelm^{r}dyne.
1568.	June 16.	Marie Shelm^{r}dyne.
1569.	April 12.	Marie Shelm^{r}dyne
1570	Sept. 7.	Robert Shelm^{r}dyne of Kenworthey
1571.	March 25	Elline Shelm^{r}dyne of ye Moore Syde.
1571	March 25.	Robert Shelm^{r}dyne of ye Mooresyde
1573.	Nov. 8.	Elizabeth Shelm^{r}dyne of Kenworthey.
1574	Aug 21.	Richard Shelm^{r}dyne of the pyper hill.
1576.	July 25	Thomas, son of John Shelm^{r}dyne
1578.	Nov 18.	Elline da of Edward Shelm^{r}dyne.
1579	Nov. 29.	John son of Edward Shelm^{r}dyne
1579	Nov 30.	Edward son of John Shelm^{r}dyne
1582.	Oct. 21.	W^{m} s of John Shelm^{r}dyne.
1585.	Oct. 3.	Elline da of John Shelm^{r}dyne
1589.	Jan 27.	Elizabeth da. of John Shelm^{r}dyne
1591.	Jan 15	Elline d. of John Shelm^{r}dyne.
1592	Nov. 3.	Edmunde Shelm^{r}dyne of Kenworthey
1593.	Nov. 8	Raphe son of John Shelm^{r}dyne
1594	Oct. 6.	James son of John Shelm^{r}dyne.
1595	Nov 8	John s of R. Shelm^{r}dyne
1595	Oct. 12	Ellinore da to William Shelm^{r}dyne.
1596.	Dec 2.	Alis da of John Shelm^{r}dyne.
1598	June 21.	John son of John Shelm^{r}dyne
1599	April 27	Elizabeth da of R. Shelm^{r}dyne.
1599.	Augt 24.	William Shelm^{r}dyne of Kenworthey.
1601	April 26.	Jane Shelm^{r}dyne of ye pyp' hill
1601.	March 2	John Shelm^{r}dyne of the pyper Hill.
1602.	Feb 4.	Elline Shelm^{r}dyne of the pyper hill
1602	M^{ch} 21	Henry Shelm^{r}dyne of the pyper hill.
1603.	April 26.	Elizabeth da. of ffrancis Shelm^{r}dyne.
1604	March 3.	Robert son of T Shelm^{r}dyne
1605.	Jan. 27.	ffrancis Shelm^{r}dyne.
1606	Jan. 18	Elline Shelm^{r}dyne of Kenworthye.
1607.	March 23.	William son of ffrancis Shelm^{r}dyne.
1608	Nov. 30.	William Shelm^{r}dyne.
1609	Sept. 10.	John Shelm^{r}dyne
1610	March 26.	Alis Shelm^{r}dyne of the piper hill
1610.	October 19.	Edward Shelm^{r}dyne.
1611.	March 19	Richard Shelm^{r}dyne
1612	April 9.	Marie da. of ffrancis S
1612	April 19.	Marie Shelm^{r}dyne of Chowlerton.
1612.	October 30.	Elizabeth Shelm^{r}dyne of Kenworthey.
1613	July 7.	Raphe Shelm^{r}dyne
1613.	Dec 29.	John Shelm^{r}dyne.
1614.	May 19	Thomas Shelm^{r}dyne.

* Communicated by T Shelmerdine, Esq.

1614. June 4 Francis son of Francis Shelm^{r}dyne.
1614 Oct. 15. Raphe Shelm^{r}dyne of Chorlton
1615 Jan. 14. William son of William Shelm^{r}dyne of Kenworthy.
1615. June 4 Francis son of ffrancis Shelm^{r}dyne.
1616. Sept. . . Alis Shelm^{r}dyne of Kenworthey.
1618. Jan. 24. Robert son of Jo Shelm^{r}dyne of Kenworthy
1619. Oct 3. Elisabeth Shelm^{r}dyne.
1621. Oct. 14. Ellenor Shelm^{r}dyne of the moorsyd
1626. Sept 10. John son of John Shelm^{r}dyne of the piper Hill.
1627 July 15. Rebecka da. of William Shelm^{r}dyne.
1627. March 26. Jane da to Robert Baxter & Jane Shelmerdine
1627. Easter. *William Shelmerdine signs as Warden this year*
1628. May 11. Edmund son of Edmund Shelmerdine.
1628. Sept 14. John son of Jo Shelmerdine of the Lane End
1628 Feb. 22 Ellen da. of Jo. Shelm^{r}dyne of the piper hill.
1629. *Edmund Shelmerdine Warden this year.*
1630. Dec. 19. Robert son of John Shelm^{r}dyne of the lane end.
1630 Feb. 13 John son of Edmund Shelm^{r}dyne.
1631. March 18. John son of William Shelm^{r}dine of North^{n}
1631. *Francis Shelmerdine Churchwarden this year.*
1632 May 20. Edmund Shelmerdine of the piper hill
1633. October 6 Elizabeth Shelmerdine of the piper hill
1633. October 27 Mary Shelmerdine of the Lane end.
1633 Dec. 22. Thomas son of Edmund Shelmerdine
1634. Feb 15 Marie da of William Shelmerdine
1635. Feb 7. Anne da of John Shelmerdine of the lane end.
1637. March 11. Edmund son of Willm Shelmerdine of Northenden.
1638. *Edmund Shelmerdine Churchwarden this year*
1654. Nov. 7. Edmund son of Edmund Shelmerdyne of Kenorday.
1654. Oct 19. Elizabeth Shelmerdyne born
1654 July 17. Elizha Shellmerdyne
1662. June 29. Mary da of William Shellmerdyne
1663 Sept 20. Elizabeth da. of Edmund Shellmerdyne
1664. . . . 19. Elijah son of Edmund Shellmerdyne.
1665. Augt 21. Robert son of William Shellmerdyne
1665. Feb. 26. Anne da. of John Shellmerdyne of piper hill
1666. May 3 Edmund son of Edmund Shellmerdyne of Northerdyne.
1666. March 9. Ester da of Mr Shellmerdyne
1667 April 12 Elizabeth da of John Shellmerdyne.
1669. —— 1 Jane da of Edmund Shellmerdyne
1671 April 24 ffrancis son of John Shelmerdine of the Piper Hill.
1671 Feb. 8. William Shelmerdine.
1672 Dec. 22. John son of Edmund Shelmerdine of Northerdine.
1673. July 12. Ellen da of William Shelmerdine the Taylor.
1674 Nov 1 William son of John Shelmerdyne of ye Piper Hill.
1676 April 30 William son of Edmund Shelmerdine of Northerden.
1678 March 19 Elizabeth da. of William Shelmerdine of Northerden
1709. Jan 15 William son of Francis Shelmerdine

This Francis had also Elizabeth, Mary, Alice, James, and Francis.

(*To be continued.*)

CORLISS.—George Corliss, or Corlis, of Devonshire (probably of Exeter) emigrated to America about 1638, and settled at Haverhill, Mass Information relative to his family is desired. Please address, Capt. A. W. CORLISS, 8th U S. Infantry, Yarmouth, Cumberland Co , Maine, U.S.

THE MONUMENTAL INSCRIPTIONS OF THE FAMILY OF HARINGTON, CO. SOMERSET,

AS WELL OF THE DAUGHTERS AS OF THE SONS OF THE HOUSE, WHICH MAY BE FOUND IN THE CATHEDRAL OF BRISTOL, THE ABBEY OF BATH, AND IN SEVERAL OTHER PARISH CHURCHES NEAR THOSE CITIES *

(*Continued from p 34.*)

M. I on a tablet at west end of Kelston Church, surmounted by arms of HARINGTON *impaling* LEY OF TEFFONT EWYAS, DORSET, *as figured in* 'Misc Gen. et H.,' Vol I (New Series), p 352 —

Diones Harington late wife of
John Harington Esq[r] and daughter
of the R[t] Hon[ble] James Earle of
Marlburgh, who died the 8th of August
Annoq. Domini 1674.

[*Note*—This unusual name (representing, I presume, Dyonisia) was introduced into the Ley family by the marriage of Henry Ley, father of the Earl, who became possessed of the Manor of Teffont by grant from Hen VIII in the 37th year of his reign, and married Dionysia de Mayne He was buried at Teffont 1574 —F J. P]

Inscription on a tablet in the wall of the churchyard near the Harington tombs and vaults.—

Hic jacet Georgius Harington
Generosus Filius Tertius Natu
Johannis Harington Militis
Qui obiit 7° die Decembar (*sic*)
Anno Domini 1665.

[*Note*—I have some grounds for believing that this gentleman resided at Fieldgrove, in the parish of Bilton, and died there, but was brought to Kelston to rest with his fathers —F. J P]

On a marble tomb in Kelston Churchyard, west of the tower —

ARMS.—*Quarterly 1st and 4th.* GIBBES OF BRISTOL AND LONDON. 2. HARINGTON. 3. SPECOT OF NORTH DEVON AND CORNWALL.

Here lyeth the body of
Harington Gibbes of the City of Bristol Merchant
who departed this life the 7th day of October
1732 aged 50 years.
He was son of Henry Gibbes Esq, sometime
Alderman of the said City,
By Elizabeth his wife, who was daughter of
John Harington of this Parish Esq.
and Mary his wife, daughter of
Peter Speccott of Thornbury Co Devon Esq
This tomb was erected by Dioness Gibbes,
his sister, as a testimony of
her great affection · and to perpetuate
the memory of her dear Brother.

The above is on the north side of the tomb, and then on the south side is inscribed—

Here lieth the Body of
Diones Gibbes
of the City of Bristol
who departed this life the 4th day
of August 1760.

* Communicated by the Rev FRANCIS J POYNTON, M A, Rector of Kelston

MONUMENTAL INSCRIPTIONS AND OTHER MEMORIALS OF HARINGTON AND ALLIED FAMILIES, FROM MARSHFIELD CHURCH, CO. GLO'STER.

In the North Aisle at Marshfield Church.

ARMS.—HARINGTON *and* GIBBES.

Here lieth the body of Elizabeth Gibbes
Relict of Henry Gibbes Alderman and Merchant
of the City of Bristol, and eldest daughter
of John Harington Esq of Kelston Co Somerset
who departed this life Octr 12th
A D 1723 aged 67.

[*Note*—This last memorial is of special value as there is no baptismal entry of this lady in the Kelston or Corston Register 1567 nor thereabouts]

Near this place lyeth the body of Mary Gostlet widow
of John Gostlet Esqr and daughter of John Harington Esqr
of Kelston in the County of Somerset by Lady Dionissa
Ley d^r & coh^s of the Right Honble James, Earl of
Marlbrough, who departed this life Octr 27th
Ann Dom. 1698 aged (?)*

Near this place lyeth the body of John Gostlet Esq.
who departed this life January 24th 1692 in the
67th year of his age

[*Note*—It appears from the above that Mary, the daughter of John Harington, Esq, of Kelston (the Parliamentarian M P. for Bath), only survived her husband six years I have learned from family memoranda that this marriage was without issue She was baptized at Corston, Somerset, 1628, where her father resided till after the death of his mother, the Lady Mary, in 1631. John Gostlett, being in the 67th year of his age when he died in 1692, must have been born 1625-6, and his wife Mary, being bapt 1628 and dying in 1698, attained the age of 70 From observation of these dates, it would seem that *Benjamin* Gostlett, whose wife's surname is not known, but whose dau'r Helena married John Harington, Esq, of Kelston, son of John the Parliamentarian, in 1678, was brother and probably younger brother of the above John Gostlet, and not his son This family is mentioned in Fosbrooke's Gloucestershire' as having purchased the lands in Marshfield once held by the Abbey of Keynsham, Somerset]

On a marble monument there.—

ARMS.—LONG *impaling* HARINGTON.

Interred near this place lieth the body
of Dionysia widow of Calthrop Long
of Whaddon in the County of Wilts Esq
and daughter of Jno Harington Esq.
of Kelston in the County of Somerset
who departed this life Decr 4th 1744
aged 86 years

[*Note*—He was Calthrop Parker at the time of their marriage They both executed a lease of property at Instow (in Devon), in the name of Parker, 27th July, 1709 (to which Elizabeth Gibbes was also a party), but on 20th May 1716, they executed as C and D Long Calthrop Parker (Long) was her 2d husband She was previously the wife of Henry Long, Esq of Stanton Prior, co Somerset (married at Kelston, 1682). Her mother was Mary Speccot (Harington)]

The Table of Benefactions records the following bequests of Mrs. Dyoness Long to the church and parish of Marshfield —

"Imprimis To the Vicar of this place for the time being an estate lying in the parish of Mangotsfield called Cleave Hill of the yearly value of one hundred pounds or thereabouts—provided he preaches or causes to be preached two sermons on every Lord's day in this Church, and reads or causes to be read on Wednesday and Friday in every week Prayers in the said Church." (This estate was purchased in the year 1731.)

* It should be seventy years.—F J P.

"Item Towards the maintenance of six poor Widows an estate lying in the parish of Iron Acton in this County (Glos'ter) of the yearly value of 20 pounds or thereabouts, purchased in the year 1731.

"Item To a Charity School towards teaching and Clothing twenty Boys, if so many can be had, an estate lying at Frampton in this County, of the yearly value of twenty-five pounds or thereabouts, purchased in the year 1731.

"Item The interest of nine hundred pounds lying in New South Sea Annuities for the use of the two last mentioned charities."

There was also given to this Church (Marshfield) by Colthrope Long, Esq, and Dyonisia his wife a set of communion plate, consisting of two large flagons, one large cup with a cover, and two large plates

---

Kelston Monuments resumed.

An Inscription which would seem to have been upon a flat stone in Kelston Church in the time of Collinson, the historian of Somerset, but is now (1877) *no longer extant, and has never been seen by the present Rector.—*

Here lyeth the Body of Dorothy
Wife of John Harington Esqr
and Daughter of William
White of Little Somerford
in the County of Wilts, who died
July 4th A D 1726
Aged 42.
"We shall rise again"

A monument on record as having once been in Kelston Churchyard, but no longer extant, nor remembered in situ *by the oldest inhabitant* (1877). *A marble table supporting a Bible —*

Near this place lyeth the body of Dr Edward Harington a faithful and diligent servant of his God, who entrusted him with Five Talents, the improvement of which was his constant care, for, so far as human nature would permit, he followed the Pattern of our Blessed Lord and Master, instructing the ignorant, comforting the afflicted, and healing the diseased Indeed he had the virtues both of Head and Heart, which made him highly esteemed and beloved, and as greatly lamented at his Death, which was the first of August 1757

His unhappy widow, sensible of his merits and her own great loss, has ordered this emblem (The Holy Bible) of his daily study to be erected.

On a tablet in the porch over the north door, Kelston.—

Near this Place lieth the Body
of
Alice, the wife of Th^{os} Facknaham
of
Marshfield in the Co of Gloucester
Daughter of John Harington Esq.
of this Parish
Who departed this life
the 2^{d} May 1742
Aged 71 Years.

[*Note*—This lady was previously married to Mr Edward (? Coward, the writing of marr entry is indistinct) Chetwynd The Rev Thos Fecknam succeeded Mr Wm Wallis as Vicar of Marshfield in 1686, and himself died in 1704—*Vide* Atkyns's 'Gloucestershire,' p 286, as to Fecknam]

In the churchyard of St. Catherine's, near Bath, on an altar tomb near the chancel door, is this inscription :—

Near this stone lyeth the body of
John Fackenham of the Parish of Marshfield
son of the Rev. T. Fackenham
and Alice his wife, daughter of John Harington
of Kelston Esqr.
He died May 3^{d} 1745
Aged 52

BRIEF INSCRIPTIONS FROM A ROW OF FLAT TOMBS PLACED TO N.E OF THE CHURCH PORCH, KELSTON

No. I. (the most Northernly).

Edward	Harington	1757
Hester	Harington	1762
Colthrop	Harington	1752

No. II.

Isabella Harington	1755

No III.

John	1725
Dorothy	1726

No. IV.

Robert	1765
Susannah	1765
John	17*

No V.

Henry Harington M D.†
died 15th Jany 1816 in the 89th year
of his age.

Martha wife of the above
died 6th March 1805 aged 76

M.I on a marble tablet erected by subscription to the memory of Dr. Hen. Harington in Bath Abbey.—

Memoriæ Sacrum
Henrici Harington M D.
ex veri nobili Haringtonorum stirpe de Kelston
in agro Somerset oriundi
Qui natus Septembris XXIX A.D MDCCXXVII
obiit Januarii XV. A.D MDCCCXVI.
Per sexaginta annos suæ Bathoniæ saluti
omnibus officiis assidue studebat
optimas artes ad municipum suorum
Delectationem et utilitatem excolens
Medicus solers et fidelis
Poeta lepidus, musicus sciens et peritus;

* The other figures are hopelessly gone, and unfortunately cannot be replaced from the Register as the entry is wanting

† This eminent musician and man of letters has a handsome monument, in marble, erected to his memory, by public subscription, in Bath Abbey It is surmounted by a sculpture of the instrument in which his heart delighted—a fine organ For the inscription on his Bath monument see following His body rests at Kelston with his ancestors

Magistratus gravis, justus, acer,
Erga suos amantissimus
Erga omnes comis et benevolus
Tantâ insuper sanctitate morum, tantâ erga Deum pietate imbutus
ut omnes animi sui facultates,
quantum humanæ vitæ ratio paterluo
Deo dicandos esse judicaret
Hoc marmor pecuniâ publice collatâ poni curaverunt
Amici dolentes.

In Bath Abbey, an inscription on a slate stone, covering a vault at the junction of the South Transept with the Nave —

In a Vault underneath this Stone
Rest the Remains of the Very Rev.
Josiah Thomas* M.A Archd[n] of Bath
who died 28th May 1820 aged 60.
Also of Susan Isabella† wife
of the above . . ‡

ADDITIONS TO THE PEDIGREE OF KERR OF ABBOTRULE.

Vol. II, page 382

1. Mary, daughter of William Kerr, second of Abbotrule, Esquire, by his second wife Mary Henry, was married in 1740 to John Rutherfoord of Knowsouth, Esquire (*son* of John Rutherfoord, of Knowsouth, Esquire, by his wife Isabella, daughter of William Scott of Raeburn, Esquire, *grandson* of Thomas Rutherfoord, of Knowsouth, Esquire, by his wife Cecil, or Cecilia, daughter of William Douglas, of Airdit, co Fife, and sister of Sir William Douglas, of Glenbervie, Baronet, *and great grandson* of John Rutherfoord, of Knowsouth, Esquire, who died in, or before, A D 1666.)
2 Charles, or Charlotte, younger daughter of William Kerr, second of Abbotrule, Esquire, by his second wife Mary Henry, was married to . . Elliot, and had a daughter who died unmarried

The children of the marriage of John Rutherfoord and Mary Kerr were —

1 Thomas Rutherfoord, of Knowsouth, Esquire, who married Miss Elliot, but all their children died s. p
2. Captain John Rutherfoord, of Knowsouth, died unmarried
1. Jean Rutherfoord, married to Thomas Scott, Esquire (a younger brother of Sir Walter Scott's father), from this marriage Scott of Milsington is descended.
2. Euphemia Rutherfoord (coheiress to her brother Capt. R), born in December, 1758; married, 14 February 1788, to John Thomson, Esquire, town-clerk of Jedburgh (*son* of William Thomson of Jedburgh, surgeon, by Anne, his wife, daughter of John and Isabella Rutherfoord, of Knowsouth, and *grandson* of Joseph Thomson, of Jedburgh, surgeon, and Agnes his wife, daughter of Thomas Davidson, the King's printer, Edinburgh)

Many descendants of John and Euphemia Thomson are now living.

J P. R.

* The Archdeacon was also Rector of Street, co Somerset, and Chaplain to the Marquis of Bath

† This lady was daughter of Dr Henry Harington, of Bath, M D, by Martha daughter of . Musgrave, of Oxford She was born 24th June 1762, and died 5th Dec 1835 æt 73 (This partly from family memoranda and partly from her monument given hereafter)

‡ The rest is lost under the pews

CHAYTOR

The following entries relating to the Chaytor family are on the fly-leaves of an old Breeches Bible, dated 1654, in my possession —DUDLEY CARY ELWES.

John and Margrit Chaytor was married the 17° day of the 2° moneth called Aprill 1670.

John Chaytor the first borne sonn of John and Margrit Chaytor was borne the 17° day of the 9th moneth 1671

Caleb the second sonn of John and Margarit Chaytor was borne the third day of the 6th moneth called August 1673

Joshua the third sonn' of John and Margaret Chaytor was borne the seaventh day of the 5th moneth called July 1676

Christopher the fourth sonn' of John and Marg^{t} Chaytor was borne the tenth day of the moneth called January 1678

James Chaytor the fifth and youngest son of John and Marg^{t} Chaytor was borne the 11th day of the mo called March 1689 or 90

John Chaytor, eldest son of John and Marg^{t} Chaytor departed this life att Heighington the 23th day of the sixth moneth called August and was buryed in the orchard belonging his grandfather Christopher Richmond the 24th day of the afforesd moneth 1681.

Joshua Chaytor the third sonn' of John and Marg^{t} Chaytor departed this life the third day of the 11th moneth called January and was buryed in the burying place of the people called Quakers in Richmond the ffouerth day of the aforesd moneth in the yeare 1684

Christopher Chaytor the 4th sonn of John and Margt Chaytor departed this life the 26th day of the first moneth and was buryed in the Burying place above mentioned the 27th day of the aforesd moneth in the year 1685.

At end of Bible occurs the following entries —

ffor want of Roome att the fore-end of this Byble where the Decease of my other Childeren was entered I am forced to bring the departure of my son Caleb hither

Caleb Chaytor the second son of John and Margaret Chaytor departed this life the 23^{d} day of the eleaventh moneth called January in the yeare 1689 and was buryed in the burying place att Richmond the 25th day of the s^{d} 11th moneth 1689

Memorand that James Chaytor the youngest son of John and Marg^{t} Chaytor was borne the eleaventh day of the first moneth called March 1689 or 1690.

Memorand that the Births and buryalls of the sonn^{s} of John and Marg^{t} Chaytor are all entered in the Record of Richmond Meeting, yet for further satisfaction are thought fitt to be entered here allso

C C Deceased the 23^{d} day of the 11th mo 1689 as on the contrary side

This of James Chaytors Birth was Entered in the forcend of this Byble, but not being very faire was thought fitt to be entered here for explanac'on.

FRENCH HOSPITAL OF LA PROVIDENCE —I append a list of the Governors, from its foundation in 1718, of the French Hospice of "La Providence" (which still pursues its useful work in the East of London), and should be obliged if any of your correspondents, versed in French heraldry, could supply information as to their armorial bearings The italics mark the names of those few Governors, whose arms are known.

1718 *Henri de Massue, Marquis de Ruvigny, Comte de Galway*
1720 Philippe Hervart, Baron d' Hunningue
1721 Jean Robethon, Conseillier Privé
1722 Guy de Vicouse, Baron de la Court
1728 Moise Pujolas
1729 Paul Buissiere
1739 Pierre Cabibel
1745 Jaques Gaultier
1748 *Jean Ligonier, Comte Ligonier*
1770 *Guillaume Bouverie, Comte de Radnor.*
1776 Jean Buissiere
1781 Jean de Blagny
1789 *Jacob Pleydell Bouverie, Comte de Radnor*
1828 *Guill Pleydell Bouverie, Comte de Radnor*
1869 *Jacob Bouverie, Comte de Radnor*

13 *Half Moon Street, Piccadilly W.* HY WAGNER.

The Pedigree of the Family of Woodrooffe,

COLLECTED FROM FAMILY PAPERS AND OTHER EVIDENCES BY SELINA MARY WOODROOFFE, 1878.

ARMS.—*Argent, a chevron between three crosses formées fitchées gules.*
CREST.—*A woodcock close proper.*
MOTTO.—"QUOD TRANSTULI RETULI."

Thomas Woodrooffe, A.M., of the house of Woodrooffe of Hope, in Derbyshire; Chaplain to the Earl of Warwick at Leighs Park, in Essex; Rector of Chartham, in Kent, 1646—1660. Buried "in woollen" at Felsted, in Essex, 29 October, 1689. = Anne, daughter and co-heiress of William Robinson, Esq., of the younger house of Robinson of Denston, in Suffolk.

Children:

1. Mary, born at Felsted.

2. Anne, born at Stanmore, Middlesex. = ... Walker.
   - 1. John Walker.
   - 2. Thomas Walker.

3. Thomas, A.M., born 4 March, 1654, at Chartham; of Trinity Coll., Cambridge, A.B. 1675; A.M. 1679. Died unmarried 13 October, 1712, at Felsted, of which parish he was Rector for 33 years. He left the Glebe (nearly 30 acres) to the parish, and £12 a year to the poor of the parish of Leighs.

4. William, B.D., born 15 Dec. 1656, at Chartham; Fellow of Queen's Coll., Cambridge. Rector of Balsham, Cambridgeshire, for 34 years. Died June 20, 1732; buried at Balsham. = 2 November, 1698, Elizabeth, second dau'r of the Rev. Nathaniel Gurdon, D.D., of Assington Hall, Suffolk, and Rector of Chelmsford, and Elizabeth his wife, dau'r of Rev. Emmanuel Arundell of Stoke, Northamptonshire. She died 26 Sept. 1741, aged 69.
   - 5. Anne, born 6 Dec. 1708, at Balsham. Died 10 Jan. 1789. = Her cousin, Rev. Brampton Gurdon, M.A., Vicar of Assington, and Rector of Milden, Suffolk. He died 21 Aug. 1780, aged 72.
     - A daughter, who died in infancy.
   - 6. Elizabeth, born 13 Nov. 1710, at Balsham. Died unmarried 3 Feb. 1764. She was of Friday Street, Cheapside, and bequeathed:—
     To the Poor of Assington, £20.
     " " Balsham, £20.
   - A

5. John, born 21 Jan. 1658, at Chartham.

6. Charles, born 2 June, 1662, in Rood's Parish in London, and baptized the same day.

7. Essex, born 16 October, 1663, at Springfield, Essex. Died 2 Jan. 1748. = George Andrewes, Esq., of Felsted. He died 6 May, 1742, aged 77.
   - 1. Margaret Andrewes, born . . October, 1703. Died unmarried 14 March, 1765.
   - 2. George Andrewes, born 7 May, 1706. Died unmarried 17 January, 1791.

8. Robert, born 6 Jan. 1665, at Leighs, and bapt. the same day.

9. John, born 17 August, 1666, at Felsted, and bapt. the same day.

10. James, born 13 May, 1672, at Felsted, and bapt. the same day.

A

1. Thomas, A.M., born 16 January, 1700, at Balsham. Vicar of Linton, Cambridgeshire, 1731–1741. Died unmarr. 25 April, 1746.

2. William, born 22 Sept. 1703, at Balsham. Died 10 Sept. 1758. = ...

3. John, A.M., born 15 April, 1705, at Balsham; Rector of Cranham, Essex, 1734-1786. Died 2 March, 1786. = Catharine, dau'r of Rev. Oliver Pocklington, Rector of Chelmsford, and Catharine, his 2nd wife, dau. of John Manwood, Esq., of Priors, in the parish of Broomfield, Essex. She died 1 May, 1783.

4. Nathaniel, born 12 July, 1707, at Balsham; hosier in Cheapside, and citizen of London. Died unmarried 27 May, 1766. He bequeathed :—

To the Society for the Propagation of the Gospel	£200.
„ „ Promoting Christian Knowledge	£200.
„ Corporation of the Sons of the Clergy - -	£100.
„ Poor of Balsham - - - - - -	£200.
„ Farringdon Ward Schools - - - -	£100.
Bethlehem Hospital - - - - - - -	£100.
Bethlehem Asylum - - - - - - -	£100.

1. William, died 8 Dec. 1760, in his 28th year.

2. Thomas, hosier and citizen of London. Died 8 October, 1771, in his 37th year. = Martha, daughter of Wm. Priaulx, a Huguenot. She married 2ndly, Ambrose Serle, Esq., of the Transport Office, Private Secretary to William, 2nd Earl Howe, with whom he went to America. Mrs. Serle died 9 Apr. 1817, aged 74.

1. Nathaniel George, M.A., born 6 April, 1766; Rector of Somerford Keynes, Wiltshire, 1803-1851. Died 30 October, 1851, at Somerford Keynes. = 27 July, 1803, at Streatham, Anne, dau. of John Cox, Esq. She was born 14 July, 1766. Authoress of 'Michael Kemp,' 'Shades of Character,' etc., etc. Died 24 March, 1830.

2. John, died without issue. He was Secretary to the Transport Board during the "Long War." = Jane Lovegrove.

3. Martha, died 1 Sept. 1852, at Beckenham, aged 83.

4. Elizabeth, died 11 July, 1840, at Beckenham, aged 69.

Emma Martha, born 30 May, 1807, at King's Square, Bristol. = Thomas Wood, Esq. 5 February, 1852, at St. Martin's-in-the-Fields. He was born 8 May, 1799, at Caversham. Died without issue Dec. 19, 1865, at Twyford Abbey, Middlesex.

Two children, who died in infancy.

1. Thomas, B.D., born 5 March, 1750, at Cranham; educated at Charter-house; B.A. 1770; 1st Senior Optime; Fellow of Clare College, Cambridge; Rector of Oving, Sussex, 1799-1814; J.P. for the County of Surrey; Rector of Ockley, Surrey, 1784-1817. Died 8 Mar. 1817, at Ockley. = 21 June, 1787, at Wandsworth, Catharine, fifth daughter of Richard Barbor, Esq., of Brentwood, and Sarah his wife, dau'r of Edmund Cooke, Esq., of East Hanney, Berkshire. She was born 17 July, 1760; died 10 Jan. 1799, at Ockley. = Married secondly, 6 Feb. 1800, at Dorking, Sarah, dau'r of . . . Barnard, Esq., of Westcott, Dorking. She died without issue, 3 Mar. 1808, aged 59.

B

2. John, born 15 Aug. 1751; died 9 March, 1752, at Cranham.

3. Anne, born 2 May, 1754, at Cranham; died 30 Mar. 1823; bur. at Borley, Essex. = 2 June, 1785, at Cranham, Rev. Wm. Herringham, B.D., Rector of Chadwell St. Mary, and of Borley, Essex; Prebendary of Mora in St. Paul's Cathedral. He died 22 Feb. 1819, aged 61; buried at Borley.

C

B C

1. Catharine Herringham, born 1786; died unmarried 22 June, 1811; buried at Borley, Essex.

2. Anna Maria Herringham, born 1787; died 5 February, 1796; buried at Chipping Ongar, Essex.

3. John Philip Herringham, A.M., born 30 Jan. 1789, at Ingatestone; died 4 Dec. 1861; buried at Borley. He was Rector of Chadwell St. Mary and of Borley. = 9 December, 1823, at Little Waltham, Susanna Jackson, daughter of Rev. Godfrey Bird and Susanna his wife, daughter of Edward Greaves, Esq. She was born 21 May, 1798, at Little Waltham, Essex.

William Walton Herringham, A.M., born 31 Dec. 1824, at Borley; of St. Peter's Coll., Cam. A.B. 1847; A.M. 1850. Curate of Borley, 1848-53; Curate of St. Nicholas, Guildford, 1854-56; Rector of Chadwell St. Mary, 1856-59; Rector of Hawksworth, Notts, 1859-73; Rector of Old Cleeve, Somerset, 1873. = 19 April, 1853, at Minstead, Matilda Anne, dau'r of Major-General John Boteler Parker, C.B., of the Royal Artillery, and Lieutenant-Governor of the Royal Military Academy, Woolwich.

1. Mary Sophia Frances Herringham, born Nov. 25, 1853, at The Ryes, Henny, Essex; died the same day.

2. Wilmot Parker Herringham, born 17 April, 1855, at Guildford; Scholar of St. Mary's Coll., Winton; Exhibitioner of Keble Coll., Oxford. B.A. 1877.

3. Mary Maud Herringham, born 23 Aug. 1857, at Chadwell.

4. Amy Herringham, born 24 Sept. 1859, at Hawksworth; died 4 Nov. 1859.

5. John Philip Herringham, born 11 July, 1863, at Hawksworth.

6. Alice Kathleen Herringham, born 21 Dec. 1864, at Hawksworth.

4. William Allan Herringham, R.N., born 9 July, 1790, at Ingatestone; entered the Royal Navy 1803; gazetted Lieut. 1810; Commander, 1818; Post Captain, 1837; Retired Rear-Admiral, 1857; Vice-Admiral, 1863. Died without issue 27 Dec. 1865; buried in Kensal Green Cemetery. = 11 October, 1849, at Branston, Lincolnshire, Barbara, dau'r of Rev. Peregrine Curtois and of Anne his wife, dau'r of Sir James W. Lake, Bart. She was born 3 Jan. 1805; died 23 June, 1873; buried in Kensal Green Cemetery.

5. Thomas Herringham, born 6 Dec. 1792, at Chipping Ongar; was in the Commissary in Chief's Office. Died without issue April 18, 1828; buried at Kensington. =

6. Samuel Taylor Herringham, b. 17 March, 1795, at Chipping Ongar; of Brentwood, Solicitor. Died 25 Dec. 1836; buried at Brentwood. = 3 Sept. 1823, at Rayne, his cousin Mary Anne, youngest daughter of Rev. Thomas Woodrooffe, B.D., Rector of Ockley, Surrey.

7. Elizabeth Mary Aletheia Herringham, born 2 Dec. 1796, at Chipping Ongar; died 1 Jan. 1812; buried at Borley.

B

A daughter still-born, in 1824.

B

3. John, born 1 Jan. 1791, at Ockley; educated at Merchant Taylors' School. Secretary to the British Gas Light Company; Liveryman of the City of London, of the Merchant Taylors' Company. Died unmarr. 10 July, 1866, at Reading; buried in Kensal Green Cemetery.

4. George Henry, b. 21 May, 1792, at Ockley; educated at Merchant Taylors' School; Lieut.-Colonel Bengal Artillery. = 7 September, 1848, at Stamford, Charlotte, youngest dau'r of Dr. Arnold, M.D. of Stamford. She was born 4 Nov. 1806.

5. Mary Anne, born 10 Nov. 1793, at Ockley. Died 1 August, 1875, at Reading; buried at Brentwood. = 3 Sept. 1823, at Rayne, her cousin, Samuel Taylor Herringham of Brentwood, Solicitor.

6. William, born 8 June, 1796; educated at Merchant Taylors' School; of New Square, Lincoln's Inn, Solicitor; died without issue 8 Dec. 1857; buried in Kensal Green Cemetery. = 23 Sept. 1819, his cousin, Clariana Isabella, youngest daughter of Robert Tindal, of Chelmsford, Solicitor. She was born 23 August, 1792; died 8 Dec. 1871; buried in Kensal Green Cemetery.

1. Catharine, born 16 Apr. 1788, at Ockley; died unmarried Mar. 24, 1819, at Rayne, Essex.

Mary Anne, eldest dau'r of Edmund Woods, Esq. of Shopwyke, near Chichester, and of Katharine his wife, dau. of John Ommanney, Esq. She was born 24 July, 1788; mar. 7 Mar. 1816, at St. James's, Westminster; d. 19 July, 1818. = 2. Thomas, M.A., born 21 July, 1789, at Ockley; educated at Merchant Taylors' School and at St. John's College, Oxford, of which he was Fellow; B.A. 1810; M.A. 1814. Ordained Deacon 1812; Priest 1814. = Sophia Brooke, eldest dau'r of John Reade, Esq. of Ipsden, Oxfordshire, and of his wife Anna Maria, dau'r of Major John Scott. She was born 22 Nov. 1799; mar. 26 July, 1820, at Ipsden; died 25 June, 1856, at Alton, Hants.

Curate of Aldingbourne and of Oving, Sussex	1813-14.
Classical Professor at the R. M. C., Sandhurst	1814-15.
Curate of Brightwell Baldwin, Oxfordshire	1816-18.
„ Crowmarsh Gifford, „	1818-19.
„ Drayton, n^r Banbury „	1820-25.
Assistant-Secretary of the Church Missionary Society	1825-32.
Minister of Wheler Chapel, Spitalfields, London	1830-32.
Rector of Calbourne, Isle of Wight	1831-45.
Canon of Winchester Cathedral	1845-78.
Rector of St. Maurice, etc., Winchester	1845-54.
Vicar of Alton, Hants	1854-62.
Rector of Peper Harow, Surrey	1862-73.

Died at Amberwood House, near Christchurch, Hants, 14 May, 1878, and was buried at Highcliffe, Christchurch, 18 May, 1878.

A son still-born, in 1818.

D

D |

1. Sophia, born 21 Nov. 1821, at Drayton; died unmar. 11 May, 1844; bur. in Highgate Cemetery. She wrote 'Poems,' 'Dramatic Poems,' and 'Stories of the Primitive Church,' which were edited and published after her death by her great-uncle, Rev. George Stanley Faber, B.D.

2. George Thomas, born 19 Aug. 1823, at Drayton; educated at Cheam and at King's College School. Of Oatlands, Walton-on-Thames, and of New Square, Lincoln's Inn, Solicitor. = 25 March, 1854, Harriet E. Burgess.

3. Mary Anne, born 25 April, 1825, at Drayton. = 28 Oct. 1847, at St. Maurice, Winchester, her cousin, William Raikes Faber, C.B., 2nd son of Rev. G. S. Faber, B.D., and of his wife Eliza Sophia, dau'r of Major John Scott. He was born 2 May, 1806. B.A. of Univ. Coll., Oxford, 1826; M.A. 1836. 2nd Lieut. 60th Rifles, 1826; Lieut. 49th Regt., 1828; Capt. 49th Regt., 1835; Major by brevet, 1842; Major 49th Regt., 1843; Lieut.-Col. 2nd West India Regt., 1848; Lieut.-Col. 35th Regt., 1854; Colonel 35th Regt., 1854; Colonel 53rd Regt., 1857; Major-General, 1863; Lieut.-General, 1871; Colonel 17th Regt. Foot, 1871; General, 1877.

Reginald Stanley Faber, M.A., born 27 October, 1848, at Sherburn, n^r^ Durham; educated at Wellington Coll. and at Univ. Coll. Oxford. B.A. 1874; M.A. 1874. = 7 August, 1873, at Wraxall, Elizabeth, second dau'r of Rev. E. P. Vaughan. She was born 12 June, 1842.

4. John Allen, born 21 Dec. 1826, at Woodford; bapt. at Walthamstow; educated at Cheltenham College; died 4 July, 1868, at Forest, Ontario, Canada; buried at Warwick, Canada. = 10 March, 1856, at Warwick, Canada, Emma Richardson. She married 2ndly Alexander Scott, Esq., M.D.

- 1. Selina Emma, b. 11 Nov. 1857.
- 2. Sophia Mary, b. 8 June, 1861.

5. Julia Anne, born 6 Sept. 1828, in London, bapt. at Wheler Chapel; died Nov. 20, 1842; bur. at Calbourne, Isle of Wight.

6. Edward, born 7 July, 1830, in London, bapt. at Wheler Chapel; died 7 May, 1832; buried at Watton, Herts.

7. William Erskine, born 17 May, 1832, in London, bapt. at Wheler Chapel; educated at Brighton College. Barrister-at-Law of the Inner Temple, 1854. Ensign Cape Mounted Rifles, 1855. Lieutenant „ „ 1858. Captain „ „ 1867. = 26 April, 1855, Amelia Maria Pyle.

- 1. William Herbert, b. 16 May, 1857; died 11 March, 1863; buried at Cape Town, South Africa.
- 2. Lilias Mary, b. 20 Nov. 1860.

8. Henry Reade, M.A., born 27 April, 1834, at Calbourne, Isle of Wight; educated at Brighton College; B.A. of Christ Church, Oxford, 1856; M.A. 1876; Ordained Deacon, 1857; Priest, 1858. Missionary of the Diocese of Grahamstown, 1854-65; Curate of Ryton, Durham, 1865-68; Rector of All Saints, Somerset East, South Africa, 1868; Canon of Grahamstown, 1876. = 14 Nov. 1866, at Isleworth, Marion Elizabeth Oak.

- 1. George Borries, b. 12 March, 1868.
- 2. Charlotte Mary, b. 12 March 1870.
- 3. Henry Waring Oak, b. 6 July, 1872.
- 4. Hilda Reade, b. 11 May, 1875.

9. Selina Mary, b. 18 May, 1836, at Calbourne.

10. Arthur Gurdon, born 5 Feb. 1840, at Calbourne; educated at Brighton College. Resident in Tasmania. = Louisa Hardwicke.

11. Edmund Auriol, born 12 April, 1842, at Calbourne; educated at Repton School. Resident in Natal.

12. Charles, born 21 May, 1845, at Calbourne; educated at Rugby; and A.B. of Emmanuel Coll. Cambridge (1868.)

EXTRACTS FROM THE REGISTERS OF BURIALS IN THE PARISH OF CHELTENHAM, GLOUCESTERSHIRE.*

(*Continued from p.* 55.)

1767.	February 19	Hester Cook, Widow.
——	June 25	Thos Hartelbury
——	July 7	Mr Edward Cox
1769.	February 4.	Mrs Jane Wells
——	June 18.	Mr Thomas Packer.
——	October 16.	Martha [? Margaret], wife of John Hays [Hayes].
1770.	March 5.	William, son of Thomas Hind.
1771	February 1.	(Dyed) Jno Roydon, son of Thos Hughes
——	May 3	Harriet, daugr of Robert Snow, Esqr.
1772.	April 19.	Thomas Wood
——	November 1.	Henry Sturmey
1773.	April 27	Rebeka, wife of Revd Anthony Freeman.
1774	January 14.	Ann Etheridge, Spinster.
1775.	August 31.	Martha, wife of Robert Snow, Esqr.
1776.	September 26.	Katherine, wife of Captn Acourt

[First wife of William Pierce Ashe A'Court, Esq, M P., who was created a baronet in 1795, and was father of William, first Baron Heytesbury The tablet is the work of Westmacott]

1777.	January 12.	Martha Jordan, Widow.
——	July 28.	Thomas [? John] Ailway.
1778.	January 11.	Mary Stokes, Widdow.
1779.	April 30.	Sarah Sargeaunt
1780.	August 14	Ann Dews [Anne Dewes], and Mary, her daughter.

[See 'The Autobiography and Correspondence of Mrs Delany' (Mary Granville), edited by Lady Llanover, vol. v., p 284, London, 1862]

1781.	January 7.	Elizabeth Chester
——	September 7	Ann Wanley Bowes.
——	September 22.	George Apthorpe, Esqr, Merchant, of London
——	October 9	John Harcourt, Esqr
1783.	February 4	Arathea [? Ann], wife of Charles Harvey
——	March 12.	Mrs Ann Benfield, Widow
——	December 5	Ann, wife of John De La Bere, Esqr
1784.	April 18	Elizabeth, wife of John Field
1786.	January 13	Lætitia Sarah Maria Harcourt.
——	October 14.	Charles Hethaway.
——	November 17.	Elizabeth, wife of Thomas Hughes, Esqr.
——	December 26	Ann Hetheway, Widow.
1788.	November 26.	Revd Joshua Kyte, D D.
1790.	January 18.	William Clarke, Gent.
——	February 3	William Cook
1792	August 14.	Mrs [Sarah] Timbrell.
——	September 24	Ann Pullen
1793	January 17	John De la Bere, Esqr.

[On the tablet '1795" is given as the year of his death.]

——	February 3	George Monk Berkeley, Esqr

[Author of 'Literary Relics,' etc, London, 1789 There is also a privately-printed volume of his 'Poems,' with a preface by his mother (who *d* November 1800), and a portrait from a painting by the Rev. W. Peters, London, 1797.]

(To be continued.)

* Communicated by the Rev BEAVER H. BLACKER, M A, Cheltenham.

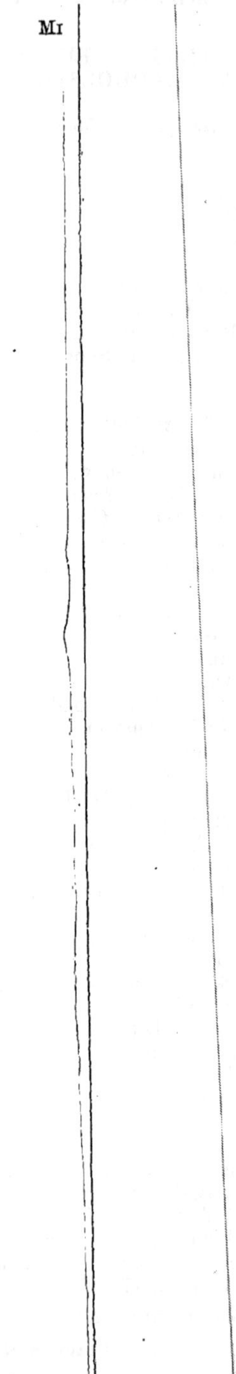
MI

EXTRACTS FROM THE REGISTERS OF BURIALS IN THE PARISH OF CHELTENHAM, GLOUCESTERSHIRE.*

(*Continued from p.* 55.)

1767.	February 19.	Hester Cook, Widow
——	June 25	Thos Hartelbury
——	July 7.	Mr Edward Cox
1769	February 4.	Mrs Jane Wells.
——	June 18	Mr Thomas Packer
——	October 16.	Martha [? Margaret], wife of John Hays [Hayes].
1770	March 5	William, son of Thomas Hind
1771.	February 1	(Dyed) Jno Roydon, son of Thos Hughes
——	May 3	Harriet, daug^r of Robert Snow, Esqr
1772.	April 19.	Thomas Wood
——	November 1.	Henry Sturmey
1773.	April 27	Rebeka, wife of Revd Anthony Freeman
1774	January 14	Ann Etheridge, Spinster
1775	August 31.	Martha, wife of Robert Snow, Esqr
1776.	September 26	Katherine, wife of Captn Acourt

[First wife of William Pierce Ashe A'Court, Esq., M.P., who was created a baronet in 1795, and was father of William, first Baron Heytesbury. The tablet is the work of Westmacott.]

1777.	January 12.	Martha Jordan, Widow
——	July 28.	Thomas [? John] Allway.
1778.	January 11.	Mary Stokes, Widdow.
1779.	April 30	Sarah Sargeaunt
1780.	August 14	Ann Dews [Anne Dewes], and Mary, her daughter.

[See 'The Autobiography and Correspondence of Mrs. Delany' (Mary Granville), edited by Lady Llanover, vol. v., p. 284, London, 1862.]

1781.	January 7	Elizabeth Chester.
——	September 7	Ann Wanley Bowes
——	September 22.	George Apthorpe, Esqr, Merchant, of London.
——	October 9	John Harcourt, Esqr.
1783.	February 4	Arathea [? Ann], wife of Charles Harvey
——	March 12.	Mrs Ann Benfield, Widow.
——	December 5	Ann, wife of John De La Bere, Esqr
1784.	April 18	Elizabeth, wife of John Field.
1786	January 13	Lætitia Sarah Maria Harcourt.
——	October 14.	Charles Hethaway
——	November 17.	Elizabeth, wife of Thomas Hughes, Esqr.
——	December 26.	Ann Hetheway, Widow.
1788.	November 26.	Revd Joshua Kyte, D.D.
1790.	January 18.	William Clarke, Gent
——	February 3.	William Cook.
1792	August 14.	M^{rs} [Sarah] Timbrell
——	September 24.	Ann Pullen
1793	January 17	John De la Bere, Esqr

[On the tablet "1795" is given as the year of his death.]

——	February 3.	George Monk Berkeley, Esqr.

[Author of 'Literary Relics,' etc., London, 1789. There is also a privately-printed volume of his 'Poems,' with a preface by his mother (who *d.* November 1800), and a portrait from a painting by the Rev. W. Peters, London, 1797.]

(*To be continued.*)

* Communicated by the Rev. BEAVER H. BLACKER, M.A., Cheltenham.

LONG OF SEMINGTON, TROWBRIDGE, WHADDON, MONKTON, &c., CO. WILTS; BECKINGTON, STRATTON, AND DOWNSIDE, CO. SOMERSET.

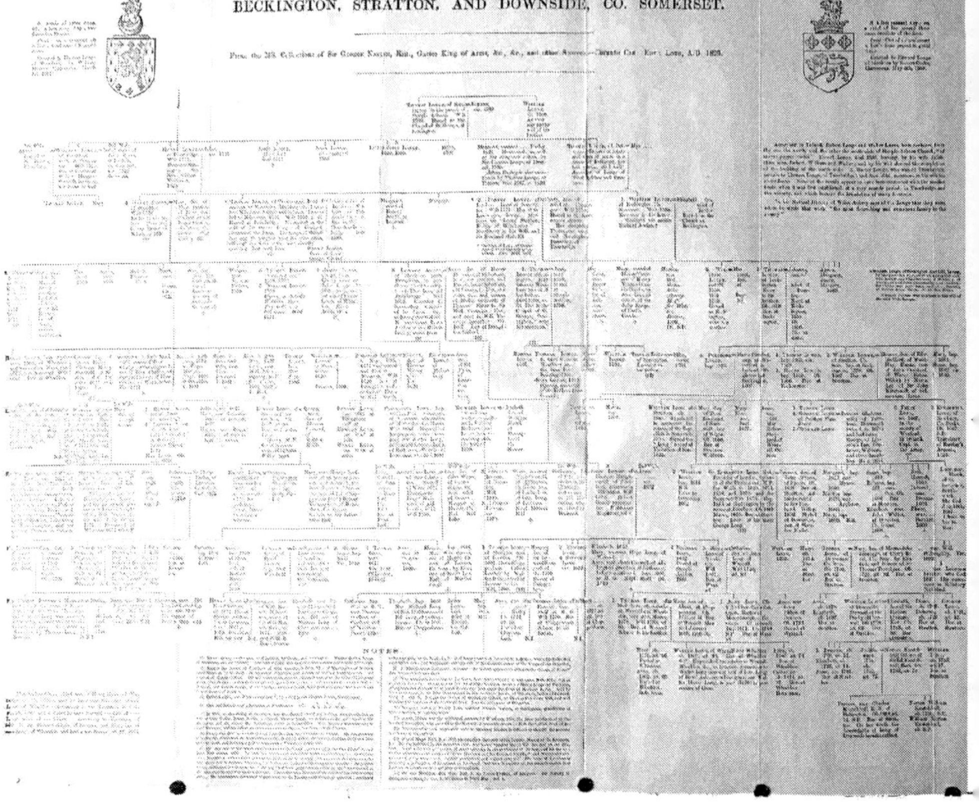

Pears or Peirce of Richmond, co. Surrey.

Compiled by Colonel Joseph Lemuel Chester, LL.D.

. . . Pears.═. . . . . living 10 Aug. 1603.

1st w. . . . . . Buried at Richmond 16 July 1604. ═ Stephen Pears, of Richmond, co. Surrey, Gent. Keeper of the Wardrobe to Q. Eliz., James I. and Charles I. Bur. at Richmond 28 Aug. 1630. Will dated 10 March, 1628-9, and proved Sept. 7, 1630. Named in his cousin Walter's will in 1603. (Mentions in his will his cousin Thos. Robinson, citizen and merchant taylor of London, and the uncle Henry Carey and grandmother Eden of his 2nd wife's children.) ═ 2nd w. Mary, only dau. of Richard Astley* (3rd son of Thomas Astley of Hillmorton, co. Warwick, Esq., by his 3rd wife Anne, dau. of . . . . Cruse of Warwick), by Margaret, dau. Sir William Stamford of Hadley, co. Middlesex, Judge of the Common Pleas 1554. She was widow of . . . . Baker. Mar. to Mr. Pears at Richmond 12 Apr. 1605. Living 10 Mar. 1628-9. (Her husband's will names her "brother Astley.")

Richard Pears, named in cousin Walter's will 10 Aug. 1603, as living "at Court." Living 10 Mar. 1628-9.

Children of . . . Pears:

- Walter Pears, of Hackney, co. Middx. gent. Will dated 10 Aug. 1603, and proved 6 June, 1604. ═ Mary, proved her husband's will 6 June, 1604.
- John Pears, living 10 Aug. 1603.

Children of Stephen Pears:

- . . . . a daughter married to . . . . Gaskyn. Issue living 10 Aug. 1603, viz., Margaret, Mary, and Anne Gaskyn.
- 1. Stephen Pears, living 1628-9. Eldest son. ═ Elizabeth, living 1628-9.
- 2. Rev. George Pears of Tiverton, co. Devon. Bapt. at Richmond 7 Dec. 1602. Called 2d son in father's will, which he proved. (He appears to have written his name *Peirce*.) His will dat. 7 Oct. and proved 29 Nov. 1679. (Mentions grands. Thos. Peirce.) Buried at Tiverton 3 Nov. 1679.† ═ . . . . . living 1679.
- 1. Anne, bapt. at Richmond 17 Apr. 1597. Evidently died young.
- 2. Dorothy, bapt. at Richmond 15 June, 1600. Married to Mark Hildersley of Hackney, co. Midx. Esq. Both living 1628-9. His will dated 15 Dec. 1659, and proved 3 April, 1660. She was bur. at Hackney 8 Dec. 1659, and he 5 Jan. following.
- 3. Elizabeth, bapt. at Richmond 12 Aug. 1604. Living 1628-9, then 2nd dau.

Children of Rev. George Pears:

- Stephen Peirce, proved father's will 22 Nov. 1679.
- Peter Peirce, living 1679.
- John Peirce, living 1679.
- Susanna, buried at Tiverton 26 April, 1638.
- Susanna, bapt. at Tiverton 23 Dec. 1641. Living 1679, wife of . . . . Chamberlaine, with a daughter Susanna.
- Jane, bapt. at Tiverton 25 Sept. 1647, and bur. there 20 Oct. 1663.

A

* Richard Astley was the younger brother of John Astley, Gent., of the Privy Chamber and Master of the Jewel House to Queen Elizabeth, and of Thomas Astley of Writtle, co. Essex, a Groom of the Privy Chamber to Queen Elizabeth. He was himself of the Jewel House.—(*Vide* supplement at Pedigrees of Stamford and of Astley.)

† "George Pierce, A.M., Rector portion of Pit in Tiverton, co. Devon, and another living in Kent, worth £160 a year." . . . . "He was bred at Eton School, and from thence elected to a Fellowship of King's College, Cambridge, in 1622, and afterwards admitted to this living in 1634. I find him articled against Dec. 11, 1646, before the standing committee of the County of Devon

A

3. Robert, bapt. at Richmond 3 April, 1606. Living as 3rd son 1628-9.*	4. Henry (twin with Mary), bapt. at Richmond 18 Sept. 1609. Living 1628-9, as 4th son. Bur. at Richmond 14 Aug. 1645.†	5. Theobald Pears, bapt. at Richmond 27 April, 1613. Living 1628-9. = Sarah Thomas mar. at St. Martin-in-the-Fields, nr London, 2nd Jan. 1639-40.‡	6. Stephen, bapt. at Richmond 11 Oct. 1614. Living 1628-9. Called 6th son and "Stephen the youngest." — 7. Joseph, bapt. at Richmond 5 March, 1615-6. Living 1628-9, as 7th son.	8. William, bapt. at Richmond 28 May, 1617. Living 1628-9, as 8th son. — 9. John, bapt. at Richmond March 25, 1619. Living 1628-9, as 9th son. Living 7 Oct. 1679.	Rev. John Weston.§ = 4. Martha, 4th dau. and eldest by 2d wife. Bapt. at Richmond 19 May, 1607. Married ante 10 March, 1628-9, and then living.	5. Mary (twin with Henry) bapt. at Richmond 18 Sept. 1609, and buried there 19 Feb. 1618-9.	6. 7. Margaret, bapt. at Richmond 11 Dec. 1610. Living 1628-9, as 4th dau. — Anne, bapt at Richmond 19 Dec. 1611. Living 1628-9, as 5th dau.	8. 9. Susan, bapt. at Richmond 3 Sept. 1620. Living 1628-1629, as 6th dau. — Mary, bapt. at Richmond 19 Sept. 1622 and buried there 4 Mar. 1627-8.

Children of Theobald Pears and Sarah Thomas:

Sarah, bapt. at Richmond 27 Jan. 1641-2.	Mary, bapt. at Richmond 13 July, and buried there 12 Oct. 1643.	Frances, bapt. at Richmond 31 Aug. 1644.	Theobald, bapt. at Richmond 31 Jan. 1646-7.	Elizabeth, bapt. at Richmond 30 Sept. 1649.

for having taken the *Cavalier's Protestation*, and for exhorting others to it." . . . . . . "He also had a temporal estate of £80 a year in London, which was likewise seized and put under sequestration." (*Vide* Walker's 'Sufferings of the Clergy,' part ii. p. 327.) Walker details the outrages from which George Pierce and his family suffered, and the privations they underwent. How long he survived the Restoration was unknown to Walker, but is above recorded. He returned to Tiverton, and became a D.D. He was an especial benefactor to the poor, and a man of singular diligence and industry in the ministry, and of great temperance and sobriety. (*Vide* also Harwood's 'Alumni Etonenses,' 1797).

* Educated at Eton, 1628.—It is stated by Harwood that he "was brother to the unfortunate and worthy George Pierce (of the year 1622)." Their father had twenty-three children by his 2nd wife, some of whom were educated at Eton and King's Coll., Cambridge, through the bounty of K. James. This Robert was a schoolmaster in Ireland.

† In the 'Alumni Etonenses,' under A.D. 1631, Car. I. 7, Harwood writes that this Henry Pierce, A.M., "was wounded at Bridgewater, and died on his passage to London."

‡ Administration was granted on the estate of Theobald Pearce of Richmond 1 May, 1656, to the relict, Sarah.

§ The Rev. John Weston, M.A., Oxon., was the only son of Dr. John Weston, D.C.L., Canon and Treasurer of Christ Church, Oxford; grandson of Dr. Robert Weston of Weeford, co. Stafford, D.C.L., Fellow of All Souls, Oxon, and the renowned Lord Chancellor of Ireland temp. Eliz., and great grandson of John Weston of Lichfield [who was descended through the family long seated at Hagley, near Rugeley, from the ancient and knightly house of Weston of Weston-under-Lyzard, co. Stafford], by Cecilia Nevill, daughter of Ralph, Lord Nevill of Raby, and sister of Ralph Nevill, who succeeded his grandfather as 4th Earl of Westmoreland. At the commencement of the Great Civil War, John Weston was the Rector of All Hallows, Lombard Street, London, and, as Newcourt records, "was for his loyalty sequestered by the rebels." He is mentioned by Walker in his 'Sufferings of the Clergy,' and Lloyd in his 'Loyal Sufferers' tells us that "because he (Weston) walked uprightly and would not creep or crouch using no Arts to gain them but pious Living and painful Labouring and because his smart Preaching made some galled back wince, they persecuted and imprisoned him." He did not survive to benefit by the restoration of the living of which he had been deprived, but died A.D. 1660. By his wife Martha, above named, he had, with other children, John, who died unmarried, and Henry, 2nd son, who married Mary, daughter of John Buckler of Radipole, in Dorsetshire, and who acquired Lane House and other property in that County, which have been retained by the family, and are now held by William Henry Purcell Weston, his direct descendant.

QUOD TRANSTULI RETULI

Pedigrees of Stamford and of Astley.

Compiled by COLONEL JOSEPH LEMUEL CHESTER, LL.D.

(*Vide ante* PEDIGREE OF PEARS OR PEIRCE.)

ARMS.—*Argent, three bars azure; on a canton or a fess sable, in chief three mascles of the last.*

(Granted by Sir Christopher Barker, Garter, to Wm. Stamford of Hadley, co. Middx., 2 May. 1542.)

Robert Stamford of Rowley, co. Stafford. = Margery dau. and heir of .... Fisher of Rowley.

William Stamford of London, mercer, 2nd son. Died ante 19 Oct. 1541. = Margaret, dau. and heir of .... Gedney of London. Her will, as late of London, widow, dated 19 Oct. 1541, and proved 7 Dec. 1542. To be buried in Islington Church, near her late father.

Sir William Stamford, 2nd son, born at Hadley, co. Middlesex, 22 Aug. 1509. Attorney General before 3 May, 1545. Queen's Serjeant-at-Law 19 Oct. 1553. Judge of the Common Pleas 1554. Knighted 27 Jan. 1554-5. Author of 'Pleas of the Crown,' etc., etc. Died 28 Aug. and buried at Hadley 1 Sept. 1558. Will dated 4 April, and proved 11 Oct. 1558. = Alice, eldest dau. of John Palmer of Kentish Town, Esq. (buried at St. Pancras.) Married ante 1541. Died 20 Sept. 1573, and buried at Hadley. = Roger Carew of Hadley, Esq. 2nd husband.

Henry Carew. Will, as of St. Andrew Wardrobe, London, gent., dated 11, and proved 13 Dec. 1626. Buried at Hadley, aged 61. (M.I.)

Richard Astley, 3rd son of Thomas Astley of Hillmorton, co. Warwick, Esq. (by his 3rd wife Anne, dau. of .... Cruse of Warwick), and younger brother of John Astley, Gent. of the Privy Chamber and Master of the Jewel House to Q. Eliz., and of Thos. Astley of Writtle, co. Essex, a Groom of the Privy Chamber to Q. Eliz. Was himself of the Jewel House. Will, as of Thetford, co. Norfolk, dated 30 Aug. 1600, and proved 20 May, 1601.* = Margaret, twin with her brother Henry. Unmarried in 1558. Living 11 Dec. 1626, as Margaret Eden. Died ante 10 March, 1628-9. = ... Eden. 2nd husb.

Drew Astley, eldest son, proved father's will. Living 3 Jan. 1639-40.

Henry Astley, youngest son. Living 1626.

.... Baker. 1st husb. = Mary Astley, only dau. evidently survived her 2nd husb. = Stephen Pears of Richmond, Esq. Keeper of the Wardrobe. (*Vide ante.*) 2nd husb.

Edward Astley, living 1639-40. (son of Drew Astley)

Mary Baker, living 1626, unmarried. (dau. of .... Baker and Mary Astley)

Children of Sir William Stamford and Alice:

Robert Stamford, son and heir. Living 20 Aug. 1600, of Pury Hall, co. Stafford, Esq.

Henry Stamford, 4th son, twin with Margaret. Will, as of Blackfriars, gent., dated 23 April, 1614, and proved 2 Nov. 1616.

Four other sons.

Frances, 2nd dau. Marr. Thos. Repington of Amington, co. Warwick, Esq., by whom Sir John Repington.

Five other daus.

* The Astleys of Hill Morton, one of the best families in Warwickshire, whose pedigree goes back to the time of King John.

THE DENNYS,

EARLS OF NORWICH, BARONS DENNY OF WALTHAM, AND BARONETS OF IRELAND

THE lineage of this very ancient family is given at length in Archdall's revised edition of 'Lodge's Peerage of Ireland' (vol i, p 298, ed. 1789), and by Sir Bernard Burke in his 'Peerage and Baronetage of Great Britain and Ireland' Traditionally it claims for a founder a knight who rendered good service to Charlemagne, but Lodge begins the pedigree with John Denny, who served Henry the Fifth in the French wars, and who, with his son John, was slain in battle and buried in France Fourth in descent from the elder brother of this last-mentioned John was Edmund Denny of Cheshunt, Baron of the Exchequer and Knight, who died in 1520, leaving with other issue a daughter Joice Denny, who marrying William Walsingham, was by him mother of Sir Francis Walsingham, Secretary of State *temp* Elizabeth, and Anthony born in 1500, the well-known favourite of Henry the Eighth He was knighted and made a Privy Councillor and Groom of the Stole to that king Fuller tells us in his quaint language that "alone of all the courtiers Sir Anthony Denny was bold and faithful enough to acquaint King Henry truly with his dying condition, to dispose his soul for another world" The learning and virtues of Sir Anthony Denny have been commemorated in the verse of Surrey and in the Latin prose of Roger Ascham. He married, says Lodge in his Biographies of Royal and Illustrious personages, "a lady of ancient lineage and great piety," Joan daughter of Sir Philip Champernoun, of Modbury, Devonshire, the aunt of Sir Walter Raleigh and Sir Humphrey Gilbert, the hero of Longfellow's ballad In a curious and beautiful epitaph on Sir Anthony Denny amongst the Harleian MSS in the British Museum he is described as a—

> "Mæcenas to the learned, an anchor to relygion,
> To these an open haven that were for Christe opprest,"

and from the narration of Anne Askew, it appears that Joan Lady Denny was one of the friends and helpers of that noble-minded martyr during her imprisonment. The Champernoun sisters appear to have been amongst the first who ventured to protect the persecuted in Devonshire under Henry the Eighth (*v.* Edwards' Life of Raleigh) Joan Lady Denny left by Sir Anthony, with other issue, two daughters, Mary, who married Thomas Astley, Groom of the Chamber, and Honora, who married Thomas Wingfield, grandson of Sir Richard Wingfield, Kt Mareschal of Calais, Privy Councillor and Ambassador and Knight of the Garter, who by his marriage with Catherine, dowager Duchess of Buckingham and Bedford, was great uncle to Henry the Eighth. In 1522 that king granted to Sir Richard the castle and manor of Kimbolton with other manors and several priories, all of which were inherited by his grandson Thomas above mentioned. He had issue, by Honora Denny, a son, Sir Edward Wingfield of Kimbolton, whose grandson, Sir Edward Maria Wingfield. sold that ancient mansion to the ancestor of the Duke of Manchester Sir Anthony Denny, besides these daughters, had also two sons, of whom it is only here necessary to mention two, viz. —I. HENRY, who married first the daughter of John Lord Grey of Pirgo, coheir to Henry Duke of Suffolk, and by her had no issue, and secondly Honora daughter of William Lord Grey of Wilton, and had with other issue a son and heir Edward, created Baron Denny of Waltham in 1605, and Earl of Norwich 24th August, 1616 Edward Denny Earl of Norwich married Lady Anne Cecil, daughter of the Earl of Exeter, by whom he had an only child and heiress Lady Honora Denny, who married James Hay, Earl of Carlisle, and left an only son, James, Earl of Carlisle, who married the daughter of the Earl of Bedford. and died s p. II EDWARD, fifth and youngest son of Sir Anthony Denny by Joan, dau of Sir Philip Champernoun, went to Ireland with his connexion Lord Grey and his cousins Raleigh and Gilbert, and served gallantly against the Irish and their Spanish and Italian allies To quote again from Fuller, "Sir Edward Denny was dubbed a knight banneret on the field of battle, and by God's favour, Queen Elizabeth's bounty, and his own valour, achieved a fair estate in the county of Kerry in Ireland, at this day enjoyed by his descendants." This estate of about seven thousand acres was portion of the immense forfeited Palatinate of Gerald, 16th Earl of Desmond, and contained the Earl's chief castle of Tralee, and several smaller castles in the west of Kerry. Sir Edward Denny married, like his father, a lady of old west of England stock, Margaret daughter of Piers Edgcumbe, Esq. of Mount Edgcumbe, ancestor of the Earls Mount Edgcumbe. Margaret Edgcumbe had been Maid of Honour to Queen Elizabeth, and soon after her marriage she accompanied her husband to Ireland, where a fierce rebellion raged. She was, with her two young children and a small garrison of the Queen's troops, at Tralee on the west coast of Kerry, when in September, 1588, the ships of the Spanish Armada were driven thither. Sir Edward Denny was absent in Dublin, and the position of his wife amidst the half-subdued wild Irish, all devoted to Spain and Catholicism, was far more perilous than that of her father in the "Edgcumbe's lofty hall" of Macaulay's fine ballad She was however equal to the occasion, and the few Spaniards who were able to effect a landing in Dingle and Tralee were made prisoners, and at once hung by her orders at the latter town Lady Denny and her husband appear to have remained in Kerry until 1589, and to have then, with their young children, returned to England in the ship of the famous sea rover, George Clifford, Earl of Cumberland, which had put into Dingle for water and provision on her perilous voyage homeward from the Azores (*v.* Hakluyt) Sir Edward Denny died on the 13th of February, 1599, and was buried in Waltham Abbey, Essex, under a fine altar tomb erected by his widow In a recess above the tomb is a slab bearing a long and quaint inscription to the memory of the knight, and, according to old histories of the county, a small stone tablet was formerly attached to the marble pillars of this recess, on which these lines were inscribed —

> "Learn curious reader, ere you pass,
> What once Sir Edward Denny was,
> A Courtier in the Chamber—a Soldier in the field,
> Whose tongue could never flatter,
> Whose heart could never yield"

Two marble effigies, a knight and lady, lie on the tomb itself, and on the stone pillow beneath the lady's head are carved these lines from the Book of Job —

"All the daies of my appointed time will I wait untill my change come"

From this it is evident that the widowed Margaret Lady Denny intended that she should be buried with her husband, but this intention was frustrated, probably by the disturbed state of the country when she died in the midst of the great Civil War of the seventeenth century The "days of her appointed time on earth" were long and changeful, and she was probably the sole survivor of that brilliant ring of fair women and brave men which encircled the throne of the last of the Tudors Of Sir Edward Denny's distinguished kindred, Gilbert had perished at sea in a manner befitting his mother's pious and noble race, Grey and Raleigh on the scaffold, through the malice of Spain and the perfidy of James the First, that king had passed away to his account, and his son was a prisoner to fall under the axe in less than a twelvemonth, when Margaret Lady Denny, the ex-maid of honour to Elizabeth, died at the age of eighty-eight years, and was buried *not* with her husband at Waltham, but in the church of Bishop's Stortford, in Hertfordshire The brass which marks her resting place, near the altar, is still in good preservation, and bears the following inscription —

"Here Lyeth interred the truelie honor'd The Ladye Margaret Dennye descended of the ancient familie of Edgcumbe of Mount Edgcumbe in Cornwall,—a Mayd of Honor in Ordinarie to Queen Elizabeth of blessed memorie, then marry'd to Sir Edward Dennye, Kt Groom of her Majesty's Privy Chamber, She departed this lyfe April 24, 1648, Aged 88 yeares, and in the 48th yeare of her widowhood."

Several monuments to her younger children, and their Hertfordshire connexions, are to be seen in the church

Her eldest son Sir Arthur Denny, Kt. seems to have returned to Ireland at the beginning of the seventeenth century He married Elizabeth daughter of Miles

Forest, Esq. of Huntingdon, and sister of Sir Anthony Forest, and, dying at his mansion house of Carrignafeely, near Tralee, in the county of Kerry, on the 4th of July, 1619, left an only son and heir, aged fourteen years and three months, as appears by an inquisition taken at Tralee, 18th April, 1622, and preserved in the Public Record Office, Dublin The wardship of Edward Denny, during his minority, was granted to Sir Robert Loftus, eldest son of Lord Loftus of Ely, Lord Justice of Ireland in 1636-40, and ancestor of the Lennard Barretts of Bell House, Essex, and the Lords Dacre. Edward Denny attained his majority in the year 1626, and the family genealogy for a hundred and twenty years after is preserved with tolerable fulness (and perfect accuracy as far as it goes), in an old MS volume, half diary, half register, in the possession of his lineal descendant the present Sir Edward Denny, Baronet, supplemented by various entries on the fly-leaves and margin of a yet more curious family relic, a black-letter Bible of the early part of the seventeenth century, which by a well-nigh miraculous succession of Providences escaped destruction in the great Irish civil wars of 1641 and 1689, when Tralee Castle was in the hands of the Irish, and innumerable churches and Bibles were burnt all over the island The original Desmond Castle, which was granted to Sir Edward in 1587, had been so dilapidated in the wars of that time that it was uninhabitable, hence the family resided for nearly fifty years at the manor house of Carrignafeely before mentioned But when Sir Edward Denny, the ward of Loftus, attained his majority, he rebuilt or restored the old Castle of Tralee, as appears by the old diary It begins with the following entries, written by him in a very clear, fine hand for the time —

"I was marryed in Roper's Rest House to Ruth Roper in Lent being the (*illegible*) 1625.

"I finished this great Castell and came with my mother to live in itt upon y[e] 22[d] of December 1627.

"Margarett Denny my daughter was born y[e] 25th of March 1627, being Wensday and dyed thursday sennight after Whit Sunday being early in y[e] morning, her Godmother were y[e] Ladye Honora Fitz Maurice and my mother the Ladye harris,* Sir Valentine Browne her Godfather

"Monday y[e] 21st of September 1629 between 11 and 12 o'clock in the day Arthur Denny was borne, his Godfather was Donough O'brian deputy of the Lord Presydent S[r] W S[t] Leger and David Earle of Barrymore who was here, his God mother was my mother

"The 20th of November 1629 my wyfe and I began housekeeping in this greate Castell"

Roper's Rest House (which seems to be an Anglicised version of Rast Haus) was, in 1625, the residence of Sir Thomas Roper, Lord Baltinglass, father of Lady Denny and collateral ancestor of Lord Teynham Part of it, with a high antique roof and massive chimney stacks, still stands in the suburbs of Dublin, amidst a crowd of warehouses, tanyards, and other vulgar companions unknown to the knightly mansion in its better days. There are some very curious legends connected with it Honora Fitz Maurice, the Godmother of the short-lived child Margaret Denny, was the wife of the nineteenth Lord Kerry, who was buried in the church of St. Giles's in the Fields, London, on the 31st of January, 1660. His wife was the daughter of Sir John Fitz Gerald of Cloyne, said by Archdall to have been "the richest commoner of his time" Honora Lady Kerry had, with other issue, a daughter Margaret married to Christopher Roper, Lord Teynham, and a son whose son and successor the twenty-first Lord Kerry, created Earl of Kerry in 1722, married Lady Anne Petty, sister of the Earl of Shelburne, and the friend of Swift, and was by her ancestor of the present Marquis of Lansdowne Honora Lady Kerry and Anne Countess of Kerry (*née* Petty) are both buried in Ardfert Cathedral, in Kerry (*v* 'Journal of the Royal Historical and Archæological Association of Ireland,' July, 1876) Sir Valentine Browne, mentioned in the above entry, was the ancestor of the present Earl of Kenmare.

M. A. H

(*To be continued*)

* The widow of Sir Arthur Denny, who married secondly Sir Thomas Harris

Pedigree of the Family of St. George.*

"The title of the Pedigree I sent into France to my cousin St. George, the nun, in Paris, together with the attestation under the Seal of the Office of Arms, viz.:—

'Stemma perantiqua Equestris Familiæ Sancti Georgiorum, modo de Hatley St. George, in Comitatu Cantabridgiæ.

'Baldwinus de Sancto Georgio 13° Henrici primi, Regis Angliæ. David de Argentine sive de Argentimago 20° Conquestoris. Teca Normanus quidam Nobilis.

'Ex Archivis Collegii Heraldorum, in Civitate Londonensi, aliisq. Scriptis et testimoniis fide dignis desumptum, et sigillo Communi Collegii prad'ci comprobatum, tertio die mensis Aprilis, a° Incarnationis Domini M°DC°LXXXVI° Regniq. Serenissimi et Potentissimi Domini nostri Jacobi Secundi, Dei Gratia, Magnæ Britanniæ, Franciæ, et Hiberniæ Regis, Fidei Defensoris Secundo.'"

(The above was written by Sir Thomas St. George, Garter King of Arms; and his "cousin, the nun in Paris," was Margaret, grand-niece of Sir Richard St. George, Norroy, he being grandson of the same. This Pedigree has been carefully continued to the present day.)

Baldwin St. George, came into England with William the Conqueror, from "Saint Georges," near Limoges.

- Baldwin, temp. William Rufus.
  - Baldwin, living 13 Hen. I.
    - William St. George, temp. Hen. II. = ... dau'r of Bancis of Kingston.
      - Baldwin St. George, 1st year of John.
        - Baldwin St. George, 1st & 12th Hen. III.
          - Dom^s Will^s St. George, 26 Hen. III.
            - A
          - Amicia, married Philip de Abington.
            - Sir William de Abington.
        - William St. George, 7 Hen. III. 2nd son.
        - Henry St. George, 7 Hen. III. 4th son. = Alicia, 33 Hen. III.
          - Alicia, married Walter Gifford.
          - Joan, married Robt. Bozon.
          - Rosamund, 33 Hen. III.
        - Robert St. George, surnamed "de Haileweston." 3rd son. Bur. at St. Neots. 2nd husband. = Agnes, daughter and heir of William de Alneto. Buried at St. Neots. = Hugo de Ardres, 1st husband.
          - (by Robert St. George) Baldwin.
          - William.
          - Albreda, 29 Hen. III.
          - Agnes, married Wm de Graffham.
          - (by Hugo de Ardres) John de Ardres.
      - Mabilia St. George, a nun in Clerkenwell.
    - Albreda St. George, a nun in Clerkenwell.

* Communicated by General Sir JOHN ST. GEORGE, K.C.B.

A

Eymond de Turenberd, 1st husband. Seized of Upton in le Cley in Notts. Constable of the Tower of London. ═ Bazilia de Soham, Lady of Mepham in Isle of Ely. (An heiress of Avenel.) ═ Dom. Baldwinus de St. George, 40 Hen. III. d. 1282. 2nd husb.

- Elizabeth, wife of Thomas de Echalers.
- Margery, wife of Roger Gynney.
- Alianora, wife of Baldwin Colne.
- Margaret, coheir of both her parents. ═ Sir William de St. George, died before 1312.

Baldwin St. George, died before his father. ═ Johanna, living 1340.

Margery, married Rob. Haringall, co. York.

Sir William St. George, Knt., of Hungre Hatley in co. Cambridge, 21 Edw. III.

Basilia St. George.

Sir Baldwin St. George, Knt., M.P. and Sheriff of cos. Cambridge and Huntingdon. ═ Elizabeth, daughter and coheir of Sir John Argentine, Knt.

- Sir Baldwin St. George, Knt., M.P. and J.P., died 18 Feb. 1425. Was buried at Hatley St. George, co. Cambridge, where there is a brass in the Church of a knt. in armour, and his name and arms. ═ Joan, dau'r and coheiress of Sir John Engaine, Knt.
- Thomas.
- Elizabeth.
- Giles, at school in 1393.
- John.

John, died in v.p. ═ Matilda, dau'r and heir of Sir William de Coggeshall, Knt.

Baldwin.

William.

Alianora, dau'r and coheir of Sir Richard Arundel, Knt. ═ Sir William St. George, Knt., M.P. for Cambridgeshire; d. 1472. ═ Katherine, daughter of Sir J. Manningham, Knt.

Thomas St. George, died unm. before his mother.

Sir Richard St. George, Knt. b. 1446; died 1485. ═ Ann, daughter of Thomas à Burgoine of Impington, co. Cambridge.

Alice, daughter of Sir John Rotherham, Lord of Somerham; died before 1512. ═ Thomas St. George of Hatley St. George, b. 1473; d. 1540. ═ Etheldreda, dau'r of Clement Higham of Giffards, Suffolk.

- Ann, mar. to John Docwra.
- Catherine, mar. to Richard Marshall.
- George St. George, mar. 1512; d.s.p. ═ Joan, dau'r of Wm Mordaunt.

Francis St. George of Hatley St. George, Esq. b. circ. 1525; mar. before he was 15. ═ Rose, dau'r of Thomas Hutton of Drydrayton, co. Cambridge.

John St. George, Esq. of Hatley St. George, co. Cambridge. ═ Mary, daughter of Peter Grey of Rugcourt, co. Bedford.

B

Sir Richard St. George, Knt. Clarenceux King of Arms. Knighted 28 Sept. 1616. Married in 1575. Died on the 17 May 1635. Bur. in the chancel of St. Andrew's Church, Holborn. ═ Elizabeth, daughter of Nicholas St. John, Esq. of Lidiard Tregoz, ancestor of the Viscounts St. John and Bolingbroke.

C

John St. George of Hatley St. George, fined £625 by the Parliament in 1648 for being in arms for the King. Buried 30 Dec. 1652. ═ Dorothy, daughter of John Legatt of Horn Court, co. Essex, Esq.

William St. George.

Henry St. George.

Peter St. George.

Thomas, died Nov. 1637. ═ Frances, daughter of John Shelbury of High Holborn, and of Perrivale, co. Middx.

Margaret, mar. Humfrey Elms. — Katherine, mar. John Sharpe, and 2nd J. Southwell. — Mary, mar. P. Lenthal.

Ann, mar. . . . Flood, 2nd . . . Fanning. — Elizabeth, mar. . . . . Cramlington.

John St. George, mar. 1st Clara Gage, who died s.p. His second wife was ═ Margaret, dau'r of Francis Perkins of Ufton, co. Berks.

Richard St. George. ═ Susanna, dau'r of Anthony Thomson of Cambridge.

Thomas. — William. — Anthony.

Baldwin. — Margaret, a Nun in Paris.

Mary, coheir, mar. F. Harris.

Margaret, mar. Segrave, d. s.p. 1720.

John, died 6 Oct. 1690. ═ Sarah, dau'r of Edward Norman of London.

Susanna, d. unmar.

Mary, d. young.

Edward St. George. ═ Alicia, dau'r of Gabriel Selden of Kinsale.

Elkin St. George.

Sarah, d. an infant.

Edward. Gabriel. George. Richard. — Died young.

Dillon, b. 21 May 1719. s.p.

Henry, b. 4 Nov. 1720. s.p.

George, b. 4 Dec. 1723. s.p.

Emelia, b. 5 May 1717. s.p.

1st son. William St. George, killed in action at Loch Foyle, temp. Eliz., aged 22.

2nd. John St. George, killed also in the Irish Wars.

3rd. Sir Henry St. George, Knt., D.C.L., Garter King of Arms, b. 27 Jan. 1581; mar. 1614; d. 5 Nov. 1644. ═ Mary, dau'r of Sir Thomas Dayrell of Lillingston Dayrell, Bucks, Kt.

4th. Sir George St. George, Knt. of Carrickdrumrusk, co. of Leitrim, born 13 Jan. 1583. M.P. Murdered at Croghan, King's County. ═ Catherine, dau'r of Captain Gifford of Castle Jordan, King's County.

Sir Thomas St. George, Knt., Garter King of Arms, of Woodford, in Essex, b. 1615; died 6 March, 1702-3. ═ Clara, dau'r of Rev. John Pymlowe, d. 1691. ═ 2nd wife, Ann, dau'r of Sir John Lawson, Kt. d. 7 Feb. 1720.

William St. George, Col. in the Army of Charles I. Killed at the storming of Leicester 21 May, 1645.

Sir Henry St. George, Knt., Garter King of Arms, d. 1715, aged 91. ═ Elizabeth Wingfield, died 1704.

Richard St. George, Ulster King of Arms died s.p. ═ Mary, dau'r of Sir Hen' Hastings of Bramston.

Thomas St. George, Esq., Lay Rector of Bexley. ═ Damaris, dau'r and coheir of Robert Renter.

Eleanor, mar. Thomas Coote of Coote Hill.

Isabella, b. 4 Sep. 1693.

A daughter, mar. . . . Wynne of little Chelsea, Esq., Serjeant-at-Law.

A daughter, and coheir, mar. Mr. Gregory of Woolthorpe, Leicestershire.

Elizabeth mar. Col. R. Bourke. — Mary, mar. Ferdinand Hastings. — Frances, mar. George Tucker. — Rebecca, mar. George Cooke.

Elinor, dau'r and heiress, mar. Thomas Dare of Taunton.

D E

D — E

Sir Oliver St. George, Bart. M.P. for Galway in 1661. = Olivia, dau'r of Michael Beresford.

Letitia, married Arthur Dillon, Esq.

Elinor, mar. Sir Arthur Gore, Bart.

Ann, mar. Sir Thomas Newcomen, Bart.

Sir George St. George, Kt., of Dunmore, M.P. for Leitrim in 1661; d. 1711. = Elizabeth, dau'r of Sir Robert Hannay, Bart.

Mary St. George, mar. Richard, Lord Colooney.

Sarah St. George, mar. Sir Henry Brooke, Bart.

Children of Sir George St. George and Elizabeth Hannay:

Richard, d. s.p. 1726. Mar. 1686, Ann, dau. of John Eyre of Eyre Court.

George, died unmar.

Elizabeth, d. s.p. 1739. m. Sir Wm. Parsons.

Amelia, m. Rev. Carleton. Died s.p. 1721.

Jane, d. 5 Aug. 1741. Mar. Dr. St. George Ashe, Bishop of Clogher.

Catherine, m. Dr. Chas. Crowe, Bishop of Cloyne.

Children of Mary St. George and Richard, Lord Colooney:

Thomas Coote, mar. Elinor, dau'r & co-heir of Sir Thomas St. George of Woodford, Essex.

Elizabeth Coote, mar. General Richard St. George.

Children of Sir Oliver St. George and Olivia Beresford:

Catherine, mar. Sir Ed. Crofton, Bart.

George, *Lord* St. George, d. 4 Aug. 1735, aged 84. = Margaret, dau'r of John, Viscount Massarene.

Oliver St. George, mar. Susanna Knox, d. s.p.

Olivia St. George, mar. 1st, Sir Richard Colvil; 2nd, Pierce, Viscount Ikerrin; 3rd, 1719, Mr. Wroth of Epsom.

Daughter of George, Lord St. George:

Honble. Mary St. George, sole heiress. Mar. John Usher, Esq., M.P. for Carrick.

Children of Mary St. George and John Usher:

St. George Usher, created Lord St. George; d. 1775. = Elizabeth Dominick.

Olivia St. George Usher, mar. 23 Jan. 1736. = Arthur French, Esq. of Tyrone House.

Daughter of St. George Usher:

Honble. Amelia Olivia St. George. = William Robert, 2nd Duke of Leinster.

Son of Olivia St. George Usher and Arthur French:

Christopher French St. George, Tyrone, mar. Ann Bingham.

Arthur French St. George, b. 1780; mar. Lady Harriet St. Lawrence, and left, *inter alia*

Christopher St. George, born 1810; died 1877, at Tyrone House, co. Galway.

D

D

5th son.

Ann, daughter of Michael Pinnock, Esq., of Turrock, co. Roscommon, mar. 1625; d. 4 Oct. 1643. Buried in Athlone. ╤ Captain Richard St. George, b. at Hatley St. George, 27 March, 1590; d. 24 Apr. 1667. Bur. in Athlone. The progenitors of all existing persons entitled to the name. ╤ Dorothy, daughter of Sir John Moore of Crogan, Knt., mar. in 1644. She was the widow of Hamon L'Estrange of Castle Strange, Roscommon.

Martha St. George, b. 1644; mar. 3 Aug. 1671. = Joseph Jackman, Captain of Horse; d. at Carrickfergus.

Captain Arthur St. George of Turrock, b. 1629, d. 1702.

Mary St. George, mar. Dec. 1655, Thos. Ashe of St. John's.

St. George Ashe, Bishop of Clogher, and other children. = Jane, dau'r of Sir George St. George of Dunmore, Knt., d. 5 Aug. 1741.

Richard, killed at the Siege of Galway 1652.

Ann, mar. Lieut. Ed[d] Wood of Cour.

Henry St. George of Athlone, b. 15 Oct. 1638; mar. 3 June 1669, at Killanure; d. 1723. Was M.P. for Athlone. ╤ Ann, daughter of Alderman Rigeley Hatfield of Dublin, d. 10 Aug. 1688, at Castle Coote. Buried at Athlone.

Richard St. George of Kilrush, b. in Athlone 28 Aug. 1670; mar. 9 Aug. 1696; d. in Dublin in Jan. 1755, without lawful issue. He was a Lieut.-General in the Army, and M.P. = Elizabeth, dau'r of Lord Coote of Colooney, and of Mary St. George, his wife.

Henry, b. 30 July 1676; d. unmar. 1723. Sheriff of Roscommon in 1717.

Arthur St. George, D.D., Dean of Ross, b. 25 Apr. 1681; d. 24 Sept. 1772, aged 91. ╤ Jane, 3rd dau'r of Sir Thomas Molyneux, Bt., m. 2 Mar. 1730, d. 30 Sep. 1788.

George St. George, born at Athlone 2 July 1682, and d. 23 Dec. 1762. ╤ Elizabeth, daughter of John Bligh of Rathmore, & sister of John, Earl of Darnley.

Richard St. George of Kilrush, mar. in 1763; died ante 1775; mar. Sarah, dau'r of Dean Handcock, who died 1820.

Richard (the minor), b. 21 Feb. 1766. Sold Kilrush to his uncle Howard. Died s.p. June, 1840.

Catherine, married Clement Wolseley, Esq. Had issue.

Thomas St. George, M.P. for Clogher, b. 1738; mar. 5 Aug. 1776; and died 1 Apr. 1785. ╤ Honble. Lucinda Acheson, dau'r of Lord Gosford.

G

Capel, d. a Capt.

Arthur, Major 62 Reg. d. s.p. mar. 1768.

Howard, D.D., b. 1744; mar. 1767. Purchased Kilrush. ╤ Mary, dau'r of Edward Lucas of Castleshane, b. 1751.

H

Rev. Henry St. George, mar. 1st, Mary, dau'r of Philip Percival, who d. 1776, leaving a son Arthur, who d. in 1845. ╤ 2nd wife, Jane, dau'r of Sir Fred. Flood, Bart., d. 1842.

I

F

G — H — I — F

Thomas Baldwin St. George, b. 12 May 1777; Capt. 80th Regt.; d. 28 Feb. 1852. No male issue now surviving.

Elinor, dau'r of Rob. Gordon, mar. 1810; d. May 1821. ╤ Acheson St. George of Wood Park, co. Armagh, b. 21 June 1778; died 3 Dec. 1855. ╤ Jane, dau'r of Hon. & Very Rev. John Hewitt Dean of Cloyne.

John St. George, Capt. 80th Regt. Lieut.-Col. Salop *Militia*; born 16 Aug. 1779, at Kilrush; d. at Birkenhead 28 Jan. 1854. ╤ Frances, dau'r of Arch[d] Campbell, M.D., of Stafford; d. 10 Oct. 1865.

Archibald St. George of Camma, b. 27 Feb. 1782; d. in Dublin 14 Nov. 1864, unmar.

William Molyneux, b. 17 Feb. 1784. Lieut. R. Navy. Was killed at Trafalgar 21 Oct. 1805, s.p.

Issue of Acheson St. George and Elinor:

Thomas Gordon St. George, Colonel in E.I.C. Service; b. 10 March 1812; died at Erchfont 22 May 1874. ╤ Sarah Straghan Caldecot.

- Norah. — Ethel Eugenie.
- Acheson Wm. Gordon. — Adela Eleanor.

Acheson St. George of Wood Park, b. 16 July 1819.

Eleanor Mary.

William. — Lucinda. — Olivia. — John. } d. s.p.

Issue of Acheson St. George and Jane:

Alicia Hewitt Caroline, m. Edward Chaloner Knox.

Issue of John St. George and Frances:

4th. George, b. 12 June 1816. H.M.C. ╤ Annie Gibson, dau'r of Richard Bryan, J.P., Esq. of Parkfield, Cheshire.

- George Edward. — Arthur Baldwin.
- Archibald Henry. — *Annie Georgina.*
- Frances Alice.

5th. Millicent, mar. Fred. Holder, Esq.

6th. Howard, Vicar of Billinge, born 12 June, 1816. ╤ Emelia, dau'r of Andrew Comber, Esq.

- Howard Comber. — Frances Emelia.
- Lucy Frances Mary, d.s.p. — Millicent Lucinda.

7th. Lucy Eliz. Georgiana, mar. Rev. W. E. Coldwell, Vicar of Sandon, Staffordshire.

- Ellinor, d. s.p. — Mary Emily.
- Wm. St. George. — Lucy Olivia.

1st son. General Sir John St. George, K.C.B., Col. Commandant Royal Artillery; born at Stafford 18 Jan. 1812; mar. 15 Aug. 1860. ╤ Elizabeth Marianne, dau'r and coheir of Thos. Evans of Lyminster, Esq., and of his wife, dau'r and sole heir of William Harris, Esq.

- Baldwin John St. George, born 16 Feb. 1862.
- Frances Millicent, b. 16 Jan. 1865.

2nd. Archibald St. George (of Camma, co. Roscommon) born 5 June 1813, mar. his cousin Kate St. George.

- William Baldwin St. George, Lieut. R.A.; d. 6 Dec. 1876.
- Mary Ann Frances. — Millicent Eleanor. — Lucy Olivia.
- Edward Whitmore, d. s.p.

3rd. William Whitmore of Clifton Park, b. 3 Dec. 1814. ╤ Mary Ann, dau'r of David Cram.

- Harriet Louisa. — Emily Agnes. — Sophie Emma.
- Acheson Whitmore, Lieut. 14th Regt. — Howard. — George Herbert. — Charles Henry.

H — I — F

John St. George.

H | I | F

1st son.
Arthur John of Kilrush House, b. May 1775; d. in 1853. = Elinor, dau'r of Theophilus Blakeney of Abbot, d. 11 Feb. 1876, aged 86.

- Howard John of Kilrush House, born 1813. Was in the 12th and 17th Lancers. Mar. in 1843. = Caroline, dau'r of Col. George Grogan of Seafield, co. Dublin.
  - Arthur.
  - Emily Elizabeth.
  - Harriet Eleanor.
  - Caroline Frances.
  - Howard Cecil.
  - Selina Ada.
  - Edith Margaret.
  - Cecilia Mary.
  - John Edward.
- Mary Henrietta.
- Margaret Elizabeth.
- Sarah Selina.
- Capel Lucas.
- Harriet.
- John Hatley, d. s.p.
- Theophilus Edward, mar. 6 Apr. 1853, Isabella, dau'r of Rev. Henry St. George.
- Arthur John, mar. Kate Nevill.

2nd.
Henry Lucas St. George, in Holy Orders; b. 1781; Rector of Dromore; d. 24 Feb. 1872. = Elizabeth, dau'r of Edw. Warren of Lodge Park, co. Kilkenny.

- Capel.
- Elizabeth, m. 28 Feb. 1837, Sir Hugh Stewart, Bart., of Ballygawley, co. Tyrone.
- Henry Lucas, mar. only child of Wm. Sterne, Esq., of Gola House, co. Fermanagh.
- Edward, d. s.p.
- Anne.
- Oliver Hatley, d. s.p.
- William Nassau, d. s.p.
- Mary, mar. H. W. Roley, Esq. of Mapperath, co. Meath.
- Henrietta, m. Hugh Lyons Montgomery, Esq.

3rd.
Thomas Belmore, b. 1782, Barrister-at-Law. = Wilhelmina, dau'r of Major Wolseley, and great grand-dau'r of Dean Arthur St. George.

- Rev. Henry St. George.
- Oliver St. George.
- Nelson of Altamont, mar. Miss Cash, and died.
- William, of Kildavin House, mar. Miss Lovel; d. s.p. in 1871.
- Jane, mar. Rev. Mr. Whitly.
- Henrietta, d. s.p.
- Isabella, mar. in 1843, Theophilus Edward St. George of Kilrush.

4th.
Richard Quintus St. George, Vicar of Crossmolina, b. 1786; d. 8 Aug. 1877, aged 92. = Henrietta Maria, dau'r of Sir Robert Langrishe, Bart., d. 25 Apr. 1877.

- Rev. Howard Boyle, born 20 June 1812; mar. 13 June 1843. Has ten children. = Jemima Grace, dau'r of Rev. Wm. Atthill, of Brandiston Hall, Norfolk.
  - Howard Henry, mar. Jane Eyre, and settled in Australia.
  - Thomas Clement Belmore, Capt. 78th Regt.; m. 1873, Jane Ellen, dau'r of the late George Baillie of the Grove, Hanwell.
  - Mary Caroline.
  - William, d. young.
  - William, d. young.
  - Richard John, drowned.
  - Wm. Augustus, d. s.p.
  - Willa Frances.
  - Mary John.
  - Edward Beauchamp.
  - Louisa Elizabeth, mar. 1863, Sedgwick S. Cowper, Esq. in Australia.
  - Arthur George, m. 1866, Sarah Ann Lee, and d. 5 Dec. 1876.
- Wm. Edward, mar. twice, and d. 7 Dec. 1876.
- Anne, mar. Rev. St. George Knox.
- Mary, mar. J. Ormsby Orme.
- Elizabeth.
- Richard, d. s.p.
- Henry Charles, d. s.p.
- Robert, d.
- Isabella.
- Charlotte Cecilia, mar. 1856, Charles Moore, Esq., of Claughton, Cheshire.
- Willa, mar. in 1863, George Orme.

F

F

Henry, b. 18 Apr. 1716. Was an M.P.; died unmar. 1763.

Sir Richard St. George, Bart., b. 1718; mar. 1764; a Bart. 1765; d. 25 Feb. 1789. = Sarah, dau'r of Robert Persse of Roxborough.

Thomas, born 13 Sept. 1720.

George, a Capt. and A.D.C. to his uncle General Bligh. = Grace Bathurst, mar. 1762.

Elizabeth, m. 24 June 1758. = ... Dowglass, Esq., co. Down.

Children of Sir Richard St. George and Sarah:

3rd. Rev. George St. George, b. 1767; died 24 Nov. 1824; married Frances Grady of Littleton.

4 and 5. Elizabeth, d. s.p. — Henry, d. s.p.

6th. Thomas Bligh St. George, mar. 1804; d. 1859. = Anna, dau'r of Sir Hercules Langrishe, d. 1851.

1st son. Sir Richard Bligh St. George, Bart., b. 1765; d. 1852. = (1) Harriet, dau'r of Justice Kelly. = (2) Bridget, dau'r of Theophilus Blakeney, Esq.

2nd. Robert St. George of Bailef Castle, b. 1766; d. 1840. = Caroline, dau'r of General Pringle.

Children of George and Grace Bathurst:

Sir Thomas Bligh St. George, C.B., K.C.H., Lieut.-General, and Colonel of 3rd R.V. Battalion; d. 1836, having mar. Elizabeth, dau'r of Charles Walker, co. Wexford.

Richard, drowned in the St. Laurence.

Children of Rev. George St. George:

A daughter, married Rev. Mr. Latouche of Duleek, co. Louth.

Fanny, mar. in 1841, Rev. Mr. Harris.

Katherine.

Children of Thomas Bligh St. George and Anna:

Hercules Langrishe St. George of Bailef Castle, b. 1810; m. Marg^t daughter of Alexander Taylor of Banffshire.

Richard Thomas.

Hannah. — Mary.

Rev. Francis de Montmorency St. George, Rector of St. Paul's, Cork, mar. Miss Edgeworth. Has issue.

Children of Sir Richard Bligh St. George and Harriet:

Frances Elizabeth, d. unmar. 1877. — Sarah Salsbury, mar. John Dillon. — Harriet Annabella, mar. Hugh Eccles.

Children of Sir Richard Bligh St. George and Bridget:

Richard Bligh, d. s.p. in 1826.

Grace Ann, mar. Rev. Ch. Caulfield of Kilcock.

Sir Theophilus John St. George, Bart., b. 1810; d. in 1857 in South Africa. = (1) Caroline Georgina Latour, mar. 1836; d. at Boulogne 1842. = (2) Maria, dau'r of John Power of Churchtown, co. Waterford.

Robert, b. 1811; mar. 1841; (of Chiswick.) = Sophia, mar. Olivia Mahon.

Wm. Oliver, b. 1813.

James Cuffe St. George of Sheene, born 1814; mar. 1856. = Jane Grey, dau'r of Arthur Loftus, Captain R. Navy.

John Henry, — Margaret. } d. s.p.

Theodosia, mar. Rev. Jas. Freke.

Children of Sir Theophilus and Caroline:

Sir Richard Latour St. George, Bart., R.H.A., d. unmar. in 1861.

William Edward, d. young in 1847.

Caroline, mar. Horatio Seftenberg Ross, E.I.C. Service.

Children of Sir Theophilus and Maria:

Sir John Edmund St. George, Bart., b. 3 Apr. 1851.

Arthur. — Theophilus.

Charles. — Alice.

Maria.

Children of Robert and Sophia:

Robert J. Ker St. George, mar. Catherine, dau'r of Christopher St. George of Tyrone House.

Josephine Louisa, mar. in 1873, H. Vesey Seymour Fitzgerald.

Elizabeth Olivia, mar. in 1874, to Charles O'Hara Trench, Esq.

Children of James Cuffe St. George and Jane Grey:

Loftus St. George, b. 28 June, 1858.

Florence Charlotte Jane St. George.

Family of Gresham.

ABSTRACT OF INQUISITIONS POST MORTEM. TITSEY LINE.

SIR JOHN GRESHAM, KT.

[Chancery Inquis. p m 3 and 4 Ph. and Mary, 1st Pt, No. 98.]

Inquisition taken at Southwark 15 Feb. 4 Ph. and Mary (1556-7), on the death of Sir John Gresham Kt. The Jurors say that the said Sir John Gresham was seised on the day of his death of the manors of Tyttesey, Lymesfelde, Brodham, Oxtede, Warlingham, Sanderstede and the Borough of Langehurst, and of Rowholtes, and Waldingham, and of the right of patronage of the rectory and vicarage of the parish Church of Sandersted, and of 26 messuages, 1000 acres of land, 200 of meadow, 600 of pasture, 300 of wood, 500 of furze and heath,* and of £5 rent with the appurtenances in Tuttesey, Lymesfelde, etc, and of the rectory of Wallingham, and of a messuage or tenement called Welcombes and Lawrence,† and of 100 acres of land, meadow and pasture, 20 of wood, 10 of furze and heath, and 6d rent, and of a messuage or tenement called Felcourte,‡ and of 60 acres of land, 30 of meadow, 40 of pasture, 60 of wood, and 20 of furze and heath, and of another messuage or tenement called Westbarnes,§ and of 100 acres of land, 40 of meadow, 100 of pasture, 20 of wood, 2 of furze and heath in Westbarnes, and that the said Sir John Gresham being thereof so seised made and declared his last will at Tittesey (here the Will is set out) They further say that the said Sir John died at Tichesey‖ seised of the said manors, that the manor of Tichesey is held of the King and Queen in socage by fealty only, and that it is worth 40*l* The manors of Lymesfeld and Brodham £21 6*s* 8*d* The manor of Oxtede £8 19*s*. The manor and rectory of Warlingham £20 The manor of Sandersted and the advowson of the rectory and vicarage of the Church of Sanderstead and the borough of Longhurst etc £20 9*s* The manor of Rowholtes 53*s*. 4*d*. The manor of Waldingham £20 The messuages called Welcombes and Laurence 50*s*. The messuage called Felcourt £18 6*s* 8*d*, Westbarnes £18 10*s* That said Sir John Gresham died on 23 Oct last, and that William Gresham Esq is his son and heir, and aged 34.

[Chancery Inquis p m 5 and 6 Ph. and Mary, 2nd Pt, No 89]

Inquisition taken at Lewisham, co Kent, 20 Sep, 5 and 6 Ph and Mary (1558), on the death of Sir John Gresham K[t] The Jurors say that the said Sir John Gresham at the time of his death was seised in his demesne as of fee of and in the manors of Westram and Etonbridge, co Kent, and of lands and tenements called Charmans¶ in Westram, and of and in the rectories and churches of Westram and Etonbridge, and of the manor of Henden, in Sundryshe, Chedyngstone, and Brasted, co Kent, and of Henden Park containing 300 acres (here the Will is set out) And that the manors of Westram and Etonbridge and the farm called Charmans, and the rectories of Westram and Edonbridge and the manor and park of Hendon, are held of the King and Queen by the service of the 20th part of a Knight's fee, and that the farms called the Courtlodge,** and Charmans with the profits of the conies are worth 23*l* 6*s* 8*d*. That the manor and rectory of Westram are worth 11*l* 13*s* 4*d* That the manor and rectory of Etonbridge are worth 16*l* That the manor and park of Henden are worth 21*l* 19*s*. 4*d* That the said Sir John Gresham died 28†† Oct 3 and 4 Phil and Mary. That William Gresham Esq is his son and heir, and was 36‡‡ years old at the time of his death

* Jampnor et bruere

† These farms were in Coulsdon parish

‡ In Lingfield

§ In the parish of Merton.

‖ This was not so, he died at his house in St. Mary Aldermanbury, London, of fever, 23 Oct 1556

¶ A farm still so called

** Still so called

†† Should be 23rd

‡‡ He was thirty-four years old at his father's death (see Inquisition preceding), having been born on 25 Ap 1522

William Gresham, Esq

[Chancery Inquis. p m 21 Eliz, 2 Pt No 14]

Inquisition taken at Deptefordestrond, co. Kent, 29 Oct 21 Eliz (1579) before Thomas Culpeper and others The Jurors say that William Gresham Esq was seised in his demesne as of fee tail to him and his heirs male of the gift of Sir John Gresham Kt, his father, of the manor of Hethenden and the lands called Henden Parke in the parishes of Sundrish, Brasted, and Chedyngstone, co Kent, in the tenure of Robert Sone, and of a farm parcel of the manor of Westram called the Curtelage of Westram, in the tenure of Anthony Saxbye, and of a tenement called Charmans with the profits of the conies, of a messuage called Rowholtes and divers lands there in the county of Surrey, of the manor of Waldyngham and divers lands, of the manor of Felcourt, of the manor or farm of Lovestede, and of a messuage in Milk Street in the city of London, and that he was seised in fee of the manor of Stangrave in Eatonbridge and of the rectory of Eatonbridge, co Kent, of the manor of Westram and certain lands there called Shotts and Hame, lately purchased of William Casingherste, of a messuage called Welcomes and Laurence with divers lands co Surrey, and of divers lands, tenements, and almshouses(?)* in Bowe Brickhill, Little Brickhill, Wandon, Calcote, Sewenestis,† and Fenny Stratforde, co. Bucks, of divers messuages, tenements, and gardens in the parish of St Giles' without Crepelgate, London, and that at the time of his death he was seised of the rectory of Westram co. Kent and of the manors of Tuttesey *alias* Tichesey, Lymsfelde, and Brodham, and of the patronage of the rectory of Lymsfelde, and of the manor of Oxstede in Brodham, and of a stable with the appurtenances in the borough of Southwark in the parish of St George, and of a tenement in Milkestreete in the city of London, and of another tenement in the parish of St Mary Aldermanbury, and of a tenement called "le Sonne" in the parish of St Alphege within Creplegate, and of divers lands in Westram lately purchased of Cuthbert Brewad (here recites his will, dated 9 Oct 1575), and gives the value of his property as follows—Henden Park 21*l*. 19*s* 1½*d* The curtelage of Westerham and Charmans 23*l* 6*s*. 8*d* Manor of Rowholts 53*s* 4*d* The manor of Waldyngham 20*l* Manor of Felcourt 13*l* 6*s*. 8*d*. Manor of Lovestede 5*l* Tenement in Milkstrete 100*s* Manor of Stangrave 16*l* 10*d* Rectory of Eatonbridge 17*l*. 10*s*. Manor of Westerham 36*l* 10*s*. 8*d* Shotts and Hames in Westerham 20*s* Wellcomes and Laurence 50*s* The messuages etc in Bowe Brickhill etc 19*l*. 8*s* 6*d* The messuage and garden in St Giles 10*l*. The rectory of Westerham 12*l*. The manor of Ticchesey 40*l* The manors of Lymesfelde and Brodeham and the advowson of Lymesfelde 50*l* 7*s* 8*d* The manor of Oxstede 8*l* 19*s* The stable in Southwark 10*s*. The tenement in Milk Street 40*s* and the tenement in St Mary Aldermanbury and "le Sonne" £3 The land bought of Cuthbert Brewood 3*l* That he died on 20 June last, and that William Gresham is his son and heir, and aged 23 and upwards.

Beatrice Gresham.

[Chancery Inquis p m. 2 Jac 1, 2 Pt No 155]

Inquisition taken at Tunbridge 21 Aug 2 Jac. I. (1604) upon the death of Beatrice Gresham, widow The Jurors say that she was seised in her demesne as of fee in the manor of Stangrave *alias* Edelmebridge, co Kent, and in the rectory or church of Etonbridge with all the tithes and emoluments thereto belonging, of lands called Shots and Hams in Westerham, of a messuage called Lusted in Cowdham, co Kent, and Tattisfield, co Surrey, of divers lands and woods called Rowholts in Chelsham, of Welcombes and Laurence in Colesden, of divers lands and tenements in Tittussie and Lymsfeld and of the manor or farm of Waldyngham, of one messuage called Bolters in Lymsfield, co Surr (Indenture recited here.) The

* Hospicis † ? Stevenage

value as follows—Stangrave and rectory of Etonbridge 16*l.* Shotts and Hames 40*s.* Lusted 5*l.* Rowholtes 53*s* 4*d.* Manor of Waldyngham 10*l* Welcombes and Lawrence 50*s.* Bolters 4*l.* That said Beatrice died on 22 May last, that Sir William Gresham Kt. is her son and heir, and of the age of 48 and upwards.

Sir Thomas Gresham, Kt.

[Chancery Inquis. p m. 6 Car I., 1st Pt No 60]

Inquisition taken at Southwark 5 Nov 6 Car. I. (1630) upon the death of Sir Thomas Gresham Kt. The Jurors say that he was seised in his demesne as of fee in the manors of Titsey, Limsfielde, Broadham, and Wouldingham, co. Surrey, and of the advowsons of the parish churches of Titsey and Limpsfield, of the manor of Westerham, co Kent, of a tenement in Westerham called Charmans and of the rectory, of three messuages and tenements in the parish of St. Mary Aldermanbury in the city of London, of a messuage and tenement in the parish of St Helen's in Bishopsgate Street, of thirty messuages and tenements and divers gardens in Beechlane, Whitecross Street, Moorelane, Grubstreet, Goulding Lane, and St Giles Alley in the parish of St. Giles without Criplegate in the suburb of the city of London and in the parish of St Alphege within Creeplegate, of one messuage in Milk Street, and of a messuage and stable in the parish of St George in the borough of Southwark (Indenture recited here) That said Sir Thomas Gresham died on 4* July at Limpsfield, that Sir John Gresham Kt is his son and heir, and of the age of 40 and upwards That the manor and rectory of Tychesey was of the value of 20*l.* Limpsfield and the rectory with Broadham 20*l.* Wouldingham 5*l* Westerham and Charmans 10*l* The rectory of Westerham 5*l* Tenements in Aldermanbury 20*s*, in Bishopsgate Street 10*s* The 30 messuages in Beechlane etc 20*s* Tenement in Milkstreet 10*s.* The messuage and stable in St George's, Southwark, 8*s*

Sir John Gresham, Kt

[Chancery Inquis. p m. Miscellaneous 20 Car. I Pt 16, No. 144.]

Inquisition taken at Limsfield, co Surrey, 3 May, 20 Car I (1644) upon the death of Sir John Gresham Kt The Jurors say that on the day of his death he was seised in demesne as of fee tail of the manors of Titsey, Limsfield, Broadham, with the advowsons of Titsey and Limpsfield, the manor of Westerham, the farm called Charmans, the rectory of Westerham, and three messuages lying in St Mary Alldermanbury, and in fee simple of the manor of Tattesfield with the advowson (Indenture recited here) That he died on 1 July† last past before the taking of this Inquisition without issue, Elizabeth his wife surviving. That Sir Edward Gresham Kt is his brother and next heir, and was of the age of 50 years at the time of the death of Sir John Gresham. Value of manor and rectory of Titsey 20*l.* Limsfield and the advowson and Broadham 20*l* Westerham and Charmans 10*l* The rectory of Westerham 5*l.* The messuages in Aldermanbury 20*s.* Manor of Tatsfield 15*l* The rectory nil because it is filled The writ for holding the Inquisiton is dated from Oxford 16 June 19 Car. I.

Scholey Family.—Richard Neale of Mansfield Woodhouse, in Nottinghamshire, who came over from Ireland with the first Duke of Newcastle, and settled at that place in the time of Charles II, married Mary Scholey, a Yorkshire heiress Information as to the descent of this lady is requested.

Highfield, Nottinghamshire. A. E Lawson Lowe.

---

* He died on 1st July, 1630

† He died at Titsey on 26 May as appears by his monument.

GRANT OF ARMS TO WILLIAM HENRY HYETT OF PAINSWICK, CO GLOUCESTER, 1813.*

To all and singular to whom these Presents shall come Sir Isaac Heard Knight Garter Principal King of Arms & George Harrison Esquire Clarenceux King of Arms of the South East and West Parts of England from the River Trent Southwards send Greeting. Whereas Frances Adams of the City of Gloucester Widow, Relict of the Reverend Henry-Cay Adams, Clerk, deceased, on behalf of her eldest Son William Henry Hyett (late Adams) now of Painswick in the County of Gloucester a Minor, hath represented unto the Most Noble Charles Duke of Norfolk Earl Marshal and Hereditary Marshal of England that His Royal Highness the Prince Regent by Warrant under His Majesty's Royal Signet and the Sign Manual of His Royal Highness in the Name & on the Behalf of his Majesty bearing date the first day of June last hath been pleased to give and grant unto Her, on behalf of her aforesaid Son, William-Henry Adams, His Majesty's Royal Licence and Authority that He may from grateful respect and affectionate Regard to the memory of Benjamin Hyett late of Painswick aforesaid Esquire deceased, take and use the Surname and Arms of Hyett only, such Arms being first duly exemplified according to the Laws of Arms and recorded in the Heralds' Office otherwise the said Royal Licence and Permission to be void and of none effect That upon an examination of the Records of the College of Arms it appears that the Armorial Ensigns borne by the said Benjamin Hyett have not been duly registered to his family so as to authorize the Exemplification thereof in obedience to the said Royal Warrant, She therefore requested the favour of his Grace's Warrant for our granting and assigning such Armorial Ensigns for Hyett as may be proper to be borne by her said Son William-Henry Hyett according to the Tenor of the said Royal Warrant and the Laws of Arms And forasmuch as the said Earl Marshall did by Warrant under his Hand and Seal bearing date the eighteenth day of June last authorize and direct Us to grant and exemplify such Armorial Ensigns accordingly Know Ye therefore that We the said Garter and Clarenceux in obedience to the Royal Command, in pursuance of his Grace's Warrant and by virtue of the Letters Patent of our several Offices to each of Us respectively granted do by these Presents grant and exemplify the Arms following for Hyett that is to say Argent a Lion rampant Azure on a chief indented Sable two Roses of the Field barbed and seeded proper And for Crest on a Wreath of the Colours A Castle proper, charged with four Pellets in Cross, issuant therefrom a Lion's Head in the Mouth a Rose Gules slipped also proper as the same are in the Margin hereof more plainly depicted to be borne and used for ever hereafter by him the said William-Henry Adams now William-Henry Hyett and his descendants according to the Tenor of the said Royal Warrant and the Laws of Arms In Witness whereof We the said Garter and Clarenceux Kings of Arms have to these Presents subscribed our Names and affixed the Seals of our several Offices the fifth day of August in the Fifty-third year of the Reign of our Sovereign Lord George the Third by the Grace of God of the United Kingdom of Great Britain and Ireland King Defender of the Faith &c and in the Year of our Lord one thousand eight hundred and thirteen.

ISAAC HEARD, Garter Principal King of Arms
GEORGE HARRISON, Clarenceux King of Arms.

BEDFORD FAMILY.—Can any of the readers of the 'Miscellanea Genealogica' give information respecting the Yorkshire family of this name, first mentioned as of Hull from early in the fourteenth to end of the fifteenth century, and of Dewsbury from about the commencement of the sixteenth to the eighteenth century? As the Bedfords of Dewsbury were probably descended from the Hull family, I shall be glad of information that may lead to the connexion, or that will in any way be useful in tracing the descent of the family, especially with regard to John Bedford, born in 1609, who was the younger son of John Bedford of Crownest, and who it is presumed resided after his father's death at Smythey Brook, near Dewsbury

Sheffield. EDWIN JACKSON BEDFORD.

* Communicated by F A HYETT Esq of Painswick

THE MONUMENTAL INSCRIPTIONS OF THE FAMILY OF HARINGTON, CO. SOMERSET.*

(*Continued from p.* 63.)

In Bath Abbey, South Transept, East wall, a small marble Tablet further confirms the inscription of the flat stone to the memory of Susanna Isabella Thomas *née* Harington. It is set up next a handsome monument, erected by subscription to the memory of the Archdeacon her husband, and runs as follows —

Sacred to the Memory of
Susanna Isabella Thomas,
Relict of the late Rev Josiah Thomas
Archdeacon of Bath
And only daughter of the late
Henry Harington M.D. of this City,
Died December 5, 1835 Aged 73 years
"I know that my Redeemer liveth" Job 19, xix, ver. 25.

In Bath Abbey, South Transept, West wall,—

Sacred to the Memory of
Esther Harington
Widow of the Revd Hen^{y} Harington D.D †
Sister to the late John Lens Esqr
King's Antient Serjeant
And Daughter-in-Law to
Henry Harington M.D. of this City
Died April 30, 1829
In the 71st year of her Age.

In the North Aisle of Chew Magna Church, co Somerset, mural Tablet near the North entrance.

Elizabeth the Wife of
Benjamin Haryngton of Corston Esq.
and daughter of William Lyde‡
of this Parish, Gent.
Changed a frail life, etc etc
ye 12th Decr An^{o} Do. 1693.

* Communicated by the Rev FRANCIS J POYNTON, M A, Rector of Kelston

† This is the editor of the 'Nugæ Antiquæ' of Harington, he died 1793, vitâ patris, at the early age of thirty-seven years

‡ The Will of Elizabeth (Lyde) Harington is (Box 147) G C P, dated Nov 20th, 1693. She was her husband's first wife, he married secondly Elizabeth Bailey (of whom see "after" on M I at Corston, and note thereon) Both Harington and his wife, Lyde, were barely of age when they married He was baptized at Corston 1673, and after his marriage went to reside at Knighton Sutton, his wife's father's home. For the Lydes are an old family of Somerset, having considerable property at Chelwood, Stanton Wick, and Sutton in the parish of Chew Magna about this date (1693) A direct descendant of William Lyde of Sutton (who was born 1576, and died 1620), viz Lionel Lyde, was created Baronet Oct 13th, 1772, but died s p 2nd July, 1791. He was owner of the manor of Ayott St Lawrence, Herts, and is now represented there by Lionel Ames, Esq

The Lyde residence at Sutton is now a farm-house, and has become the property of Sir Edward Strachey, of Sutton Court, Bart

Elizabeth Harington *née* Lyde's will cites articles of agreement on marriage, dated Sept 25th (these are virtually her will), "made between John Harington the elder, of Kelston, Esq, and Benjamin Harrington my husband, *eldest* son (*i e* surviving son) of said John Harington, on one part, and Joseph Langton, of Newton St Loc, Esq, my father, William Lyde the elder of Knighton Sutton, my brother, William Lyde the younger, son of William Lyde the elder, of London, Gent Samuel Prig (or Trig), of Stanton Drew, Clerk, Robert Kening of Kelston Clerk, and me, the said Elizabeth Harington, by the name of Elizabeth Lyde, daughter of said

MONUMENTS TO HARINGTON IN CORSTON CHURCH, CO SOMERSET

I. *On Eastern wall of the Chancel, north of the window a marble tablet, surmounted by arms of* HARINGTON, *sable a fret argent, impaling* BAILEY *of* WILTS, *or on a fesse engrailed (? azure), three fleurs-de-lis of the first, between three nags' heads erased of the second*

Near this place lyeth buried
The Body of Benjamin Harington Esqr
[eldest* son of John Harington Esqr of Kelston]
who departed this life the first X^ber†
Anno Dom 1711
in the 39th year of his age
leaving issue two sons John and William
and two daughters Abigail and Elizabeth

Also of Mary who dyed
5th June 1708

II IN CORSTON CHURCH, ON EASTERN WALL, SOUTH SIDE OF CHANCEL WINDOW.

The arms on this monument both above and below are effaced by damp.

Near this place lies interred
The Body of Mary the wife of
John Harington Esqr of this Parish
Who departed this life ye 16th April
1732 aged 25.

Will Lyde the elder, on the other part, my share in the estate of Richard Jones, Esq,[1] deceased, and my own personal estate I give to my husband, my plate to my father, to my kinswomen, Mary York and Susannah Lyde, my linen, to my kinswoman Ann Chiswell, daughter of John, Chiswell, deceased, £10, to my kinswoman, Mary Stephens, £10, to Jane Reddick (or Ruddock), £10 Residue to my brother Wm Lyde, executor, to my sister-in-law, Rebecca Harington, my best dresses, etc "—Proved by Will Lyde, June 2nd, 1791

* This should have been eldest *surviving* son, Benjamin was the first son of his father's third marriage with Alice Snow The eldest son by his first wife Mary Specot, viz John, died vitâ patris, and is buried at Kelston (M I has been given before) After his marriage with Miss Bailey, Benjamin purchased Corston Manor of his father, and residing there, transferred the eldest male line to Corston, whilst the eldest son of the father's fourth marriage, and his heirs, succeeded to the original family seat at Kelston This is curious, and worthy of note in the history of the family

The old manor house, the residence of the Haringtons at Corston, is now used as a farm-house It has a spacious entrance hall, with garden court in front In the rear is an old gate-way leading to the church, and it is reported traditionally that on a stone removed from that gateway was once the date 1627 The house is in substantial repair, but denuded of any Harington traces, such as arms or stained glass, or ornamental work of any sort The rooms are large, have stone floors down stairs, and are half wainscoated It is said (I know not with what truth) that a sketch of this manor house was given in the 'Illustrated London News' some years ago It seems to be later than the time of Elizabeth, is, perhaps, of the time of Charles I It was used as a boarding school at the close of the last century, to which the Poet Southey was sent at the age of six years and he alludes to it at some length in his Recollections' Of the features impressed on his memory a few still remain, for instance, the balls on the pillars of the entrance gates, and some of the trees of the avenue It was purchased from the Haringtons by Joseph Langton, Esq, of Newton Park, whose daughter and sole heir (Bridget) married Colonel William Gore, of Barron Gurney, who subsequently took the additional name of Langton, and in his representatives it still remains

† By the Register of Corston he was buried 28th November, a slight discrepancy probably caused by a confusion of his day of death and burial Say—died 28th November, buried 1st December, 1711 —F. J P

---

1 Elizabeth's mother was Sarah Jones, of the family of Jones of Stowey House, benefactors to several parishes in that neighbourhood, and notably to Newton-St-Loe, Stowey and Chew Magna The same family became subsequently Jones Burdetts, and under that name are well known, Mr Wm Jones Burdett younger brother of Sir Francis Burdett, M P, died 1810

Also near this place lieth the Body
of Elizabeth,* Widow & Relict
of Benjamin Harington
of this Parish Esqr, who
Died 28th Decr 1735 aged 55 years.

Also of John Harington, son of
the above Elizth &
Benjn Harington
qui obiit 1st May
1763. Ætat 61

In the chancel of Corston Church, North wall

S. M of
William Harington Esqr
Born 5th July 1705
Died 10th May 1780.

S. M of
Mrs Elizabeth Harington
Who died in the 90th year
Of her age upon the
17th Novr 1797
Born 21st Decr 1707.

An Inscription in Corston Church.

Recorded by Dr Henry Harington as extant in his day, but query if still there, 1877.

Here lyeth the Body of Rebecca Harington†
daughter of John Harington Esqr of Kelston & sister
of Benjamin Harington of this Parish Esqr who
dyed March 28th Anno Dom : 1747.

Bequest to the Parishes of Newton St Loe and Corston, Somerset

"William Harington late of Newton St Loe Esqr by Will dated 6th April 1780 gave the Interest of £612 10, which at that time purchased £1000 Stock vested in the 3 per Cent Consolidated Annuities to be applied to the following Charities —One moiety to be applied to the relief of the necessitous poor of this Parish, and the other to the necessitous poor of Newton aforesaid, at the discretion of the Trustees of the said Will"

M I. at Kington St. Michael, co. Wilts.

South-west (in the churchyard), on a raised tomb (from Wilts' 'Archl. Magazine,' vol. iv., p 88).

Here lieth the body of Wm. Harington
Vicar of this Parish 34 years
Who departed this life July 13 1751
In the 64th year of his age

* * * * * *

* This lady was coheiress with two sisters of Bailey of Westbury, Wilts, whose widow was Sarah —Of these coheiresses one married into the Elton family, another married Tarver, the third (as above) married Harington Of the order of these sisters in age I have not as yet been informed, as I had hoped to have been from the Westbury Register —F J P

† This lady is named in her sister-in-law's will, 1693—'Elizabeth H.'s' (*née* Lyde), which see before.

He was son* of Jn° Harington of Kelston
C° Somerset by his 4th Wife Helena
daughter of Benjamin Gostlett
of Marshfield, C° Gloucest.
And was baptized at Kelston
His wife Sarah was daughter
& co-heiress of Thomas Harrison of Bath
and had no issue.—
Mrs Mary Webbe 29th May 1773
aged 80

FROM BITTON CHURCHYARD, CO GLOUCESTER.

Inscriptions as given by Bigland in his 'History of Gloucestershire,' vol. i, p. 205

Among the M I s to the Family of Goodman on an old altar tomb, North side of the Church

Elizabeth† wife of George Harrington, Gent,
Grand-daughter of the said
Francis Goodman, died Jany 23d
1743, aged 28 years.

Among the gravestones to the Foords·—

John Harrington Gent‡
died Oct 16, 1714 aged 41.

Betty the wife of George Harrington Yeoman
died Sept. 15th 1773 aged 69

Ann daughter of John Harrington Gent
by Mary his Wife died Jany 7th
1771 aged 66

George Harrington, Gent
died Feby 14th 1781 aged 77.

(From Bigland's 'History,' p. 206)

Inscriptions on two altar tombs in the churchyard of Kelston, side by side, within rails, near the chancel door —

Tomb I

In memory of
The Revd Edward Harington
Eldest son of
Sir Edward Harington Kt
Who died 3d June 1811
Aged 33 years
This tomb is erected by his Widow
Frances Harington
Daughter and sole Heiress of
John Boote Esqr
Of Fifield House, Oxfordshire.

* He was fourth son of six by his father's fourth marriage, the two younger than he being Robert and Edward. He graduated from Corpus College, Oxford

† This lady's maiden name was Bush She was the daughter of Samuel Bush of North Stoke and Bitton, by Elizabeth his wife, daughter of Francis and Elizabeth Goodman of Upton Cheney, parish of Bitton This information was given me by the Rev H. T Ellacombe of Clyst St George, and many years Vicar of Bitton I would add that the family of Bush is widely scattered in the district They are to be traced at Doynton, Tracy Park, Upton Cheney, North Stoke, and Kelston, besides being very numerous in Bitton, and members of the family are settled both in Bath and Bristol —F J P

‡ He was son of William and Anne Harington of Kelston, and baptized there 3rd March, 1672-3.

Also to the memory of
Anne Elizabeth Harington*
Daughter of the above Rev[d] Edward Harington
and Frances his Wife
Who died March 20th 1870
Aged 63 years

Tomb II

To the Memory of
Lady Harington
Wife of
Sir Edward Harington
Died May 11th 1796
Aged 44 years

IN THE CHURCHYARD, KELSTON

At the foot of a cross, in white marble, near the rest of the family tombs:—

To the beloved memory
of
The Rev[d] Edward Templer Harington
Vicar of Axmouth, Devon
who entered into rest
May 11th 1874 aged 45

MONUMENTAL INSCRIPTION AT CHILCOMPTON, NEAR RADSTOCK, SOMERSET †

Given by Collinson in his history of this Parish

Mary Wife of Benjamin Harington Gent.
Second daughter of Anthony Stocker Esq.
& Margaret Capel his wife
She died Dec[r] 1649.

(*To be continued.*)

PARKINSON, R.N.—William Hammond, of St. Alban's Court, co Kent, married 1692, Elizabeth, daughter of John Kingsford, of Oxney, co. Kent His sister Anne Hammond married Dr. Wotton, whose daughter Anne married William Clarke, of Haghmon Abbey, co Salop, Chancellor of Chichester Cathedral, 1770 their son, Edward Clarke, afterwards Rector of Buxted, married 1763, Anne Grenfield, of Guildford, co Surrey, by whom he had four children,—J. S. Clarke, D D., Chaplain to King William y[e] 4th, E. D. Clarke, the traveller, afterwards Rector of Yeldham, co Essex, died 1822, George Clarke, Capt. R N., drowned in the Thames in 1805, and one daughter, Anne, who married Captain Parkinson, R.N., one of Admiral Lord Nelson's officers Can any of your readers inform me to what family this Captain Parkinson belonged? C. J. B.

---

* This lady died in Exeter, at the house of her brother, the Rev the Chancellor of Exeter Cathedral, but is buried at Kelston

† This monument was surmounted by Arms—Harington and Stocker.

We believe this Benjamin Harington was a younger son of *Francis* Harington (son of John Harington, Esq, of Stepney and Kelston), and was therefore a nephew of Sir John Harington, Knt, and not a direct descendant, although the arms, as described by Collinson, have no mark of difference for a second son Sir John had no son named Benjamin, and any lower descendant from his line would be out of date with the M I.

MEMORANDA RELATING TO THE HYETT FAMILY

COPIED FROM AN OLD BIBLE PRINTED IN 1682, BUT BOUND UP WITH A PRAYER BOOK PRINTED IN 1726 *

The leaf on which the entries appear seems to correspond with paper of the former, as if the Prayer Book was interpolated

Beniamin Hyett the Son of John Hyett of Dursley was borne at Dursley the 30th day of March, 1651, being Easterday. He dyed March 12, 1711

Elizabeth Morwent daughter of Joseph Morwent of Tetbury was borne at Tetbury the — of Aprill, 1653, being Good Friday. She dyed Novr 21, 1708

Beniamin Hyett and Elizabeth Morwent were married at Oldbury super Montem the 10th day of August, 1674

Charles son of Beniamin & Elizabeth Hyett was borne in the parishe of St Trinity in the City of Gloccester the 10th of Aprill A° Dni 1676.

John Hyett their second Son was borne in the parishe of St Mary de Grace September 14th 1677, he dyed May 1st 1682

Wm Hyett their 3rd Son was borne the 11th of Aprill, 1680, he dyed 29th Sepr 1705.

Elizabeth their daughter was borne the 12th April, 1681, she dyed July 19th 1683

Mary their second Daughter was borne the 13th of April, 1682, shee dyed May the 3rd 1682, and was buried with her brother John in one coffin

Robert their fourth Son was borne in the parishe of St Michaell the 8th day June 1683, and dyed 25th July, 1683

Joseph their fifth Son was borne there July 18th 1684, he died April 5th 1686

Sarah their third daughter was borne there Septr 16, 1685; she dyed Janry 16, 1692 aged 7 yrs 4 months.

Beniamin their sixth son was borne in the parishe of St Nicholas 21st day of Novr 1686, he married Jane Nedham of Gadsby, Lincolnshire, dyed in London 1725, left one son who dyed about 1760

Elizabeth their fourth daughter was borne Dec. 21, 1687; marryed Edward James of Gloster, dyed April, 1739, and is buryed in the family vault, had one son who dyed before her.

Mary their fifth daughter was borne there Aprill 23, 1689, she dyed Feb 11, 1712

Wm the above mentioned third Son Marryed with Elizabeth Oldisworth of Hackney near London, the 1st Jany, 1705, And dyed without Issue the 29th Sept following, and was brought from Hackney & buryed in the Cathedrall of Gloster with the rest of his brothers and sisters

Charles the eldest son of Benjamin & Elizabeth was marryed to Anna Webb of Gloccester at the Cathll of Gloster March 11th 1707

Elizabeth the wife of the said Benjamin the father, dyed Novr 21st 1708, and was buryed the 24th November, 1708.

Benjamin the first son of Charles & Anna was Born in the Parish of St Nicholas Decr 17th 1708, and christened at Church, St John's day after, and dyed Dec 15, 1762, and was buryed in the family vault.

Nicholas their second son was Born there Decr 6, 1709, and christened at home on the morrow

Benjamin Hyett the father dyed March 12, 1711, and was buryed March 21, 1711, in a vault then made for the family in the Cathedrall of Glo'ster

Charles the 3rd Son of Charles & Anna was Born Saturday, 28th Novr 1713, and dyed Augst 20 following

1728 Anna the wife of Charles Hyett dyed Octr 20, 1728

* Communicated by F. A. HYETT Esq

1738. Charles Hyett, Husband of Anna died Febry 17, 1738, and both buried in the Vault in the Cathedral of Glo'ster.

1744. Benjamin the first Son of Charles & Anna was married to Francess only daughter of Sir Thos Snell, Knight, of London, merchant, May 15th 1744.

1745. Francess the daughter of the above Benjamin and Francess was Born in the Parish of St Nicholas in the Citty of Glo'ster May 17th 1745, dyed an infant & buryed in ye family vault

1762. Decr 15, Benjamin Hyett son of Charles Hyett dyed and was buryed in the family vault in the Cathedral Church at Glo'ster aged 53.

Armorial Bookplates.

HYETT.

William Henry Hyett of Painswick House, Stroud, co. Gloucester, formerly M.P. for Stroud. Born 2 September, 1795 He married 25 October, 1821, Anne Jane, daughter of Joseph Seymour Biscoe, Esq.

Mr. Hyett, on succeeding to the estates of Benjamin Hyett of Painswick, assumed in 1813 the surname of Hyett, in lieu of that of Adams He died 10 March, 1877, and was buried at Painswick

He was succeeded by his only surviving son, Francis Adams Hyett, born 18 November, 1844, who married 12 July, 1870, Ellen Maria, daughter of Charles Carpenter, Esq of Brighton, and has issue three daughters

---

ARMYTAGE PEDIGREE —Who was the Mr John Armytage who was brought up at Brussels by Lady Mornington, and was taught with Wellington by M Goubert there?

Penzance. G. B. MILLETT.

FICKLIN FAMILY.—Wanted information relative to the Ficklin family They lived during the last century at or near Hadleigh in Suffolk, and intermarried with the family of Farewell, whose pedigree I am also anxious to trace The arms of Ficklin are described to me as Azure on a saltire argent 5 bezants, but I should be glad of some confirmation. BETA

COLLIER FAMILY (Vol II, p 187) —I am endeavouring to work up a pedigree of Sir George Collier, Knight, born 11 May, 1732 (? 1730), Knighted 27 January, 1775, and was then described as of Froyle, co Hants, Vice-Admiral of the Blue, M.P. for Honiton, 1784 Sir George Collier married, and had issue He died 6 April, 1795, and was buried at St Marylebone Parish Church 16 April, 1795 Lysons speaks of the tablet to his memory in St Marylebone Church, from which it appears he was aged 65 He had a brother, Theodosius Benjamin Collier, who married, and died 1803 at Bath, leaving issue Sir George Collier had an uncle, Benjamin Collier, of Red Lion Square, London, who married Lætitia, youngest daughter of Mark Weyland. Benjamin Collier had property in Suffolk, which he left to his great nephew, George Collier, son of Sir George Collier Benjamin Collier died 12 March, 1791, and was buried 21 March, 1791, at Groton, Suffolk I cannot discover the names of the brothers and sisters of Benjamin Collier, or the names of his parents, neither do I know which of Benjamin Collier's brothers was Sir George Collier's father

15 *Markham Square, S.W.* REGINALD STEWART BODDINGTON

EXTRACTS FROM CHURCH REGISTERS RELATING TO THE FAMILY OF SHELMERDINE.*

(*Continued from p.* 58.)

NORTHENDEN.

Marriages

1575.	May 22.	Jeffrey Shelm^{r}dyne & Joane Greefie
1578.	August 3.	William Whitelegge & Elizabeth Shelm^{r}dyne.
1582	June 12.	Raphe Shelm^{r}dyne & Marie Coppocke.
1594.	September 8.	Robert Shelm^{r}dyne & Jane Houlome.
1594.	October 14	Thomas Linney & Elline Shelm^{r}dyne.
1595.	October 19.	John Boothe & Elline Shelm^{r}dyne
1596.	December 16	James Shelm^{r}dyne & Margaret Harison.
1596.	January 16.	William Williamson & Elizabeth Shelm^{r}dyne.
1601.	May 2.	Richard Brownhill & Alis Shelm^{r}dyne.
1602.	February 20.	ffrauncis Shelm^{r}dyne & Elline Williamson.
1606.	June 18.	Jeffrey Shelm^{r}dyne & Anne Leighe.
1606.	December 22	John Shelm^{r}dyne & Elizabeth Barrett.
1608.	October 2.	William Shelm^{r}dyne & Maude Baxter.
1613.	May 6	Thomas Shelm^{r}dyne & Ellyne Alcocke
1618.	September 16.	William Shelm^{r}dyne & Ann Tomlinson.
1621.	June 26	Thomas Norbury & Ellnor Shelm^{r}dyne
1625.	October 24.	John Shelm^{r}dyne & Margrate Brownhill
1628	January 17.	John Reade & Margaret Shelm^{r}dyne
1632	July 1.	John Burscough & Alice Shelm^{r}dyne both of the parish of Ormskirke, by a certificate from the Curate & Churchwarden of Ormskirk.
1634	July 6.	John Bulling of fflixton & Alice Shelm^{r}dyne of this parish, by a certificate from Mr. Edward Woolmes, Curate.
1659.	April 6.	*William* ? Shelmerdyne & Mary Knight.
1662.	June 10	Edmund Shellmerdyne & Mary Gee.
1663.	May 14.	John Shellmerdyne & Elizabeth Kelsall
1664–6.		Edward Kinsey & Mary Shellmerdyne.
1670–9.		William Shelmerdine & Katherine Devonport.

Burials

1569.	Sept 23.	Mary Shelm^{r}dyne of Kenworthey
1578.	October 27.	William son of Henry Shelm^{r}dyne
1579	Jan. 16.	Thomas wch dwelt once with Henry Shelm^{r}dyne
1591.	May 31.	Robert Shelm^{r}dyne of Kenworthey.
1596	November 17	The wife of Henry Shelm^{r}dyne
1605	July 10.	Thomas Shelm^{r}dyne
1605	January 26.	The wife of Jeffrey Shelm^{r}dyne.
1606.	April —	Humfrey Shelm^{r}dyne.
1606	June 23	James Shelm^{r}dyne.
1606.	October 26.	Robert Shelm^{r}dyne & John Shelm^{r}dyne
1607.	Novr 30.	Jeffrey Shelm^{r}dyne.
1608.	July 29.	Edward Shelm^{r}dyne
1610	June 21	Elizabeth da. of Francis Shelm^{r}dyne
1612.	March 31.	The wife of Humfrye Shelm^{r}dyne.
1612.	August 19	Ellyne da of Francis Shelm^{r}dyne
1616	April 14.	Henry Shelm^{r}dyne de morelyd
1617	Oct 16	William son of Francis Shelm^{r}dyne.
1617	Nov 1.	Elin wife to John Shelm^{r}dyne of the Pyper Hill

* Communicated by T SHELMERDINE, Esq

1618. July 23. John Shelm^{r}dyne of Kano^{r}they.
1618 August 17. Elne Shelm^{r}dine of Kanorthey widow.
1618 September 23. Robert Shelm^{r}dyne of the Pyper Hill
1618 March 2 Ann Shelm^{r}dyne, widow.
1619. August 14. Margaret Shelm^{r}dyne of the Morefyd, widow
1621. July 16 Alis servant to William Shelm^{r}dyne of Kenorthey.
1622. May 27 John Shelm^{r}dyne of Pyp' hill.
1629 March 18. John son of William Shelm^{r}dyne of Northen.
1630 January 2 A childe, still born of William Shelm^{r}dine.
1632. October 22. Edmund Shelmerdine of the pip' hill.
1632 Feb 10 John son of William Shelmerdine
1634. January 17 Elizabeth wife to Edmund Shelmerdine of Kenworthie.
1635. April 23. Thomas son to Ed Shelmerdine
1638 May 3 Elizabeth da. to Edmund Shelmerdine
1638 September 13 John son of Edmund Shelmerdine.
1640 April 27. Maudlin Shelmerdin.

In a list of Mortuaries paid in the year 1639 the following entry occurs, but the record of the Burial does not appear in the Register.

Received from ye Executors of William Shelmerdine of Kenardy for a mortuary 10s

1653. Dec. 19. Edmund Shelmerdyne of Kenorday died 17 December
1653 February 20 Robert Shelmerdyne
1655. February 22 Ann Shelmerdyne, widdowe
1656. —— 9. Elizabeth Shelmerdyne, widow
1657 November 3. Mary wife to William Shelmerdyne.
1659. January 3. Margrett Shelmerdyne
1660 December 20 Ellen Shellmerdyne
1662. Oct. — Ellen Shelmerdyne
1666. April 20. Anne Shellmerdyne.
1668. June 12. John Shellmerdyne.
1668. June 15. William Shellmerdyne
1669. Nov. 14. Joane Shellmerdyne
1670. March 4 Margaret wife of Edward Shelmerdine Taylor.
1671. Feb 20. William son to Wm Shelmerdine the younger of Northerden
1672 Nov. 18. John Shelmerdine of the Piper hill
1672 February 20. Elizabeth Shelmerdine.
1674 April 10. Mr Francis Shelmerdine of the Chamber.
1674 Dec 22 Edmund son and heir to Edmund Shelm^{r}dine of Kenorthy.
1676 May 15 William Shelm'dine of Northerden, webster.
1676. Oct 2 Mary wife to Edmund Shelmerdyne of Northerden.
1676 Dec 27 William son of Edmund Shelmerdine.
1681. March 26. William Shelmerdine

SANDBACH.

Baptisms.

1746 March 26. Francis son of William Shelmerdine.
1774. November 12. Elijah son of Francis Shelmerdine

Marriage.

1765 April 22. Francis Shelmerdine and Anne Hodson

Burials.

1768. August 4. William Shelmerdine of Kennedy, aged 60.
1769 November 10 Lydia wife of William Shelmerdine, aged 53.
1814. January 22. Ann wife of William Shelmerdine, aged 68.
1825. February 8. William Shelmerdine, aged 77
1839 May 11. Mary Shelmerdine, aged 72.

GRANT OF CREST AND CONFIRMATION OF ARMS TO NICHOLAS MOSLEY, ALDERMAN OF LONDON, 1592 *

To all and singler as well Nobles, as others, to whome these Presents shall come, Robert Cooke Esquire, alias Clarencieulx Principal Herauld and King of Armes of the South, East, and West Partes of this Realme of England from the Ryver of Trent Southwardes sendeth Greetinge in our Lord God everlasting Whereas auncientlly from the beginnige the valiant and vertuous Actes of excellent Persons have been commended to the World with sundry Monumentes and remembrances of their good desertes, emongest the which the chefyest and most usuall hath been the bearinge of Signes in Shildes called Armes, which are evident demonstracions of prowes and valour diversly distributed according to the quallities and desceartes of the persons meritinge ye same, which order as it was prudently devised in the beginninge to stirre and kindell the heartes of men to the imytacion of vertue and nobleness, even so hath the same bene and yett is continually observed, to the Intent that such as have done commendable Service to their Prince or Country in Warre or Peace might thereby receave due honor in their lyves, and also leave the same in Succession to their Posteritie for ever. And being required by Nicholas Mosley of the City of London Esquire and Alderman of the same, the Sonne of Edward Mosley of Hough'send in ye county of Lancaster Gentillman, which Edward was son of James Mosley gentilman, which James was sonne of Jenkyn Mosley of the same place and County gentilman, to make Searche in the Registers and Recordes of myne Office for the auncient Armes of that name and Family whereof he is descended, Whereupon I have made Search accordingly, and doe find that he may lawfully bear, as his Ancestors heretofore have borne, these Armes hereafter followinge, that is to saye, the first for Mosley, Sables, a Cheveron between three Battle axes silver, the Second for† . . , Gold, a Fess between three Eglets displayed Sables, and so quarterley. And for that I find no Creast or Cognoysance to the same Armes belonginge, as to many ancient Armes there is none, therefore, at the Request of ye said Nicholas Mosley, I ye said Clarencieulx Kinge of Armes have added and assigned unto his auncient Armes this Creast or Cognoysance hereafter specifyed, that is to saye, Upon the Healme, on a Wreathe Silver and Sables, an Eagle display'd Ermynes, Mantiled Gules, doubled Silver, as more plainly appeareth depicted in the Margent hereof; which Creast or Cognoysance I the said Clarencieulx King of Armes, by vertue of myne Office, and by power and auctoritie to me commytted by Letters Patentes under the Great Seale of England, doe give, graunte, ratyfie, and confirme unto the said Nicholas Mosley Esquire, and to his posteritie for ever, so that he and they the same with all Furnitures and Ornaments thereunto belonginge shall and may use, beare and shewforthe in all places and at all times hereafter, according to the auncient Lawes of Armes, without lett, impediment, or interruption of any person or persons whatsoever. In Witnesse whereof I the said Clarencieulx King of Armes have hereunto subscribed my name, and likewise putt the Seale of myne Office, the xvijth daye of Februarye, in the yere of our Lord God 1592, and in the xxxvth yere of the Reigne of our most gracious Soueraigne Lady Queene Elizabeth.

ROBT COOKE, alias Clarencieulx,
Roy Darmes.

BALL FAMILY (Vol II, p. 324)—From a Papillon family MS, I obtain the following information—Mary, wife of George Papillon, was the eldest daughter of Thomas Nicholson by Phœbe his wife, and was baptized 15 April, 1635, at St Mary's Church, Cambridge. Samuel Ball, who was a Hamburg merchant, married 20 Nov., 1682, Mary, daughter of George Papillon, by Mary (Nicholson) his wife.

REGINALD STEWART BODDINGTON.

---

* Communicated by CHARLES JACKSON, Esq

† Blank in the Copy

ARMITAGE FAMILY.

Copy of notes from the collection and in the handwriting of the late Mr. WILLIAM RADCLYFFE, *Rouge Croix.*

The Family of Armytage is of great Antiquity in the County of York, as proved by many undoubted authorities

1. Ricardo de Heimitagio occurs with several of the principal men of the County of York as a Witness to a Charter of Edmund de Lasey Constable of Chester to the Monastry of St John of Pontefret dat 2 May 1258. (Monasterium Sci Joh'i de Kirkby fol. 4^b^).
2 Adam de Armitage occurs with several others as witness to a Charter of Adam son of Ward de Meltham dat in the feast of St Scholaste the Virgin A D 1395
3. And to a deed of Roger de Rowley 6 April 9 Hen 5.
4 Willm del Ermitage & Adam del Ermitage held lands &c in Meltham of John or Elyas de Puton A.D 1426. (Dods'w. Vol.)
5 Thomas Armytage ten ter &c mess Joh'is Armytage et redd 11^d^
6. Thomas del Heimitage was constituted Att^y^ by Ric' Beaumont & others to deliver seizen &c of Lands &c in Meltham to Thos Harrington & others 1 July A^o^ 7 Hen 6.
7 Margerita Armitage nuper uxor Thome Armitage de Armitage in Co Ebor' Obligat Thome Wombwell Arm^o^ Ric'o Beamont arm' et Henrico Beaumont in decem marcis dat 18 Feb A^o^ 20 Hen 6 (Dods MSS.)

NOTES ON LONG *

FROM THE REGISTERS OF STANTON-PRIOR IN THE COUNTY OF SOMERSET.

Baptisms —Matthew Longe the sonne of John Longe was baptized the 20th day of March 1650

Sarah the daughter of John & Sarah Long was baptized May 9th 1653

Jane the daughter of John & Sarah Long was baptized the second day of June 1662.

Marriage —Elizabeth Poole, servant to Robert Long, Esq of this Parish was married the 2nd day of February 1662-3

Burials.—Sarah Long, the daughter of John & Sarah was buryed the 3^d^ day of October 1662

Richard Eaton, servant to Collonel Thomas Long was buried (no date, but it comes between 1664—1667)

Jane Long daughter of John & Sarah Long was buried February 14th 1668.

Marriage.—George Stedman of Midsomer Norton Esq. & Mis Mary Long† were married on the one & thirtieth day of August 1671

Burials —Sarah Long, Widdowe, the mother of Matthew Long was buried ye 3^d^ day of November Anno Dom' 1681

Collonell Thomas Long‡ of Stanton Pryor Esq was buried the six and twentieth day of May Anno Domini 1682. (To this is added, in another hand, " Aged 82.")

Robert Long Esq was buried March 3rd 1697-8 aged 91.

Marriage.—William Long and Elizabeth (no name) his wife were married September ye 20th 1735.

* Communicated by Rev. F J POYNTON

† She re-married Thomas Bere of Huntsham, co Devon, was exor to her father

‡ He was the fourth son, and Robert the third son, of Henry Long of Whaddon, both of them being brothers of Sir Walter Long of Whaddon Bart

Baptism.—John son of John Long and Mary his wife was baptized Aprill ye 17th 1741.

Mary Long was buryed Nov. ye 24th 1742.

Marriage.—James Class and Mary Long* both of this Parish were married March 26, 1778.

As to the age and state of the Register, it goes back to 1572 with the entries of Baptisms, Marriages, and Burials entered in different parts There are no Weddings entered between 1642 and 1653, nor between 1656 and 1662 Under the Weddings 1653, is the following appointment of John Long to be Marriage Registrar.

"I doe approve of John Long for Register of the Parish of Stanton Prior, chosen by the Inhabitants thereof for this Parish, and he was accordingly sworn the 10th day of Jan 1653 by me

"Rob Long

"ffebruary y^e^
"ffirst 1653."

In 1670 there is entry of a "Briefe for captived seamen by the Turks." Coll. Thomas Long gave 5^s^, and Long Esq. 1^s^, and Matthew Long 3^d^.

In 1672, 1673, 1680, Matthew Long was Churchwarden

In 1680, to a Collection made "for the redemption of Captives out of Turkey," Thomas Long Esq. gave £1, Robert Long Esq 5^s^, Matthew Long 6^d^, and John Long 2^d^

In 1689, "A Brief was got at for the Swiss Protestants," to which Robert Long gave £4 and Matthew Long 1^s^.

(The whole Parochial Collection was £5 12^s^ 10^d^.)

In 1695, Robert Long Esq gave "ye sum of four pounds towards ye Briefe for ye fire of Warwick."

Monument to Robert Longe, on the north side of the Tower of Stanton Prior Church —

Marmor Hoc Sepulchrale
In Eternam
Merito Consecratur Memoriam
ROBERTI LONG
Armigeri
Qui Pius atque Probus, necnon bene Notus Egenis
Fautor, ad extremum perstitit usque Diem
Tanti morte viri quid non amisimus, unde
Quod doleat Pietas, Pauper, amicus habet.

Annorum pariter ac laudum
Plenus
Terram Cœlis mutavit
Februarii Die Decimo Nono
suæ
Anno Ætatis Nonagesimo
Primo
Salutis Vero
1697.

* This Mary Long signed the entry with a "X" in lieu of signature From which incident, coupled with observation of the Pedigree of Long, published in the June number of 'Miscellanea Genealogica et Heraldica,' *i e* comparing the names which occur in it with the additional ones that are given here it may fairly be inferred that these extra names were Longs at Stanton-Prior, coeval indeed with those of the Pedigree, but in a humbler sphere of life, and that the name has been handed down in the parish to much later date by the latter and poorer Longs

GENEALOGICAL MEMORANDA RELATING TO THE MITCHELL FAMILY *

Written on the fly-leaves of a Bible, dated Oxford. Printed by Thomas Baskett, Printer to the University, MDCCLIII.

Daniel Mitchell was born in the pish of St James Westm^r 25th day of March 1746.

Edward Charles Mitchell was born in the pish of St Ann Soho, 10th July 1749

Anthony Mitchell was born at Enstone in Oxfordshire 15th Augt 1750

Ann Barroughby Mitchell was born at Great Tew 15th May 1752

Sarrah (*sic*) Compton Mitchell was born at Great Tew the 17th Decem^r 1753

Elizabeth Mitchell was born at Great Tew the 10th June 1755

John Warburton Mitchell was born at Great Tew the fourth day of November 1756

William Mitchell was born the first day of May 1758 at Great Tew

Alexander Mitchell was born on Sunday the 26th day of August 1759 at Great Tew

Rebecca Mitchell was born on Monday the 7th June 1761 at Great Tew

Joseph Mitchell was born at Great Tew on Saturday the 27th November 1762

Benjamin Mitchell was born at Great Tew on Monday the 17th December 1764

The above entries of the names of his children are in the handwriting of John Mitchell, of the parish of St. James, Westminster, and afterwards of Great Tew, South Weston and Tetsworth, in the county of Oxford

John Mitchell died 25th November 1790

A certificate of the marriage of John Mitchell, first with Mary, and afterwards with Elizabeth, is wanted

Elizabeth, his second wife, was buried at South Weston, in Oxfordshire, 29th October, 1786.

(*Another Leaf.*)

Benjamin Mitchell ma. April 1792 Frances da. of Joseph Cooper of London

Joseph Theophilus Mitchell, born at Ware in Hertfordshire 20 February 1793

Benjamin John Lawrence, born at Ware 1797

Edward Charles, born at Ware 15 Decr 1800

Frederick Young Harman, born at Ware 3 June 1802

(*Another Leaf.*)

Joseph Theophilus Mitchell ma 4 Apr 1835 Isabella da. of James Young of Lee Kent

James William Mitchell, born at Lee Monday 7th November 1836

Theophilus, born at Lee Monday 8 April 1839

Isabella Boyd, born at Lee Monday 12 April 1841

Edward Charles, born at Lee Saturday 29 Oct. 1842

John Francis, born at Lee Tuesday night 3 June 1845

Katherine Rose, born at Lee 18 September 1846 at night Died 1 January 1847

The above is in the handwriting of Joseph Theophilus Mitchell, who died 29th March, 1849.

The names as under are written on the fly-leaves of a Bible which belonged to a family of Sykes, of Ackworth, in the West Riding of Yorkshire The title page, and as far as the Book of Numbers, is lost; at the end there is a Table of Contents, which has the following date —Imprinted at London by the Deputies of Christopher Barker, Printers to the Queenes most excellent Majestie 1599 cum privilegio

Richard Shepley. Booke
God giue him grace on it to Looke

* Communicated by J. W. MITCHELL, Esq , of Audley, Sidmouth, Devon

And soe to practise in his Race
That Heauen may be his dwelling Place
Richard Shepleys Booke
June ye 4th (1691) I Bor[d] this booke

Jno. Thompson was born the 26th of December 1729 Lived eight weeks and two days.

Elizabeth Thompson was born ye 14th of June 1733 Baptized ye 14th of July 1733

Rachel Sikes Samuel Sikes 1743.

(*On another leaf*)

Rachel Baynes was born February ye 12 1714
Rachel Sykes died February ye 7 day 1772
old Samuel Sickes was born June ye 2 1715
Samuel Sickes and Rachel was maried June ye 8th 1741
Isack Sickes was born August ye 2nd day att Six o'clock in the morning 1742
Rachel Sikes was born Aug. the 30 day att 9 at night 1744
Joseph Sikes was born December the 8 day att Six o'clock in the morning 1746
Rachel Sikes died, April ye 03 1747
Bengman Sikes was born April ye 1st day 1754 about half a houer after five
13 May 1757 Rachel was born 30 minets past 8 att night

(*On another leaf.*)

Hannah Sikes was born Monday ye 11 day May at 3 quarter past 8 at night In the year of our Lord 1749

Hannah Sikes died April 25 1751

Samuel Sikes was born November 23, 1751 at 15 menets after 4 a clok Saturday morn

Isaac Sikes His Book
God give him grace on it to look
but not to look but understand
that learning is better than house and land
but . . . . house and land it . .
go (*The rest is illegible*)

EXTRACTS FROM PARISH REGISTERS *

Ackworth, Yorkshire

Baptisms.

	Born.	Baptized	
1742		21 August	Isaak Sykes son of Samuel.
1747		7 January	Joseph Sykes son of Samuel.
1748		1 January	Sarah Sykes
1749		11 June	Hannah Sykes
1754	1 April	1 May	Benjamin Sykes of Samuel and Rachel
1777		20 January	Ann Sykes.
1778	10 Nov.	28 December	William Sykes of Joseph and Martha
1779		28 August	John Hunter Sykes
1780		13 February	Mary Sykes
1781		5 March	Isaac Sykes
1781		4 April	Rachel Sykes
1783		4 March	Hannah Sykes.

* These extracts from the Registers were made in order to prove a Sykes pedigree, there are likely to be many other Sykes Registers at Ackworth, and the other parishes named I wish to find the baptism of Samuel Sykes of Ackworth, who was born 2nd June, 1715 He is supposed to have come from Wortley—Qy near Leeds or Sheffield.

	Born	Baptized	
1783	18 April	29 May	Joseph Sykes of Joseph and Martha.
1785		1 February	Hannah Sykes.
1785		1 May	James Sykes.
1785	1 May	22 May	Philip Street Sykes of Joseph and Martha
1787	26 July	27 July	Samuel Sykes of Joseph and Martha
1814		5 June	William Sykes of William and Jane
1816		3 March	Joseph Sykes of William and Jane
1820		28 May	George Henry Sykes of William and Jane
1822		3 June	Martha Sykes of William and Jane
1826		3 September	Thomas Sykes of William and Jane.
1828		29 June	Mary Sykes of William and Jane
1856	1 July	25 July	Annie Tilburn Sykes of Thomas and Ann
1858	8 April	30 May	Mary Emily Sykes of Thomas and Ann.

Marriages.

Joseph Sykes and Ann Butler of Ackworth, 24 November 1772.
Joseph Sykes and Martha Street of Ackworth, 29 September 1776
their eldest son
William Sykes and Jane Wilkinson of Ackworth, 28 November 1813
their fifth son
Thomas Sykes and Ann Tilburn of Ackworth, 23 August 1855

Burials

Rachel Sykes, 10 February 1772, aged 57 years.
Ann Sykes, 2 May 1774, aged 35 years
Samuel Sykes, 4 January 1789, aged 74 years.
Joseph Sykes, 23 October 1814, aged 68 years
Martha Sykes, 6 November 1814, aged 64 years
William Sykes, 2 January 1862, aged 84 years.
Jane Sykes, 15 December 1861, aged 75 years

Beeston, in the Parish of Leeds, Yorkshire

Baptisms

Samuel, ye son of Will Sykes, 10 December 1727.

Church of St Peter, Leeds, Yorkshire.

Marriage.

Samuel Sykes and Rachel Baynes of Ackworth, 8 June 1741.

Doncaster, Yorkshire.

Marriage.

Samuel Sykes, Ackworth, and Ann Clark, Doncaster, 28 October 1774.

Penistone, Yorkshire.

Baptism.

Martha, of John Street, 29 July 1750

St. Mary-Church, Devon.

Burial

Thomas Sykes, 3 November 1859, aged 33 years.

Chapelries in the Parish of Leeds, Yorkshire.

Baptisms.

At Beeston, William Sykes, a son, Jona. (Qy Jonathan), 2 February 1717.
At Farnley, Ralph Sykes, a daughter, Mary, 21 March 1714
At Beeston, William Sykes, a daughter, Mary, 4 April 1725.
At Farnley, Sylvanus Sykes, a daughter, Elizabeth, 10 Oct 1725.

At Beeston, William Sykes, a son, Samuel, 10 Dec 1727
At Farnley, Ralph Sykes, a daughter, Sarah, 30 July 1727.
At Hunslet, John Sykes, two sons, Thomas and John, 17 July 1730.
At Beeston, William Sykes, a daughter, Dorothy, 28th Oct. 1730
At Farnley, Ralph Sykes, a daughter, Hannah, 21 June 1730.

WILL OF ROBERT LONG, 1669.

In the name of God Amen I Robert Long* of Staunton Prior in the County of Somersett Esquire being of a sound and good memory for which I render to Almighty God the praise and honour yett minding my age and mortality doe this eight and twentyeth day of January in the yeare of our Lord God one thousand six hundred ninety and six make and declare this my last Will and Testament in manner following hereby revokeing all former Wills by me made ffirst and principally I bequeath my soule to God my Creator with hopes of eternall life by his infinite free grace and mercy thro the meritts and mediation of my alsufficient and alone Saviour Jesus Christ And my body I comitt to the earth to be buryed in such manner and place as my Executrix herein after named shall thinke fitt Alsoe I give unto the Poore of Staunton aforesaid Ten pounds And Ten pounds to the poore of Priston to be disposed of at the discretion of my executrix And whereas I have by deed dated the eleaventh day of November last past granted and assigned unto my son in law Thomas Beref† of Huntsham in the County of Devon, Joseph Langton‡ of Newton Park in the said County of Somersett and Colthrop Parker§ of London Esq[rs] and to William Webb of the City of Bath Gentleman All that my yearly rent or sum of ffoure score pounds granted by S[r] Robert Vyner‖ Baronett unto my brother Thomas Long¶ Esq[r] since deceased and to his Heires and Assignes for ever and issueing and payable out of the hereditary Revenues of Excise to and for the severall uses in the said Deed menc'oned and expressed I doe hereby confirme the

* Robert Long, third son of Henry Long of Whaddon, Wilts and of Priston, Somerset, by Rebecca Bailey, daughter of Christopher Bailey

Robert's wife is set down in Burke and other printed works as Alice Coward, daughter of Thomas Coward of Wilton (?) Any information upon this family of Coward, if published in 'Miscellanea Genealogica et Heraldica,' would oblige and interest several of its supporters, as also would an answer to the question, if this Robert Long be not the same with the M P for Somerset, 1654 1656?

† Thomas Bere the second husband of Mary, Robert's daughter, she married firstly Geo. Stedman of Midsummer Norton, Esq co Somerset

‡ The line of this Joseph Langton ran out in daughters and coheirs, we believe they were two only surviving at the time of his death, March 17th, 1719 He was then in the 82nd year of his age, and was buried at Newton St Lo in the Church His sons (of whom Henry is mentioned further on in this Will), and all his daughters, except Ann, and (perhaps) one other, died in the lifetime of their father Ann married *firstly*, Sir Geo Cobb of Adderbury Oxon, *secondly* her cousin, Joseph Langton, Esq, of Brislington, son of Sir Thomas Langton, Knight From this marriage came Joseph Langton of Brislington and Newton St Lo, who dying 10th February, 1779, ætat 72, left a daughter and sole heir, Bridget, by his second wife Bridget married Col William Gore of Barrow-Gurney, Somerset, who added to Gore the name of Langton, was M P for East Somerset for many years, and dying in London 14th March, was buried at Newton on the 26th March, 1847 From him the present family of Gore-Langton of Newton Park descends The name Bridget was brought into the family of Gore by the marriage of Bridget Harington, fifth daughter of Sir James Harington, Bart of Ridlington, with Sir John Gore of Gilston Herts, it was brought to the family of Gore-Langton by Bridget Langton, as shewn above, whose mother (second wife to Joseph Langton) was Bridget Glanville, daughter of Evylyn Glanville, Esq of Sinclair, co Kent

§ Colthrope Parker, afterwards Parker Long (see 'Miscellanea Genealogica et Heraldica,' Vol III, No 5, pp 60 61) He married Dionysia, the widow of Testator's only son, Henry Long, 1682

‖ Sir Robert Vyner of London, Bart, 10th May, 1666, died s p 1688 The Testator's grandfather had a cousin, Mary Long, married to Henry Viner of Castle Combe, so probably the London Viners came from Wilts

¶ Thomas Long, commonly known in his day as Col Long (So entered in Stanton Prior Registers)

said Deed and desire the said Thomas Bere Joseph Langton Colthrop Parker and William Webb to performe the Trusts thereby in them reposed Alsoe I give unto the said Colthrop Parker my Nephew Mr ffrancis* Knight and to my cozen Mr William Hall† All that my Messuage or tenement with the appurtenances wherein I now dwell in Staunton aforesaid And all Lands Meadowes Pastures Com'ons Woods Priviledges and Comodityes whatsoever to the same belonging or in any wise apertaining And alsoe all that my Capitall Messuage or Tenement and ffarme in Priston aforesaid called Priston ffarme and all Lands Meadowes Pastures Com'ons Woods Profitts Priviledges and appurtenances whatsoever to the same belonging or in any wise appertaining for the severall termes and estates I have therein Upon this speciall trust and confidence neverthelcss that is to say That they the said Colthrop Parker ffrancis Knight and William Hall and the survivor and survivors of them and Executors and Adm'strators of such survivor shall permitt and suffer my dear daughter Mary Bere and her Assignes to hold and enjoy the said severall Messuages ffarmes Lands and Tenements with their and every of their appurtenances and to receive the rents issues and profitts thereof to her own proper use and benefitt for soe many yeares of the said severall termes as she shall live And from and after her decease shall permitt Charles Bere (one of the sons of the said Thomas Bere) his Executors Adm'strators and Assignes to hold and enjoy the same for the remainder of the said severall termes which shall be then thereon to come and unexpired to whom after the decease of my said Daughter I give the same Alsoe I give unto my said Nephew ffrancis Knight one hundred pounds To my neice Mrs Rachell Cross ffifty pounds To her daughter Rachell Twenty pounds To Latymer Cross son of my said Neice Twenty pounds To my Cozen Robert Cooke son of Edward Cooke Dr in Phisick twenty pounds To Jane and Mary two daughters of my cozen Roger Knight of Greenham I give twenty pounds apeice To my cozen Phillip Caldecott And to my cozen Lovelace Bigg‡ I give ffifty pounds apeice And to my cozen§ William Hall twenty pounds All which said legacies I will shall be paid in lawfull money of England within twelve moneths after my decease I forgive unto my cozen Edward Knight of Ireland all the moneys which he owes me on bond or otherwise Alsoe I give unto the daughters of my cozen Mr Thomas Sambourne‖ that shall be liveing at the time of my decease twenty pounds apeice to be paid as they shall respectively attaine the severall ages of eighteene yeares or marry which shall first happen And I will that the share of any dying shall goe and remaine to the survivors of them But if my Executrix shall thinke proper soe as it be for the said Childrens advantage or the advantage of any or either of them she shall be at liberty to pay then and either of their legacie or legacies sooner and the receipt of her soe receiving shall be a sufficient discharge to my Executrix for soe much To the children sons and daughters of my cozen Rebecca Collyer I give twenty

* Robert's sister Martha married Roger Knight of Greenham, Berks

† William Hall, probably William Hall of Bradford-on-Avon, *vide* Wilts Magazine, vol v, 360 Some of this family were settled at Weston, near Bath, and one of them was Rector of Kelston Their property at Weston has, we believe, passed to the Sambourne family.

‡ Testator's sister Mary Long = Timothy Wade of London, Merch[t]

Edward Cooke, 1[st] =	Mary Wade =	2[ndly] Richard Bigg =	1st Lady Phœbe Ley
M D. "My cozen, Robert Cooke, son of Edward, etc"	dau'r & sole heir of her father	of Haine's Hill, n[r] Wokingham	dau of James Ley, 1st Earl of Marlborough
Robert Cooke named in this Will		Lovelace Bigg of Chilton Follyat named also in this Will	

§ "My cozen William" Hall This kinship was, we believe, through the Baileys, above referred to

‖ Probably one of the Samborne family chronicled in 'Somersetshire Visitation,' 1623

pounds apeice To be paid to the Boyes to put them out apprentices or at their respective ages of one and twenty yeares which shall first happen and to the Daughters at their respective ages of eighteene yeares or be married which shall first happen. To Thomas Browne son of my cozen Elizabeth Browne widow I alsoe give twenty pounds to put him out apprentice or to be paid at his age of one and twenty yeares which shall first happen. To my cozen Martha the wife of M[r] John Price Clerke I forgive a debt of thirty pounds due to me on bond And her children sons and daughters I give twenty pounds apiece to bė paid in such manner as I have appointed for the sons and daughters of my cozen Collyer. To my daughter in law M[rs] Dyoness Parker wife of my said cozen Colthrop Parker for the great respect love and kindness she hath alwayes shewne me for which I leave her my thanks and I give her twenty guineas which I desire her to accept as a token of my love and respect to her to buy a ring to weare in remembrance of me. To my cozen ffrances Richmond Widow I give five pounds. To my Godson M[r] Henry Langton* I give Ten guineas to buy him a ring. And to my Godsons Robert Harrington† and Henry Long Gibbs‡ I give Ten pounds apeice or to each of them a peice of plate of Ten pounds value. To my servant Tobit Reed I give all my wearing apparell both Lynnen and Woollen And one Hundred and Twenty pounds of Lawfull money of England And to whatever other servants I may have at my death that have lived with me twelve moneths or upwards before either Men or Maides I give to each of them twenty shillings But if any or either of them shall have lived with me for the space of two yeares or more next before my death Then to each such servant I give twenty shillings over and above for each yeare he she or they hath or have soe lived in my service next before my death (except Mary Charles to whom I give ffive pounds only) To the said William Webb of Bath I give Ten pounds And I desire that he'el assist my Executrix in getting in the debts oweing me for which I leave her to reward him. Alsoe I give to my saide deare Daughter Bere as a particuler token of my love that little old gold I shall leave behind me at my decease To whom alsoe I give the rest residue and remainder of my estate reall and personall not herein before otherwise disposed of But I desire that notwithstanding her coverture that she may be at liberty at any time during her life or by her last Will and Testam[t] to dispose of one thousand pounds of my estate to such uses as she shall thinke fitt And I desire my son in law the said M[r] Thomas Bere to consent thereto and not to obstruct the true meaning of this Will And I doe hereby make and constitute my said Daughter Bere sole Executrix of this my last Will and Testament In witness whereof I have to this my last Will and Testament written in one whole sheet of paper to which I have put my name and parte of this to which I have put my hand and seale dated the day and yeare first above written ROB. LONG.

Signed sealed published and declared in the presence of Thomas Sambourne, W[m] Webb, W[m] ffisher.

* This was the only son of Joseph above named that lived to any age. Thomas, John, Joseph, and Borlase all died young, this Henry, born about 1660, died vitâ patris, 10th September, 1701, and was the last of his father's male issue.

† Robert Harington, fifth son of John and Helena, baptized at Kelston July 23, 1689.

‡ Henry Long Gibbs.—The connection between the Longs and Gibbs was through the Haringtons. Elizabeth Harington and Dionysia were sisters, and both of them daughters of John Harington by Mary Specott, his first wife. The former married Henry Gibbs, Mayor of Bristol. The latter married into the Long and Parker Long families, as *vide* the Pedigree of Long of Semington, Stanton Prior, etc., etc., Vol. III., No. 4.

Proved at London March 30, 1698 by Mary Bere (wife of Thomas Bere Esq.) dau. & Executrix of the said Robert Long.

Adm'on granted July 15, 1701 to Thomas Bere Esq. husband & administrator of Mary Bere, deceased, the dau. & Ex'trix of the said Robert Long.

HUBBARD OF BARLEYTHORPE, RUTLAND.

ARMS.—*Gules, on a bend sable three annulets or.*
CREST.—*A wolf's head erased.*

Richard Hubbard of Barleythorpe, yeoman. Will proved at Peterborough 4 April, 1722. = Jane.

Children:

- John Hubbard, yeoman.
- James Hubbard of Barleythorpe, yeoman. Will dated 12 Oct. 1766, proved at Peterborough 10 April, 1767. = Rose.
- Mary. = Harris. A widow in 1722.
- Mabel. = Thomas Broom.

Children of James Hubbard and Rose:

- James Hubbard of Barleythorpe, yeoman. Will dat. 15 June, 1800. Died 20 March, 1801, and buried at Oakham. = Elizabeth.
- Mary.
- Elizabeth.
- Rose Ellingworth, bapt. at Oakham 24 Oct. 1732. = Wm. Hayes.

Children of James Hubbard and Elizabeth:

- John Hubbard of Bloxholme in Lincolnshire. Will dated 21 Feb. 1800, and proved at Lincoln 16 May, 1800. Died 21 Feb. 1800, aged 38 years, and buried at Bloxholme. = Mary Dickinson. She married 2dly. Robert Graves of Ashby. Died 25 June, 1850, aged 82 years, and was buried at Bloxholme.
- Dove.
- Elizabeth. = Nathaniel Moss of Digby.
- Ann. = John Hubbard of Langham, Rutland.
- Mary. = Henry Snow of Wellingore.

Children of John Hubbard and Mary Dickinson:

- Richard Hubbard.
- James Hubbard, died 13 June, 1808, aged 12 years, buried at Bloxholme.
- William Dickinson Hubbard of Sleaford, merchant. Died 13 July, 1846, aged 47 years, and bur. at Bloxholme. Will dated 12 July, 1846, and proved at Lincoln. = Mary Redshaw, born 20 Sept. 1804; mar. at Bourne 14 Oct. 1828; living 1878.
  - A
- Mary. = John Hall.
- Elizabeth, died 26 Nov. 1814, aged 22 years, unmarried, and buried at Bloxholme.

| A

James Hubbard of Ewerby Thorpe, merchant & farmer, born 29 June, 1832. Living 1878. = Fanny Sharpe, married 1864, at Leverington. Living 1878.	Marian, born 14 Jan. 1830. = John Sutton Sharpe of Bardney Manor.	Sarah, born 29 Dec. 1833. = Edmund Clements of Sleaford.	Maria, born 9 Sept. 1839; died 18 April, 1877. = James Rusby, F.R.Hist:Soc: of London.

Charles William, born 1866.	Henry Hubert, born 1868.	Ernest James, born 1871.	Marian, born 1865.

NOTES RELATING TO THE WOODHOUSE FAMILY.

FROM THE FLY-LEAF OF A MS. VOLUME OF COLLECTIONS RELATING TO ST. PANCRAS.

"Wm Woodhouse 1699."

Under the signature is inserted the following shield of arms drawn on vellum, Sable a chevron between three lions passant or, impaling argent on a chevron between three trefoils gules two mullets of the first.

Crest, a lion passant or. Motto, "Quod verum atque decens."

The Register of ye children of William Woodhouse and Dorothea his Wife January 24th 1703-4.

Hulbert was Born Jan. 8, 1703-4 about 9 in ye morning. Baptized January 23^d 1703-4 at Rearsby in Leicestershire.

Ann ye Daughter of William & Dorothea Woodehouse was Born April 1 about 2 in ye Evening and bapt. April 21, 1706 at Rearsby. She Dyed Novr 1708.

Mary ye Daughter of William & Dorothea Woodehouse was Born May 15 Between 3 and 4 of the Clock in the Evening & Bapt. the 25th at Rearsby in the year of our Lord 1707.

John the son of William & Dorothea Woodehouse was Born Dec. 21st between the Hours of 7 & 8 in the morning, Bapt. the same Day at Gainsboro in Lincolnshire in the year of our Lord 1709.

William the son of William & Dorothea Woodehouse was Born March 5th between the hours of 3 and 4 in the morning was Bapt. on the 15 day of March at Highgate in the year of our Lord 1711. He dyed at Tetuan in Barbary March 11, 1731.

My Pious & prudent wife Dyed Nov. 21, 1739 buried in Reresby church.

On a plain stone in Rearsby Church. In Memory of William Woodehouse Gent. who died February 24, 1742-3 aged 84.

The Revd William Woodehouse was rector of Rearsby in Leicestershire whose granddaughter Elizabeth married the Rev. Dr Whitaker of Leeds whose daughter Catherine is my wife.

Saml. Crompton.

JACKSON FAMILY.—Information is requested respecting the ancestry of James Jackson, Vicar of Farnham, who died in 1791. He married Phillis Steer, and left six sons—John, a solicitor at Brighton; George, of Petworth; James, who died abroad; William, a Chaplain to the Prince of Wales; Richard, a surgeon at Petworth; and Edward, who died young.—E. J. BEDFORD.

Family of Gresham.

ABSTRACTS OF INQUISITIONS POST MORTEM.

EDMUND GRESHAM, ESQ

[Chancery Inquis. p m 29 Eliz, 1st Pt, No 47].

Inquisition taken at Norwich in 'Le Sheirehowse' 7 June 29 Eliz. (1558) upon the death of Edmund Gresham late of Thorpmarket, co. Norf, Esq deceased The Jurors say that upon the day of his death he was seised in his demesne as of fee of the manors of Thorpmarket and Bruserds in Thorpe with the right of one fold course* for 360 sheep on Oldfield Heath, co Norf And of divers other lands and tenements in Thorpemarket lately bought of Robert Cotrell, and of the fee farm of Coxford Priors in Thorp, and of 30 acres lately bought of Martin Burney Esq., of a tenement called Cottons and of a close called Parrowe Close in Hunworth and Thorp lately bought of Edmund Windham Gent., and of the Manor of Kidlams and divers lands and tenements in Roughton, Hunworthe, Felbrigg, Systrond, Cromer, Antingham, and Bradfield co Norf and of a tenement with divers lands in Holt, of the Manor and Rectory of Warlingham and divers lands there, of the Manor of Sanderstead and of the Advowson of the Church, and of the Boro' of Langhurst co Surrey, and of a messuage in Milk Street in the City of London. (Here the will is set out) That the manors of Thorp and Bruserds were held of the late Earl of Surrey now of the Earl of Arundel by the service of one Knight's fee and were worth £13 6*s.* 4*d* The Manor of Coxford was held in fee farm by rent of 40 shillings The tenements called Cottons and Parrow Close were held of the Queen in chief by the service of the hundreth part of a Knight's fee and were worth 10*s.* Kydlams and the other lands were late held of the Duke of Norfolk now of the Earl of Arundel by the service of one Knight's fee, and were worth 13*s.* 4*d* The lands in Holt were held of Sir William Heydon Knt. as of his Manor of Holt, in socage, and were worth five marks The Manor and Rectory of Warlingham were held of the Queen in chief by the service of the twentieth part of a Knight's fee and were worth £10. The Manor of Sanderstead with the Advowson, and the Boro' of Langhurst were held of the Queen by the service of one Knight's fee and were worth £10 The Messuage in Milk Street was held of the Lord Mayor in free burgage and was worth five marks That the said Edmund Gresham died on the last day of August last past and that Richard Gresham was his son and heir and of the age of twenty-one years and one month

THOMAS GRESHAM, ESQ.

[Chancery Inquis. p m. 18 Jac I, 1st Pt No. 61.]

Inquisition taken at Folkingham, co. Lincoln, 9 Jan., 18 Jac I, upon the death of Thomas Gresham, Esq The Jurors say that he was seised in his demesne as of fee in two parts of 2 messuages, 1 toft, 1 dovehouse, 4 gardens, 40 acres of land, 200 of meadow, 100 of pasture, 10 of wood, 200 of furze and heath, and 30 of salt marsh, and of common of pasture for all beasts in Tetney and Tetney Grange, co Lincoln, and of the tithes of corn and hay in Tetney and of a close there called Holme alias Skerneholme (Here part of his will is set out) † That said Thomas Gresham died on 6 July last—that the 2 parts of the said lands were held of the King in chief by Knight's service and were worth £6 That the tithes were held of the King as of his Manor of East Greenwich, co Kent, in free socage by fealty only and were worth 20 shillings, that the close called Skerneholme was worth 20 shillings That Judith his wife survived him and was then living, and that John Gresham was his son and heir and was of the age of nine years and nine months at the time of his father's death.

* Cursus foldagi

† See *ante*, Vol II, p 455

[Chancery Inquis. p m 19 Jac. I., 1st Pt., No. 19]

Inquisition taken in the parish of St Clement's Danes upon the death of Thomas Gresham of Fulham Esq The Jurors say that he was seised in fee of 1 messuage, 1 toft, 1 dovehouse, 2 gardens, 2 orchards, and 10 acres of land meadow and pasture thereto belonging at Fulham co Midd and of 2 closes called Kittecloses in Fulham containing 7 acres, and of 1 close called Bradbrakes containing 10 acres [Here part of his will is set out *ut ante*] That the said premises in Fulham were held of the Bishop of London as of his Manor of Fulham by fealty and were worth 60*s.* per annum. That said Thomas died on 6 July 18 Jac I., that Judith his wife survived him, and that John Gresham was his son and heir (*ut ante*).

GENEALOGICAL MEMORANDA RELATING TO THE FAMILY OF POTTER, OF THE CO DOWN, IRELAND.*

Copy Entries of Births and Marriages of the Potter Family, taken out of the old Ballymacarron Bible, 10 December, 1815, by R. Potter.†

Thos Potter & Mrs Jane Read were married in Greyabby by Mr Williamson 8th May 1731.

Their son John was born 31 March 1732.

Thos Potter the Father of the Thos above died 10th January 1733.‡

Thos Potter married 2dly 23 July 1736 Mrs Cathrine Marshell in Killinchy by Revd Thos Brinton (?)§ their son Hugh Born 7th November 1738 their son James was Born 20 Novemr 1740.

Also my son Thomas was Born 11th February 1743

My Daughter Mary was Born in Sept. 1745

My son Marshell was Born 9th December, 1746

My son Joseph was Born 11th February, 1750.

My Daughter Jane was Born May 5, 1755

Deaths of the Potter Family of Ballymacarron.

John Potter Died 31 March 1761 ||

Hugh Potter died 3 November, 1796 ||

Joseph Potter died 2d January 1770.||

Jane Potter died 3d February 1772 ||

James Potter died 26 Octr 1779.¶

Thos Potter Senr died 25 December 1782.||

Thos Potter Junr died 26 July 1785 ||

Cathrine Potter Died 11 August 1794. She was Marshall.||

Rose Widow of Thos Potter Junr died 24 March 1816 ||

* Communicated by WALTON GRAHAM BERRY, Broomfield, Fixby, Yorkshire

† See 'Miscellanea Genealogica et Heraldica,' N S Vol II., p 570

‡ The date of his death is here given as 1733, whereas he was living when his father made his will dated 10 August, 1747 Probably a mistake for 1753

§ This name is not quite clear

|| Buried at Killinchy, co Down

¶ James Potter of Mount Potter, co Down, married in 1773 Dorothea Josepha, only daughter and eventual coheiress of William Shaw, Esq , of Ballytweedy, co Antrim (by his wife Charlotte Dorothea Finiston), by whom he had issue —

I Thomas, of Ballymacarron, co Down died 1803, left issue now represented by John Hart, Esq , Barrister at Law, of Ballymacarron House

II William Henry, a Lieutenant in the Madras Native Infantry, died at Madras

III Charlotte, married John M'Connell, Esq , of Belfast, and had issue now represented by John M'Connell Higginson Esq , J P of Carnalea House co Down

Mr Potter died 26th Oct , 1779, and was buried in the burying ground of the Shaw family at Carmevy, co Antrim His widow married secondly Thomas Potter, Esq , J P of Ardview, co Down, by whom he had issue

HAWKINS.

ADDITIONAL PEDIGREE OF THE FAMILY OF HAWKINS, SHEWING THE DESCENTS OF ESTATES AT NETHERSEALE, COUNTY OF LEICESTER, TO THE PRESENT TIME.*

Seal of JOSEPH MUCCLESTON, Esq.—Muccleston and Hawkins, quarterly. In the emblazoned pedigree from which this is taken, in the arms of Hawkins, the chief is party per pale, gules and sable, the griffin ermine, the escallop shells on the chevron argent, the cinquefoils azure.

William Hawkins of Burton-upon-Trent, co. of Stafford. Will dated 23 Sept. 1724. Buried at Newport, co. Salop. = Katherine, dau. of John Gisborne, of Derby. Will dated 18 Oct. 29 Geo. II., proved at Doctors' Commons 3 Sept. 1760.

William Hawkins, died unmarried.

Isaac Hawkins, possessed of great wealth, is said, in some law proceedings at Peniarth, to have given £200,000 to the East India Compy, owner of the estates at Netherseale, now vested in his representatives; founded and endowed a chapel at Burton-upon-Trent; married Anne, one of the daughters of the Rev. James Gisborne, Prebendary of Durham, and Rector of Staveley, co. Derby, but died 6 Feb. 1800, s.p.; buried at Burton-upon-Trent. Marriage covenants dated 18 June, 1759. She died in 1782.

Philip, married, but died in the lifetime of Isaac.

Catherine Hawkins. = Joseph Muccleston, bapt. 17 Dec. 1699; died 15 July, 1757; bur. at Shrewsbury.

Catherine, married 14 Feb. 1753, to Samuel Griffiths, but died s.p., in April, 1766.

Jane. = John Holland, buried at Shrewsbury.

John Coghill, of Coghill Hall, co. of York. = Jane, only dau. and heir.

George Mowbray of Sunderland, died in June, 1799. = Jane, only dau. and heir. (Oct. 9, 1802, signs her name as "Jane Mowbray.") = John White, 2nd husb. Living in 1804.

George Mowbray, living 1804.

Thomas, living 1804.

A daughter, living in 1804.

A large portion of the Netherseale estates, formerly owned by Isaac Hawkins above, is still vested in the Mowbrays, and it is believed that the Gisbornes possess another portion.

Richard Muccleston,† of Stoke Newington, brother of Joseph, bapt. 28 May, 1708, died Oct. 20, 1773, buried at Hillingdon, Middlesex. The grandmother of Richard Muccleston was Mary, dau. of Wm. Hawkins, of Newport Isle. She died Sept. 21, 1730, aged 71. Her husband was bapt. 24 Feb. 1671, and died June 25, 1730. The arms of Hawkins of Newport Isle were the same as those of Wm. Hawkins above, as were those quartered by the late Isaac Hawkins Browne, M.P. = Mary Hawkins, born 30 May, 1717, died 29 Dec. 1778, buried at Hillingdon, co. of Middlesex.

Joseph Muccleston of Walford and Prescot, co. of Salop, and of Netherseale, devisee under the will of his uncle Isaac, who was possessed under the settlement of his father, Wm. Hawkins. Born Jan. 28, 1754, and Sheriff of Shropshire 1788. He was of very frugal habits, and died very wealthy 11 Nov. 1730, unmarried.

William Hawkins Muccleston, M.D., born 15 July, 1755, died in 1787. = Frances, dau. of Thomas Presland of Shrewsbury.

Several other children, who died infants.

Elizabeth, only child and heiress, born 19 Dec. 1784, married 7 Feb. 1811, died in July, 1847, buried at Baschurch. = Robert Aglionby Slaney, Esq., of Hatton Grange, co. Salop, for many years M.P. for Shrewsbury; died 19 May, 1862, buried at Shiffnal. = Catherine Anne, 2nd wife, dau. of George Buckstone, of Bradbourne, co. Derby, relict of Graves Archer, of Mount John, co. Wicklow. Now living.

A

* From an illuminated pedigree in the possession of Mrs. Kenyon Slaney, and the muniments of the Netherseale Estate at Peniarth.

† Richard Muccleston, son of Joseph, admitted freeman of Shrewsbury 7 May, 1735.

| A

Thomas Campbell Eyton of Eyton in the Wildmores, co. Salop. Now living. =	Elizabeth Frances, dau. and coheir, born 31 Oct. 1813.	Mary, dau. and coheir, born 4 March, 1817, died 17 May, 1866, buried at Llanegryn. =	Wm. Watkin Edw. Wynne of Peniarth, co. of Merioneth, M.P. for that co. from 1852 to 1865. Constable of the Castle of Harlech. Now living.	Frances Catherine, now living, youngest dau. and coheir. =	Lieut.-Col. Kenyon Slaney, 2nd surviving son of the Hon. Th. Kenyon. See Peerage. Assumed the name of Slaney after that of Kenyon. Now living.

Wm. Robert Maurice Wynne, late Ensign and Lieut. Scots Fusilier Guards, M.P. for co. of Merioneth from 1865 to 1868; owner, by settlement, of a considerable portion of the Netherseale estates owned by Isaac Hawkins above. Now living.	Owen Slaney Wynne, 2nd son, late of Christ Church, Oxford, A.M. Now living. =	Mary, 2nd dau. of Edw. Owen, of Garthangharad, co. Merioneth, and relict of Francis Parry Davies, of Barmouth. Now living.

STRENGFELLOW NOTES (Vol. II., p. 545).—Frances Strengfellow of Parish of Camberwell, co. Surrey, Widow, signed her will 17 May, 1738. She names grandnephew Henry Vognell; grandnieces Christiana Frances Vognell and Elizabeth Vognell. Testatrix had property at or near Croydon, co. Surrey, and at or near Warfield, co. Berks. Gift to poor of village of Openshaw, in the parish of Manchester, where her late husband, the Rev. William Strengfellow, was born, and a gift to poor of the parish of Warfield, co. Berks, where testatrix was born. Testatrix names Mary, widow of John Strengfellow, and their son and daughter, James Strengfellow and Frances Strengfellow; late husband's cousins, Elizabeth and Sarah, daughters of William Strengfellow, deceased, brother of Joshua Strengfellow, testatrix's late husband's heir-at-law; late husband's cousin, Hannah Shuttleworth; John Strengfellow of Coleman Street, Barber, his wife, his sister Hannah Strengfellow, his children William and Frances Strengfellow; .... wife of Capt. Warden and her sister, Elizabeth Sumner; testatrix's God-daughter, Catherine Warden; Samuel and Mary Patteson; daughter of .... Pitt of Kensington; Thomas Boardman, pewterer; Susannah Strengfellow, sister of Captain Strengfellow; cousin William Hercy, his wife, and his sister Mrs. Parminton (? Parminter); cousin Frances Langley; cousin Mary Miller, wife of .... Miller, weaver; cousin Thomas Boddington, weaver, and his sister .... Sedgley; cousins Richard and Sarah West; son and daughter of late cousin Ann Mitchell; ... Hamlett; Agar Legg, his brother .... Agar, and his sister .... Legg; Frederick Vognell; Henry, Ann, Sophia, and Amelia, son and daughters of Anthony Furstenan; God-daughter Christian Toderhurst, and her sister Mary Toderhurst; and Miss Ann Hercy. Appoints as executors Henry Vognell of London, merchant, and John Welles of Abchurchyard, London, Gent.

Codicil dated 15 Aug., 1739, names Thomas Quincy of Walbrook, London.

Further codicil dated 20 January, 1742. Administration with will annexed, granted 13 Nov., 1747, to Christiana Frances Pakenham, heretofore Vognell, wife of George Edward Pakenham or Packenham, John Welles, the surviving executor, first renouncing.

Tablet in church of St. Dunstan in the East, London, to memory of Rev. William Strengfellow, successively Curate, Lecturer, and Rector of St. Dunstan in the East, appointed Rector 1698; died 19 June, 1731, aged 73 (intestate). Also to memory of his widow Frances, daughter of William Boddington, of this City, merchant, who died 25 August, 1747, aged 69.

William Boddington the father of Frances, wife of Rev. William Strengfellow, at page 545 of Vol. II., should be given as the son of William Boddington, whose wife's name is undiscovered, and grandson of William Boddington of Brinklow. The Rev. William Strengfellow died s. p., and therefore the marriage of his supposed daughter Frances with Frederick Vognell, as given at Vol. II., p. 545, is entirely incorrect. Is anything known of this family of Strengfellow?

REGINALD STEWART BODDINGTON.

THE DENNYS,

Earls of Norwich, Barons Denny of Waltham, and Baronets of Ireland.

(*Continued from* p 76)

Donogh O'Brian, the godfather of Arthur Denny born in Tralee Castle 21st of September, 1629, was grandson of the first Earl of Thomond He married Honora, daughter of Richard Wingfield, ancestor of Lord Powerscourt, and from this marriage descends the present Lord Inchiquin The Wingfields of Kimbolton, as we have seen, were nearly related to the Dennys Donogh O'Brian and Sir Valentine Browne (who was sponsor to Margaret Denny, born in 1627) were both Roman Catholics. Their intimacy and connection with the Wingfields and Dennys are a few out of many proofs to be found in the bye-ways of history, family records, and genealogies, which "distinguished" writers over-mindful sometimes of the "dignity of history," as the phrase goes, are too apt to ignore, shewing that the Irish and Anglo-Irish of different creeds lived on excellent terms with one another in the early part of the seventeenth century, before the "thorough" policy of Strafford and continental influences revived racial and religious strifes The next entries in the old diary or register kept by Sir Edward Denny are as follows —

"Ye 25th March, 1630, I began chapters* after dinner and suppers.

"Monday, ye 15th of November, 1630, Edward(*a*) Denny was borne between six and seven at night; his godfathers were William Steere, Lorde Bishop of Kerrye, and Sir Charles Harrys, Knt., his godmother Mrs Joane Crosbye

"Ye 20th of Aprill, 1632, being fryday betweene six and seven of the clock in the morning, Anthony Denny(*b*) was borne, his godfathers were Mr Robert Blennerhassett and Ensign John Wyse, his godmother Mrs Anne Baden

"Anne Denny(*c*) was borne uponn Sunday night att one of ye clocke ye 28th of Aprill, 1633, her godmother Mrs 'Hassett for the Lady Baltinglas, and Mrs Steere ye Bishop of Kerry's wife, her godfather Sr Walter Crosbie

"Thomas Denny(*d*) my sonne was borne upon Wensday morning, betweene nine and tenn o'clock, ye 16th of July, 1634, att Roper's Rest House neare Dublin, his godfathers the Lord Viscount Baltinglas and Sir Charles Coote, ye Ladye Tresham his godmother.

"Ye 23d of July, 1633, ye Lord Viscount Wentworth came to Ireland to governe ye Kingdom as Deputie Many men feare

"Elizabeth Denny(*e*) was borne uponn thursday early in the morning, about six o'clocke, ye 25th of Februarie 1635, her godmother my mother and my cosen Martha 'Hassett, her godfather Mr Edmond Harrys

"Lucius Denny(*f*) was born uponn Wensday at break of day being ye 21st of June 1637, his godfathers were ye Deane Gray and Mr Thomas Denny his godmother Mrs Vaucher.

"William Denny(*g*) was borne on teusday morning ye 11th of September 1638 his godfathers William St Leger and Anthony Stoughton Esquires, the Deane's wyfe Mrs Gray his godmother.

"Ruth Denny(*h*) was borne on Monday ye 13th of September (between six and seven o'clock in the morning) 1641 her godmother my sister in law Mary Roper and Mrs Barbara (illegible) and Philip Percivall."

This record of his youngest child's birth in September, 1641, was the last entry made in the old MS. volume by Sir Edward Denny, the great-grandson of Sir Anthony. The three words "many men feare," following the note of Wentworth's arrival, have a sad significance read by the light of subsequent events in this, as in many another family history. In 1634 Sir Edward Denny was High Sheriff of Kerry, and from that year until 1641 he and Sir Valentine Browne, before men-

* Chapters let in hope of the old Bible so carefully preserved by his descendants

tioned, represented the county in parliament In 1639 Wentworth, in order to raise money for the King, compelled Sir Edward, and several other Kerry landowners, to take out new letters patent, confirming them in the possession of their estates, and to pay heavy fines A clause in Denny's letters (and a similar one, I believe, appears in the rest) bound him to bring in on his estate within a twelve month, under pain of forfeiture, eight free tenants of the "British race and blood," in addition to those already planted there The carrying out of this clause would, of course, involve the eviction of great numbers of the Irish of the native blood, who had been for several years living peacefully as tenants on the estate It revived, in fact, the old odious distinctions (which were gradually dying out, and which a statute of James the First had ostensibly abolished) between the Anglo-Irish, that is, the Irish descended from English colonists of Ireland, and the Irish descended from the Celtic inhabitants before 1172, or the "mere Irish," as they were contemptuously styled in legal and common parlance, until the beginning of the seventeenth century Sir Edward paid the fine for his new letters patent, but it is very doubtful that he ever carried out the clause respecting the new tenants The twelve months allotted to him in which to do so were hardly over before the island was filled with rumours of coming trouble, and in six weeks after he had made the above entry of his daughter's birth it was once more in open rebellion

Sir Edward Denny and Sir Valentine Browne, the Protestant and the Catholic members for the county of Kerry, were both of the King's party in Ireland, but that party was divided against itself Sir Valentine was a loyal Catholic, while Sir Edward Denny belonged to that section of the Cavaliers who are described by Macaulay as fighting "not for an intolerant Church and a tyrannical King, but for the old English banner which waved over their ranks, and for the altars at which they had received the hands of their brides" He sent his wife and young children to England, and leaving his Castle of Tralee to be defended by his stepfather, Sir Thomas Harris, and a chosen band of two hundred Irish and English tenants, he joined Sir William St Leger, Lord President of Munster, who was maintaining the royal cause in Waterford county A letter in one of the pamphlets of the year 1642 in the King's Library, British Museum, mentions Sir Edward Denny as a Captain commanding four hundred soldiers in a skirmish near Dublin The letter is said to have been written by the Earl of Antrim to his connexion the Earl of Rutland We have no further account of Sir Edward Denny's movements, nor any record of the time of his death. Meantime his Castle of Tralee was closely besieged by the Irish Catholic forces A number of Protestants from the town of Tralee and the country around it, amongst them two clergymen of the Reformed Church, the Reverend Nathaniel Harrison and the Reverend William Fell, and a surgeon named Elkanah Knight, crowded for shelter into the old fortress, which was badly provisioned The food and water ran short, while the besiegers received fresh reinforcements, and laid the country under contribution Dr Elkanah Knight, with his hands full, assisting in the defence and attending the daily increasing number of sick, found time to keep a journal of events within and outside the walls of the castle from day to day, and this very curious and interesting record, which threw much light on one or two points in the history of the rebellion of 1641, about which there has been much disputing, was amongst the Denny family papers until the last dozen years, when it appears to have been borrowed by some one who "*forgot*" to return it If recovered, it would be well worth the attention of the Historical Manuscript Commission, but I fear the chances are small of its being returned to its lawful owner The siege lasted nearly two years, and might have lasted longer, but that the brave commander of the little garrison, Sir Thomas Harris, died, worn out with fatigue and ceaseless anxiety, and poisoned by the corrupt water. When the besieged found themselves quite destitute of ammunition and food, they surrendered upon quarter, and on delivering up their arms were allowed to pass to the north side of the county, where they were protected, for a time at least, by Colonel David Crosbie in a little island fortress near the mouth of the Shannon. The Castle of Tralee was partly destroyed, and the church and town ruined and plundered. Two memorials of the church, however, were spared by the insurgents, the old grey marble font, presented to it in 1623 by the Provost of Tralee, John Cirlestone, which remains to this day as perfect as when it was first placed within the sacred building, and the old black-letter Bible already alluded to (*v ante*, p 76) The steel plaques remain with holes pierced in them, through which a chain was passed to fasten the volume to the reading desk in the aisle. It is probable that this is the only one of the English Bibles printed before 1641, and used in the country churches of Munster, which escaped destruction in that calamitous year. Both font and Bible were destined, however, to pass unscathed through another great civil war, as we shall hereafter see.

M. A. H.

(*a*) Edward Denny whose birth is here recorded as the second son of Sir Edward Denny by Ruth, daughter of Lord Baltinglas, married Lady Katherine Barry, daughter of David, first Earl of Barrymore, by Lady Alice Boyle, dau of Richard first Earl of Cork (*v Lodge's Peerage, revised by Rev Mervyn Archdall*, vol i, p 298, ed 1789) Edward Denny left issue by Lady Katherine two sons Barry and John who died unmarried a captain in the army. Barry Denny eldest son, M P for Tralee in 1697, married Catherine, dau of Sir Boyle Maynard, Knt, of Curryglass county Cork, and had issue Edward, M P for Doneraile in 1695, died s p, and Anne, married the Rev Maurice O'Connor, and had issue Barry, Catherine and Jane, who married as we shall hereafter see her cousin, the Reverend Barry Denny. William Steere, the godfather of Edward Denny, was Bishop of Kerry, or rather of Ardfert and Aghadoe, from 1628 to 1637. The following is from the Book of Funeral Entries in the Record Tower of Dublin Castle —'The Right Reverend Father in God William Steere, late Lord Bishop of Ardfert and Aghadoe in y[e] County Kerrye, was second sonne of William Steere Parson of Barmesby (*sic*) by London in Kent in y[e] Kingdom of Englande. He tooke to wyfe Elinor, daughter of Randall Maynwaring, second sonne of Sir Randall Maynwaring of Peever in Cheshire, in y[e] said Kingdom of England, Knt, and relict of William Gunn of Lymerick, parson, by whom the said Lorde Bishop had no issue. The s[d] Lorde Bishop departed this mortall lyfe at Ardfert, y[e] 21st of January, 1637, and was interred in y[e] Cathedrall Church of Ardfert aforesaid. The truth of these premises is testified by the subscription of the said Ellinor, relict and executrix of y[e] said Bishop, who hath returned this Certificate into my office to be there recorded. Thomas Preston Ulcester King of Arms, 23[d] May 1638.' Sir Charles Harris, the second sponsor of Edward Denny, was the grandson of Sir Thomas Harris of Corworthen, Devon, who had married Elizabeth, widow of Arthur Denny and daughter of Miles Forest, Esq (*v ante*, p 76) Joan Crosbie, the child's godmother, was the younger daughter of Colonel David Crosbie of Ardfert, second son of John Crosbie, Bishop of Ardfert from 1600 to 1621, ancestor of the Earls of Glandore (extinct) of Sir John Crosbie, Bart, of William Talbot Crosbie, D L of Ardfert Abbey and in the female line of Lord Dacre. Joan Crosbie married Gerard Ryeves son of James Ryeves by Alice daughter of Captain Thomas Spring (ancestor of Lord Monteagle), and had a son Thomas Ryeves (who went to France with the Irish regiments after the surrender of Limerick in 1691 and died in exile) and three daughters Alice married William Carrig of Coolmines in Clare, and had a son, whose daughter married Finucane of Ailine in Clare, Catherine married Francis Brudenell of Limerick and died without issue, and Elizabeth married Walter Langdon, son of Walter Langdon by Catherine Hickson. This last mentioned Walter was son of Nathaniel Langdon, Dean of Ardfert before 1641' (*MS Genealogies by Captain John Blennerhassett written between* 1688 *and* 1736)

(*b*) Anthony Denny died unmarried. His godfather Robert Blennerhassett, was the first settler of his name at Ballyseedy in Kerry, and the ancestor of Arthur Blennerhassett now of Ballyseedy, High Sheriff of that county, of Rowland Ponsonby Blennerhassett at present M P for the same, and of the Blennerhassetts of Riddelstown in Limerick county. Robert Blennerhassett was M P for the then newly-created borough of Tralee in 1613. Mrs Anne Baden, the godmother of Anthony Denny, was the wife of the Dean of Ardfert (*MS* 1688, *Diocesan Records*, 1633 *State Papers*)

(*c*) Anne Denny died unmarried. Her godmother, Mrs 'Hassett, was the wife of Robert the Blennerhassett mentioned in the preceding note, and the daughter of Jenkin Conway of Castle Conway, or Killorglin, County Kerry. Sir Walter Crosbie was the eldest son of Bishop Crosbie, and the ancestor of the Crosbie, Barts, of the Queen's County

(*d*) Thomas Denny died unmarried. His godfather, Sir Charles Coote, was the first baronet of his name ancestor of the Earls of Mountrath (extinct) Lady Tresham was I believe, a niece or sister of the Lord Baltinglas

(*e*) Elizabeth Denny married John Blennerhassett of Ballyseedy (marriage settlements dated 1651), grandson of Robert Blennerhassett mentioned in note (*b*), and son of John Blennerhassett by Martha Lyn. John Blennerhassett left issue by his wife, Elizabeth Denny two sons and a daughter, viz —

1 Arthur, married Anne, daughter of Sir Boyle Maynard, and died s p

2 John, married Margaret Crosbie, and was by her ancestor of Arthur Blennerhassett, Esq, present owner of Ballyseedy and High Sheriff of Kerry (son of Charles Blennerhassett, Esq, by Mary Anne, daughter of John Hickson, Esq, D L of the Grove, county Kerry), of Lord Headley, and

of Jemmett Browne, Esq, of Riverston, county Cork, and Cornwall Gardens, London This last-mentioned gentleman is the representative in the female line of the elder branch of the Blennerhassetts of Ballyseedy, descended from John Blennerhassett, eldest son of John by Margaret Crosbie above mentioned, who married his cousin, Jane Denny, as hereafter mentioned

3 Ruth, only daughter of John Blennerhassett and Elizabeth Denny, married first (before 1677) Thomas Browne of Guiteendrohid, county Cork, and secondly, her cousin, Thomas Blennerhassett, son of Arthur Blennerhassett by Mary Fitzgerald of Ballynard, county Limerick, and had two daughters, Sarah married Richard Hall, son of Rev John Hall, Prebendary of St Finbarr's, and Mary, married George Rowan and had with other issue two sons, 1 John Rowan married Sarah, daughter of James Leslie of Tarbert House, county Kerry and sister of James Leslie, Bishop of Limerick and Ardfert from 1756 to 1770 and had a son George, married Jane Usher, of Mount Usher, county Wicklow (v Mrs Delany's 'Letters and Memoirs'), and a daughter Mary married Rev Edward Day, Rector of Tralee in 1758, and had a son, Rev James Day, Rector of Tralee in 1809, and Vicar-General of Ardfert, who by Margaret, daughter of the MacGillicuddy of the Reeks, hath with other issue three sons Reverend Edward Day, Rector of Kilgobbin, married and had a numerous issue James Leslie Day, Major in the Bengal Army, died s p, John Sealy Day, Captain in the 87th Regt, served throughout the Peninsular and Burmese Wars, and died s p, and Sarah, married John James Hickson, and had surviving issue, James married his cousin, Deborah Godfrey Day, and had issue, John died unmarried, and Mary Agnes Hickson 2 George Rowan second son of George Rowan and Mary Blennerhassett before mentioned, married Margaret, daughter of Richard Chute of Chute Hall and had with other issue a son George, who married Gorham, and had with other issue a son William, who married his cousin Letitia, daughter of Sir Barry Denny, Bart, as hereafter mentioned, and had a son Rev Arthur Blennerhassett Rowan, D D, Archdeacon of Ardfert, who by his wife Alicia, daughter of Peter Thompson, Esq, had a son William, now of Belmont, county Kerry, married twice, and has issue, and two daughters, Anne and Ora Martha Hassett, the godmother of Elizabeth Denny, was the wife of John Blennerhassett, eldest son of Robert, the first settler at Ballyseedy, Martha Hassett was the niece of the mother of Mary Forrest, the mother of Sir Edward Denny (*MS Pedigrees of the Seventeenth Century, Marriage Settlements, and Diocesan Records*)

(*f*) Lucius Denny died unmarried His godmother, Mrs Vaucher was the wife of a Captain Edward Vaucher, an officer of Huguenot descent serving in the English army in Ireland, who had settled in Kerry His deposition detailing his sufferings and losses in 1641-2 at the hands of "Walter Hussey of Castle Gregory O Sullivan More of Dunkerron, Florence MacCarthy, Esquires, Daniel MacMoriarty, Garret Fitz James Gerald Christopher Hickson of Knockglass, gentlemen," and other 'Papists and rebels (as he styles them), is in Trinity College Library, Dublin

(*g*) William Denny According to Archdall in his revised edition of 'Lodge's Peerage,' vol i p 300, *note* William Denny married in 1664 Elizabeth, daughter of Richard Clarke, Esq, and died in 1665, and his widow remarried in 1671 the Rev Richard Synge of Cork Sir William St Leger, godfather of William Denny, was the son of Sir Warham St Leger, the brother officer of Raleigh, Gilbert, and Sir Edward Denny (the elder) in the Elizabethan wars, and the grandfather of the first Viscount Doneraile Anthony Stoughton was the ancestor of the family of his name, now of Owlpen, Gloucestershire, and Ballyhorgan, county Kerry

(*h*) Ruth Denny died unmarried Her godfather, Philip Percival, was the ancestor of the Earl of Egmont (*v Archdall's 'Lodge,'* vol ii, p 238)

(*To be continued.*)

EXTRACTS FROM THE PARISH REGISTER OF ILKLEY, IN THE COUNTY OF YORKSHIRE, AND DEANERY OF CRAVEN *

The register commences in 1597. The following extracts relate chiefly to the family of Langfellow, sometimes written Langfelley, and once or twice Longfellow, one of whom emigrated to America towards the close of the seventeenth century, and became the ancestor of the poet, Mr. Henry Wadsworth Longfellow

The late Vicar of Ilkley, the Rev John Snowdon, by whose permission I made these extracts, and my grateful sense of whose kindness I wish here to record, had in his possession a letter from Mr. Somerby, a friend of the poet, written in April, 1858

I gather from it that William Longfellow, the American settler, emigrated to Newbury, Massachusetts, that he there married Anne Sewell, 10th of November, 1676, that he became an officer in the Essex regiment, and that he was drowned at Cape Breton in 1690, being upon an expedition against the French and Indians.

* Communicated by HUGH F BOYD, Esq

His children were William, Stephen, Anne, Elizabeth, and Matthew. I venture to hope that some American genealogist will send you the descent from them down to the present time.

I hoped that I had found the baptismal entry of the settler in William, son of Francis Longfellow, who was baptized the 10th of November, 1650; but on turning to the burials, I find William, son of Francis Longfellow, was buried the first of September, 1654. The register from 1650 to 1656 is miserably defective, and there is an absolute cessation of entries from 1656 to 1674.

I give also a few extracts relating to a branch of the Hebers of Marton, settled at Hollinghall in the parish of Ilkley—*vide* Whitaker's 'Craven,' p. 71. It will be seen from a glance at the pedigree that either the wife of Reginald Heber did not die in 1615, or that he married a second time subsequently to that date.

Parochiæ Olicanæ Baptismata.

1599. Richardus filius Will'mi Langfellow baptizatus fuit Maij decimo.
1600–1. Joh'es filius Richardi Longfellow bap. Februarij vicesimo.
1601. Will'mus filius Will'mi Langfellowe baptiz. Maij septimo.
1602–3. Willm'us filius Richardi Langfelley bap. Januarij decimo sexto.
1602–3. Georgius filius Ric. Langfelley junior bap. Martij tertio.
1603. Margareta filia Jacobi Langfelley ba. Augusti nono.
1604. Rob'tus filius Will'mi Langfelley baptiz. Junij decimo.
1606–7. Isabella filia Will'mi Langfellowe bap. Martij primo.
1608. .... filia Richardi Langfellowe baptiz. Junij ....
1608. Maria filia Richardi Langfellowe bapt. Augusti ....
1609. Brianus filius Richardi Langfellowe bapt. Junij 25.
1609–10. Jana filia Will'mi Langfellowe bap. fuit Jan. 28.
1611–12. Isabella filia Richardi Langfellowe de Ilkley baptiz. fuit Januarij duodecimo.
1615. Franciscus, filius Jacobi Langfellow de Ilkley baptiz. Julij vicesimo tertio.
1616. Isabella, filia Edwardi Langfellow de Ilkley baptiz. Aprilis primo.
1616–17. Agnes, filia Jacobi Langfellow de Ilkley baptiz. Martij vicesimo primo.
1617. Franciscus, filius Richardi Langfellow de Ilkley baptiz. fuit Julij vicesimo nono.
1618. Thomas, filius Edwardi Langfellow de Ilkley bapt. fuit Martij vicesimo nono.
1620. Elizabetha, filia Edwardi Langfellow baptiz. Septembris decimo septimo.
1621. Johannes, fil. M[ri] Reginaldi Heber de Austby baptiz. Septembris secundo.
1623. Henricus, filius Edwardi Langfellow de Ilkley baptiz. Maij quarto.
1623. Christopherus, filius Reginaldi Heber de Austby baptiz. Julij vicesimo septimo.
1625–6. Dorothea, filia Richardi Langfellow de Ilkley baptiz. Januarij decimo nono.
1625–6. Anna, filia Reginaldi Heber de Austby baptiz. Februarij decimo nono.
1626–7. Robertus, filius Edwardi Langfellow de Ilkley baptiz. Martij decimo octavo.
1628–9. Martha, filia Reginaldi Heber de Holling Hall baptizata fuit Martij vicesimo primo.
1631. Letitia, filia Reginaldi Heber de Holling Hall baptiz. fuit Octobris secundo.
1632. Maria, filia Johannis Langfellow de Ilkley baptiz. fuit Octobris vicesimo octavo.
1633. Helena, filia Edwardi Langfellow de Ilkley baptiz. fuit Octobris sexto.
1634. Reginaldus, filius Reginaldi Heber baptizat. fuit Aprilis octavo.
1634–5. Gulielmus, filius Johannis Langfellow de Ilkley baptiz. fuit Februarij vicesimo secundo.
1636. Maria, filia Georgii Langfellow de Ilkley baptiz. fuit Septembris vicesimo quinto.
1637–8. Jana, filia Georgii Langfellow de Ilkley baptiz. fuit Martij quarto.
1640–1. Thomas, filius Johannis Heber de Holling Hall gen. bapt. duodecimo die Martij.
1641. Maria filia Francisci Langfellow bapt. Augusti tricesimo.
1643–4. Richardus, filius Francisci Langfellow bapt. Martij vicesimo quarto.
1647–8. Robertus, filius Wil'mi Langfellow vicesimo tertio Januarij.

1648. Tho filius Joh'is Langfellow bapt. vicesimo quinto Aprilis.
1648. Edward, fil Tho Langfellow bapt quarto die Maij
1650. Will'mus, filius Francisci Longfellow bapt decimo Novembris.
1651. Margareta, filia Henrici Longfellow bapt vicesimo [Aprilis]
1651 Maria, filia Rob'ti Langfellow bapt Augusti .
1654 John of Francis Langfellow of Ilkley bapt August . . .
1685. Reginaldus, filius Johannis Heber de Holling Hall Gen baptiz vicesimo octavo Aprilis.

Nuptiae

1600 Inter Richardū Langfellow et Marg'tam Hutt Maij decimo nono
1602 Inter Richardū Langfellow junior et Dorotheam Hutt Junij
1606. Inter Johannem Rosendale et Elizabetham Langfellow Maij
1612 Inter Franciscū Holmes et Mariā Langfellow Novembris vicesimo quarto
1613 Inter Jacobū Langfellow et Dorotheam Barrose secundo Novembris
1615 Inter Edwardū Langfellow et Janam Harrison Junij decimo nono
1622 Inter Thomam Harrison p'ochiæ de Otley et Elizabethā Langfellow Maij vicesimo primo
1629 Inter Christoferum Hardwick et Dorotheam Langfellow Decembris primo.
1635. Inter Georgium Langfellow et Janam Armistead Octobris vicesimo sexto
1640–1 Inter Georgiū Butler et Janā Langfellow Jan decimo quarto
1641 Inter Franciscum Langfellow et Janā Gaunt Maij tertio die
1642 Inter Franciscum Langfellow et Annā Robinson nono die Junij
1642 Inter Tho Langfellow et Susannā Moone primo Sept
1648–9 Inter Henricū Constantine et Annā Heber vicesimo die Martij

Sepulturæ

1597 Elizabetha, filia Jacobi Langfellow sepulta Aprilis quarto
1597–8 Richardus Langfellow senex sepultus Martij vicesimo
1600. Richardus fil Will'mi Langfellow sepult Maij xxiº.
1608 filia Richardi Longfellow sepulta Junij xxix
1611 Elizabetha, uxor Jacobi Langfellow de Ilkley sepult fuit Septembris primo.
1611 Johannes Langfellow de Ilkley sepultus fuit Septemb decimo tertio
1612 Jana, filia Richardi Langfellowe de Ilkley sepult. fuit Augusti decimo tertio
1612. Margareta Langfellow, sepulta fuit Decembris vicesimo primo
1613–14 * filia Jacobi Langfellow sep Feb. vicesimo octavo
1627 Jacobus Langfellow de Ilkley sepult Octobris decimo sexto
1627–8 Gulielmus Langfellow de Ilkley Januarij vicesimo primo
1635 Edwardus Langfellow sepult fuit Junij decimo
1635. Isabella Langfellow sepult fuit Augusti decimo
1637–8 Jana, uxor Georgii Langfellow de Ilkley sepult fuit Martij tertio
1638 Gulielmus Langfellow de Ilkley Augusti vicesimo
1638–9 Agnes Langfellow de Ilkley Januarij quarto
1640–1. Jana uxor Johannis Heber gen sepult decimo secundo die Martij
1643 Elizabetha uxor Will'mi Langfellow sepult primo Aprilis
1643 . . Langfellow octavo die Julij
1643 Anna Langfellow vidua sepulta decimo quinto Septembris
1647–8 Willm's Langfellow sepult decimo nono Januarij
1648 Margareta Langfellow sepulta vicesimo Decembris
1649 Johannes Heber sepult decimo octavo Aprilis
1649 Letitia Heber sepult vicesimo nono Aprilis
1649 Christopher† Heber sepult [decimo] tertio Maij
1650–51 Franciscus Langfellow sepult Februarij septimo die
16[illegible] Bryan Langfellow of Ilkley sepult June the xxiv^th
16[illegible] filia Henry Langfellow sepult July 27th
1654 Will'm of Francis Langfellow of Ilkley sepult September first.

(*To be continued*)

* No name given

† The inscription on the brass to him in the chancel says that he died on the 8th of May Perhaps the Register should read decimo tertio

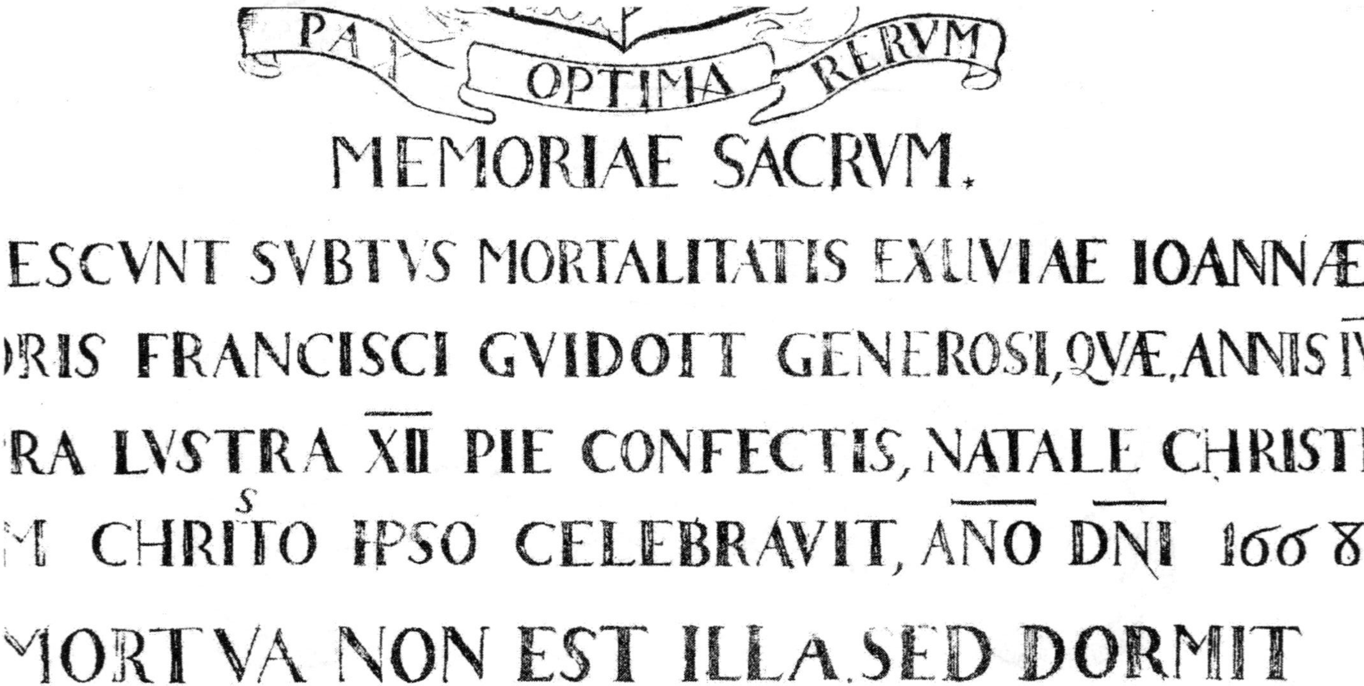

PA OPTIMA RERVM

MEMORIAE SACRVM.

ESCVNT SVBTVS MORTALITATIS EXUVIAE IOANNÆ

RIS FRANCISCI GVIDOTT GENEROSI, QVÆ, ANNIS IV

RA LVSTRA XII PIE CONFECTIS, NATALE CHRISTI

M CHRI^S^TO IPSO CELEBRAVIT, ANO DNI 1668.

MORTVA NON EST ILLA SED DORMIT

IPRESSION FROM A BRASS PLATE FORMERLY IN THE NORTH AISLE OF LYMINGTON CHURCH, HAMPSHIRE, BUT REMOVED FROM THENCE A FEW YEARS AGO ON THE FLOORING BEING RENEWED AND RELAID.

THE ORIGINAL PLATE IS NOW IN THE POSSESSION OF EDWARD KING, ESQ., OF LYMINGTON.

GEORGE AND ROGER HARINGTON, ALDERMEN OF BRISTOL. WERE THEY MEMBERS OF THE KELSTON FAMILY?

HAVING already given the monumental inscriptions of all undoubted Haringtons of Kelston which may be found in Bristol and the neighbourhood, it becomes necessary now to speak of a monument to Harington extant in the city of Bristol which has not been included in the Kelston category, and to discuss the grounds on which it has been rejected from the good company of the others. The monument referred to is set up in St Peter's Church, Bristol, at the east end of the north aisle, where the organ is now fitted in (1878). It is a mural one, of somewhat costly character, on which are represented an alderman and his lady, both kneeling at a desk in prayer beneath an arched canopy, with this inscription:—

> "To the Memory of the Worshipfull Mr. George Harrington Sometime Mayor and Alderman of this Citie, who departed this life the Second of Janvarie 1639."

This gentleman was Mayor of Bristol in 1617, and it is recorded of him, during his mayoralty, that he went through the city trying the weights and measures, and removed all that were faulty. Moreover, he tried all the colliers sacks, cutting to pieces those that did not hold their measure. Again, that when butter had been dear, he bought it out of the ships that were outward bound, and had it sold in the market at a reasonable price to the poor. We learn from his Will that his wife (the lady who kneels with him as above described), was named Thomazine, and was left his executrix, and from a legacy being left in it to his brother's children, and no mention made of any of his own children, we safely conclude he died without issue.

But to pass on to the *real* point under discussion. Was he a Harington of Kelston by extraction or not? Has any wrong been done to his memory in rejecting him from being a member of that house, and that more especially when we may see from the notes of the family, collected by Dr Henry Harington of Bath some eighty years ago, that the Doctor was disposed to admit the Mayor to his family connection? We say, then, that George Harington, Mayor of Bristol, was *not* a Harington of Kelston. Firstly, because his monument is surmounted by arms, or something akin to arms, which are not the arms of Harington of Kelston, indeed, they no nearer resemble them than a barrel is like a true-lover's knot, and few persons, I presume, would contend for the closeness of that resemblance. George Harington was a wealthy brewer by trade (and so was his brother Roger Harrington, in the parish of Temple, Bristol). The Arms on his monument look like a chevron between three tuns. This is scarcely Harington of Kelston, 1568!

Again, if a Harington of Kelston, he must by his date (a mayor of Bristol in 1617) be descended from John of Stepney. And *à fortiori* his brother Roger, who died in 1600 (a married man), must have been, at latest, of the same generation as Sir John Harington, Knt (*i.e.*, the *son* of John of Stepney), who died in 1612. But who has ever heard of such brothers of Sir John Harington as Roger and George? And what is more, this George Harrington leaves his "*brother John*"* by his will (1638) £20, when Sir John of Kelston had long been dead. This altogether militates against his family connection with Sir John. But some may inquire, How did Dr Henry Harington treat the possibility of some family connection existing with him? Well! he supposed that *George* Harrington, the Mayor of Bristol, might have been the son of Francis Harington, younger brother of Sir John. But the Doctor does not appear to have had any knowledge of the perplexing "Roger" of this case, the other brother, who dying a married merchant in 1600 could never have been the *son of Francis younger* brother of Sir John who died in 1612. Now that Roger and George *were* brothers is clear from their Baldwin relationship,† and other points disclosed in their wills. On *these* grounds then we have excluded the Bristol Haringtons from the Kelston stock, but shall heartily appreciate the gift of any new data on the point, whichever way it may lead. As a general confirmation of our argument and case, the wills of Roger and George Harrington are subjoined in brief.

Will (Coventry, 27) G. C. P.

George Harrington, Alderman of Bristol, March* 20, 1638. To MY BROTHER JOHN H.* £20—my *kinsman Thomas Bishop, Brewer,* £500 at the *decease of Thomasine my wife—my Brother's children* (their *names* not mentioned)—my *sister's children,* except *the above Thomas Bishop,* £5 each—to *Church of Wellington, Salop, for repayring and beautifying it,* £10, and £5 to *the Poor of the same Parish*—my *sister Margery Bevan of Cardiff*—MY SISTER† *Baldwin* and *her d. Margaret*—my *Cosin Darby and his wife*—my *Sister Atwood* and *my Sister Carde* (? Carde or Cave)—my *cousin John Vaeen* and *his wife*—residue to *my wife Thomasin H.*, Ex.

Proved by her. *Feb.* 6, 1639–40

Will (Wallop, 38) G. C. P.

Roger Harrington, of Par. of Temple, Bristol (Brewer)

Dated June 11th, 1600.

*My Brother John** & George Harrington — *My Brother† William Baldwyn* — my Mother Margaret — my Wife Anne

Proved Aug 4, 1600.

BENTLEY OF STAFFORDSHIRE

(And subsequently of Northwich, co Chester)

ARMS —*Argent, three bendlets sable*
CREST —*A hound statant argent*

AUTHORITIES — Dugdale's 'Visitation of Cheshire. 1663-4', Ormerod's 'History of Cheshire,' iii, 92, 'Parish Registers of Witton, in the county of Chester' (commencing 1561), Heralds' College, C 10, 67 Vis Staff C 38, 50.

William Bentley = of Hungry Bentley, co Stafford

William Bentley, = Anne, daughter second son living in the second year of the reign of Henry IV [1401-2] | and heiress of Robert Bilston

Henry Bentley, = Jane (or Joan), living in the seventh year of the reign of Henry VI [1429-30] | daughter of . . Plint

James Bentley = daughter of Ashenhurst, of Ashenhurst

A

BENTLEY OF BREADSALL, CO. DERBY

ARMS —*Argent, three bendlets sable*
CREST —*A hound statant argent*

[The Arms are given however by Lysons as, —*On three bendlets sable*, and the Crest—*A lion statant argent* *]

* The figure, however, is given as a dog in the Heralds' College

AUTHORITIES —From Heralds' College, C 4-42, I 22-59? Lysons's 'Magna Britannia,' vol v, cxviii, 67, 261

John Bentley = dau of of Bentley, co Stafford | Harper of Rushall

B

A

John Bentley, living in the reign of Edward VI. [1547-1553.] = Anne, daughter of Sutton of Marston, co. Montgomery.

William Bentley. = ... daughter of Swinton of Knutsford, co. Chester.

Hugh Bentley. = Margaret, daughter and heiress of Roger Stapleton of Upton.

William Bentley. = Anne, daughter of John Masterson (of Nantwich, co. Chester ?)

John Bentley, of the Ashes, n[r] Leek, co. Stafford, living in 1614. = Ellen, daughter of William Bowyer of Knipersly

Richard Bentley. (Query Churchwarden of Witton, co. Chester, in 1625, and bur. at Witton Nov. 13, 1638.)* = Margaret, widow (or daughter ?) of Thomas Strethill (of Mobberley ?) (? buried at Witton, co. Chester, May 16, 1631.)

Ursula, "dau. and heiress." = John Bellott of (Great) Moreton co. Chester.

Margaret, [married at Witton, co. Chester, May 30, 1627.] = Robert Okell of Denwall.

1. Elizabeth, dau. or widow of Thomas Clutton of Nantwich. = William Bentley, a Physician at Northwich, born 1601-2, [? bapt. at Witton, co. Chester, April 28, 1602.] (Mar. also a third time.) Died Sept. 13, 1680, and buried Sept. 16, 1680-81, at Witton, co. Chester, leaving daughters only surviving. See Ormerod's 'History of Cheshire,' iii., 92; also Registers of Witton, co. Chester. = 2. Mary, dau. of George Venables of Agden.

?

B

William Bentley of the Ashes, co. Stafford. = ... daughter of . . . . Blunt of Kedermister sive Kinlet.

Humphrey Bentley of Derby. = Ellen, daughter of Thomas Grosvenor of Belloparte, co. Salop.

Frances, dau. of Nicholas Bagshaw of Farwall, co. Stafford, and relict of Thomas Sutton of Overhadden. = Sir John Bentley of Breadsall Park co. Derby. Died Feb. 1, 1621-22, and was buried in the Chapel of Stanley, near Derby. = Maria, daughter of Thomas Leigh of Adlington, co. Chester.

Maria, born about 1599.

Elizabeth, born about 1601. Died in 1623-4. = Sir Gervase Cutler of Stanbar Hall, co. York.

* The Registers of Witton, though very imperfectly kept, contain a great number of entries of the name of Bentley between 1600 and 1700. The family of Bentley of Cound [whose pedigree appears in the 'Miscellanea Genealogica' for August, 1878] is supposed to be descended from the Bentleys of Staffordshire in the seventeenth century.

STAFFORD.—In the church of St. Bride's, Fleet Street, London, there is a mural monument commemorating Mr. Carey Stafford, many years Master of the Glass Manufactory in White Friars. He died Aug. 14, 1778, aged 54. The shield of arms above the inscription may be thus described: Quarterly—1 and 4. Argent on a bend sable three roses of the field. 2 and 3. Or on a chevron gules three bezants. I should be glad to know whether there are any representatives of this family.

H.

GRANT OF ARMS TO EDWARD BENTLEY OF ELY PLACE, 1834.

To All and Singular to whom these presents shall come Sir RALPH BIGLAND Knight GARTER Principal King of Arms and Sir WILLIAM WOODS Knight CLARENCEUX King of Arms of the South East and West parts of England from the River Trent Southwards send greeting **Whereas** EDWARD BENTLEY of Ely Place in the parish of St Andrew Holborn in the County of Middlesex Gentleman hath represented unto the most noble Bernard Edward Duke of Norfolk Earl Marshal and Hereditary Marshal of England one of his Majesty's most Honourable Privy Council that being uncertain of Armorial Ensigns pertaining to his family He therefore requested the favor of His Grace's warrant for our granting and assigning such as may be proper to be borne by him and his descendants according to the Laws of Arms **And Forasmuch** as the said Earl Marshal did by Warrant under his hand and seal bearing date the fifteenth day of July instant authorize and direct Us to grant and assign such armorial Ensigns accordingly Know ye therefore that We the said GARTER and CLARENCEUX in pursuance of His Grace's Warrant and by virtue of the Letters Patent of our several offices to each of Us respectively granted do by these presents grant and assign unto him the said EDWARD BENTLEY the arms following that is to say OR A BEND VAIR BETWEEN TWO BENDLETS ENGRAILED SABLE and for Crest On a wreath of the colours A TALBOT PASSANT ARGENT THE DEXTER FORE-FOOT RESTING UPON AN ANCIENT SHIELD VAIR CHARGED WITH AN ANNULET OR as the same are in the margin hereof more plainly depicted to be borne and used for ever hereafter by him the said EDWARD BENTLEY and his descendants with due and proper differences according to the Laws of Arms In Witness whereof We the said GARTER and CLARENCEUX Kings of Arms have to these presents subscribed our names and affixed the seals of our several offices this eighteenth day of July in the Fifth year of the reign of Our Sovereign Lord William the Fourth by the grace of God of the United Kingdom of Great Britain and Ireland King Defender of the Faith &c And in the year of our Lord one Thousand eight hundred and thirty four.

Signed

RALPH BIGLAND Garter WILLIAM WOODS Clarenceux

(*Endorsed*) Recorded in the College of Arms, London, this 22nd day of July 1834

(Signed) CHAS GEO YOUNG,
York Herald and Register

NOTES RELATING TO THE FAMILIES OF GREEN AND ARMITAGE

From the collections of Mr WILLIAM RADCLYFFE, *Rouge Croix*

Uncle John Green Died in 1765 Buried at Kirkburton
Uncle Chris^{t} Green died Ap^{l} 1780 Buried at Holmfirth
Uncle Benjn Green Died—I am not quite certain nor can I get better informed as to the time—1797 Buried at Denby.
Uncle Anthony Green Died March 1798 Buried at Holmfirth.
Uncle Nathan Armytage Died 16 Decr 1778 aged 76 Buried at Meltham
Aunt Martha His wife Died [illegible] Jan 1742 aged [illegible] Buried at Do
Christ^{n} Name of Aunt Benjn Green was Martha
Chris^{n} Name of Cousin Mrs Chris^{r} Green is Mary Daug^{r} of Mr Isaac Lees of Linthwaite in Saddleworth, she is now living

Chris[n] Name of M[rs] James Green Son of Cousin Antho is Mary & D[r] of M[r] W[m] Roebuck of Hinchliffe Mill, has Issue

Chris[n] Name of M[rs] Jos[a] Green Son of Cousin Anthony is Martha & D[r] of the late M[r] Thos Wimpenny of Cartworth both living & has Issue

---

ARMITAGE FAMILY.

Copy of notes from the collection and in the handwriting of the late Mr. WILLIAM RADCLYFFE, *Rouge Croix*

The Family of Armytage is of great Antiquity in the County of York, as proved by many undoubted authorities

1 Ricardo de Hermitagio occurs with several of the principal men of the County of York as a Witness to a Charter of Edmund de Lasey Constable of Chester to the Monastry of S[t] John of Pontefret dat 2 May 1258. (Monasterium Sci Joh'i de Kirkby fol 4[b]).

2 Adam de Armitage occurs with several others as witness to a Charter of Adam son of Ward de Meltham dat in the feast of S[t] Scholaste the Virgin A D 1395.

3. And to a deed of Roger de Rowley 6 April 9 Hen 5

4 Will[m] del Ermitage & Adam del Ermitage held lands &c in Meltham of John or Elyas de Puton A D. 1426 (Dods.)

5 Thomas Armytage ten ter &c mess Joh'is Armytage et redd 11[d]

6. Thomas del Hermitage was constituted Att[y] by Ric' Beaumont & others to deliver seizen &c of Lands &c in Meltham to Thos Harrington & others 4 July A[o] 7 Hen 6

7 Margerita Armitage nuper uxor Thome Armitage de Armitage in Co Ebor' Obligat Thome Wombwell Arm[o] Ric'o Beamont arm' et Henrico Beaumont in decem marcis dat 18 Feb. A[o] 20 Hen 6 (Dods. MSS)

FAMILY OF STOPES.*

Taken from the fly-leaf of a small royal octavo Bible, printed at London by the Company of Stationers in 1619

Jacobus Stopes Filius Johannis Stopes, Clerici Baptizatus erat Nov 29, 1623
Anne Daughter of M[r] John Mariott was baptized March 29, 1628.

James Stopes Clerke } maryed April y[e] 2[d] 1650.
M[rs] Anne Mariott }

The names of the children of { James Stopes Clerk / Anne y[e] daughter of M[r] John Mariott }
and the Time of their Births and Baptizings:

John then eldest child was borne July 5 being Munday between one and two of the clock in y[e] Afternoon. And Baptized July 22, 1652. He dyed on y[e] Lord's day being Oct. 6. 30. And was buried Nov 3, 1653
James was borne Sept 22 being Thursday Baptized Octob 6, 1653
John was borne March 5 being Munday, and baptized March 15, 1654.
Mariott was borne Aug. 20 Baptized Aug 28, 1656
Judeth was borne Feb 23 Baptized March 4, 1657
Anne was borne Sept 22. Baptized Octob 6, 1659
Rebecka was borne July 26. Baptized August 1, 1661
Mary Baptized March 29, 1663.
Martha Baptized Octob 7, 1666.

* Communicated by A. E. WOOLRYCH, Esq

Mariott Stopes dyed at Winchester College May 4 being Sunday at 7 of ye clock at night and was buryed in ye Cloysters May 6 at 4 in ye afternoon being Tuesday, 1673, being Twelve dayes before Whitsunday, ye day of his burial, being Tuesday being one of the Twelve dayes. He was one of the Foundation.

GYBBON QUERY.—I should be much obliged if any correspondent would give me information concerning the pedigree of Gibbon or Gybbon. They seem to have held lands in Rolvenden, co. Kent, as early as 1340. The Hole estate in Rolvenden temp. Henry VIII. became the property of this family, in which it continued until about the end of the last century, when it passed into the Monypenny family. (Hasted, vol. iii., pp. 86, 87, 88.) There was also a branch of this family at Pumphouse in Benenden (an adjoining parish), the representatives of which are now living at Cheriton, Lucas County, United States, who trace their descent to Edmond Gibbon of Benenden, co. Kent, England. I wish to find how the Gybbons of Pumphouse were connected with those of the Hole.—There were two other branches of this family, one of Frid in Bethersden (which, according to the same authority, was a younger branch of those of the Hole), and the other of Westcliffe (which was also a younger branch of those of the Hole, Berry's 'Kentish Genealogies,' 410). Berry gives at length the pedigrees of both of these branches, but altogether leaves out the family from which they are admitted originally to have sprung.

CHARLES NEVE.

Benenden, Staplehurst.

BEANLANDS OF MORTON, CO. YORK.—Since the beginning of the sixteenth century there has been settled a family of the above name in and around the village of Morton in Skyrack, co. York. In the York Registers is the will of John Benlande of Morton 151—, Allan Beanlandes of Morton 1561, his wife Isabelle Beanlande 1570, his son Christopher 1589, etc. Prior to John, no mention whatever of the name in any Yorkshire papers have I been able to find. From Christopher the registers of the parish church of Bingley contain a complete descent, with several branches settled in the same parish, of the Beanlands of Morton down to the beginning of the present century. Now the only trace of any family of this somewhat singular name that I have been able to find is in connection with Herefordshire, Gloucestershire, and the Welsh Marches. In 'Plac. de quo Warr.,' p. 250, Rot. 8—"et *Johannes Benlonde* et alii undecim jur' in recordo nominati," etc. This is with reference to the rights of Abbot de Hayes to some land at Wynchcombe, co. Gloucester (temp. Ed. I.). Again, from 'Rot. Originales,' temp. Edw. III.—"Johannes de Banlande de Botelsford capellanus." And in 'Calendarium Inq. post mort.,' pp. 145–8, among the list of tenants of "Johannes de Mowbray dux Norfolc' dominus de Mowbray," I find, under "Hereford et March, Wall."—"Perschenet et Herkerdeston i. feod. milit' per Matheum Beenland."

Is there any trace of the name existing now in these counties? Can any of your subscribers give me further, or rather earlier, notice of the Yorkshire family? I believe two of the name are in the list of Craven men who fought at Flodden. What were their names? It is quite within the bounds of possibility that during the Wars of the Roses some individual of that name may have been stranded in Yorkshire after one of the great battles (*e.g.* Towton) and settled in that county.

That all of the name now existing in Yorkshire have originally come from the Morton stock is, I think, from the registers, pretty evident. The members of this family were of that class of yeomen and small landowners so common in the West Riding of Yorkshire. Any information will be very acceptable to

"ULTIMUS SUORUM."

Pedigree of the Family of Collier.

Communicated by REGINALD STEWART BODDINGTON, Esq.

ADMIRAL H. T. B. COLLIER.

Henry Collier of parish of St. Mary Matfellon *alias* Whitechapel, Gent. Will dated 7 August 1701, proved by his relict and his son Jabez Collier 5 August 1710. P.C.C. Smith, 176. = Sarah, daughter of . . . .

Their issue:

1. Henry Collier. His father states in his will that he had set him up in business, but that he was in August, 1701, in difficulties.

2. Jabez Collier, Solicitor in Chancery, of Symond's Inn. Marr. prior to Aug. 1701, as his father states in his will he made a settlement in his favour on his marriage. Had property in co. Cambridge. Died 21 March, 1732. *See* 'Gent.'s Mag.' Will dated 17 Feb. 1730, proved by relict 29 March, 1732. P.C.C. Bedford, 67. = Elizabeth, daughter of . . . . Had a sister Anne Pope, who query marr. Robert Moody. Will dat. 3 May, 1747, and then of Cheshunt, co. Herts. Will proved 26 May, 1747. P.C.C. Potter, 122.

3. John Collier, living 21 Feb. 1735, the date of his nephew Henry Collier's will.

4. Edward Collier.

5. Ebenezer Collier, Clerk in Chancery. Will dated 13 Dec. 1722. Died before 7 May, 1723. Will proved by relict 12 June, 1723. P.C.C. Richmond, 117. Letters of Administration to son Benjamin Collier 6 Dec. 1759. = Sarah, daughter and 12th child of George Boddington, Turkey Merchant, M.P. for Wilton, co. Wilts, Director of the Bank of England on its first starting, 1694, Governor of the Greenland Company. Born 16 Sept. 1690. Married 22 Feb. 1710-11, at S. Helen's Church, City of London. Will dat. 3 Feb. 1738, proved 30 March, 1743. P.C.C. Boycott, 70. Died 26 March, 1743. Buried at Bunhill Fields.

(Issue of Ebenezer Collier continued at A and B.)

Daughters of Henry Collier:

1. Elizabeth marr. prior to Aug. 1701, as her father names in his will he had settled money on her on her marriage. = Samuel Cullier.

2. Sarah.

3. Mary.

One of these married . . . . Lloyd, living 1717.

4. Anne, marr. prior to 13 Dec. 1722, the date of will of Ebenezer Collier. = Thomas Steele.

A B

A | B

Henry Collier, Property in co. Cambridge and at Rainham and West Ham, co. Essex. Of Red Lion Square. Will dated 21 Feb. 1735, proved 15 Oct. 1743, by his mother, sole executrix. Died 13 Aug. 1743. *See* Gent.'s Mag.

James Collier of March, Isle of Ely, High Sheriff of counties Cambridge and Huntingdon, 1769. J.P. for Isle of Ely. Brought up a dissenter, but ornamented and fitted up parish church of March. Property at Bray, co. Berks. Will dated 3 Jan. 1771, codicil 22 Nov. 1771, proved 8 March, 1773. P.C.C. Steevens, 99. *See* Add. MS. 5804, fol. 12b, etc.; Coles's MS., vol. iii., British Museum,—"Friday 19 Feb. 1773, died after a lingering illness of two years James Collyer, Esq., High Sheriff 1769, etc."

Watty Collier.

1. Elizabeth.=Jonathan Fawconer.

2. Rebecca, married 11 Nov. 1746. *See* Gent.'s Mag.=Anthony Allen, Master in Chancery.

Children of Jonathan Fawconer and Elizabeth:

- Henry Fawconer, one of the executors, who proved his uncle James Collier's will 8 March, 1773.
- James Fawconer.
- John Fawconer.
- 1. Pope, a daughter.

3. Sarah, died prior to Jan. 1771.=Philip Hollingsworth or Hollingworth of Lombard Street, Banker. (Son of Philip Hollingsworth or Hollingworth of Maiden Lane, Covent Garden, whose will was proved 19 May, 1747. P.C.C. Potter, 127.)

4. Margaret, marr. 30 July, 1751, at Enfield Church, co. Middlesex. Died 8 Oct. 1768, aged 49. Buried in Dutch Church, Austin friars London. M.I.=Herman Meyer of London, Hamburg Merchant. On occasion of his marriage all the foreign ships displayed their colours. *See* Gent.'s Mag. Died 27 April, 1784, aged 69. Buried in Dutch Church, Austinfriars. M.I.

Children of Philip Hollingsworth and Sarah:

- Philip Hollingsworth or Hollingworth, one of the executors, who proved his uncle James Collier's will 8 March, 1773. Died 31 Jan. 1818. M.I. at Thundridge.
- 6th son. Richard Hollingsworth or Hollingworth of Queen Square, Westminster and Thundridge, co. Herts. Died 12 January, 1812. M.I. at Thundridge.=Joanna. of Stondon Place, co. Essex. Died 12 April, 1824. M.I. at Thundridge.

Children of Herman Meyer and Margaret:

- 1. Catharina, born 23 June, 1752. Died 2 June, 1807, at Forty Hall. Bur. in Dutch Church, Austinfriars. M.I.
- 2. Herman Meyer, b. 15 Nov. 1753. Died 19 Dec. 1754, and bur. in Mr. Collier's vault in Bunhill Fields.
- 3. James Meyer, b. 4 Sept. 1755. Purchased Nov. 1799, for £11,940 Forty Hall, Enfield, and resided there. His business in Leadenhall Street. Died 11 Feb. 1826. M.I. Dutch Ch., Austinfriars.
- 4. Christian Paul Meyer, b. 20 July, 1757. Twin with Herman Meyer. Died 26 April, 1790. Buried in Dutch Church, Austinfriars. M.I. Partner in Firm of Grote and Co., Hamburg Merchants.=Ann, eldest dau. of Isaac Solly of Jeffreys Square, City of London, by his wife Elizabeth Neal, born 28 Oct. 1765. Marr. 2 Nov. 1789, at Walthamstow, Essex. Died 9 Feb. 1841. M.I. Dutch Church, Austinfriars.
- 5. Herman Meyer, born 20 July, 1757. Twin wth Christian Paul Meyer of Forty Hall, Enfield, co. Middlesex. Died 20 June, 1832. M.I. Dutch Church, Austinfriars.

C | B

C | B

Louisa, 3rd daughter of Rawson Hart Boddam, born 23 Oct. 1794; married 5 April, 1813, at Bath. Died 21 June, 1822. Buried in Dutch Church, Austinfriars. M.I. 1st wife. ╤ Christian Paul Meyer, born 8 Oct. 1790, posthumous. Died 13 Mar. 1857, at Little Laver, co. Essex. = Mary, eldest daughter of William Walton, married 4 Aug. 1827. Died 26 Feb. 1829, in Cavendish Square. Buried at Enfield. *See* Gent.'s Mag. 2nd wife. ╤ Anna Maria, daughter of John Lindegren, married at Brighton. Died 28 June, 1851, aged 58, at Brighton. M.I. Dutch Church, Austinfriars. 3rd wife.

1. Christian Paul Meyer, born 28 Mar. 1814. Died 25 May, 1832. M.I. Dutch Church, Austinfriars.

2. James Meyer, b. 24 May, 1815. For marriage, etc. *see* Walford's 'County Families,' Meyer of Forty Hall, Enfield, co. Middlesex.

3. Louisa Joanna, born 5 Sept. 1816. Died 9 July, 1843. M.I. Dutch Church, Austinfriars.

4. Ann Sophia, born 5 April, 1818. Died 28 Feb. 1838. M.I. Dutch Church, Austinfriars.

5. Philip Herman Meyer, born 6 March, 1820. Died 14 Nov. 1870, s.p. Query marr. Marianne, 2nd dau. of Robert Smart Watlin, who married 2ndly, 1874, Capt. Francis James Baker. *See* Walford's 'County Families.'

6. Eliza Mary, born 15 Feb. 1822. Died 25 Feb. 1843.

7. Anna Maria, born 16 Jan. 1832.

8. Christian Paul Meyer, born .... Died 27 July, 1835, aged 11 months. M.I. Dutch Church, Austinfriars.

9. Herman Paul David Meyer, born 15 Nov. 1837. Of The Grange, Little Laver, Essex. *See* Walford's 'County Families.' ╤ Constance, 4th daughter of P. S. Feake Martin of Rawcliffe, near York. Married 20 Sept. 1864, at Skelton, near York. *See* Gent.'s Mag.

1. A daughter, born 18 July, 1865. *See* Gent.'s Mag.

2. A son, born 29 July, 1866. *See* Gent.'s Mag.

1. George Collier, born 18 Dec. 1711. His wife referred to in his mother's will, but no Christian name given. ╤ .... dau. of ....

2. Hannah, born 11 June, 1713. Living 30 Mar. 1743.

3. Isaac Collier, born 4 Sept. and died 20 Dec. 1714. Buried at Bunhill Fields.

4. Benjamin Collier, born 24 June, 1716. Of Red Lion Square. Died 12 March, 1791, s.p. Will dated 16 May, 1787. Had property in Suffolk. Buried 21 March, 1791, at Groton, co. Suffolk. = Letitia, youngest daughter of Mark Weyland. *See* Burke's 'Landed Gentry.'

5. Sarah, born 2 Nov. 1718.

6. Theodosia, named in the will of each of her parents.

Christiana, daughter of Richard Gwyn of Middleton Hall, co. Carmarthen, by his wife Elizabeth, formerly Elizabeth Fuller. Married 17 July, 1763. *See* B. P. xv. College of Arms, 328. ╤ George Collier, born 11 May, 1732, according to an entry in an old Boddington MS. book, Vice-Admiral of the Blue, Knighted 27 Jan. 1775. M.P. for Honiton, 1784. Died 6 April, 1795. Buried at Marylebone Parish Church. M.I. ╤ Elizabeth, daughter of William Fryer, Merchant, of Exeter. Marr. 19 July, 1781, at Exeter, by special licence. Died 24 May, 1831, at Paris. *See* A xxi. 539, College of Arms.

Theodosius Benjamin Collier. Will dated 1 July, 1771, and then of Oxford Road, St. Marylebone. Died at Bath. ╤ Mary. Proved her husband's will 2 June, 1803.

1. Benjamin Collier. Died in India.

1. Theodosia Henrietta. ╤ .... Egan.

2. Sophia, died 6 April, 1804, at Bath, unmarr. *See* Gent.'s Mag.

3. Mary. ╤ Capt. .... White.

D | E

D | E |

1. William George Collier, Capt. 9th Regt., Assistant Collector Inland Revenue, Mauritius, in 1821. Born 23 June, 1769. Died 9 June, 1832. ═ Frances Mary, daughter of .... Born 16 July, 1784. Died 31 Jan. 1832. Query 2nd wife.

Daughter, living June, 1765. Died before 11 March, 1772. B. P. xv. College of Arms.

1. William George Collier, b. 11 June, 1813, bapt. 1813, at S. John's, Clerkenwell. Died 30 Jan. 1839, in Jermyn St., S. James's, aged 25. Bur. at S. James's, Piccadilly. ═ Mary Ann, only dau. of Joseph Vaughan of Jermyn Street, marr. at S. James's, Piccadilly, May 28, 1833. Died Oct. 1870. Bur. at Brompton Cemetery.

1. Letitia Christiana, born 29 March, 1808, bapt. 1813 at S. John's, Clerkenwell. Marr. 16 Sept. 1829. Died 26 July, 1835, in the Mauritius. ═ Charles Ingham, M.D., Surgeon to H.M.'s 29th Regt.

2. Georgiana Clementina, born 14 Dec. 1809. Bapt. 1813, at S. John's, Clerkenwell. Marr. 5 Nov. 1829. ═ .... Shearman, Lieutenant Staff Corps.

3. Sophia Matilda, born 3 Feb. 1811. Bapt. 1813, at S. John's, Clerkenwell. ═ Uriah Boyd, Lieut. H.M.'s 54th Regt.

Charles William Gwyn Collier, born 5 March, 1835, in Jermyn St., S. James's. Bapt. at S. James's, Piccadilly.

Daughter. Died young.

Mary Frances, born on voyage to Cape of Good Hope, bapt. 9 Oct. 1830, at Cape Town. Died when 16 months old.

2. George Collier, Lieut.-Col. Coldstream Guards. His uncle Benjamin Collier left him his property in Suffolk. Died 10 May, 1814, of wounds before Bayonne. *See* Gent.'s Mag.

.... daughter of .... Osborn of Antigua. 1st wife. ═ 3. Francis Augustus Collier, C.B. 8 Dec. 1815; Knighted 28 July, 1830; K.C.H. 31 Jan. 1833; Appointed 1837, Naval Aide de Camp to Her Majesty the Queen; Knight of the Persian Order of the Lion and the Sun; Superintendent of Woolwich Dockyard; appointed Commissioner at Greenwich, 1845; Admiral. Died 28 Oct. 1849. Bur. at Victoria, Hong Kong. ═ Katherine, daughter of Thomas Thistlethwayte of Southwick Park, Hants. *See* Burke's 'Landed Gentry.' Marr. 14 March, 1831. *See* Walford's 'County Families,' Lady Collier. 2nd wife.

1. Augusta.

2. Frances Isabella, marr. 19 July, 1850, at Wickham, co. Hants. *See* Gent.'s Mag. ═ J. F. B. Wainwright, Commander R.N., youngest son of late Capt. John Wainwright, R.N., C.B.

3. Ellen, marr. 10 April, 1850, at Stinsford, co. Dorset. *See* Gent.'s Mag. ═ Frederick English, Capt. 35th Regt., eldest son of late Lieut.-Col. English, R.E.

Alexander Thistlethwayte Collier, died 17 April, 1861, aged 21, at Hayward's Heath.

Selina Catherine, married 20 Oct. 1864, at Wickham, co. Hants. *See* Gent.'s Mag. ═ Carr Stuart Glyn, born 25 Nov. 1835. Capt. Royal Dragoons. *See* Burke's Baronetage, Glyn of Gaunts.

E

E

4. Henry Theodosius Browne Collier, R.N. Admiral. Died 10 Sept. 1872, in Ryder Street, St. James's, London. = Harriet, 4th daughter of Robert Nicholas, M.P., of Ashton Keynes, co. Wilts. Married 26 June, 1816. *See* Gent.'s Mag. Died 22 Oct. 1850, in Upper Grosvenor Street, London. Bur. at Hove, near Brighton. *See* Burke's 'Landed Gentry.'

2. Georgiana, died . . . . = ... Aidé, a Greek. Died . . . .

Hamilton Aidé, sole surviving issue.

3. Louisa, died unmarried.

1. George Baring Browne Collier, Capt. R.N. Retired 1 July, 1864. = Justina Maria Stepney, youngest dau. of Joseph Gulston of Derwydd, co. Carmarthen, & Grosvenor Sq., London. Marr. 18 Feb. 1846, at S. George's, Hanover Sq. *See* Burke's 'Landed Gentry.'

2. Clarence Augustus Collier, Lieut.-Colonel Bombay Staff Corps. Retired on full pay with rank of Colonel.

3. Herbert Cromwell Collier. At date of marriage, late 8th Hussars. In 1878, Capt. 21st Hussars. = Blanche Frances, only child of Major General Bonner of Great Cumberland Place. Married 22 June, 1865, at St. George's, Hanover Square. *See* Gent.'s Mag.

1. Ernest Alan Collier. 2. Meynell Cromwell Collier. Reginald de la Roche Collier. Three daughters.

1. Gertrude Barbara Rich, married 11 Sept. 1847, at Ryde. *See* Gent.'s Mag. = Charles Tennant of Cadoxton Lodge, co. Glamorgan. *See* Burke's 'Landed Gentry.'

Adeline. = Col. . . . . Gordon.

Henrietta, marr. 20 Aug. 1855, at St. George's, Hanover Square. *See* Gent.'s Mag. = Sir Alexander Campbell, Bart. of Barcaldine. *See* Burke's 'Baronetage.'

Clementina Frances, marr. 6 June, 1855, at S. George's, Hanover Square. *See* Gent.'s Mag. = Frederick Erskine Johnston, Capt. R.N., son of late Right Honble. Sir Alexander Johnston of Carnsallock, co. Dumfries. *See* Burke's 'Landed Gentry.'

Ebenezer Collier admitted as one of the Sworn Clerks in Chancery 2 March, 1710, and surrendered his appointment 8 January, 1723.

James Collier of March gave Communion plate to that Church, Sept. 1752.

A portrait is given in 'Naval Chronicle,' vol. xxxii., page 265, etc. (1814), of Sir George Collier, Knight, Vice-Admiral of the Blue.

According to one account, Sir George Collier married his first wife 3 September, 1763, at St. James's, Westminster.

Christian Meyer, Merchant, married 2 April, 1767, Miss Herman. *See* Gent.'s Mag.

In Dutch Church, Austinfriars, lie buried besides those of the family of Meyer before given, Christian Meyer, who died 7 June, 1799, aged 74; also Hannah, his widow, who died 30 November, 1799, aged 74.

In the 'Topographer and Genealogist,' edited by John Gough Nichols, F.S.A., etc., vol. iii., Mr. Thompson Cooper, of Cambridge, gives a long account of the family of Collier of Darlaston, co. Stafford, who entered their pedigree in the Visitation of co. Stafford, 1663.

The family of Collier of Steeple Langford, co. Wilts, is referred to in Hoare's 'History of Wiltshire,' and one of this family is named at page 269 of the 'Westminster Abbey Registers,' edited by Col. J. L. Chester, etc.

Sir Edward Collier, Admiral, J.P. and D.L. co. Worcester, K.C.B. 1865, of Blockley, born 1783, died 5 August, 1872.

Sir George Ralph Collier, Capt. R.N., K.C.B., was created a Baronet 23 July, 1814, but died s.p. 21 March, 1824. *See* Burke's 'Extinct Baronetage.'

Families of Collier have long been resident at Witney, co. Oxford; at Blockley, co. Worcester; Plymouth, and Grimston Hall, near Plymouth.

I seek for information as to any families of Collier, and particularly as to that whose short and imperfect pedigree is given here.

15 *Markham Square,*
Chelsea, London, S.W.
REGINALD STEWART BODDINGTON.

THE PRINCIPAL MONUMENTAL INSCRIPTIONS IN THE CHURCH AND CHURCHYARD OF KELSTON, SOMERSET,

Which have not already appeared, either in the "Notes on the Rectors" of that Church, or in the Memorials of the Hawkins, Hudleston, and Harington Families of Kelston.

On a head-stone in the churchyard, broken and almost defaced

Sacred to the Memory
of
Thomas Dwelly
Who died Novr 29th 1781
Aged 56 years
Also to the Memory
of
Alice
Wife of the above
Thos Dwelly
Who died July 17, 1816
Aged 89 years
This stone was placed here in remembrance
of the best of Parents
by their only and affectionate son
Thomas Dwelly
Whose family grave is in the Burial Ground
of St. George's, Hanover Square, London.

On a flat stone in the church porch

Here lies the Body of Anne Thomas
Widow of Col Wm Thomas
of the Island of Antigua
who departed this life
30th Day of December 1741
aged 58.

Plain marble tablet in the entrance porch

Sacred to the Memory
of that truly good and Virtuous man
Samuel Nott, A M
Prebendary of Winchester*
And Chaplain in Ordinary to His Majesty
He died beloved, &c.
Aged 53 May 27th 1793.

A ✠ Ω

In the north-east corner of the churchyard, on raised tombs

Here lieth The Remains of
The Revd Samuel Nott A.M
late Prebendary of Winchester
He died at Bath the xxviith of May
MDCCXCIII
Aged LIII years

* This gentleman was also Rector of Houghton, co Hants, and Vicar of Blandford, Dorset No doubt he came to Bath for his health, but not recovering, and being connected with the Hawkins family by marriage, was buried at Kelston upon his decease

Arms of Mitchell

OF BANDETH IN THE COUNTY OF STIRLING,
AND OF WESTSHORE IN ZETLAND.

And on the side of this tomb is the further inscription—

In the same vault are deposited
The Remains of Charlotte Georgina Augusta
Daughter of the above Sam[l] & Augusta Nott
She was born June MDCCLXVII
Died Oct XII. MDCCCXXXVII.

A ✠ Ω
Here lieth the Remains of Augusta
The well beloved wife of
The Rev[d] Samuel Nott, M.A
She died at Bath
The VIIth day of April MDCCCXIII
Aged 67 years

On a small tablet in the porch

S M.
of
Henry the fifth son of
Stephen Harding and Ann his wife
of this Parish
who departed this life
March 12th 1816 aged 6 years.
"Suffer the little children to come unto me," etc., etc.

M I. inside the church porch, surmounted by arms which are effaced

To the memory of Isaac Hillier Esq[r] of Holt
in the County of Wilts.
Who died the 6th day of December
1808 aged 68 years.
This Monument is erected by his afflicted Children.

On a plain tablet near the above.

In the same vault are deposited
The Remains of Harriet Hillier
youngest daughter of Isaac Hillier Esq.
who died the 21st of Novr 1825 aged 47.
Also of Elizabeth Ann Bradford
widow of James Bradford Esq. of Dublin
who died the 13th Jany 1820
Aged 58.

M.I in the tower.

Hic
Deponuntur exuviae Dom · Johannis Fenn
hujus parochiae, qui morti obiit octavo Jan
Anno Dom: 169⅔ ætatis suæ (? 59).

"Death unexpect me snatcht away
And house'd my Body in the Clay
Reader, look on, and learn to die
For time with rapid wings doth fly."

Marble tablet with inscription on north wall in the church

Near this place are deposited
The Remains of
Frances Anna Shuttleworth
Whose innocent and useful life
Was suddenly terminated by a fatal accident*
on the 10th day of Feby 1816
In the 37 year of her age.

On an altar tomb beneath the yew tree in the churchyard to the memory of the same lady and other members of the Shuttleworth family

Frances Anna Shuttleworth
Died Feby 10th 1816
Caroline Shuttleworth
Died Octr 15th 1827
Here also lie the Remains
of
The Revd Richard
Henry Shuttleworth B D.
who died Decr 20 1829
Aged 49.
(In St. James's Square, Bath.)

A marble tablet on north wall of the church

In the Churchyard adjoining are
interred the remains of Arthur Weston
Late Major in his Majesty's
3rd Regt of Dragoon Guards
who died at Bath on the
5th April 1831
His services with that Regiment in
the Peninsular War
are noticed with high distinction
in the public despatches
relative to those events
As a faithful, tender & affectionate
Husband, an indulgent, kind
and attached Father, as a firm
zealous & sincere friend he will
never be surpassed
This tablet is placed here by his afflicted Widow
as a small tribute to departed worth
and a testimony of her lasting regret
& sincere affection.

Also in Memory of
Anne Elizabeth Weston, the affectionate Widow of
the above, who died at No 2 Royal Crescent, Bath
May 6th 1866 aged 72
Beloved & regretted

---

* This alludes to her being thrown from her horse and killed in Gay Street, Bath She is buried beneath the yew tree in Kelston Churchyard with M I. there also.

M I in an angle of the church near the tower.

M S.
Roberti Halifax, qui Georgii Augusti
Serenissimi Walliæ Principis
E Medicis ordinariis
Per annos fere quadraginta Artem Medicam
Londini feliciter exercuit
Id autem illi imprimis laudi erat
Quod et sibi hæreditarium pientissimè agnovit
Vitam integram scelerisque puram servâsse
Erga omnes præterea, quibuscum interfuerat
Erga necessarios præcipue, nihil humani
a se alienum putavit.
Natus XII. Julii MDCCXXXV Mansfeldiæ
in agro Notts
Obiit Bathoniæ XVII Septr
MDCCCX.

On a gravestone in the churchyard south-west of the tower

In memory of
Sir Henry White, Knt
late of Portsmouth
Who died at Bath
July 13th 1823
Aged 61 years.

(*To be continued*)

EXTRACTS FROM CHURCH REGISTERS RELATING TO THE FAMILY OF SHELMERDINE

(*Continued from p 97.*)

MUCCLESTONE

Baptisms.

1801	November	1.	John son of James Shelmerdine.
1809	March	31.	John son of Elijah Shelmerdine
1812.	July	19.	James son of James Shelmerdine
1833.	.	.	Elijah Shelmerdine.

Marriages.

1799	April	1.	James Shelmerdine & Judy Tinsley.
1803.	Dec.	29.	Elijah Shelmerdine & Mary Minor
1831	Dec.	29	Thomas Broster & Judith Shelmerdine
1833	Jan	29	Thomas Shelmerdine & Elizabeth Platt.
1840	Feb	18	John Shelmerdine & Ann Dunn.

Burials

1808.	Oct	1	Francis Shelmerdine

WOORE

1840.	Oct.	25.	Thomas son of John Shelmerdine bapt

Market Drayton.

Baptisms.

1847. November. John Shelmerdine.
1849. August. Kate Shelmerdine.
1842. August. Elizabeth Shelmerdine.
1845. July. Mary Shelmerdine.

Burials.

1865. August 13. John Shelmerdine aged 55.
1850. John Shelmerdine (son of the above) died April 10, 1850, aged 2 years.

Brown Edge, Norton on the Moors.

1862. March 20. Esther Shelmerdine } bapt.
1863. Nov[r] 10. Thomas Shelmerdine } bapt.

Langport.

Baptisms.

1871. Jan. 16. Anne Leah da: of Thomas Shelmerdine.
1873. April 20. Kate Elizabeth da: of Thomas Shelmerdine.
1874. Nov: 14. Mabel Lucy da: of Thomas Shelmerdine.
1876. Sept. 9. Edmund John son of Thomas Shelmerdine.

Marriage.

1869. Dec. 23. Thomas Shelmerdine & Lucy Jane Payn.

Ashley.

1823. Feb. 23. Elijah Shelmerdine aged 58.
1824. May 7. Mary Shelmerdine aged 51.

Bowdon, Cheshire.

Marriage.

1823. Oct. 4. John Shelmerdine, Esq., to Sarah Mort.

Burial.

1846. Dec. 3. John Shelmerdine Solicitor died 21 Nov[r].

Trent Vale.

1861. April 15. Elijah Shelmerdine of Clayton & Sarah Matthews, Spinster, of Stoke.

Wrenbury.

1846. Dec. 27. James Shelmerdine aged 74.

Lymm.

1627. Edmund Shelmerdine, Parson of the Moiety of this church, was buried at Warburton.

Arms of Shelmerdine.

These Arms were represented quarterly with those of Leigh of Oughtrington on a Hatchment formerly in Lymm Church, and which was placed there in 1761.

A CRITICAL EXAMINATION OF THE GENEALOGY OF MASTERTON OF THAT ILK, PARKMILL, ETC

Published in Douglas's 'Baronage of Scotland,' and Craufurd's 'Memorials of Alloa.'

THIS pedigree is a good instance of the way in which fact and fiction are interwoven, and notices of several different families thrown into one so as to compose a long pedigree.

Crawford begins by the statement that the Mastertons of Parkmill "were probably the most ancient landed proprietors in Clackmannanshire, the traditional account of their origin being that one of the chief architects at the building of the Abbey of Dunfermline obtained from Malcolm Canmore the lands of Masterton, in Fifeshire, from which he and his posterity assumed their surname"

The church of the Holy Trinity and St Margaret, at Dunfermline is believed to have been founded soon after the marriage of Malcolm and Margaret, the Abbey probably dates from the reign of their son David.

Malcolm IV (1153-65), granted the lands of Ledmacdunegil, afterwards called Masterton, as formerly held by *Magister Ailricus cementarius*, to the Abbey church of Dunfermline. Ailric's designation has perhaps formed the ground of the fable of the architect, and it is evident that the lands not being then called Masterton could not have given a name to their owner.

The first we find is

I Hugo de Villa Magistri, who about 1250 witnesses a charter of Petrus de Rupe, there is nothing to suggest a descent from the *cementarius*

II William de Maystertun, son and heir of Hugh, in 1272 enters into an agreement with Symon Abbot of Dunfermline as to the multures of his lands of Maystertun, he being a vassal of the Abbey, in 1278 and later, he is a witness to several charters, and in 1296 as "William de Meistreton del Comté de Feyf," he swears fealty to Edward I

III. Duncan de Maysterton in 1316 witnessed the homage of Duncan, Earl of Fife, to the Abbot of Dunfermline, for lands held of the Abbey.

IV Symon de Maysterton, in the reign of David II (1329-71), witnesses the resignation of the lands of Wythker to the Abbey by Alan de Lyburton

V John de Maisterton was dead 23 March, 1419, when his son and heir

VI William de Maisterton has sasine of the Villa de Maisterton, as formerly held of the Abbots of Dunfermline by his ancestors In 1540 James II granted to the Abbot and Convent of Dunfermline a Charter of Confirmation of all their possessions, including Mastirtone, the gift of King Malcolm 1455, William Maistertoun was a Canon of Cambuskenneth, in 1471, Thomas Mastertoun was a member of that chapter, and at an earlier period John Mastertoun was a monk there

VII. William Maistertoun was on an assize at Dunfermline, 1491.

Of these seven successive owners of Masterton, the only one mentioned in the published pedigree is (II.) William, and his homage to King Edward, there is, however, a statement which seems to be quite groundless, that William Masterton of that Ilk in 1442 "made a donation to the Abbey of Dunfermline out of his lands of Masterton *pro salute anime sue*," this is not to be found in the chartulary He is stated in the Baronage to have been father of Alexander Masterton of that Ilk, whose son and heir John Masterton had a crown charter in 1528 of the Mains of Bothkennar in Stirlingshire, to him and Grizel Mure his spouse

The charter is merely to John "filio et filio et haeredi Alexandri Masterton" not of that Ilk Crawford calls his wife "Dame Grisel Mure of Glenderston," but she could not be a daughter of that family, the first of which was at this time a youth

There is not only nothing to connect these Mastertons of Bothkennar with the family of that Ilk, but their succession can be traced, and it differs from the alleged pedigree making them ancestors of the Parkmill branch Thus,

Alexander Masterton.

John, and Grizel Mure his wife, 1528.

Robert.

John, portioner of Bothkennar, 1579. Married Marjory Forrester.

George, writer in Edinburgh in 1662, was heir to his father's lands at Bothkennar, and also succeeded to his mother in property in the same parish.

George, was served heir of his father in 1697, and died in Sep. 1709.

Adam Masterton, of Bothkennar, heir of his brother, and the last of that family.

The Mastertons of Masterton probably sold or lost their ancient patrimony at or shortly before the Reformation. A great part of the Fifeshire lands of the Abbey of Dunfermline are included in a charter to Mr. John Pitcairn of that Ilk, among them Maistertoun. In the rental of the Abbey lands, 1561, it is set down at £26 6s. 4d., and why the Mastertons should figure among the Barons of Scotland at all it is not easy to see.

They held the lands from which they took their surname as vassals of the Abbots of Dunfermline, and Parkmill, the property for about two centuries of the family claiming to represent the older race, was not held of the Crown at all, but under the Earls of Mar.

The lands of Masterton soon passed out of the hands of the Pitcairns, and were feued out in small portions, Robert Lundy getting one fourth, and persons of the name of Mudie, Durie, Kent, Stenhouse, Kellok, and Cunnand, each one eighth.

The descendants of some of these retained their shares for several generations, but the greater part of the lands about the middle of the seventeenth century belonged to Sir Henry Wardlaw of Pitreavie, baronet, who in 1675 founded an almshouse in the village of Masterton for the support of four widows, each of whom has a room, £2 a year, and half a boll of meal monthly.

Masterton now belongs to Miss Caroline Augusta Madox-Blackwood of Pitreavie, and is a farm of 338 acres rented at £600.

But while the main line thus disappears, we find persons of the name acquiring parts of the possessions of the Abbey of Dunfermline.

Robert Maisterton and his wife have a charter of two salt pans, probably about 1570, and in 1588 he has a lease of his part of the teinds of the lands of Balsusny and Smetoun.

John Walwod and Grizel Maisterton his wife have a feu charter before 1583 of half of the lands and mill of Touch; their descendant is the present Allan Maconochie-Welwood of Pitliver and Meadowbank.

In 1594 James Masterton was one of the surviving monks of Couper Abbey.

S * * *

(*To be continued.*)

MOLESWORTH.—William Molesworth, Esq., 3rd son of Robert Viscount Molesworth by Letitia his wife, sister to Richard Earl of Bellamont, by his will dated in 1769, after referring to other children, adds the names of two daughters, *i.e.*, Elizabeth, wife of Richard Holmes, Esq., of Dublin, and Julia, the wife of Captain Herbert. Information as to the descendants (if any) of these marriages will be esteemed a favour.

A. J. H.

EXTRACTS FROM AN OLD MS *PENES* LIEUT-COLONEL JOHN PHILIP OSBALDESTON MITFORD OF MITFORD CASTLE, CO NORTHUMBERLAND *

The several marriages and issue of ye Mitfords soe high as at p'sent can be made both out of the Heralds' College and by writeings

Bertram Mitford married Margaret daughter of Lisle of ffelton, & had issue Gawin Mitford and two daughters (vizt) Margaret married to Geo. Parkinson & Joane marryed to Ayton

Gawin Mitford marryed one of ye sisters of Sr Thos Foster of Etherston Knt & had issue Cuthbert Mitford.

Cuthbert Mitford maryed Anne daughter to Wallis of Akeild, and had issue Robert Mitford & three daughters (vizt) Jane marryed to Thos Hudspeth of Corbridge, Margaret to Thos Pye of Newminster Abbey, & Isabel to Cuthbert Ogle of Chappington.

Robert Mitford † was son & heir to Cuthbert, & lived all the Reign of Queen Eliz & K James, and dyed in ye first year of K Charles ye first, he being then a very old man of about 88 yrs of age, & dyed at Gillingwood & was buryed in Gilling Church This Robt had issue Cuthbert, who dyed in ye lifetime of his said Father Robt. Cuthbert left his only son Robert, now alive

Robert Mitford of Mitford, Esq married Philadelphia, one of ye daughters of Humphrey Wharton of Gillingwood in the county of York, Esq, and had issue six sons & five daughters (vizt) Humphrey, Cuthbert, John, Edward, Wm & Michael, Barbara, Margt, Ann, Elinor & Elizabeth Cuthbert ye 2d son was senior ffellow of Caius College in Cambridge, and afterwards Rector of ye parsonage of Ingram, where he dyed and was buryed in the Chancel there 1662 Jno ye 3d son is now a mercht in Newcastle, Edward ye 4th son is now a Batchelor of physick & at p'sent studyes ye same at London, Wm ye 5th son is now a student in ye College of Glascow in Scotland, and Michael ye 6th son is not as yet disposed on Barbara ye eldest daughter marryed to George Reeveley of Thriple, now both dead, & lye buryed in the Chancel of Mitford Church, and left four children, two boys and two girls, Mary ye 2d daughter marryed to Geo Tunstall, Dr of physick, and now both liveing in Newcastle, Ann ye 3d daughter marryed to Patricke Crow of Roseden, and now both liveing at ye Hermitage near Hexam, Elinor & Elizabeth both yet unmarryed

Humphrey, eldest son of ye sd Robt, marryed ffrances eldest daughter of Sir George Vaine of Rogerley in the County of Durham, upon Valentine Day 1661, in Stanhope Church, and had issue three sons and eight daughters (viz.) Robt, Elizth, Philadelphia, Ann, Margt, George, John, Barbara, ffrances, Mary & Sarah

Robert Mitford, eldest son of ye sd Humphrey, marryed Ann eldest daughter of John Ashton of Burne, Esqr, second son of Sr Ralph Ashton of Midleton in Lancashire, Bart, upon the 19th Decr 1681, and had issue five sons and one daughter (vizt) Robert, John, Edward, Humphrey, Elizabeth and William.

Robert Mitford, eldest son of the aforesaid Robert, was born the eighth day of

* There are two copies at Mitford, one dated 1666, and the other 1717 The latter is a transcript of the former, with some variations and additions and has the following title — "Collected out of Evidences Newminster Abbey Register Book & other Records by ye late Worthy Humphrey Mitford of Mitford Esq Councellr at Law The matter within written being transcribed from his own entire Collection & handwriting by his grandson Robt in ye Year 1717"

† Robert Mitford [son of Cuthbert Mitford] marryed Anne (Jane), daughter to John Mitford of Seghill, and had issue, Cuthbert, John and Wm, and four daughters, viz Barbara marryed to Geo ffenwicke of Langshaw, Elinor to Daniel Collingwood of Branton, Margaret to Nicholas Heron, and Isabel to Richd Rosemotherley, Jno ye 2d son lived at Mitford all his life, Wm ye 3d son was ffellow of Clare Hall, Cambridge, and now Parson of Kirby overshaw [Kirby overblow] in Yorkshire

Cuthbert Mitford marryed Mary, daughter and heir of Christopher Wharton of Ufferton in ye County of Durham and had issue Robert Mitford They both dyed in one day at Mitford, leaveing only ye said Robert

Aug[t] 1686, about four a clock in the morning at Burne, his great uncle Lyonell Vane, Esq , and his grandfather John Ashton, Esq , godfathers, and Philadelphia Mitford his great grandmother, godmother

John Mitford,* second son, was born at Burne July 9th 1687, about two a clock in the morning, S[r] Henry Herbert, Baronet, and .... godfathers, and his Aunt Crow, godmother

Edward, the third son, was born at Burne Dec[r] 4th 1689, about seven a clock in y[e] morning, his great uncle Edw[d] ffleetwood, Esq., and his great uncle George Vane, Esq , godfathers, and godmother

Humphrey, the fourth son, was born at Burne the seventh day of ffeb[y] 1690, about two a clock in y[e] morning, his great uncle W[m] Mitford and his uncle George Mitford, godfathers and godmother

Elizabeth, only daughter of the said Robert, was born at York June 7th 1696, about five a clock in the afternoon, S[r] Humfrey Herbert, Bart , godfather, her grandmother Ashton and her great aunt Betty Vane, godmothers

William, youngest son, was born at Burne ffeb[y] 10th 169$\frac{8}{9}$, about two a clock in the afternoon, W[m] Rawstorne of Preston in Lancashire, Esq , and W[m] Reeveley of Newby Wisk, godfathers, and his Aunt Stradling, godmother. (In another copy, his Aunt Redman, godmother)

(*In another handwriting*)

Robert Mitford, the eldest son, married Mary, one of the daughters of S[r] Richard Osbaldeston late of Osbaldeston in Lancashire, but now of Hunmanby near Scarborough, in Yorkshire, and has issue four sons and three daughters (to wit) Robert, Philadelphia, John, ffrances, Humphrey, Richard and Mary

John, second son, apprentice to S[r] George Meritins in Cornhill, London, Banker, and married a daughter of S[r] George's, and has one son and one daughter, Robert and Philadelphia

Edward,† third son, dyed at ffort S[t] George in India in his first voyage to the East Indies

Humphrey, fourth son, dyed very young

Elizabeth married one Pomfret of Lond[n], wine marc[ht]

William, the youngest, married a Lady in Petworth in y[e] County of Sussex, where he resides

(*To be continued.*)

LASCELLES FAMILY—In the Pontefract Registers there is an entry of the marriage in 1715 of the Rev. Francis Lascells to Hannah, fourth daughter of the Rev. Samuel Drake, Vicar of Pontefract By this marriage there were several children, Thomas, Francis, Hannah (subsequently married to the Rev John Sturdy), and two other children The Rev Francis was buried at Pontefract 19 April, 1753, and the Hon (?) Col Thomas Lascelles was buried 1 Nov 1751 I am wishful to ascertain to what branch of the Lascelles family these persons belonged On referring to the Lascelles Pedigrees, to which I have access, I find first in Jones' 'Harewood,' Daniel Lascelles of Stank was born in 1655 By his first wife he had George (born 1681), Henry (born 1690), Francis, said to have died young (born 1674, *i e*, when his father was 19 !), Thomas, also said to have died young (born 1688) In Foster's 'Yorkshire Pedigrees,' Francis is said to be born in 1664, or when his father was 9 years old A similar mistake occurs in Whitaker's 'Leeds' I suppose that these two entries really mean that Francis was born in 1681 Can it be that these are the two gentlemen whose deaths we have recorded in the Pontefract registers? G. W T.

* In a later handwriting a note is added to the MS of 1666, viz , "dyed in London, 1713"

† Note in MS of 1666 "Edward Mitford was bound apprentice y[e] six of Aug[st] 1703, to an East India Merch[t] and dyed y[e] first Voyage at China"

THE PRINCIPAL MONUMENTAL INSCRIPTIONS IN THE CHURCH AND CHURCHYARD OF KELSTON, SOMERSET,

Which have not already appeared either in the "Notes on the Rectors" of that Church, or in the Memorials of the Hawkins, Hudleston, and Harington Families of Kelston

(*Continued from p.* 133.)

On a flat stone of white marble

Here lieth the body
of
Mrs Alicia Jones who died
Decr 21th 1777 aged 44 years
She was daughter of Charles Valence Jones Esqr
And Mary his Wife
And was niece to the late R^t^ Hon
Philip Yorke Earl of Hardwick
Lord High Chancellor of Great Britain.

Mrs Elizabeth Jones inscribes this to the Memory
of
An affectionate Sister a sincere friend
And pious Christian

Also Elizabeth Jones
Sister of the above Alicia
Who died Jany 8th 1790
Aged 67.

In the churchyard under the yew tree near the west gate (tomb enclosed with rails)

Here lieth the Body of
Elizabeth Ellen Duncan,
Born June 13th 1764, Died Decr 25, 1852.

Also the body of
Frances Duncan
Born 1768 died May 7th 1855.

Adjoining the above is this M I on a tomb enclosed with iron rails

James Richard Miller*
Obiit 16th December 1825 aged 81

On an altar-tomb (enclosed by rails) in the churchyard

Beneath
are laid the Remains of
The Revd William Meyrick A M.
He died at Bath May 13th 1842
in the 74th year of his age
The family are of Bôdaugan, Anglesea.
This tomb was erected by his Children
to his Cherished Memory
Through long and deep affliction he found
Comfort and support in the Gospel
&c &c

* I have been told that this gentleman was resident at Weston juxta Bath, when he died, and was previously of Castle Court, Budge Row, London

Also of Mary Lucy eldest daughter
of the above
She died March 23[d] 1846
Aged 47
And is buried at Weston
n[r] Bath.

In the church, on the north wall, a marble tablet

Sacred to the Memory
of
Charlotte, relict of the late Henry
Taylor Esq. of the Madras Civil Service
4th daughter of the Rev[d] Robert
Andrews D D *
She died Nov[r] 12. 1837.
Aged 67 years
Deeply & deservedly lamented by
her affectionate Children, who have
raised this tablet, as a tribute
of their gratitude, duty & affection

Near the grave where she is
interred lie the remains of
Otway her Grandson,
Son of Charles Otway Mayne Esq[r]†
by Emma his wife, who died
Feb[y] 8th 1820 aged 3 years

In the churchyard on a flat stone, north-west of the tower

To the Memory of
Elizabeth daughter of
The Rev[d] Edw[d] Warneford
formerly Rector of
Winterbourne, Gloucestershire
who died at Partis College
March 9th 1830
aged 60

And also of her Sister
Frances Matilda Younge,
Widow of Ralph Younge Esq[r]
who died in the same College
Aug. 28, 1854.

In the churchyard Inscription on a flat stone south of the tower

Matilda Louisa Barbara
Villiers‡
Died June 1st 1808
Aged 17.

(*To be continued.*)

* On the flat stone which covers her grave Robert Andrews is simply styled "Rev[d]" Query whether he did or did not ever take his Doctor's degree We think not

† The Otway Maynes were of Bellevue, Kent

‡ The Hon Matilda Villiers was buried at Kelston, July 29, 1820 This is from the Register, as she has no monumental inscription to her memory at Kelston

A CRITICAL EXAMINATION OF THE GENEALOGY OF MASTERTON OF THAT ILK, PARKMILL, ETC.

Published in Douglas's 'Baronage of Scotland, and Craufurd's 'Memorials of Alloa'

(*Continued from p* 136.)

Alexander Masterton and Catherine his wife obtained a feu charter of their lands of Beath, called Masterton-Beath, and of four-sevenths of the lands of Grange, Alexander seems to have been son of Robert of Beath, and father of Andrew of Beath, living in 1593 Adam Maistertoune, probably of this family, is a witness 1568

Before 1669 Masterton-Beath had been acquired by Wardlaw of Wester Luscar, but Easter Grange was retained by Adam Masterton, probably son of the above-named Andrew. In 1662 John Masterton was served heir of his father Adam in the lands of Easter Grange, and about 1673 Adam Masterton of Grange (? son of John) registered arms, Argent, a chevron between two crescents in chief, and a mullet in base gules, on a chief azure an eagle displayed or, crest, a dexter hand holding a scymetar proper, motto, *Pro Deo et rege* In 1690 he appears as tutor of John Philp, nephew and heir of Mr John Philp, minister of Queensferry, who had died in 1688 a prisoner in the Bass, having been deprived of his benefice and fined in 1681

We now come to the modern family of Masterton of Parkmill, which has been set up as representative of Masterton 1616 is the first appearance of them in the Acts of Parliament

I Alexander and Janet Couston his wife had in 1547 a charter of the lands of Millerwood and Cumlybank, afterwards called Parkmill, in the county of Clackmannan, from John Lord Erskine, they are also stated to have been infeft in the lands of Bad in Perthshire, in 1544

II Ronald Masterton of Parkmill had a charter from John, Earl of Mar, 1570, married Marjory Bruce, of the Clackmannan family, daughter of Robert of Lintmill Gilbert Masterton, who figures 1595–96 as a dependant of the Earl of Mar, was probably of this family. Mr John Colville writes to Robert Bowes that he is to be there one of these days with Highland men from Mar, and later David Foulis advises Lord Burleigh that Gilbert is not presently in England.

III Robert Masterton of Parkmill 1599, a member of the Committee of War, 1646, married Agnes, daughter of John Douglas of Rennieston in Fife

IV John Masterton of Parkmill was Sheriff Depute of Clackmannanshire, and a member of the Committee of War 1648, Robert, bailie of Clackmannan, is at the time on the Committee, and may have been his brother John, who had a charter of Parkmill in 1632, married Mary, daughter of Mr. William Lindsay

V Francis Masterton of Parkmill, a graduate of Edinburgh University 1663, also Sheriff Depute of the county, appears as a Commissioner of Supply 1667-1701, married Christian, daughter of John Kerrie of Gogar, in the parish of Blairlogie, and county of Perth, of a family originally belonging to Alloa, who had a grant of Arms 20th June, 1673 Argent, a fess counter-embattled between two cinquefoils in chief, and a cross crosslet fitchee in base gules Crest, a hand holding a rose slipped proper, motto, *Virtute Viget*

John Kerrie, then designed "Servant to the Earl of Mar," married Isobel, daughter of Mr John Craigingelt, minister of Alloa. Francis Masterton also registered arms about the same time, Argent, a chevron gules and a chief azure, crest, A stag courant, bearing on his attyre an oakslip fructed proper, motto, *Per ardua*

The history of the variations of the arms of the family is nearly as singular as the construction of their pedigree

The seal of William appended to his Deed of Homage, 1296, bears a lion rampant, the next authority is an illuminated MS of the middle of the sixteenth century, which gives, Argent, a chevron gules, on a chief of the second a crescent or

The seal of Robert Masterton of Bad, appended to a resignation of the lands of Ken in favour of Edward Brown, 1588, has an eagle displayed, impaling a chevron with a crescent in chief, or on a chief. This Robert of Bad does not fit into Sir Robert Douglas' pedigree at all, as it is stated that Alexander of Bad, 1514, had one son Ronald, and one daughter

A later MS has, Mastertoune of that Ilk, Per fess azure and argent, in chief a crescent, or, and in base, a chevron gules, impaling or, an eagle displayed sable.

Sir James Balfour has, gules, a unicorn trippant argent armed and unguled, or, while Porteus 1661 gives, argent, a chevron, and on a chief gules three crescents of the first

Francis and Christian had issue,

1 Charles

2 John, Merchant in Edinburgh, father of Colonel James Masterton, M P for the Stirling Burghs It is added in Burke's *Landed Gentry*, that James acted as Aide-de camp to H R H the Duke of Cumberland at Culloden, and had a sister Katherine, who married James Laurie of Burngrange, and had issue

VI Charles Masterton of Parkmill graduated at the University of Edinburgh 1697, married his cousin Mary, daughter of John Kerrie of Gogar and Catherine his wife, daughter of Mr Robert Wright, minister of Clackmannan, by Mary Craigingelt, whose sister was wife of John Kerrie of Gogar,

They had issue a daughter Katherine, who married James Christie, writer in Sterling, and one surviving son

VII Francis Masterton of Parkmill and Gogar who married Margaret, daughter of James Graeme of Braco co Perth, and Katherine his wife, daughter of Sir William Stirling of Ardoch, Bart, and had issue.

Charles

James.

Katherine

Mary

Thus far Douglas, who makes Francis the tenth in succession from William, living in 1422 inclusive Crawford adds that the last of the family, John, died at Leyden at an advanced age and childless, about the end of last century, and that Parkmill became the property of the Mar family Francis in 1720 was, along with his uncle Francis Kerrie, served heir of provision general of his grandfather John Kerrie, younger of Gogar, in 1747 he was served heir general of his father, Charles of Parkmill, in 1764 he was served heir of provision general of his cousin Edward Wright, of Kersie, co Stirling, M D, son of James Wright of Kersie and Janet, daughter of Mr Robert Wright, minister of Clackmannan, finally, in 1766, being then styled of Gogar, he was heir of provision general of his cousin Mary, daughter of Mr Robert Wright, minister of Culross, who was brother of Mrs Wright, of Kersie, and of Mrs Kerrie of Gogar

Francis had apparently succeeded to Gogar after the death of his uncles Charles Kerrie of Gogar and Francis Kerrie.

Francis Masterton, of Parkmill and Gogar, registered over again in his own name, 21 July, 1777, the arms recorded a hundred years before by his ancestor, and died 1795 in his 79th year, his widow died in 1806

In 1791 James Masterton, Merchant in Madeira, was served heir of his brother Charles of Aucklandskyes, in Perthshire, Captain 31st regiment of foot, who died in June, 1789, these might be the two sons of Francis

John Masterton of Braco, Perth, who has been stated to be a son of Francis and Margaret Graeme, married Anne Amelia Murdoch, who died 1806

James Masterton of Braco Castle (their son?) had an only daughter Margaret Seymour, who married in 1823 Captain Elliot, eldest son of the Right Hon. Hugh Elliot, Governor of Madras.

James William Mitchell.

Other persons of the name were Dewar Masterton, Advocate, who married in 1789 Helen, only child of Sir John Gibson, of Pentland, Bart., and died without issue in 1797, aged 31.

John Masterton, glazier to the King, had an Act in his favour in 1681 declaring that he should be free from all taxes, stent, etc., the name appears a hundred years before this in Edinburgh, borne by merchant burgesses of good position.

There are also lands in the county of Edinburgh named Masterton, and it is possible that they may have given name to a family in that quarter, who, however, never were owners of the estate. Robert I. granted a charter of half Masterton, near Newbottle, to the Abbot and Convent of Newbottle, on the resignation of Nigel de Carrick and Marion his spouse, and of Gilbert de Aytoun and Ada de Rossine his spouse, a subsequent charter conveyed the patronage of the church of Masterton to the Abbey. David II. granted half of Masterton to Walter Dispensa, Masterton was included in the great estate which was acquired by Mark Ker, last Abbot of Newbottle, as a hereditary barony, and was held by his descendants the Earls of Lothian till the middle of the seventeenth century, when it belonged to Thomas Meggat and descended to his heirs.

S * * *

Armorial Bookplate.

ARMS.—MITCHELL IMPALING SYKES.*

James William Mitchell of Audley, Sidmouth, Devon, late a Lieutenant in the 42nd Royal Highland and 17th Regiments of Foot, eldest son of Joseph Theophilus Mitchell, late of Lee, Kent (see page 101 'Miscellanea Genealogica'), married 8th April, 1871, at St. Mary Church, Devon, Annie Tilburn, elder daughter of Thomas Sykes of Ackworth, Yorkshire (see her baptism, page 103 'Miscellanea Genealogica'), and has issue Edward Charles Halliburton Mitchell, born at Sidmouth 2 June, 1876, and Isabel Beatrix, born at Sidmouth 28 December, 1874.

BENTLEY.

EXTRACTS OF THE NAME OF BENTLEY FROM THE REGISTERS OF THE PAROCHIAL CHAPEL OF WITTON IN THE COUNTY OF CHESTER, FROM THEIR FIRST COMMENCEMENT IN 1561 TO 1700.

1599 March 6 Will'm fil Ricard Bentley bapt.
1602. April 28 Will'm fil Richardi Bentley bapt.
1602. June 23. Will'm Bentley and Margreta Tomlinson married.
(Register very defective from 1601 to 1610.)
1610. April 26 Elizabeth da. of Rich[d] Bentley bapt.
1610 Feb 4 William Bentley & Jane More married.
(Registers still defective, no entries in 1611, few in 1612, none in 1613.)
1616 Dec 18 Joanna fil Thom Bentley bapt
1616 June 20 Fil Ricar Bentley sepult
1616. Febr 6 Jana fil Thom Bentley sepult
No entries of Burials or Weddings in 1618, no entries of Baptisms in 1619.
1620 Jan. 28 Edward fil Edward Bentley bapt
1625. *Richard Bentley was churchwarden in this year.*
1627 May 30 Robert Okell & Margaretta Bentley marr[d]

* Registered in the Heralds' College.

1631. May 16. Margeri uxor. Rici Bentley de Lach Green

Lach Green or Lach Dennis is a hamlet within the Lostock Graham Division of Witton Chapelry.

1632 July 2. Nicholas Bentley & Margaret Barrow marr^{d}
1633. October 6. Maria fil Will'mi Bentley bapt
1633 Feb 6 Will'm Bentley buried
1634 Oct 21 Richard Bentley & Marg Gregory married
1635 March 6. Gulielmus fil Gulielmi Bentley bapt.
1638 Nov 13 Ricardus Bentley bur^{d}
1640. Sept. 13. Ricardus fil Gulielmi Bentley bapt

(*The Registers very defective with very few entries from* 1641 *to* 1658.)

1648 April 9 Margaret da of William Bentley bapt.
1658 Oct 13 Johannes Bentley de Lostocke sepult
1662 May 4 Guelilme fill Guelilmi Bentley bapt
1664 Oct 3. Willam fil John Bentley bapt
1665 Dec. 25 Johannes fil Johannis Bentley de Northwich bapt
1667 Oct 22. Olave fill Johannis Bentley de Northwich bapt.
1673 May 21 Petrus fil Joh Bentley bapt
1673–4 Feb 18 Elizab fil Joh Bentley J^{r} de Hulse

Hulse is a hamlet in the Lostock division of Witton Chapelry

1676. July 4 Margreta uxor Johannis Bentley sepult
1678–9 April 23 Ricardus Bentley & Maria Burton married.
1678–9 Jan 30 Johannes Bentley & Annah Pries married
1680–1 Sept 16 Gulielmus Bentley, medicus, bur^{d}

His tomb was recently taken away, and the handsome old mausoleum which contained it converted into a greenhouse by the present possessor of what formerly was his garden

1680–1 Mar 12. Emm Bentley, Vid bur^{d}
1680 Aug 23 Petrus Buckley & Maria Bentley marr^{d}
1681. Sept 23. Daniel fil Johannis Bentley bur^{d}
1681 Dec 12 Ricardus Bentley bur^{d}.
" Dec 22 Maria uxor Will'mi Bentley sepult apud Peover Inferiora
1686 October 9 William Bentley & Margaret Siddely marr^{d}
1691. July 11 Sarah fil Will'mi Bentley de Lostock Gralam bapt
1691 July 21 Sarah fil Gulielmi Bentley de Lostocke Gralam bur^{d}
1691 June 16 Will'mus Bentley & Elizabetha Travis marr^{d}
1692 June 26. Maria fil Will'mi Bentley de Northwich Salificis bapt
1692 *Willimus Bentley one of the guardians during this year*
1695. Dec 6 Jacobus fil Gulielmi Bentley de Northwich Salificis bapt.
1698 July 21 Elizabetha fil Wil'mi Bentley de Northwich Laboratoris bapt
1699. March 7 Maria Bentley de Lostock Gralam vidua bur^{d}

CROMWELL DESBROW.—A boy bearing these very distinctive names was at Merchant Taylors' School in 1681 He might perhaps be the same as Cromwell Desborow (son of Benjamin, the 7th son of Colonel Desborow and Jane Cromwell), who died 4 March, 1717–18, in his 44th year, and was buried in the Abbey Church, Bath More probably he may be identified with Cromwell Disbrowe of Bombay, administration to whose effects was granted in 1730 to Platt Disbrowe, his brother, and further administration in 1757 to Mary Desmadryl (wife of John Charles D) sister of deceased, on behalf of Cornelia Disbrowe, widow, mother of deceased I should be glad to learn more of Cromwell Desborow, and also of Thomas Desborow (born Aug 1644), who entered M T. School in 1652.

West Hackney Rectory, N CHARLES J. ROBINSON.

CHURCH NOTES AT GRASMERE, WESTMORELAND.

Taken September 3rd, 1878, *by* CHARLES JACKSON.

MEMORIÆ SACRVM.*

GVILIELMI FLEMING DE CONISTONE ARMIGERI
QVI QVICQVID MORTALE HABVIT DEPOSVIT AD 9
CALENDAS IVNII. ANNO ÆRÆ CHRISTIANÆ
CIↃ . IↃC . LIII† ÆTAT SVÆ 41
IN EODEM TVMVLO VNÀ IACENT CINERES IPSIVS & AVIÆ
SIC,

Hæc capit Vrna duos, auiam natumq sepulchrum
Iungit idem viuos iunxerat unus amor.
Vincula non soluit uitæ mors Matris in alui,‡
Vnde oritur cineres filius inde redit
Sic cinis es genitor, cineris sed fama superstes,
Chara mihi in tumulo, nescia mortis erit.
Iusta tibi numeris non fas est soluere Iusta
Sic quæ non linguæ est soluere, soluet amor.
HÆC AMORIS ET OBSERVANTIÆ
ERGÒ POSVIT
Daniell Fleming FILIVS
ET HÆRES

BARBARÆ FLEMING*
HENRICI FLETCHER de Hutton in Comitatu Cumbriæ Baroti
et CATHARINÆ uxoris ejus (filiæ primogenitæ GEORGII DALSTON
de Dalston in eodem Comitatu Equitis aurati) filiæ natu max
et DANIELIS FLEMING de Rydall in Comitatu Westmorlandiæ
Armigeri, amantissimæ, amabilissimæ, fidelissimæq Conjugi,
in ipso ætatis flore morte immaturâ præreptæ,
Quæ
ob felicissimam Indolem, insignem Pietatem,
ingentem Charitatem, singularem Modestiam,
summam Probitatem, generosam Hospitalitatem,
vigilantem bonæ parentis curam,
Moresq suavissimos,
magnum sui apud omnes desiderium relinquens,
Corpus humo, Amorem Sponso, et Amicis,
Benedictionem quatuordecem Liberis
(decem nempe Pueris, ac quatuor Puellis)
Cœloq Animam legavit,
Monumentum hoc, Amoris & Mœroris perpetuum testem,
charissimus posuit Maritus.
Nata est apud Hutton xxv Julij A Dni MDCXXXIV.
Nupta ibidem xxvii Aug A Dni MDCLV
Confirmata apud Wathersiack xxii Junij MDCLXXI.
Mortua apud Rydall (de xvta prole) xiii Apr MDCLXXV
Sepulta in hoc Templo xiv Apr A D MDCLXXV.
LECTOR,
Si Lugere nescius, (quod præstat) Æmulare.

* On brasses framed in wood, against the east wall, within the Communion railing
† 24th May, 1653
‡ *Sic* orig., but should be alvo

MS D DANIELIS FLEMING Equitis Aur qui in Aula Lancastriensium Regiomontana, (vulgo Coningston Hall) patris et proavorum sede antiqua, natus Julii die 24, A D MDCXXXIII Inter deflendas gentis patriæ miserias, hoc unicum habuit ætatis juvenilioris solamen quod in uxorem duxerat BARBARAM D HEN FLETCHER Bar filiam plurimis amoris pignoribus undecim filiis, quatuorque filiabus, charissimam redeunti Anglorum Astreæ A D MDCLX Fasces prætulit, primus Cumbriæ vicecomes In ordinem merito receptus equestrem A D MDCLXXXI, in senatorium MDCLXXXV Tandem magistratum simul incorruptum animamque immaculatam demisit Mai 25, A D. MDCCI ætatis suæ LXVII In beatam cujus memoriam monumentum hoc filius posuit quintus, reverendus admodum in Christo pater D. GEORGIUS FLEMING Baronettus Episcopus Carliolensis

To the memory of SIR MICHAEL LE FLEMING fourth baronet, M P of Rydal Hall, Westmoreland. Born 10th December 1718, died 19th May 1806 Also of his wife LADY DIANA, only child of Thomas Howard, 14th Earl of Suffolk and Berkshire, who died 20th June 1816. And of their only child Ann Frederica Elizabeth, relict of Sir Daniel Fleming fifth baronet, died at Rydal Hall 5th April 1861, aged 77.

ARMS.—FLEMING with 14 quarterings MOTTO —*Pax Copia Sapientiæ.*

In memory of three sisters whose remains are here interred Mrs Barbara Fleming of Cowmire Hall, departed this life the 17th of Novr 1781, aged 81 years Mrs Anne Fleming died Septr 2d 1763, aged 61 years. Mrs Isabel Fleming died May 4th 1777, aged 73 years These ladies passed thro' life much respected by their acquaintance, and died in hopes of an happy resurrection.

To the memory of Edward Burton Esq, who departed this life March 7th A D. 1834, aged 26 This tablet is erected by his affectionate and afflicted widow

Flos ante diem flebilis occidit

(To be continued.)

Family of Gresham.

ABSTRACTS OF INQUISITIONS POST MORTEM

SIR RICHARD GRESHAM, KT

[Chancery Inquis p m 4 Ed VI, 2nd Pt No 56]

Inquisition taken at Norwich in 'Le Shirehowse' 8 March 4 Ed VI (1550) upon the death of Sir Richard Gresham Kt The Jurors say that he was seised in his demesne as of fee of the manors of Hardwike Swaynestrop Keswicke Intwood Swardeston and Mulberton with the appurtenances and of the advowsons of Swainestropp and Keswick (Here his Will is set out) That the manor of Hardwike was held of the King by the fourth part of a knight's fee and was of the clear annual value of £13 6*s* 8*d*, that the manor of Swainestropp was held by the sixteenth part of a knight's fee and was worth £23 12*s* 5*d*, that the manor of Keswick was held of the heirs of Hubert de Multon and was worth £25 2*s* 10½*d*, that the manor of Mulberton was held of Robert Benhale by the service of one knight's fee and was worth £39 14*s* 4*d*, that the manors of Intwood and Swardeston were held of the King as of the Duchy of Lancaster by the service of a fourth part and a twelfth part of a knight's fee and were worth £49 That the said Sir Richard Gresham died on 21 Feb 3 Ed VI, that Sir John Gresham the younger Kt is his son and next heir and of the age of thirty years and upwards. They say further that he was seised of a Watermill in Tasbrough and Freton worth £5 a year. That the Lady Isabella Gresham widow late the wife of the said Sir Richard takes the rents and profits of Mulberton for the term of her life.

[Chancery Inquis. p m 4 Ed VI, 2nd Pt. No 77]

Inquisition taken at Bungaye, co Suffolk, 5 March 4 Ed VI (1550) upon the death of Sir Richard Gresham Kt The Jurors say that he was seised in his demesne as of fee of the manors of Rokells Rawlyns and Battisforde late of the Bishop of Norwich and of the manor or Comandry of St John of Battisforde and of the manor of Bavent Combes and of the advowsons of Ryngsell and of the Vicarage of Battisforde and of 60 messuages 500 acres of land 200 of meadow 100 of pasture 100 of wood 20 of moor furze and heath and of £20 14s rent in Ryngsell Charles Rokelles Rawlyns Battisforde St Johns of Battisforde Combes Wattesham Bavent-combes Barkyng Badleycombes Fynborowe Ryngsell parva Brysett magna and Flocton in the County of Suffolk (Here his Will is set out) That the manors of Ryngsell Charles Rokells Rawlyns and the premises in the same Battesforde Combes Waltesham and Barkyng were held of the King by the service of one knight's fee and the eighth part of a knight's fee and were worth £101 7s 11½d That the manor of Bavent Combes with the appurtenances was held by the service of the sixtieth part of a knight's fee and by the rent of 12 shillings yearly and was worth £13 12s 10d That the premises in Battisforde, Badley, Combes, Fynborowe, parva Ryngsell, Brysett magna Wattesham and Flocton were held of the King by the service of the sixtieth part of a knight's fee and by rent of *25s 1½d* and were worth £18 0s 10d That the manor of Battesforde late of the Bishop of Norwich was held of the King by the service of the fortieth part of a knight's fee and by rent of *27s 11½d* and was worth £35 and no more Further that he bequeathed to his kinsman Richard Billingforde and to such wife as he should happen to marry for the term of their lives an annual rent of £10 issuing out of his manor of Battisforde and that the said Richard is still living at Bungaye That the said Sir Richard Gresham died on 21 Feb 3 Ed VI, that Sir John Gresham Kt is his son and heir and was at the time of the taking of this Inquisition thirty years old and upwards

[Chancery Inquis p m 5 Ed VI, 1st Pt No. 50]

Inquisition taken at the Castle of York 7 April 5 Ed VI (1551) upon the death of Sir Richard Gresham Kt The Jurors say that he was seised of the manors of Bremben *alias* Brembery Benley in Ellerdale and Eldborough Malham Lytton Kylnesey Merkington *alias* Morker Lound upon the wold Sutton *alias* Sutton Grange Bordeley *alias* Bordeley baronye with the rights tithes and appurtenances in the County of York, and of a moiety of the Manor and Church of Nonkelyng and of the Rectors of Swyne with the chapel, and of one messuage and of the site of the late Monastery of Fountaynes and the Barkehowse, and of 500 messuages 8 water mills 4 dove houses 5000 acres of land 800 acres of meadow 4000 acres of pasture 2000 acres of wood 5000 acres of moor 10,000 acres of furze and heath and of £6 10s rent with the appurtenances in Brembery Massam Kyrby Malsharte Taufelde Malham Lound on the Wold Ryppen Stanley Beverley in Netherdale Arnclyffe Horton in Rybblesdale Burnshale Kyrby in Mallam dale Nonkelyng Swyne and Spaldyngton (Here the Will is set out) Recites a Fine made in Hilary Term 1 & 2 Ed VI whereby Sir Richard Gresham and Isabella his wife conveyed to Sir John Gresham Kt his son the manor of Sutton and divers tenements in Ryppon, the Rectory of Swyne, a moiety of the Rectory and Manor of Nonkelyng, for the term of his life with divers remainders over They further say that all the premises with the site of Fountaynes, the Manors of Brember Massam Kyrkbye Malshart Taufeld Morker *alias* Merkyngton Beverley in Netherdale Aldburghe Malham Bordeley Kylnsey Lytton Sutton the Rectory of Swyne and a moiety of the Manor and Rectory of Nonkelyng (the premises separately purchased of the Earl of Rutland Sir Ralph Ellerker Kt and Edmund Wryght only excepted) were held of the King in chief by knight's service by a Rent to the King and his successors of £57 19s. 0¾d. annually at the feast of St. Michael and were of the annual value of £579 11s. 3¼d.; that the manor of Lound and tenements in Lound bought of Sir Ralph Ellerker Kt. were held of the King as of his Manor of Topclyf by knight's service and were worth £16 14s. 4d. That the tenements in Lounde bought of the Earl of Rutland of Thomas Johnson and of Edmund Wright were held of the King as of his manor of Topclyf by knight's service and were worth £6. That said Sir Richard Gresham Kt. died on 21 Feb. 3 Ed. VI., that Sir John Gresham Kt. is his son and heir and was of the age of thirty-four years at the time of the taking of this Inquisition.

BENTLEY OF STAFFORDSHIRE.—The following facts may assist any inquirer into the early history of this family.—Shaw ('Hist. of Staffordshire,' ii., 93) says, "The first we meet with is Gervase de Bentley, *who had issue* Roger de Bentley, who by a deed without date grants to Roger his son and his heirs all Bentley, etc." No authority is given for the statement that Gervase was father of Roger. He might have been *predecessor of some other family*, and some genealogists, after the manner of compiling pedigrees formerly, have set him down as father. The pedigree of Bentley is unbroken and authoritatively made out from the first Roger. Wm. de Bentley, who died 4 Edw. I., leaving William, a son and heir, æt. 21, mentions "Roger avus suus temp. John" (Testa de Nevill). To all this must be added the important fact that Robert de Broc, Marshal of the King, gave to *Roger Helias* alias de Bentley, temp. Ric. I., his lands in Nether Shugborough, co. Warwick (Shaw, ii., 93). In the Heraldic Dictionaries three bends are given as the coat of Helias. One of the coats of Bentley was *Azure, a mermaid Or* (Dugdale's 'Warwickshire,' p. 351), and existed in Kineton Church, co. Warwick. Now in connection with this coat these facts are remarkable:—Byron, who early bore three bends, had for crest a mermaid. The mermaid was the ancient coat of Prestwick of Prestwick, co. Lancashire. In 1301 we find Adam de P., John de P., Sir John Byron and others witnesses to a charter granted by Thomas de Grelley (which family also bore three bends). Furthermore, 1322, Richard Fitz Elias was manucaptor of Robert Byron, Knight for Rutlandshire. And 20 Edw. I. Sir John Elyas, with Sir John Byron and other knights, were named in a commission of inquiry (Hundred Rolls).

Sir Roger Alis, temp. John, descended from Sir Wm. Alis, who in Domesday is mentioned as the tenant *in capite* of Ellatune olim Auditon hodie Allington, co. Hants, in South Stoneham parish, it is probable is the same person as "Roger Helias alias de Bentley," for Alis was often spelt Elias and fitz-Elias, and his benefactor or grantor De Broc was connected with the Hampshire families of Croc, Bendinges, etc. Now the mermaid was the coat of the Hampshire family of Wallop. Mathew de W. was witness to a charter of Wm. Alis temp. Hen. II. (Record Office Augmentation Deeds, C. 33). Roger Alis, 1217, had seisin of lands in Wellhope. Again, the mermaid is on a seal of Wm. Brewer, temp. John, and is figured in Mr. Moule's 'Heraldry of Fish.' This was a Hampshire family.

This interesting badge, device or crest of the mermaid was also borne as a coat of arms by the Shropshire family of Gros at an early period, and is quartered by Corbet (Harl. MSS. 1396, and Add. MSS. 21,017). Two mermaids appear as supporters on the seal of Thomas de Berkley, who died 1361, and on the seal of James de B., who died 1463. The mermaid, as crest or as a charge, was also borne by a dozen other families, and more than once in both senses by families of the name of Elys and Ellys. And the unique crest of a naked female was very early borne by the ancient family of Elys, of Kiddall Hall, near Leeds, supposed to be derived from Alis of Hampshire, and early written fitz-Elias, Eliz, etc.

W. S. E.

THE PRINCIPAL MONUMENTAL INSCRIPTIONS IN THE CHURCH AND CHURCHYARD OF KELSTON, SOMERSET,

Which have not already appeared, either in the "Notes on the Rectors" of that Church, or in the Memorials of the Hawkins, Hudleston, and Harington Families of Kelston

(*Continued from p* 140.)

On the top stone of an altar-tomb in the churchyard, near the north gate

Matilda Surtees
died December 28th 1811
aged 21 years
"Blessed are the pure in heart," &c.

Wm Surtees
died Jany 4th 1832
aged 82 years

Arthur Surtees
died April 17th 1833
aged 20 years

M I on a marble tomb recumbent upon a stone base

(The marble bears a full-length floriated cross in relief)

"Resting in hope"

Mary the beloved wife
of
The Revd Francis John Poynton
Rector of this Parish
Died March 20, 1863
Aged 33 years

Mary Brune Poynton the beloved
Sister of the Same Rector
Died April 22d 1877
aged 61 years

On a raised tomb in the churchyard, south of the church.

Here are deposited the Remains
of Harriotte Bowers
(Daughter of the late Maunsell
Bowers of Waterford, Ireland)
Who died on the 8th of April 1816
Aged 25

Also
Julia Spence,
Relict of Captn Spence
(of the 87th Regt), Sister
of the above
Died 25th May 1852
Aged 62 years

In the wall of Kelston churchyard, south of the chancel

(1) In Memory of Bethiah
The wife of John Smallcombe of this Parish
Died the 14th day of Novr 1711
aged 71 years

Also John the Son of Thomas and
Katharine Smallcombe
of the Parish of North Stoke
Who died the 14th day of April
1747 aged 19 years

(2) Also here lye the Bodies of
James & Hannah Smallcombe
The beloved son & daughter of
Thomas & Katharine Smallcombe
of the Parish of Northstoke James died
2d day of June 1747 aged 2 years. Hannah
died the 8th day of the same month & year
aged 14 years.

(3) By the side of this tomb lyeth
The body of Thomas Smallcombe
of the Parish of Northstoke, Yeoman
Who died the 20th of December
1767 aged 63.

(4) In Memory of Catherine
Wife of the said Thomas Smallcombe
of the Parish of Northstoke, Yeoman
Who died the 22th August 1773
Aged 70 years

To the south of chancel, on a flat stone

Here lieth the body of Ann
Wife of Moses Smallcombe of the Parish of Northstoke
and daughter of Robert Whittington
of the Parish of Bitton, who died 6th day of March
1771 age 35 years

Also Ann their daughter, who died in her Infancy.

Also the said Moses Smallcombe of this Parish
Son of Thomas and Katherine Smallcombe
of Northstoke, who died the 11th July 1797
aged 60 years.

Also Sarah daughter of Thomas & Rebecca Smallcombe
of Bitton who died 24th Jany 1806
aged 16 days

Also Rachel daughter of Thomas & Rebecca Smallcombe
of Bitton, who died 28th Jany. 1806 aged 20 days

Also Jane daughter of the Same who died
9th April 1810 aged 17 weeks

On a flat stone beside the last

A vault near this spot contains the remains of
Thomas Smallcombe of Fieldgrove
In the Parish of Bitton & County of Gloucester, Gent
Who died on the 20th day of November 1818

S

TAG

W. C. 18

Arms nroe, in Co.
ds of Shanro

Crest ie, Gent., on
, and then ov
Motto f Silloo, Co. M
, Co. Monag
te. He endu

Rev. Thomas Car
eldest son. Ma
Nov. 4, 1715.
naghan, amon
Granted premi
Co. Donegal, b
nolly, on June
session of his re
Curate of Errig

Catherine S
George S
Co. Mona
Jane, dau
Barlow, E
was High
County, 1

s Barkley, of Limerick, = *Elizabeth Fosberry*,
but whose family was daughter of Geo.
d in Co. Clare. Fosberry, of Kil-
cooley, Co. Limerick, Esq., by
Bridget, his wife.

In the wall of Kelston churchyard, south of the chancel

(1) In Memory of Bethiah
The wife of John Smallcombe of this Parish
Died the 14th day of Novr 1744
aged 71 years.

Also John the Son of Thomas and
Katharine Smallcombe
of the Parish of North Stoke
Who died the 14th day of April
1747 aged 19 years.

(2) Also here lye the Bodies of
James & Hannah Smallcombe
The beloved son & daughter of
Thomas & Katharine Smallcombe
of the Parish of Northstoke James died
2d day of June 1747 aged 2 years Hannah
died the 8th day of the same month & year
aged 14 years

(3) By the side of this tomb lyeth
The body of Thomas Smallcombe
of the Parish of Northstoke, Yeoman
Who died the 20th of December
1767 aged 63

(4) In Memory of Catherine
Wife of the said Thomas Smallcombe
of the Parish of Northstoke, Yeoman
Who died the 22th August 1773
Aged 70 years

To the south of chancel, on a flat stone

Here lieth the body of Ann
Wife of Moses Smallcombe of the Parish of Northstoke
and daughter of Robert Whittington
of the Parish of Bitton, who died 6th day of March
1771 age 35 years

Also Ann their daughter, who died in her Infancy.

Also the said Moses Smallcombe of this Parish
Son of Thomas and Katherine Smallcombe
of Northstoke, who died the 11th July 1797
aged 60 years

Also Sarah daughter of Thomas & Rebecca Smallcombe
of Bitton who died 24th Jany 1806
aged 16 days

Also Rachel daughter of Thomas & Rebecca Smallcombe
of Bitton, who died 28th Jany 1806 aged 20 days

Also Jane daughter of the Same who died
9th April 1810 aged 17 weeks.

On a flat stone beside the last

A vault near this spot contains the remains of
Thomas Smallcombe of Fieldgrove
In the Parish of Bitton & County of Gloucester, Gent
Who died on the 20th day of November 1818.

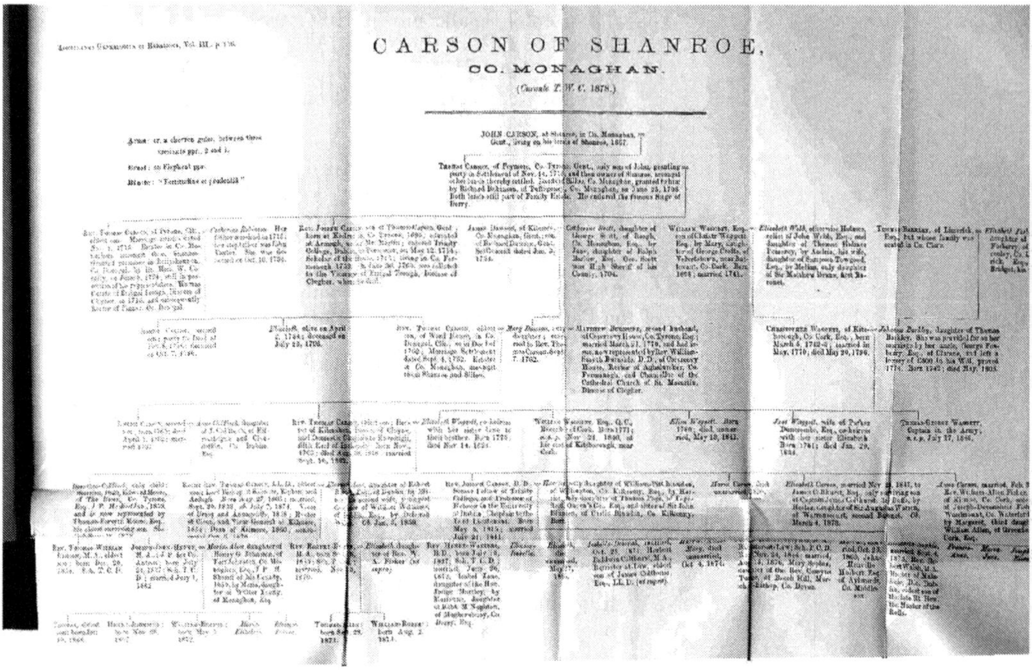
CARSON OF SHANROE,
CO. MONAGHAN.
(Curante T. W. C. 1878.)
JOHN CARSON,
Motto: "Fortitudine et prudentiâ"

Also the remains of Rebecca his wife
Daughter of James Hooper Esq of Lameridge
in the county of Somerset.
Who died the 25 day of December following
aged 49 years
Leaving Seven Children to deplore their loss

Also the remains of Moses, second son of
the above Thomas & Rebecca Smallcombe
Who died October 15th 1824 aged 22 years

Also the Remains of Rebecca, third daughter
of the said Thos & Rebecca Smallcombe
Who died Oct 21st 1837 aged 33 years.

Also the Remains of Thomas Eldest Son
of Thomas & Rebecca Smallcombe
who died July 31st 1845

To the Memory of
Elizabeth Smallcombe daughter of Moses & Anne Smallcombe
who died April 16, 1840, aged 71

Thomas Jones Hamerton, late of Dublin
Died Aug 15 1858, aged 50 years

EXTRACTS FROM AN OLD MS *PENES* LIEUT-COLONEL JOHN PHILIP OSBALDESTON MITFORD OF MITFORD CASTLE, CO NORTHUMBERLAND

(*Continued from page* 138)

(*In a later handwriting*)

Robert Mitford, eldest son of Robert Mitford, was born at Brayton Hall at Mr Pockley's the 24 of July 1717 or 1718, but who were his godfathers he knows not He married Anna Lewis, daughter of John Lewis, Esq , of the Island of Jamaica, and has issue by her five sons and two daughters, Anna, Robert, Robert John, Bertram, John, Mary, William Henry, Sybill Anna Knight, four more dyed under Robert Clement buried in Mitford Church Two boys twins buried within the first two days of their Birth at Aix la Chapelle He had by the above mentioned Anna Lewis his wife Nineteen children She died May 6th 1763, aged 38 years, and was buried in the Chancel of Brayton Church in Yorkshire, the Burying place of this family since Robt married Miss Ashton, by whom he got the Burn estate

Humphrey, son of the above Robert Mitford, married He was born the 20th March 1720 •

Philadelphia, daughter of the above Robert Mitford, married the Rev Mr Wickin of Petworth, where she now resides

From the older MS

Robert Mitford was born att Rogerley the last day of October abt two of the Clock in the morning 1662, his grandfather Mitford and his uncle Reeveley godfathers, and his great grandmother the Lady Ann Maddison his godmother

Elizabeth Mitford was born att Newcastle the 29th day of Sept abt 5 Clock in ye morning being Michaelmas Day 1663, her uncle Dr Geo Tunstall being her godfather, and her grandmother Lady Eliz Vaine and her aunt Elinor Mitford her godmothers.

Philadelphia Mitford was born att Newcastle 13 day of Sept abt one of ye clock in ye morning 1664, her uncle Reeveley being her godfather, and her grandmother Philadelphia Mitford and her Aunt Vaine her godmothers

Ann Mitford was born at Rogerley the 5th day of Nov ab^t 6 a clock in the morning 1665, my cosen Lyonell Maddison of Scutwelside being her godfather, and her grandmother the Lady Eliz Vaine and her aunt Ann Vaine her godmothers

Margaret Mitford was born at the same time and dyed ab^t a fortnight after, and was buried in Stanhope Church in the County of Durham

George Mitford was born att Mitford the day of Oct betwixt 5 & 6 of ye clock att night 1666, his grandfather Sr Geo Vaine and my coz W^m ffenwick his godfathers, and his aunt Eliz Mitford his godmother

John Mitford was born att Mitford the sixth day of June 1668, ab^t 5 of ye clock in ye morning, his uncle John Mitford and his uncle Patricke Crow godfathers, and his aunt Camilla Vane his godmother.

Barbara Mitford was born att Mitford ye 20th day of Nov 1669, ab^t 7 of the clock att night her Aunt Crow and Martha Reeveley godmothers, and Jno Dasteney of Dalton godfather

Frances Mitford was born at Mitford the 31st day of July 1671, ab^t 12 a clock at noone ffrances Reevely and Philadelphia Tunstall godmothers, and her uncle Herbert godfather.

*Mary Mitford** was born at Mitford ye 21st Sept 1672, ¼ of an hour before 2 in ye afternoone. The Lady Mary ffenwick her grandmother Mitford godmothers, her uncle Herbert godfather Dyed May 29th 1702 att London

Sarah Mitford,† youngest daughter of Humphrey Esq, defunct, was born att Mitford ab^t 2 months after her ffather's death being in ye year 1674

ffrances Mitford, Relict of Hump Mitford, dyed att Lond ye . . day of . . . 1675.

Robert Mitford, eldest son of ye said Humphrey Mitford, marryed Ann eldest daughter of J^no Ashton of Burn in ye County of York, Esq,‡ upon the nineteenth of Decr 1681, and had issue five sons and one daughter (viz) *ut prius*.

On a detached sheet, endorsed "Genealogie of MITFORD De Mitford of Northumberland from before W^m ye Conqueror to this p'sent year 1663"

John, the 2^d son, married Ann, daughter of Doct^r Cradock who had issue, Bulmer, John and Cuthbert, Dorothy, May, Ann, ffrances, Hellen

William, ye 3^d son of Robert, married Jane, daughter of Dr Henry Banks de Settrington, who had issue Henry, Matthew and Edward, Mary, Margarett, ffrances and Helyen, and William who died young

Henry, son of William, married Ann, daughter of William Staveley of Rippon Parke, Esq. Matthew married Mary, daughter of John Woodward of Wrelton, gent, who had issue by her, Anne, Mary and William, Jane, Matthew and Edward, Susanna, Anthony, Henry

Edward, 3^d son of William, married Mary, daughter of Mr Crawduk of Dover Mary married ffrancis Aislaby of South Dalton, gent, who had issue by her Martha, who died young, and John Margarett married Henry Strangways of Sneaton, gent, who had issue, James, Thomas, Henry, John, Charles and William, Mary, Margarett, Dorothy, Jane

Frances married Wm Nesfield of Scarborough, mariner, who had issue William

Hellen, ye youngest daughter of William, married Richard Tate, minister, who had issue William, dead

A Parchment slip, being the admission to the freedom of the City of London of John Midford, son of Wm Midford of Newcastle upon Tyne, mariner, who was app to Abraham Coleman, citizen and glover of London, dated 17 April 1710

* Mary Mitford married to Wm Heyington of Durham, whoe are both dead and left issue one son named Humphrey The father was killed in a Duell at Rochester, as some say, and others say he was run through ye back cowardly and she dyed at Lond^n in 1702

† Sarah Mitford marryed one Knightley Vicar of Byfield in Northamptonshire, by whom she has severall sons and daughters

‡ John Ashton was 2nd surviving son of Ralph Ashton of Middleton, Esq, and brother (*not son*) of Sir Ralph Ashton, Bart He married Elizabeth dau of John Fleetwood of Penwortham, co Lanc [C J R]

CHURCH NOTES AT GRASMERE, WESTMORELAND.

Taken September 3rd, 1878, by CHARLES JACKSON

(*Concluded from p* 146.)

TO THE MEMORY OF
WILLIAM WORDSWORTH,
A TRUE PHILOSOPHER AND POET,
WHO, BY THE SPECIAL GIFT AND CALLING OF
ALMIGHTY GOD,
WHETHER HE DISCOURSED ON MAN OR NATURE,
FAILED NOT TO LIFT UP THE HEART
TO HOLY THINGS
TIRED NOT OF MAINTAINING THE CAUSE
OF THE POOR AND SIMPLE,
AND SO, IN PERILOUS TIMES WAS RAISED UP
TO BE A CHIEF MINISTER,
NOT ONLY OF NOBLEST POESY,
BUT OF HIGH AND SACRED TRUTH

THIS MEMORIAL
IS PLACED HERE BY HIS FRIENDS AND NEIGHBOURS,
IN TESTIMONY OF
RESPECT, AFFECTION, AND GRATITUDE
ANNO MDCCCLI

Below the above is a medallion likeness of the poet

Michael Knott Esq of Rydall, died August 28th 1772, aged 76 years Susannah, wife of Michael Knott, died December 16th 1767, aged 56 years Edward, son of Michael Knott, died November 2d 1766, aged 25 years

In the Burial Ground
of this church are deposited the remains of
JEMIMA ANNE DEBORAH,
second daughter of
Sir Egerton Brydges of Denton Court, Kent, Bart,
She departed this life at the Ivy Cottage, Rydal,
May 25th 1822, aged 28 years.

This memorial is erected by her husband Edward Quillinan

These vales were saddened with no common gloom
When good Jemima perished in her bloom ,
When such the awful will of Heaven, she died
By flames breathed on her from her own fireside *
On earth we dimly see, and but in part
We know, yet Faith sustains the sorrowing heart
And she, the pure the patient, and the meek,
Might have fit epitaph could feelings speak ,
If words could tell, and monuments record,
How treasures lost are inwardly deplored,
No name by grief's fond eloquence adorned
More than Jemima's would be praised and mourned
The tender virtues of her blameless life,
Bright in the Daughter, brighter in the Wife,
And in the cheerful Mother brightest shone —
That light hath passed away—the will of God be done

* She died from the accident of her dress catching fire

In memory of Octavia Kearsley, daughter of John Kearsley Esquire of Manchester, who departed this life at Ambleside September 8th 1827, aged 41 years. Her mortal remains are deposited in the burial ground of this parish Through life she was much beloved and respected by her numerous relatives and friends Her affectionate mother, in remembrance of her filial piety, hath caused this tablet to be erected

To the memory of M[rs] Laetitia Pritchard, late of Croft Lodge in the township of Loughrigg, in this parish, who died on the 18th day of January A D 1827, in the 71st year of her age Her life was devoted to the offices of Charity, the claims of Friendship, and the duties of Religion.

(*Medallion likeness*)

Sacred to the memory of Elizabeth, wife of the late Archibald Fletcher Esq[re], Advocate of Edinburgh She was born on the 15th of January 1770, and died at Lanerigg, in this parish, on the 5th of February 1858.

"Her children arise up and call her blessed"

Proverbs, C xxxi., v. 28.

Within the Communion railing are four hatchments of the Fleming family —

1 Gules, a fret argent Crest —A snake nowed holding in its mouth a garland. Motto.—*Pax copia sapientiae*
2 Same, with, on an escutcheon of pretence, HOWARD, with sundry quarterings
3 Same in a lozenge
4 Same, with, on an escutcheon of pretence, FLEMING quartering HOWARD, etc.

The poor box bears the the date of 1648. Two old oak chairs within the rails on one, I L 1677, and the other M B. 1703

The first page of the oldest register is illegible, but it appears to commence in or about 1570

Benefactors —Edward Partridge of Grasmere, and others 1680 Rev John Ambrose, rector 1680 Anthony Dawson of Grasmere. 1796. William Waters of Thornyhow 1807 William and Eleanor Waters of the same 1812 M[rs] Dorothy Knott of Ambleside 1817 Vincent G Dowling esq 1852. John Watson of Winterseeds in Grasmere, yeoman

There are no inscriptions on the floor of the church, which up to 1840 consisted merely of the bare earth, and this it was the custom to strew with rushes immediately after the hay-harvest in each year From this practice arose the village festival of the "Rush-Bearing," which takes place annually on the last Saturday but one in July.

The Church, which is of great antiquity, is dedicated to S[t] Oswald, and the present rector is the Rev Henry M Fletcher.

In the Churchyard are memorials for —

Louisa Ann, wife of James Wrigley esq and only dau of John Clark Langmead esq and Louisa Ann his wife, of Plymouth. May, 1812

Octavius Kearsley, Sept 8, 1827, aged 4.

Rev Thomas Jackson, rector of this parish, 13 Dec 1821, aged 65

Jane Elizabeth, widow of Charles Gibson of Quernmore park, Lancashire, esq. Sept 20, 1862, aged 65

Isabella, wife of John Prince Halton, F R C S, Nov 20, 1871, aged 72. J P Halton, Jan 27, 1873, aged 75

Rev Edward Rowlandson, minister of this parish for nearly 50 years, Jan 20, 1811, aged 77 Mary, his widow, 13 Feb 1817, æt 76

Rev Jos Sympson, 1807

Elinor, wife of John Philipps Philipps, esq Commander R N Aug 17, 1866, the said J P Philipps, Aug 8, 1875, aged 82

Anne Clough, a native of Pontefract, widow of James Butler Clough of Liverpool, died at Eller How, Ambleside, 12 June, 1860, aged 65

WILLIAM
THOMAS
CARSON
FORTITUDINE ET PRUDENTIA

In memory of Octavia Kearsley, daughter of John Kearsley Esquire of Manchester, who departed this life at Ambleside September 8th 1827, aged 41 years. Her mortal remains are deposited in the burial ground of this parish. Through life she was much beloved and respected by her numerous relatives and friends. Her affectionate mother, in remembrance of her filial piety, hath caused this tablet to be erected.

To the memory of Mrs Lætitia Pritchard, late of Croft Lodge in the township of Loughrigg, in this parish, who died on the 18th day of January A.D. 1827, in the 71st year of her age. Her life was devoted to the offices of Charity, the claims of Friendship, and the duties of Religion.

(*Medallion likeness.*)

Sacred to the memory of Elizabeth, wife of the late Archibald Fletcher Esqre, Advocate of Edinburgh. She was born on the 15th of January 1770, and died at Lanerigg, in this parish, on the 5th of February 1858.

"Her children arise up and call her blessed."

Proverbs, C. xxxi., v. 28.

Within the Communion railing are four hatchments of the Fleming family:—

1. Gules, a fret argent. Crest.—A snake nowed holding in its mouth a garland. Motto.—*Pax copia sapientiæ.*
2. Same, with, on an escutcheon of pretence, HOWARD, with sundry quarterings.
3. Same in a lozenge.
4. Same, with, on an escutcheon of pretence, FLEMING quartering HOWARD, etc.

The poor box bears the the date of 1648. Two old oak chairs within the rails: on one, I.L. 1677; and the other M.B. 1703.

The first page of the oldest register is illegible, but it appears to commence in or about 1570.

Benefactors.—Edward Partridge of Grasmere, and others. 1680. Rev. John Ambrose, rector. 1680. Anthony Dawson of Grasmere. 1796. William Waters of Thornyhow. 1807. William and Eleanor Waters of the same. 1812. Mrs Dorothy Knott of Ambleside. 1817. Vincent G. Dowling esq. 1852. John Watson of Winterseeds in Grasmere, yeoman.

There are no inscriptions on the floor of the church, which up to 1840 consisted merely of the bare earth, and this it was the custom to strew with rushes immediately after the hay-harvest in each year. From this practice arose the village festival of the "Rush-Bearing," which takes place annually on the last Saturday but one in July.

The Church, which is of great antiquity, is dedicated to St Oswald, and the present rector is the Rev. Henry M. Fletcher.

In the Churchyard are memorials for:—

Louisa Ann, wife of James Wrigley esq. and only dau. of John Clark Langmead esq. and Louisa Ann his wife, of Plymouth. May, 1812.

Octavius Kearsley, Sept. 8, 1827, aged 4.

Rev. Thomas Jackson, rector of this parish, 13 Dec. 1821, aged 65.

Jane Elizabeth, widow of Charles Gibson of Quernmore park, Lancashire, esq. Sept. 20, 1862, aged 65.

Isabella, wife of John Prince Halton, F.R.C.S., Nov. 20, 1871, aged 72. J. P. Halton, Jan. 27, 1873, aged 75.

Rev. Edward Rowlandson, minister of this parish for nearly 50 years, Jan. 20, 1811, aged 77. Mary, his widow, 13 Feb. 1817, æt. 76.

Rev. Jos. Sympson, 1807.

Elinor, wife of John Philipps Philipps, esq. Commander R.N. Aug. 17, 1866; the said J. P. Philipps, Aug. 8, 1875, aged 82.

Anne Clough, a native of Pontefract, widow of James Butler Clough of Liverpool, died at Eller How, Ambleside, 12 June, 1860, aged 65.

foldout
here

Arthur Hugh Clough, Fellow of Oriel College, Oxford, son of J. B and Anne Clough, buried in the Swiss Cemetery, Florence, where he died Nov. 13, 1861, aged 42.

Rev John Milson, late of Ambleside, and formerly minister of this place, 6 April, 1791, ætat 63

Lieut James Stewart, 88th Regt, son of the late Lieut-General James Stewart, Jan. 3, 1809, aged 24

James Cookson of Clappersgate, April 18, 1849, aged 84. Mary, his wife, Dec 1829, æt 41. Dorothy Tyson, Jan 12, 1858, aged 62, and others of the name

Rev Isaac Green, M A of Queen's College, Cambridge, 38 years second master of Sedbergh Grammar School, and 38 years incumbent of Howgill, born at Grasmere Feb 1, 1804, died at Sedbergh Sept 25, 1875. Caroline Bella, his second wife, dau of Julius C Ibbetson of Masham, landscape painter, died Nov. 5, 1865. Caroline their dau Sept 24, 1859

William Wordsworth, 1850 Dorothy Wordsworth, 1855 Mary Wordsworth, 1859. Dora Quillinan, 9th July, 1817. Edward Quillinan, born at Oporto Aug 12th 1791, died at Loughrigg Holme July 8th 1851 Rotha Quillinan, died at Loughrigg Holme, Rydal, 1st Feb 1876, aged 54. Jemima Anne D. Quillinan, died May 25th 1822, aged 27 Dora, dau of Wm and Mary Wordsworth of Rydal Mount, wife of Edward Quillinan, born 16th August, 1804; married 11th May, 1841, died 9th July, 1847

Sarah Hutchinson, born at Penrith 1st Jan 1775; died at Rydal 23rd June, 1835.

William Wordsworth, born at Cockermouth 7th April, 1770, died at Rydal 23rd April, 1850 Dorothy Wordsworth, born at Cockermouth 25th Dec 1771, died at Rydall 25th Jan 1855 Mary Wordsworth, wife of Wm Wordsworth and sister of Sarah Hutchinson, born at Penrith August 16th 1770, died at Rydal Mount Jan 17, 1859 Catharine, dau of Wm and Mary Wordsworth, born Sept. 6th 1808, died June 4th 1812 Thomas, son of the same, died 1st Dec. 1812. William, infant son of William and Fanny Wordsworth, born July 13, died at Carlisle Oct 5th 1851.

John Wordsworth, Staff Assistant Surgeon to H.M Forces in the Ionian Islands, only son of the late Richard Wordsworth of Sockbridge in this county, and nephew of William Wordsworth of Rydal Mount, died at Ambleside 18 Aug 1846, aged 31. Sara Cookson died Sept 4th 1875 Elizabeth Cookson of How Foot, Grasmere, Nov 5th 1868, æt 94, widow of Thomas Cookson of Kendal, who died Oct. 20th 1833, aged 62, at Ramsey, Isle of Man Hartley Coleridge born Sept XIX A.D. mdccxcvi, deceased Jan VIth A D mdcccxlix.

Charles Frederick Younge of Forrest Side, youngest son of late Simon Andrews Younge of Sheffield, died 17 Nov 1866, aged 71 John Wordsworth Faber Harrison, son of Benson and Dorothy Harrison of Green Bank, Ambleside, born Sept. 25, 1835, died Oct. 8th 1849

Ford North of Ambleside, and Sarah his wife He died Feb. 11th 1812, aged 77 By a steady course of generous, firm, and courteous bearing, throughout all the transactions and duties of life, he had gained the sincere respect of all who knew him She died Dec. 23rd 1829, aged 60 By a heart to feel for every one's distresses, and an ever active endeavour to relieve them, she had won the neighbourhood's unaffected love Henry, son of Ford and Sarah North, died Jan 4th 1809

Sir John Richardson, born at Dumfries Nov 5, 1787, died at Langrigg June 5, 1865 Josephine Fanny Richardson, born 5th June, 1836, died 6 Sept 1856. Anna Deborah Richardson, born 22d Feb at Newcastle-on-Tyne died 5 Aug 1872.

James Airey, many years parish clerk and postmaster, and previously schoolmaster of Grasmere, June 18, 1864, aged 60 Sarah, his widow, April 24, 1868, aged 65

William Ross of Manchester and Grasmere, Dec 14, 1872, aged 73

Charles Henry Binstead, 18 Dec 1871, aged 36

David Huddlestone of Ulterwater hall, 27 Oct 1831, aged 65. David and John his sons, and others of his family

Henry Tyson, esq. Astronomer and Mathematician, formerly author of the Kendal Diary, and for many years Manager of the Bank of Westmoreland, March 27, 1852, aged 53

John Walker, aged 28, George Thompson, aged 27, Isaac Tyson, aged 20, Thomas Garnett, aged 20, fellow workmen, carpenters, upset in a sail boat on Lake Windermere, 13 July, 1851

Robert Carlyle of Kirkallans, Grasmere, Oct. 21, 1874; born Oct. 21, 1800. *In cruce salus.*

Frances, wife of Rev Isaac Green, Feb 20, 1836, aged 31 Mary Ann, their dau Oct 21, 1832, aged 3 Thomas Green, M B., April 26, 1876, aged 54, and others of the name.

Edward Brown, late of the Prince of Wales Hotel, Grasmere, Nov 17, 1865, aged 54 Jane, his widow, June 10, 1869, aged 52. Mary, their dau. Jan. 31, 1861, aged 13

Mary, widow of Thomas Hutchinson, formerly of Prinsop Court, Herefordshire, Nov 17, 1858, aged 71

Thomas King, esq of Cossington, Leicestershire, and Hollin Grove, Grasmere, 17 Nov 1831, aged 59 His grandson Thomas King, 4 Oct. 1832. Also his only son Thomas Marshall King, esq Nov 6, 1834, aged 34

With names of Atkinson, Backhouse, Carter, Coward, Dowling, Dixon, Fleming, Greenwood, Gillbanks Heelis, Hodgson, Holmes, Holme, Jones, Mason, Newsham, Pearson, Pask, Robinson, Roughsedge, Sharpe, Stanley, Satterthwaite, Walker, Youdell, etc.

Armorial Bookplate.

ARMS—CARSON OF SHANROE, CO. MONAGHAN.

The Rev. Thomas W Carson, M A, of Beaumont, Terenure, co. Dublin, was born 20 Dec 1834, and is the eldest son of the late Right Rev. Thomas Carson, LL D, Lord Bishop of Kilmore, Elphin, and Ardagh (*see* accompanying Pedigree)

Mr Carson is also co-representative, with his cousin Nicholas Dunscombe of King William's Town, co Cork, Esq. J P, of the elder branch of the family of Waggett of Cork

The Plate was designed by John Leighton, Esq, F S A.

GRANT OF ARMS TO DANIEL BURR OF HOLM LACY, CO. HEREFORD, 1822.*

To all and singular to whom these Presents shall come Sir George Nayler Knight Garter Principal King of Arms and Ralph Bigland Esquire Clarenceux King of Arms of the South East and West Parts of England from the River Trent Southwards send greeting Whereas Daniel Burr of Hom Lacy in the County of Hereford and of Portland Place in the County of Middlesex Esquire, Lieutenant General in the Army in the East Indies, only surviving Son and Heir of Daniel Burr late of Ramsey in the County of Essex Esquire deceased by Elizabeth his Wife only Child of John Davall also of Ramsey aforesaid Esquire deceased hath represented unto Henry Thomas Howard-Molyneux-Howard Esquire commonly called the Right Honourable Lord Henry Thomas Howard-Molyneux-Howard Deputy (with the Royal Approbation) to his Brother the Most Noble Bernard Edward Duke of Norfolk Earl Marshall and Hereditary Marshal of England that he and his Ancestors have hitherto borne for Armorial Ensigns On a Chief indented two Lions Rampant which Arms appear annexed to the Pedigree of a Family of the same Name recorded

* Copied from the original grant in the possession of Higford Burr, Esq

D. Higford D. Burr.

at the Heralds Visitation of London made in the Year 1633 but being at present unable to shew his Descent from the said Family owing to the emigration of his Ancestors to Holland And finding also that the Arms of Davall hitherto used by the Family of his late honoured Mother have not been duly established He therefore requested the favour of his Lordship's Warrant for Our granting and assigning such Armorial Ensigns for Burr and Davall as may be proper to be borne by him and his Descendants and that the Arms of Burr may bear allusion to the Services rendered by him in the East Indies more especially to the Capture of the Island of Ternate on the 21st of June 1801 by the Forces under his Command after an arduous Blockade by Sea and Land of fifty-two Days, And the Memorialist having intermarried with Mary youngest Daughter and Coheir of James Davis late of Chepstow in the County of Monmouth Esquire deceased who was the son of Francis Davis of the same Place by Anne his Wife Daughter of James Higford of Alvington in the County of Gloucester Esquire who was the Great Grandson of John Higford of Dixton in the same County by Frances his Wife sister of John the first Lord Viscount Scudamore, He further requested the favour of His Lordship's Warrant for Our granting and assigning in the same Patent Arms for Davis to be borne by his said Wife and her Descendants according to the Laws of Arms And forasmuch as His Lordship did by Warrant under his Hand and Seal bearing date the Eleventh day of June Instant authorize and direct Us to grant and exemplify such Armorial Ensigns accordingly Know ye therefore that We the said Garter and Clarenceux in pursuance of His Lordship's Warrant and by virtue of the Letters Patent of Our several Offices to each of Us respectively granted do by these Presents grant and exemplify unto the said Daniel Burr the Arms following that is to say Quarterly First and Fourth Ermine on a Mount Vert within a park paling and a Gate of three Bars proper a Lion rampant Or holding in the Dexter paw a Scymetar, and in the Sinister a Sheaf of seven Arrows points upwards also proper, a chief indented Sable thereon two Lions rampant Argent for Burr Second and Third Gules a Lion rampant within an Orle of eight Fleurs de lis Argent supporting in the forepaws a ducal Crown Or for Davall And for the Crest Out of a Mural Crown Argent inscribed with the Word TERNATE Sable a Demi-Malay Soldier habited and armed with a Kreese the dexter Arm supporting a Standard intended to represent that taken at the Capture of the aforesaid Island of Ternate by the said Lieutenant General Burr, all proper, the sinister hand resting on the Mural Crown as the same are in the Margin hereof more plainly depicted to be borne and used for ever hereafter by him the said Daniel Burr and by his Descendants with due and proper differences according to the Laws of Arms And we do hereby further grant and assign the Arms following for Davis vizt Gules on a bend Ermine a Lion passant Sable, in the sinister Canton a Rose Argent barbed and seeded proper as the same are on the Escocheon of Pretence in the Margin hereof also depicted to be borne and used for ever hereafter by the said Mary Burr and her Descendants according to the Laws of Arms In Witness whereof We the said Garter and Clarenceux Kings of Arms have to these Presents subscribed Our Names and affixed the Seals of Our several Offices this thirteenth day of June in the third Year of the Reign of Our Sovereign Lord George the Fourth by the Grace of God of the United Kingdom of Great Britain and Ireland King Defender of the Faith etc. and in the Year of Our Lord one thousand eight hundred and twenty-two

In behalf of Sir George Nayler, RALPH BIGLAND Clarenceux Deputy Garter.

RALPH BIGLAND, Clarenceux King of Arms.

JOHN SAVAGE married Mary, eldest daughter of Henry Pincke of North Waltham, co Hants, about the year 1766 From which branch of the Savage family was he descended? In the will of Henry Pincke, proved at Winchester Sept. 22, 1768, he is called "John Savage the younger"

Leigh, Lancashire. W. D. PINK.

THE DENNYS,

EARLS OF NORWICH, BARONS DENNY OF WALTHAM, AND BARONETS OF IRELAND

(*Continued from page* 116)

The County of Kerry, after the taking of Sir Edward Denny's Castle in 1642, continued entirely in the hands of the Irish Catholics until 1650, when it was reduced for the parliament by Ludlow, Sir Hardress Waller, and Colonels Le Hunte and Sadlier Sir Edward Denny seems to have died before the latter year, and his son and heir, Arthur, born in 1629 (*v ante* pp. 76 and 113), submitted outwardly at least to the Cromwellian Government He was just twenty-two years of age when he married the Lady Ellen Barry, daughter of David, first Earl of Barrymore, by the Lady Alice Boyle, daughter of the first Earl of Cork, and began another page of the old diary (which his father had left off keeping in the memorable autumn of 1641), with the following entries —

"Ye Ende of one Generation and ye Beginning of another"

"I was marry'd upon ye 9th of September, 1651, to the Lady Ellen Barry daughter to ye Earle of Barrymore

(*Signed*) "ARTHUR DENNY"

"Edward Denny, my heire was born att Castle Lyons uponn ye 10th of Februarie 1652, between eleaven and twelve o'Clock in ye Morning, his godmother ye Lady Broghil,(*a*) his godfather ye Earle of Cork(*b*) and Mr Percy Smith (*c*)

"I began to keep howse in this greate Castell of Tralye, November (illegible) 1653

"Arthur Denny(*d*) was born att Castle Lyons ye 2d of January att 2 of the Clock on Wensdaye morning, 1660, his grandmother was Martha Countess of Barrymore, his godfathers ffrancis Lord Viscount Shannon and John Jephson of Moyalloe Esq.

"William Denny(*e*) was born att Tralye January 16th, 1663, his godfather was William Lord Baron of Kerry and John Blennerhassett Esq. ye son of Robert Blennerhassett and Mrs Honora Stoughton, my sister Elizabeth 'Hassett his godmother

"Ellen Denny(*f*) was born att Tralye, Aprill 3d 1665, her godfathers were my brother Lucius Denny and my cosen Francis Lynn, her godmothers Mrs Isabella Vaukher and Mrs Joane Comyns."

This is the last entry made by Arthur Denny He was High Sheriff of Kerry in 1656, and was returned M P for the county in the year after the Restoration On the death of his first wife, Lady Ellen Denny, he married in or about 1670, Frances, daughter of Sir Richard Kerle or Kyrle, by whom he had no issue. He died in March, 1672, and was buried with his first wife in the family vault in Tralee Church. His eldest son Edward made no entries in the old MS diary, so that I cannot fix the dates of his marriage and of the births of his numerous children In the fly-leaf of the old Bible mentioned at page 115, there is the following entry made, apparently, by the Rev. William Stanford, the then Rector or Curate of Tralee

"1686 The 7th of January died in Traly, that worthy and ingenuous Gentleman, Arthur Blennerhassett, Esq of Ballyseedy, one of his Majestye's Justices of the Peace, and was buryed in Ballycarthy, being the Parish Church where his family are interred, to the great Griefe of all that knew him being a Gentleman of exquisite parts"

This Arthur Blennerhassett was the eldest son of John Blennerhassett, who had married in 1654, Elizabeth Denny (*v ante*, p 115, note *e*), and therefore the first cousin of Edward Denny, eldest son of Arthur and Lady Ellen Edward Denny in his father's lifetime, or soon after his death, married Mary daughter of Sir Boyle Maynard, Knt of Curryglass, in the county Cork One of the sisters of Mary Maynard had married the above mentioned Arthur Blennerhassett, who died s. p probably at the castle of his cousin and brother-in-law, while another sister married Barry Denny, son of Edward of Castle Lyons, mentioned at p 115, note *a*. Within little more than two years after the rector of Tralee had made the above record of Arthur Blennerhassett's untimely death, and while Edward Denny's children were still young, another great civil war broke out all over Ireland, and at once, as in 1642, the Roman Catholic party became dominant in Kerry A great number of Protestants, as Macaulay and Froude have told us, fled from the country to England, dreading a repetition of the miseries of 1641–2, but a few, Edward Denny amongst the rest, remained, seemingly reluctant to desert the cause of James the Second, although they had good reason to fear that its success would prove their ruin The name of Edward Denny is not mentioned in the black list of thirty-two Kerry estate owners who were marked down for attainder by the Irish Convention of 1689, unless they submitted by the 10th of August or 1st of October in that year to the Stuart king, but that of Barry Denny appears in it. Edward Rice and John Hussey were the M P s for Tralee in 1689, while Nicholas Browne, ancestor of Lord Kenmare, represented the County The Jacobites continued in possession of Kerry until 1691, when Brigadier Levison with seven hundred Williamite horse entered it, and was opposed by the troops under Lord Brittas and Sir James Cotter. The latter was a neighbour and old acquaintance of the Maynard family in Cork, and it appears that Edward and Mrs Denny (*née* Maynard) opened a negotiation with Sir James, giving him a sum of money on his promising not to destroy Tralee Castle. There was nothing strictly speaking dishonourable to either party in the proposal or acceptance of such an offer, as Edward Denny had remained neutral in the civil strife, and had not been attainted by the Convention, which would have gained nothing by the destruction of his castle He appears to have left it, probably to place his wife and children in safety at Cork or Dublin, and the Reverend William Stanford remained in rather a perilous position, watching over his Church and the few Protestant parishioners who had not been able to leave the little town The following entries in the fly-leaves of the old Bible tell the state of affairs in Tralee in 1689–1691 graphically enough —

"Traly Church Bible, 20th May, 1689, being then put into my custody.—W S

"Ye 2d of September, 1691, the Castle of Traly, the seat of that worthy, constant, and loyall gentleman, Edward Denny, Esq , was burnte by Colonel Rutte, by order of Sir James Cotter, who was then Governor of the County Kerrye, after he had received a good sum from Madam Denny to save it, and engaged his Hand and Faith to the performance thereof, but he not like a Gentleman broke his engagement "

"The Destroyer is destroyed and we are preserved, so they that sow in Tears shall reape in Joye

(*Signed*) "WILLIAM STANFORD"

The last entry was probably written in October, 1691, when Brigadier Levison's troops, having been reinforced by a detachment sent by Ginkel from Limerick, and some volunteers from that county, headed by the Hon William Fitz Maurice, ancestor of Lord Muskerry, and second son of the 20th Lord Kerry (by Constance dau of William Long of York), reduced Kerry for King William Smith, in his 'History of Kerry,' published in 1758, a work to which Macaulay expressed himself indebted, says that Tralee Castle and town were burned by Captains Navarre and Houlahan, serving under Sir James Cotter,(*g*) and that Ginkel ordered them to be hung, but that they were pardoned at the intercession of Edward Denny The following entry was made in the old Bible by him on his return to Tralee —

"This Bible was preserved by the care of William Stanford all the tyme of the War, more especially when this Town was burnte in August and September, 1691. Given under my hand this 10th of October, 1691 Tralye County Kerrye"

(*a*) Lady Broghill was the Lady Margaret Howard, daughter of the 2nd Earl of Suffolk, (grandson of the 4th Duke of Norfolk) who had married Roger Boyle (fifth son of the 1st Earl of Cork), created Lord Broghill at the age of six years and Earl of Orrery by Charles the Second He was the grand-uncle of the infant heir of Arthur and Lady Ellen Denny, for whom his wife stood sponsor

(*b*) Richard, 2nd Earl of Cork He was brother of the Earl of Orrery, Lord Broghill of the preceding note, and therefore his godson's grand-uncle He married Lady Elizabeth Clifford, daughter and eventually heiress of Henry Earl of Cumberland, and granddaughter maternally of Robert Cecil, Earl of Salisbury, whose niece Lady Mary Cecil had married Edward Denny, Earl of Norwich (*v ante*, p 74) Richard Earl of Cork was created Earl of Burlington in 1663 His great grandson Richard, 4th Earl of Cork and 3rd Earl of Burlington claimed and was allowed the Barony of Clifford, but dying without male issue, the English Earldom expired, while the Barony devolved on his daughter Charlotte, who married the 4th Duke of Devonshire, for whose third son by her the Earldom of Burlington was revived, while the Irish Earldom of Cork passed to the great-grandson of Roger, Earl of Orrery, Baron Broghill above mentioned

(*c*) Percy Smith of Ballynytray, in the County Waterford, was the nephew maternally of the first Earl of Cork (*v Burke's 'Landed Gentry'*)

(*d*) Arthur Denny died unmarried Castle Lyons, where he and his elder brother were born, was the mansion of the Earls of Barrymore In 1789, Archdall describes it as still "a stately fabric in the county of Cork," but the ruinous prodigality of the two last Earls caused it and most of the ancient possessions of this long-descended family to pass away to strangers Hooker's translation of Cambrensis, dedicated to Sir Walter Raleigh describes the Barrys as then, in the seventeenth century, "in nothing degenerate from their first ancestor (Philip De Barry of 1172), noble and valiant gentlemen who for their fidelity and good sense were advanced to honour and made Viscounts, but would to God' he adds, "they were not so misled, rooted, and altogether seized in Irishrie, their name and honours onlie beinge Englishe alle the reste for the most parte Irishe!" Martha, Countess of Barrymore (the 2nd wife of Richard, 2nd Earl), the child's godmother, was however an Englishwoman, the daughter of Henry Lawrence, Esq, an English Roman Catholic, who seems to have been an agent of Glamorgan's, and who played a curious part at the siege of Tralee Castle in 1642, of which I shall have more to say hereafter when giving some papers found on him at the time he was made prisoner by the garrison Lord Shannon, the child's godfather was the 6th son of the 1st Earl of Cork, and John Jephson of Moyalloe (Mallow) was his son-in-law, and the ancestor of the present Sir Denham Jephson Norreys, Baronet, of Mallow Castle

(*e*) William Denny died unmarried. His godfather William, 20th Lord Kerry, was father of Thomas, created Earl of Kerry, ancestor of Lords Lansdowne and Orkney John Blennerhassett (who died unmarried) was the son of Robert Blennerhassett of Littur, county Kerry (younger brother of the owner of Ballyseedy) by Honora Stoughton, grand-daughter maternally of Dermot O'Brien fifth Baron of Inchiquin From this Robert and Honora descends in the female line Rowland Ponsonby Blennerhassett Esq, M P for Kerry The wife of the fifth Baron of Inchiquin Dame Ellen Fitz Gerald of Cloyne, was the great-great-granddaughter of James Fitz Gerald, 11th Earl of Desmond, thus the present M P for Kerry above mentioned descends from the extinct Earls of Desmond and the O'Briens, Lords Inchiquin Elizabeth 'Hassett or Blennerhassett was the wife of John of Ballyseedy, mentioned at p 115, note *e*

(*f*) Ellen Denny married John Carrique, Esq, of Glandine, county Kerry Francis Lynn seems to have been a relative of William Lynn, who married Mary Forest, sister of the wife of Arthur Denny (*v ante* p 76) and Mrs Vaukher, or Vaucher, was probably the daughter of the Huguenot officer mentioned at p 116 note *f*

(*g*) It is but fair to Sir James Cotter to observe that he was very probably unable to restrain his troops from burning the Castle of Tralee The two Captains whom Smith mentions as its destroyers were strangers, one a Frenchman Sir James was included in the Articles of Limerick, and the Parliament paid for the rebuilding of the castle

M. A. H.

(*To be continued*)

NOTES RELATING TO THE FAMILY OF ANDREWS,*

TAKEN FROM A CHURCH SERVICE BOOK CONTAINING THE COMMON PRAYER, 1682, THE NEW TESTAMENT, 1679, THE METRICAL VERSION OF THE PSALMS BY STERNHOLD AND HOPKINS, 1684, ETC

[This book is in the possession of William Long, Esq, F S.A, of West Hay, Wrington, 1878]

Births

My son John, born June ye 24th (16)96 between 5 & 6 in ye morn Christened about 10 ye same Evening, being Wednesday

My son Hildebrand born Aug^st 21 being Satterday (16)97 about 10 in ye morn Christened Satterday 28° of the same

My son Richard, born Decb^r 13° being tuesday 1698 between 1 & 2 in ye morn baptized ye 20th ditto.

My daughter Mary, born Decr 14°, being thursday, 1699 about 3 in ye morn baptiz'd ye 20th ditto

* Contributed by Rev F J. POYNTON

My son Richard, born March ye 21st 1700 [query error for 1701 See previous birth] being friday, a few minutes before 8 at night baptized Tuesday 25th ditto

My daughter Elizabeth born Sept ye 15th being Tuesday about 4 in ye morn baptized ye 22 Foll 1702

My son Robert born Sept. 3d (being friday) 1703 abt 11° in the morn baptized ye 5° Foll being Sunday

My son Thomas, born friday ffeby 1° 1705 abt 4 in the morn baptiz'd ye same Evening

My son Hugh, born tuesday Xber 23° 1707 abt 6 in ye Evening at Hodnet Hall in Shropshire Baptiz'd ye 29° foll

My son Henry, born Tuesday May 29° 1711 a quarter after 2 in ye morn at Hodnet hall in Shropshire. Baptized ye 2° of June ffoll.

Obituary.

Bro. John dyed ye 26th of feby 1695–6 being Wednesday.

My son John dye'd Jany 26° 1696 about 8 of ye Clock in ye morn being tuesday

My dear childe Hildebrand dye'd June ye 29° being Thursday between 12 & 1 in ye morn 1699.

My dear childe Richard dye'd at Cheam July ye 5° being Friday about 10 at night & was buried in ye Parish Church aforesaid on Sunday ye 7° ditto 1700

My daughter Elizabeth dye'd at Cheam Sepr 26° 1702 being Satterday abt 2 afternoon and was buryed in ye Parish Church aforesaid on Monday ye 28 ditto

My son Thomas dy'd at Hampsted ffriday April 12° 1706 and was buried in Hampsted Churchyard ye 13° instant

My son Henry dye'd at Hodnet hall June 9° abt 11 at night being Satterday Buried in Hodnet Chancell Munday Evening foll being ye 11° instant

*My ffather dyed November 11th 1734 about 10 at night aged 70 ye 24 Augst then last past in Great Russell Street, Bloomsbury & was interred in the vaults under Grosvenor Chappell. Entd p Robt Andrews

*My mother dyed in Great Russell Street 17th Decr 1749 aged 86 & was buried in my vault at Hanwell R Andrews

*My Bror Richd dyed in Great Russell Street 20th of Decr 1751 and was buried in Hillingdon Churchyard by his own desire † (R Andrews)

‡My uncle Hugh Andrews died at Rugeley in Staffordshire 1779 and was bur. there

‡My Aunt Mary Andrews died Novr ye 6th 1781§ in Mount Street and was buried in the vaults at Grosvenor Chapel the 10th day of the same month

(*To be continued.*)

HUBBARD PEDIGREE, Vol. III, pp 107, 108 —In Castor Church, Northants, is a flat stone thus inscribed —Here lieth the body of Mary, wife of William Hubbard, of Langham in the county of Rutland, daughter of William and Mary Serjeant of Castor. She died Nov 19, 1742, aged 22 Adjoining is a marble tablet to her father and mother he ob 22 July, 1744, aged 53, and she 31 Jan 1765, aged 68 Near to is another to Mary, wife of Mr Wright Serjeant, dau of Henry Dove, esq died 24 Aug 1750, aged 25, and her husband, 11 Feb 1787, aged 59 She was the eldest dau of Henry Dove, esq (bur at Tinwell, Rutland, 3 Oct 1766), descended from Tho Dove, Bishop of Peterborough, d 30 Aug 1630 She was b 26, bapt 28 Dec 1724, at Castor, and was mar 26 May, 1750, to Wright Serjeant. I may add that Langham and Barleythorpe are but a short mile apart.

JUSTIN SIMPSON

---

* These three entries made by Robert Andrews of the Inner Temple, continuing his father's (Richard Andrews) obituary list

† This is the second Richard, as is evident from observation of the above dates

‡ These two entries marked ‡ are in a lady's handwriting, which would seem to be that of Catharine Nott (*née* Andrews), who handed on the book to her daughter Elizabeth, whose name is inscribed over the vignette on its title page

§ This date is indistinct. It may possibly be 1785

NOTES ON THE FAMILY OF PROWSE, OF COMPTON BISHOP, CO SOMERSET.

Communicated by EDWARD FRY WADE, ESQ, *Axbridge, Somerset*

FROM AXBRIDGE CHURCH.

Anna Deo et Chara et cura marito Joanni Prowse generoso conjux peramata et pia patri Guil'mo Spearing istius Burgi ter Maori Agnitiq' uxori ejus filia unica postquam bene vixisset hic latère voluit in virtutes in aliis singula in ea emicuissent singulares longœua q^d bona paucos exegit dies multos habuit annos virtutis optimum et monumentum et munimentum Ingenio clara innocentia candida corpus morti triumphatum animam Deo triumphantem reddidit et victrix et victa mors eternum captiva exuvias depromet in gloria Præijt not perijt resurget Obijt die mens. May Anno Dom 1668, ætat suæ 23

ARMS —*Sable, three lions rampant argent*
CREST —*Out of a ducal coronet a demi-lion rampant.*

Near this Pillar lyeth the body of William Spearing, Gent, four times Mayor of this Town, who died in the Year of our Lord 1690 and in the 74th year of his age

Also near this Monument lieth the Body of John Andrews, Gent, three times Mayor of this Town, who departed this life ye last day of December in the year of our Lord 1720, in the 83rd year of his age. He was Nephew, Heir, and Executor of the above-said Wm Spearing

Likewise near this place (under the same stone) are deposited the remains of John Andrews, Gent (son of the above-named John Andrews), who died 16th October 1728 aged 55 And of Sarah his Wife (daughter of William Boulting of Theale Esqre), who departed this life 19th January 1740 aged 52.

ARMS.—*Argent, a bend cottised sable*

M P Q S. Guelimus Prowse* generosus juris (si quisalius) peritus etiam et probus natus apud Simonsborough in agro Damnon'iorn domum incluta majorum serie insignitam apud Axbridge in agro Sommersetensi denatus et hic sepultus est Prid callend April anno salutis nostræ MDCCLXX Ætatis suæ LXXX°.

Sacræ memoriæ monumentum piæ Gratitudinis Testimonium posuit et consecravit pronepos et exalse hæres Joannes Prowse Armiger

ARMS AND CREST —PROWSE, as before

[NOTE —I cannot vouch for the correctness of the grammar in these two Latin inscriptions but they are copied *verbatim* from the originals The first contains the figure of a woman (in wood) kneeling before a desk in prayer The second is the half-length figure of a man habited in the dress of the period]

In hopes of a blessed resurrection here lyes the body of John Prowse, late of this Town of Axbridge Esqr His father was John Prowse Esqre, who died in June 1688, and lies buried in the Parish Church of Compton Bishop, Nephew and Heir of William Prowse Esqre, whose Monument is seen in this Church, and his mother was Anne eldest daughter and coheiress of Roger Newborough of Barkley in this County Esqre. He had two wives, his first was Margaret daughter of William Bragge of Sadborough in the County of Devon Esqre, who died in Child-bed in December 1702, and was buried at Compton Bishop And his second was Abigail daughter of George Lord Bishop of this Diocese, by whom he had Thomas, yet living, his only child He had the Honour to serve the Queen in his County as Justice of the Peace and Colonel of the Bath Regiment, and to be unanimously elected Knight of the Shire for the Parliament called in the year 1708 And in

* I shall be glad if any correspondent can give me the parentage of this William Prowse Will a reference to Halstead Genealogists afford the information?

the diligent and faithful attendance on that Service he died of the Small Pox at Westminster on the 4th day of April 1710, and in the 34th year of his age, much lamented To the Memory of her very affectionate and dearly beloved Husband, Abigail, his sorrowful Widow and Executrix, erected this Monument in the year 1712

ARMS —*Quarterly, sable, three lions rampant argent,* PROWSE; *or, three bends azure within a bordure engrailed gules,* NEWBOROUGH, *impaling on the dexter side arg, a chevron vert, between three bulls passant gules,* BRAGGE, *On the sinister side, gyronny of eight, or and ermine, a castle triple towered sable,* HOOPER *

Sacred to the Memory of Abigail Prowse, widow of John Prowse Esq[re] and daughter of the Rev[d] D[r] George Hooper, who was Bishop of this Diocese She was one of the most accomplished Women of her time, admired for her excellent Understanding, extensive Knowledge and agreeable Manners, and beloved for her eminent and exemplary Piety The early part of her life was dedicated to the care and education of her Son, and she lived to see the happy effects of that care in him and in his Children She died 15th Nov[r] 1763, in the 80th year of her age

ARMS.—PROWSE AND NEWBOROUGH, *quarterly, on an escutcheon of pretence,* HOOPER

(*To be continued*)

MONUMENTAL INSCRIPTIONS AT WILFORD, NOTTINGHAMSHIRE

Communicated by CAPTAIN A E. LAWSON LOWE, F S A

Upon a large mural monument on the north wall of the chancel (now concealed behind the organ) —

Near this Place
Lieth interred the Body of
The Rev[d] John Woods,([a]) M A
Late Rector of this Parish and
of Costlingstock, in this County
He married Catherine the Daughter of
John Bridges, Esq[r], of Barton,
In the County of Northampton,
By whom He left two Daughters
He died Feb[y] 29th, 1752 Aged 73.
She died Jan[ry] 29th, 1732
Aged LII

ARMS —*Quarterly, 1 and 4 Argent, an eagle with wings expanded sable, preying upon an infant swaddled of the last, banded or, face proper 2 and 3 Gules, three ancient drinking-cups argent*—for RISLEY CREST —*Upon an oak tree vert, fructed or, a raven sable* MOTTO —Fato prudentia Major ([b])

Upon another mural monument on the opposite side of the chancel —

Near this place
Lies y[e] Body of y[e] Rev[d] Henry Woods,([c]) M A
late Rector of Lambley & of Stanford,
In this County, who died March y[e] 24th, 1755
In the 66th year of his age.

* Bedford, in his 'Blazon of Episcopacy,' gives these arms to Bishop Hooper, but Cassan in his 'Lives of the Bishops of Bath and Wells' says Hooper had ' no right to arms, none being recorded at the Heralds College, London, at Ulster's, or Lord Lyon's offices " He died in 1727 For Monument, see 'Gentleman's Magazine,' vol lxii, p. 596

As he fulfilled his Ministerial Charge
with great Sufficiency and Credit,
so was he in other important Relations of Life
not less eminent
He was a kind Master, an obliging Neighbour,
an affectionate Friend and an agreeable Companion
But above all He adorned the Married State,
in which he lived near Twenty Years,
in the most perfect Union and Harmony
with Her
who, in memory of One so dear to herself
and so much esteemed by others,
caused this Monument to be erected A D 1755
By his side lies his Infant Son.

Also the Remains of
Sarah Woods
Relict of the Revd Henry Woods.

ARMS —As upon the last-named monument.

Upon a floor-stone on the south side of the chancel —

Here lyeth Interred y^e^
Body of Henery,
Son of ye Rev^nd^ Henery
Woods(^d^) and Sarah his
Wife, who departed
This Life December 29,
Aged 2 Years.
1736

(^a^) "Mr John Woods, Clerk, Rector of this Parish, buried March 5th, 1732"—*Parish Register* He was the eldest son of Hamlet Woods of West Leigh, and afterwards of Risley, co Lancaster, Esq, by his marriage (at Winwick May the 23rd 1678) with Elizabeth, only daughter of John Risley of Risley, Esq In 1702, he inherited the Risley and Broseley estates under the will of his cousin, John Risley Esq, who died that year and was buried at Winwick (*vide* 'Misc Gen et Heraldica,' Vol II p 275) In 1732, the rectory of Wilford having become vacant by the death of the Rev Benjamin Carter, he was presented to that benefice by Sir Robert Clifton, Bart, and he also held the rectory of Cortlingstock now called Costock There are entries in the Wilford registers of the marriages of his daughters and coheiresses, namely, "Mr Richard Arnold, Clerk Rect^r^ of Thurkinson (*Thurcaston*) in the County of Leicester and Mrs Catherine Woods of this Parish married Nov 6 1735," and "Mr Joseph Milner Clerk Rector of Barton, and Mrs Elizabeth Woods of this Parish married by License May 30, 1750" His wife appears to have been interred elsewhere as no entry of her burial is to be found in the Wilford registers

(^b^) These arms are those of the Risley family, which appear to have been assumed by the children of Hamlet Woods, Esq and Elizabeth his wife In the Visitation of Lancashire made in 1665, the arms of the Risleys of Risley, in that county, are described by Sir William Dugdale as—Argent, a tree sable with a raven perched thereon It is however, doubtful if such arms were ever borne by the family, though their crest was a raven perching upon an oak tree In the second and third quarters, birds seem to have been not unfrequently substituted by the Risleys themselves for the peculiar charges which appear upon the arms on the monuments at Wilford The seal of John Risley Esq, who died in 1682 (an engraving of which is given in the 'Misc Gen et Heraldica,' Vol II, p 274), furnishes an example of this

(^c^) "Mr Henry Woods, Rector of Lambley, buried 29th March, 1755"—*Parish Register* He was a younger brother of the above-named John Woods and the fifth son of Hamlet Woods, Esq and Elizabeth his wife Besides Lambley, he was also rector of Stanford, near Loughborough, to which benefice he was presented by Charles Lewis, Esq in 1722 His widow survived him for upwards of thirteen years, and her interment is thus recorded in the Wilford registers "Sarah, Widow of the late Revd Henry Woods, Rector of Lamley in this County, buried in the Chancel June 29th, 1768"

(^d^) "Henry, son of Henry Woods, Clerk, and Sarah his wife, buried Dec 30th, 1736"—*Parish Register.*

(*To be continued.*)

NOTES ON THE FAMILY OF PROWSE, OF COMPTON BISHOP, CO SOMERSET *

(*Continued from page* 163.)

FROM AXBRIDGE CHURCH.

Sacred to the Memory of Thomas Prowse Esqre, the only son of John Prowse and Abigail his Wife He was five times unanimously chosen Knight of the Shire for the County of Somerset, and discharged his duty in Parliament with ability, integrity and honour Though frequently solicited he never could be prevailed on to accept any office in the State He loved his Country, and thought he could better serve it in his private independent Station He was perfectly from Vanity or Ambition, not conscious himself of those accomplishments and that distinguished merit which acquired for him the Esteem of all who knew him And ever attentive rather to promote the Interest and Happiness of others than his own, He knew how to suffer Adversity or to enjoy Prosperity with the same truly Christian Spirit and to make the proper use of both He was blessed with many opportunities of doing good, and met with uncommon returns of Gratitude from those of all ranks who experienced his generous Friendship and extensive Charity No Flattery shall stain his Monument, but it would be unpardonable to lay down in Silence one who was an Ornament and a Blessing not only to his Family, but to his Country After a long series of ill-health and patient suffering, in sure and certain hope of a blessed Resurrection, he calmly resigned his Soul into the Hands of God on the 1st of Jany 1767, aged 59 Few have lived so greatly beloved or died so universally lamented. He married Elizabeth daughter of John Sharp Esqre of Grafton Park in Northamptonshire, and by her had Eight Children, six of whom he buried near him —Elizth, born Oct 30th 1736, died Jany 21st 1742, Elizabeth, born March 10th 1744, died March 19th 1746, Charles, born Jany 21st 1747, died June 15th 1756, Susan, born May 29th 1742, died Feby 17th 1758 John, who inherited his Father's Virtues, soon followed his beloved Sister He died Feby 27th 1758, in the 24th year of his age George, the only surviving son of Thomas Prowse, died Augt 25th 1767 After a blameless life of Thirty years, he married Elizabeth† daughter of the Revd Dr Thomas Sharp, Archdeacon of Northumberland, but had no child Elizabeth, relict of Thomas Prowse, died June 18th 1780, aged 68. Her praise is anticipated by the above Memorial, composed by herself to the merits of her Family. She left this small space to be filled by her surviving Children, who complying with her desire forbear any other Tribute to the Piety and Virtue of which her Life and death exhibited the most shining example

ARMS —*Quarterly*, 1*st and* 4*th*, PROWSE. 2*nd and* 3*rd*, NEWBOROUGH *On an escutcheon of pretence, quarterly*, 1*st and* 4*th, azure, a pheon within a bordure or, entoyre of torteaux.* SHARP. 2*nd and* 3*rd, party per bend sinister ermine, and ermines a lion rampant, or* HOSIER

CREST —PROWSE, *as before*

[Thomas Prowse was Recorder of Wells from 1745 to 1752, when he resigned, also Recorder of Axbridge]

In memory of Mary, the eldest sister of Dame Elizabeth Mordaunt, and co-heiress with her of the property of their family She was married in 1783 to the Revd John Methuen Rogers (afterwards Rector of Berkley), and was buried there in the year 1800 Considerable estates in that place and its vicinity belonged to her, to which also Lady Mordaunt's grandson, now a minor, is heir In these two sisters (whose paternal and maternal ancestors were Dr George Hooper, Bishop of this Diocese, and Dr John Sharp, Archbishop of York) their own family name of Prowse became extinct, but the Christian virtues that adorned the lives and characters of each, and the use they made of the ample means they inherited for being "rich in

* Communicated by EDWARD FRY WADE, Esq Axbridge, Somerset

† She never remarried, and dying Feb 23rd, 1810, aged 77, was buried at Fulham, co Middlesex, in which churchyard there is a tomb erected to her memory as also to that of her brother William Sharp, Esq, who died March 17th, 1810, aged 81

good works," bespoke them worthy of so respectable an ancestry, and will embalm their memories in general esteem.

In memory of Dame Elizabeth Mordaunt, Widow of Sir John Mordaunt of Walton in the county of Warwick, Bart., whom she survived 20 years She was the youngest daughter of Thomas Prowse, Esq[re], and Elizabeth his wife, and dying at Hampstead on the 6th October, 1826, was buried at Walton on the 14th of the same month, aged 77 This lady, in whom terminated a long line of highly respected ancestry, possessed within herself a character far superior to all that names or titles on monumental tablets can bestow It was that of a sincere Christian, acting on genuine Christian principles in all the relations of life Her peculiar characteristic indeed was that of unbounded liberality without ostentation, to such of the poor as were most proper and deserving objects of her bounty. On her decease a fair inheritance in this vicinity and in Northamptonshire devolved to her grandson Sir John Mordaunt, Bart

COMPTON BISHOP

On a flat stone in the chancel is a partially obliterated inscription to the memory of William Prowse, who died in June (or July) 1677.

On another

Here lyeth the body of Mary davghter of John Prowse of this parish Esq[re] who dyed the Fovrth day of April in the eighth Moneth of her age Anno Dom MDCLXXXI. And also the body of Thomas Prowse, son of the said John, who dyed the Fovrteenth day of September in the yeare aforesaid and in the Third yeare of his age

---

Here lies the body of John Prowse Esq[re] of this parish, who died in the year 1688, as also of Anne* his wife, daughter and co-heiress of Roger Newborough of Berkley in this county, Esq[re] She died in the year 1740 They had seven children, Newborough, Thomas, William, and Mary, died young, Elizabeth in 1725, and Ann in 1729, and are all buried in this church John, their second son, who succeeded his father, lies buried at Axbridge Margaret, his first wife (daughter of William Bragg of Sadborough in the county of Devon, Esq[re]), was buried here with a still-born daughter in the year 1702 Thomas Prowse, Esq[re], only son of the aforesaid John Prowse, erected this monument to their memory in the year 1751

ARMS —PROWSE *impaling* NEWBOROUGH

WELLS CATHEDRAL (IN CLOISTERS)

In hope of a blessed resurrection near this place rests the body of Abigail, daughter of Richard Guilford, Gent, and wife of D[r] George Hooper, late Lord Bishop of this Diocese She lived 46 years and had 9 children, of which two sons and five daughters dying young, were buried in the Church of Lambeth, Surrey She died Sept[r] 24th, 1726, in the 71st year of her age Near her lyeth the remains of Rebecca, her youngest daughter, who died June 4, 1716, in the 21st year of her age As does also the body of Charles Guilford, Gent, her brother, who died in April, 1707, in the 42nd year of his age Erected 1728 by Abigail Prowse, their fourth and only surviving daughter.

WELLS CATHEDRAL

Here lyeth the body of M[rs] Mary Prowse, wife of Charles Prowse† of Croydon in this county, Esq[re], and daughter of Thomas Carew, late of Cannington, Esq, who departed this life 3rd day of May 1733, in the 30th year of her age

ARMS —PROWSE *impaling three lioncels passant* CAREW

In memory of Elizabeth Carew, daughter of Thomas Carew of Cannington, .. 1733

EXTRACTS FROM REGISTERS, AXBRIDGE CHURCH.

Baptisms

1672	Mch 19th	Newborough son of John Prowse Esq[re]
1674.	Mch 24th	Ann daughter of John Prowse Esq[re]
1676	Mch. 11th	John son of John Prowse Esq[re].

* They were married at Berkley in the year 1670

† I do not know that this man was a connection of the Axbridge and Compton Bishop Family

1678. Jany 10th. Thomas son of John Prowse Esqre.
1617. July 13. Frances the daughter of James Jeffrey.
1646. March 3rd. Anne daughter of William and Agnes Spearing.

Burials.

1666. Octr 22nd. Mrs Francis wife of Mr Wm Prowse of West Street.
1667. May 21st. Mrs Anne wife of Mr John Prowse.
1670. March 31st. Mr Wm Prowse Gent.
1710. Ap^{l} 10th. The Honourable Colonel John Prowse Esqre.
1742. Jany 24. Mrs Elizabeth daughter of Thomas Prowse Esqre.
1746. March 27. Mrs Elizabeth daughter of Thomas Prowse Esqre.
1758. Feby 24th. Mrs Susanna daughter of Thomas Prowse Esqre.
1758. Mch. 9th. Mr John Prowse son of Thomas Prowse Esqre.
1763. Novr 24th. Mrs Abigail Prowse, Widow, aged 80.
1767. Jany 12. The Honourable Thomas Prowse Esqre one of ye Members for ye County and Major of the Militia.
1767. Septr 3rd. Mr George Prowse son of Thomas Prowse Esqre.

Marriages.

1645. Novr 20. Mr William Prowse and Frances Jeffery.
1665. Feby 10th. Mr John Prowse and Mrs Ann Spearing.

COMPTON BISHOP CHURCH REGISTERS.

William Prowse Gent. was buried ye 2nd July 1677.
. . . . Prowse sonne of John Prowse Esqre . . . . his wife was buried 5th February 1685.
Mad^{m}* Jane Prowse was buried ye 19th day of December 1702.
Mrs Anne Prowse, Widow, was buried March 21st 1739.

PROWSE OF COMPTON HOUSE, COMPTON BISHOP, CO. SOMERSET.

ARMS.—*Sable, three lions rampant argent.*
CREST.—*Out of a ducal coronet a demi-lion rampant.*

Prowse.

Prowse. Prowse.

William Prowse,† b. at Simonsborough, co. Devon. Buried at Axbridge, co. Somerset, 31 March, 1670, aged 80. = Frances d. of James Jeffrey of Axbridge. Mar. 5 Nov. 1645. Bur. Oct. 22, 1666.

John. Susan = . . . Salter. Agnes = William Spearing. John Prowse, late of Simonsborough. Dead in 1667.

A B

* This is evidently meant for Margaret Prowse; *vide* monument.

† Will of William Prowse of the West Street of Axbridge within the parish of Compton Bishop in the county of Somerset gent., whereby he makes the following devises and bequests. To the poor of Compton Bishop Axbridge Congresbury Winscombe Weeke St. Lawrence Weeke Badgworth and Nempnett, to each parish 40s. Unto my brother John Prowse if living at my death, £40, and to each of his children then living £10. Unto my sister Susan Salter and unto her son and daughter, if living, £10 each. Unto my cosen Henry Trood, if living, £10. Unto my cosen Alexander Gready and his sister my cosen Joan Blackmore if living £10 each. Unto my cosen Edward Thurston and to every one of his brothers and sisters forty shillings a piece to be bestowed by them in gould rings. Unto my cousen Thomas Prowse and William Prowse sons of my cousen John Prowse late of Symondsborowe in the parish of Hennocke in the county of Devon deceased £200 a piece. Unto my brother-in-law Mr. James Jeffery 40s. and to my cosens James and Frances his son and daughter 40s. a piece. Unto my brother-in-law Mr. William Sperring and my sister his wife 40s. a piece. Unto my cosen Mr. John Jeffery £5 if he survives me. Unto Mrs. Mary Cox daughter of Mr. Samuel Cox deceased and to Mr. Joseph Cox £10 each if living. Item I give and devise unto my cosen John Prowse now of Axbridge, eldest son of my said cosen John Prowse late of Symondsborow deceased and to his heirs and assigns for ever my manour of Compton Magna and Badgworth &c. in the said county of Somersett situate

A | B |

1st wife Anna, dau. of William Spearing of Axbridge, Gent Mar. Feb. 10, 1665. Obiit May 21, 1668, æt. 23. = John Prowse of Compton House, Axbridge, & Compton Bishop, obiit 1688. Bur. at Compton Bishop. * "Pronepos et hæres" to William Prowse, above mentioned. = 2nd wife Anne, dau. of Roger Newborough of Berkley, co. Somerset, Esq. Married at Berkley 1670. Bur. at Compton Bishop 1740.

Arms.—*Or, three bends azure within a bordure engrailed gules.*

Thos. — Wm.

Newborough, bap. March 19, 1672. — Thomas, bap. Jan. 10, 1678. — William, bur. at Compton Bishop 1677.

Mary. — Elizabeth, obiit 1725. — Ann, bap. March 24, 1675. Obiit 1729.

All died young.

1st wife Margaret, dau. of William Bragge of Sadborough, co. Devon, Esq. Bur. at Compton Bishop 1702.

Arms.—*Argent, a chevron vert between three bulls passant gules.*

= John Prowse of Compton Bishop, bap. March 11, 1676. Bur. at Axbridge April 10, 1710. M.P. for Somerset 1708. = 2nd wife Abigail, dau. of George Hooper, D.D., Lord Bishop of Bath and Wells, and Abigail his wife, dau. of Richard Guilford, Gent. Obiit Nov. 24, 1763, æt. 80.

Arms.—*Gyronny of eight or and ermine, a tower triple-towered sable.*

Thomas Prowse of Compton Bishop, Esq., son and heir. M.P. for Somerset 1740 to 1767. Bap. Jan. 10, 1678. Bur. at Axbridge Jan. 12, 1767. = Elizabeth, dau. of John Sharpe of Grafton Park, co. Northampton, Esq., and Anna Maria his wife, dau. and coheiress of Charles Hosier of Wicken Park, Northampton, Esq. Bur. at Axbridge June, 1780.

Arms.—*Azure, a pheon argent within a bordure entoyre of torteaux, quartering party per bend sinister ermine and ermines a lion rampant or.* Hosier.

Mary, dau. and coheir. Born 23 Aug. 1745. Marr. 1783. Obiit April, 1800. = Rev. John Methuen Rogers, Rector of Berkley, Somerset. Ob. 22 Aug. 1834, aged 85.

A son died an infant.

Elizabeth, dau. and coheiress. Born 25 Sept. 1749. Marr. 3rd Jan. 1769. Ob. at Hampstead 5 Oct. 1826, aged 77. = John Mordaunt, Esq. (afterwards Sir John Mordaunt, 7th Bart.). Obiit at Walton 18th Novr. 1806, aged 73.

C

lying and being within the parishes of Compton Bishopp Badgworth Wedmore Weare Biddesham Allerton Morte (Mark) South Brent Lympsham Weston Super Mare Winscombe Banwell Congresbury Weeke St. Lawrence Portishead Nempnet Well (Wells) Wookey Claston Spaxton Cannington Otterhampton Stogursey Stockline Lovell and Fiddington in the said county of Somersett. And I doe hereby declare that the said John Prowse is my next heire at lawe to whom all the said manours and lands would in right have descended after my death if I should not in my lifetime have otherwise disposed of them. But my will is and I doe require and charge my said cosen John Prowse & his heirs to ratifie and confirme all leases and estates heretofore made or granted of any of the said premises by me or any other wherewith the land was charged when I bought it and whereof I had my notice when I bought the same. The residue of goods chattels & estate unto my said cosen John Prowse son of said cosen John Prowse. Appoints said John Prowse executor. Forgives cousin Edward Thurston £100 which his father owed me, upon condition that he pays his brothers and two sisters £10 each, and retains £50 for his own use.

Witnesses: William Sperring Jo. Jeffery The mark of William Hill.

Proved in the Strand, Middlesex, and Admon. &c. granted to John Prowse the Exor. on the 15th Feb. 1670-1. Further Admon. granted 7th July 1690 to Anne Prowse to whom had been granted the Admon. of the effects of John Prowse deceased, who was the Exor. of William Prowse deceased &c.

1688-9. John Prowse. On the 29th January 1688-9 Admon. &c. was granted to Anne Prowse the Relict, of the goods and effects of John Prowse of Compton Bishop co. Somerset, gent. (Act Book 1689 fo. 3 B.)

* A reference to the will shews that he was a "cousin."

| c

Elizabeth, born Oct. 30, 1736. Buried 24 Jan. 1742. — Elizabeth, b. Mar. 10, 1744. Buried Mar. 27, 1746. — Susanna, born May 27, 1742. Buried Feb. 24, 1758.	Charles, born Jan. 21, 1747. Obiit June 15th, 1756. — John, obiit 27 Feb. 1758, æt. 24.	George Prowse= of Compton Bishop, Esq. Bur. at Axbridge Sept. 3, 1767, æt. 30.	=Elizabeth, d. of the Rev. Dr. Thomas Sharpe, Archdeacon of Northumberland, by Judith his wife, 16th dau. of Sir George Wheeler, Preb. of Durham. Ob. at Fulham, co. Middx., 23 Feb. 1810, aged 77, and buried there. ARMS.—SHARPE, *as before*.

NOTES ON THE FAMILY OF ANDREWS.*

(*Continued from p.* 161.)

The following genealogical memoranda relating to the Andrews family are copied from a Book of Common Prayer, printed at Cambridge by John Hayes, Printer to the University, 1683.

I.

On the outside of the cover are stamped in gold the initials J.A. within a wreath. Inside is written,—

"This Book was Given me by my Dear mother Mrs Eliz^th^ Andrews.
Robt Andrews."

And by the side of the armorial bookplate of Robert Andrews (a facsimile of which is here given), is written this further memorandum marking the devolution of the Book of Prayer to the hands of William Long, Esq., of Wrington, co. Somerset, through Elizabeth Hare Joliffe, his late wife, who received it from her aunt, *i.e.* from Elizabeth Nott, sister to Diana Joliffe. The last named were both of them granddaughters of the above Robert Andrews.

II.

Then secondly upon the fly-leaves of the same book are entries made as follow:—

"September 3^d^ 1726. I Robert Andrews was married at Eccleston church near Eaton in the County of Chester (by the Revd Mr Aubury) to Marg^t^ Pigot second Daughter of Robt. Pigot of Eaton aforesaid Esqr.; I being this day 23 years of age, & my wife Marg^t^ 23 years of age the 30th of August last past.

"(1st) Diana Andrews daughter of Robert and Margaret Andrews was born on the 10th day of June 1727 being Saturday at $\frac{1}{4}$ after three in the Afternoon in Great Russell Street Bloomsbury. She was Baptized 15th of the same month by the Rev^nd^ Mr Saunders Curate of the Parish of St Giles' in the Fields. Sir Richard Grosvenor being Godfather & his Lady Diana Grosvenor & Mrs Anne Grosvenor his Sister being Godmothers (who were represented).

"(2.) Thomas Andrews Son of the abovesaid Robert & Margaret Andrews was born on the 7th day of ffebruary 172$\frac{8}{9}$ being fryday at Nine in the morning, in Great Russell Street Bloomsbury. Was baptized privately by the Reverend Mr Saunders (Curate of the Parish of St Giles' in the fields) on Thursday the 20th of the same month, & afterwards viz. on Monday 3^d^ of March 1728 publickly. Thos. Grosvenor Esqr & Robt Grosvenor Esqr being Godfathers & Mrs Grizel Manwayring Godmother (who stood in person).

"(3.) Elizabeth Andrews Daughter of Robt & Margaret Andrews was born on the fifth day of ffebruary 17$\frac{29}{30}$ being thursday about $\frac{1}{4}$ after 7 in the morning in Great Russell Street Bloomsbury & was baptized on Thursday the 19th of the same month by Mr Burnett Curate of St Giles' my mother Elizabeth Andrews & my sister Elizabeth Pigot standing Godmothers in person with my Good friend Mr Partington for Godfather.†

* Contributed by Rev. F. J. POYNTON.

† This Mr. Edward Partington of City of Chester.

"(4) Margarett Andrews daughter of Robert & Margarett Andrews was born on the Monday 19th July 1731 about a quarter before 10 at night in Grosvenor Street in the P'sh of St George Hanover Square and was baptized on Tuesday the 27th day of the same July by the Revnd Mr Newton afternoon Preacher at Grosvenor Chappell, my sister Harleston & my sister Molly Andrews being Godmothers & my Bro^{r} Tom Pigot Godfather, Mrs Harleston was represented by my sister Betty Pigot, & Tom Pigot by my Father Andrews

"(5) Robert Andrews, Son of the aforesaid Robert and Margaret Andrews was born on Friday the 1st day of September 1732 about a q^{r} before Six in the Morning in Grosvenor Street in the Parish of St George's Hanover Square & was baptized on Monday the 24th day of the same September by the Reverend Mr Trebeck Rector of the s^{d} Parish of St George's Hanover Square, Robert Myddelton of Chirk Castle in the County of Denbigh Esqr & Charles Harleston of Newton in the County of Chester being Godfathers & Mrs Jane Grosvenor wife of Robt Grosvenor Esqr Godmother who were represented *viz* Mr Mydd^{ton} by Thos Warre Esqr Mr Harleston by myself, & Mrs Grosvenor by Mrs Warre

"(6) Margaret Andrews Daughter of the aforesaid Robt & Marg^{t} Andrews was born on ffriday the 28th Day of December 1733 about five minutes before 8 o'clock in the morning in Grosvenor Street in the Parish of St George Hanover Square, & was Baptized on Thursday the 17th day of January following by the Revd Mr Trebeck Rector of the said Parish. My sister Molly Andrews & Mrs Gertrude Partington wife of Mr Edward Partington of the City of Chester (who was represented by my mother) being Godmother, & my brother Charles Pigot (who was represented by myself) being Godfather

"(7 & 8) Richard Andrews son of the aforesaid Robt & Marg^{t} Andrews and Mary Andrews daughter of the aforesaid Robt & Marg^{t} Andrews were both born on Tuesday 28th Jany 1734 Richard about a quarter before 7 in the morning, and Mary about an hour & a half afterwards in Grosvenor Street in the parish of St George Hanover Sq^{r} They were both privately baptized on Friday 31st of same Jany by the Revd Mr Trebeck Rector of the s^{d} parish Richard died on the same Friday 31st Jany 1734 about 9 in the morning Mary was afterwards baptized publickly by s^{d} Mr Trebeck on Sunday 16th feb^{y} 1734 Mrs Manwayring standing Godmother in person, & Mrs Harleston (by my sister Molly) and my Father Pigot Godfather (by me)

"(9.) Catherine Andrews, Daughter of the aforesaid Robt & Marg^{t} Andrews was born on Tuesday the 1st day of June 1736 a ¼ before 10 in ye Morning in Grosvenor Street in ye p'sh of St George Hanover Square, & was baptized on Friday ye 11th day of June following by the Revnd Mr Trebeck Rector of the s^{d} parish, Mrs Catherine Walker of Whitehall & my sister Molly Andrews being Godmothers, & my good friend Mr Isaac Hornor Godfather

"(10.) Jane Andrews Daughter of the aforesaid Robert & Margaret Andrews was born on Tuesday July the 19th 1737 ab^{t} ¼ before 5 in the morning in Grosvenor St in the Parish of St George Hanover Sq & was baptized on ffriday the 12th day of August following by the Revd Mr Palmer one of the Curates of the s^{d} parish, Mrs Jane Marten, Wife of the Revd Edmund Marten D D being Godmother (represented by Mrs Manwayring) & my own Mother (represented by my sister) being Godmothers, and my Father Robt Pigot Esq (represented by myself) Godfather

"(11) Maria Charlotta Andrews Daughter of the aforesaid Robert & Margaret Andrews was born on Monday the 31st day of Jany 1742 about ¼ before 7 in the evening in Grosvenor Street in the parish of Saint George Hanover Square, and was baptized on Friday the 18th Day of Febr^{ry} following By the Rev Dr Andrew Trebeck Rector of the said Parish The Honble Mrs Anna Maria Egerton being one of her Godmothers (represented by Miss Jane Trebeck) and Miss Charlotte Addison being her other Godmother (represented by Miss Margarett Lloyd) and my Bro^{r} in Law Mr Charles Mytton (represented by myself) being her Godfather"

III.

Thirdly, on the plain leaves at the end of the same Book of Common Prayer the entries made are.—

Robert Andrews
of the Inner Temple Gen.t

"My son Thomas dyed July 2^d 1729 aged 5 Months & 4 days of the Small Pox & was buried the 3^d of July at night in St Giles' Churchyard under a Window on the South Side

"My Daughter Margaret died Novr 18th 1731 of Convulsions at Putney about nine in the Morning and was buried in the Churchyard at Putney on Saturday the 20th of the same month Aged 4 mo^s wanting 1 day

"My son Richard died Jany 31st 1734 in Grosvenor Street aged 3 days, & was buried in the best burying Ground belonging to the Parish of St George Hanover Square Feby 1st 1734

"My Daughter Mary died July 23^d 1735 at Nurse in Markett Street Westminster & was buried in the new burying ground belonging to the parish of St John the Evangelist Westm^r July 25th 1735 aged six months wanting 5 days

"My daughter Jane died at Nurse at Putney in the county of Surry Sept 6th 1737 aged 7 weeks & was buried in the Churchyard at Putney near her sister Margaret on Thursday the 8th of the same month

"My Daughter Maria Charlotta dyed ffeb^y 24th 1742 in Grosvenor street aged 3 weeks & 4 days & was buried in the best burying ground belonging to the parish of St. George Hanover Sq^r on 26th of same month

"My Dear Dear Dau^r Eliz was married to Mr Thos Partington eldest son of my late worthy ffriend & her Godfather Edward Partington of the City of Chester Gent July 10th 1754 to whom she brought a son in July 1755, who died in the month, as did its dear Mother on the 2^d day of August following to the unspeakable Grief of her Parents She was buried in my vault in Hanwell Churchyard the 9th Day of the same August, & her little infant removed from the place where it was interred & put into the same vault with her."

Here follow in a different hand six entries (doubtless the writing of Catharine Andrews afterwards Nott) —

"(1) My dear Father died at his house at East Acton in the County of Middlesex on Saturday ye 27th Day of August 1763 and was interred on Friday the second of September in his own Vault at Hanwell.

"(2) My dear Mother died May ye 23^d 1779 in Grosvenor st & was buried on the 28th Day of same month in my Father's vault in Hanwell Churchyard.

"(3) My dear Sister Margaret Ashcroft died April 10th 1782.

"(4.) My *Sister-in-law Sarah Andrews*, wife of my Brother the Revd Robert Andrews died in April 1785 at St Omer* in France and was buried there

"(5) My dear Brother Robert Andrews died of a Paralytic stroke on Monday March ye 25th 1793 at 12 o'clock at night, at his house at Great Ealing Middx. & was buried on Tuesday April 2^d in the Vault at Grosvenor Chapel

"(6) My sister Diana Andrews died of a long & painful illness on Thursday May 8th 1800 at half-past nine in the morning at her house at Great Ealing Middx and was buried on Friday May 16th in the Family Vault at Hanwell"

Here is again a change of handwriting, and the family obituary is continued by Elizabeth Nott (dau'r of the preceding writer) as follows —

"My dear Mother Catherine Nott late Andrews died after a long & painful illness on Friday Aug^st 8th 1817 at 4 o'clock in the morning at Bathford near Bath where she went for change of air and was buried on Friday Aug 15th in Bathford churchyard, near the south side of the Chancel The last survivor of the Family"

In the same hand is stated "Omitted to be entered—Catherine Andrews married June 29th 1766 to Captn John Neale Pleydell Nott, R N of Braydon, Cricklade, Co Wilts who was killed in action while Commanding the Centaur off Martinique, West Indies Ap^l 1791"

* The Rev Robert Andrews, as I have been informed, was previously Rector of Great Ealing, Midx , but about this time either resigned the living, or retired from the active discharge of its duties, adjourning to St Omer where his two youngest children were born, and where as we see from this entry, his wife (*née* Sarah Hawkins, dau'r of the 1st Bart of Kelston) died

MONUMENTAL INSCRIPTIONS AT WILFORD, NOTTINGHAMSHIRE.

Communicated by CAPTAIN A. E. LAWSON LOWE, F.S.A.

(*Continued from p* 164.)

Upon another tablet on the north wall of the chancel:—

Near this place
are Deposited the Remains
of
George Sinclair,(e)
M.A.
late Rector of this Parish,
who Died the 12th of June
1775
Aged 46 years.

ARMS.—*Quarterly* 1. *Azure, a ship at anchor, oars in saltire and sails furled, (within a double tressure flory counter-flory) or.* 2 *and* 3. *Or, a lion rampant gules.* 4. *Azure, a ship under sail or; over all, dividing the quarters, a cross engrailed sable*—for SINCLAIR; *impaling, Argent, a chevron between three roses gules, on a chief azure as many mullets of the first*—(for STEVENSON ?) CREST.—*A cock proper.* MOTTO.—Commit thy Works to God.

Upon a plain marble slab on the south side of the chancel:—

To the memory of
the late
Revd Owen Dinsdale, M.A.(f)
son of George Dinsdale, Esqre,
of Nappa Hall,
in the County of York.
He departed this life
November 5th 1818, aged 78,
having been Rector of this Parish
upwards of 37 years.

The east window of the chancel is filled with modern stained glass, representing the Resurrection, and along the bottom of the window runs the following inscription:—

"Ad Dei Gloriam et in piam memoriam Thomæ Thorp, A.M. per annos XLVI hujus ecclesiæ Rectoris qui obiit die xxvo Februarii MDCCCLXIV. æt. LXXIV. Hanc fenestram vitilis ornavit H. J. Peach, A.M., ecclesiæ de Tutbury Vicarius."

A window on the south side of the chancel has been filled with stained glass as a memorial of the poet Henry Kirke White, who resided for a time at Wilford, and expressed a wish that his burial-place should be in this churchyard. At the west end of the chancel, near the chancel-arch, is a good medallion bust by Halle, simply inscribed:—

Henry Kirke White
Born 1785 + Died 1806.

On the pavement, near the reading-desk, is a large slab (now partly hidden beneath the pews), which bears the following inscription:—

Here lie ye Bodies of Gervase Handley, Gentn(g), and Katherine his Wife. Also ye Bodies of their Son Gervase and two Daughters, Katherine and Dorothy. Ye last departed this Life November ye 12th, 1724. Aged 74 Yeares.

In the south aisle, upon a small lozenge-shaped tablet —

Near
this Place lie
the Remains of
Ann Cradock,
Relict of Joseph Cradock, Esq^{r}(h)
of Leicester,
who died the 18th day of Sep^{t}
1774
Aged 56
Years

Upon a large marble tablet in the same aisle —

"Near this Place lies the Body of William Lee, Gent, who departed this Life February 8th, 1792, in the 84th year of his Age Also the Body of Elizabeth Catherine Lee, Daughter of the above by Ann his Wife, who died February 26th, 1792, in the 48th year of her Age In the same Vault are deposited the Remains of Sarah Lee, Relict of the above Willm Lee She died May 1th, 1793, in the 73rd year of her Age

Upon a floor-stone —

To the Memory of Richard Handley, Gent,(i) of Wilford, who died 23rd Jan^{ry}, 1740 Aged 48 Also Thos Hodgkin(j), of Nottingham, who died May 9th, 1805 Aged 68 Years Likewise Three Sons(k) and One Daughter of Thos and Mary Hodgkin Also Richard Son of Thos and Mary Hodgkin who died June 25th, 1807, in the 29th Year of his Age. And Dorothy Daughter of Thos and Mary Hodgkin who died Feb 10th, 1810 Aged 33 Years

Upon a large brass plate, at the west end of the south aisle —

To the endeared memory of Henry Smith, Esqre, of Wilford House, 3rd son of Samuel Smith, Esqre, M P of Woodhall Park, Herts Born December 12, 1791 Died February 7, 1874 Also of his beloved wife the Lady Lucy Smith eldest daughter of Alexander, 8th Earl of Leven and Melville Born January 26, 1794 Died December 23, 1865 One in the Lord they lived for the Glory of God and the welfare of His Church While renouncing all merit of their own and having a deep and abiding sense of their sinfulness by the blessed teaching of the Holy Ghost, they enjoyed through His anointing the most firm confidence in the Sovereign Grace and Love of God in Christ toward them And having perfect peace through the cleansing of the blood of Jesus they died resting on the Covenant Faithfulness of the Triune Jehovah.

Also to the memory of their children Robert Melville Born May 3, 1827. Died April 15, 1828 Lucy Jane Born July 6, 1828, who fell asleep in Jesus May 14, 1842 Marianne Born July 30, 1829 Died May 6, 1830 Their bodies lie in the family vault beneath the centre of the nave

Upon a tablet in the north aisle

In affectionate remembrance of
George Barnard
who departed this life September 28th, 1819
in the 43rd year of his age
Also of Elizabeth Ann
wife of John Cox, of Wilford
and sister of the above George Barnard
who departed this life January 6th, 1852
Aged 67 years

In this aisle is an ancient sepulchral slab, apparently of the fifteenth century, bearing an incised cross entwined with a scroll There are also two old alabaster slabs near the north door, exhibiting traces of incised effigies with marginal inscriptions Upon one of these slabs the date—"vij[th] day of December, 1582"—alone is legible, whilst upon the other—"in day of October"—is all that remains.

In the churchyard, at the east end of the chancel, upon the upper slab of a large square monument —

+
In Memory of
Thomas Wybert, Gent (l)
who was thirty years Gentlem[n] to
Thomas
Duke of Norfolk
Earl Marshall of England
Ob 7 Decemb, 1735
Æt 65
Requiescat in Pace

Upon a square monument, enclosed by iron railings, on the south side of the church —

Here lieth the Body of John Deane, Esqre, (m)
who from the year 1714 to 1720 commanded a ship of War
in the Czar of Muscovy's service, after which, being
appointed by his Britanick Majesty Consul for the Ports
of Flanders and Ostend, He resided there many years
& by his Majesty's leave retired to this village in y[e] year 1738,
Where he died August the 18th, 1761
In the 82nd Year of his Age
His Lady, Sarah Deane, lies here also interr'd
Who departed this Life August the 17th, 1761. Aged 81

Upon a large stone slab, underbuilt with masonry —

Here Lieth the
Body of Phebe Slack(n) who departed this
Life Aug[t] the 27th, 1737
Aged 26 years

Upon another monument —

Sacred
to the Memory of
John Cox, Esq[re],
who departed this life
on the 10th of May, 1831
in the 62nd year of his age.
As a Man and a Christian he was unostentasiously upright
and sincere; as a Husband faithful and affectionate,
his Wife, who deeply laments her loss
testifies her affection and soothes her
sorrow by this brief memorial
of his virtues

On the outside of the chancel, beneath the east window, are two slate slabs thus inscribed —

This Tablet commemorates
the many virtues and the early loss
of a beloved wife and mother
the premature orphanage of her surviving children
and the anguish of her bereaved husband
Eliza,
the wife of Charles Robinson, of Wilford
and daughter of Richard Wells, of Nottingham.
She died February 14, 1836, aged 36 years

Here also lie the remains of
Charles Espin Robinson, their first-born child,
and Ellen Sutton Robinson, their only daughter,
the former died March 13, 1831, aged 20 months,
the latter died at the age of 10 months
on the third day after her lamented mother
and lies buried in her arms

Sacred
to the memory of
an affectionate and much-beloved parent
Charles Robinson, (°)
who for upwards of thirty years
was Master of the Free School
in this village
He was born at Kingston-upon-Hull
11th May, 1793
and died at Wilford 14th August, 1852.

(e) "The Revd George Sinclair, Rector of this Parish, buried June 23rd, 1775"—*Parish Register*

(f) The Rev Owen Dinsdale was of Trinity College, Cambridge where he graduated as B A in 1762, and M A in 1782 In 1767, he was presented to the rectory of Eastwood, in Nottinghamshire, by John Plumptre, Esq, and in 1781, he became rector of Wilford on the presentation of Sir Gervase Clifton, Bart, holding both benefices until his decease

(g) Richard Handley, the first of this family who settled at Wilford, is stated in the pedigree given in the Visitation of Nottinghamshire, made in 1614, to have been descended from a Somersetshire family By his will, dated September the 9th, 1592 and proved in the Prerogative Court of York, that same year, he desired to be buried at Wilford, "withoute the chauncell dore and soe nere thereunto as conveniently may be" He left four daughters and two sons, of whom Henry the elder, settled at Bramcote in Nottinghamshire, at which place he was married, April the 6th 1592, to Elizabeth daughter of Thomas Bray of Sheffield, in Yorkshire and sister of Francis Bray, Alderman of Nottingham His wife was buried at Bramcote, February the 20th, 1596, and he himself was buried there November the 12th, 1608 The issue of this marriage was a son Henry, who obtained a Patent of Armorial Bearings from Sir William Segar, Garter, June the 21st, 1612, and died without surviving issue, and was buried at Bramcote June the 11th, 1650, and a daughter Alice, who was married at Sandiacre, in Derbyshire, October the 28th, 1611, to Nicholas Charlton, Esq, of that place but died without issue, and was buried at Sandiacre, June the 25th, 1615 Gervase Handley of Wilford the younger son of Richard Handley, married Anne, daughter of Jerome Brand, of Staunton, in Nottinghamshire (by Bridget, his wife, the daughter of Anthony Staunton of Staunton, Esq), and by her he had five sons and three daughters His second son, Gervase, had a son of his own name whose place of interment is marked by the above-mentioned slab This last-named Gervase was married at Radford, July the 12th, 1641, to Katherine daughter of Thomas Wartey, otherwise Wharton, rector of Wilford by whom he had a son and two daughters He died intestate and was buried at Wilford, July the 28th, 1659 and his widow was buried there July the 8th 1664 The earlier portion of the Wilford Registers has been lost, and as the burials of Gervase the son of Gervase and Katherine Handley and of Katherine, their daughter, are not found in the existing Registers, which only date from the year 1659, it is presumable that their deaths occurred before that time The burial of the other daughter is thus recorded, "Mrs Dorothy Handley buried Novr 15th, 1724"

(h) "Anne Craddock buried September 14th, 1774"—*Parish Register* This lady was the only daughter of Richard Ludlam, M B, and was the second wife of Joseph Cradock of Leicester, and of Gumley in that county Esq by whom she had four sons and one daughter, all of whom died in their infancy and a son Joseph who inherited the Gumley property Her husband Joseph Cradock, Esq, was the third son of Edmund Cradock, Mayor of Leicester in 1702, and grandson of another Edmund Cradock, who was Mayor of Leicester in 1615 and 1637 He died April the 20th, 1759, and was buried in St Martin's Church, Leicester (Nichols' 'Hist and Antiq of Leicestershire' vol iii p 1119)

(i) "Mr Richard Handley buried Janry 23rd 1740,"—*Parish Register* This Richard Handley was the eldest son of Huntingdon Handley, of Wilford, by his marriage (at Bilborough, October the 20th, 1691) with Margaret Bainbridge His father was the only son of Huntingdon Handley, who (according to the pedigree in the Visitation of 1614) was the youngest son of Gervase Handley, of Wilford, by Anne his wife daughter of Jerome Brand, of Staunton Richard Handley was baptised at Wilford, October the 18th 1692 He was first married (at Wilford by license, April the 14th, 1727) to Mrs Hannah Parkes who was buried at Wilford, June the 4th 1728 By his second wife, Sarah Jackson (to whom he was married at Wilford, August the 15th, 1739), he had a son of his own name and a daughter Mary married to Thomas Hodgkin, of Nottingham. His widow was afterwards married to John Jackson, of Nottingham

(j) "Yesterday afternoon, aged 67, died Mr Hodgskin, breeches-maker, of Swine's Green in this town."—*Nottingham Journal*, May 10th, 1805.

(k) "Monday, died Mr Thomas Hodgkin, son of Mr Hodgkin, Breeches-maker, on Swine's Green in this town. On Thursday his remains were deposited in a vault belonging to the ancient family of the Handleys, from whom he was lineally descended by his mother's side."—*Nottingham Journal*, April 24th, 1784.

(l) "Mr Thomas Wybert buried Decr 10th, 1735."—*Parish Register*.

(m) "John Deane, Esqr, and Sarah his Wife buried Augst 21st, 1761."—*Parish Register*.

(n) "Mrs Phebe Slack buried Augst 28, 1737."—*Parish Register*.

(o) According to 'Notes and Queries,' 1st s., vol. xii., pp. 491, 492; 2nd s., vol. i., pp. 81, 170, this Mr. Charles Robinson was maternally descended from John Bunyan, and had a Bible and other relics of the great allegorist in his possession.

MITFORD AND ASHTON.—The statement made by the compiler of the old Mitford Pedigree with respect to the marriage of Robert Mitford and Anne Ashton has been repeated by Sir B. Burke in his 'Landed Gentry,' and accepted as the fact. There can, however, be no doubt that the compiler was in error, though it is certainly strange that such should have been the case. The father of Anne Ashton was brother, not son, of Sir Ralph Ashton or Assheton, as will be best seen by the accompanying extract from Collins's 'Baronetage' (1741), which agrees with the Visitation Pedigree, and is confirmed by the Mitford notes, wherein mention is made of "great-uncle, Edward Fleetwood."

Ralphe Assheton of Middleton, Esq., High Sheriff co. Lanc. 8 Car. I., died 17 Feb. 1650, bur. at Middleton. = Elizabeth, sole dau. of John Kaye of Woodsome, co. Ebor. died 22 Mar. 1662. M.I. with effigies in alabaster in St. Botolph, Aldersgate.

1. Richard, died young, 25 March, 1631.	2. Ralph, mar. Anne, dau. of Sir Ralph A. of Whalley, Bart. and was himself created 1st Baronet of Middleton, 1660.	3. John, resided at Burne, co. Ebor, and mar. Elizabeth dau. of John Fleetwood of Penwortham, co. Lanc.	Elizabeth, mar. Adam Beaumont of Whitby.	Mary, mar. Christopher Bannister.

CHARLES J. ROBINSON.

COLBY.—I shall be pleased if any heraldic reader can correctly appropriate the following arms:—Party per bend sinister gules and azure a lion rampant arg. They appear upon a tombstone in Benacre Church, Suffolk, impaled with the arms of Edward North, Esq., who died 16 Dec. 1701, whose wife was Ann, relict of John Colby of Banham in Norfolk, Esq. Now the wife of John Colby was Ann, daughter and heir of John Arthur of Wigenhall St. Mary, in Norfolk, which John Arthur was buried at Wigenhall 1 Dec. 1655. Mary, one of the daughters and coheirs of this John Colby and Ann his wife, married Thomas Carthew, Esq., Serjeant-at-law, and on a silver cup still in the possession of the Carthew family is engraved a shield with the arms of Carthew impaling Colby and his quarterings, and in the place where the quartering of Arthur would properly come is the same coat as that I have mentioned. It must therefore have been adopted for the coat of Arthur; but I cannot find it so attributed in any ordinary of arms or heralds' visitation that I have been able to consult, or indeed to any other family whatever. A branch of the family of Arthur of Somersetshire did settle at Wisbech, on the borders of Norfolk, and near Wigenhall, a century earlier, but I have not been able to affiliate John Arthur of Wigenhall to it, or any other family of the name. Had he any right to that coat? If not, who had?

G. A. C.

SUTTON OF SUTTON, CO. YORK.—Is there any pedigree extant of such a family, and where is it to be met with? They bore for arms—*Gules, on a castle or a stork proper*. This coat is given in Berry's 'Encyclopædia Heraldica' for "Sutton of Kittismore, Yorkshire." Where is that place?

Doncaster. CHARLES JACKSON.

Descent of the Andrews, Pigott, and Nott Families.

ARMS.

ANDREWS.—*Argent, on a chevron engrailed gules three mullets or between three trefoils slipped vert.* CREST.—*On a wreath a blackamoor's head.*
NOTT.—*Azure, on a bend between three leopards' faces as many martlets gules.* (Arms granted in 1587.) CREST.—*A martlet argent, ducally crowned or, holding in beak an olive branch vert.**
PIGOT OF SALOP:—*Erm. three lozenges in fesse sa.?* (Burke's G. Ar.)

Hugh Pigot of Peploe, co. Salop, died 28th Aug. 1697, ætat. 67. = Elizabeth Dicken, died 27 June 1727, æt. 90. (Betham's Baronetage.)

Andrews, dead before 1696, or his name would no doubt have been entered in the family book by Richard his son, who commenced to chronicle at that date in the s[d] book. =

In all, 12 children of Hugh and Eliz. Pigot.

1 Thomas Pigot. Died 1662. — 2 Henry. — 4 Hugh. — 5 Walter.

3 Robert Pigot of Eaton, co. Cest. Sponsor for his grandchild Mary Andrews 16 Feb. 1734, by proxy, and for Jane, her sister, 12 Aug. 1737. Died 1749. = Margaret, dau'r of Walley, co. Cest. (A)

Elizabeth Pigot, born 1664, died 1749, Dec. 17. Buried in the family vault of her son at Hanwell, Middx. ætat. 86. = Richard Andrews, Esq. of Great Russell St., Bloomsbury, born 1664. He died 14 Nov. 1734, aged 70, in Great Russell St. Bur. in Grosvenor Chapel 18 Nov. (B)

Charles Pigot. — Susanna. — Margaret. — Evan. — Lucy.

11 Richard Pigot of Westminster, bapt. at Hodnet 6 Oct. 1769, died 31 Dec. 1729, bur. St. Martins in the Fields. = Frances, dau. of Peter Godde of Westminster, b. 12 Jan. and bap. at S. James's, Piccadilly, 2 Feb. 1694-5. Died 29 Dec. 1769, bur. at St. Martins.

John Andrews,† died 26 Feb. 1695-6.

? if other children of this generation.

Children of Richard Pigot and Frances:

George, created Baron Pigot,‡ of Patshull, 1765. Bart. 1764. Ob. s.p. in India. With remainder, in default of lawful issue, to his brother, as to the baronetcy.

Sir Robert (Brigadier General), 2nd Bart.§ Died 1796. =

Hugh, Vice-Admiral. Twice marr. Left issue.

Margaret, m. 10 Apr. 1755, at St. Anne's, Soho. = Thos. Fisher, Esq.

* Arms are ascribed to Nott in Stow's 'Survey of London,' p. 554 (edition 1632). John Nott (1363) and (1367) then Lord Mayor, who was also Sheriff in 1350,—*Quarterly ermine and azure, in the second and third an eagle rising or.*

† This John Andrews is no doubt the "J. A." within a wreath, stamped and gilded on the large Book of Common Prayer, and he the original owner of the book, which contained the family memoranda of Andrews made in it after John's death, when it became the property of his brother Richard; which Richard commenced the obituary, and was followed up by his son Robert.

‡ Lord Pigot by his will and codicil thereto, 1777, left among many legacies £300 to Mr. Robert Andrews.

§ The Barony expired with George being childless.

Authorities of this Pedigree are—

A Pedigree of Pigot *penes* Henry Wagner, Esq., F.S.A., founded on Betham's Baronetage, Extracts from Registers, and data in the family Bible of Godde. MS. entries in Books of Common Prayer belonging to the Andrews family. A Pedigree of Nott of Braydon among the family papers in the collection of Wm. Long, Esq. The Registers and Monumental Inscriptions of Kelston, Somerset; and St. George's, Hanover Square. The personal information afforded by members of the Hawkins and Andrews' families to the Rev. F. J. Poynton whilst compiling this Pedigree.

A | B |

Richard Pigot.

Thomas (sponsor to Marg[t] Andrews 1731.)

Charles Pigot, Capt. E.I.S. (Living in Jan. 1734.) = Sarah, da. of Capt. Thomas Hill.
Issue eleven children.

Susanna (or another Elizabeth), mar. before 1731. = Charles Hurleston of Newton, co. Chester, Esq.

Elizabeth, 3 da. not mar. in Feb. 1729, when she stood sponsor to her niece Elizab. Andrews; mar. at Hodnet 18 Feb. 1733. = Chas. Milton (or ? Mytton, who was a sponsor at bapt. of M. Charlotte Andrews, Feb. 18, 1742.)

I am informed by Mr. Wagner that there was issue of this marriage a son Charles Milton (or Mytton), clerk, of Christleton, co. Cest.

Margaret Pigot, 2[d] dau'r. was 23 years of age when married. Born 30 Aug. 1703, marr. 3 Sept. 1726, at Eccleston, n[r] Eaton, died 23 May, 1779, in Grosvenor Street, bur. at Hanwell, Middx. = Robert Andrews, Esq., of the Inner Temple, 2nd surviving son, b. 3 Sept. Xtened 5th, 1703. Marr. on his birthday when 23 years of age, 1726. Died 27 Aug. 1763, at East Acton, co. Middx. Bur. at Hanwell. Comptroller of the Cash in the Excise Office.

1. John Andrews eldest son by birth, born 24 June, 1696, died 26 July following, or 26 Jan. 1697. (In any case died infant.)

2. Hildebrand, born 21 Aug. 1697, died 29 June 1699.

3. Richard, born 13 Dec. 1698, died 5 July, 1700, at Cheam, and buried there on 7th.

4. Mary, born 14 Dec. 1699, bapt. 20th. Died in Mount Street 6 Nov. 1781, bur. on the 10th in the Vaults, Grosvenor Chapel.

5. Richard, eldest surviving son, b. 21 March, 1701, bapt. 25 Mar. Died in Gt. Russell Street 20 Dec. 1754, bur. at Hillingdon, Middx. by his own desire.

6. Elizabeth, born 15 Sept. 1702, bapt. 22nd. Died at Cheam 26 Sept. and bur. there 28, 1702.

8. Thomas, born 1st Feb. 1705, and bapt. Died at Hampstead Apr. 12th, 1706, and was buried there on 13th.

9. Hugh, born 23 Dec. 1707, at Hodnet Hall, co. Salop. Died 1779, at Rugeley in Staffordshire, buried there.

10. Henry, born at Hodnet Hall 29 May, 1711, bapt. 2nd June, died 9th, bur. there 11th, in the Chancel.

Issue eleven children.

HAWKINS, co. Salop.

Cæsar Hawkins, Esq. born 1688, died 1752. = Anne Bright Nov. 9th, 1710.
Amongst other children.

2. Pennell Hawkins, Esq. Body Surgeon to Geo. II. and Serjeant Surgeon to Geo. III. Born 16 May, 1716. = Sarah, da. of Thomas Chetle, Esq. Died 25 Dec. 1791.
D

1. Sir Cæsar Hawkins, 1st Bart. of Kelston, Som't, born 10 Jan. 1711. Created Bart. 25 July, 1788. Buried at Kelston Feb. 19, 1786. = Sarah, da. of John Coxe, Esq. of London.
E

2nd h. Sir Herbert Perrott Packington, Bart. = Elizabeth Hawkins, died 23 Feb. 1812. = 1st h. Herbert Wilde, Esq. of Ludlow.

Elizabeth, the mother of Lord Hampton.
C

E Libris
Isaac Savnders Leadam A·M
Avl: Reg: et Coll: de Brasenose. Oxon: Socii.
Harry Soane. del 1875

D | E | C

George Hawkins.=

Augusta Hawkins, died in Bath 7th April, 1813, aged 66, by the Kelston Register. Bur. at Kelston 14 April, with tomb in the churchyard, on w^h her age is given as 67.=Rev. Samuel Nott, M.A., Rector of Houghton, Hants, and Vicar of Blandford, Dorset, Preb. of Winchester Cath. and Chaplain in ordinary to H.M. Geo. III. Died in Gay St., Bath, May 27, 1793, aged 53. Bur. at Kelston May 31, 1793. Has M.I. at Kelston.

Mary Ann Hawkins.=Geo. Thornhill, Esq. of Diddington, Hunts.

2. Rev. Robert Andrews, eldest surviving son. Born 1732 (Sept. 1st). At Westminster School 1751. M.A. 1758. Vicar of Wartling and Westling, co. Sussex, and at last Rector of Ealing. Died at his house at Great Ealing, Middx. of paralysis, 25th March, 1793. Buried in the vaults, Grosvenor Chapel, 2nd April, 1793.=Sarah Hawkins, da. of Sir Cæsar Hawkins, 1st Bart. of Kelston, Som't. Marr. 25th Apr. 1758, at St. James's, Westminster. Died at St. Omer in France, April, 1785. Buried there.

Geo. Frederick Nott, D.D., b. 14 May, 1768, Fellow of All Souls' College, Oxford, Rector of Harrietsham and of Woodchurch, Kent, Canon of Winchester, and Sub-Preceptor to the Princess Charlotte; a man of considerable talent and much taste, who took interest in the repairing of Win. Cath. in 1816, during which he sustained a severe accident. Died unmar. Oct. 23, 1841. Bur. in Winchester Cathedral, with M.I.

Charlotte Georgina Augusta Nott, born June 5, 1767. Died Oct 12, at Weston, n^r Bath, unmarried. Buried at Kelston Oct. 19, 1837.

George Thornhill, Esq. M.P. co. Hunts.

Frances Thornhill.=1st. Wm. Russell, Esq., brother of Lord Hampton.
=2nd. Jno. Harding, Esq.

One son, died s.p.

Issue 14 children.

1. Diana Andrews, eldest dau'r, b. 10 June, 1727. Died unmar. at her house at Great Ealing, 8 May, 1800. Buried at Hanwell in the family vault on 16 May, 1800.

1. Thomas, 1st son, b. 7 Feb. 1728-9, died 2 July, 1729, aged 5 months and 4 days.

2. Elizab. born 5 Feb. 1729, d. 2 Aug. 1755 (having been married on July 10, 1754), bur. at Hanwell 9 Aug. 1755.=Thos. Walley Partington, Esq. son of Edward Partington of the City of Chester, gent. and Gertrude his wife. Purchased y^e estate at Offham, co. Sussex, 1785. Marr. 2ndly Miss Trebeck, and left issue Thomas. Died March, 1791, and buried at Hamsey.

Issue, a son who died in a month after birth.

3 da. Margaret, born 19 July, 1731, d. Nov. 18, 1731, infant.

4 da. (2nd of name) Margaret Andrews, born 28 Dec. 1733, died April 10, 1782.=Richard Ashcroft, Esq. of Thorn, Yorks, n^r Doncaster; but his family of Huntingdonsh.

Anthony Ashcroft.

F | C

F — C

7 | 8 — 3 son and 5 da. Richard and Mary Andrews, twins, born 28 Jan. 1734. Richard died on 31st, Mary 23rd July, 1735.

9 — Catharine Andrews, 6 da., born 1 June, 1736, bapt. 11 June, St. George's, Hanover Square. Marr. June 29, 1766. Died at Bathford, near Bath, Aug. 8th, 1817, bur. 15th in the church-yard there. = John Neale Pleydell Nott, Capt. R.N., of Braydon Lodge, Cricklade, co. Wilts, 1763. Killed in action off Martinique, April, 1791. He was son of John Nott, Esq., of Braydon aforesaid by Elizabeth Neale, dau'r of Henry Neale of Allesley Park, co. Warw., and Anna Maria (Hanbury), his wife.

10 — Jane, 7 da., born 19 July, 1737, bapt. 12 Aug., died 6 Sept. at Putney, and bur. there in the ch.-yard Sept. 8.

11 — Maria Charlotta, 8 da. and last child, b. 31 Jan. 1742, bap. 18 Feb. at St. George's, Hanover Square. Died 24 Feb. 1742.

Children of John Neale Pleydell Nott and Catharine Andrews:

- John Nott, Lieut. in R.N., born Feb. 24, 1771. Died unmarried in Jamaica of Yellow Fever Aug. 18, 1794.
- Edward Nott, clerk, Rector of Weeke, Hants, born 15 March, 1774, died April 22, 1842. = Mary Messman of Reading, April 10, 1799. She died 26 March, 1851.
  - 1 John. 2 Edward. 3 Geo. 4 Henry. Mary. Catherine. Eliza.
- George, a midshipman in R.N.
- Diana Nott, mar. Oct. 24, 1800. = Jas. Hare Joliffe, Esq. qui ob. May 21, 1836.
  - Elizab. Hare Joliffe. = Wm. Long, Esq. M.A., Ball. Coll., Oxford. J.P. for Somerset.
- Elizabeth, died unmar. Nov. 5, 1858.
- Three dau'rs, died young.

1 son. Robert Andrews, 3rd child, b. Nov. 3, 1762. Of the Madras Civil Service. (F. M.) Died unmarried in India circ. 1824.

George, 2nd son, 5th child, b. Jan. 22, 1765. (F. M.)

John, 3rd son, born May 30, 1769. (F. M.)

Cæsar, 4th son, born Oct. 10, (1770), St. Geo., Hanover Sq. Went to the Cape of Good Hope, and mar. there. =

Children of the marriage, amongst others,

- Cæsar Andrews, living at Port Elizabeth, Algoa Bay, 1879.
- Mary Andrews = Fleming, Esq.

Hugh, 5th son, born Nov. 8, 1772. (F. M.) In the Par. of St. James's, Westminster. Died of Yellow Fever in the West Indies [as did another brother, but ? which].

Henry, 6th son, b. Nov. 8, 1773, in parish of St. George's, Hanover Square.

Frederick, 7th son, b. 2 March, 1775.

Note.—Of the sons of this family, only Cæsar and Augustus are believed to have married. This information is from their niece, Mrs. Harding of Guildford, 1878.

Augustus Andrews, 8th son, 14th and youngest child, b. at St. Omer, in France; became General Andrews, C.B., and built "Vellore," Bath, afterwards the residence of the Rev. Prebendary Kemble, Rector of the Abbey Church. General Andrews died at his residence, Vellore, 3rd March, 1858, ætat. 79, and was buried with M.I. in the churchyard at Bathampton, Bath. He had the custody of Tippoo Saib's children at Vellore, after the conquest of Seringapatam, and was there during the mutiny (1806), hence the name of his Bath residence. = Maria, da. of Chas. Conolly, Esq., owner of Midford Castle. She died s.p. at Bath, 26th May, 1855.

Sarah Andrews, b. May 31, 1760, in parish of St. George's, Hanover Square. Died March 28, 1763. Infant.

Elizabeth, 2nd da., born Oct. 6, 1761, in same parish. Died at Bath Oct. 21, 1837. (F. M.) = 1st, Rev. Richard Farrer (his 2nd w. s.p., but his 1st wife had 2 sons), co. Leicester. = 2ndly, Col. Warne (also his 2nd wife), H.E.I.C.S. s.p. His 1st wife was Barbara Harwood of Norwich, who died in March, 1823. The Colonel died 17 July, 1845, aged 92. M.I. in Woolley Church says he distinguished himself at Seringaptam.

F

F

4. Catherine, 3rd da., born Feb. 23, 1764. = Ansell, Esq., M.R.C.S.

Issue one son, 2 dau'rs, of whom the son died young (F.M.), and 1st da. Sarah married Col. Gillespie, s.p. 2nd da. Catherine marr. Chas. May Lushington, Esq., with issue.

6. Charlotte Andrews, 4th da., born March 28, 1766, in parish of St. George's, Hanover Sq. Died Nov. 12, in Russel St., Bath, 1837, and buried at Kelston, co. Somerset, Nov. 20. = Harry Taylor, of the Madras Civil Service. Married at St. Mary's, Fort St. George, 1795.

7. Sarah, 5th da., born Aug. 18, 1767. = Edw. Atkinson, Esq.

13. Marianne, youngest da., born at St. Omer in France, to which place her parents retired from Great Ealing, Middx. = 1st h. Loder. 2ndly ?

Issue of Sarah and Edw. Atkinson:

1. Edw. Atkinson, in Navy. Died unmarried.

2. Henry William Atkinson, living 1878.

1. Caroline Sarah.

2. Elizabeth Mary.

3. Frances Helen.

4. Laura Rosa, married 1863. = Evan Thos. Williams, who died in Sydney Place, Bath, 1st Apr. 1875.

5. Emily Graham, marr. 1 Dec. 1864, living 1878. = O. T. Barlow, Esq., Postmaster of Bath.

6. Emma Isabella.

Issue of Charlotte and Harry Taylor:

Charlotte Taylor, 2nd da. Died 1856. (F.M.) = Edward Holden Cruttenden, Esq. s.p.

Mary Ann, 3rd da. Died 1870. = Col. Chas. Graham.
Issue, six children.

Louisa, 4th da. = Bannatyne Macleod, Esq.
Seven children.

Harriet, 5th da. died young.

Elizabeth Taylor, 6th dau'r, and twin child with Thomas, the 5th son, 2nd wife. Living at Guildford, Surrey, 1878. = John Harding, Esq. Died at Dawlish, Devon, 1872. Bur. at Mamhead, Devon. = 1st wife, Mrs. Russell (*née* Frances Thornhill), widow of an elder brother of the Right Hon. John Somerset Russell Pakington, raised to the Peerage as Lord Hampton. Mr. Russell has an M.I. in Exeter Cathedral. She died in Pulteney St., Bath. Buried at Kelston **25 Jan. 1827, as Frances Harding.**

Issue, a dau'r Blanche. (by 2nd wife)

A son, who died s.p. (by 1st wife)

Note.—The issue of Harry and Charlotte Taylor were all born in India. Their father died just before embarking for home (circ. 1805), and left eleven children, of whom the eldest was only nine years old.

Emma Taylor, 1st dau'r. mar. about 1816. Died 1870. = Capt. Chas. Otway Mayne, R.N., of Bellevue, Kent.
Ten children, of whom a son, Otway was bur. at Kelston, 16 Feb. 1820, age 3.

Henry Taylor, 1st son. Died unmarried in India.

2. Robert, died about 1843. = 1st, Sarah Keys. = 2nd, Charlotte Delpratt.

3. John, died cælebs in India.

4. William. = Agnes Edwards.
Five children.

Thomas, 5th son, and twin with Elizabeth. = Eliza Lockett.
Issue, six children.

Armorial Bookplate.

ARMS OF WAGGETT OF CORK

William Waggett, Esq, Q C., and Recorder of Cork, was born in 1771, being the eldest son of Christopher Waggett, Esq, Sheriff of the City of Cork in 1786 He was elected to the Recordership of the City of Cork in 1808, and died unmarried at his seat, Kitsborough, near Cork, in Nov 1840 His brother Captain Waggett having died without issue in July, 1818, with him ended the direct male line of the elder branch of this family, which is now jointly represented by Nicholas Dunscombe of King William's Town, co Cork, Esq, J.P, and the Rev. Thomas W Carson, M A., of Beaumont, Terenure, co Dublin. (See accompanying pedigree of Waggett, and that of Carson of Shanroe in 'M G et H., Vol III, p 156.)

A marble tablet with the following inscription stands affixed to the wall of the Court House, Cork.—

"The Mayor, Sheriffs, and Commonalty of the City of Cork have erected this Tablet to perpetuate the memory of William Waggett, Esq, Q C, their late Recorder.

"Eminently gifted with Eloquence and Genius, possessed of sound knowledge and Experience, the high and ennobling qualities of his Mind commanded the respect and the benevolent affections of his Heart secured the esteem of all within the sphere of their influence Purity and Integrity shone conspicuous in his Judicial character. Fondly beloved as a friend, devotedly revered as a Public Functionary, he for thirty-two years ardently devoted himself to the duties of his station, and died amidst the regrets of his friends and fellow citizens 23rd November 1840."

NOTE ON THE NAME OF LEADAM

This name is a corruption, probably of very old date, of the name Leetham or Leatham The following appear to have been variations of the same name, the soft sounds of dh and d belonging probably to the South, the harder th (but pronounced soft, as in "though" or "fathom") to the North Letham (Scotland and Lancashire), Lethem, Lethom, Leathom, Lathom, Latham, Leadham, Leedham, Ledham, Ledhenham, Ledenham, Ledeham, Lideham, etc The following are examples of some of these variations of spelling —In the Rolls of Parliament 6 Ed. I., Isabella de Hautencote presents a petition for compensation for the manor of Lideham or Ledeham, which has been taken from her This manor of Lideham is perhaps the manor of Leadenham in Lincolnshire, mentioned in the Abbreviatio Placitorum temp Ric I, in which Alan de Bosco appears as Plaintiff in respect of land in this manor. So Browne Willis's 'History of Cathedrals,' vol. iii p 213, "Thomas Ledham or Ledhenham or Leedham held the Prebend of Louth in Lincoln Cathedral 1446–1451, and was buried in the Cathedral with this Inscription 'Hic jacet Thomas de Ledenham quondam Canonicus hujus ecclesiæ'" The Southern dh appears in the Domesday of 1282, "Robertus de Leedham tenet in Pampesworth dimid Feodi et valet per annum et debet sect" (Pampsford, co Cambridge) And in a certain Chancery suit temp. Elizabeth, Thomas Ledham and others are plaintiffs in respect of a tennis court and premises devised to them by a testator who held them by lease from the Dean and Chapter of Saint Paul's, the tennis court being near Paul's chain On the other hand, we have in Yorkshire, 30° Elizth. (vol iii of the Calendar to the Pleadings in the Duchy of Lancaster), Richard Lathom, otherwise Lethom or Ledam, plaintiff, against Anthony Leathom, defendant, as to lands in Carleton, Tanshelf, and Pomfret. There was a border manor of

William Waggett.

Letham, the Escheat Rolls of Edwd III mentioning Edwardus de Letham as lord of the manor of Letham and other lands in Berwick-on-Tweed A religious house called Letham, but qu whether in the same place, is also mentioned in vol ii of the Calendar to the Pleadings of the Duchy of Lancaster (22 Hen VIII.) as a cell to the Priory of Durham It may be added as an illustration that the names of Leatham and Latham have at some time been recognised as identical, that Mr Leatham, the present M P for Huddersfield, bears the Latham and Stanley crest, the eagle and child

The name of which, as has been said, Leetham is perhaps the oldest form is of very ancient origin The glossary at the end of vol ii of Thorpe's 'Ancient Laws and Institutes of England,' under the word "Laet," which forms the first syllable of the name, is as follows —

"Laet—Litus, Lidus, Letus One of a class between servile and free. According to Legg. Langobard Car Magn 83, equivalent with 'fiscalinus' —'Aldiones câ lege vivant in Italiâ, in servitute dominorum suorum quâ *fiscalini vel liti* vivunt in Franciâ' The following passages will serve to shew the distinction between litus and servus —'Si quis servum suum tributarium aut litum fecerit'—Lex Rip 62 'Inter exx homines, nobiles et ingenuos, similiter et litos, servum et ancillam eidem ecclesiæ tribuant.'—Cap. de part Sax. 15 'Qui hominem ingenuum occiderit solidos cc, qui lidum solidos c., qui servum solidos l componat'—Cap. Car an. 813 By the Frisic law cap 15, the composition for a noble was eleven pounds, for a freeman five pounds six ounces, for a litus two pounds nine ounces, for a slave one pound four and a half ounces These particulars are noticed because, according to some traditions, Kent was settled in part by Frisians These Læti or Leti were Germans who voluntarily placed themselves under the Roman Government, and received lands (terræ leticæ) to cultivate, for which they probably paid rent, and were obligated to perform military service If the enactment of Ethb 26 be genuine, and not servilely copied from some Germanic code by the compiler of these laws, the question presents itself, at what period came this class of persons into Kent? The most obvious solution seems to be that they must have been foreigners, or their descendants settled here under the Roman Government, and that the high value set upon their lives was in consequence of their consanguinity with the Germanic conquerors of the country See Grimm's D R A, pp 305–9, Graff's Sprachschatz, vol ii p 190; Eichhorn, vol. i p 319 (edit 1834), Palgrave, i p 354"

The word "Leet" in the phrase "Court-Leet" is probably the same, and Thorpe also notices the word Laed or Lathe as a name of divisions or districts peculiar to the County of Kent Leetham, therefore, is almost equivalent to Frankland *

The form of spelling the name in use by the writer and his family is, he believes, exclusively confined to them The family of Leadam were for many generations before the close of the last century owners of land in and in the neighbourhood of Walkington, East Yorks. They probably belonged to the class of substantial yeomen, though usually described in wills and deeds as "gentlemen," and occasionally even in contrast with other parties who are described as "yeomen," and though they seem to have retained the use of a crest, a demi-griffin proper with a feather in its beak, it was perhaps scarcely customary among yeomen proper. It happens unfortunately that the Parish Registers of Walkington were carried up to London about the year 1754 as evidence in a law suit between the Rev Randle Hancock, then Rector of Walkington, and the Corporation of Beverley, and never returned The present Rector, the Rev Douglas Ferguson, to whose courtesy I am much indebted, informs me that "the books are reported to have been seen by Poulson, who was searching when busy writing his History of Beverley' I have however succeeded by the means of tombstones, wills, the transcripts (very imperfect) of the Walkington Registers, preserved in the Diocesan Registry at York, the Registers of

* The writer has the authority of the late Professor Bosworth for this derivation

Land Transfers, etc., in reconstructing the pedigree as far back as one Emma Leadam, who was buried at Walkington Nov. 22, 1661. The name therefore appears not to have varied in spelling for more than two hundred years. About the beginning of the last century, one John Leadam the younger, gentleman, of Walkington, owned freeholds and copyholds in the parishes of Walkington, Heddon, Coningston, Bishop Burton, Willerby, Swanland, Ebberston, and Snainton, besides land and houses in Hull. A younger branch of the paternal generation had settled in Beverley, but also owned land in Walkington. This branch, however, became extinct on the death of William Leadam "of Hull and Beverley, merchant," without issue in 1752. All present bearers of the name are, therefore, descended from John Leadam the younger, "of Walkington and Willerby, gentleman," born 1699, died 1752, and buried at Walkington. He was the father of ten children, and not long after his death the family possessions were sold, and the family dispersed. His eldest son appears to have settled at Beverley, and to have fallen into comparatively poor circumstances. His male descendants are believed to have become extinct before 1815. The last female descendant of this son married in 1815, George Fielding, Esq., Surgeon, of Hull. The second and third sons of John Leadam the younger, William and Robert Leadam, emigrated to Virginia. It is believed that some of their descendants are still existing in America, and that one of them is a surgeon or physician, and the writer would be glad to be brought into communication with them. The fourth son died young. The fifth son and tenth child, Christopher Leadam, great grandfather of the writer, came to London, and practised as a surgeon. He was the last male of the family buried at Walkington (1793). His male descendants down to and including the present eldest son, William Ward Leadam, M.D., have all been surgeons or physicians.

The family politics appear to have been Whig, if one may judge from the fact that the two brothers, John Leadam the younger of Walkington and Robert Leadam of Walkington and Beverley, both supported Fox, the first Lord Holland, in 1741.

The Coat is—*Gu., a cross ermine between two crescents in chief or.*
Crest.—*A griffin's head between two wings, holding a feather proper.*

In conclusion, should any of your readers meet with my spelling of the name of a date later than the Commonwealth, or with any near variation prior to that date, I should be obliged by a communication.

Isaac Saunders Leadam, M.A.,
Late Fellow of Brasenose College, Oxford; of Lincoln's Inn, Barrister-at-Law.

Jan. 20, 1879.

MEMORANDA RELATING TO THE BALL AND LAVENDER FAMILIES.

.... Ball 1st husband.=Ann dau. of ....=.... Benbridge 2nd husband.

Samuel Ball, citizen and salter of London. Will dated 28 May, 1661. Property at Newington Green; Hollingbury, Kent; Chadwell, Essex; and in Ireland. Will proved 2 July, 1661, by relict Anne, sole executrix. P.C.C. May, 104.	= Anne dau. of Thomas Lavender by his wife .... dau. of .... Living 28 May, 1661. Her parents living 28 May, 1661. A	Thomas Ball, citizen and leatherseller of London. Will dated 14 Oct. 1679. Property at Basted, Kent. Will proved 6 Nov. 1679 by one of the executors, Benjamin Williams, his son in law. P.C.C. King, 138.	= Frances dau. of .... B	Samuel Benbridge of Canterbury.

A | B

1. Samuel Ball citizen = Mary, dau. of George Papillon. Married 20 Nov. 1682. and salter of London. See Vol. I., p. 315. | 2. John Ball. | Frances. = Benjamin Williams.

1. Anne. 2. Elizabeth. 3. Sarah. 4. Mary. 5. Margaret. 6. Martha.

Will of Richard Ball, citizen and clothworker of London, dated 1 July 1613. Wife Anne, mother Elizabeth Ball, eldest *son* John Ball, property at Wellingborough; sons Richard and William Ball, brothers John Ball and *his* wife Avis, and George Ball, *cousin* (niece) Elizabeth, dau. of brother John Ball; *cousins* Philip and Richard Ball, mother Mrs. Barbara Burnell, brothers Thomas Morley, Thomas Burnell, and William Burnell. Proved by relict Anne Ball 3 June 1617. (P.C.C. Weldon 59.)

Will of Nicholas Ball dated 23 Aug. 1638. Names wife Ellen Ball, brother John Ball and *his* sons John and Nicholas Ball, sister Mary, Alice Coles and her boy. Proved 29 Aug. 1638, by relict Ellen Ball, sole executrix. (P.C.C. Lee 98.)

Will of Anne Ball of London, widow, dated 13 March 1653. Bury. at P'ish Church of S. Dunstan's in the East, as near as may be to late husband (the above Richard Ball). Poor of Stanmore Magna and Harrow-on-the-Hill; dau. Anne Young, son-in-law John Cooke and his son, Richard Cooke, son of my dau. (*deceased*) Mary (Cooke); grandson Thomas Ball and *his* brother and sister; sons John Ball and Richard Ball who was March 1653 *married*, dau.-in-law Susan Ball, dau. Barbara and her husband Thomas Reeve, dau. Jane and her husband William Pindar, dau. Margaret Allott, dau. Elizabeth and her husband James Gough, son-in-law William Ro*bb*inson (no wife named), grandchild Anne Pindar, cousin Cicely Gilbert, brother Thomas Burnell and his wife. Proved 9 Oct. 1654, by Anne Young, sole executrix. (P.C.C. Alchin 46.)

Will of Samuel Ball, citizen and salter of London, dated 28 May, 1661. Property at Newington Green in parish of Islington; Hollingbury, Kent; Chadwell, Essex; and in Ireland. Names his wife Anne, his mother Ann Benbridge, his father in law Thomas Lavender and his wife, his children Samuel, John, Anne, Elizabeth, Sarah, Mary, Margaret, and Martha (children not 21), his brother Thomas Ball and his wife, his brothers in law Thomas *Kem*, William Rymer, James Wroth, Matthew Meriton, Nathaniel Greenell, John Lavender, Thomas Brewer, and each of their wives. Proved 2 July, 1661, by relict Anne, sole executrix. (P.C.C. May, 104.)

1672. 30 April. Date of Will of John Ball, citizen and carpenter of London. Brother Thomas Ball alone mentioned. Proved 4 June 1673. (P.C.C. Pye 72.)

Will of Thomas Ball, citizen and leatherseller of London, dated 14 October, 1679. Property at Basted, Kent. Names his wife Frances, his dau. Frances the wife of Benjamin Williams, his brother Samuel Benbridge of Canterbury, his nephew Samuel Ball and his *three* sisters his nieces, his brother and sister Thomas and Elizabeth Brewer, his three sisters Sarah Brewer, Dennis Brewer, and Martha Brewer, his kinsman Thomas Brewer, yeoman, his cousin John Brewer, a Doctor Benbridge, cousin Williams, Minister, a William Drope, Bridewell Hospital, and the parish of St. Margaret Moses, Friday Street. Proved 6 November, 1679, by son-in-law Benjamin Williams. (P.C.C. King, 138.)

Will of Richard Ball, D.D., Master of the Temple.* To be buried in Temple Church. Eldest (? elder) dau. Elizabeth, wife of Francis Purley; youngest

* See Clutterbuck's 'Co. Herts,' third vol.:—Helen, dau. of James Willymott, bapt. 28 Jan. 1633, married Richard Ball, D.D., Master of the Temple.

Rev. Richard Ball, D.D., Fellow of Pembroke Hall, Cam., Rector of Wilby and Westerfield in Suffolk. Installed as a Prebendary of Ely 22 Sept. 1660, and *same* month installed as a Prebendary of Lincoln. Rector of S. Mary, Woolchurch, London, Chaplain in Ordinary to Charles II., and Rector of Bluntisham, co. Hunts, 18 August, 1662. Died in the Temple, London, of which he was Master, 6 April, 1684, aged 86.

(? younger) dau. Helen Ball. Property at Baddingham, Framlingham, etc., and in Shotly in Suffolk, widow of son Thomas Ball, brother John Ball, *Esq.*, son William Ball, sister Aylet, Serjeant Hampson, niece Anne Browne, nephew John Ball, son of eldest brother John Ball; *goddau.* Elizabeth Purley. Tes'tor born at Stanmore Magna. Will dated 31 Oct. 1683, and proved 1 Dec. 1684, by Anne Browne, power reserved to Eliza Purley. (P.C.C. Hare 159.)

Will of Samuel Ball,* citizen and salter of London, dated 1 May, 1738, and proved 14 October, 1741, by testator's two sons Papillon Ball and Benjamin Ball. (P.C.C. Spurway, 252.)

Richard Lavinder of Felmersham, co. Bedford. = Anne, dau. of . . . . Risely of Risely, co. Bed.

- 1. William Lavinder of town of Bedford.
- 2. John Lavinder.
- 3. Thomas Lavinder of London a° 1634. = Margaret,† dau. of Ambrose Salisbury of Ravenston, co. Leicester.
    - 1. Thomas Lavinder, æt. 4 in a° 1634.
    - 1. Elizabeth.
    - 2. Margaret.
    - 3. Mary.
    - 4. Anne.
    - 5. Sarah.
- 4. Richard Lavinder of Felmersham, co. Bedford.
- 1. Anne. = Henry Jay of Bedford.

Harl. MS. 1476, page 414.
Visitation of London, 1634.

Will of Thomas Lav*e*nder, citizen and grocer of London, dated 1 Sept. 1661. Property in Essex, at Highbury, and a house in Bread Street. Names wife Margaret, son John Lav*e*nder, son-in-law Thomas *Came*, and all his grandchildren. Proved 29 September, 1664. (P.C.C. Bruce, 102.)

I shall be much indebted for any information as to these families of Ball, or as to any of those who are named in the wills, from which I give very short extracts.

REGINALD STEWART BODDINGTON.

15 *Markham Square, Chelsea, S.W.*

Family of Gresham.

INQUISITION POST MORTEM.

SIR THOMAS GRESHAM, KT.

[Chancery Inquis. p.m. 22 Eliz., 2nd Pt. No. 36.]

Writ to John Southcott one of the Justices of the Pleas William Fleetewood Esq. William Gerrard Esq. Jeronimus Hawley Esq. William Necton Gent. to

* Samuel Ball took up the freedom of London by patrimony, May, 1690. His patrimony vouchers were members of the Salters' Company, and from the records in the Chamberlain's Court of the City of London it appears he was born 7 April, 17 Charles I., at Newington Green, co. Middlesex. He went on to the Livery of the Salters' Company 27 May, 1691, was chosen on the Court of Assistants 12 May, 1709, and subsequently served the offices of Junior Warden, Upper Warden, and Master of that Company. He paid £400 and twenty marks into the Chamber of the City of London, June. 1731, as his fines for exemption from serving the office of Sheriff of the City of London and County of Middlesex.

Mary, daughter of Samuel Ball, merchant, bur. at St. John's Church, Hackney, 16 Aug. 1715.

Samuel Ball, died 13 and buried 19 September, 1741, at Hackney.

† In 'Visitation of Co. Leicester' and Nichols' 'History of co. Leicester,' under pedigree of Salisbury of Ravenston, appears the marriage of Margaret, eldest dau. of Ambrose Salisbury of Ravenston by his wife Elizabeth, dau. of George Hopkins of Wednesbury, co. Stafford, with Thomas Lavender, grocer in Wood Street, London.

ORK.

m Bowers. Mar-
at Cloyne, dated
33.

= George Crofts, of Churchtown, Co. Cork. Marriage Bond at Cloyne, dated Feb. 28, 1719.

March, 1744; = *Eliza Sealy*, daughter of G
., 1778; Mayor of Barleyfield, near Band
93; died Sept. Esq., and Anne, otherwi
his wife.

George-Sealy, Sheriff Thomas, Rector =

(? younger) dau. Helen Ball. Property at Baddingham, Framlingham, etc., and in Shotly in Suffolk, widow of son Thomas Ball, brother John Ball, *Esq.*, son William Ball, sister Aylet, Serjeant Hampson, niece Anne Browne, nephew John Ball, son of eldest brother John Ball; *goddau.* Elizabeth Purley. Tes'tor born at Stanmore Magna. Will dated 31 Oct. 1683, and proved 1 Dec. 1684, by Anne Browne, power reserved to Eliza Purley. (P.C.C. Hare 159.)

Will of Samuel Ball,* citizen and salter of London, dated 1 May, 1738, and proved 14 October, 1741, by testator's two sons Papillon Ball and Benjamin Ball. (P.C.C. Spurway, 252.)

Richard Lavinder of Felmersham, co. Bedford. = Anne, dau. of . . . . Risely of Risely, co. Bed.

Children:
1. William Lavinder of town of Bedford.
2. John Lavinder.
3. Thomas Lavinder of London a° 1634. = Margaret,† dau. of Ambrose Salisbury of Ravenston, co. Leicester.
4. Richard Lavinder of Felmersham, co. Bedford.
1. Anne. = Henry Jay of Bedford.

Children of Thomas and Margaret:
1. Thomas Lavinder, æt. 4 in a° 1634.
1. Elizabeth.
2. Margaret.
3. Mary.
4. Anne.
5. Sarah.

Harl. MS. 1476, page 414.
Visitation of London, 1634.

Will of Thomas Lavender, citizen and grocer of London, dated 1 Sept. 1661. Property in Essex, at Highbury, and a house in Bread Street. Names wife Margaret, son John Lavender, son-in-law Thomas *Came*, and all his grandchildren. Proved 29 September, 1664. (P.C.C. Bruce, 102.)

I shall be much indebted for any information as to these families of Ball, or as to any of those who are named in the wills, from which I give very short extracts.

REGINALD STEWART BODDINGTON.

15 *Markham Square, Chelsea, S.W.*

Family of Gresham.

INQUISITION POST MORTEM.

SIR THOMAS GRESHAM, KT.

[Chancery Inquis. p.m. 22 Eliz., 2nd Pt. No. 36.]

Writ to John Southcott one of the Justices of the Pleas William Fleetewood Esq. William Gerrard Esq. Jeronimus Hawley Esq. William Necton Gent. to

* Samuel Ball took up the freedom of London by patrimony, May, 1690. His patrimony vouchers were members of the Salters' Company, and from the records in the Chamberlain's Court of the City of London it appears he was born 7 April, 17 Charles I., at Newington Green, co. Middlesex. He went on to the Livery of the Salters' Company 27 May, 1691, was chosen on the Court of Assistants 12 May, 1709, and subsequently served the offices of Junior Warden, Upper Warden, and Master of that Company. He paid £400 and twenty marks into the Chamber of the City of London, June. 1731, as his fines for exemption from serving the office of Sheriff of the City of London and County of Middlesex.

Mary, daughter of Samuel Ball, merchant, bur. at St. John's Church, Hackney, 16 Aug. 1715. Samuel Ball, died 13 and buried 19 September, 1741, at Hackney.

† In 'Visitation of Co. Leicester' and Nichols' 'History of co. Leicester,' under pedigree of Salisbury of Ravenston, appears the marriage of Margaret, eldest dau. of Ambrose Salisbury of Ravenston by his wife Elizabeth, dau. of George Hopkins of Wednesbury, co. Stafford, with Thomas Lavender, grocer in Wood Street, London.

WAGGETT OF CORK.

(Curante N. D.)

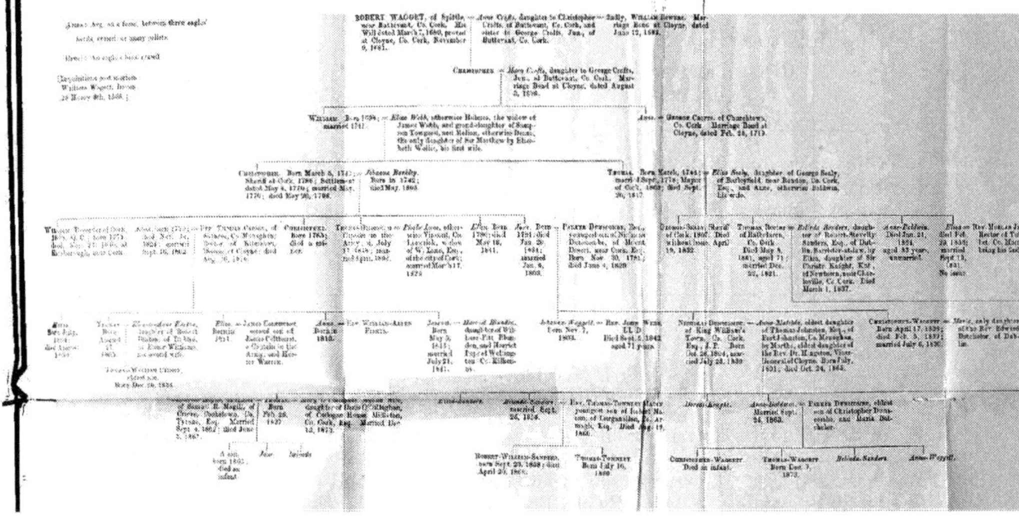

enquire what lands and tenements Thomas Gresham Knight held in chief or in service in the County of Middlesex at the time of his death and who was his next heir Dated at Westminster 12 March 22 Eliz.

Inquisition taken at Westminster 22 March 22 Eliz before John Southcote one of the Justices of the Queen and others The Jurors say that long before his death Thomas Gresham was seised in his demesne as of fee of the Manors of Heston Wike Osterley and Burston in the County of Middlesex and in forty messuages forty gardens 3000 acres of land 500 of meadow 2000 of pasture 500 of wood 1000 of furze and heath and £20 rent with the appurtenances in Osterley Heston Wike Norwood Isleworth Braynford Ashford Bedfont Laleham Irene* Staynes and Howneslowe, and also of the Park of Osterley co Midd (Recites an Indenture of 20 May 17 Eliz whereby the above premises were conveyed to Trustees to the use of Sir Thomas Gresham and Anne his wife for the term of their lives with divers remainders over) That Sir Thomas Gresham died on 21 Nov 22 Eliz without any issue by Anne his wife, that at the time of his death Henry Nevell Junior was his kinsman and next heir as being son and heir of Elizabeth late the wife of Sir Henry Nevell Knight, the daughter and heir of Sir John Gresham Knight deceased late brother of Sir Thomas Gresham Knight That the said Henry Nevell was on the 21st March last past of the age of 16 years 11 months and 10 days and is now living That Anne late wife of Thomas Gresham is still living and at Osterley That the Manor of Heston is held of the Queen by the service of the 20th part of a Knight's fee and is worth £22 16s. 5d yearly—that the Manors of Osterley Wike and Burston and the other premises are worth £87 5s 1d. yearly but of whom held they know not

[Chancery Inquis p m. 23 Eliz, 1st Pt No 11]

Inquisition taken at Norwich Castle 11 July 23 Eliz before Sir William Paston Knight and others upon the death of Sir Thomas Gresham Knight The Jurors say that the said Sir Thomas Gresham long before his death was seised in his demesne as of fee of the Manors of Westacre Eastwalton Narford Lakenham Tasburghe Bynham in Great Walsingham, Great Walsingham Little Walsingham Botts Cullinghams Fennes Marshes Wells Ousthorpe Magna Massingham Massingham Debtford Burrowghall in Holkham *alias* Holekombe Hardingham Myleham Beston *alias* Biston Lympnow Castellacre Arundell Castellacre Priory Heringshall Dyckwood Egmer Hemesby Luddon Bacon Therlyng co Norf And of the Manors of Greatover Littleover and Fyndeine and of the Manors of Nunkelyng and of Sutton and of the Rectory of Swyne and of the Rectory and Advowson of Nunkelynge and of a moiety of the Manor of Estbalk co York and of the Manors of Mayghfeild and Wadhurst co Sussex and of the Manor of Wedmor co Somerset and of the Manors of Ashmorehall and Erlestonham *alias* Stonham Comitis co Suffolk and of the Manor of Thirling co Cantab' and of the Manors of Heston Wike Osterley and Burston co Midd and of a capital messuage and house in the Parish of St Helen near Bishopsgate Street and of St Peter le pore in the City of London and of divers other messuages gardens shops cellars &c in the Parishes of St Helen St Peter le pore St Michaell in Basinghall Street St Bartholomew and St Michael in Cornhill in the City of London and of the Manors of Stranton Staton Carew and Newborne Grewe in the County Palatine of Durham and of the Manors of Cantercelly *alias* Cantrecelly and Brentley and the Castle of Brentley and of the Advowson of the Church of Llandvrenachet† co Brecon in Wales and of 14 acres and 3 roods of marsh in Erith co. Kent (Recites an Indenture of 1 Sep 12 Eliz. by which the said manors and lands were conveyed by Sir Thomas Gresham and Anne his wife to Anthony Strynger and Thomas Cely in trust to the use of themselves for life with divers remainders over)

[The rest of the Inquisition is illegible]

---

* Iveney † Llandvrenech

WORDSWORTHIANA GRASMERE CHURCHYARD.

Permit me to rescue from the mere summary of names of those to whose memory tombstones are erected in Grasmere Churchyard, four whose holders, I think, merit that their monumental inscriptions should be recorded with others, many of whom are much less worthy of the honour conferred upon them in your number for January There are three plain slate upright stones standing side by side on the one we read, "Gathered to the side of kindred whom in their declining years she faithfully and affectionately tended, here lies the Body of Elizabeth Satterthwaite, late of Loughrigg Holme She died at Stanwix, near Carlisle, the 11th day of March, 1849, aged 35 years This stone is erected in grateful remembrance of her and Elizabeth Youdell, who died at Rydal 12th Jany 1831, aged 67 years, and of Jonathan Youdell, who died at Rydal 28th Nov 1841, aged 79 years." This is the pair of whom Wordsworth says in 'The Excursion' —

> "High in the mountain where they long have dwelt
> A wedded pair in childless solitude"

It was poor old Betty who

> ' Drawn from her cottage on that aery height,
> Bearing a lantern in her hand, she stood
> Or paced the ground to guide her husband home"

She was also the heroine of Southey's story of "The Terrible Knitters of Dent," given in 'The Doctor'

The central slab is "In memory of John Carter of Loughrigg Holme, Ambleside, who died 28th January, 1863, aged 67 years He was the confidential clerk and much valued friend of the late William Wordsworth, Esq, P L, of Rydal Mount, with whose family he was connected by mutual ties of gratitude and sincere affection for a period of fifty years" Of him it is said in 'Wordsworth's Life,' vol ii p. 5, "Justice would not be done, and Wordsworth's feelings would be wronged, if his own name went down to posterity unaccompanied by that of one who served him faithfully, zealously, and efficiently for thirty-seven years, and by thus serving him as he did, conferred a benefit on the world"

How profound was the admiration inspired by the great poet in the breast of his friend is evidenced by a letter before me, dated Stanwix, April 23rd, 1850, in which he informs a correspondent of the death of Wordsworth, "The glory is departed from Israel! the good old man, our dear friend, expired at a quarter to twelve to-day"

The third slab is "In affectionate remembrance of James Dixon, born 19th July, 1797, died 4th April, 1873 He was for thirty-three years the faithful servant of Mr and Mrs Wordsworth of Rydal Mount, and for upwards of half a century the much valued friend of their family"

A fourth plain upright slate is "Sacred to the memory of James Greenwood of The Wyke, who died 2nd May, 1845, aged 57 years, also of Ann Greenwood, who died 12th May, 1852, aged 62 years also of Richard Jones Greenwood, son of the above, who died in Liverpool 10th Sept 1842, aged 17 years Vita ut herba" James Greenwood was the friend of Wordsworth, Hartley Coleridge, and Professor Wilson He assisted Wordsworth and Mr Barber in planting the yew trees which flourish near their respective graves (Works, ed 1857, vol. vi. p. 7) He it was for whom "The Westmoreland Girl" (Sarah Mackereth),

> ' fulfilling her sire's office,
> Rang alone the far-heard knell,
> Tribute, by her hand in sorrow,
> Paid to one who loved her well
>
> "When his spirit was departed,
> On that service she went forth,
> Nor did fail the like to render
> When his corse was laid in earth"

Fleatham House, Saint Bees WM JACKSON.

GARE LE PIED FORT
John Bedford

Pedigree of the Bedfords of Hull, Dewsbury, Penistone, etc., co. York.(1)

Compiled by EDWIN JACKSON BEDFORD.

ANCIENT ARMORIAL BEARINGS OF BEDFORD.—*Argent, three lions' or bears' paws couped within a bordure engrailed sable.* These arms were granted probably to one of the Bedfords of Hull previous to the establishment of the Heralds' College. They have frequently been borne by later generations of the family.

ARMS OF BEDFORD OF OUGHTIBRIDGE.—*Per chevron argent and sable, four bears' paws erased, three in chief and one in base, within a bordure engrailed, all counterchanged. Quartering,* 2. GRAYSON. 3. HALL.

CREST.—*In front of a bear's paw erased sable, holding a terrestrial globe proper, an annulet argent.*

MOTTO.—GARE LE PIED FORT.

(Granted Nov. 19th, 1878, to John Bedford of Birley House and Oughtibridge, and his descendants.)

John de Bedford, Sheriff of Hull in 1332 and 1333. King Edward III. passed through Hull in 1332, when he created William de la Pole a knight banneret and first Mayor of Hull, and made Stephen de Begholm and John de Bedford Sheriffs or "Bayliffs." ═ . . . .

. . . . de Bedford of Hull. ═ . . . .

John Bedford, Mayor of Hull in 1412, 1414, 1420, 1428, 1435, and 1443. Alderman for White Fryers Ward. Possessed property in Hull, Beverley, etc. [*vide* Ex. Reg. Prop. Bev. l. 2, p. 78b.] Will dated Dec. 23, 1450. Proved at York, May 14, 1451. On the 18th March, 1414, the King wrote to him from Kenilworth, demanding assistance from him and the principal burgesses of Hull in procuring shipping and stores to aid him in his wars with France, Scotland, and other powers. This was unanimously granted by them. ═ Agnes, dau. of . . . . Will dated Sept. 14, 1459. Proved at York, Oct. 18, 1459.

Children:

- Richard Bedford, eldest son, he inherited lands at Estcroft and Molescroft, near Beverley, at Supelwalde and Horkestowe, co. Lincoln; also property in Yule Street and Starle Lane in Kingston-upon-Hull. ═ . . . .
  - Elizabeth.
  - Anne.
- Nicholas Bedford, inherited property in Ball Street, Denton Lane, and Henkil Street, in Kingston-upon-Hull. ═ . . . .
  - John Bedford, named in his grandfather's will.(2)
- John Bedford.
- Hellen ═ . . . . Eare.
- Elizabeth ═ John Dalton.

William Bedford of Womersley. Will dat. Aug. 10, 1637. Proved at York, May 27, 1639. ═ Ellen, dau. of . . . .

A

John Bedford of Dewsbury, living 1480-1527. ═ Johanna, dau. of . . . . Administration granted to her and to Robert Bedford her son, Sept. 12, 1527.

Children:

- Robert Bedford of Dewsbury, son and heir. Bur. at Dewsbury, Sept. 16, 1582. ═ . . . . Bur. at Dewsbury, Feb. 5, 1579.
  - B
- Elizabeth.
- Marion.
- Johanna.
- Alice.
- John Bedford of Emley. Will dated July 1, 1571. Proved at York, Oct. . . 1571. Died s.p. Leaves 12d. to every householder in Emley parish.
- William Bedford of Hemsworth. Will dated May 10, 1574. Proved at York, April 20, 1575. Leaves land at Hemsworth to Richard Heaton, his servant. Died s.p.

A

William Bedford, son and heir. Executor by his father's will. ═ . . . .

Henry Bedford, to whom his father left the sum of 20s.

William Bedford, lord of the manor of Cridlingstubs, leaves land there and at Norton to Mary his wife, and William Savile, gent., on trust for his wife and children. Will dated Nov. 13, 1689.(3) ═ Mary, dau. of . . . . Administration granted to her March 1, 1693. Dead before Jan. 22, 1701, when administration was granted to Ann Hutton, in trust for her children, being minors.

Joshua, eldest son. — William, 2nd son. — Thomas. — Ann.

[All under age in 1701.]

B

Robert Bedford of Dewsbury, had property there. *Vide* Court Rolls. Buried at Dewsbury Jan. 20, 1627. Was churchwarden in 1571, when he was styled Robert Bedford, Junr. See Church Register. (H.C.) ═ . . . . Buried at Dewsbury Oct. 26, 1597.

John Bedford of Crownest, in Dewsbury, son and heir, born before July 1, 1571, being named in the will of John Bedford of Emley, of that date, as "my godson, John Bedford, son of Robert Bedford of Dewsburie." Bur. at Dewsbury, Feb. 1636. Will dated Feb. 13, 1636. Proved at York Aug. 26, 1637. Leaves to Alice, his wife, Crownest and other property in Dewsbury, and £50 to Sir John Savile of Lupsett, Knt., in trust for his younger son John. (H.C.) (4) ═ Alice, dau. and sole heiress of Robert Savile of Snydale, son of Thomas Savile of Stanley Hall, near Wakefield. Marr. at Dewsbury Nov. 22, 1603.(5) ═ 2nd husb. Robert Nettleton. Marr. at Dewsbury April . . . 1637.

Edward Bedford, bap. at Dewsbury June 16, 1577. Bur. there Feb. 6, 1614. Died s. p. ═ Jennet, dau. of . . . . Forrest. Marr. at Dewsbury April 25, 1614. ═ 2nd husb. Michael Speight. Marr. at Dewsbury Feb. 9, 1623.

Grace, bap. at Dewsbury, Feb. 26, 1565.

Robert Bedford, son and heir, bap. at Dewsbury Dec. 11, 1605. Buried there January 21, 1659. See Dewsbury Rectorial Manor Court Rolls, etc. (H.C.) ═ Ann, dau. of . . . . Bur. at Dewsbury Dec. . . 1651.

John Bedford, bap. at Dewsbury April 23, 1609, most probably identical with John Bedford, living at Smythey Brook, near Dewsbury, 1642-1658.(6) (H.C.) ═ ? Elizabeth dau. of . . . . Leatham. Married at Thornhill Nov. 9, 1641.

John Bedford, bap. at Dewsbury Nov. 16, 1630. ═ . . . . — C

Robert Bedford of Crownest, bapt. at Dewsbury Dec. 28, 1631. Dead before April 20, 1661. *Vide* Court Rolls. (H.C.) ═ Isabel, dau. of [? William] Riche of Bull House, par. of Penistone. Mar. at Dewsbury Jan. 9, 1653. — D

Edward Bedford, bap. at Dewsbury, Sept. 1650.

Elizabeth, bap. Sept. . . 1636.

Mary, bap. May . . 1634.

Mary, bap. at Thornhill Sept. 18, 1642.

Robert Bedford of Smythey Brook, bap. at Thornhill, March 1, 1652. Marr. at Dewsbury, January 2, 1681. Bur. at Thornhill, June 19, 1686. (H.C.) ═ Martha, dau. of . . . Fowleson of Dewsbury. Bur. at Thornhill, Mar. 11, 1699. — E

John, bap. at Thornhill, Feb. 24, 1655. Buried there Feb. 25, 1658.

C | D | E

Thomas Bedford of Crownest. Died unmar. in 1748, aged 80. Bur. at Dewsbury. Will dat. Nov. 15, 1743. He sold Crownest. Left £500 to found a charity school at Dewsbury.(7) (H.C.)

Robert Bedford of Crownest. Died in 1712. (8) (H.C.) = Ann, dau. of . . . . Calverley of Leeds. = 2nd husb. Robert Wynne.

John Bedford of Thornhill = Mary, dau. of . . . Briggs. A Major in the army. He and Sir George Armytage, Bart., jointly gave £200 to the chapel of Rastrick. Ob. s. p.(9) (H.C.) — Mary: Will dat. Dec. 13, 1735. Left £200 to the Charity School at Dewsbury.(7)

Robert Bedford = ... of Smythey Brook, born circa 1682. Living there 1702-1708. (H.C.)

John, died young.

Mary, bap. at Thornhill, Jan. 18, 1684.

Robert, bap. at Dewsbury, Nov. 1653.

John, bap. at Dewsbury, Feb. 4, 1655.

Elizabeth, bap. at Dewsbury, Jan. 20, 1660. Bur. there Aug. 2, 1662.

Thomas, bap. at Dewsbury, Oct. 29, 1663.

Sarah, bap. at Dewsbury, April 6, 1670.

Mary, bap. at Dewsbury, June 1, 1676.

Sarah, dau. of . . . . Squires of Leeds. 1st wife. = John Bedford of Leeds, merchant. (H.C.) = Anne, dau. of . . . . 2nd wife.

Anne. (H.C.) Mary. (H.C.)

Elizabeth. (H.C.) = ... Wrigglesworth of Winlayton, co. Durham.

Robert Bedford, died at Madras, unmarried. (H.C.)

John Bedford of Huntingdon. Married at All Saints' Church, Huntingdon, Aug. 9, 1768. (H.C.) = Elizabeth, dau. and sole heiress of Walter Thong of Huntingdon, by Eliz. dau. of John Ferrar of Huntingdon, Alderman.

Elizabeth. (H.C.) = Thomas Glover.

Sarah. (H.C.) = William Turner.

Ann, bap. at Thornhill, Jan. 3, 1702.

John Bedford, bap. at Thornhill, June 21, 1704. Living afterwards at Ponds in par. of Penistone, where he died May 7, 1791, aged 87. Bur. at Peniston. See M.I. there. (H.C.) = Mary, dau. of John Pashley of Oxspring Lodge, par. of Penistone, son of John Pashley, son of Thomas Pashley, all of Oxspring Lodge. Bap. at Penistone Dec. 20, 1715. Died Jan. 1, 1800. Buried at Penistone. See M.I.

David, bap. at Thornhill, Nov. 3, 1708.

John Bedford of Ponds, bap. at Penistone, Oct. 29, 1747. Marr. Dec. 14, 1774. Died Oct. 23, 1809. Bur. at Penistone. See M.I. (H.C.) = Martha, dau. of Abraham Crossley of Handbank, par. of Penistone. Died Dec. 6, 1834. Buried at Penistone.

Mary, o. s.p. = John Robinson of Wakefield.

Frances.

William Bedford of Threadneedle Street, London, Insurance Broker, bap. at Penistone, June 23, 1778. Died in London c. 1849. (H.C.) = ... dau. of . . . . of London.

Hannah. Eliza. Mary Ann. Clara. Julia. [All unmarried.]

Joseph Bedford of Oxspring and Penistone, b. at Ponds, Jan. 24, 1782. Died Jan. 31, 1845. Bur. at Penistone. (H.C.) = Dorothy, dau. of Thomas Wain of Birchen Lee, co. Derby, b. April 12, 1770. Died Sept. 30, 1840. Bur. at Penistone.

G

Mary, born June 16, 1784. Died March 17, 1813, unmarried.

F

F

G

Mary, born Nov. . . 1800. = John Parkin, of Middlewood, n^r Sheffield, died s.p.

Ann, born . . . 1802. Died . . . 1874. = John Senior Crossley of Water Hall, Penistone.

Martha, born . . . 1804. Died Oct. 24, 1839. No issue living. = George Brown, timber merch^t, Bankside, London.

John Bedford of Penistone, born March 10, 1806. D. May 10, 1873. Bu. at Penistone. = Mary, dau. of Joseph Swift of Hoylandswaine, b. March . . 1807. D. Apr. 3, 1853. Bur. at Penistone.

Jane, born . . . 1808. D. . . 1871. Buried at Penistone. = James Mitchell of Penistone.

Children of John Bedford and Mary Swift:

Charles Henry, eldest son, born Aug. 8, 1831. Died Oct. 25, 1876, unmarried.

John, now of New York, U.S., born Jan. 22, 1835. = Mary, dau. of Thomas Davies of Manchester.

Joseph.

Benjamin Swift.

Walter.

Mary.

Children of John and Mary Davies:

Charles Henry, died young.

John Richard.

John Bedford of Ponds and Oughtibridge, bap. at Penistone, Dec. 4, 1786. Mar. May 26, 1814. Died Jan. 18, 1839. Bur. at Bradfield. He sold "The Ponds." (H.C.) = Ann, dau. and heiress of George Grayson of Oughtibridge, by Martha, his wife, dau. and heiress of Joseph Hall of Oughtibridge. Born Nov. 10, 1787. Died Dec. 2, 1860. Bur. at Bradfield.(10)

Thomas Bedford of Liverpool, West India merchant, bap. at Penistone, Aug. 22, 1793. Died at sea, Aug. 28, 1825. Unmarried. (H.C.)

Children of John Bedford and Ann Grayson:

Dorothy, born . . . 1810. = ... Marsh of Penistone.

Joseph Bedford of Penistone, born Dec. 22, 1813. Mar. at Petworth, Oct. 2, 1839. Died Oct. 14, 1848. Buried at Penistone. = Harriet Elliot, dau. and eventual coheir of George Jackson of Petworth, eldest son of Rev. James Jackson, Vicar of Farnham. Born Jan. 25, 1813.

John Bedford of Birley House & Oughtibridge, merchant, born May 26, 1815. Marr. at Ecclesfield, Nov. 1844. (H.C.) = Harriet, dau. and coheir of George Hawksley of Owlerton, born Nov. 14, 1821.

Mary, born Oct. . 1816. Died May 5, 1844. Unmarried.

Sarah, born . . . 1820. Died Oct. 4, 1851. Unmarried.

Child of Joseph Bedford and Harriet Elliot:

Edwin Jackson Bedford, born at Water Hall, Penistone, June 21, 1840. Marr. at St. Mary's, Stoke Newington, Oct. 5, 1876. = Eliza Mary, dau. and coheiress of Charles Ledger of Stoke Newington, born Sept. 23, 1847.

Children of Edwin Jackson Bedford and Eliza Mary:

Eleanor Gundreda, born Oct. 1, 1877.

Adela Maud, born Nov. 23, 1878.

Children of John Bedford and Harriet Hawksley:

John George Hawksley, born Sept. 25, 1845.

Henry Hall, born April 17, 1847. Marr. at Filey, Feb. 20, 1879. = Lucy, dau. and coheiress of Joseph Danby of Hibaldstow, co. Lincoln, born Mar. 31, 1855.

William James, born June 8, 1849.

Anne, born Dec. 2, 1856.

NOTES

(1) The above pedigree has been carefully compiled from wills, court rolls, records in the College of Arms, parish registers, family documents, and local histories Where the letters H C are affixed, they denote that the names of those persons are entered at the Heralds' College, though all the information here given may not be found there

(2) There appears to be no further record of the Bedfords of Hull Whether one of the family settled in Dewsbury or not, we have no proof If as is surmised, this was the case the first John Bedford recorded as living at Dewsbury between 1480-1527 might have been the son of John Bedford of Hull, here named The perpetuation of the name John suggests a relationship

(3) The following is extracted from the will of William Bedford of Cridlingstubs, in com Ebor, gent —"My manor and lordship of Cridlingstubs and my land at Norton to Mary Bedford, my wife, and William Savile gent on trust that my wife have one-third as her portion for life, the rest to my children' viz, Joshua, his eldest son and William, his second son He also leaves 'to my younger children Thomas Bedford and Ann Bedford, each £150, to be raised out of the property above on their attaining twenty-one years of age' The seal affixed to the signature of William Bedford bears for a crest "an owl," probably the seal of William Savile, named in the will

(4) The following are extracts from the will of John Bedford the elder, of Crownest, in the par of Dewsbury, in com Ebor, yeoman —' To Alice Bedford, my wife, my house at Crownest, and a house at Dewsbury, wherein Samuel Pearson minister, now dwelleth' "To Robert Bedford and John Bedford, my grandchildren those two iron ranges standing in the hall and kitchen at Crownest, provided Alice my wife shall have them for her life To Robert Bedford my son all the glasse and wainscott about Crownest and one corslett with the pike hereto belonging' "Fifty pounds to be payd to Sir John Savile, of Lupsett, Knight, in truste for the use and maintenance of John Bedford, my younger son' Leaves Alice Bedford his wife, ex trix

(5) Thomas Savile was great-great-grandson of Henry Savile of Thornhill and his wife Elizabeth, dau and heiress of Sir Simon Thornhill of Thornhill whose mother Joan was dau of John Fitzwilliam of Emley, descended from Sir William Fitzwilliam of Emley, and his wife Ella, dau of William Earl of Warren and Surrey, great grandson of William the Conqueror

(6) There is much evidence in favour of this identity, though legal proof is as yet wanting We find no record of John Bedford in Dewsbury after his father's death in 1636, and the first of the Bedfords of Smythey Brook, mentioned in the Thornhill Registers, bears this name Sir John Savile, being left his trustee, it seems very probable he would place him in some farm on his estate, Smythey Brook which is about two and half miles from Dewsbury, being then the property of the Saviles, as it is at the present time We also find his nephew, Robert Bedford of Crownest, married one of the Riches of Bull House, in par of Penistone and Robert, grandson of John, of Smythey Brook, places his son John in the 'Ponds Farm' near Penistone, previously in the possession of Josias Rich, a descendant of the Bull House family This would suggest a family connection, and account for the settlement of John Bedford, last named, in the bleak district of 'the Ponds' It is also worthy of notice that the family names of John and Robert were still retained almost exclusively for several generations, the name of John being still common in the family

(7) For a complete account of these charities, see Greenwood's 'History of Dewsbury' They were for building a schoolhouse and educating fifty poor children

(8) A deed signed by Robert Bedford, dated April 23 1702, and in the possession of the compiler of this pedigree, gives full particulars of the property comprised in the Crownest estate

(9) The communion plate in the Parish Church at Dewsbury was presented by John Bedford of Thornhill Briggs He probably died about 1730, when his elder brother Thomas became the last of the family living at Dewsbury

(10) There is a pedigree of the family of Hall of Oughtibridge recorded in the Heralds' College, commencing in the sixteenth century

---

VINCENT —Thomas Vincent, J P. for co Surrey, Alderman of London, married Joanna, dau of Thomas Burgess. She died 1654, and was buried at Camberwell, having been married twenty years They had five sons and nine daughters The sons appear to have died young, of the daughters, Elizabeth married Richard, Lord Blayney, Sarah married George Blount, another married Jeffrey Paul

In Playfair's 'Irish Baronetage,' Barbara, wife of Thomas Esmonde, is said to be a daughter of the above-named Thomas Vincent, and a sister of Alderman Vincent of Limerick I think there is a mistake here

Thomas Vincent was High Sheriff of Meath 1656, M P for Monaghan 1661, died 1666 After the death of his wife Joanna, he appears to have married secondly Elizabeth? He mentions in his will an only son Nathaniel, who I suppose was grandfather to Richard Vincent of New Abbey, M P for Clogher, 1733

I want to find out the connection of these Vincents and Alderman John Vincent, Sheriff of Limerick 1696, and Mayor 1703 and 1727.—W C VINCENT.

EXTRACTS FROM THE REGISTERS OF THE PARISHES OF KELSTON AND CORSTON, SOMERSET, AND FROM BITTON IN GLOUCESTERSHIRE, RELATING TO THE FAMILY OF HARINGTON

Kelston Registers.

Baptisms.

1577	13 Jan.	Eliz d of Tho Harington
1579	8 March	Mary, d of Tho Harington.
1580	3 Dec	John, s of Tho. Harington.
1585	31 Jan	Tho. s of Tho Harington
1591.	3 May	Ellina, d of Jo Harington
1594	3 Aug.	Robert, s of Jo Harington, Esq.
1600	21 Sept	Mary, d of Sir John Harington.
1602	29 June	Robert, s. of Sir John Harington
1607	29 Aug	Thomas, s of Francis Harington.
1624.	8 July.	John, s of Jno. Harington, Esq.
1627	19 May	John, s of Jno Harington, Esq
1630	20 April	Edward, s of Geo Harington.
1637	6 July	Phœbe, d of Jno Harington, Esq and the honourable Lady Dionyssa his wife
1672	3 March.	John, son of Mr Will Harington & Anne his wife
1674	2 Nov.	James, s of M^r^ W Harington & Anne his wife
1675	7 Sept	James, s. of Jno Harington, Esq
1676	6 Dec	Dionyse, d of Mr Will Harington and Anne his wife
1680	1 Jan	John, s of John Harington, Esq and Helena his wife
1680	9 Aug	Mary & Eliz dau'rs of Mr Will Harington and Anne his wife.
1681	11 Feb	Helena, d of John Harington, Esq and Helena his wife (Born Feb 10)
1682	16 May.	Gostlett, s of John Harington, Esq and Helena his wife.
1682	12 Oct	Phœbe, d of M^r^ W Harington and Anne his w
1683	20 March.	Mary, d of John Harington, Esq and Helena his w
1685	7 April	Isabella, d of John Harington, Esq and Helena his w.
1686	13 July.	Henry, s of John Harington, Esq and Helena his w
1687	26 Oct	William, s of John Harington, Esq and Helena his wife.
1689	23 July	Robert, s of John Harington, Esq. and Helena his wife.
1693	16 Oct	Mary, d. of John Harington, Esq and Helena his wife
1696	2 Nov.	Edward, son of John Harington, Esq and Helena his wife.
1715	2 Jan.	James, the son of Mr James Harington.
1716	15 March.	William, the son of Mr James Harington.
1717	27 Nov	George, the son of Mr James Harington
$17\frac{18}{19}$	13 Jan.	John, the son of Mr James Harington
1723	28 March.	Dorothy & Phœbe, the twin dau'rs of Mr James Harington.

[N B —This entry of TWINS is the final entry of Harington baptisms at Kelston —F J P.]

Marriages.

1604	7 June.	Richard Davis=Marie Harington
1606	15 Nov.	Fraunces Harington=Joane Baylie
1613	21 Jan	John Roberts=Jane Harington
1620	26 Oct	Doctor Chetwind,* Dean of Bristoll=Helena Harington
1631	3 Nov	Mr Richard Digge of Marlborough=Mrs Elizab Harrington.
1678	6 Aug	John Harington, Esq =Mrs Helena Gostlett
1682	13 June	Mr Henry Long of Staunton Prior=Mrs Dyoness Harington of Kelston

* Dr Chetwynd, Dean of Bristol died 13th May 1639, and was buried in the Choir of his Cathedral, near his wife, who died 9th Nov 1628 aged 39

1706
Gostlete Harington of Marshfeild
in the Coun: of Glocester Gent:

1692 18 Oct Mr Edward Chetwind of Bristol=Mrs Alice Harington *
1700 20 May. Mr David Masey (Macie)=Mrs Amye Harington.†
1701 24 April Mr John Brittain of Corston=Mrs Phœbe Harrington ‡
1711. 19 Feb. Lawson Hudleston=Helena Harington

[Note —No Harington marriage in Kelston books after this]

Burials

1605. 30 March Rob Harrington
—— 7 April Marie Harington.
1611 15 Feb Sidnam Harington
1612. 1 Dec Sir John Harington, Knyght
1615 7 Feb Joane Harington.§
1616 2 Feb. Thomas Harrington, late Parson of Kelston.
1622. 15 Dec Ralphe, s of Francis Harington.
1624 8 July John, s of John Harington, Esq
1632. 8 Feb Margaret Harington, widow ||
1634 10 Dec The Lady Mary Harington, widowe
1636. 10 June. Edward, s of John Harington, Esq
1665. 4 Dec Mr George Harington.
1673. 8 March. Mrs Mary Harington, widow.
1674. 11 Aug Lady Dyonesse Harington.
1675 22 Feb Mr John Harrington the younger.
1675. 23 Sept. James, s. of John Harington, Esq
1675 31 Dec Alice, w of John Harington, Esq.
1676 24 Nov. Mrs Mary Harington, d. of John Harington, Esq.
1682 23 Nov Eliz Harington
1686 13 Sept. Mary Harington
1693. 10 Oct. Mary Harington.
—— 25 Nov. Mary Harington
1700 16 April. John Harington, Esq
170½ 20 March Will Harington, Gent.
1705. 26 Nov Gostlett Harington, Esq
1707 21 Aug Mrs Ann Harington.
1718 12 Aug. Helena Harington, the Relict of John Harington, Esq
1725 29 June John Harington, Esq
1726 7 July Dorothy, the Relict of John Harington, Esq.
1731. (No day entered ¶) Mary, the wife of Henry Harington, Esq
1731 June 3 Mary the wife of Mr James Harington.
1737 June 10 Mr James Harington
1743. April 19 James Harington
1752 August 29. Colthrop, son of Dr Edward & Mrs Hester Harington.
1755 July 5 Mrs Isabella Harington of Bristol
1757 August 8 Dr Edward Harington
1762. May 17 Mrs Hester Harington, widow of Dr Edward Harington.
1763 Jan 15. Grace Harington
1765. March 9. Mrs Susannah Harington, w. of Mr Robert Harington.

* This lady afterwards was re-married to the Rev Thos Fecknabam or Facknam, Vicar of Marshfield, and is named in her sister Phœbe's will

† This lady afterwards was married to   Hall of   She was sole executrix of her sister Phœbe's will, to which William Hall was one of the attesting witnesses—the said William being, as I have little doubt, father of the Rev Dr Hall Rector of Kelston

‡ This Phœbe H was the youngest dau r of William and Ann Harington, which William was the 2nd surviving son of his father John, the (Parliamentarian) M P for Bath, by the Hon Dioness Ley

§ This probably the wife of Francis Harington, *née* Bayley of Kelston

|| I am not able to say of which Harington this lady was the widow, but conjecture either of the Rector, Thomas Harington, or one of his sons —F J P

¶ She died in May

1765.	May 16.	Mr Robert Harington
1769	May 23.	Henry Harington, Esq.
1774.	May 1.	Mr Wm Harington, late of Bristol
1781.	August 23.	Mrs Helena Harington, late of Bath
1783	Feb 16	Constancia, d of Mr Edward & Mrs Harington of Bath, an infant.
1788	Jan 23	William, son of Mr Edw and Mrs Harington of Bath, an infant
1792	May 5	Mis Dionis Harington of Bath, spinster.
1796	May 18	Lady Ann Harington, w of Sir Edward Harington, Knt, of Bath
1805	March 12.	Martha Harington of Bath, aged 76
1811.	June 17.	The Rev Edward Harington, aged 35
1816.	Jan 23	Henry Harington, M D, aged 89
1870	March 26.	Anne Elizabeth Harington, the Cathedral Close, Exeter, 63
1874.	May 14.	Rev Edward Temple Harington, Rector of Axmouth, aged 45

CORSTON REGISTERS.*

Christenings

1628.	Oct. 14	Mary the daughter of John Harington, Esq
1631	June 18.	William the sonne of John Harington, Esq.
1634	July 21	Edward the sonne of John Harington, Esq and the Ladye Dyonis his wife, was baptized
1660.	Sept. 6.	Mary the daughter of John Harington, Esq and Mary his wife
1666.	Aug. 30.	Phœbe ye daughter of John Harington, Esq and Mrs Alice his wife
1667.	—— day	Janet† ye daughter (same as previous entry)
1668.	Aug 20.	Virtue ye daughter, etc (same parents).
1669	Nov. 5	James ye sonne of, etc. (same parents)
167$\frac{0}{1}$	Jan 3.	Amy ye daughter of, etc (same parents)
1671	Dec 27	Alice ye daughter of same parents
1673.	May 6	Benjamin ye sonne, etc (same parents)
1702.	April 10	John the son of Benjamin Harington, gent and Mis Elizabeth his wife.
1703	May 10	Abigail, the daughter of, etc (same parents).
1704	May 14.	Mary the daughter of Benjamin Harington, Gentleman, and Mrs Elizabeth his wife, was baptized
1705	July 5	William the son of Benjamin and Elizabeth (as before)
1708	Jan. 1	Elizabeth the d of (same parents)
1732.	March 26	John son of John Harington, Esq and Mary his wife, was born, and was privately baptized on Easter Day April 9th, and June 1st was publickly ratifyed.
1747	April 5	Benjamin, son of John Harington, Esq. and Mary his wife, was baptized.
1749	June 18	Elizabeth, dau'r of John H etc (as before).

Marriages ‡

(Entered among the Xtenings' stand)

1726.	Sept 10.	John Harington, Esq and Mrs Mary Bushell of Bath, married
17$\frac{40}{41}$.	Jan 15	Were married the Revd Mr Hudson Martin, A M., of Saltford, and Mis Abigail Harington§ of Corston
1781.	October 2.	Benjamin Harington of the Parish of Corston and Hannah Vele or Vile of same parish, spinster, were married

* The Baptismal Register of this parish commences in 1568, but no Harington entry occurs before 1628

† Buried same year

‡ The Marriage Register of Corston Parish commences 1586

§ This lady, by vote of Vestry held July 31, 1760, had "permission to erect a new seat in the Parish Church by the South door for her separate use" John Harington (one of the signatories)

*Burials.**

1667.	(No day stated)	Jane ye daughter of Jno Harington, Esq. and Mrs Alice his wife
1707.	4 June.	Mary ye daughter of Mr Benjn Harrington, was buried.
1711.	Nov. 28.	Benjamin Harrington, Esq was buried.
1732.	April 16	Dyed Mary the wife of John Harington, Esq. and mother of the sd infant (i e John, born March 26, vid entry), aged 25.
1734.	Dec 28, Sunday	Dyed Mrs Harrington of Corston, Relict of Benjamin Harington, Esq and was buried Dec 31st aged 55
1747.	April 1.	Mrs Rebecca Harington was buried
1763.	May 6.	John Harington, Esq was buried
1773	August 9	Abigail Martin (*née* Harington) was buried
1781	———	William Harington of Newton St Loe, buried.
1786	March 23.	Mrs Mary Harington buried
1797.	Nov. 24.	Elizabeth Harington buried
1806.	Aug 26.	Hannah Harington, aged 60

(*To be continued*)

THE DENNYS,

Earls of Norwich, Barons Denny of Waltham, and Baronets of Ireland

(*Continued from page 160*)

Edward Denny was returned M P for Kerry in 1692 and in 1695 (his cousin Barry being High Sheriff of the County in the latter year) and died in 1712, leaving issue one son, Edward and eight daughters, viz, Anne, Ellen, and Alice, died young, Angel and Anne, died unmarried, Catherine, married William Sprigg, Esq, of Clenvoe, King's County, M P. for Tralee in 1723, Mary, married Thomas Crosbie, Esq, and Jane, married in 1713 her cousin John Blennerhassett, Esq, of Ballyseedy, heir by survival to his brother Arthur, who died as before mentioned in 1686

Edward Denny, the brother of these eight sisters, had married in 1699 Lady Letitia Coningsby, daughter of Thomas, Earl Coningsby The following entries, the next in order on the fly-leaves of the old Bible, are in the writing of the Rev. W. Stanford —

"October 3d 1700. Madam Letitia Denny ye daughter of ye Right Honble Thomas, Lord Coningsby, made her entry here with divers Gentlemenn of Quality, and about three hundred Horsemenn of ye Tenants, and she and her Husband were received with much Joye in ye Castell of Tralye by theire father, Colonel Edward Denny and theire mother Madam Denny, and by all ye noble Relations"

"8th June, 1701 Ye younge Ladye Letitia Denny was brought to bed of a Daughter, about one of ye Clocke in ye Morning, being Sundaye, who that Afternoon was Christened by Dean John Richards and named Frances Lucia Godfathers Thomas Lord Coningsby (presented by Mr Barry Denny) and Colonel Edward Denny, Godmothers ye Ladye Wharton (presented by Mrs Mary Denny) and ye Lady Coningsby by Miss Ursula Coningsby"

Edward Denny represented the county of Kerry in Parliament from 1703 until 1713, and in 1715 was returned for the borough of Askeaton He died in 1727, leaving issue by his wife Lady Letitia, with the daughter Lucia Frances above-mentioned (who married Arthur, younger son of John Blennerhassett, Esq, of Ballyseedy, and had no issue), seven sons and three daughters, viz 1. Edward, High Sheriff of Kerry in 1723, died unmarried *vitâ patris*; 2 Arthur, heir by survival; 3 Thomas, died young, 4 Thomas, who succeeded his brother Arthur,

* The Burial Register of Corston Parish commences 1569.

5 Barry, in Holy Orders, Treasurer of the Cathedral Church of Ardfert (married his cousin Jane, daughter of the Reverend Maurice O'Connor, *v ante* page 115), and died in September, 1751, leaving two daughters and four sons, viz, Arthur and Barry, of whom hereafter, as successors to their cousins, Edward (*a*) and Maynard (*b*); Ursula (*c*) and Arabella (*d*), 6. William, died young, 7 George, died young, 8. Lucia Frances above-mentioned, 9 Mary, died young, 10. Barbara, died young On the death of Edward Denny in 1727, he was succeeded by his son Arthur above-mentioned, who was chosen M P for Kerry in the same year He married, in August, 1725, the Lady Arabella Fitz-Maurice, second dau of the Earl of Kerry by Lady Anne Petty, sister of the Earl of Shelburne, and died s p in 1742 His widow, Lady Arabella Denny, survived him a half-century, and then passed away, honoured and lamented by thousands, on the 18th of March, 1792, at the great age of eighty-four, preserving her clear intellect to the last Like her husband's ancestress, Joan Champernoun, the protectress of the martyred Anne Askew (*v ante*, p 71), Lady Arabella Denny was no less distinguished by her ancient lineage than by her deep piety and Christian benevolence. She founded the Magdalen Asylum in Leeson Street, Dublin, and an almshouse in Tralee, and was throughout her long life the supporter and patroness of innumerable good works in different parts of Ireland The Corporations of Dublin and Cork presented her with the freedom of their cities for her exertions on behalf of their workhouses, hospitals, and schools Her husband, who freely supported all her generous plans, and provided her with the large sums necessary for carrying them out, was succeeded in the estates by his next brother Thomas Denny, before mentioned, who was knighted by the Duke of Devonshire, the Viceroy of Ireland, in 1743 Sir Thomas Denny took up again the broken thread of the family history in the old diary, and wrote as follows —

"I was marry'd the 13th of 9ber, 1740, to my Cousin Agnes Blennerhassett, daughter of John Blennerhassett of Ballyshedee (*e*)

"THOMAS DENNY.

"I had a son born ye 10th of 7ber, 1741, called Thomas Coningsby, he died at about six weekes old

"My second son Anthony Arthur, was born ye 16th of 7ber, 1742, at three o'clock in the afternoon, his godfathers, William, Earl of Kerry, (*f*) and my cousin Thomas, Lord Southwell, (*g*) his godmother the Lady Arabella Denny my sister-in-law.

"My daughter Letitia Denny was born ye 6th of October, 1743.

"My third son William Denny was born ye 23rd of January, 1744–5, at Prospect Hall (*h*)

"My fourth son Thomas was born ye 25th of June, 1746, at Prospect Hall

"My fifth son Thomas was born at Prospect Hall, ye 6th of July, at one o'clock in ye morning, 1747, his godfathers the Lord Kenmare, and Rowland Bateman, Esqr, his godmothers my cousin Helena Hedges Eyre, (*i*) and my Aunt Maynard.

"My daughter Jane Denny was born ye 28th of August on Sunday morning at 8 o'clock, 1748, her godfathers Sir Maurice Crosbie, and my father-in-law, her godmothers my sisters Denny and Ponsonby

"My daughter Mary Denny was born at eight o'clock on Thursday morning ye 20th of July, 1749

"My sixth son Robert Maynard Denny was born in Aungier Street, Dublin, the 2nd of January, 1750–1, in the morning, his godfather my cousin Robert Maynard, Esqr of Hammersmith, and Arthur Crosbie, Esqr, his godmother my Aunt Catherine Sprigg, he dyed in Dublin the fourth of March, 1752 (new stile), and was buryed in St Peter's Churchyard God preserve ye rest to me

"My daughter Frances was born ye 28th of March,1752, and dyed at nine days old.

"My seventh son Edward Denny was born ye 9th of May, new stile, 1753"

This is the last entry in the old diary begun in 1625. Sir Thomas Denny died in 1761. Two only of his seven sons, William and Thomas, and two daughters, Letitia (*j*) and Jane, survived him.

M. A. H.

(*a*) Edward Denny, third son of the Reverend Barry Denny, by his wife Jane O Connor, married Mary, daughter of Bind, Esq of Fermanagh and had issue Edward, died unmarried, Anthony, married his cousin Frances Blennerhassett, and had issue two sons and one daughter, viz 1 Edward an officer in the 3rd Buffs, married his first cousin Georgina, daughter of Arthur Blennerhassett, Esq, of Ballyseedy, and had issue, Anthony, an officer in the 71st regiment who married Sarah, daughter of Rev J Lockwood and had issue, living in 1868 three sons, Edward, Anthony, and Arthur 2 William, Colonel in the 71st regiment, married Everetta, dau of the Hon J Richardson of Montreal 3 Mary, married Charles O'Malley, Q C, of Hawthorn Lodge, co Mayo, and had issue

(*b*) Maynard Denny was in Holy Orders and Rector of Church Hill near Tralee He married Penelope, daughter of Anthony Stoughton, Esq of Rattoo co Kerry, high sheriff of that county in 1717, great grandson of Anthony Stoughton and Honora O'Brien, daughter of Lord Inchiquin (*v ante* p 160), and had issue five sons and four daughters, viz 1 Barry, in Holy Orders Rector of Church Hill, married Helen, daughter of Richard Townshend Herbert, Esq of Cahirnane, and had four sons and two daughters viz Maynard, Richard, major in the 58th regiment died unmarried, Barry, in Holy Orders died unmarried, Arthur, married and has no issue Penelope married Delmege Esq, and Helena, died unmarried 2 Thomas died unmarried 3 Anthony, married Patience Mary daughter and co-heiress of Admiral Lord Collingwood, and had issue two sons and one daughter, viz Collingwood, of Barham Wood, Herts, married and has issue a son and daughter Arthur, married his first cousin Penelope Herbert of Cahirnane, and has issue a daughter, and two sons officers in the army Sarah Blackett, only daughter of Anthony Denny, and his wife the Hon Sarah Collingwood, married Sir John Stephen Robinson, Bart, of Rokeby Hall co Louth, and has issue 4 Edward Maynard, in Holy Orders, Rector of Listowel married first Millicent Blennerhassett, and had issue an only daughter Penelope (married Richard younger son of Sir Richard O'Donnell Bart), secondly, Jane, daughter of Townsend Gun, Esq, of Rattoo co Kerry and had issue two sons, Maynard, now in Australia, William an officer in the Royal Artillery, and a daughter 5 Arthur an officer in the army died unmarried 6 Elizabeth, married Captain Robert Steers of Yorkshire, and had issue 7 Jane, married Rev Arthur Herbert, of Cahirnane and had issue several sons and a daughter, married her cousin Arthur Denny as above mentioned 8 Arabella, married Francis Chute, Esq, of Chute Hall, co Kerry, and had issue two sons, Francis died unmarried, Arthur, Penelope died unmarried, and Arabella 9 Penelope, youngest daughter of the Rev Maynard Denny and his wife Penelope Stoughton, died unmarried

(*c*) Ursula Denny married Samuel Morris, Esq, of Ballybeggan, co Kerry, great grandson of Samuel Morris, of same place, by his wife Elizabeth Southwell, daughter of Richard Southwell of Callow (son of Sir Richard Southwell, Bart of Barham Hall Suffolk, and Court Mattrass, co Limerick), M P for Askeaton in 1661 by his wife Lady Elizabeth O Brien dau of the Earl of Inchiquin Ursula Denny and Samuel Morris had issue, with an elder son Samuel, who married Sarah dau of Townsend Gun, Esq (and had issue two sons, Maynard and Townsend, an officer in the army, who both died *s p*, and four daughters, Georgina, married Capt De Ravigny Sarah and Jane, died unmarried, and Elizabeth, married Rev Davis), a younger son George, Colonel in the 3rd Regiment K C B, Usher of the Black Rod, Dublin Castle, who married and left an only child, Theodosia

(*d*) Arabella Denny married George Gun, Esq, and had, with a son Barry whose only son George died *s p*, two daughters Jane, married Capt Cashel and secondly, William Hickman, Esq, and Arabella, married John Watts, Esq, and had issue

(*e*) This is the true Irish pronunciation of the name of the Blennerhassett's estate and residence in Kerry The meaning of the word is the place or abode of the fairies, *sidhe* (sheedy) being the Irish name for those imaginary creatures The Blennerhassets came hither from Flimby, in Cumberland, in 1587 and one of the old divisions or farms of their Irish estate bears the name of Flimby in remembrance of their English home before that date

(*f*) William Earl of Kerry, the brother of Lady Arabella Denny

(*g*) Thomas third Baron and first Viscount Southwell son of the second Baron by Mary dau of Thomas Coke, Esq, of Melbourne, co Derby and grandson of the first Baron, who had married Lady Meliora Coningsby, dau of Thomas Lord Coningsby and sister of Lady Letitia Denny

(*h*) Prospect Hall, of which no trace now remains, stood on the shore of the lower Lake of Killarney Dr Smith, writing in 1759, notices the exquisite view of the lake from this Hall, then occupied by a Mr Supple

(*i*) Helena dau of Edward Herbert of Kilcow, Esq, and his wife Frances, dau of Nicholas Brown, Viscount Kenmare, married Richard Hedges Eyre, Esq of Macroom Castle (grandson maternally of Edward Eyre, Esq of Galway, by Jane, dau of Sir William Maynard, Bart) and had with other issue two daughters, Frances, who married Simon White, Esq, and by him was mother of the first Earl of Bantry, and Helena, married the Rev George Maunsell, D D, Dean of Leighlin The last-mentioned lady must have been the godmother of the son of Sir Thomas Denny, who was her cousin through his Maynard ancestors

(*j*) Letitia Denny married Rowland Bateman, Esq, of Oak Park, co Kerry, High Sheriff of same county in 1759, and had by him an elder son, who married his first cousin, Arabella dau of Sir Barry Denny, Bart, as hereafter mentioned

(*To be continued*)

TALBOT AND BRADDYLL MEMORANDA *

In the Calendar of an illuminated MS Breviary, fifteenth century, in the possession of John Ingilby, Esq , of Austwick, co. York, are the following entries —

Marcius	11.	Anne Talbotte borne this day in ye morninge 1595 being Tuesday and dyed when she was eleven weekes oulde
„	23.	Eli Talbott borne this day beinge Wednesday 1613 being foure in ye morninge
„	25.	Jo Talbot sonne of Go Talbott borne anno 1571 about 11 of ye clocke at nup^{t} beinge Sonday
„	26	Anne Talbott borne anno 1601 about five of ye clocke in the morninge
Aprilis	17.	Margarett Talbott borne anno 1602, six of ye clocke in ye morninge being Saturday.
Maius	2	George Talbott was borne anno 1597 hora quasi octava vespere beinge Monday
„	10	Circa horam ante meridie' . nata fuit Joh'na filia Joh'is Bradyll a^{o} d^{ni} 1581 et a^{o} Eliz 26, 10 Maij.
„	20.	Natus erat Edwardi filius Joh'is Braddyll circa horam quarta' post meredie 1583 (Elizabeth 25)
„	24	Tho Talbott borne anno 1603 aboute foure of ye clocke in ye morninge beinge tuesdaye
Julius	2.	†Dorethy Bradill maried to John Talbott ann' 1595.
„	12	this day M^{r} braddyll was bourne 1602
„	25	Edwarde Talbott was borne anno 1599 post meridiem hora quasi secunda beinge Wednesdaye
„	25	Frances Talbott ye same daye prima hora post meridiem anno 1610.
Augustus	2	Marie Talbott borne anno 1606 about twoo of y^{e} clocke in the morning beinge Saturday.
September	17.	John Braddill bourne a^{o} dom 1599 being Monday.
„	24	Briget Talbott borne anno 1612 about three of y^{e} clocke in y^{e} morninge being Thursday.
October	3	Doretty $doughte^{r}$ of Ed Bradyll borne 1572.
„	6	‡Anne Braddyll mariage being Monday a^{o} dom 1584
December	13	John Talbott sonne of Jo was borne anno 1607 about three of y^{e} clocke in the morninge in the greate froste beinge Sunday.
„	19	Nup^{t} Lawrence Tomli'son et Ann Smyth 1615

In die martis viz. secundo die decembris 1628 et $Carol^{s}$ 4° in aurora natus fuit Thome Whyt filius Ro Whyt de Magna inter horam sextam et septimam . . diei.

STROTHER —In Berry's 'Heraldry, vol. iv , the following Arms are recorded — Strother [Scotland], ar. three piles issuing from the base, az in chief an eagle's head erased, sa betw two fleurs-de-lis vert Crest a martlet sa

Query What connection is there, if any, between this Scottish family and the ancient Northumbrian family of Strother of Kirknewton?

Roborough, S Devon JAMES B. STROTHER, Vicar of Shaugh Prior

---

* Communicated by JOHN FOSTER, Esq , Jun

† Dorothy Bradill, d of Edward Bradyll, mar John Talbot of Carr She was born 3 Oct, 1572 (J F)

‡ Anne Bradyll mar Thomas Southworth

Pedigree of Rugeley of Dunton, co. Warwick.

FROM THE HERALDS' VISITATION OF THE COUNTY OF WARWICK, MADE IN THE YEAR 1682.

ARMS.—*Argent, a chevron between three roses gules.*

Coleshill, 1 Sept., 1682.

Nicholas Rugeley.([a]) ═

Nicholas Rugeley of Dunton, in com. War., 33 H. 6. ═

1. Wm. Rugeley of Dunton, in Arden. ═ . . . da. of Massey.
2. James Rugeley of Warwick, Genⁿ, 14 H. 7. ═ Isabell. [Pedigree continued in the Visitⁿ of Warwick 1619.]

John Rugeley of Dunton. ═ Joyce,([b]) d. of William Sheldon of Beoley in com. Worcester.

Ralph Rugeley of Dunton. ═ Rebecka,([c]) da. of Rowland Rugeley of Shenston, in com. Stafford.

- 3. Henry Rugeley of Coleshill, in com. War. ═ . . . da. of . . . Stepings.
- Sarah, wife of Henry Cooper of Coleshill.
- Mary, wife of . . . Barber of Tamworth, Gen.
- 1. Sir Rowland Rugeley of Dunton, Knᵗ, ob. 1629.([d]) ═ Elizabeth,([e]) da. & coheir of Sir Tho. Knowles, Knᵗ, younger brother to Wm. Earl of Banbury. A
- 2. John Rugeley married in Wales and died s.p.

Children of Sir Rowland Rugeley:

- Wᵐ Rugeley, of Dunton, Esq. ob. 21 Sep. 1655.([f]) ═ Mary, da. of John Wirley of Dodford in com. North'on, Esq.
- 1. Katherine, wife of Arthur Warren,([g]) eldest son to Sʳ Arnold Warren of Thorpe Arnold in com. Leic.
- 2. Dorothy, wife of Sir Arthur Smithies, Knᵗ.
- 3. Mary, wife of . . . Wiseman of Broadoaks in com. Essex, Esq.
- John Rugeley of yᵉ citty of London. ═ — issue: John.

Children of Wᵐ Rugeley and Mary Wirley:

- Hugh* Hutching Rugeley of Coleshill in com. War. æt. 36 in May 1682. ═ Eliz. da. & sole heir of Faux Nobold of Bilton, in co. War., Gen. — issue: Thomas æt. 5. Anne. Lettice. Elizabeth. Mary.
- 1. Mary, wife of Alexander Jones, Clerk, Rector of Ashby de la Zouch, in com. Leic., afterwards mar. to Gilbert Woodward, Clerk, Minister of Onelip, in com. Leic.
- 2. Goditha, wife of . . . Nottley, in Virginia, ob. 1682.
- 3. Dorothy died unmarᵈ.
- John* Rugeley of Dunton, Esq. now living æt. 50 an. 1682. ═ Ann, da. & coheir of Edward Wagstaffe, B.M. a younger brother of . . . Wagstaffe of Harbury in com. War.
- Wᵐ Rugeley, Citizen of London. ═ Grace, da. of . . . Heathcot of Culthrop Hall in co. Derby. — issue: John, æt. 23. Wirley, æt. 19, 1682.

Children of John Rugeley and Ann Wagstaffe:

- 1. Raphe Rugeley of Dunton, son & heir apparent, æt. 20, 1682. ═ Eliz. da. of John Rugeley of Partney in com. Lincoln. — issue: Elizabeth, æt. 1 an, 1682.
- 2. John, æt. 15.
- 3. Rowland, æt. 4.
- 1. Anne, wife of Wᵐ Wood of Pedimore in com. War.
- 2. Mary.
- 3. Bridget.
- 4. Gertrude.

Extracted by me, G. E. COKAYNE, Lancaster Herald,
25 March, 1879.

* Signed by "John Rugeley."
"Hu. Rugeley."

[*Notes continued on next page.*

([a]) He was of Hawkesheard, co Stafford, 10 Hen V, and married Edith, da of Waldief, by whom he had three sons—(1) Nicholas who continued the line (2) William, living 20 Ed IV and (3) Thomas whose only da and heir Edith married Richard Thickness of Sutton Cheney (see note page 318 to Harwood's edition of Erdeswick's 'Survey of Staffordshire,' 1820) According to Erdeswick (page 171 *ibid.*), Humphrey Rugeley was owner of Hawkesharde, temp Ed III who has issue Thomas, who had issue Nicholas who lived 7 Hen VI etc

([b]) She was the da of Ralph (not of *William*) Sheldon of Beoley and Aberton, co Worcester, by Philippa, da and coheir of Baldwin Heath of Foordhall in Wootton She married 30 Nov, 1542 at Beoley and is mentioned in her father's will proved 1646, together with her husband After his death she married Thomas Baskerville of Cudworth These facts are correctly recorded in the pedigree of Sheldon, entered at the College of Arms in 'Norfolk vj'"

([c]) Her mother was Ellen, da and heir of James Thirkald of Smallwood co Stafford, by Jane da of Sir Lewis Bagot Knt Her brother, William Rugeley of Shenston, entered his pedigree in the Heralds' Visitation of the County of Stafford in 1583 being then the father of ten children Shenstone Hall was built by the Rugeleys from whom it passed to the Brandreths, who temp Queen Anne sold it to Samuel Hill

([d]) He was knighted in Ireland by the Lord Deputy (Arthur Chichester Lord Belfast) on 5 Nov 1611 Admon of his goods in C P C, wherein he is described as Sir Rowland Ridgeley late of Clengham co Carmarthen was granted 7 Oct, 1629, to Humphrey Bracebridge, "consanguineo" during the minority of his children, Lettice, Odiley, Catherine, Isabel George, Penelope Devereux, Dorothy, John and Mary

([e]) She was married 20 Dec 1604 at St Clement Danes Westminster and must have died before 1629 in her husband's lifetime Of her father, Sir Thomas Knollys, little is known excepting that he was a mourner at the funeral of his father in Aug 1596, and that he married Odelia da and heir of John de Merula, Margrave of Bergen op Zoom (a scion of the house of Nassau and uncle to the Prince of Orange) by Maria, da and heir of Anthony Margrave of Bergen op Zoom in Brabant

([f]) He was probably twenty four at his father's death in 1629 at all events he was of full age as he is not mentioned among the minor children of his father in the admon of 1629

([g]) Arthur Warren, or Waring, born 18 Jan and bap 3 Feb 1617, at Thorpe Arnold co Leicester, died at St James's Clerkenwell, and was buried at St Marylebone, 26 Nov, 1678 His wife had died before him Their son another Arthur Warren was of Stapleford, Notts and (by his wife the coheir of the family of Borlase Barts) was great-grandfather of Admiral the Right Hon Sir John Borlase Warren, Bart K B, etc

---

MONUMENTAL INSCRIPTIONS, WITH NOTES, FROM THE CHURCH AND CHURCHYARD OF AXBRIDGE, CO. SOMERSET.

BY EDWARD FRY WADE

On Monuments in the Church —

1 Near this place were interred the bodies of Mr John Tuthill Three times Mayor of this Corporation and Grace his Wife, He died 30th Decr 1716 aged 63 years, She died ye 10th November 1712 aged 54 years.

2 M S Thomas Welsh Gent interred Decr 13th A D 1675 ætatis suæ 58. Also William Welsh Gent. his beloved son interred Octr 30th A.D 1691 ætatis suæ 22

Who living was a true epitome,
Of Virtue, candour, ingenuitie.
Whose Generous soul to charitie inclined,
Courteous he was and of a pious mind
His body near this marble, *and*
His pious soul resigned unto God's hand
Now with the quire of angels sings
Sweet Hallelujahs to the King of Kings

ARMS —*Az, six mullets or, 3, 2, and* 1

3 To the memory of Richard Chapman of this parish Gentleman who departed this life the 29th day of April 1790 aged 49, Also of Elizabeth Chapman daughter of the said Richard Chapman who departed this life the 23rd day of September 1784 aged 16 years and of Mary Chapman Wife of the said Richard Chapman who departed this life the 20th March 1824 aged 83, Also of Adden son of the above

named Richard and Mary Chapman who died the 19th Jany 1715 aged 79 and of Sarah his wife who died the 6th September 1814 aged 38 years.

ARMS.—*Party per chev. ar. and gules, a crescent counterchanged, on a canton of the second, three fleurs-de-lis or, all within a bordure gobonated ar. and az.*

4 Near this place in hopes of a blessed resurrection lie the remains of the Reverend Elias Robotier who was rector of this parish 42 years and died the 19th December 1765 aged 88 years. He was born at St John de Gardonenque in the Cevennes in the province of Languedock and during the great persecution of protestants in France fled from that place and left his family fortune and friends to seek after the most pure and reformed religion of the Church of England He followed his studies for some time in Greece, Holland, and Germany, and after enduring many hardships and vicissitudes of fortune he came to England where he was by that great and good Prelate George Hooper Lord Bishop of Bath and Wells taken into his palace as chaplain and promoted to many favours in the Church by his Lordship Here also lyeth the Remains of Elizabeth the Wife of the said Elias Robotier who died the 20th February 1766 aged 74 years

5 In the Chancel of this Church are deposited the remains of Solomon Pain Gentleman Born 28th October 1761 Died 18th October 1836 Ursula his Wife born 26 July 1761 died 11th April 1840, and Amy Ann their daughter Born 16 January 1787 died 1st February 1818 This monument is erected to their beloved memory as a Tribute of affection by their surviving children.

ARMS.—*Gules, three crosses botonnée, on a chief ar. two escallops*

6 To the Memory of Mary Tratham who lived 40 years a faithful servant in the family of Thomas Prowse Esqre. She had the care of Mr John Prowse in his infancy and by her own desire is buried near him, She died 20 March 1776 in the 71th year of her age

7 In a vault near this place are deposited the remains of Levi West Gent Attorney at Law who departed this life January 13th 1797 aged 36, Also of Sarah Wife of the above named Levi West who departed this life 2nd Feby 1799 aged 48 years, This Tablet is erected by Sarah Matilda Coombe* their daughter, as a Tribute of affection and respect to perpetuate the memory of her beloved parents

ARMS.—*Erm. a bend indented sable*

CREST.—*A lion rampant sable*

8 Sacred to the memory of Peter Fry† of Compton House Esqre who departed this life on the 19th Decr 1816 aged 78 Also of Joanna his Wife who died on the same day aged 79 Also of their children Frederick Yeatman Fry who died on the 15 October 1819 aged 21 years, Fanny Fry on the 22 June 1815 aged 43 years, James Henry Fry on the 26 Novr 1825 aged 22 years, Charlotte Fry on the 14 January 1832 aged 27 years, Katherine Long Rosetta Fry on the 3rd Decr 1822 aged 15 years

ARMS.—*Vert, three horses courant*

CREST.—*An arm embowed in armour, holding a dagger enfiled by a Moor's head.*

9. In Memory of Peter Wickens Fry Esqre of Montague Street, Russell Square, London‡ Eldest Son of Peter Fry Esqre of Compton House Axbridge died on the 29th August 1860 aged 65 years

* Of the family of Coombe of North Petherton, co Somerset. Levi West was Town Clerk of Axbridge

† In Winscombe Church, co Somerset, there is a monument to his ancestor, John Fry and Ann his Wife She died 20th August, 1745, in the 37th year of her age, he died the 13th August, 1774, in the 73rd year of his age William, their eldest son, died Sept 4th, 1775, in the 46th year of his age

‡ In Compton Bishop Church co Somerset, there is a monument erected to the memory of another son, Charles Edward Fry of Compton House, Esq who died 6 Nov, 1867 Mary Morris, his wife, died 2nd Feb, 1864 Peter William, their eldest son died 23rd Aug, 1871 Arthur Robert, their youngest son, died March, 1867 Bruges Fry another son of Peter Fry, died 23rd Sept, 1865, and buried in Axbridge Churchyard. Thomas Homfray Fry, last surviving son, died 20th Nov, 1878, aged 78, buried at Winscombe

10 Sacred to the Memory of Rachel Fry Wife of Peter Fry of this Town and daughter of the Revd Samuel Male Rector of Wishaw in the County of Warwick. She died 3rd July 1823 aged 57 and lies near this place. Also to the above named Peter Fry who died 13th February 1856 aged 77 much esteemed and lamented. Also in Memory of Margaret the Relict of the above named Peter Fry and Fifth and last surviving daughter of William Dyne Esqre late of Milton next Sittingbourne Kent who died 19 Septr 1863 aged 89

11. Sacred to the Memory of Amy youngest daughter of William Dyne Gentleman and of Effield his Wife of Milton next Sittingbourne Kent obiit 8 July 1817 aged 69 years. This monument is erected to her memory by her affectionate Sister Margaret Fry.

12 To the Memory of Peter Fry who resigned his spirit into the hands of his redeemer 21st Septr 1787 aged 52.

13 In memory of Elizabeth Fry who died on the 24th Decr 1814 aged 93 years, She was Widow of Peter Fry who died on the 21st Septr 1787 aged 52 Also Elizabeth daughter of the above Peter and Elizabeth Fry and Wife of the Revd Edward Crosse M.A. formerly of Halberton in the County of Devon and perpetual curate of Hay in the County of Essex who died the 3rd Novr 1852 aged 71 Also Samuel Lund Fry youngest son of Peter and Elizabeth Fry who died on the 8th April 1871 aged 83 years

14. Sacred to the memory of Charles Day of this Town who died 23rd June 1843 aged 92 years

15. Sacred to the memory of William Ogbourn twice Mayor of this Corporation who died the 16th April 1773 aged 48 years and was interred near this place. Also Katherine his daughter who died the 30th June 1777 in the 5th year of her age Also Ann Wife of the aforesaid William Ogbourn who died 6th August 1782 aged 45 years

16. Sacred to the Memory of Sexa Wife of William Robert James of the City of Bristol Merchant and late only surviving daughter of William Ogbourn of this Town died Septr 6th 1798 at the age of 29 years William Ogbourn James her son aged 3 months died same year William Robert James obiit 28th Feby 1805 aged 39 years.

17. Sacred to the Memory of John Flower Surgeon and Apothecary of this Town who died Novr 6th 1789 aged 73 years.

18 To the Memory of John Gaisford Gent. Three Times Mayor of this Corporation who died 11th February 1775 aged 48.

19 In Memory of John Maggs who died Novr 1st 1817 aged 85 yrs. Also of John Maggs his son who died January 24th 1821 aged 46 yrs And of Ann Maggs his Widow who died Novr 30th 1858 aged 93 years Also of James Maggs who died July 15th 1829 aged 27 years Charles Maggs who died Novr 8th 1833 aged 36 years And of John Maggs who died June 11th 1857 aged 60 years sons of the above named John Maggs the younger and Ann his Wife.

MONUMENTAL INSCRIPTIONS FROM TUDDENHAM CHURCH, CO. SUFFOLK.*

Chancel, South Side.

ARMS.—Az., three sickles interlocked in point arg, handles or, impaling gules, two chevrons arg.

Here lyes the bodyes of John Sicklemor, Gen. Lord of this Mannor & Elizabeth his wife who together had issue seaven sonns & seaven daughters & they left surviving them six sonns & fovre Daughters namely Mary, Thomas, John, Tobias, Martha, Nicholas, Elizab Samuel, Alice & Jonathan Obijt Johannes 9no Jan 1644 Johannes filius hoc Dedicavit.

* Communicated by W. H. RICHARDSON, M.A., Esq.

Chancel, North side.

Rich Keble.

Arms.—Quarterly of six—1 Barry unduly of six, arg. and sa, a canton gu; 2. Fusily arg. and sa, 3 Arg two chevrons gu. within a bordure sa, 4 Arg. on a chevron sa, three . . . , 5. Gules, three chevrons arg, 6. Gules, a griffin segreant or

Crest.—A lion's head (?) erased, gu

Above the shield of Keble appear these crests —Dexter a demi-eagle, wings expanded or, banded unduly sa for Keble Sinister a demi salient sa

Below appear these arms —Barry unduly of six, arg and sa, a canton gu, impaling per chevron arg and sa. in chief two sickles of the second, in base a cock or

Roydon Hall
16 nec flatu nec fluctu. 53

There be low lie In terred Rich[d] Keble Esq[r] and Mary his wife with Thomas Mary & Elizabeth their children.

Its sure we Dye to live else tell me why
We mortals rather chuse to live than dye

In grateful remembrance of the best of wives Isabella Wratislaw died the XXI February MDCCCXII in her XX year. Blessed are the dead which die in the Lord.

Nave, South Side.

The Reverend Benjamin Young, M A. Vicar of this Parish. Born April 25, 1797. Died April 1, 1813

George John Young eldest son of the Reverend Benjamin Young Born 16 September 1827, died 12 June 1831. Also his fourth son the Rev Frederic Clement Young, M A Rector of Chetwynd, Salop, who fell asleep in Jesus, December 8, 1872.

Elizabeth Margaret, youngest daughter of the late Rev. Benjamin Young, born May 8th, 1838, died December 5th, 1857, and Mary Ann, his second daughter, wife of the Rev F. S. Clark Born January 7th, 1833. Died October 25th, 1869

In the same vault with those of the Rev. B. Young and George John Young are deposited the remains of Harriot relict of John Peter Holloway, Esq died 27th March, 1857, aged 84 This tablet is erected by her children

Churchyard, South Side.

Mary Ann wife of Rev F. S Clarke & daughter of Rev. B. Young. Fell asleep Oct. 25th, 1869, aged 36 years

---

Frederic Clement Young, Priest, Rector of Chetwynd, Shropshire. Born March 15, 1840 Died December 8, 1872

Churchyard, East End

Within an iron railing, on a raised tomb —In memory of William Charles Fonnereau, Esq. of Ch Ch Park in Ipswich, who died XXXI July MDCCCLV. Aged L years

---

Upon a table tomb, a shield bearing a snake entwining a pillar —M S Rev[di] Gulielmi Minter Coll S Petri apud Cantabrigienses Socii Virtute et modestia ornatus nec non amicis carus Die 25 Januarii A.D 1787, Ætatis 25 cum summo suorum luctu decessit Etiamque M.S. Patris ejus Gulielmi Minter Generosi Qui Anno Ætatis suæ 77, obiit Die 4 Aug[ti], 1788

Armorial Bookplate.

WHITE.

This plate—for the fine impression of which the subscribers to the 'Miscellanea' are indebted to its owner—has been recently designed and engraved for Captain Edward Arthur White, of Old Elvet, co Durham, F S A, Honorary Secretary to the Archæological Society of Durham and Northumberland, by Mr. J H Le Keux, of Durham, not the least talented of the trio of eminent engravers of this name

INSCRIPTIONS, ETC., RELATING TO THE FAMILY OF ASHBURNER.

The following inscriptions are to be found on three table-tombstones in the churchyard of the demolished church of St. Lawrence Pountney, Cannon Street The tombstones are in fairly good order, and the inscriptions are perfectly legible.

(No. 1.)

To the memory of Miss Mary Ashburner daughter of Mr Will & M. Mary Ashburner of Bombay in the East Indies Died 29 December 1777, aged 6 years.

(No. 2)

In memory of Mr Thomas Ashburner of Lawrence Pountney Lane died 24th of Octo^r 1747, aged 47 years Also Dor^y Ashburner of Cannon Street wife of the above said Thos Ashburner died 8th of Sep^t 1765, aged 57 years Also John Butterworth who died 5 of Nov 1772, aged 3 years & 4 months. This ground was purchased and tomb erected by Mr Joseph Butterworth of Cannon Street, London, who marry'd Elizabeth, daughter of the above said Thos & Dor^y Ashburner.

(No 3)

Underneath is (*sic*) deposited the remains of M Elizabeth the wife of Mr Joseph Butterworth of the parish of S Mary Abchurch who died the 24 of July 1779, aged 19 years. Also the above said Mr Joseph Butterworth who died the 9th of June 1782, in the 69th year of his age

The marriage allegation of Thomas and Dorothy Ashburner is in substance as follows —

(Copy)

Faculty Office. 6 February, 1729

Thomas Ashburner of the Parish of St Ethelburgh in the City of London Merchant aged 29 years Bachelor, and Dorothy Taylor of Latham in the County of Lancaster aged 23 years Spinster.

To marry in Parish church of Croston or Goosnagh in the County of Lancaster.

WILLS.

Thomas Ashburner of St Laurence Pountney, Merchant, mentions as Executors his wife Dorothy, his brother-in-law Peter Woosey of Ormskirk in the County Palatine of Lancaster, Gentleman, and Thomas Walker of Willstreet, St Mary Magdalen, Bermondsey, Surrey, Brewer. Will proved 21 March 1750

Dorothy Ashburner of the Parish of St Mary Abchurch, Widow, mentions her daughter Elizabeth, etc, and as Executors Mr John Le Gros of Bishopsgate Street, London, and Oliver Toulmin of Crutched Fryars, London. Will proved 25th Sept. 1765.

I should be glad of any information as to the families of Thomas Ashburner and Dorothy Taylor, his wife

54 Pembridge Villas, W. GEORGE ASHBURNER.

EXTRACTS FROM PARISH REGISTERS, ETC.*

Marriage Licences

Vicar General's Office

1674. 30 June. George Boddington of Islington, Middlesex, aged about 27, Widower, and Hannah Cope of St. Mary Bothaw, London, aged about 18, Spinster, with the consent of her Mother, Hannah Venning *alias* Cope, Widow To marry at Allhallows in the Wall, St Botolph Bishopgate, or St Margaret Lothbury, London.

1675 30 October. John Steere of Wootton, co Surrey, Gent, Bachelor, about 26, son of John Steere of same, Gent, who alleges, and Mrs. Fiducia Lee of Kinford, co Sussex, Spinster, about 16, with consent of her Parents To marry at St. Mildred, Bread Street or (*blank*)

1693 4 April John Gould of Allhallows the Great, Merchant, Bachelor, about 27, and Rachel Gilstorpe of St Andrew's, Holborn, about 20, Spinster, with her Father's consent To marry at St. Andrew, Holborn

1699 21 April George Caswall of Allhallows, Lombard Street, London, Citizen and Haberdasher, aged 23, Bachelor, and Mary Brassey of the same Parish, aged above 16, Spinster, with consent of John Brassey, her Father To marry at Allhallows in the Wall, London.

1799 15 June Jonathan Raine, Esq of Lincoln's Inn, co Middlesex, Bachelor, aged upwards of 21, and Elizabeth Price of Kensington, in the same county, Spinster, aged upwards of 21 To marry in Parish Church of Kensington.

Faculty Office

1671 11 December George Boddington of St Margaret, Lothbury, London, Bachelor, aged about 25, and Mary Steele of St Andrew, Holborn, a maiden, aged about 19, daughter of William Steele of the same place, who is consenting To marry at St Andrew, Holborn, Allhallows in the Wall, London, or St James, Clerkenwell, co Middlesex

1697 13 October Samuel Papillon of St Peter, Cornhill, London, aged above 21, Bachelor, and Fiducia Steere of St Martin, Ironmonger Lane, London, aged about 19, Spinster, with consent of Fiducia Steere *alias* Raper, now the wife of Matthew Raper, Merchant, her Mother. To marry at St Martin, Ironmonger Lane

1701 14 August Jabez Collier of Symond's Inn, London, Widower, aged 21, and Elizabeth Pope of Camberwell co Surrey, Spinster, aged 22 and upwards To marry in the Parish Church of Camberwell

1707 17 October Joseph Townsend of St Giles, Cripplegate, co Middlesex, aged above 30, Widower, and Mrs Anne Beacon of the same Parish, aged above 21 To marry at St Michael, Cornhill, or St Marylebone

1707-8 28 February. Samuel Raymond of St Olave, Old Jewry, London, aged 32, Bachelor, and Anne Skinner of Hackney, co Middlesex, aged above 21, Spinster To marry at St John, Hackney, or St Giles, Cripplegate

1712. 4 July. Francis St John of Longthorp, co Northants, Bachelor, aged 34, and Mary Gould of Newington Stoke, co Middlesex, Spinster, aged 20 and upwards, with consent of Nathaniel Gould, her Father To marry at St Andrew, Holborn

1724. 21 August John Gould, junior, of Hackney, co. Middlesex, Bachelor, aged upwards of 28, and Mary Bulkeley of Mortlake, co Surrey, Spinster, aged upwards of 22 To marry at Somerset Chapel.

1735 18 November John Raymond of St Ann, Limehouse, co Middlesex, Esq, aged above 22 Bachelor, and Britannia Lambe of St John, Hackney, co Middlesex, aged above 20, Spinster. To marry at St Antholin, London, or St. John, Hackney.

* For the Extracts from Parish Registers I am indebted to the kindness of Colonel Chester.

1738 1 March Henry Rogerson of St. John the Baptist, London, Watchmaker, aged about 25, Bachelor, and Mary Fido of St Andrew, Holborn, aged above 21, Spinster. To marry at St Nicholas Cole Abbey, London

1742 21 September Benjamin Ball of Hackney, co Middlesex, Bachelor, aged 30, and Sarah Wilkinson of the same place, Spinster, aged 24 To marry at St George, Bloomsbury

1744 17 May. Philip Hollingworth the younger, of St Edmund the King, London, Widower, and Sarah Collier of St Andrew, Holborn, aged upwards of 21, Spinster To marry in the Chapel in Bedford Row, in Parish of St Andrew, Holborn.

1755 11 June. Joseph Hurlock, Esq., of St. Stephen, Coleman Street, London, aged 21 and upwards, Bachelor, and *Sarah* Hartopp of Epsom, Surrey, aged 21 and upwards, Spinster To marry at St. Stephen Coleman Street

1804 10 November Luke Ashburner, Esq, of Paddington, co Middlesex, Widower, and Sarah Price Morgan of the same Parish, Spinster, aged 19 and upwards, with consent of Ann Morgan, Widow, the Mother and Testamentary Guardian, under Will of George Cadogan Morgan, Esq, whilst living the Father To marry in the Parish Church of Paddington

MARRIAGE REGISTER OF ALLHALLOWS, LONDON WALL

1674 July George Bodington Hannah Pope 2°

This Pope should be Cope, as appears in Marriage Licence and in a Boddington MS. book kept at the time

Marriage at Bridewell Hospital Chapel

1693 April 18. John Gold and Rachell Gilstorpe

Marriage at Parish Church, Kensington

1799. 21 June. Jonathan Raine and Elizabeth Price

REGISTERS OF ALLHALLOWS, LOMBARD STREET

Baptisms

1684	Nov. 12.	Daniel, son of John and Mary Brassey
1686	July 1.	Elizabeth, dau ,, ,,
$168\frac{8}{9}$	January 28	*Born* Sarah dau. of ,, ,,
1691.	December 27	Daniel, son of ,, ,,
1694	April 29.	Rebecca, dau of ,, ,,
1695.	Nov. 10	Daniel, son of ,, ,,
1700	Aug. 11	*Born* John, son of ,, ,,
$170\frac{1}{2}$	Feb 8.	*Born* John, son of George and Mary Caswall
1703.	Nov. 20	*Born* Mary, dau of ,, ,,
1706.	May 24.	*Born* and *bapt* George, son of ,,
1707.	Nov. 25.	*Born* and *bapt* Ann, dau of ,,

Burial

1737. Nov. 27. Mrs. Mary Brassey, in North Aisle

Marriage at Parish Church, Kensington

1799 24 June. Jonathan Raine and Elizabeth Price

Burial at St. Andrew, Holborn

1719. 18 June Peter Gelsthorpe, M.D.

M I. at Hillingdon, co Middlesex, to Ann, wife of Peter Gelsthorpe, M D, 1716, and to Mary, sister of Ann Gelsthorpe, wife of Gideon Harvey, M D, 1725.

Marriage at Temple Church, London

1717 August 1 Mr. Lee Steere of Wootton, Surrey, and Martha Sorocold, dau of the Worshipful Deputy Sorocold, Citizen and Mercer of London

Burial at Hackney.

1753. 20 January. Lee Steere.

Marriage at St Giles, Cripplegate

$170\frac{7}{8}$ March 2. Samuel Raymond and Ann Skinner

Registers of Parish of Hackney.

Baptisms.

1699. 25 July. Mary, dau. of Disney Stanyforth.

1702. 25 May Jonathan, son of „

Burials

$170\frac{6}{7}$ 24 January. Anna, infant dau of Disney Stanyforth, Merchant, of St. Botolph, Bishopsgate, London.

1712. 4 April. Nicholas, son of Disney Stanyforth, an infant.

1715. 16 Sept Nicholas, son of „ „ an infant

1725 7 May. Anne, dau. of „ „ aged 16.

$17\frac{39}{40}$. 18 January. Disney Stanyforth

Registers of Parish of Hackney

Baptism.

1708 25 Nov. John, son of Mr Samuel and Ann Raymond.

Burials.

$170\frac{5}{6}$ 1 March. Nicholas Skinner, in Chancel

1708 25 Dec John Raymond, infant

1712. 8 Aug Mrs Ann, wife of Mr Samuel Raymond, Merchant, in South Chancel

$17\frac{12}{13}$ 14 March. Mr Samuel Raymond, a child, in South Chancel

1719. 4 August John Raymond, a nurse child

1722 21 Dec Mary Skinner, widow

$172\frac{3}{4}$ 14 March Zachariah Skinner, Esq, bachelor

1725. 24 July Mr. William Raymond, a Barbadoes Merchant, carried to Bristol

1727. 27 Dec. Mr. James Lambe, hosier, in the new vault

1743 9 May Mrs Britannia Raymond, wife

Registers of Allhallows, Lombard Street, London

Baptism.

1732 3 August. William, son of Chauncey and Bridget Townshend, born same day

Burial.

1732 19 Aug. William Towns*h*end, infant, in Churchyard.

Registers of St. Christopher le Stocks, London

Baptisms

$173\frac{6}{7}$. 8 Feb James, son of Chauncey and Bridget Town*send*

1738 25 March. Judith, dau of *same*, born 7th

1739. 27 April Joseph, son of *same*, born 1th

Burials.

1734. 13 August Richard, son of Chauncey and Bridget Town*send*

1735 31 July. Thomas, son of *same*.

$174\frac{1}{2}$. 21 January. Wilhelmina, dau. of Chauncey and Bridget Townsend, died 12th.

1762. 24 January. Bridget Townsend
1770 4 April Chauncey Townsend
1772. 27 January. Mrs Elizabeth Townsend

Registers of St. Peter le Poer, London.

Baptisms

1741. 19 Nov Wilhelmina, dau of Chauncey and Bridget Townsend
174⅚ 9 January. Sarah, dau of *same*

Marriages.

1672 27 June. Thomas Hayes, D D., and Jane Townsend.
1758. 17 January John Wordsworth of St Dunstan in the East, London, Esq, Bachelor, and Judith Townsend of this Parish, Spinster, a minor, by Licence Witnesses, Chauncey Townsend, John Knight
1771. 3 January. Thomas Hawes (? Hawe*rs*), Clerk, of Aldwincle, co Northants, Bachelor, and Judith Wordsworth of this Parish, Widow, by Licence.
1784 17 May Rev Thomas Biddulph, Vicar of Padstow, Cornwall, and Sarah Townsend of this parish, Spinster, Licence.

Burial.

1669. 23 Oct Doctor Townsend.

In Churchyard of St. Augustine's, Hackney

Here lyeth ye body of James Lambe, Esq, who departed this life December ye 18th, 1727, aged 62 years Here also lieth the body of Elizabeth his wife, who after Mr. Lambe deceased, married ye Rev John Barker, and who departed this life January 21st, 1756, in the 75th year of her age In this Vault also are deposited the remains of ye Rev Mr John Barker, who departed this life May 31st, 1762, in the 77th year of his age Elizabeth, wife of Charles Raymond-Barker, Esq, of Blandford Street, Portman Square, who died 8th January, 1825, aged 39 years James Raymond-Barber, Esq, died 25 May, 1832, aged 61 years Britannia Raymond, wife of John Raymond, Esq, died May 2nd, 1713, aged 25 years John Raymond, Esq, son (query son-in-law) of the above James and Elizabeth Lambe, died January 20th, 1782, aged 70 years Mrs Mary Raymond died 7th of April, 1795, aged 82 years Mrs Sarah Wansey, daughter of John and Mary Raymond, died 8 November, 1802, aged 53 years Emma Wansey, daughter of Henry and Elizabeth Wansey of Warminster, Wilts, died 6 May, 1805, aged 3 years 7 months Mr John Wansey died 2nd May, 1820, in his 72nd year Mr John Wansey, son of the above, died 12th Dec, 1832, aged 18 Sarah Wansey, daughter of John and Sarah Wansey, died December 18th, 1837, aged 62 years

Firbeck, co York.

Mary, widow of Disney Stanyforth, died 19 Dec, 1756, aged 76, buried at Firbeck
Jonathan Stanyforth, died 8 Dec 1779, aged 77, bur. at Firbeck.
Mary, dau of Disney Stanyforth, died 19 April, 1781, aged 80, buried at Firbeck
Henrietta, dau. of Disney Stanyforth, died 20 Aug. 1787, aged 65, buried at Firbeck.
Amelia, dau. of Disney Stanyforth, died 22 January, 1792, buried at Firbeck.

Register of St. James, Clerkenwell.

Marriage.

1671. 19 December. Master George Boddington and Mistress Mary Steele was marryed by consent.

Marriage at Somerset House Chapel.

1724. 21 August. John Gould to Mary Bulkley

REGISTER OF ST. GEORGE'S, BLOOMSBURY.

Marriage.

1742. 23 Sept. Benjamin Ball and Sarah Wilkinson

REGISTER OF ST NICHOLAS, COLE ABBEY, LONDON.

1738. 4 March. Henry Rogerson and Mary Fido married by licence

REGISTER OF ST ANTHOLIN, LONDON.

Marriage

1735 20 Nov John Raymond of St Ann, Limehouse, co Midd, bachelor, and Britannia Lambe of St John's, Hackney, Spinster, married by Licence by Mr Newcombe.

REGISTER OF ST ANDREW, HOLBORN.

Marriage.

1744. 18 May. Philip Hollingworth the younger, of St. Edmund the King, London, Widower, and Sarah Collier of this parish, Spinster

Possibly this marriage took place in Bedford Row Chapel

$172\frac{0}{1}$ 2 January. Died Sir Charles Cooke, Knighted as Sheriff of London 21 January $17\frac{16}{17}$, and following 29 January elected Alderman of Bassishaw Ward, M P for Grampound in Cornwall 1715, appointed 8 June 1720 Commissioner of Trade and Plantations

1721. 8 Aug Died the wife of Sir George Caswall, Knt

1722 11 Aug Sir George Caswall of London, Knt, married to Mrs Milburne

$172\frac{1}{2}$ 7 March. Thomas Cooke of Newington, co Middlesex, married only dau of Sir Nathaniel Gould of the same place

1723 3 Oct. Died Dr Gilsthorpe, an eminent Physician at Welwyn, co. Herts

1728. 21 April. Died Sir Daniel Dolings of Hackney, co Middlesex, knighted 19 May, 1722, J.P. for co. Middlesex, and D L of the Tower Hamlets

1728 29 Oct. Died Joseph Townsend, and buried 7 Nov at Bunhill Fields, aged 58

1733 18 Aug. Died Mr. Raymond, Brewer, at Ratcliff Cross

1736. Dec Died the wife of Sir George Caswall, M.P for Leominster

1737 9 Dec Died Humphry Thayer, one of the Commissioners of Excise.

1743. 12 July Died Daniel Dolins of Hackney, Esq

1746 19 Nov Died James Cooke, Turkey Merchant

A James Cooke of London, Merchant, M P for Tregony in Cornwall 1722

1748 19 June Died Matthew Raper, a Bank Director

1755. 23 February. Died John Bance of Challow, co. Berks, Bank Director, M P. for Westbury, co Wilts, 1734, for Wallingford, co Berks, 1741, and for Westbury 1747

1770. 28 March Died Chauncey Townsend, Merchant in Austin Friars, London. M P. for Westbury, co. Wilts, 1747 and two succeeding Parliaments, and then for Wigton Burgh in Scotland

1782. 21 January. Died John Raymond, Esq, who for these 24 years last past held the office of Brewer to the Board of Victualling John Raymond of Hatchlands, co Surrey, M P. for Weymouth and Melcombe Regis 1741 to 1747.

1787. 1 July. Died at Bruce Castle, Tottenham, Alderman James Townsend, Lord Mayor of London $177\frac{2}{3}$, M P. for West Looe, Cornwall 1762, and succeeding Parliament.

WILLS.

Francis Cooke the elder of Kingsthorpe, co Northants, dated 12 May, 1658. Wife Sarah Cooke, sons Francis Cooke, George Cooke, John Cooke, and Thomas Cooke, son Timothy Wade, son William Pritchard and his wife; four Brothers in law, Lawrence Coles, Samuel Coles, James Coles, and Benjamin Coles, sisters Polsteed and Throckmorton. Son Francis Cooke sole Executor Proved 14 Feb. 1658–9 by sole Executor.—P C C. Pell, 127

The above Testator's son George Cooke married 1stly, Mary, dau. of . . . died 6 Oct. 1695, aged 57, buried at Eltham, Kent, and married 2ndly, Amy dau of . Osborne, who on her husband's death, 3 June, 1699 (buried at Eltham), married 2ndly the Rev Samuel Barton, D D, Prebendary of Westminster, and died 19 January 1737–8, aged 68, and a tablet erected to her memory at Eltham by her brother Andrew Osborne.

George Papillon of London, Merchant, dated 11 March, 1682–3 Property in co. Leicester and at Great Bentley, Essex, son Samuel Papillon, daus. Mary, wife of Samuel Ball, Phœbe, wife of Benjamin Smith, and Anne, Brother Thomas Papillon and Cousin Charles Chambrelan (*sic*) Executors.—Proved 26 February, 1683–4 —P C C Cann, 128

Nicholas Skinner of London, Merchant. To be buried at Parish Church, Hackney Settlement on marriage 20 and 21 May 1678, the parties being Nicholas Skinner, John Skinner, late of London, Merchant, now deceased, Thomas Owen of Gray's Inn, Esq, and my now wife by her then name of Mary Worth, Father in law Thomas Owen, and Mary his wife, brother Matthew Skinner, sister in law Susannah relict of deceased, brother John Skinner Testator born at Enfield, aunt Mrs Anna Berry and her dau Anne Berry, dau. Anna Skinner, wife Mary Skinner, brother in law Thomas Owen, Jun., Esq son in law Disney Stanyforth, nephew Nicholas Skinner, son of late brother John Skinner, Executors. Dated 8 August, 1702. Proved 8 March, 1705-6 —P C C. Eedes, 71

Peter Gelsthorp, Citizen and Apothecary of London To be buried in South Vault under Chancel of St Andrew, Holborn, where he wife and youngest dau. Elizabeth, son Dr. Peter Gelsthorp, dau Mary, married Richard Hind, in July 1716, deceased, Grand dau Elizabeth Hind, Grandson Peter Hind, the eldest of late Richard Hind's sons; dau. Rachel, wife of John Gould of London, Merchant, to take property at Headcorn and Frittenden, Kent, Grandson Robert Gelsthorp, grand dau Mrs Frances Cannes Property at Turners Hill, co Herts, and in Hatton Garden, London Testator born at Granby, co Notts. John Gould and Mary Hinde Executors Dated 3 July, 1716, 1st. Codicil 15 Dec 1716, 2nd Codicil 8 May, 1719, in which is named Kinswoman Mrs Frances Gelsthorp, living at Nottingham Proved 19 June, 1719 —P C C Browning, 105

Mary Skinner of Hackney, co Middlesex, Widow of Nicholas Skinner of London, Merchant, dated 18 October, 1721. To be buried in Parish Church of Hackney near late Husband, son Zachary Skinner, son in law Samuel Raymond and his son John Raymond, dau Mary, wife of Disney Stanyforth, and their children, Jonathan Stanyforth, Mary Stanyforth, Anna Stanyforth and Henrietta Stanyforth, Mother Mary Owen Brother Thomas Owen of Gray's Inn, and John Conder, Executors. Proved 10 January, 1722–3 —P C.C. Richmond, 17.

Zachary Skinner of St John's, Hackney, Esq, dated 3 January, 1722–3, Brother in law Samuel Raymond, sister Ann Stanyforth Executrix Proved 7 March, 1722–3 —P.C C. Richmond, 60

Margaret Cooke of Stoke Newington, widow of Thomas Cooke of Hackney. Dated 14 June, 1721. Leasehold houses in Basinghall Street to grand-dau. Margaret Cooke Sole Executor and residuary legatee son James Cooke To be buried at Hackney near late Husband. Son James Cooke sole Executor. Proved 7 Sept 1723.—P C.C. Richmond, 186.

Sir Charles Cooke, dated 12 May, 1703, and then of Smyrna. In partnership at

Smyrna with Pelatia Barnardiston, Mother Margaret Cooke, residue, cousin James Winstanley; Executors, Brother John Cooke and Samuel Barnardiston, both of Smyrna Administration with will annexed 7 Sept 1723, to James Cooke, son and Executor named in Will of Margaret Cooke, Widow, Mother and residuary legatee of Sir Charles Cooke —P C C. Richmond, 186

Peter Gelsthorp of Welwyn, co Herts, M D To be buried at Welwyn. Son Robert Gelsthorp Executor, brother and sister Gould brother Robert King, Esq, sister Hind Dated 12 July, 1722 Proved 26 October, 1723 —P C C Richmond, 207

Samuel Papillon, Citizen and Fishmonger of London, residing at Hackney Mother Raper, son John Papillon, brothers in law Lee Steere and his wife, Samuel Ball, John Gledhill (his wife Anne, Testator s sister, dead), and his issue, sister Phœbe deceased, late wife of Benjamin Smith, left issue, Phœbe, wife of William Voyce of Cornhill, London, Linendraper, and Elizabeth, widow of . . Hippisley nephew William Voyce sole Executor Dated 7 Oct 1725 Proved 2 Dec 1725 —P C C Romney, 257

William Raymond of Bristol, Merchant, now resident in London To be buried at St Augustine, Bristol, brothers Samuel Raymond, Edward Raymond, Rev Dr. Anthony Raymond, James Raymond, sister Elizabeth Thornhill, and her sons Richard Thornhill, William Thornhill, Francis Thornhill, and Edward Thornhilll, and her daus. Ann and Grace Son Anthony Raymond died under 21, Brother in law William Lane, deceased William Lane s sister Mary, wife of William Swymmer, nephew William Raymond, son of brother Edward Raymond, Edward Thornhill, Richard Morgan, and Richard Mansell, the two latter of the Kingdom of Ireland, Poor of St Augustine, Bristol, and of Michaels Town in Ireland. Brother Edward Raymond sole Executor. Dated 11 July, 1725 Witnesses, Philip Raymond, Dan Cullinan, and Fr Harding Proved 19 July 1726 —P C C Plymouth, 152.

James Lambe, Citizen and Haberdasher of London, wife Elizabeth, dau of late Thomas Cole, Citizen of London, whose other dau Mary married Henry Lovell: son James Lambe, sister, widow of my brother Bazill Lambe, dau Elizabeth, wife of John Bance, daus Mary and Britannia, unmarried, cousins Sarah Newton, Rebecca Pepper, Robert Lambe, Sarah Elmes, Alicia Lambe, Sellers and her husband, James Henry Lambe, Mary Boyce and her husband, Mary Chauvin and her husband, Ann Lambe, Elizabeth Lambe, Sophia White and her husband, and Arthur Lambe. Wife Elizabeth Lambe, and son James Lambe, Executors Dated 18 Nov 1727 Proved 17 January, 1727-8 —P C C Brook, 17

Joseph Townsend, Citizen and Brewer of London To be buried at Bunhill Fields, near first wife Mary, 2nd wife Anne Beacon had an only child, Thomas Beacon Townsend, 3rd wife Mary, son Joseph Townsend, dau. Mary, wife of Robert Ferguson, dau Elizabeth, wife of Abraham Reynardson Testator lived in Winchester Street, City of London Settlement on marriage with 2nd wife Anne Beacon dated 17 Oct 1707, and on marriage with 3rd wife Mary, 1 Dec 1714 Brewhouse in Old Street, St Giles, Cripplegate Sister Susannah, wife of Samuel Roberts; Nieces Elizabeth Swanwicke and Hannah Swanwicke, Executors, Wife Mary Townsend, Thomas Beacon of Ilford, Essex, and son in law Robert Ferguson of Lyme Street, City of London, Merchant, dated 6 May 1725 Proved 12 Dec 1728 —P C C Brook, 365

Sir Daniel Dolins of St John's, Hackney, Knight. To be buried at Hackney. Lady Player named, son Daniel Dolins, dau Margaret, brothers in law Thomas Cooke of Stoke Newington, co Middlesex, and James Cooke of Ashtead, co Surrey Wife Margaret sole Executrix Dated 26 May 1727 Proved 7 May 1728 Further grant 17 May, 1713, to dau Margaret Dolins, Spinster —P C C Brook, 113

Lovelace Hercy of Crutchfield, in Parish of Bray, co Berks To be buried at Winkfield, co. Berks. 2nd wife Rebecca, son William Hercy, dau Mary, wife of Joseph Parmenter and their dau Mary, dau Ann by second wife, son William Hercy sole Executor, dated 20 August, 1728. Proved 9 June, 1730.—P C.C. Auber, 161.

Samuel Raymond of St. Giles in the Fields, co. Middlesex, Esq. Mother living; son John Raymond, brother Joseph Raymond sole Executor, sister Elizabeth Angier Dated 16 Feb 1722–3 Administration with Will annexed 13 June, 1733, to son John Raymond, brother Joseph Raymond renouncing —P C C Price, 183

Edward Raymond of Carraughanna, co. Cork, Gent Dated 1 March, 1728. Wife living, sons William Raymond and Samuel Raymond, dau Elizabeth, Property in Barbadoes. Mary Cullinan, Margaret Cullinan, Julian Cullinan, Derby Cullinan, Daniel Cullinan, Friends Edward Thornhill, Devereux Spratt, and Harmon Bond, Executors A memo, dated 26 March, 1729. Proved 28 June, 1733 —P C C Price, 183

Joseph Raymond Citizen and Brewer of London Sister Elizabeth Angier, Nephew John Raymond sole Executor, dated 27 May, 1732. Proved 29 August, 1733 —P C C. Price, 229

Toby Chauncy of St Andrew, Holborn, Brewer, dated 28 Oct 1735. Married, but at date of Will no child. brother Richard Chauncy sole Executor. Proved 30 Dec 1736 —P C C Derby, 264

1736 13 Dec Died Tobias Chauncy in Hatton Garden, a Brewer, worth £40,000

Thomas Beacon of Ilford, co Essex, dated 9 Feb 1736–7 To be buried at Barking Sister Joyce, wife of Richard Drury, and their son Thomas Drury, one of the Six Clerks in Chancery, sister Elizabeth Beacon, Spinster, nephews Thomas Beacon Townsend and Thomas Drury Executors Codicil 16 Feb 1736–7 Died 23 April, 1737, Proved 26 April, 1737 —P C C Wake, 76

Thomas Beacon Townsend of London If die within 10 miles of London to be buried at Bunhill Fields Sister Mary, wife of Robert Ferguson, sister Elizabeth, wife of Abraham Reynardson cousins Thomas Drury, one of the Six Clerks in Chancery, and Major Swanwick, Cousin Chauncy Townsend, Aunts Hannah Parish, and Martha Hammon, Elizabeth Swanwick, Hannah Voice, and Mary Parish, daughters of Aunt Parish, six children of late Aunt Roberts Executors, brother Joseph Townsend and Robert Ferguson. Dated 25 June 1737 Proved 16 July, 1737 —P.C C Wake, 171

Humphry Thayer of Hatton Garden, co Middlesex, Citizen and Skinner. Wife Elizabeth Thayer living, dau Jane, wife of Nathaniel Gould, son in law Richard Knollys and his son Frances Knollys, brothers Thomas Thayer, John Thayer, Samuel Thayer and Edward Barber Nathaniel Gould Sole Executor, dated 28 May, 1735 Proved 16 Dec 1737 4 May, 1746, Administration with Will annexed granted to Francis Knollys, grandson of Testator, Elizabeth Thayer relict of deceased renouncing 18 March, 1811, further grant, Jane Gould, afterwards wife of Richard Madan, dying intestate 6 May, 1824, further grant —P C C Wake, 288

Francis Knollys, created a Bart. 1 April, 1754, married, but died s p 29 June, 1772

Rebecca Hercy of Winkfield, co Berks, widow of Lovelace Hercy of Crutchfield, co Berks, nephew Richard West of London, three children of niece Anne, wife of Mitchell, Frances, widow of Rev William Stringfellow, Sarah, daughter of Richard West, grand-daughter of Richard West by his daughter Frances ., Joseph Parmenter, his wife Mary, and their two sons, daughter in law Anne Hercy, William Hercy and Elizabeth his wife, and their children, Frederick Vognell and his children Richard West sole Executor Proved 12 May, 1738.—P C C. Brodrepp 121

James Townsend, Citizen and Bowyer of London, dated 25 August, 1738 To be buried at Hanwell, Middlesex, where wife lies, nephew or kinsman Thomas Holford, and niece Mary, his wife, cousin Thomas Hopkins of London, cousin James Boddington, niece Ann, his wife, and their sons James Boddington and Josias Boddington, late cousin Thomas Dawkins, James Holford, Thomas Holford, Josiah Holford, John Holford, William Holford, Charles Holford, Margaret Holford, and Mary Holford, late nephew Francis Fox, cousins Martha Fox, Mary Park,

Josiah Boddell, Jerome Knapp and wife, Henry Bowman and Barbara Errick Names Matthew Raper. Thomas Holford sole Executor Property at Brentford Proved 9 January, 1740-1 —P.C.C Spurway, 21.

'Gent Mag' 1740, 29 Dec Died James Townsend, eminent hosier in Cheapside, and one of the Governors of St Thomas's Hospital

James Cooke of Ashtead, co Surrey, dated 10 August, 1733 To be buried in Ashtead Churchyard Wife Anne sole Executrix Proved 8 Dec 1746 Appeared Elizabeth, wife of Crayle Crayle of St George's, Hanover Square, and William Skrine of St. James, Westminster, 1 Dec 1746, and spoke to handwriting Administration granted 6 May, 1747, to William Skrine, son and Administrator of said Anne Cooke the Executrix —P C C Edmunds, 346

James Cooke, Turkey Merchant, died 19 Nov 1746

1743. 15 Dec Crayle Crayle of Beechwood, Herts, married Miss Skreen of Ashtead, near Epsom, with £10,000.

Matthew Raper of Newington Green, co Middlesex Marriage articles on marriage with Elizabeth, daughter of John Billers, Citizen and Haberdasher of London, dated 18 Dec 1704, Testator in 1704 a Silkman and son and heir of Matthew Raper, whose will dated 5 August, 1710. Sons Matthew, Moses, John, William, George, and Henry Raper, daughter Elizabeth Raper, brother Moses Raper Names Sir William Billers, Knt, and Alderman of London Wife Elizabeth Raper and brother Moses Raper Executors, dated 3 March, 1740-1 Codicil dated 20 April, 1743, refers to death of son Moses Raper Proved 6 July, 1748, by Elizabeth Raper, relict and surviving Executor —P C C Strahan, 222

John Bance of Challow, co Berks, and of London, Merchant, sister in law Mary, wife of John Raymond, kinsman John Shipway of Froom Hall, co. Gloucester, Executor Dated 27 August, 1754 Proved 15 March, 1755. Administration with Will annexed 31 May, 1769, to Nathaniel Beard, one of the Executors of John Shipway, deceased —P C C Paul, 67

Elizabeth Barker, late Elizabeth Lambe, relict of James Lambe of Hackney, son James Lambe married, daughter Mary Raymond and her daughter Mary, late daughter Britannia Raymond and her children John Raymond, Britannia and Elizabeth, John Raymond of Ratcliff Cross, co Middlesex, Brewer; Rev John Barker, present husband, sole Executor Dated 23 April, 1751 Proved 10 Feb. 1756.—P.C.C Glazier, 28

James Lambe of Fairford, co Gloucester Settlement on Marriage 6 and 7 July, 1730. Brother John Bance, cousins Robert Lambe and Mrs Anne Massey. Wife Esther Lambe sole Executrix Dated 12 April, 1753. 1st Codicil 16 July, 1756, 2nd Codicil 15 Aug 1759 Proved 11 April, 1761 —P C C Cheslyn, 138

John Barker of Clapham, co Surrey, Gent Nathaniel Neal, sole Executor Nephew Samuel Barker, son in law Mr Daniel of Colchester, grand-daughter Mary Raymond, Mrs. Mary Raymond residue Dated 10 Nov. 1761 Proved 5 June, 1762 —P C.C. St Eloy, 235

Chauncy Townsend Dated 7 March, 1765 Sons James Townsend and Joseph Townsend, son James Townsend, and daughters Elizabeth, wife of John Smith, Charlotte Townsend, and Sarah Townsend, the last not of age, March 1765, Executors Grandson Charles Smith, daughter Judith Wordsworth, late of Parish of St Peter le Poor, London Proved 5 May, 1770,—P C C Jenner, 211.

John Raymond of Tower Hill, co Middlesex, Brewer Wife Mary Raymond sole Executrix. Dated 16 Sept. 1762 Codicil 1 March, 1781 Proved 4 Feb 1782 —P C C Gostling, 96.

James Townsend of Conduit Street, co Middlesex. Wife Henrietta Rosa Peregrina Townsend and Samuel Phipps, Esq, Executors Dated 18 Dec 1761 12 Sept 1767, Administration with Will annexed granted to Henry Hare Townsend, son of deceased Samuel Phipps of Lincoln's Inn, Esq, surviving Executor, renouncing —P C.C Major, 431

Esther Lambe of Fairford, daughter of Samuel Barker by his wife Frances. Grandfather John Hibbert, formerly of Hampstead, co Middlesex. To be buried near late husband James Lambe at Fairford, Nieces Mary Warren, Ann Coates, Elizabeth wife of Thomas Lane, and Britannia, wife of Charles Turel Morgan, nephew John Raymond to take Fairford, etc, and assume name and arms of Barker, and the sole Executor Dated 19 March, 1776 Proved with four codicils 29 April, 1789 —P C C Macham, 209

Mary Raymond of Clapham, co Surrey, Widow Son in law Mr John Warren and his wife Mary, daughter Sarah, wife of John Wansey, son in law William Cotes Names Elizabeth Raymond of Barton Court in Kintbury, co Berks John Warren and Mr John Harrison, Executors Dated 3 April 1790. Codicil 1 Dec 1794. Proved 15 June, 1795,—P C C Newcastle, 407

I should be glad of any additions touching any of the families named, and especially as to the Raymond ancestry.

15 *Markham Square, Chelsea, S W.* REGINALD STEWART BODDINGTON.

Family of Gresham.

Inquis. p m of ANNE LADY GRESHAM, 1597.

[Chancery Inquis. p m 39 Eliz., 1st Pt, No 57]

Writ directed to Michael Stanhope Esq Richard Candler Esq & William Necton Esq to inquire what land Anne Lady Gresham widow late wife of Sir Thomas Gresham Kt deceased held in the County of Middlesex, what day she died, and who was her next heir. Dated at Westminster 1 May 39 Eliz.

Inquisition taken at Westminster 9 May 39 Eliz before Michael Stanhopp Richard Candler and William Necton upon the death of Ann Lady Gresham late wife of Sir Thomas Gresham Kt deceased The Jurors say that long before her death the said Anne Gresham was seised in her demesne as of fee of and in the Manors of Osterley Burston and Heston with the appurtenances co Midd and in 40 messuages 40 gardens 2000 acres of land 500 of meadow 2000 of pasture 500 of wood 2000 of furze and heath 200 of marsh and of £2 rent in Osterley Heston Wyke Norwoodde Isleworth Braynceford Ashford Bedfounte Laleham Iveney Stanes and Hounceslowe co Midd. and in the park of Osterley, and in the Manors of Great Massingham Massingham Dettforde and of the advowson of the Church of Great Massingham co Norff, and in the Manors of Great and Little Walsingham Bynham in Walsingham Botts Collinghams Fennes Marshes Hatchewood graunges Wells Boroughall in Holkham *alias* Holcombe Estwalton with the advowson of the Church Lakenham with the advowson of the Church Narford Herryngeshall and Dickwoodde co. Norff And in the Rectory of Swyne with all lands tenements and Tithes thereto belonging, and in a moiety of the Manor and of the Rectory and advowson of Nunkelynge co. Ebor. and of the Manor of Erlestonham co. Suff Recites an indenture of 7 March 29 Eliz between Dame Anne Gresham widow Sir Thomas Cecill of Burghley Kt and Mildred Cecill his second daughter and William Reade Esq son and heir apparent of said Dame Anne and Thomas Reade his son and heir apparent being a settlement on the marriage of the said Thomas Reade and Mildred Cecill upon him of the Rectory of Swyne the moiety of the Manor of Nunkelyng with all lands in the said Parishes thereto belonging, the Manor of Erlestonham, the Manor of Heston, the capital and great dwelling house called Osterley and Osterley Park, and all her lands tenements and hereditaments in Norfolk except the Manor of Estwalton, and except the Manors of Thirling and Upwell co Cambridge The Jurors further say that the said Anne Gresham was seised in demesne as of fee of a messuage in the Parish of Great Saint Helen's in Bishopsgate Street lately bought of John Ellyott mercer and of another messuage in Broad Street in the Parish of St Peter le poor formerly called the Foxtail and now the Rose, and of the Manors of Great Over

Little Over and Fynderne co Derby, and of the Manor of Wedmore co. Somerset, and of the Manor of Thurling co Cantab, and of the Manors of Cantrecellie Brentleys and Brentleys Castle, and of the Forest or Wood called Coydyforth, and of the advowson of the Church of Llanveneche co Brecon, and of 14 acres 3 roods of marsh in Erith co Kent That the said Anne Gresham died at Osterley on 23 Nov 39 Eliz That the Manor of Heston was of the yearly value of 16*l* 0*s* 1*d*, the tenements in Wyke 6*l* 17*s* 4*d*, Osterley together with all the other lands in Middlesex 77*l* 5*s* 1*d*, Estwalton 11*l* 9*s* 2*d*, Lakenham 32*l* 16*s* 8*d*, Walsingham and other lands in Norfolk 61*l*, Brnham 3*l* 10*s* 9½*d*, Narford 6*l* 0*s*. 2¼*d*, Massingham 35*l*, Boroughall 24*l*, Herringshall 16*l*, lands in Intwood Swardeston and elsewhere 40*s*., the messuage in Bishopgate Street 60*s*, the messuage in Broadstreet 3*l*, Great and Little Over and Fynderne 63*l*., Nunkelyng 21*l* 9*s* ¾*d*, Rectory of Nunkelyng 10*l*, Rectory of Swyne 26*l* 18*s*. 8*d*, Manor of Wedmore 10*l*, Manor of Thurling 5*l*, the lands in Brecon 20*l*, the 14 acres of Marsh in Erith 13*s* 1*d* That William Reade is son and heir of said Anne Gresham widow of Sir Thomas Gresham Kt and formerly wife of William Reade of London Esq deceased father of the said William Reade and that he was of the age of 58 years and upwards at the time of the taking of this Inquisition.

MEMORANDA IN A MS VOLUME OF PRAYERS, ETC, IN THE POSSESSION OF REV F. BROWN, OF BECKENHAM *

On the inside of cover

Mary Bunbury given her by her Father

On the fly leaf

Sarah Lydall

Sister Fonnereau married April 1728

I came to live at Bolton May 1711

I went to Houghton Tower July 21st 1712 & came back July 26

My Bro & his wife came to see me 1713

I went to London & Catworth June 1714

Lady Boughton & her sister Boughton & Lucy Houghton lay at Bolton.

Sunday Nov 13, 1715 ye day Preston Fight was

I went to ye Isle of Man Aug 11, 1716 & returned 18.

Charles Bunbury was baptized sayes ye Stoake register Feb 22, 1656

Jenney went from Poolton to London Aug 5, 1718

Hannah Johnson came to live with me Aug 15, 1718

My brother & his son Will came to Poolton May 25, 1730 & went away June 3

I went to Houghton Tower July 4 & came back ye 9, 1720

I saw ye Bp of Down & Connor & Lady & coz. Jack Skeffington at Chester as I went to Alton Aug 14.

The prodigious high tyde Sunday 18 of Dec. 1720.

* The Book apparently belonged to Mary Bunbury Strong, having been given her by her father, who has written many of the prayers and reflections and the family memoranda She was born at Hargrave Dec 6, 1751, and died July 12, 1776, aged 24 She was the daughter of Rev Thomas Strong of Spaldwich Hunts who married at Brampton, Feb 2, 1749, Mary Bunbury, who was sister of Rev William Bunbury, Vicar of Brampton, Hunts (died Jan 17, 1754, aged 37), and daughter of Rev William Bunbury Rector of Great Catworth, Hunts He was born May 18, 1664 and was summoned to take the oath of allegiance to King George, June 15 1722 This Rev William Bunbury and his brother Charles Bunbury baptized at Stoke Feb 22, 1656, were sons of William Bunbury, by Mary Skeffington, the sister of Sir John Skeffington 1st Viscount Massereene Clothworthy Skeffington, 2nd Viscount Massereene married March, 1684, Rachel, daughter of Sir Edward Hungerford He died 1713 She died Feb 2, 1731 Their daughter Mary Skeffington married, April, 1710 Dr E Smyth, Bishop of Down and Connor, who died Oct 16, 1720 Mary Skeffington, a daughter of the 1st Viscount Massereene married 1676 Sir Charles Houghton of Houghton Tower, Bart, who died June 10, 1710 aged 67 Their son, Sir Henry Houghton, Bart., married Mary, the daughter of Sir William Boughton, Bart.

My father died Oct 23, 1676

I went to Oxford Nov 1, 77

After I had fix'd my Bro at Oxford I took him to London where he staid at my sisters till ye middle of Ap & then returned to Oxford

In 1685 my Mother & I went to London & my Bro met us at ye Coronation of King James 2d

Wm Bunbury born May 18, 1664, 4 o'clock my mother died Apr 22, 1711 Sunday evening

June 18, 1722 I was legally summonded to . this day to take the Oaths to Kg George.

July 10, 22 I was convict. at the Quarter Sessions for refusing to take ye Oaths to Kg George

A prayer taken from my Uncle William Skeffington's will

Miss Betty Fonnereau died of the Small Pox the day after her Grandmother, aged 9

1748 Dec 16 on Friday about 10 o'clock (aged 82) my Dear Father Departed this life, as did also my Dear Bro. Charles (aged 29) on Tuesday June ye 6 about one o'clock in ye morning 1749

My Dear Bror W Bunbury departed this life Jan. 17, 1754 in ye 37 yr of his Age

MARY STRONG.

Thomas Strong (clerk) of Spaldwick Huntingdonshire & Mary Bunbury Daughter of the Revd Wm Bunbury (late Rector of Great Catworth in ye same county were married at Brampton by her Brother W Bunbury Vicar of Brampton on Friday ye 2 of Febry 1749 old stile

Mary Bunbury Daughter of Thomas & Mary Strong was born at Hargrave Dec 6, 1751 (ye last year of ye Old Stile) about 5 o'clock in ye Afternoon, & baptized by her Father Jan 1, 1752 (ye first year of ye New Stile) Mrs Fonnereau, Mrs Bunbury of Brampton & Mr Will Strong were her sponsors

My dear Polly went to Stamford on Tuesday July 9, 1765 Returned Sept 11 1766

Our Dear Daughter departed this life on Friday July ye 12th about 1 o'clock in ye afternoon & was buried on Wednesday ye 17th 1776 Aged 24 yrs

---

EXTRACTS FROM THE REGISTERS OF THE PARISHES OF CHILCOMPTON, SOMERSET, AND FROM BITTON IN GLOUCESTERSHIRE, RELATING TO THE FAMILY OF HARINGTON

(*Continued from p 197.*)

BITTON REGISTER

Baptisms.

1702 Sept. 17 William the son of John Harington, Gent. by Mary his wife, was baptized.

1703. Aug 30 George the son of John Harington, Gent. by Mary his wife, was baptized

Marriage.

1767 Robert Bush of the Parish of St Mary-le-Port in the City of Bristol, widower, and Ann Harington of this Parish, spinster, were married in this Church by License the 17th day of February, 1767, by me Henry Hawes, Curate.

Burials.

163$\frac{8}{9}$. Francis Harington,* Gent. was buried January xxii.

1714. Oct. y[e] 19. M[r] John Harington† was buried.

1743. No register entry of burial, but on an altar tomb, on north side of Bitton, Church, "Elizabeth the wife of George Harington, Gent., who died aged 28."

CHILCOMPTON REGISTER.

Burial.

1670. Benjamin Harington‡ was buried in ye Church of Chilcompton, Oct. 27th.

THE LADY MARY HARINGTON'S PEDIGREE (*née* ROGERS OF CANNINGTON, SOMERSET),

Given in illustration of the preceding Registers, and other data on the connection of Rogers with Harington.

ARMS.—Argent, a chevron between three bucks passant sable. These arms appear on a tomb at Cannington.

[Note.—The manor of Cannington, etc., was granted to Edward Rogers, Esq., 30 Hen. VIII., on the suppression of the monastery. It continued with the Rogers to 1670, the date of Henry Rogers's decease, when it escheated to the Crown.]

Alexander Sidenham. Will proved Oct. 19, 1523. = Agnes, relict of Popham.

Children:
- John Sidenham, Junior, of Chelworthy, Som't.
- John Sidenham, Senior, of Leigh, Som't. s. and h. His will proved Aug. 27, 1547; = Joan. her will, Jan. 28, 1549-50.
- Silvester Sidenham. = Joan.

Daughter of Silvester: Eleanor Sidenham. = Edmund Wynter of Cleeve, Som't. Will proved Feb. 23, 1550-1.

Sir Geo. Rogers of Cannington, son of Edward Rogers. Will proved Nov. 6, 1582. Marriage settlement dated March 16, 1551. = Jane Wynter. Will dated Sept. 24, 1598, proved May 20, 1601.

Children:
- Catherine Popham. = 1. Edward, died Sept. 3, 1627.
- 2. William, buried in Westminster Abbey, June 18, 1593.
- Mary Rogers. Will proved Feb. 23, 1636-7. = Sir John Harington of Kelston, Kt. circa 1585.

[N.B.—For much of the filling up in precise detail of the above illustrative pedigree, the writer on the Haringtons of Somerset acknowledges with sincere thanks his indebtedness to the Rev. Frederick Brown, F.S.A., whose stores of Somerset genealogy are very rich, and are often opened for the benefit of others with great liberality.]

* Francis Harington received a bequest, under the will of his sister-in-law, Dame Mary Harington (proved 1636), widow of Sir John, K[t] (who died 1612), of all her "interest in a Lease of Fieldgrove in the Parish of Bitton." Though we do not know the date of this gentleman's birth, yet, since his eldest brother John was born 1561, as we gather from his entrance at College, we may fairly assume that he was born about 1563, and would therefore be about 70 years of age (not younger) when he received this bequest. We are not, therefore, surprised to find from the date of burial that he did not long enjoy it. His history has always been unknown, and hitherto no register of him discovered. I am glad to be able to set it now before the public.—F. J. P.

† This the son of Wm. and Ann Harington.

‡ This gentleman was son of Francis Harington, the brother of Sir John, Kt., by Mary, daughter of Antony Stocker, Esq., of Chilcompton, and Margaret Capel his wife. He resided at Weymouth (Melcombe Regis), co. Dorset, and probably died there, though brought to rest with his wife and her relatives at Chilcompton. He left an only son John, matriculated at Trin. Coll. Oxford, 10th July, 1668, about whom more information is earnestly desired.

A letter (not before published) from Sir John Harington, Knt., to his mother-in-law, the Lady Jane Rogers, on presenting her with his "Orlando Furioso."

"To the Right Virtuous and kind Mother-in-law The Ladie Jane Rogers.

"Madam,—I have sent you my long promised Orlando, and that it may properly belonge to you and your heire female, I have added to it as many of the toyes I have formerly written to you and your daughter, as I could collect out of my scattered papers, supposing (though you have scene some of them long since) that now to review them againe and remember the kynde and sometimes unkynde occasions on which some of them were written will not be unpleasant and because there was spare roome I have added a few others that were showed to our Soveraigne Lady and some that I durst never show any ladie,* but you two And so wishing you to lock me up as safe in your love, as I know you will lay up this booke safe in your chest, I commend me to you

"Your son in law and in love
"(signed) JOHN HARINGTON.

"19 December
"1600."

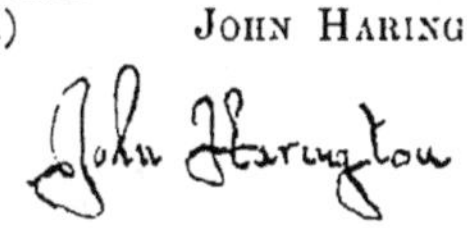

(Facsimile of Autograph in 1599.)

(*To be continued.*)

PARR FAMILY OF POWDERHAM, EXETER.—Can any one help me to the ancestry of John Parr, who married Elizabeth Williton (both were of Powderham, Exeter) in 1775, of Thomas Parr, who married Esther Woollacott (both of Powderham) in 1780, and of William Parr, who was living at Powderham, and married in 1785? I cannot trace the Parr family of Powderham prior to the year 1775

Ledbury FRANK JOHN PARR.

NATHANIEL MAXEY.—Can any of your readers afford me any information as to the direct ancestors of this gentleman? He was a merchant in London, and married the daughter of Sir Rowland Crispe, by whom he had issue two daughters, Martha, married to Elwes Robinson, and who died in 1726 without issue, and Mary, who died in 1770, having married James Pattison of Congleton and London, by whom she left issue Nathaniel Maxey had a brother Joseph Maxey, and a sister Martha, married to John Bockett Joseph Maxey had two sons, William Seele Maxey and Nathaniel Edward Maxey, and a daughter Mary, wife of Samuel Bridgeman Nathaniel Maxey bore the same arms as the Maxeys of Salinghall, co Essex, and is believed to have been an offshoot of that family He died in 1708 Any information regarding the ancestors of Nathaniel Maxey, or of his son-in-law James Pattison, would be acceptable

---

THE LEIGH PEERAGE.—In 'Notes and Queries,' vol v, March 26, 1870, page 316, appeared the following query —

"BARON LEIGH.—Can any of your readers furnish me with the date and place of the marriage of Thomas, second Baron Leigh, with the daughter of Lord Rockingham? It took place somewhere about the year 1680 Also any information respecting Thomas, eldest son of the said second Baron, who was baptized at Stoneleigh, March 10, 1682, and is usually stated to have died young, but of whom it was proved on the trial of the Leigh peerage case before the House of Lords in 1828, that no register of his burial could be found. It is strongly suspected that he survived many years, and even outlived his father."

The marriage certificate referred to has been found. Can any reader of the 'Miscellanea Genealogica' give the required information respecting the said son Thomas? The smallest contribution will oblige

S John's College, Cambridge J HENRY WHITEHEAD.

* Queen Elizabeth's lesson on this point, in 1590, seems to have lingered in his mind? (See 'Nugæ Antiquæ.')

PETER GODDE,* traditionally a Huguenot Refugee, d. intestate 1716. Letters of admon. granted June, 1716, to Francis and Richard Pigot. = Mary, d. of . . . . d. before 1716.

Frances Godde, b. 12 Jan. 1694-1695, bapt. Feb. 2, at S. James', Piccadilly; d. 29 Dec. 1769. = Richard Pigot, bapt. at Hodnet, co. Salop, 6 Oct. 1679; d. 31 Dec. 1729.†

Mary Godde, b. 14 Feb. 1698-9, bapt. 19 Feb. at S. James'.

Henry Godde, b. 16 April, 1702, d. 24 Sept. 1764, at Clewer; buried at S. Anne's, Soho, "under the middle aisle." 3 Oct. Will dated 1763. Sole ex'or his s. Henry. = Anna, d. of John Jackson of S. Anne's, Westminster, b. 24 Feb. 1701-2, bapt. 16 March; died in childbirth, and bur. at S. Anne's, 7 Oct. 1739.

Ann Godde, born 4 Nov. 1704.

William, born 8 Mar. 1706.
—
John, twin with William.

Richard Godde, b. Dec. [?] 1707. Of H.E.I. Co.'s ship the "Bedford." Died abroad or at Sea. Will dat. 1739. Proved Sept. 1742.

Elizabeth Godde, b. Feb. 13, 1712.

George Godde, b. 25 Jan. 1729, bapt. 11 Feb. at S. Martin's in Fields, & there bur. 3 Jan. 1730.

Mary Wilhelmina Godde, b. 3 Nov. 1731, bapt. 22 Nov., at S. Martin's in Fields; mar. at S. John's, Hampstead, 9 June, 1748; d. 14 Jan. 1808; bur. at Lee, co. Kent. = George Wagner, b. 4 Dec. 1722, d. 7 Dec. 1796, bur. at Lee, co. Kent. Godson of George I. Will proved 30 Dec. 1796. Ex'ors, his relict, (her cousin-in-law) Dr. Samuel Smith, Headmaster of Westminster School, Rev. S. S. Bale, and T. W. Partington, Esq.

William Godde, b. . . Sept. 1732. Bur. 29 August, 1733, at S. Anne's, Soho.

Louisa Godde, b. . . Nov. 1733, bapt. 26 Nov., at S. Martin's. = Rev. Sackville Spencer Bale, Rector of Withyham, co. Sussex, 1749-78; and of Chiddingstone, co. Kent, 1755. See 'Alumni Westm.' p. 326.

Issue of George Wagner and Mary Wilhelmina Godde:

Melchior Henry Wagner, b. Dec. 19, 1749, d. 17 Feb. 1811. Bur. in family vault, at Lee, co. Kent. = Anne Elizabeth,‡ d. of Rev. Henry Michell, Vicar of Brighton, and Rector of Maresfield, co. Sussex; b. 22 Dec. 1757, bapt. at Brighton 11 Jan. 1758; there mar. 27 May, 1784; d. 27 Aug. 1844; bur. at Brighton.

A

Rev. George Wagner, Rector of Mursley, co. Bucks, 1790, b. 1764, d. 1836, unmar. Buried at Fulham. Sponsors, Lord Pigot and †Thos. Walley Partington, Esq.

Other issue.

Issue of Rev. Sackville Spencer Bale and Louisa Godde:

Rev. Sackville Stephens Bale, LL.D., Rector of Withyham, co. Sussex, 1778; and also (by dispensation granted in 1783) of Chiddingstone, co. Kent; d. 2 Sept. 1836, æt. 83; bur. at Withyham. See 'Alumni Westm.' p. 393. = Alicia, d. & coheiress of Francis Otway, Esq., of Riverhill, nr Sevenoaks; mar. at Sevenoaks, 29 Dec. 1788.

Louisa Bale, b. 17 May, 1755, d. 12 Oct. 1831, æt. 76.

Issue of Rev. Sackville Stephens Bale and Alicia Otway:

Sackville Bale, b. 21 Oct. 1789, bapt. at Withyham, 2 Dec. See 'Alumni Westm.,' p. 462. 5th Regt. Bengal Nat. Inf. D. at Calcutta, June, 1812.

Otway Bale, bapt. at Withyham, 2 Feb. 1791.

Rev. George Bale, b. 25 Feb. 1792, bapt. at Withyham, 22 May. At Westm. and Ch. Ch., Oxford. Rector of Odcombe, co. Somerset, 1836. Died unm. 2 July, 1875, æt. 84. Odcombe Church, rebuilt at his cost, reopened 10 March, 1876.

Charles Sackville Bale, bapt. at Withyham, 23 July, 1793; at Westm. and Ch. Ch. Oxford. Of 71 Cambridge Terrace, W. [Waagen's 'Art Treasures,' ii. 329–32, iv. 116–21.]

B

The dates of birth are derived from an old family Bible (of 1679), which on the death of Selina Frances Godde—the last of her name—in 1850, passed to Miss Maria Clayfield, and was given by the latter, in 1862, to the compiler of these notes, by whom further information is sought.

* There were two other Refugees in London of this name, viz., Benjamin Godde, who m. Magdalene Chapret, and left children, of whom the eldest, Peter, was born in 1690; and Philip Godde, who m. Marie Menanteau, and died, leaving issue, in 1725. No direct evidence has been found to connect them with Peter; but it may be noted, as at least a curious coincidence, that the name of Francis Duroure appears in two of these Godde wills in 1779, while the two brothers, Generals Scipio and Alexander Duroure, were successively Governors of St. Mawes' Castle till 1765, and Sir Robert Pigot and Henry Godde are found, not long after, as Keeper and Deputy-Keeper of the same remote post.

† Cf. p. 177-9.

‡ Grand-dau. of John Michell and Eliz. Hamshar, his wife, cf. p. 56. See also Lower's 'Sussex Worthies,' p. 229, 30. Her brother, the Rev. John Henry Michell, Rector of Buckland and Kelsall, co. Herts, m. Margaret Wagner (her husband's sister), and left issue, William Anthony Michell, who d. 23 Dec. 1819, æt. 13, and Margaret Henrietta, who d. 29 May, 1859, wife of Major Francis John Swayne Hepburn, of the 60th Rifles.

A | B

Frances Godde ═ James Ireland of Brislington, Sheriff for co. Somerset 1782. Born 1724, d. 1814. — Frances Godde b. 3 Nov. 1734, mar. 1771, died 1805.

Sarah Godde, born Oct. 30, 1735. Will dated Feb. 1767, pr. Aug. same year.

William Augustus Godde, born Oct. 5, 1737. ? dead in 1763, since not named in father's will.

Elizabeth Godde, b. Oct. 22, 1738, of Brompton; d. of decline, at Lisbon, 6 April, 1766. Will dat. 1765, pr. June, 1766.

Henry Godde, b. 23 Sept. 1739. In the R.N. Somewhile Lieut. Governor of S. Mawes' Castle, co. Cornwall. Died 24 March, 1809. Buried in Clifton Parish Church. ═ Ann Elizabeth, d. of . . . . Short, m. 1769, d. . . . 1775.

Frances Constance, elder dau. and coheir, b. . . . m. 1795, d. 1812. ═ Edward Rolle Clayfield of Brislington, J.P. and D.L. for co. Somerset. Died 1825.

Louisa Frederica, younger dau. and coheir, b. . . . . m. 1799, died s.p. in Paris, 20 Sept. 1854, æt. about 75. ═ Sir Richard Vaughan, Kt. of Redland Court, near Bristol.

Selina Frances Godde, born Sept. 23, 1770. Died unm. at Clifton, 21 May, 1850, æt. 79.

Hugh Henry Godde, born Aug. 18, 1771; died abroad.

Charles, b. Jan. 9, 1774, d. May, 1775.

Sidney, b. Jan. 1775, d. month following.

Edward Ireland Clayfield, of Dowrich House, co. Devon, b. 1798, d. 1862, s.p. Mar. Charlotte L., da. of Capt. William Cox, of the Coldstream Guards.

James Ireland Clayfield-Ireland (assumed in 1827, by Royal license, additional name and arms of Ireland) of Brislington Hall, b. 1804, d. 1864. ═
See 'Landed Gentry,' under Clayfield-Ireland of Brislington Hall, and of Dowrich House.

Louisa Godde Clayfield, d. at Exmouth, 3 March, 1841, æt. 32. ═ Rev. Nathaniel Hole, Rector of Broadwood Kelly, Devon, m. 1836.
Louisa Sophia Hole, only child, d. 18 Oct. 1857, æt. 20.

Maria Vaughan Clayfield, d. unm. at Clifton, 12 Feb. 1871, æt. 61.

Richard. — Frances. d. infants.

George Pigot, b. 4 May, 1719, bapt. 31 May, at S. Martin's. Governor of Fort S. George, Madras. Created Bart. 1764; a Peer of Ireland, as Baron Pigot of Patshull, 1766. Died 17 April, 1777, at Madras (? a violent death).

Left issue, b. out of wedlock, of whom were General Pigot, Col. 4th Dragoon Guards; Sir Hugh Pigot, K.C.B., K.C.H., Admiral of the White, who d. 30 July, 1857, æt. 82; and Sophia, who m. 1776, the Hon. Edward Monckton, and had by him 8 sons & 4 daus.

Sir Robert Pigot, Bart., b. 24 Sept. 1720, bapt. 16 Oct. at S. Martin's. Brigadier-General. Succeeded his brother as 2nd Bart. 1777. Highly distinguished during American War. Governor or Keeper of St. Mawes' Castle, co. Cornwall, 1795. Died 1 Aug. 1796. ═ Anne, sister of Sir Allen Johnson Walsh, and Gen. Sir Henry Johnson, both created Barts. Mar. 18 Feb. 1765; d. . . . 1772.

Elizabeth, d. of Peter Le Neve, Esq. 1st w. ═ Hugh Pigot, b. 28 May, 1722, bapt. 7 June, at S. Martin's, Vice-Admiral R.N.; M.P. for Bridgenorth. Died . . . . 1793. ═ Frances, d. of Very Rev. Sir R. Wrottesley, Bart. & Dean of Worcester, by Lady Mary, his wife, d. of 1st Earl Gower. Died 13 Apr. 1811. 2nd w.

Margaret Pigot, m. 10 Apr. 1755, at S. Anne's, Soho. ═ Thomas Fisher, Esq., of Acton, co. Middx., d. 29 Dec. 1767, bur. at Ealing.

Frances.

Caroline, b. . . . . m. 1800, d. 1835. ═ Rev. Lord Henry Fitzroy (her first cousin), son of the third Duke of Grafton, Preby. of Westminster, b. 1770, d. 1828.

Isabella, b. 5 Nov. 1750.

Sir Henry Pigot, K.C.M.G., b. 25 Dec. 1752. General Officer, to whom Malta was surrendered: Col. of (?) 30th Regt. Died 6 June, ═ Frances.

Anne, m. 1787, d. 1816, bur. at Waresley. ═ Francis Jack, 12th Viscount and 1st Earl of Kilmorey, d. 1832, buried at Adderley, Salop.

Margaret, m. 29 Apr. 1794. 2 w. ═ Henry Vernon, Esq., of Hilton Park, co. Staffs. d. 21 Oct. 1814.

[illegible] 'Landed Gentry' under Vernon

UNPUBLISHED WILLS AND NOTICES OF KENTISH FAMILIES.

Will of Katherine Turner* of Ashford co Kent widow. Notices Bond of Edmund Ellice whereby £20 is payable after her decease—to her cousin Ellis Ellice [of Stoneacre in Otham near Maidstone] 20s for a ring—Bequests to servants—To my god-daughter Mary Cawtrey [Hawtrey] a ring of gold which was some time her grandmother's—John Cawtrey (*sic*) of Ashford sole Exor —Dated 2 Nov 1625, proved 24 Oct 1626 at Canterbury by John Hawtrey. A sentence of the Court is annexed in which are mentioned John Hawtrey gent Exor, and Ellis Ellis parishioner of Otham, and Thomas Ellis of Hothfield parishioner, " prope consanguineos† predicte Cath Turner vidue"

Will dated 9 March, 1467, of JOANNES ELYS of Willesborough [co Kent] "jacens in extremis." To be bur in cemetery of W. Alice my wife, William and Richard my sons Last will made 9 Mch 7 Edw IV John Rolffe, John Bray, John Goldhall, Stephen Poynaut my feoffees. Messuage at Lacton to Alice my wife for life, then to right heirs, and a principal messuage at Swatford. Also his lands called Estfyld, Bromlands and Eston in Rokyng to be sold Son William to have lands in Sevington (under 20), Richard his br also under 20, lands in Swatford, Alice their mother, to Thomas br of testator 5 marcs. Bequests to trustees and for good of souls, etc [Pr at Canterbury]

Will pr in the Consistory Court at Canterbury, A.D Mill'cccc quinquagesimo sexto xi die mensis Januarii [11 Jan. 1456] Ego RICARDUS ELYS to be bur in cemeterio of Willesborough Bequests to church of W. and high altar and to church of Hinxhill Rest of effects to Joanna my wife She and Robert Wylde exors Witn. Peter Burgh vicar of W, Richard Raynold and others Last will — I will that Joanna my wife have my manor of Southertons in Wyvilsbergh, with appurtenances in W, Hinxhill, Ashford and Wye, ad terminum vite suæ. Also a rent of 10s from Henry atte Mille, and 3 acres of pasture near the mill at Ashford, remainder manor of Sothertons to the heirs of our bodies. Mentions a debt of £22 post decessum matris meæ

(At Somerset House, Godyn, 199) Will of JOHN ELYS esquire of Otham [co Kent] dated 24 Aug 1467 John my son under 21 Elizabeth my wife. Peter Elys clericus and another, exors. 4 or 5 feoffees, int al the said P E. Dau'rs Margaret, Elizabeth and Alianor, under 18 Peter Elys my br 40s Margaret my sister 20s. Margaret *her* dau'r, 20s Prior of Ledys 10s. Friars at Aylesford legatees Names int al Tatteshain and Hadd Long and important will in Latin $4\frac{1}{2}$ p Proved at Lambeth 5 Aug 1468. Devises lands in Lenham, Leedes, Harrietsham, Stockbury, Smerden, Bersted, Thurnham, Detlyng, Alyngton, Northfleet, Ifield, Upchurch, Halstow, Langley, Hunton, Luddenham, Fredynden, Chart, etc.‡

The will of Edward Cayley of Lamberhurst yeo dated 26 Feb 1668, is at Somerset House (Coke, 51) He therein mentions his dau'rs Judith and Mary, his dau r Catherine ux Valentine Ellis [son of Tho Ellis of Pembury, qui ob 1650], his dau'rs Gibbons and Woodgate, and his sons Josias and William The said William of Lamberhurst made his will 3 Mch 1693 (Box, 97) and therein mentions his cousins Larkin and Martin of Pembury his sister Catharine Ellis, his sister

* She was d of Stephen Ellis of Burton in Kennington, gent

† These two were brothers and *distant* cousins Her nephew Tho Ellis of Burton gent, the last owner of that property, alive in 1609, was then doubtless dead There was a Tho Ellis of Headcorne, gent, at this time who was the same as Tho Ellis of Hothfield, who died at Canewden, co Essex, 1636, leaving an only d Dorothy His will is at Somerset House

‡ These three ancient wills rectify some mistakes in Hasted's History,' followed in 'Notices of the Ellises' Hasted presumed the John Elys of Willesborough qui ob 1467, was the same person as John Elys of Otham, who died the same year The latter was probably son of Thomas Elys, the Sheriff, though he does not appear to have inherited any property in Kennington or East Kent Hasted also misread the date of the will of Richard Elys, making it 1471. The affiliation of these three testators cannot at present be correctly made

Mary Martin, his brother Joseph deceased, his nephews Woodgate, and his kinsman Wm Eldridge of London and his wife Anne.*

Will of John Hawtrey of Ashford co Kent, gent. To John H. my son 2 houses in A. Philip my son—My five daughters Ursula, Joan, Elizabeth, Susan, & Barbara, £100 each. Dated 24 Aug. 1637. Proved at Canterbury (Masters, 199).

Will d. 14 July 1645 of Stephen Barton of West Peckham, yeo.—To his wife Elizabeth Rent Charge of 20s. bequeathed by his late father John Barton—Also Goods and Chattels and to be Ex'x—My friend Thomas Furner gent. and brother-in-law John Snowe overseers. Pr. 8 Nov. 1645 at Rochester.

Will d. 29 Dec. 1663 of Walter Barton senior of Hadlowe, yeo. "aged." Silver Bowle to Walter Barton son of his son Tho. Barton—Releases bond of £20 of his youngest son Walter Barton—Said Tho. B. eldest son, Executor, to whom personal estate. My worthy friend and kinsman Mr John Knill, and my good friend Mr Geo. Hooper, overseers. Witnesses, John Knill, Robert Dewhurst, Geo. Hooper. Pr. 27 May, 1668, at Rochester.

Will of John Barton of Poulters in Hadlow, yeo.—To Elizabeth Oliver god-daughter 20s.—To Jane ux. Wm Coyfe son in law £5—To Elizabeth Thorpe, god-daughter, dau. of Wm Thorpe 20s.—To wife of Thomas Barton's son £1.—To Jane, Testator's wife 40s.—to son Thomas, Poulters etc. D. 12 Sep. 1690. Proved 30 Apl. 1695, at Rochester.

Will of Thomas Barton of Poulters, yeo., dated 2 May 1713. To eldest son John 4 pieces of land called Cardens—To his four daughters Elizabeth, Alice, Jane, and Sarah, £50 each at 21—Poulters containing 120 acres to four sons equally between them, viz., John, Thomas, Henry, and Charles. Wife Jane and son John Exors. Proved 9 Aug. at Rochester.

Will of Thomas Barton of Hadlow, senior, cordwainer, "old & infirm," d. 11 July 1718—2 Dau's Margaret ux., Robert Hayes, and Elizabeth ux. John Humphry—Son Thomas Barton. Witnesses,—Henry Barton, Geo. Hooper, and another. Pr. Jan. 3, 1720, at Rochester.

Will of Walter Barton of Hadlow, yeo., d. 6 Nov. 1725—To Thomas and John his sons he had advanced already of considerable value—messuage and lands wherein I dwell to wife Jane for jointure—4 sons, Walter, Thomas, John and George. Pr. 14 May 1725-6 at R.

Will of James Barton of Bexley, senior, yeo., "old."—To eldest son James B. £150—£20 each to his 2 children and Testator's grandchildren at 21 or marriage, viz., Richard and Mary—son Richard B. exor. and 2 acres of meadow land in Bexley and rest of personalty—To youngest son John £150—To d. Mary Holden £5. Pr. at Doctors' Commons 1703.

Will of Charles Barton [at Somerset House, Rudd, 118], of East Peckham, co. Kent, yeo. To the poor of E. P., West Peckham, Hadlow, and Mereworth—My god-daughter Elizabeth B., d. of my br. John B.—Godson, Tho. B., son of my br. Tho. B.—my goddau. Elizabeth d. of Henry Fenner—my cosen John Standen—my wife Elizabeth sole Ex. [mar. at Titsey, Surrey, Charles Barton and Elizabeth Valentyne 4 Aug. 1606, d. of Humphrey V. bap. there 22 Nov. 1582]—Anthony B. and Walter B. my brothers—my four sons, Richard, John, Wm, and George—brothers

* The said Catharine Ellis was bur. at Lamberhurst April 10, 1695. She had issue by her said husband 1 son and 2 dau'rs, bapt. at Goudhurst, but there is reason to believe she had other children previously bapt. elsewhere. She was not married at Lamberhurst. Tho. Cayley of Heathfield, co. Sussex, yeo. (brother of the aforesaid Edward Cayley), made his will 21 Feb. 1692 (Coker, 39), being "aged, weak, and infirm." It is very lengthy, and the testator therein devises several farms in Heathfield and other parishes to his son, dau'rs, and grandchildren, one of which was jointly occupied by Thomas Ellis and himself. The will is attested by six witnesses, int. al. Sarah Ellis, Thomas Ellis, and Tho. Ellis junior, apparently the issue of Valentine Ellis and his wife. These would seem to constitute the link between the Ellises of Pembury, Marden, and Heathfield, mentioned in 'Notices of the Ellises.' Wm Valentine of Tattesfield and Westerham made his will 1633 (Sadler, 83), and therein mentions his sister Eliz. ux. Charles Barton, and his wife Anne, and dau. Elizabeth. Anne remarried Tho. Ellis of Pembury aforesaid, and the latter, æt. 11, 1633, was the wife of Richard Hayward of Tattesfield.

Tho and Anthony, overseers—my br John B, Solomon Newman my uncle—a bequest to my br Walter on the day of his marriage—mentions a recent purchase of 100 a of land Dated 5 June 1615, Pr 4 July, s y Witnesses, Tho. Barton, Sol Newman, John Barton, Nicholas Hooper, sen, Writer

Will of Antone Barton [at Som Ho Barrington, 85], of Great Peckham, co Kent, yeo —my godson Anthony Swan 20s —to Geo Barton, son of my br Charles B £7 at 21—my daurs. Anne and Elizabeth—my br Walter B and my first wife's br. Wm Fayreman to be exors during nonage of my children Dated 4 Aug 1624. Witnesses,— Edmund Porter, Wryter, Wm Raynes, his marke

Richard Barton of Marden, co Kent, gent, married twice By Mary, dau of James Alchorne of Tunbridge, he had John B of Lydd, gent, his s and h His second wife was Elizabeth —Peter Maplesden of Brookland, Kent, mar. Joan sister of the aforesaid Mary, as appears by deed between him and the said Rich. Barton, A.D 1640 (deeds)

Will of John Barton [at Som Ho Skynner, 95] of East Peckham, co Kent, yeo Dated 5 June, 1626—wife Alice—Daurs Anne & Elizabeth—To John B, son of my br Charles £5 at 21—Tho son of my bro Tho B —John Richardson and his bro Tho R, my sister's sons—Richard Fenner my sister s son—wife Alice, Ex'ix—my brothers Tho and Walter B, overseers—lands in Hadlow. Witnesses, Daniel Pinckney, churchwarden of Tunbridge, John Hooper, notary publick—Pr. 17 Oct 1627

Thomas Barton of East Peckham yeo made his will 13 Apl 1630 (Scroop, 104) wherein he mentions his dau'r Susan ux John Keeble, his dau'r Margaret, his d Elizabeth, John B his nephew, his son Tho Barton, his br. Mr Tho. Oliver of Layborne and his kinsman Mr Robert Oliver his son Pr 18 Nov 1630.

John Barton of the Bourne in Hadlow yeo made his will 20 Nov 1628 (Ridley, 102) He therein mentions Richard son of his brother Henry, and John br of the said Richard. His son Stephen B, his eldest son Henry B and his wife Hellen, also his kinsman Tho Barton of Court Lodge in Hadlow, and Richard and Henry the two sons of his br Henry B Pr. 4 Nov. 1629

Thomas Barton of the Court Lodge in Hadlow yeo made his will 11 Oct 1662, wherein he mentions his wife Elizabeth, and his dau'r Elizabeth, Tho and Alice Newman his wife's children, his brother-in-law Mr John Kirrell, his sons Walter and Thomas, and his br-in-law Henry Barton of the Bourne Proved at Rochester 5 Jan. 1672.

John Derbie of Horsmonden made his will 1653 (Alchin, 306) and therein mentions his sister Joane ux — Barton, and their issue,—Thomas, James, Walter, John, and Peter

A branch of Barton of Hadlow is settled at Watton co. Norfolk, of whom an account is given in Burke's 'Landed Gentry,' ed. 1858

Wills at Rochester

1600 Barton Richard, Southfleet
1602 ,, John, Hadlow.
1614 ,, Thomas, Hadlow
1629 ,, Joanna, Chelsfield.
1645 ,, Stephen, Peckham
1665 ,, Thomas, Rochester
1668 ,, Walter, Hadlow
1671 ,, William, Charlton
1672 ,, Thomas, Hadlow
1674 ,, John, Brenchley
1677 ,, Walter, Farleigh
1693 ,, Peter, Pembury (Admon)
1695 ,, John, Hadlow.
1713 ,, Thomas, Hadlow

1720 Barton Thomas, Hadlow.
1733 „ Jane, Hadlow (A.)
1737 „ Jane, Hadlow.
1740 „ Jane, Hadlow.
1741 „ Henry, Hadlow (A.)
1742 „ Thomas, Hadlow (A.)
1725 „ Walter, Hadlow.
1738 „ John, Hadlow (A.)
1744 „ George, Hadlow (A.)
1745 „ Thomas, Milton near Gravesend.
1766 „ John, Hadlow.
1660–1703. None at Doctors' Commons of Barton of Kent—sed quære.

Charlwood, Surrey. W. S. Ellis.

(*To be continued.*)

Armorial Bookplate.

WALTERS.

Quarterings: 1. Walters. 2. Robnet. 3. Blanchard. 4. Smith. 5. Skynner. 6. Melmoth. 7. Sidebottom. 8. Helm.

William Melmoth Walters of Lincoln's Inn and Ewell, Surrey, eldest son of John Eldad Walters, Esq., of the same places, by Eleanor his wife, dau'r and coheiress of the late Alexander Radclyffe Sidebottom, Esq., of Lincoln's Inn (descended from the Radclyffes of Foxdenton in Lancashire), was born 28 Jan. 1835, and married 17 July, 1860, Marian Eleanor, eldest child of Alfred Leggatt, Esq., of 13 William Street, Lowndes Square, by whom he has issue Percy Melmoth Walters, born at Ewell 30 Sept. 1863, and two other sons and six daughters.

WALTERS PEDIGREE.

Arms.—*Azure, a squirrel séjant devouring a nut or.*
Crest.—*On a wreath or and azure a squirrel séjant, devouring a nut proper.*

John Walter of Piercefield, Monmouthsh. descended from John Walter of Persfielde (in 1470). = Bridget, daughter and coheiress of John Robnet. Arms (2nd quartering).—*Azure, three pairs of keys in saltire or.*

Male issue extinct.

Susanna, = Her cousin, Edmond Walters of Cophill Howick, who d. 1651. [Arms.—*Azure, a squirrel séjant devouring a nut or.*]

Eldad Walters of Batheaston, Somersetshire, b. 1640, m. 1666, d. Sept. 24, 1706. = (2nd wife) Mary, only child of Henry Blanchard of Batheaston, d. 1685. Arms (3rd quartering).—*Gules, a chevron or, in chief two bezants, in base a griffin's head erased of the second.*

Henry Walters, High Sheriff of Somersetshire (1715), b. 1667, d. 1753. = Mary, daughter of Joseph Houlton of Farleigh Castle, Trowbridge, Wilts, b. 1679, d. Aug. 6, 1752.

Henry Walters, Dep. Lieut. for Somersetshire, and Col. of Militia during French War, b. 1722, m. 1745, d. 1797. = Anne, daughter and coheiress of Thomas Smith of Nottingham, elder brother of Abel Smith (from whom is descended Lord Carrington); b. 1725; d. 1788. Arms (4th quartering).—*Or, a chevron cotised between three demi-griffins, the two in chief respectant each other sable.*

A

W. Melmoth Walters.

A

Thomas Walters of Batheaston, sometime of the R.N., served in Lord Rodney's action in East Indies, b. May 15, 1757, m. 1792, d. July 1, 1847. = Sophia, daughter and coheiress of Rev. John Skynner, Public Orator of Cambridge, and Rector of Easton and Blatherwick in Lincolnshire, and Sub-Dean of York, b. 1771, d. May 20, 1836.

Arms (5th and 6th quarterings).—*Sa., a chevron or between three griffins' heads erased argent;* quartering the coat of his maternal grandfather, William Melmoth, King's Counsel and Bencher of Lincoln's Inn, who died 1743, viz.:—*Argent, a fess gules betw. three griffins' heads erased sable.*

Other issue.

John Eldad Walters of Lincoln's Inn, and Ewell, Surrey, born Sept. 12, 1797, mar. 21 Dec. 1831. = Eleanor, daughter and coheiress of Alexander Radclyffe Sidebottom of Lincoln's Inn (descended from the Radclyffes of Foxdenton, Lancashire), b. March 21, 1807.

Arms (7th and 8th quarterings).—*Argent, a chevron between three lions rampant azure;* quartering the arms of her mother Catharine, da. and coheiress of Richard Helm, Esq., viz.:—*Vair, argent and sable, a bend gules.*

Wm. Melmoth Walters of Lincoln's Inn, and Ewell, Surrey, b. 28 Jan. 1835, m. 17 July, 1860. = Marian Eleanor, eldest daughter of Alfred Leggatt, Esq., of William Street, Lowndes Square, b. 20 March, 1840.

Other issue.

Edith Marian, b. 14 May, 1861.

Alice Mary, b. 31 Aug., 1862.

Percy Melmoth, b. 30 Sept. 1863.

Arthur Melmoth, b. 26 Jan. 1865.

Gertrude Hamilton, b. 25 Sept. 1866.

Hugh Melmoth, b. 7 April, 1868.

Guy Melmoth, b. and d. 10 July, 1869.

Constance Maud, b. 11 Aug. 1870.

Nora Mackenzie, b. 8 Oct. 1873.

Katharine Eleanor, born 9 Mar. 1877.

DE-LA-PRYME AND BLAYDES.

The following notes I copied from the fly-leaves of a small Bible, 16mo, imprinted at London by Robert Barker, 1638, in the possession of H. S. Blaydes, Esq.

1672.	Ap. 3rd.	Peter Prim, born.
„	Sept. 14th.	Franceas Wood, born. m. 25 July 1695.
1696.	July 26th.	Mary, born. Buried 3rd August sa. year.
1697.	Sept. 6th.	Matthew, born.
1699.	feb. 21.	Abram & Sarah were born.
„	Ap. 19.	the afsd. Sarah buried.
1702.	Ap. 13.	Francis born.
1704.	March 14.	Bete was born.
1707.	July 12.	Frances the wife of Peter Pryme dyed.
1724.	Nov. 25.	Peter Pryme died.
1729.	X^ber 5th.	Sarah the widow of Matt. Pryme died.

Hugh Blaydes & Elizabeth Prime married ye 28th Aprill 1728.
Hugh Blaydes born ye 29th Jan. 1728-9, & was buried 20th of feb. 1728-9.
Elizabeth Blaydes born ye 26th March 1729-30, died Sept. 10 day 1734.
Francias was born Aprill the 10 day 1731.
Benjamin was born 26 August 1732 & died December ye 26th day 1733.
The seckond Ben. wass born 5 day of March 1735-6.
Peter wass Born May ye 26th 1737 & died Aprill 1 day 1738.
Ben. Blaydes married Kitty Scott 1775 at Mary-le-bon and had Ben. Blaydes born 5th August 1776 at Melton, etc., etc.

B. A. F.

ABSTRACT OF WILLS RELATING TO THE FAMILY OF HARINGTON

(*Continued from page 220*)

Summary of the Will of Lady Jane Rogers, of Cannington, Somerset.
Dated 24 Sept 1598 G. C. P. (Montague 13)

Francis, son of Edward Rogers,* Esq to have the manor of Bodmin, he not to alienate it for more than three lives, etc, if he do, or if he die without lawful issue, then the said manor to go to George Harington, son of John Harington, Esq, and his heirs male, and if he alienate, etc, then to James, another son of the said John Harington, if he should alienate, etc, then to George Rogers, another son of said Edward Rogers, and if he alienate, etc, or die issueless, then to testatrix heirs for ever Said manor of Bodmin charged with £200 to each of the five daughters of said Edward Rogers.

To John Harington, my godson, son of John, Esq, the manor of Trebarveth, in parish of Tyndagell, and his heirs male, but not to alienate, otherwise to go to said Geo Rogers This manor, charged with 'one hundred and three score pounds, to the Four Dau'rs of said John Harington—Fraunces, Jane, Ellen, Elizabeth—to be equally divided among them"

To James Harington, son of John Harington, Esq, the manors of Trembelthee, St. Jennes, Westmeadon, and Kilkhampton, in the counties of Cornwall and Devon To him the Demaine and Barton of Allercombe, he not to alienate, if otherwise, then to George Rogers aforesaid and his heirs, etc. This property charged with £10 yearly to "my daughter Marie Harington, £10 to Jane Harington, Allercombe (in certain events) to go to James Harington, charged as above," etc

Certain Cornish manors to Geo Rogers, if he alienate, etc, then to Francis Rogers, Marie Harington, my dau'r, to be executor, and Francis Rogers another executor To be buried, if I die at Cannyngton, "by my husband Sir Geo Rogers," to be buried, if at Bath, "by John and Robert Harington," to be buried, if in London, "by Sir Edward Rogers and my sonne Wm Rogers" Proved May 20, 1602 Francis Rogers was a minor at the time of his appointment to executorship

Abstract of the Will of Dame Marie Harington (*née* Rogers) of Kelston, Somerset, Widow

Will (Goare 33) made 1st June, 1634

To be buried in Kelston Church by my mother £5 to my son John Harington, my son George, my dau'r Lady Frances Egerton,† my dau'r Jane, wife of John Roberts, my chaplain George Ivey, Clerke, £20, to my brother-in-law Francis Harington £5, and my lease of Fillgrove, in parish of Bitton, my furniture, etc, at Kelston, all furniture in my house at Bath, lease of the (?) Tennis Court adjoining to the Crosse Bowe Inn, to my daughter Elizabeth. Proved Feb 23, 1636

A sententia follows on the Will, in which Elizabeth Harington, executrix, is called Digge. Lady Frances Egerton disputed the Will, not being satisfied with a mere pecuniary legacy she received. Decision is given for its validity

Abstract of the Will of William Harington,‡ of Kelston, co Somerset.

(From the Court of Probate, Wells) Will dated 9th Sept, 1701

To be buried at Kelston. Gives to his son *John* certain plate, to his son *James* certain other plate, to daughter Dionis £100 and a silver tankard; to his daughter

* In Calendar of State Papers, Domestic vol 1619-23 A D, p 566, mention is made of a Star Chamber Cause (Breviat), 1601, between Edw Rogers and Sir John Harington Francis Rogers accuses Sir John of conveying away plate etc, from Cannington

† Can any genealogist say who was Sir Raphe (*sic*) Egerton, the husband of this Lady Frances Egerton? Their marriage is entered in the Register of Richmond, in Surrey, Dec 21, 1606, and they had a daughter, Helena or Eleanor, bapt at Kelston 1st Oct 1615

‡ This William Harington was the second surviving son of John Harington, Esq (the Parliamentarian), and the Hon Lady Dioness Ley Can any clergyman or genealogist contribute to the knowledge of Harington history, by furnishing the Register of Marriage of William and *Ann* Harington, whereby her maiden-name may be ascertained? Such a communication to 'Miscellanea Genealogica et Heraldica' would greatly oblige

Phœbe Britton, wife of John Britton, plate. Lastly makes his wife Ann sole executrix. One of the witnesses of this Will was John Broad. The Will was proved by Anne his Relict, 12th May, 1702.

Abstract of the Will of Ann Harington, of Kelweston, Widow of the preceding William Harington

(From the Court of Probate at Wells, Somerset.) Will dated 17th July, 1707.

After specifying as to burial, and after a religious clause in usual terms of that day, she adds, "To my son John 5s., to my dau'r Diones, wife of William Hopper, one broad piece of gold, to my dau'r Phabey (Phœbe), wife of John Britton, best bed, etc.," and names "my grandchild *William* Harington,* my grandchild Anne Harington,* my grandchildren William Hopper and Mary Hopper, my grandchildren John and Mary Britton.† All residue to James my son, he to be sole executor." One of the witnesses, John Broad. Proved 8th Sept. 1707.

Abstract of the Will of Miss Phœbe Harington,‡ of Weston-near-Bath

(From the Court of Probate, Wells, Somerset.) Will dated 1704, 25th Feb.

My sister Helena Harington 20s. for a ring. To Mary, Vertue, Arabella, Elizabeth, four daughters of my sister Vertue Higginson, of Marshfield, £10 each at 16 years. John and Amy, son and daughter of my sister Alice Fecknaham, of Marshfield, £5 each at 16 years. Geo. Adams, my godson, 40s. Sarah Pexstone, wife of Thos. Pexstone,§ my sister Amy Macie‖ to be sole executrix. Will proved 7th Nov., 1709, by Amy, her executrix. Was witnessed *inter alios testes* by Wm. Hall.

Abstract of the Will of Miss Rebecca Harington, of Corston, co. Somerset

(From the Court of Probate at Wells.) Will dated 10th Dec., 1731.

"My nephew John Harington, of Corston, Esq." to have a certain estate for term of years in lands, etc., called "Babers," and a chief rent at Corston (spelt Coston) of 5s. 6d. per annum, on three messuages at Corston, to him, his heirs and assigns for ever. "My nephew Wm. Harington of the City of Bristol, Gent.," to have lands and tenements in Weston, in the possession of the proprietors of the Brass Batteries at Weston, his heirs and assigns for ever. "My *sister Elizabeth Harington*,¶ Widow, and *Mrs. Mary Harington*,¶ £1 1s. each in gold, to buy a ring. My sisters,** Amy Hall and Alice Facknam, £10 each. My three nieces,†† Mary Bennet, Vertue Osborne, Arabella Bryant, £5 each. To the poor of Corston, £5. My niece, Abigail Harington,‡‡ spinster, a diamond ring. Residue to my two nieces, Abigail and Elizabeth Harington,§§ to be equally divided, and they to be joint executors. Proved — day — 1749, by said Abigail and Elizabeth.

(*To be continued.*)

* These were the children of John Harington, of Bitton, her eldest son.

† The testatrix's daughter Phœbe married Mr. John Britton, of Corston, at Kelston, 24th April 1701, so these legatees were quite young in 1707.

‡ This testatrix was youngest dau'r of William and Ann Harington, and grand-daughter of John Harington, Esq. and the Hon. Lady Dioness his wife.

§ This family of Pexstone descended from Thomas Pexstone, Vicar of Weston-near-Bath, 1599, who made a copy of the early registers of the Parish, a thing to be recorded of him.

‖ She afterwards married a *Hall*. The Macies descended from John Macie, Vicar of Weston, qui ob. Jan. 1595-6.

¶ "My sister Elizabeth." This was Elizabeth, the second wife of testatrix's brother Benjamin, *née* Elizabeth Bushell. My *sister, Mary Harington* was testatrix's half sister, the eldest daughter of her father's fourth marriage with Helena Gostlett.

** My sister, Amy Hall. This lady had first married David Macie, Esq. vicar of Weston-near-Bath from 1698 to 1701, he died probably that year, sometime after May 11th. My sister, Alice Facknam. She was wife of the Rev. Thos. Fecknaham, Vicar of Marshfield, co. Glo'ster, whom she married after the death of her first husband Mr. Edward Chetwynd.

†† The maiden-name of all these young married ladies was Higginson. Their father was a barrister, Mr. Joshua Higginson, connected with Marshfield.

‡‡ My niece, Abigail Harington, *Spinster*. Her single state did not long continue; in 1740-41 she married the Rev. Mr. Martin Hudson, Rector of Saltford, co. Somerset.

§§ Elizabeth remained *Elizabeth Harington* for the long period of 90 years, dying in 1708.

ADAMS

ARMS.—*Argent, on a cross gules five mullets or.* CREST.—*Out of a ducal coronet or a demi-lion affrontée gules.* MOTTO.—*Sub Cruce Salus.*

In the 'New England Historical and Genealogical Register,' (Boston, Mass.) vol. vii. (1853), p. 39, is found a very ancient and apparently well-authenticated pedigree of Adams, furnished by William Downing Bruce, Esq., F.S.A., of the Middle Temple, London, from the original "discovered among the papers of the late Edward Hamlin Adams, Esq., M.P. for the county of Carmarthen, and now (1853) in the possession of his son Edward Adams, Esq., of Middleton Hall, said county."

This pedigree traces seventeen generations from —— Ap Adam, who "came out of the Marches of Wales," and had a son Sir John Ap Adam, Kt., Lord Ap Adam, who mar. Elizabeth, dau. of John Lord Gourney of Beverston, co. Gloucester, and was summoned to Parliament as a Baron of the Realm, from 1296 to 1307.

William, of the fifteenth generation, as appears, mar. —— daughter of —— "Borington (?)," and had sons, George, Lieut. in the service of Charles I., who m. —— dau. of Mr. Conrad Streetbolt,* merchant of London, and d. in Barbadoes in 1647, leaving sons Conrad, George, and John, "living in 1680."

"Henry, d. in Braintree in New England 1646," leaving sons Henry, Sam., Joseph, omas, Peter, and Edward, all "living in 1680."

Ambrose, "m. and had issue."

John, m. and had issue.

As early as 1645, a George Adams, "a glover," with wife Frances, settled in Watertown, Mass., and had issue, at least, six children, as appears by Bond's 'Genealogies of Watertown,' Paige's 'History of Cambridge,' and Hudson's 'History of Lexington.' In 1664, he sold to John Chinery "my house in Watertown and land adjoining," and removed to "Cambridge Farms," then an adjoining town, now Lexington. He was killed in Watertown, Oct. 10, 1696, "by the fall of a rock."

John Adams, a settler in Cambridge, as early as 1650 then adjoining Watertown, has been supposed by some to have been a brother of George; but positive proof is wanting to establish such relationship.

Henry Adams is known to have been the ancestor of the second and sixth Presidents of the United States, John and John Quincy Adams, and several others of the name noted in American history.

An "Ambross" Adams was an inhabitant of St. Michael's, Barbadoes, in 1680 (See Hotten's Lists, p. 443.)

I trace my lineage through seven successive generations from George and Frances of Watertown. That they emigrated hither, and that they were married prior to their coming, there can be no doubt; and that they married but a short time before their arrival seems probable, as all of their children were born in Watertown (the eldest, John, b. 6 Aug. 1645) prior to removal to Lexington.

The presumptive evidence, considering dates, names, etc., is strangely in favour of George of Watertown having been a son of Lieut. George of Barbadoes, and a nephew of Henry of Braintree.

I have in preparation a genealogy of the Adams family of this line, and am very desirous of connecting with our English ancestry, and therefore invite the co-operation of all concerned.

Washington, D.C., U.S.A. NELSON D. ADAMS.

BARNES.—Can any of your readers give me any information concerning the parents of Henry Barnes, who was filacer for London and Middlesex? He was born circ. 1670, and died at Hampstead 1731, where he was buried. Any information concerning the family of Barne or Barnes, bearing the arms—Az., three leopards' faces or,—would be most acceptable.

Univ. Coll., Oxon. G. S. BARNES.

* Was not Mr. Streetbolt a glover and hosier?

TURNER.—I am anxious to trace the descent of John Turner, citizen and merchant of London, will dated 18th June, 1691, who mar. a Cartwright of Leicester, and was grandfather of Sir Edward Turner, Bart., of Ambrosden, co. Oxon. In all the books I have consulted he is said to be descended from an ancient Leicestershire family; but as yet I have been unable to trace the connection. Subjoined is a portion of a parchment roll pedigree, compiled circa 1818, by Charles Murray Lane, Chester Herald. It will be observed that there is a link wanting to connect John Turner of London with the Turners written above. If any of your readers can supply me with dates, names, etc., to fill in the blanks I should be greatly obliged. Also I want to learn particulars as to birth, marriage, etc., of Ambrose, Freelove, Page, the children of Gregory Page, who was father of the 1st Sir Gregory Page of Greenwich, Bart. These Pages are in the same pedigree said to be descended from the pages of Hampshire. Where can I find a pedigree of such a family? Any notes relative to the above family will be gratefully received by

The Lodge, Hockliffe, Leighton Buzzard. F. A. BLAYDES.

Richard Turner of Sutton Colefield in the co. of Warwick, Barrister of the Temple, London, and Chamber fellow to Sir James Dier, Lord Chief Justice of the Court of Common Pleas. ⊤ Mary, da. of . . . . Masterton of the co. Palatine of Chester, and coheir of John Masterton, of an ancient family seated in that co.

William Turner of Sutton Colefield, in the county of Warwick. ⊤ Margaret, da. of Christopher Breton of Tecon, co. Northampton.

Richard, 2nd son. | John, 3rd son. | Edward Turner of Leicester, son and heir, living anno 1619. ⊤ Joice, da. of Levy Chamberlain of Leicester. | Joice. = Edward Hume of Marston Trussel, co. Northants.

Edward, 2nd son, living anno 1619. | William Turner, eldest son and heir, living anno 1619. | Elizabeth, eldest da., living anno 1619.

John Turner of London, merchant, citizen and vintner; had lands at Prittlewell in the par. of Prittlewell, co. Essex; also in Bishopsgate Without in London, and at Radcliffe in the par. of Stepney, co. Middlesex, and by purchase at Chestonals, Cheshunt, co. Hertford. Will dated 18 June, 1691, proved 4th October following. Buried at Stepney. ⊤ . . . . Cartwright of Leicester, as appears from a manuscript in the possession of the family.

Elias Turner. | Edward Turner. — William Turner. | John Turner of London. ⊤ Elizabeth, da. of . . . Caplin of London. | Elizabeth Turner, = Capt. Abr. Dawes. | Mary Turner, = Chas. Atherstone, Esq.

John Turner, = Anne da. of . . . Manners. | William Turner. | Sir Edward Turner, Bart. of Ambrosden, co. Oxon. Chairman of the Court of Directors of the H.E.I.C.S. in 1733. Ob. 19 June, 1735. ⊤ Mary, eldest da. of Sir Gregory Page, Bart., of Blackheath, co. Kent. | Mary or Elizabeth, = . . . Guy. | Elizabeth or Mary, = ... Withers.

FELL.—John Fell (commonly called Capt.), bur. at Poplar 1754, æt. 97. By his wife Constant [what was her surname?], ob. 1724, had a son John, ob. s.p., and a daughter Sarah, ob. 1769, who married Joseph Croucher 1718, churchwarden of St. George's in the East in 1729, where bur. 1752; his arms were—*Argent, on a pale invected sable three crosses patée or, a martlet for difference.* Both had considerable property in the East of London. Wanted, information concerning their families, etc. What arms did the former bear?—A. S.

RUGELEY PEDIGREE.

('Mis. Gen. et Heraldica,' Vol. III., pp. 17, 201.)

Richard Bickley of Halloughton in com Warr obijt circa an 1666, ætat 82	= Sarah,* dau and one of the two coheirs of John Rugeley, 2nd brother to Rafe Rugeley of Dunton in com Warr Esq, and uncle of Sir Rowland Rugeley, Knt She is now living, ætat 82 et ampl	Eliz, 2nd wife to Sir Rowland Rugeley of Dunton in com Warr Knt, whom she survived

From a pedigree of Bickley of Halloughton, in the College of Arms. (Vis of War, 1683[? 6], Reg K 3, 170)

Nou'int vniu'si p' p'sentes nos Sara Cowper de Coleshull in Com Warr viduam Rolandu' Rudgley de donton in com Warr p'd Ar' Joh'em Rudgley de drayton in Com Staff gen' et Thoma' Rudgley de Coleshull p'd in Com Warr p'd gen' Teneri et firmit' Obligari, etc etc.

(Signed) Sar' Cuper
Row Rugeley.
John Ruggeley
Thomas Rudgeley

From an old bond, dated Dec. 21st, 1613 (11 Jas. I) in the possession of

Y B

DUGDALE.—1 Christopher Dugdale, Rector of Coulston 1569, Rector of Codford St Peter (both co Wilts) 1609, ob 1633

2 Thomas Dugdale, senior (of Seend, co. Wilts), sepultus Ap 30, A D 1669, æt 85, his wife Elizabeth Ap 26, 1664, æt 70. [There is a monument in Seend Church to Thomas Dugdale, second of that name in this parish of Seend, ob. 1681, and to his wife Prosper, ob 1676. ARMS.—DUGDALE *impaling* AWDRY.]

3 Thomas Dugdale, civis Londinensis [Jane, the wife of Tho Dugdale, civis Londini, d of Ambrose Audry of Melksham (co Wilts), is buried in St Lawrence Jewry, ob Sept 17, 1692.]

These three are mentioned on a flat stone in Seend Church, great part of which is illegible or covered by the pews, the words "John (?) Dugdale of Coventry and . Dugdale eques auratus de comitatu Warvicensi" also occur

Can any of your correspondents place these names in the pedigree of the Warwickshire Dugdales, or give some information as to enable me to do so? The parish registers tell me nothing of their origin.—A S.

BATE OF ASHBY DE LA ZOUCH (see Vol II., N.S, page 490).—I have been able to procure a copy of the tablet formerly placed over the door of the library, given to the Vicar of Ashby and his successors by the Rev Thomas Bate. The stone is now built into a wall at the Vicarage, and as part of the inscription is hidden by the spouts, I have restored the missing letters in italics.—J. P R

D. O. M. Gloria
*Be*ne feliciterq vortat
*Ecc*lesiæ bonisq. Literis
*Biblio*thecam hanc donavit
*T*homs Bate, S T B
*L*icentiâ surrexit Ædificium
*An*no salutis Humanæ
CIƆDCCXXX

* Anne, the other dau. and coheir, mar to John Jesson of Rotherith juxta Southwark in Surrey

THE ARMS OF NOTT, granted in 1587. (See Edmondson's 'Heraldry.') ARMS.—*Azure, on a bend between three leopards' faces or, as many martlets gules.* CREST.—*A martlet argent, ducally crowned or, holding in beak an olive branch vert.* But Arms are ascribed to Nott in Stow's 'Survey of London,' p. 554 (edition 1632), to John Nott, 1363, Lord Mayor. He was Sheriff, 1350 (page 552).

EARLY DATA OF NOTT.—John Nott, citizen and pepperer, twice Lord Mayor of London, 1363—1367, temp. Edw. III. John, the son of John Nott of Aynford or Ashford, in Kent, 1587. The original Nott Motto was "Nil desperandum," changed to "Pacem sed Coronatam." The Crest and Motto were changed temp. Charles II.

Roger Nott, citizen of London, a younger son of the Notts of Kent.=

(1) Sir Thomas Nott, eldest son; father of Thos. Nott of Obden, co. Worcester, Esq. Living at time of the co. Visitation of Gloucester. Marked K 5 in the College of Arms as certified by Isaac Heard (Lanc^r^).

(2) Edward Nott of Bradon, in com. Wilts. Living, ætat. 70, 1683.=Elizabeth, dau'r of Edward Sewster, co. Huntingdon.

Roger Nott, student at Oxford. Died unm. | Edward Nott of Minty, co. Glos. ætat. 42 and upwards (1683).=Anne, dau'r of Wm. Webb, alias Richmond of Lideard Milicent, co. Wilts, widow of Edmund Webb of Minty.= | Thomas, died at Suratta, in East India, cœlebs. | Rebecca Nott, mar. Thos. Horne, citizen and jeweller of London. | Susannah, wife of Thos. Rich of North Cerney, co. Glouc. | Mary, wife of Augustine Kinchin of Southington, Par. Overton, co. Hants. | Several others who died young.

Ann, aged about 6 years, 1683. | Elizabeth and Susanna, twins, aged about 13, 1683. | Edward Nott, eldest son, æt. about 17, 1683. | Joseph Nott, was afterwards of Minty, co. Glouc., and buried there; aged about 12 y^rs^, 1683.=Arabella, dau'r of Chas. Pleydell of Midgshall, co. Wilts, quæ ob. 19 Aug. 1744.=2nd husb. Thos. Brown of Minty, gent. qui ob. June 5, 1738, buried at Minty. | Philip Nott, aged about 8 y^rs^, 1683.= | Mary Webb, dau'r and sole heir of Edmund Webb; wife of Thomas Brocas of Beaurepaire, co. Southants, Esq., d. s.p.

Elizab. Pleydell Nott, married Richd Franklin of Wroughton, co. Wilts, Esq. s.p. | Lettice Nott, wife of Rev. Dr. Butterfield of Mid. Claydon, co. Bucks, s.p. | John Nott, Esq., of Braydon, co. Wilts, qui ob. 24 June, 1763, bur. at Cricklade.=Elizabeth, dau'r of Hen. Neale of Allesley, co. Warwick, and grand-dau. of John Neale, Esq., of Dean, and Anna, dau'r of Henry Cromwell of Upwood, co. Huntingdon (1641).

A

Arabella Brown.=Wm. Calley, Esq., of Burderop, co. Wilts.

Philip Nott, a Bristol merch^t^.=

Joseph Nott (Jamaica).

Thos. Brown Calley, Esq.=1778, Elizab., only dau'r of John Rowls, Esq. of Burderop.

Thomas Calley, Esq., of Burderop.=20th July, 1802, Elizabeth Anne Keck of Stoughton Grange, co. Leic. inter alios

Eliz. Ann Benet Calley, died 20th Aug. 1827. (Burke's 'Com^s^,' vol. iv.)=12th May, 1827, John Neale Nott, Esq., R.N. (See other line Nott, marked A.)

A

John Neale Pleydell Nott of Braydon, Capt. R.N. Born July 3, 1732. = Catherine, dau'r of Robert Andrews, Esq., of Lower Grosvenor Street, London. Born June 12, 1736; died Aug. 8, 1817, aged 81.

Joseph Nott, a Surgeon. Twice married. Died at Madras, s.p., Nov. 1769.

Roger Nott, Surgeon in Jamaica. = Sarah Lowle, dau'r of Rev. Doctor Lowle of Stone, co. Gloucester.

- John Neale Nott.
- Arabella.
- Edward Lowle Nott.

(All living and infants in 1765.)

Several died young.

Children of John Neale Pleydell Nott and Catherine:

- John Nott, born Feb. 24, 1771. Lieut. R.N. Died unmarried in Jamaica of yellow fever Aug. 18, 1794.
- Edward Nott, clerk, Rector of Weeke, Hants, born March 15, 1774; died April 22, 1842. = Mary Messman, then of Reading, but of French extraction (Monsieur Messman of Nismes quitted France after the Edict of Nantes, and settled in London as a silk manufacturer), born 19 March, 1769; married 10 April, 1799; died 28 March, 1851.
- George Nott, midshipman R.N., born 24 July, 1778; died unmar. of yellow fever, 18 Aug. 1795.
- Diana Nott, mar. Oct. 24, 1800. = Jas. Hare Joliffe, Esq. qui ob. May 21, 1836.
  - Elizab. Hare Joliffe. = Wm. Long, Esq., M.A. Oxon. J.P. co. Somerset. 2nd son of Walter Long, Esq., of Preshaw House, Hants, and of Muchelney, co. Somerset. Living 1879.
    - William Long, eldest son. = (issue)
    - John Neale Henry Long.
    - Elizab. M. D. Long.
- Elizab. Nott, died unmar. Nov. 5, 1858.
- Three children, died young.

Children of Edward Nott and Mary Messman:

2nd, Mary E. R., eldest dau'r of Sir Wm. Burnett, M.D. and K.C.B. s.p. = 1. John Neale Nott, Capt. R.N., born 14 Aug. 1800; died 20 Oct. 1849. = 1st. Elizab. Ann Benet, dau'r of Thos. Calley, Esq., of Burderop Park, Wilts, married May 12, 1827.

2nd, Mary Bargrave Bridges of Eastry Court, Kent, died Nov. 10, 1878. = 2. Edward Bunbury Nott, born March 4, 1802, Capt. R.N. Died July 9, 1875. = 1st, Miss Reid of St. Helena, dau'r of Dr. Reid, mar. 1829.

Children of Edward Bunbury Nott and Miss Reid:

- Edward Thos. Nott, Capt. R.N., born Sept. 7, 1831; mar. 31 Oct. 1861; died Oct. 26th, 1874. = Mary Harriette Bazely.
  - Grace Catherine Neale, born 25 July, 1863.
  - St. Leger Luard Neale.
  - Percy Pleydell Neale, born 8 May, 1871.
- 3. Hollis Henry Nott, Capt. in Marine Artillery, born Dec. 21. 1834; died 1875.
- Geo. Frederick Nott, born Sept. 8, 1836, Married 8 Sept. 1836, Anne Eliza Glasse.
- 5. Bunbury Augustus, b. 23 Nov. 1837; d. in childhood.
- 2. Maria Elizabeth, born Feb. 28, 1833; died 22 Dec. 1878. = Albert Segram, Lieut. 1st Royal Regt.
  - Beatrice Eleanor Longstaff, born 24 Nov. 1861.
  - Cecil Montagu Bunbury, born 5 April, 1863.
  - Charles Cuningham.
  - Dudley.
  - Muriel.
  - Two other children, died young.
- 6. Cecilia, born July 4, 1840.
- 7. Sarah Mary, born Sept. 1841; died in childhood.
- Mary Emma, born March 31st, 1847.

B

B

3. George Nott, Major-General, born Jan. 19, 1805. Married at Madras, 19 April, 1826; and 2ndly, Mrs. W. Hood Wason, da. of Prosper de Mestre. ═ Jane, da. of Anthony Robinson Sheppard of Youghal, co. Cork, Ireland.

4. Henry Nott, Lieut.-General, born July 14, 1810; married 1850. ═ Sophia, dau'r of Rev. Robinson Elsdale, D.D. No issue.

Edw. Henry Nott, b. 25 April, 1828; d. 29 Oct. 1876.

John, born 7 Dec. 1830. Com^r R.N. ═ Dau'r of Rev. Mr. Brownrigg, co. Wicklow, in Ireland.

1 dau., Mary, born 25 Dec. 1831. ═ Major W. C. P. Haines, Madras Staff Corps. Died . . . .

2 dau., Emelie Jane, born 20 Aug. 1834; died May, 1857. ═ Major-General Sir Chas. Doyley, Bart.

John George Latham, born 5 May, 1871.

Vera Elise, born 21 August, 1872.

William George, born 28 Aug. 1855; Ceylon Civil Service.

Mary Catharine, b. 27 May, 1857.

Mary Lushington, born July, 1856; mar. Arthur F. Bernard of Combe Raleigh, Honiton.

1 dau., Mary Ann, born June 7, 1802; mar. July 26, 1827; died Feb. 11, 1875. ═ Wm. Alex. Willis, Capt. R.N.

2 dau., Catherine, b. March 3, 1808; mar. 5 Aug. 1851; d. Jan. 15, 1865. ═ Major-General John Maxwell Glasse of Bombay Artillery. Died . . . .

3 dau., Elizabeth Jane Nott, b. Aug. 13, 1813; married 4 July, 1839; living 1878. ═ Edwin Henry Atkinson, 19th Madras N.I. Major-General in Indian Army. Living 1878, at Lower Walmer, Deal. Son of Stephen Atkinson, Esq., of Beaminster.

Alexander Paul, born 29 April, 1833; died April, 1853.

William Wynch George Back, born 3 Oct. 1838; Major Retired, Royal Marines.

James Legge, born 29 April, 1841; Major Bengal Staff Corps.

George Harry Rickard, born 7 May, 1846; Commander R.N., Retired.

Arthur Clevedon, born 10 June, 1851.

Georgina Flora, born 20 May, 1828; mar. Rev. Mr. Elton.

Mary Anne Francis, born 23 October, 1839.

Catherine Anne, born 25 May, 1842; mar. 2 June, 1870, William, son of Joseph Phelps of Madeira.

Charles Edward, Capt. H.M.'s 103^d Regt., born 6 Dec. 1843; mar. 10 Jan. 1873, Harriette Montgomery, da. of Wm. Brock.

Emily Mary, born 7 July, 1846; mar. 5 May, 1871, Charles Martin, son of Rev. Edward Russell.

Anne Eliza, born 28 Oct. 1848; mar. 29 Aug. 1872, George Frederick Nott, son of Capt. Edward Bunbury Nott.

Louisa Margaret, born 14 May, 1840; died 18 May, 1857.

Stephen Edward, born 22 Sept. 1841. Major Madras Staff Corps.

Alice Mary, born 6 Feb. 1844. Mar. to Captain Edw. Harden, H.M.'s 109th Regt.

Jane Elizabeth, born 6 Aug. 1845. Married P. H. Osborne, Esq.

Edwin George, born 16 Dec. 1846.

William, born 23 August, 1848.

John Mcomass, born 15 April, 1851.

Mary Sophia, born 11 Dec. 1853; died 21 April, 1855.

A BRIEF ACCOUNT OF THE RE-GRANTS MADE BY K. HEN. VIII. AND Q. ELIZABETH TO THE

Haringtons of Wolphege,

CO. NORTHANTS, AND OF KELSTON, CO. SOMERSET, OF CERTAIN LANDS IN THE NORTH OF ENGLAND, WHICH WERE BOTH GAINED AND LOST BY ATTAINDERS PASSED DURING THE WARS OF THE ROSES; AND NOTABLY BY THE ATTAINDERS OF SIR RICHARD TUNSTALL, KT., AND OF SIR JAMES HARINGTON OF BRIERLEY IN FALKIRK, CO. EBOR.; THE LITIGATIONS WHICH ENSUED THEREON TEMP. Q. ELIZ. WITH THE REPRESENTATIVES OF STANLEY, LORD MOUNTEAGLE, THE VALUATION OF THOSE LANDS AT THE TIME, TOGETHER WITH AN EXACT COPY OF THE PEDIGREE OF HARINGTON, PUT IN AT THE SUIT BEFORE SIR WM. CORDELL, MASTER OF THE ROLLS.

Taken from the Harington Papers in possession of Capt. RICH. HARINGTON *of Bath, R.N.*

(*Continued from page* 229.)

TABLE A, BEING AN EXACT COPY OF A MS. PRESERVED IN THE FAMILY OF HARINGTON AT BATH.

(Given irrespective of any error or deficiency which might be corrected or supplied.)

"Yorkshire Line as far as concerned Sir James Harington's Lands."

Nicholas Harington.

- Sr William Harington, obiit 29 H. 6th. = Margaret Nevil, ux.
  - Sir Thomas Harington obiit 29 H. 6th, ætate 40 et amplius. } { Elizabeth ux. Thom. obiit 8mo Aprilis 2 R. 3.
    - Sir John Harington, died without issue male vitâ patris. } { Matilda Dudley, ux. exist.
      - Anna ux. Ed. Stanley Mil. the Ld Mounteagle.
      - Elizabeth, ux. John Stanley, Armig.
- Sir James Harington, obiit 5 H. 5th.
  - Sir Richard Harington, obiit 2d Edw. 4th et Inq. Capt. 7th E. 4th.
    - Sir James Harington, attainted 1 Hen. 7th.
      - John Harington, died without issue male.
    - Sir Robert Harington, attainted 1 H. 7th.
      - James Harington, Dean of York.
    - 1. Margaret. 2. Jane. 3. Anne.
    - 4. Katherine. 5. Agnes.
    - Sir William Harington.
      - Jas. Harington.
        - William, drowned, without issue.
      - Nicholas.
        - James Harington, ye 1st pattentee.
          - Thomas.
          - Henry.
          - Stephen.
  - John Harington.
- Nicholas Harington.

"This was a MS. to prove the descent in order to obtain the forfeited lands. Thease be the names of the mannors and lordships appertainynge unto the heyre males of Sir *Wm.** Harington, and for fawlte of such yssue male to the heyre males

* Sir Wm. of Hornby, qui ob. 29 Hen. VI., and whose line ran out in two dau'rs.

of Sir *James** Harington, brother to the said Sir Wm. Harington as appeareth by fyne and feoffment, as namely:—The Manore of Broughton, Bolton upon the Moore, Ashton, Shevington, Heth Chornock, Chorely, Chagley, Garstange, Hotton or Hoton, Lancaster, Kellet, Boulton in Lonnesdale, Elatt, Caton, Farelton in Lonnesdale, Farlton in Kendale, Bighall, and all other messuages, lands, and tent^s in the County Lanc^ter, York^re, Westmorel., Cumbr., Huntingdon, and Cambridgeshire."

Note.—This MS. is endorsed by the same person on the back of it.

"A trew Petigree of the Haringtons."

A List and Valuation of the Forfeited Lands of Sir James Harington,

According to a MS. in the handwriting of Jno. Harington, Esq., of Kelston, preserved by his Grandson, Dr. Henry Harington of Bath.

		£	s.	d.
By special words in the Letters Patent These 4 Manors in Yorkshire.	The Manor of Brierley, with its Appurt^s	97	18	4
	" " Sedbergh	11	3	6
	" " Langar in Dent	4	5	3
	" " Grinlington in Bowland	2	0	0
By special words in Letters Patent.	" " Farleton in Kendal	18	5	3
	" " Farleton in Lonsdale	23	7	3
In a Fine acknowledged at Lancaster 3^d Ed. IV. (1464)	" " Tatham	55	1	10
	" " Heisham	14	14	2
Expressed in Sir Jas. Harington's Will, Made 22^d Edw. IV. (1483) These 8 Manors entailed to the heyres male. In the Records of the Tower.	" " Over Kellet in Lonsdale	22	18	5
	" " Caton	26	15	4
	" " Neyther Hutton or Priest Hutton	15	6	10
	" " Ellat	19	11	2
	" " Heth Charnock and Chorley	28	7	6
	" " Shevington	3	3	0
	" " Whittington and Newton	7	11	9
	" " Asheton	7	3	4
	" " Bolton-super-Moor	4	15	11
These two in sundry old rentals.	" " Broughton	17	9	2
	" " Gressingham	6	12	6
These two be also entayled.	" " Harington Park alias Foxton	3	3	4
	" " Chawley or Chageley	3	0	0
	Lands and Tenements in the town of Lancaster	1	11	8
These be in old rentals.	The Manor of Burton in Kendale	10	13	0
	" " Mansarke (Mansergh ?)	3	3	11
	" " Penrith	1	6	8
		£411	7	7

A Letter from the 'Nugæ Antiquæ' of Harington,

In which Sir Robert Sydney writes to Sir John Harington, K^nt, of Kelston, A.D. 1600, as follows:—

"I hear you have taken possession of Harington Park. Our Lawyers say your title is well grounded in conscience; But that strict law doth not countenance your Recovering those lands of your ancestors as the Queen's right is somewhat exstinguished by your Cosins Stephen,† & James‡ who left issue. And hereby it comyth not straight to the Queen, whose good will toward you is ever apparent.

"I have seen ancient records wherein it appeareth that Sir James Harington, slain in Bosworth Field, did give by will all these lands to his Brother Sir Robert."

(*To be continued.*)

* Sir James (bro. of Sir Wm., qui ob. 5 Hen. V.), whose line ran out in Stephen Harington, and who was living 1558.

† This Stephen was third son of James Harington of Wolphege, Clerk of the Bakehouse, and he died s.p., having previously sold his rights (according to Sir John of Kelston) to him (Sir J.).

‡ This James is Sir James of Wolphege, who left issue a son William (who died s.p. 1490) and eleven daughters.

(Confer the Ped. of the Harleian MS. 1549; but in this Sir James is not mentioned.)

UNPUBLISHED WILLS AND NOTICES OF KENTISH FAMILIES.

(*Continued from p.* 226.)

Subsidy Roll

3 Charles I Hadlow.
Thomas Barton Goods, £1—21s 4d.
John Barton, lands £4—32s
Walter Barton, lands 40s —16s
Mr Tho. Barton, Clarke £3—24s

16 Charles I., Hollingbourne
Henry Barton 30s —12s

16 Car I, Hadlow.
Helen Barton widow, for self and son Henry, Lands £3—24s.
Walter Barton, Lands 40s —16s
Alice Barton, widow—20s.—8s
Thomas Barton—£3—24s

39 Eliz, East Peckham
Henry Barton, lands 40s —8s
Richard Barton, goods £4—10s 8d.

(Same date), Hadlow.
John Barton, lands 40s —8s.
John Barton, sen, — 20s —4s.
Henry Barton, 20s —4s.
Tho Barton, Goods £5—13s. 4d.

Hearth Tax, 1673

Hadlow,	Henry Barton, 6
West Farleigh,	Walter Barton, 4
Bidborough,	John Barton, 3
Hadlow,	Tho. Barton, 4
Hadlow,	Tho Barton, 4
Hadlow,	Tho Barton, 1
Elherst Boro',	Tho. Barton, 3

Miscellaneous Notices

Goldwell in Hadlow was sold by Sir Geo Chowne after the death of Charles I. to Thomas Barton, gent (qui ob. 1662, æt 57), whose d Alice mar John Kerriel, Esq At her death he devised it to her son John Kerriel, and his son John sold it John Barton in the 17th cent was Rector of Harrietsham Queen Eliz granted part of the Manor of Maidstone int al to Richard Barton David Barton was Curate of Bromley 1667 — Barton was Vicar of Kemsing 1650 Walter Barton, gent had the manor of Hadlow jure uxoris (Mary or Eliz d and coh of John France, living 1699-1725) His son John Barton afterwards owned it, as did *his* son Walter Barton *alias* May John Iden ob. seized 4 Hen VIII of Cheney's Court in Chart Sutton, a coh of this family mar — Barton (Hasted's Kent)

Thomas Barton, D D, was Rector of Westmeston, co Sussex He mar Benedict d of Walter Dobell, of Street Place, co Sussex, whose sister Mary was wife of Robert Olliver of Leybourne, co Kent *

Bur Dr Tho. Barton, late Rector, March 25, 1682
Bur. Mary d of Tho Barton, Rector, March 23, 1633
Bap Mary d of ditto Oct 15, 1639
Mar Mr Christopher Morland of Strood in Kent, and Mrs Elizabeth Colvil, grandd of Tho Barton, D D, Rector, Feb 14, 1677 —*Westmeston Reg*
Mar Mr John Barton and Mrs Margaret Dickenson, Nov 11, 1624 —*Hurstmonceux Reg*

* Thomas Oliver, *alias* Quinton, of Leybourne, t Eliz, had 2 d, viz Eliz ux Tho Barton of Peckham, and Joan ux Tho Barton (Berry's Kent Gen, p. 393)

John Neale Pleydell Nott Esq.

Great Lodge Braydon Forest Wilts. 176[illegible]

Walter Barton, sen., of Hadlow yeo., aged, will d. 1663, pr. 1668, "Kinsman Mr Jno. Kirriel." ═

Thomas Barton, gent. of Hadlow, ob. 12 April, 1662, æt. suæ 57. ═ Alice ob. 16 May, 1653.

Thomas Barton, 1663. ═ | Walter, 1663. | Alice d. and h. ux. John Kirriel.

Walter Barton of Hadlow, yeo., will d. and pr. 1725. ═ Jane, 1725.

John Kirriel.* | John Kirriel.

Alice, d. of John K. of Hadlow, ux. Thomas Lake of Taywell, qui ob. 1725, æt. 74.

Tho. Barton of Sevenoaks, nephew of Mr Geo. Putland, of Tunbridge, who left him the manor of Mascalls in Brenchley.

Walter Barton of Court Lodge in Hadlow. ═ Sarah, d. of John France, mar. 26 July, 1722.

John — George

Tho. Barton of Hadlow bo. 13 Oct. 1726. ═ Susannah, d. of Jeremiah Ellis of North Walsham, co. Norf.

John Barton, bo. 23 June, 1723. ═ Jane, d. of Richard May, Esq.

Walter Barton.
|
Tho. Barton.
|
Thomas Edward Walter Barton, of Threxton House, Watton, Norf., born 1811 (Burke's 'Landed Gentry').

Walter Barton May, ob. 1825.
|
Walter Barton May, of Hadlow Castle, ob. 1855.
|
Walter Horatio May.
|
Walter Edmund May.

Henry Barton of Folkestone, gent., ob. 1725. Had one son and three dau'rs. ═ Frances, d. of Tho. Kirriel of Hadlow, gent., ob. 1714, bur. at Hadlow.

Kirriel Barton, ob. 1713, bur. at Brookland. | Alice, ob. 1719, bur. at B.

Frances, d. and coh., ux. John Jordan.

Catherine, d. and coh. ═ Rev. Tho. Barton, jure ux. lord of the manor of Hoptons in Alkham. He bore *azure 3 bars ermine.*

Thomas. | Henry. | John. | Catherine.

* The arms of John Kirriel, Esq., of Sevenoaks in Kent are engraved in Budgen's Map of Sussex, 1724, (all these coats are blazoned in an article on the subject, by the present writer, in *Sussex Archæological Collections*, vol. xxv.), and are, Argent 2 chevrons and a canton gules, *quartering*—Ermine, on a fess gules 3 annulets or [Barton], over all on an escotcheon of pretence, party per chevron arg. and sable, in chief 2 eagles displayed, in base a fleur de lis.

The arms of Kiriell are the same as those of the ancient baronial and knightly family of Criol of Kent, and are derived from the family of Albini, who early obtained them from a match with De Clare. Croxton-Criol, co. Leic. was held of D'Albini of Belvoir Castle. Sir Thomas Kiriell, descended from Bertram De Crioll living 1247, was the last male of the chief line, and was slain at the battle of St. Albans, leaving a daughter and heiress, married to John Fogg, Esq.

There is no pedigree of Barton in the Kentish Visitations, but they bore for arms *Ermine on a fess gules 3 annulets or*, the arms of the ancient family of Barton of Yorkshire.*

Charlwood, Surrey W. S. ELLIS.

BARNES.—The following may interest your correspondent, Mr Barnes. An old "*Breviarium Romanum*," MDCXLVI (penes me), bearing the signatures of "Richd. Barnes London, A.D. 1648," "Jacob Barnes an° 1660," and lastly "Ex libris Thomæ Barnes Armig.," contains in a Kalendar of all the Saints these entries, which are written under the printed heading of the several months:—

Janvarivs	8	De Octaua. "Henry Barnes ob 1631, æt. 96."
	28	Agnetis secundo. "Mrs Barnes dyed 1663."
		"Conversio S Pauli. Mary Barnes was born $173\frac{5}{6}$."
Febvarivs	10	"Natus fuit Ricardus Barnes 1660. Hen Arondell & my ladye Willoghby goddfath^r and moth^r."
Martivs.		"die 5° Martii natus & Baptizatus fuit Henricus Barnes $171\frac{9}{1}$ fil. me Thom B. Sr Henry Tichburn & Miss Bellasis sponsors."
	22	"Dorothie Barnes obiit 1616 ætat 19 an."
Aprilis	4.	"Obit Richardus Barnes 1643 ætat 66."
Maivs	19	Pudentianæ virginis "natus Rychardus Barnes 1625. My ld Dormer & Mis stanhoppe by proxyes Mr Dormer & yonge mistresse Curson."
Junivs	1	"Natus & baptizs fuit Ricardus Barnes 1700 fil Ric. S^t ffr: Jernham & Mrs Plowden sponsors & Mr Arundell & Miss Bedingfeild Proxies."
Julivs	3	De Octaua Apostolorum. "Richard son of Richard Barnes born 1726 at one a m."
September	23.	Lini Papæ & Martyris. S. Theclæ virginis & Martyris. "Ob. Richd Barnes senior esq^r 1715 æt 85 an."
October	29	"Richard Barnes Borne 1769."
December	4	Barbaræ virginis & martyris. "Barbara Barnes nat. 1627."

I shall be glad of any information from church registers, etc., relating to this family. I should add that the book contains an excellent pen and ink drawn book-plate, the blazon of the Arms being—Quarterly, or and vert, a crescent gules. Crest: a cubit arm grasping a crescent gules. On a riband "Richard Barnes, Esqr 1703." It also contains some curious private notes, including mem. of names of women to whom alms were to be given, such as "Goody Brown, Goody Mawson, Goody Smythe, Goody Selbye," etc. Its last possessor at the latter end of last century was Richard Barnes, gentleman, of St James's, Westminster, of an ancient Roman Catholic family (of large estate in Middlesex and Surrey), often mixed up in the "popish plots" of the sixteenth and seventeenth centuries.

Lincoln's Inn. T. HELSBY.

FELTOE.—Information required respecting the Feltoe Genealogy. The family supposed to be of Wiltshire origin.

Glenwood, Thames Ditton. CHARLES TEIT FELTOE.

* The arms of Thomas Barton, gent. of Carter's Corner, viz., Ermine on a fess gemelle gules, 3 annulets argent, are engraved on Budgen's Map of Sussex before mentioned.

The name (in Kent) seems to have been originally written *Berton* or *Burton*. Alex De Bertona held one knight's fee in that county of Walter Mammot 1166. He was the same person probably as Alex. De Berton, who occurs 22 Hen. II. in the Pipe Roll for Oxon, and in that reign gave, with his son and heir Sir Wm de B. the church of Burton in that county to the monks of Eynsham. Odo de B. occurs 1166 in Oxon.; his son Humphrey de B. held one knight's fee of Philip de Hampton and he had a brother Elyas. In the first year of Richard the Second John Barton, son of Alexander Barton, proved his age (Prob. Ætatis, Kent, No 107).

EXTRACTS FROM THE PARISH REGISTERS OF LEIGHTON BUZZARD, CO BEDS *

Baptisms

1561.	Aug 17.	Robertus, filius Robert Sewell.
1564.	Dec. 13	Alice, filia Tho Chester
1565.	Mar. 16.	†Isabell Ellingham, filia Tho Ellingha
1568	Nov 18	Anna, filia Magistri Jonson
1575	Oct 25	‡Gulielmus, filius Anthonij Slater.
1577.	June 24	Marie, filia Anthonij Slater
1578	May 11	§ Joice, filia Clement Duncombe
1578.	May 21.	‖Johannes, filius Johannis Wilkes
1578	Aug 6	Marie, filia Anthonij Slater
1579	Jan 10	Edwardus, filius Johannis Wilkes
1579	April 5	Johannes, filius Mr Clement Duncombe
1580	June 5	Maria, filia Edwardi Amias
1580.	July 31.	Johannes, filius Anthonij Slater
1580.	Mar 31	Anna, filia Mr Clement Duncombe.
1581	May 4	Katherine, filia Mr „
1582.	May 27.	Johannes, filius Johannis Wilkes
1582	July 26.	Sara, filia Anthonij Slater
1583.	Feb 27.	Maria, filia Clement Duncome
1584	June 15	Maria, filia Johannis Wilkes
1584	Sept 13	Christopher, filius Anthonij Slatior.
1584	Nov 5	Edmundus, filius Edwardi Amias.
1585	May 26.	Jane, filia Magister Girdler
1585	Nov 14.	Wm Dier, filius Richardi Dier
1585.	Mar 14	Elizabeth, filia Clement Duncombe
1585	Mar 25.	Agnes Dier, filia Richardi Dier.
1586.	June 15.	Susan, filia Clement Duncome, gener
1586	Oct 16	Susan, filia Tho Gyrdler
1586	Nov. 30	Maria, filia Johannis Wilkes
1588.	Sept 29	Elizabeth, filia Anthonij Slatior
1589.	June 22	Elizabeth, filia Johannis Wilkes
1590	Sept 4.	Clement, filius Clement Duncome
1591.	Dec 31	Sara, filia „ „
1593	April 6.	Clement, filius „ „
1597	Oct. 18	Regnald, filius Robert Jackeman
1601	April 26	George, filius Robert Wingate
1601.	July 5	ffranc, filius Edward Wingate
1603	April 19.	Jane, filia „ „
1604	May 31.	Wm, filius Gabriel Jackeman
1605	Aug 18.	Marie, filia Edward Wicke [? *Wilkes*]
1606.	Mar 15.	Johannes, filius Edward Wilkes
1607.	Feb 19	¶Edward, filius Thome Hodesdo.
1608.	Nov. 13	Edward, filius Edward Wilkes
1609.	June 13	Francis, filius Edwardi Ames
1610	Dec. 26	**Matthew, filius Edwardi Wilkes

* Communicated by F A BLAYDES, Esq , Hockliffe Lodge, Leighton Buzzard

† A family of this name was formerly possessed of the manor of Morells in the parish of Stanbridge

‡ Anthony Sclater, D D , Vicar of Leighton, and successively Vicar of Walsall, and Pitminster

§ A branch of the Duncombes of Ivinghoe

‖ Founded an almshouse at Leighton in 1630

¶ The Hodesdons formerly held the Manor of Leighton under lease from the College of Windsor It eventually came into the Leigh family by the marriage of Ursula, da and heiress of Christopher Hodesdon, to John Leigh, Esq

** Matthew, eld s of Edward Wilkes, mar Frances, da of Peter Dayrell of Lillingstone Dayrell, Esq. He died 29 Mar. 1693, æt 83, s p

1611	Nov 8	Joshua, filius Thom Amies
1612.	July 5	Edward, filius Johannis Slatier.
1612	Dec 19.	Maria, filia Edvardi Amias, de Leighton
1612	Mar 7	Marcus, filius Edvardi Wilkes.
1613	April 4	Richardus, filius Georgij Bury de Leighton, generosi.
1613	Mar 26.	Lucas, filius Eduardi Wilkes
		*For y[e] names of those y[t] were Baptized between y[e] years 1615 and 1653 look in y[e] other books.
1648.	June 9.	Susanna, filia Roberti Downs, nata.
1651	Nov 9.	Sanders, filius ,, ,, natus
1656	April 18	Mary, da of Giles Duncombe, born
1656	June 3	Rebecca, da of Will Iremonger, born
1656	Aug. 29.	Elizabeth, da of M[r] Clarke, Minister, born ; bapt. Sept 7.
1656	Dec 1	Daniel, y[e] son of John Marsh, bapt.
1656.	Jan. 3	Sarah, y[e] Daughter of Robt Downes, born
1656	Mar 5.	Elizabetha, filia Samuelı Ironsides, baptizat*us* fuit March 5th, 1656
1661.	Aug 16	Daniel, y[e] son of John Marsh, borne
1622	Aug 8	Francisca, filia Christopheri Sclater baptizata fuit, nata 4[to] ej[dm].
1622	Nov. 28	Thomas, filius Edwardi Wilks, bapt fuit
1622	July 17	Maria, filia Tho Leigh, militis, baptiz.
1657	Nov 4	The daughter of M[r] Iremonger borne
1660.	Oct 19	Debborah, da of Samuel Ironsides, borne.
1660	Oct 26	Deborah, filia Samuelı Ironsides generosus bapt fuit
1661	Oct 15	Richardus, filius Samueli et Judeth Ironsides, bapt fuit
1662.	April 17	Robertus filius Roberti Downes, bapt fuit
1663	Dec 4	Judeth, filia Samueli Ironsides, generosus baptizata fuit p. me R K
1663	Sept 17.	Blandinah, filia Johan. Marsh, generosus baptizata fuit.
1664	Dec 22	Elizabetha, filia Johannis Marsh ,, ,,
1665	Aug 20	Johannes, filius Johannis Thresher Vicarij de Laighton
1665	Nov 23	†Edvardus, filius Edvardi Hargrave
1665.	Jan. 11	Maria, filia Magistri Johannis Marsh.
1666	April 8	‡Henery, filius Magistri Roberti Downes.
1666	Nov 14	§Maria, filia Jeremie Brandriff (Brandreth)
1667.	May 5.	Johannes, filius Johannis Thresher
1669	May 19	Gulielmus, fil Edvardi Hargrave
1669	May 27.	Henricus, filius Josephi Brandreth.
1669	Sept 26	Edwardus, filius Johannis Thresher, cleric.
1671.	Aug 6.	Katherina, filia ,, ,, ,,
1671.	Nov. 8	Corina, filia Johannis Vaux de Heath, gener.
1672	May 5	Anne, filia Roberti Downes.
1672	Jan 26	Francisca, filia Johannis Vaux de Heath, gener
1673.	July 22	Daniel. filius Johannis Thresher, gener.
1674	July 22.	Johannes, filius Johannis Vaux de Heath, gener
1674	Nov. 29	Phillis, filia Edvardi Hargrave, gener
1675	Jan 6.	Maria, filia Johannis Vaux de Heath, gener
1676	April 8	Maria, filia Gulielmi Whitehead.
1676.	Mar 28	Gulielmus, filius Gulielmi Duncombe.
1677.	April 29	Georgius. filius Gulielmi Whitehead

* These books are missing

† Edward Hargrave, A M, of a Yorkshire family, Curate of Linslade, in com Bucks, and Rector of Fleet Marston in the same county

‡ Afterwards became successively Killaloe, Elphin, Meath, and Derry Died Jan 14, 1734-5, and was buried in Saint Mary's Church, Dublin

§ The family of Brandreth has for some considerable time past been seated at Houghton Regis

1677	June 10	Robertus, filius Johannis Vaux de Heath
1678.	Oct. 29.	Maria, filia Gulielmi Duncombe
1678.	Dec. 26.	Edvardus, filius Gulielmi Whitehead
1680	July 11.	Robertus, filius Ric Owen
1680	Oct 27.	Francisca, filia ,, ,,
1680	Dec. 30	Percey, filius Edwardus Marsh.
1682	July 16	Elizabeth, filia Gulielmi Whitehead.
1682.	Aug 8	Annis, filia Josephi Owen, gener
1682	Nov 11.	Carolus, filius Caroli Pymbe [? *Pym*].
1684	Nov 20	Maria, filia Thomæ Vere, gent
1684	Dec. 21	Elizabetha, Rebecca, Agnes, et Josephus, fil Thomæ Vere, gener.
1689	Dec 6.	Elizabetha, filia Egidii Duncombe
1690	Feb 20	Maria, filia ,, ,,
1693	Jan 15	Egidius et Edmundus, filii Egidii Duncombe
1699	May 15.	Edward, the son of Edw Simmes, born at Peterborough, now a vagabond, was baptized Edward Browne of Waterbery in Oxfordsheire and James Burt of Northampton being his godfathers
1702	Feb. 22.	John, s of John Painteur, Physician, bapt Feb 2, 1703
1711.	Sept. 27	Elizabeth, da of Joshua Pulford, Vicar
1712	Mar 4	W^m, s of Mr John Roe, Clerke
1714.	Feb 28	Gaudercy, ye son of Mr John Roe, clerke
1715	May 31	Gaudercy, ye son of ,, ,,
1717	Aug 24.	Thos, s of Mr Willm Whip, Vicar, and Penelope his wife, borne July 26
1728	Aug 15	Catherine, da of the Rev. Mr Thomas Snow, Vicar, and Hannah his wife
1728	Nov 28	John, s of Mr Edward Rowley and Mary his wife
1729	April 24	Sarah, da of John Roe and Mary his wife
1729.	Feb 4	Mary, da. of the Rev. Mr Thos Snow, Vicar, and Hannah his wife
1730.	July 9	Mary, the daughter of Edward Rowley and Mary his wife.

(*To be continued*)

A FLY-LEAF FORMERLY BELONGING TO THE LATE SIR MARTIN CRAWLEY BOEVEY, BART, OF FLAXLEY ABBEY, GLOUC

Tho Crawley Boevey(1) and Susanna Lloyd(2) were marryed Munday the 2^d Feb 1701–2, at Great St Bartholomews, by M Wilcocks, and J B (3) gave her

W B C,(4) born the 27 October being Tuesday at 2 in the morning 1702 Dyed the 12th November at 7 at night, and buried the 14th in Foster Lane Christened the 1st November being Sunday at night by Mr Bullin Mad^m Boevey godmother, and Mr Tho. Crawley Sen^r(5) and Mr John Lloyd(6) Senr godfathers

Catherine Crawley,(4) born the 12 October, 1704, being Thursday at 12 a clock at noon Christened the . October, being at night, by Mr Abbott, Madam Boevey(7) and Madam Lloyd(8) godmothers, and Mr John Crawley(9) godfather Mrs Lucy Lloyd(10) stood for Mad^m Boevey and M^r Wm Lloyd(11) for J. Crawley

Susanna Crawley,(12) born the 7th Sept 1705, being fryday a 2 a clock in the morning Christened the 18 do being Tuesday at night by Mr Abbott, Mad^m Crawley,(13) Mrs Lucy Lloyd(10) and Mr Tho Crawley Sen^r(5) Gossops Mr John Lloyd(6) Senr represented Mr Tho Crawley Senr, and Mad^m Lloyd(8) Mad^m Crawley Senr

Mary Crawley, born the 23 Sept. 1706, being Munday ¼ before 12 a clock noon Christened the 26 do being Thursday afternoon by Mr Abbott, Mrs Foster(14) and Sister Crawley,(15) and Bro Wm. Lloyd(11) Gossops Sis^r Lucy(10) st^d for Sis Crawley (Mad^m Boevey(7) present)

Thomas Crawley and a girl born the 26th August, 1708, being Thursday at 5 a clock in the morning Thomas was christened presently after his birth, but the girl lived nott to it, they both dyed the same day, and were buryed by Mr Thache att St Michael's Church the same night.

Thomas Crawley,(16) the second, born the 11th September, 1709, being Sunday at 5 at night Christened Tuesday ye 20th September by M Thatch Madam Boevey(7) godmother, and Mr John Lloyd(6) Senr and Mr John Lloyd(17) Junr godfathers

John Crawley,(18) born the 7th Novem 1710, being Tuesday at Tenn in the morning. Christened Wednesday the 22d do by Mr Thadtch Madm M Crawley(13) godmother, Mr Riches(19) and Mr John Lloyd Senr(6) godfathers Mrs Pope(20) stood for Madam Mary Crawley and Mr Veyney for Mr Riches He went to nurse Thursday ye 14th Decem 1710 to Mrs Owen

Wm Crawley,(21) born the 12th Octo 1711 Christened by Mr Thatch Mr Charles, Mr Alderman Thos. Webb, and Mr Aylway(22) [*sic*] gossops

Robert Crawley, born the 20 Sept 1713, being Sunday about 5 in the morning Christened Tuesday the 22 by Mr Thatch Madm Boevey,(7) John Lloyd Junr,(17) and Robert Longden(23) gossops

Cornelia Crawley,(24) born the 14th January, 1714

James and Lucy, born Saturday the 12th May, 1716, in ye morning & Xnd private the same day by Mr Thache Mr John Lloyd and Robert Longden(23) godfathers, &

(1) Thomas Crawley inherited Flaxley Abbey under the will of William Boevey (dated 1692), by whose desire he "wrote himself" Boevey, as did the successive heirs of the estate, but till lately they were always *called* Crawley

(2) Daughter of John Lloyd of London merchant (erm on a saltire gu a crescent or), and Susanna his wife, daughter of Thos Holliar

(3) Query James Boevey, brother of William (?)

(4) William Boevey Crawley The younger sons and daughters were both called, and wrote themselves, Crawley only

(5) Thomas Crawley (father of Thomas Crawley Boevey) of London and Twickenham, died March, 1714

(6) John Lloyd above mentioned He d April 8, 1716

(7) Katharine daughter of John Riches of London, merchant (ar, 3 fountains az), married in 1685, to William Boevey above mentioned She is said to be the "widow" mentioned in the 'Spectator' as the inexorable love of Sir Roger de Coverley She d 1726 M I at Flaxley and in Westminster Abbey

(8) Susanna Lloyd above mentioned She d July 11 1726

(9) Elder brother of Thomas Crawley Boevey

(10) Sister of Mrs Crawley Boevey She married Robert Longden of Gloucester, and was buried at Flaxley Dec 21, 1730

(11) Her brother William afterwards Rector of Stowe-nine-Churches, co Northampton He d cœlebs July 1, 1751 Buried at Flaxley

(12) Married May 14, 1745, to Dr John Lloyd, afterwards Rector of Stowe aforesaid She d March, 1762

(13) Mary, wife of Thos Crawley aforesaid, daughter of David Bonnell by Anne his wife, daughter of Andrew Boevey

(14) Mary Holliar, sister of Susanna Lloyd, married a Mr Foster

(15) Cornelia, afterwards wife of Petley Ley of Deptford

(16) Father of the first Baronet of the name He was married May 14, 1743, to his cousin Susanna Lloyd Buried at Flaxley Dec 1, 1769

(17) John Lloyd of London and Gloucester merchant, born 1680 Married Susanna daughter of John White by Susanna (Ayleway), his 2nd wife Buried in Christchurch, Newgate Street, Nov 6, 1744

(18) John Crawley was an attorney, and died unmarried

(19) 'Madam Boevey,' was then aged 46, and this was probably John Riches her father

(20) A daughter of John Pope of Bristol merchant and Margaret his wife, and half-sister to Charles Barrow of St Kitts father of Sir Charles Barrow, Bart, M P for Gloucester, whose baronetcy was granted with remainder to Mr Thomas Crawley Boevey She died March 24, 1746 aged 81

(21) William Crawley was Incumbent of Flaxley, co Glouc, and died unmarried, buried there Dec 3, 1780

(22) Probably *Mrs* Ayleway, that is to say, Anne, sister of Mrs John White (17) and aunt of Mrs John Lloyd, junr She died at Gloucester, 1720 Will proved Dec 3 It *may*, however, have been one of her brothers, *Mr* " Charles being in that case an error

(23) Robert Longden of Gloucester,(10) born 1674, died 1724

(24) Wife of James Heywood of London, merchant.

Pedigree of the Huguenot Refugee Family of Debonnaire.

Communicated by HENRY WAGNER, Esq., F.S.A.

ARMS.—*Gules, on a fess or three mullets azure between a tower argent in chief and a lion rampant of the second in base.*
CREST.—*On a wreath or and gules a tower argent.* MOTTO.—*Dux mihi Veritas.*

Matthieu St. Amant.=Marie Bourguignon.

Marie de la Cour.=Jean Debonnaire,=2 w. Esther L'Epine, fille d'Isaac L'Epine, et de Marie Le Nain, de St. Quentin, m. at the Walloon Church, in Threadneedle Street, 16 April, 1688.
"veuf du lien de St. Quentin."

Rachel St. Amant.=Paul Bouillé, late of Tours.

Esther St. Amant,=Pierre Debonnaire, "natif de St. Quentin." Naturalised 1706. Silkweaver, of Mill End, co. Middlesex; d. 1732.
"Native de Paris," m. in Threadneedle Street, 27 March, 1686-7; d. 1712.

David Debonnaire.=Catherine Hesse.

Marie Debonnere, bap. Threadneedle Street, 11 Aug. 1689; sponsors, Jean Debonnere and Catherine Hesse.

Elizabeth Debonnaire.=Jean Milon, "natif de Bohain, en Picardie, fils de feu Jean Milon et de Susanne Fagé."

Elizabeth, bapt. 9 Oct. 1691, at S. John's, Spitalfields. "Eliz. Milot of Jean & Eliz. Bonnair." Sponsors, Daniel Milo & Esther Lespine.

Marie Debonnaire, bapt. 15 Feb. 1687-8, at Walloon Church. Sponsors, Jean Debonnaire and Marie Bourguignon.*

Esther Debonnaire, bapt. 23 Dec. 1688, at Walloon Church. Sponsor, Paul "Bouilly."

Peter Debonnaire, bapt. 17 May, 1691, at Walloon Church. Sponsors, Matthieu St. Amant and Esther "Lespaine." Merchant of London, in par. of S. Lawrence. Died 26 Jan. 1732-3, in Lawrence Lane. Bur. at Bow. Will dat. 2 Jan., pr. . . Feb. 1732-3.=Susanna, dau. of John Le Keux and Susanna Didier, b. . . April, and bapt. 2 Nov. 1690, at Walloon Church. Sponsors, Benjamin and Eliz. Didier. Died Nov. 1760. Will made same year. Directs to be buried in same vault with husband at Bow.

John Debonnaire of Bromley, co. Kent, distiller. Will dated 19 June, and pr. Aug. 1747. Ex'or, Peter Lefebure, Esq. Bur. near the Church porch in Bromley Churchyard, where lies also a Peter Lefebure, bur. in 1787.=Hannah, dau. of . . . . Anson, of S. Mary, Stratford. Will† dat. 23 Jan. 1760, pr. 1764.

A B

Esther Debonnaire,=Paul Nicholas Savignac.‡
mar. at S. Martin Orgar's.

5 Feb. 1710-11.—"Paul Nicholas Savignan (chamoiseur), fils de Jean S. de la paroisse de St. Olive en Sendrick et Ester Debonair fille de Pierre D. ouvrier en soye dans le Spitalfields."

Elizabeth Debonnaire,=Peter Lefebure§ of Westham, co. Essex, cornfactor.
m. at S. Olave's, Southwark, 6 Jan. 1715-16, by lic.

* Probably she married Jeremy Dupré. Cf. Registers of S. John's, Spitalfields. Bapt. 5 Jan. 1707, Rachel Dupré, dau. of Jeremie Dupré and Marie Debonnaire. Sponsors, Isaac Wasselard and Rachel Bisseux.

† Directs to be buried in the same vault with her husband, "without funeral pomp, but only a hearse with 6, and 3 coaches with 4, horses." . . . . No public auction of my goods on any account, except of my coach and horses. To brother Samuel Anson, annuity of sixteen guineas.

‡ At S. Martin Orgar's were (1) m. 22 Dec. 1716, Benjamin Savignac of Stepney and Susanne Mouchet; and (2) bap. 2 Sept. 1717, Jean Jacob Savignac fils de Jean. A John Savignac died in 1715; a Paul Savignac in 1723. Lysons, in his 'Environs of London,' (1796) mentions Mr. Savignac's leather and parchment mills at Carshalton; and the Registers of S. Anne's, Soho, record the marriage in Nov. 1743, of Mary Bowker and Jacob Savignac, who seems to have been presented the same year to the Rectory of Snelland, co. Linc.

§ Naturalized in 1682,—Peter Lefebure, Jeanne, wife, Peter and John, sons; Marino Lefubure (*sic*), Mary, wife, Peter and Mark Antony, sons; and others of this name.

A | B

Samuel Debonnaire, probably dead in 1764.

John Debonnaire,* of Bromley, co. Kent. D. . . . 1795. = Ann, d. of . . . . Tennant, m. at S. Dionis Backchurch 16 Mar. 1764, by lic.

Sarah Debonnaire, m. 1747. = William Jellicoe.

Hannah Debonnaire, = Charles Smith.

Elizabeth Debonnaire, mar. at S. George's, Bloomsbury, 16 July, 1772. = Paul George Elers, Esq., Lieut. 70th Regt. [His sister m. R. L. Edgeworth, Esq., and was mother of Maria Edgeworth, the Authoress.]

. . . . sister of Rev. John Wylde, R. of Aldridge, co. Staff. D. in Harley Street, 8 Aug. 1798, and bur. at Shenston. = William Tennant of Little Aston Hall, co. Staff. Lord of the Manor of Shenston, etc. = Anne Debonnaire, m. at Bromley, by special licence, Sept. . . 1799.

John. Hannah. Sarah.

William Tennant of Little Aston Hall, only son. M. 1804. = Hon. Maria Charlotte, 3rd dau. of 1st Baron Yarborough by his lady, Sophia, dau. and heir of George Aufrere, Esq., of Chelsea.

. . . . Elers, Major 43rd Foot, d. 1811, s.p.

George Elers, Capt. 12th Foot, d. 1841, unm.

Edward Elers, Lieut. R.N., d. 1814. = Elizabeth, dau. of George Younghusband, Lieut. R.N., d. 19 Dec. 1857. = Rear-Admiral Sir Charles Napier, K.C.B., G.C.I.S., K.M.I., K.S.G., Count of Cape St. Vincent, etc., of Merchistoun Hall, Hants, b. 6 Mar. 1786, d. 5 Nov. 1860.

The children assumed the name of Napier on their mother's second marriage.

Edward Hungerford Delavel Elers Napier,† Major-General in Army, b. 1808. = Eliza Louisa Daniel, niece of Sir Alexr Johnston, and coz. to Admiral Napier.

Charles. Sybil, m.

George Charles Elers Napier, b. 1812. Entered the Navy 7 Dec. 1825, and won distinction under his step-father. Was lost in H.M. frigate, "Avenger," 20 Dec. 1847.

Charles Stewart Napier, d. æt. 5, 1821. Buried in Paris, at Père la Chaise.

Eloise Fanny, only d. and heir (Countess of Cape St. Vincent), m. 1843. = Rev. Henry Jodrell, Rector of Gisleham, co. Norfolk, and of Merchistoun Hall, Hants.

Peter Debonnaire, bapt. at S. Peter ad Vincula (in the Tower of London), 16 July, 1717. Died before 1733.

John Debonnaire,‡ merchant at Lisbon and in E. Indies. D. . . . 1786, at the Cape of Good Hope. = Jane, dau. of . . . . Jones, of . . . . Wales.

C

Susanna Debonnaire, d. 1809, s.p. = James Winch of Chelsea.

A

* That this John was the father of Anne Tennant is certain: that this marriage, recorded in the printed Registers of S. Dionis, was his, is probable, but not proven.

† Author of '*Scenes and Sports in Foreign Lands*,' '*Reminiscences of Syria*,' '*Life and Correspondence of Admiral Sir Charles Napier*,' *etc.*

‡ His first cousin James Marriette (son of Francois Marriette and Jeanne Le Keux) m. at the Fleet, 11 Feb. 1753, Alice Jones, probably of the same family with Jane Debonnaire, and related to Edmund Jones and Jane his wife, *née* Mariscaux, who appear as sponsors at Le Keux baptisms in the Walloon Church in 1687-8 and 1689-90.

C | A |

Leah Debonnaire, b. . . . . 1722; mar. at S. Helen's, Bishopsgate, 21 Feb. 1744-1745; d. 17 June, 1749; bur. in the Wagner vault at Lee, co. Kent. 1st wife. = Anthony Wagner, b. 18 Mar. 1711. Killed by a fall from his horse, opposite S. James' Palace, 2 July, 1761. Bur. in Dupuis vault at Fulham. s.p. (Brother to George Wagner, p. 221, *ante*.) = Anna, d. of Abraham Dupuis, by his wife Anna Stainsby, bapt. at Twickenham 28 Aug. 1723; m. to first husband at S. James', Piccadilly, 4 Dec. 1749; bur. at Fulham 9 May, 1804, æt. 82. = Francis Cooke, Capt. in 2nd Regt. of Dragoon Guards. (Brother to Dr. Cooke, Provost of King's Coll. Cambridge, and Dean of Ely.) D. 1816, æt. 93. Her second husb.

Mary Debonnaire, b. . . . . 1726; died 27 March, 1809, æt. 83. Bur. at Lee, co. Kent. = Mark Haggard,* of Stratford-le-Bow, merchant.

Mark Haggard of Stoke Newington, d. 19 April, 1829. = Susannah Jones, d. 17 Sept. 1835.

Mary Haggard, d. 23 Nov. 1833, æt. 75. Bur. at Lee, co. Kent. = Harry Hale of Birchin Lane, merchant.

Hannah Haggard, d. 21 March, 1820, æt. 60. Bur. at Lee, co. Kent.

Mary Frances Clifton of Silk Willoughby, co. Lincoln. b. 1782; d. 1818. = William Debonnaire Haggard of the Bank of England; then of Brunswick Road, Brighton. F.S.A. Born 2 Feb. 1787; d. . . . . = Jane Copner of Barnstaple, 2nd wife, d. 5 April, 1824, æt. 26. = Elizabeth Nodes, d. of Louis Henry Le Cren (by his w. Catherine Mary, d. of Samuel Jaumard) of Greenwich. 3rd wife.

A son William Debonnaire, and two daughters.

Two sons: Mark, Frederick Thomas.

John Haggard, b. 11 May, 1783, twin with Mark.

Mark Haggard, b. 11 May, 1783, d. 25 Mar. 1809.

Samuel Haggard, d. 28 Jan. 1818, at sea.

Susannah Rachel Haggard. = C. Sanderson of . . . . London, stockbroker.

Three children.

Major John Smith, mar. 1776, d. 1778. = Susannah Sophia Selina Debonnaire, b. . . . . in Wales, 8 April, 1756; d. 10 Sept. 1815. = Thomas Theophilus Metcalfe, Director of the Hon. E.I. Co., of Ham Common, and M.P. for Abingdon. 1796-1807. Cr. a Baronet, 21 Dec. 1802. Died in Portland Place, 17 Nov. 1813.

Sarah Debonnaire, born 1758.

A son, d. young.

Sir Theophilus John Metcalfe, 2nd Bart., President of the Select Committee at Canton, b. 19 Sept. 1783; d. at Fern Hill, Berks, 15 Aug. 1822. = Hannah, dau. of Thomas Russell, Esq., of Dover, and niece of Sir Henry Russell, 1st Bart. d. 1809.

The only child, Eliza Debonnaire Metcalfe, died 19 Jan. 1833, having m. 8 June, 1826, Peter Hesketh, who in 1831, assumed the additional name of Fleetwood. He was the founder of the town of that name; was created a Baronet in 1838, and died in 1866, when the title became extinct.

Right Hon. Sir Charles Theophilus Metcalfe, of Fern Hill, Berks, 3rd Bart., P.C., G.C.B. After a brilliant career of 38 years in India, appointed Governor of Jamaica in 1838, and Governor General of Canada, 1843-5. Cr. Baron Metcalfe, 1845. With his death in Sept. of the following year, s.p., the Barony became extinct.

Sir Charles Theophilus Metcalfe, 4th Bart., Judge of the Delhi Territory; b. 2 Jan. 1795; d. . . . . 1853. He married 1st, Grace, dau. of Alexander Clarke, Esq. = Felicité Anne,† eldest d. of J. Browne, Esq., of the Bengal Medical Board; d. Sept. 1842.

See Baronetage.

E | D |

* Grandson of John Haggard and Hannah Aungier; and younger and only brother of John, whose grandson, William Henry Haggard of Bradenham Hall, Norfolk, married into the Huguenot family of Amyand. (See 'Landed Gentry.')

† Query if of the family of Felicia Hemans, the poetess, who was dau. of George Browne, Esq., by Felicité, his wife, daughter of Benedict Park Wagner, Austrian Consul-General at Liverpool.

E | D

Henry Theophilus, b. 12 Feb. 1796; d. Aug. 1802.

Emily Theophila, his second wife, mar. 22 June, 1812. ╤ Henry Jeffrey Flower, 4th Viscount Ashbrook, b. 1776, d. 1847.

The only surviving dau. Charlotte Augusta Flower, m. 1846, George, 5th Duke of Marlborough, and died 1850, leaving issue.

Georgiana Theophila, m. 1822, d. 5 Feb. 1864. ╤ Rev. Thomas Scott Smyth of S. Anstell, co. Cornwall. D. before 1864.

Charles. | Emily Smyth, living unm.

Jane Debonnaire, b. at Madras, March, 1765; m. at Cawnpore, 1793; d. . . . 1808. ╤ John Richardson of ye Hon. E.I. Co.'s Service, and of Mount Panther, co. Down. Died May, 1829.

Anne Debonnaire, born at Madras, 30 Jan. 1768. M. in Calcutta, 10 Jan. 1786. D. at Chart Lodge, co. Kent, Feb. 1841. Bur. at Kemsing, 6 March. ╤ Hon. William Monson, 4th son of John 2nd Lord Monson, b. 15 Dec. 1760. D. 26 Dec. 1807.

Anne Sophia Richardson, b. 1795. ╤ John Charles Bristow, Esq., of Ensemere Hill, Ulleswater, Westmoreland, son of John Bristow, President of the Board of Trade at Calcutta, by Emilia, dau. of William Wrangham, Esq. D. 1856.

Anne Richardson, b. 1796. Living unmarried.

Louisa Richardson, b. 1797. ╤ Rev. Daniel Henry Maunsell. (See 'Landed Gentry,' M. of Bally-William.)

William John, 6th Lord Monson, of Burton Hall, near Lincoln; and Gatton Park, near Reigate. B. 14 May, 1796. D. 17 Dec. 1862. ╤ Eliza, dau. of Edmund Larken, Esq., of Bedford Square, London, m. 8 May, 1828. D. 22 Jan. 1863.

See Peerage.

John William Bristow of Ensemere Hill. ╤ Mary Ann Barbara, eldest d. of Major Sebastian Nash, of the Bengal Light Cavalry.

Arthur. — Ernest. | Theodore, in Holy Orders. D. | Ellen. — Georgina.

Henry Daniel. | Frederick Richard, Lieut.-Col. R.E., C.B. | John. | Jane, mar. Frederic Brine, Lieut.-Col. R.E. | Louisa, mar. Rev. . . . . Medlicott.

John Charles. | Arthur Nash. | Amy Anne Theophila. | Kathleen Lyttelton.

Notes relating to others of the name who have not found their place in the foregoing Pedigree.

Jacob Debonnaire "de St. Quentin, demeurant dans la paroisse de Chardiche," had, by his wife Susanne Betembos, (1) Isaac, bap. 18 March, 1694-5, at the Church de la Patente, for whom Pierre Faquet and Jeanne Debonnaire were sponsors, and (2) Marthe, bapt. at same place. 18 Jan. 1698-9.

Arnaud Standau (called elsewhere Renaux Estando) had, by his wife Jeanne Debonnaire, (1) Susanne, bap. 18 Sept. 1698, at S. Jean, Spitalfields, whose sponsors were Jacob Debonnaire and Suzanne Stando; (2) Jacob, bapt. 29 Nov. 1702, at ditto; sponsors, Jacob Standau and Marie Debonnaire; (3) Marie Anne, bap. 22 Oct. 1710, at ditto; sponsors, Abram and Marie Commenche; and (4) Judith, bap. 8 May, 1715, at ditto; sponsors, Jean Debonnaire and Marie Standau.

Daniel Debonnaire had, by his wife Susanne Blondin, (1) Jaques, bap. 1 March, 1729-30, at the Walloon Church; (2) Pierre, bap. 17 April, 1722, at ditto; sponsors, Pierre Debonnaire and Eliz. Sauvage; and (3) Henry, bap. 3 April, 1732, at ditto.

Possibly another Refugee settled in Switzerland, as several of the name lie buried at St. Maurice, in the Rhone Valley.

Huguenot Refugee Family of Dupuis.

Communicated by HENRY WAGNER, Esq., F.S.A.

. . . . Dupuis, traditionally of Bordeaux.

Philip Dupuis,* of Pall Mall. Bur. 27 March, 1706-7, at S. Martin's in Fields. = Margaret (? Walker). Bur. at S. Martin's in Fields 22 Nov. 1716.‡ "Ex paroch. S'ti Jacobi Westmins' in com. Middxiæ vidua." Adm'on granted, 1716, to son Abraham.

Stephen Dupuis, living 1716.

John Dupuis.

Hester. = ... Pullain.

A dau. = ... Boucher.

Mary. Possibly identical with Mad. Boucher.

Abraham Dupuis,† of Pall Mall. Said to have fought in 1715 at the battle of Dumblain, a medal for which has come down to his descendants, and called *Captain* in the Twickenham Register. Died 1737. = Anna, dau. of . . . . Stainsby. Born . . . . 1684; died 24 Nov. 1756, æt. 72, bur. at Fulham.

Margaret,‡ bapt. 19 June, 1692, at S. Martin's in Fields.

Mary,‡ born 18 Oct. 1693, bapt. 22 Oct, at S. Martin's in Fields.

John Dupuis,‡ born 4 Nov. bapt. 5 Nov. 1695, at S. Martin's in Fields.

Philip Dupuis,‡ born 26 April, bapt. 9 May, 1697. (A Philip Dupuis mar. in 1730 Anne Dod.)

Mary.

Jacob. — Philip.

Magdalen. = . . . Lambert.

Abraham Dupuis, American Merchant, of Gracechurch Street, and of Percy's (Pursers') Cross, Fulham. D. and there bur. Oct. 1777. Will dat. 10 July, 1753, with four codicils. Executors therein named, Frances (his widow), Anthony Wagner, and John Batchelor. = Frances, dau. of . . . . Batchelor. Mar. in Chapel of Hampton Court Palace: died and bur. 5 Feb. 1810, in family vault at Fulham.

A

Leah, dau. of Peter Debonnaire, of Stratford le Bow. Mar. at S. Helen's, Bishopsgate, 21 Feb. 1744-5; died 27 June, 1745, æt. 23, bur. at Lee. = Anthony Wagner, born 18 March and bapt. at S. Anne's, Soho, 15 April, 1718; died 2 July, 1761, æt. 43, bur. at Fulham. Brother to George Wagner, p. 221, *ante*. = Anna Dupuis, bapt. at Twickenham 28 Aug. 1723; mar. to her first husband at S. James', Piccadilly, 4 Dec. 1746; died at Hillingdon, æt. 82, and bur. at Fulham 9 May, 1804. = Francis Cooke, her second husband, Capt. 2nd Dragoon Guards, brother to Dr. Cooke, Dean of Ely, and Provost of King's Coll., Camb. Died 1816, æt. 93.

* Will of Philip Dupuis, or "Depuis," dated 18 June, 1705; pr. July, 1707, by his widow, Margaret, sole executrix. Names his son Abraham, his brothers John and Stephen Dupuis, sister Mary, sister Hester Pullain and her daughter Mary, and nephews and niece Jacob, Philip, and Magdalen Boucher.

† Will of Abraham Dupuis, gentleman, of Pall Mall, dated 1716. Made probably upon his mother's death and his own marriage. Pr. July, 1737, by Anna, his widow, sole executrix. Names his uncles Stephen and John Dupuis, his aunt Esther "Pulley," widow, and her dau. Mary, his cousin Magdalen Lambert, and uncle Thomas Walker of Durham Yard, parish of S. Martin.

‡ In S. Martin's Registers "Dupee." The name, in its varying forms of Dupuis, Dupuy, Depuy, Depee, etc., occurs frequently in many Registers which the Compiler has had occasion to consult. It may also, possibly, have been Anglicized into Wells.

The following few extracts may not improbably relate to this family:—

1702–3. March. S. Anne's, Soho. Bur. James Depuy.
1712. 12 Dec. Do. do. John Depee.
1730. Do. Philip Dupuis mar. Anne Dod.
1731–2. Spring Garden. Philipe Rousseau de St. Dunstan à Stepney à Jeanne Dupuis de la Paroisse de St. Jaques, Westminster.
1736. Walloon Church. John Bauchet mar. Marianne Dupuis, and had issue Anne, Madelaine, and Jean Bauché (*sic*), bapt. 1737–9.

A

George Dupuis, bapt. at S. Benet, Gracechurch, 1 April, 1754; died young.

Anne, bapt. at St. Benet, Gracechurch, 5 May, 1756; died and bur. 17 March, 1766, at Fulham.

Frances, bapt. at Fulham 26 Sept. 1766.

Rev. George Dupuis, bapt. at S. Benet, Gracechurch, 7 July, 1757. An Oppidan at Eton, and matric. Merton College, Oxon. 25 June, 1776. Rector of Wendlebury, co. Oxford, 1789-1839. Died 1839, æt. 81. = Caroline Elizabeth, only dau. and heir of E. Stevens, Esq., Architect, who died and was buried in Rome 1774, by his wife Rachel Kishere, who died and was buried at Wendlebury. Born 1770; mar. 1793; died 1845.

Richard Dupuis, Lieut.-Colonel 2nd Dragoon Guards. Bapt. at S. Benet, Gracechurch, 8 Sept. 1763. Died s.p. 1837, bur. at S. Matthew's, Ipswich. = Rebecca Mary, dau. of Samuel Kilderbee, Esq., of Ipswich.

Rev. George John Dupuis. At Eton, and Fellow of King's Coll., Cam. B.A. 1819, M.A. 1822. Assist. and Lower Master at Eton Coll. till 1838, when appointed a Fellow. Vice Provost 18 . Rector of Hemingby, co. Linc., 1831–40; Rector of Creeting, Suffolk, 1840–62; Rector of Worplesdon, Surrey, 1862–78. = Julia Maria, dau. of Rev. W. Roberts, Vice Provost of Eton College and Rector of Worplesdon (son of Rev. Wm. Hayward Roberts, D.D., Provost of Eton, 1781-21).

Eliza Anne, born 1797; died 1878. = C. Price, Esq., of Westbury, Bucks.

Frances Anna, born 1798; died (about) 1865. = Rev. Charles William Stocker, D.D., R. of Draycott le Moors, Staff.

Caroline, born 1800; died 1852.

Julia Caroline, born 1832.

Rev. George Richard Dupuis, born 1835. Fellow of King's Coll. Cam. Assistant Master at Eton, 1858-75. Vicar of Sturminster Marshall, 1875-7. Rector of Sessay, co. York, 1877. = Annette Lætitia, dau. of . . . . Lloyd, Capt. 52nd Regt.

Adela Harriette, born 1837; mar. 20 April, 1858. = John Patterson Cobbold, eldest son of John Chevallier Cobbold, of The Holywells, co. Suffolk, M.P. for Ipswich 1847-68. Born 12 July, 1831; M.P. for Ipswich 18 . Died 9 Dec. 1875.

Arthur Edward Dupuis, Captain R.N. Born 1838. = Laura Sarah, dau. of W. M. McCay, of Dublin. Died at Torquay 20 July, 1873, æt. 24.

Rev. Edward John Gore Dupuis, Exeter Coll. Oxford, B.A. 1867. Conduct of Eton Coll. and Curate of Eton, 1870-75. Born 1843. = Sophia Letitia, dau. of Rev. Samuel John Heathcote, P.C. of Williton, co. Somerset.

George, born and died 1861. — Alice Jane, born 1862.

William George, born and died 1863. — Arthur George Lloyd, born 1864.

Julia Harriett, born 1866. — Annette Caroline, born 1867.

Georgina Catherine, born 1870. — Frederick John, born 1872. — Laura, born 1873.

John Richard, born and died 1875. — Margaret Ellen, born 1877.

John Dupuis Cobbold, born 1861.

Seven others.

A dau.

General Sir John Edward Dupuis. Entered Royal Artillery 1825. Received, for his war services, the Crimean Medal and four clasps, Indian Medal, Sardinian Medals, and the Orders of San Fernando of Spain, Legion of Honour, and the Medjidie. C.B. 1856; K.C.B. 1865; General, 1868. Died 25 Nov. 1876.

Edward Dupuis, born 1802; d. 1827. — Lucy Ann, born 1803; died 29 Nov. 1810. M.I. at Wendlebury. — Mary, born 1804; died young.

Louisa, born 1806; died 1875. = Rev. Robert Waller, Rector of Bourton, co. Glouc.

Rev. Harry Dupuis, born 1808; died 1867. Vicar of Richmond, Surrey, 1852-67. = Catherine Rosalie, dau. of Col. Godfrey T. Greene, C.B. Died 1875.

Right Hon. Sir Charles Jasper Selwyn, Lord Justice of Appeal in Chancery. M.P. for Univ. of Cambridge 1859-68. P.C. Of Pagoda House, Richmond. Born 13 Oct. 1814; died 11 Aug. 1869. = Hughes Hallett Royal Artillery.

Constance. Godfrey A. S. Herbert. Charles. Rachel.

Harry Jasper Selwyn, born

John Dupuis.* = Susanna (? Hadnock.†)

John Dupuis, b. 20 Jan. 1728.

William Dupuis, b. 28 July, 1731.

Thomas Sanders Dupuis,‡ Mus. Doc., b. 5 Nov. 1733; educated in the Chapel Royal, under Dr. Bernard Gates, whose principal heir he finally became; appointed Organist and Composer to the Chapel Royal, 1779; Mus. Doc. of Oxford, 1790; d. in King's Row, Park Lane, 17 July, 1796; bur. in W. Cloister of Westminster Abbey. = Martha,§ dau. of .... Skelton; bur. at Fulham.

Mary, b. 12 Sept. 1726. ? died before 1736.

Mary Dupuis, b. 12 Jan. 1736.

Rev. Thomas Skelton Dupuis, of Gray's, Essex, b. 23 Jan. 1766; d. 19 Dec. 1795, s.p. = Letitia, dau. of ....

George Dupuis, b. 22 Aug. 1767, d. aged 19 days.

Charles Dupuis, of Mount Street, Grosvenor Sq., b. 8 Feb. 1770, d. ... bur. at S. Mary, Lambeth, 1824. = Eliza, dau. of .... Wentworth, of Oxford, m. 17 Sept. 1796.

Rev. Charles Sanders Skelton Dupuis, b. 8 Nov., and bapt. at S. Mary the Virgin, Oxford, 22 Nov. 1797. Matric. at Oxford from Pembroke Coll. 4 Nov. 1814, æt. 16; B.A. 28 May, 1818; M.A. 8 Feb. 1821; Fellow of Pembr. Coll. .... R. of Binton, co. Warwick, 1836-74. Died 17 Aug. 1874. = Emma, dau. of Rev. Charles Crane, D.D., Vicar of Paddington, b. .... d. 8 Feb. 1876, æt. 69.

Rev. Theodore Crane Dupuis, born 1830. Pembr. Coll., Oxon. B.A. 1854; M.A. 1856. Vicar of Burnham, Bridgewater, 1867.

Charles Seymour Dupuis, b. 1849. Linc. Coll., Oxon. B.A. 1872; M.A. 1874. R. of Binton, co. Warwick, 1874.

Eliza, b. 1835, m. 31 Dec. 1863. = Willoughby John Trevelyan, of Perran-Uthnoe, Cornwall, b. 1839, d. 25 Aug. 1867.

Eliza Caroline, b. .... 1864.

Walter John, b. 28 Jan. 1866. [Heir presumptive to baronetcy of Trevelyan, of Nettlecombe.]

* John Dupuis is said to have occupied some position about the Court. He probably was either the brother or son of Philip Dupuis, the patriarch of the preceding pedigree, as it is mentioned in the family records that Abraham Dupuis and the Composer were related; but the link of connection is no longer known. Information is asked for.

† Authority: the record of a gift to Thomas S. Dupuis from his grandmother, Mrs. Mary Hadnock, Nov. the 1st, (?) 1751.

‡ A monumental tablet erected in the West Cloister gives the following Arms:—Or, an eagle rising from a mount ppr.,—impaling, for Skelton, Az., on a fesse between 3 fleurs de lis or, a Cornish chough sa.

§ The following entries appear to belong to Mrs. Dupuis's family:—

In Registers of S. Anne's, Soho.—Bapt. 10 Nov. 1699, Grace Skelton of John and Martha.

In Fulham Registers.—Marr. 25 Sept. 1773, by lic. Henry Collins and Mary Skelton. Witnesses, Jno. Ashurst, Martha Dupuis.

ADDITIONS TO THE WALTERS PEDIGREE.*

Henry Walters of Batheaston, eldest son of Henry Walters of Batheaston by Mary, da. of Joseph Houlton, Esq., of Farleigh Castle, co. Wilts, born 1722, m. 1745. D.L. for Somersetshire, and Lieut.-Col. of Militia during the French War. He died in 1797. = Anne, daughter and coheiress of Thomas Smith of Nottingham.

Thomas Walters of Batheaston, = Sophia, daughter and coheiress of Rev. John Skynner.

- Melmoth Walters, b. Ap. 14, 1793, d. July 28, 1868.
- 1st, Jemima Littlejohn, b. May, 1801, d. Oct. 1820. = Henry Walters, b. Sept. 29, 1794, m. . . . . d. Mar. 13, 1869. = 2nd, Eleonora Campbell, b. 1810, d. 1856.
- Thomas Walters, b. Dec. 1795, d. April, 1819.
- John Eldad Walters, b. Sept. 12, 1797. =
- Sophia, b. Feb. 1799, d. 1848.

Children of Henry Walters and 2nd, Eleonora Campbell:

- Melmoth Campbell Walters, b. Jan. 1830, m. H. A. Parker Nov. 1860, and has issue one dau.
- Sophia Jemima.
- John Skynner Walters, b. Feb. 1834, m. Sophia Lloyd, 1858, and has issue one son and two dau'rs.
- Eleanor Margaret, b. July, 1839, d. July, 1870.
- Flora Bistowe, b. 6 Jan. 1845.
- Launcelot Walters, b. 1852.

Children of Henry Walters and 1st, Jemima Littlejohn:

- Melmoth Thomas Walters, b. 1818, d. 1818.
- The Rev. Thomas D'Oyly Walters, b. June 21, 1819, m. Oct. 18, 1842, d. June 21, 1849. = Emma Elizabeth Hippisley, dau. of Rev. H. Hippisley of Lamborne Place, Berks, b. May 18, 1815.
- The Rev. Henry Littlejohn Walters, b. Oct. 1820, m. June 16, 1853. = Harriett Mitchell, dau. of Rev. C. Mitchell, Petersfield, Hants.

Children of the Rev. Henry Littlejohn Walters and Harriett Mitchell:

- Charles Walters, b. Dec. 21, 1857.
- Arthur Walters, b. Sept. 6, 1863.
- Amy, b. Apr. 1854.
- Lucy, b. Jan. 1856.
- Florence, b. July, 1861.
- Alice, b. Apr. 1868.

Children of the Rev. Thomas D'Oyly Walters and Emma Elizabeth Hippisley:

- Henry Edward Walters, b. Apr. 27, 1845, entered R. Navy in 1859, and still serving.
- Edmond Walters, b. Aug. 2, 1848, m. at Sydenham, Oxford, July 23, 1873, now Rector of March Baldon, Oxon. = Annie Elizabeth, dau. of Col. St. John Browne, R.A.
- Frances Sophia, b. Oct. 22, 1843, m. Aug. 7, 1873, E. R. Gayer, Esq., of Lincoln's Inn, Barrister-at-Law.
- Annie Jemima, b. July 27, 1846, m. Dec. 18, 1873, F. Neison, Esq.

Children of Edmond Walters and Annie Elizabeth:

- Henry R. St. Arvans Walters, b. Oct. 24, 1875.
- Arthur Lionel Walters, b. Dec. 21, 1878.
- Agnes St. John, b. July 13, 1874.
- Eleanor Margaret, b. Nov. 1876.
- Isabel Marion, b. Nov. 1877.

HENRY E. WALTERS.

MONUMENTAL INSCRIPTIONS, WITH NOTES, FROM THE CHURCH AND CHURCHYARD OF AXBRIDGE, CO. SOMERSET.†

(*Continued from p.* 204.)

On flat stones.

20\. . . . . Ann the Wife of Edward Jones of the City of Bristol Ironmonger who departed this life the 7th April 1762.

Edward Jones died the 20th Decr 1776 aged 63 years and Elizabeth daughter of Edward and Ann Jones departed this life the 7th April 1778 aged 19.

21\. Here lyes the Body of Mr Gyles Dunster who departed this life the 8th of Feby 1708. And also the Body of Mrs. Mary Dunster his Wife who died the 18th

* Communicated by HENRY E. WALTERS, Esq., R.N.

† Communicated by EDWARD FRY WADE, Esq.

SAPIENTIA

Decr 1728 And also the Body of Ann his daughter and also the Body of Rachel Fry Wife of Peter Fry (*Vide* Monument No 10)

22 Elizabeth daughter of William Bennett was here buried Novr 28, 1606 (or 96)

23 Here lyeth the Body of John Tuthill Gent. thrice Mayor of this Corporation who departed this life the 12th day of Novr 1688 aged 63 y^rs. Also Ann Tuthill his daughter deceased the 12th day of Decr 1688 aged 20 years Dorothy ye Wife of John Tuthill above named was buried August 24th 1711 aged 80 years Grace ye Wife of John son of John Tuthill above was buried Novr 30th 1712 aged 51 years

24 Hic Jacet Johannis Wrentmore Maoris Hujus Burg Filii Jasperi Wrentmore qui obiit Jany 3rd 1642 Martha Wife of George Wrentmore Wollen Draper son of the said John Wrentmore buried here Feb 21, 1661, aged 33

25. Here lies the Body of John Andrews Gent who departed this life 16th Octr 1728 Sarah Andrews died 19th Jany 1740.

26. Here lyeth the Body of Eli Andrews who was twice Mayor of this Corporation. He died the 8th March 1785 aged 74. Also here lyeth the Body of Mary his Wife who died the 15th Septr 1787 aged 84 years

27. Here lyeth the Body of William Pett Wolling Draper who was Thrice Mayor of this Borough and deceased the 5th October in the 77th year of his age A D 1650

28. In Memory of Thomas Robins Junr of Sidcot Attorney at law who died Decr 28th 1785 aged 33 years Also of Thomas Robins Father of the said Thomas Robins who died Novr 19th 1787 aged 83. Also Henry son of the said Thomas Robins Junr Who died March 2nd 1791 aged 15 years Also Mary daughter of the said Thomas Robins Junr who died 4th December 1792 aged 13 years. John their Brother who died an infant Also of Thomas Robins of Wells Attorney at law son of the said Thomas Robins Junr who died July 18th 1832 aged 55 years.

29. Here lyeth the Body of John Arnel of this p'ish who departed this life March 16th 17½? aged 51 years Here also lyeth the Body of Hannah Wife of Peter Cook of this p'ish who died Octr 1st A D 1715 aged 54 years And also Here lyeth the Body of Elizabeth daughter of Peter and Hannah Cook who died Septr 21st A D 1715 aged 20 years.

30. Here lyeth the Body of Francis Tonkins the son of Edward Tonkins Gent who departed this life 30th January (rest obliterated, probably between 1600 and 1700)

31. Here lyeth the Body of Thomas Hooper of Axbridge Gent who died 6th day of February 1626 And also Here lyeth the Body of Edith the Wife of Peter Veel Gent who deceased the 4th Novr A D 1634 Here also lyeth the Body of Ann the Wife of the said Peter Veel Gent who dyed the 9th day of April A D 1695.

32 In Memory of William S bery (Sadbery) Gent of this Borough (probably Mayor) who . . March 1690 ætatis .

33 Here lyeth the Body of Sarah Wife of William Sadbery who died Novr 3rd A.D. 1709 ætatis suæ 17°

Oh death, why dealt thou so unkind,
To part us two most in our prime?
Memento Mori

34. Here lyeth the Body of . . ter who dyed July 24th 1665 ætatis 55 (or 65)

35 Here lyeth the Body of Thomas Gilling Gent. who was twice Mayor of this Corporation dyed 6th Jany A D 1704 aged 68 Also Thomas Gilling Gent son of the abovesaid who dyed 14th Septr 1724 aged 57. Also near this place lie the remains of Thomas Gilling Grandson of the abovesaid who dyed 13th August 1726 aged 40 years Also Here lyeth the Body of Samuel Gilling Grandson of the abovesaid who died 16th August 1776 aged 70 years. William Gilling Gent. brother of the abovesaid lies buried at Cheddar Here also lyeth the Body of Richard Gilling (rest obliterated)

36. To the Memory of the Reverend William Bacon Cattell only son of Mr William Cattell of Bath Surgeon and Rector of the parish of Winnall in the County of Hants and for many years Curate of the parish churches of Axbridge and Wedmore in the County of Somerset in all which parishes he faithfully performed the duties of a good divine. He died 24th Septr 1827 in the 69th year of his age. In the

adjoining grave—on the right of this—are deposited the remains of Mary Cattell his Widow who departed this life May 24th 1831 in the 74th year of her age.

In the Middle Aisle.

37. In Memory of Sarah daughter of George Wrentmore Gent. of this Borough she died 12th Novr 1715 aged 31 years.

38. In Memory of . . . . Shippard . . . . John Shippard.

39. Here lyeth the Body of Thomas Wrentmore Gent. who took possession of his everlasting rest 24th Feby 1668.

40. Here lyeth the Bodyes of Elizabeth and her childe Wife and daughter of Richard Durban of Chedder deceased 25th Decr 1665.

MEMORANDA RELATING TO THE FAMILIES ALLIED TO THAT OF BODDINGTON.

Thomas Holford, Cit. and Baker of London; was a Freeman of his Company in 1624–5; on the Livery in 1630, and first came upon the Court in 1640. Upper Warden in 1653 with Colonel Nathaniel Whetham, Governor of Portsmouth and M.P.; fined in 1655 and 1658 for not serving the offices of Master and Warden. Living 1663, but deceased ante 1668.

John Holford of Idbury, co. Oxon, yeoman 1657.

John Holford was married and in business as a Baker before 1664; admitted free of the Merchant Taylors' Company in Aug. of that year.

John Holford, named in his brother's will, 1700.

1 wife. Mary da. of . . . . Living 1683. Deceased ante 1695.

Thomas Holford of Aldermanbury in the Par. of St. Lawrence Jewry, Cit. and Baker of London, sometime also of Forscott, nr Churchill, co. Oxon. Bound apprentice to Tho. Holford, Cit. and Baker, for 10 years, from 3 June, 1657, and admd a Freeman sometime before 1670. A Liveryman, and voted at the election in 1700. Held a farm and lands at Tradding-ton, co. Worc. Will dat. 1 Feb. 1703; cod. 29 Aug. 1705; pr. 8 Sept. follg. Bur. in the middle aisle of St. Lawrence Jewry, 9 Sept. 1705.

2 wife. Mary Bacon of Christ Church, London, widow. Lic. for her mar. at Chelsea, co. Middx. dat. 7 May, 1695, and therein stated to be above 30 years of age. Marr. articles dat. 16 Apr. 1695. Living 1703.

Thomas Holford, bapt. at St. Lawrence Jewry 6 Oct. 1672. Died young.

Hannah, bapt. at St. Lawrence Jewry 1 Feb. 1673; marr. by lic. dated 22 Mar. 1691, to John Willett. Both living 1701.

3 children 1703.

John Holford, bapt. at St. Lawrence Jewry 6 Aug. 1676. Bur. there 20 Dec. 1681.

Martha, bapt. at St. Lawrence Jewry 21 Apr. 1678, bur. there 17 Jan. 1681–2.

Thomas Holford, bapt. at St. Lawrence Jewry 10, & bur. there 27 July, 1681.

A

A

1 husb.
John Roberts of the co. of Denbigh, Cit. & Distiller of London. Will dated 5 Aug., and proved 16 Aug. 1699. The escocheons used at his funeral had an impalement of the ancient Coat of Holford. = Mary, marr. to John Roberts by lic. dated 23 Feb. 1692-3, and to Edw. Buxton by lic. dated 18 June, 1701. Will (in which she is described of St. Luke's, co. Middx.) dated 29 July, 1740; cod. 24 Nov., and pr. 9 Jan. following. Names cousin Hannah Laite of Bleddington, co. Glouc. = 2 husb. Edward Buxton of St. Mary Magdalen, Milk Street, and of Brassington, Cit. & Distiller of London, æt. 31 years, 1710. Will dated 1 Nov., and pr. 9 Dec. 1729.

Children of John Roberts:
- Thomas Roberts, 1699.
- Elizabeth, 1699.

Children of Edward Buxton:
- Edward Buxton and two other children, 1703. All died ante 1710.
- Mary only child æt. 3 years 1710. Unmar. 1729 and 1740.

Called cousins by Mary Buxton.

- John Holford.
- Elizabeth, marr. . . . Floyd of . . . . 1740.

Extract from the will of Daniel Berry of London, merchant, dated 30 April, 1696, proved 20 March, 1698. Cozen Elizabeth, wife of John Boddington, and her children.

. . . . Townsend of . . . . = ... dau. of . . . .

- Jonathan Townsend of Brentford, co. Middx. Admon. first granted Feb. 1720, and again 10 Nov. 1741. = ... dau. of . . . . d. before her husb.
- James Townsend of Brentford aforesaid, Citizen and Bowyer of London, formerly of St. Mary Magdalen, Milk St., London, hosier, æt. 28 years, and cœl. 20 Nov. 1693. Will (in wch he directs to be buried at Hanwell) dated 25 Aug. 1738, pr. 9 Jan. 1740–1. (See Vol. III., page 214.) = Margaret, dau. of Jerome Clutterbuck, Citizen and Haberdasher of London. Marr. by lic. dat. 20 Nov. 1693, then æt. circ. 19. Died before her husb. Bur. at Hanwell.

Thomas Holford of St. Lawrence Jewry, London, Cit. and Haberdasher, bapt. at St. Lawrence Jewry 1 Apr. 1683. Apprentice to James Lamb, Cit. and Haberdasher, 18 Oct. 1700. Adm[d] Free. 15 Oct. 1708. Died 27 Jan. 1740–1. Will dat. 21 Aug. 1740, pr. 5 Feb. following. 'Gent.'s Mag.', 27 Jan. 1741, died M[r] Holford an eminent Hosier, Cheapside. = Mary, dau. and at length coheir. Ex'trix of her first husb. 1741. Articles before marriage with her second husband dat. Dec. 18, 1741; marr. next day. Will dat. 17 Apr. 1766, pr. 3 Apr. 1767. = John Stephenson of Brentford aforesaid, and of the City of Lond. merchant. Living 1760. Adm[r] to his wife 1767.

B C

B | C

James Townsend, a minor 1720. Died s.p.

Anne, dau. and coh. = James Boddington. a minor 1720. Died 24 April, 1767. (See Vol. I., p. 428, and Vol. II., p. 548.)

1. Thomas Holford of Manchester. (Burke's 'Landed Gentry.') = Mary, dau. of . . . Bateman.

2. James Holford, of Berkeley Square. Died unmarried.

3. Josiah Holford, of Hampstead, etc. See Burke's 'Landed Gentry.'

4. Charles Holford, Died unmarried.

5. John Holford, of G. P. O. Died unmarried.

1. Margaret. = Capt. Cockburn.

2. Mary, marr. at Swithins. 2 wife. (First wife d. 1760.) = Charles Gardiner of Lockleys, in the parish of Welwyn, co. Herts., born 18 Mar. 1721–2, in the par. of St. Clement's Danes; died 8 Nov. 1780; bur. at Welwyn. 'Gent.'s Mag.'—2 Nov. 1780, at Lockleys, Herts, Charles Gardiner, Esq.

Charles Gardiner, only surviving son and heir, born in the par. of St. Clement's Danes 12 July, 1763.

1. James Holford. = Sarah, dau. of Rev. Humphry Owen of Manchester, Chaplain of the Collegiate Church.

1. Mary.

2. Anne, d. unmar.

3. Frances Ellen, d. unmarried.

4. Margaret Elizabeth, d. unmarried.

Thomas Holford, d. unmarried.

James Holford of Manchester and Holford House, Regent's Park, b. 17 Feb. 1788.

John Holford of Rushall, near Manchester, b. 26 May, 1789. = ... dau. of John Shaw of Rushall.

John James Holford. And others.

To my kinsman and godson George Boddington. Will of Thomas Townsend, the elder of the parish of St. Martin's in the Fields, co. Middlesex, gent., dated 13 July, 1699. A George Boddington one of the Witnesses. 100 Edes. P.C.C.

Mar. Lic. Fac. 28 Mch, 1700.

Daniel Dolins, bach[r], 21, son of Abraham Dolins of Hackney, Middx., Esq. (who alleges), and Margaret Cooke of Hackney, Spinster, 17, dau. of Margaret Cooke, widow, also consents, to marry at St. Paul's, Covent Garden, or [blank.]

EXTRACTS FROM PARISH REGISTERS OF HACKNEY, MIDDLESEX.

Baptized

1701	Oct	14.	Abraham, son of Daniel and Margaret Dolins (born.)
$170\frac{3}{4}$	Feb.	3.	Mary, dau of same, born 2[d]
1713	Apl.	3.	Daniel, son of Daniel Dolins, Esq , and Margaret, born 2[d], bap[d] by M[r] Matthew Henry, as certified
1715	Aug	5.	Margaret, dau of same, born 1st

Buried

1706	Oct	4	Abraham Dolins, Esq , buried in London.
$17\frac{19}{20}$.	Feb	24.	Mrs Mary Dolins, Spinster, in family Vault
1720	Oct.	13	Mr Abraham Dolins, æt 19, in y[e] Vault
1728	Apl.	30	Sir Daniel Dolins, Kt , in his own Vault
1740	June	13	Dame Margaret Dolins, widow
1743	July	20.	Daniel Dolins, Esq

On a tomb with iron rails in old churchyard of St Augustine's, Hackney —

The Vault of
Sir Daniel Dolins, Knight
the last of whose family
Margary
the widow of John Berney
of
Brecon Ash, Norfolk, Esq[re]
died the Fourth
and was buried here
the Tenth of March
1801
aged 87 years

Will of Abraham Dolins, late of London, and now of Hackney, co Midd , Esq[r], dat. 15 Dec 1704, pr. 10 Oct 1706, by Anne Dolins the relict, and Daniel Dolins the son

To be bur[d] in St Andrew Undershaft (the corner Church of St Mary Axe, London), in the chancel vault where my father, mother, and 2 sons are bur[d]

To the Dutch Church, Austin Friars £50, and to the poor of same £50 Poor of St. Andrew Undershaft £10 Poor of Hackney £10

My wife Ann.

Ind're bet me Abraham Dolins and Ann my wife, Tho. Marriot of Lincoln's Inn, Esq[r], and Margaret Cooke of Hackney, widow, and my son Daniel Dolins and Margaret his wife, d of the s[d] Marg[t] Cooke

My s[d] wife to have her living and a servant to attend her, in my house at Hackney, for a year after my death My s[d] wife to be bur[d] at Wormely, co. Herts, in case she shall so order, and my son Daniel to be chargeable for the cost.

My s[d] son Daniel Dolins £10,000

My da Mary, wife of Pheasant Crispe.

My da Rebecca, wife of Richard Edwards, Esq[r], and their children Abraham and Rebecca, under age

My s[d] wife and my son Daniel, Exors.

Sums for mourning to my sister Cooke, my friend Tho[s] Marriot, my brother and sister Hatley, my sister ffalkenham, my cousin Collett and her husb , and my cousin Judith Dolins.

Sir W[m] Pridgett, Sir Gabriel Roberts, Sir Sam[l] Moyer, Francis Tysen, Esq[r], Sam Powell, Esq[r], Edw[d] Bastom, Esq , Mr. Edw[d] Antony, and Mr. Joseph Thomson to be Pallbearers.

Henry Gray of Enfield, co. Middlesex, Esq. Will dat. 20 Feb. 1682-3, proved 19 Nov. 1683. Desires to be buried in the burying ground in St. Nicholas Lane, London. ╤ Mary, living 20 Feb. 168$\frac{2}{3}$.

Peter Gray | Joseph Gray | James Boddington (See Vol. II., p. 548.) ╤ Sarah. (See Vol. II., p. 548.)

Henry Gray. Mary. Peter Gray. (children of Peter Gray)
Elizabeth. Mary. (children of Joseph Gray)
Henry Boddington. (See Vol. II., p. 548.) Hannah. Mary. (children of James Boddington and Sarah)

Note.—The sons, daughter, and her husband, and all the grandchildren living 20 Feb. 1682-3.

Will of John Voyce of Sudbury, co. Suffolk, dat. 11 Dec. 1752, proved at London 26 July, 1753, by Wm Voyce and Roger Starlin, power reserved to the others.

To my wife Anna Maria £20 for mourning.
To my da. Mary fferguson Voyce £200.
To my da. Elizabeth Voyce £200.
To my da. Hannah Voyce £200.
Residue to my sd 3 dau'rs equally.

My sd wife, my sd da. Mary fferguson Voyce, my friend Thos. Fonnereau, Esq., of Ipswich, co. Suff., my 2 brothers Roger* Voyce of London and Wm Voyce of Sudbury, and my friend Roger Starlin of Sudbury, son of Richard, joint ex'ors.

S. Mary Aldermary, London, Parish Registers.

Marriage.

1707. October 28. William Strengfellow, Bachelor, Rector of St Dunstan's in the East, and Frances Boddington of the same parish, Spinster. By licence.

I am indebted to Col. Chester, the late Mr. Charles Bridger, and Mr. J. Eedes for the notes here given, and I shall be very grateful for any *additions*.

Reginald Stewart Boddington.
15 *Markham Square, Chelsea, S.W.*

EXTRACTS FROM THE PARISH REGISTERS OF LEIGHTON BUZZARD, CO. BEDS.†

(*Continued from p.* 243.)

Baptisms.

1562.	June 7.	. . . . . filius Okley	
1564.	Nov. 12.	Tho. Oke, filius Johan Oke [? Okley].	
1565.	May 10.	Georgius Bolesworthe, filius Edmundi Bolesworth.	
1566.	July 27.	. . . . . *Boles*worthe, filia	„ „
1569.	June 5.	Alce Bolesworthe, filia	„ „
1570.	Nov. 1.	Tho. Bolesworthe, filius	„ „
1571.	July 8.	Jone Ockley, fil*ii* Franc. Okely.	
1572.	Sept. 13.	Elizabeth Bolesworthe, fili*us* Edmundi Bolesworth.	
1573.	Feb. 14.	Banister Bolesworthe, filius	„ „

* Called *Robert* Voyce in the probate.
† Communicated by F. A. Blaydes, Esq., Hockliffe Lodge, Leighton Buzzard.

1574. Nov. 2. Mary Oklye, filia ffranc Okely
1575 May 13. Edmund Boleswortlie, filius Edmundi Bolesworth.
1577. Sept. 15 ffrancis Okelye, fil. ffranc Okely
1580. Aug. 7. Elizabethe Okelye, filia ffranc Okelye.
1582 Dec. 5 Jane Withers, filia Roberti Withers
1583 May 19. Anne Okelye, filia ffranc Okely.
1585 Feb. 20. Agneta Okely, filia ffrancisca Okely.
1587 Nov 5 Richard Berry, filius Thom Berrye
1587 Mar 25. Ellina Okely, filia ffrancisca Okelye
1592. Nov 26 Edmund Bolesworthe, filius Georgei Bolesworthe.
1593. April 22 Agneta Bolesworthe, filia Johannis Bolesworthe.
1593 Aug. 26. Agneta Bolesworthe, filia Roberti Bolesworthe.
1594. Nov 30 Agneta Bolesworthe, filia Georgii Bolesworthe.
1595 Feb. 4. Rose Bolesworthe, filia Roberti Bolesworthe.
1596. Feb 19. Sara Bolesworthe, filia Georgii Bolesworthe.
1598. April 17 Easther Bolesworthe, filius Georgii Bolesworthe.
1598 July 16. Edmundus Bolesworthe, filius Roberti Bolesworthe
1598. Aug. 27 Elizabeth Wethers, filia Randoll Wethers (Withers)
1600. July 5 Edmundus Bolesworth filius Johannes Bolesworthe.
1600 Mar 22. Jone Bolesworthe, filia Roberti Bolesworthe
1602. Jan 30. ffrancis Bolesworthe, filius Johannis Bolesworthe.
1602. Mar 28 Jane Withers, filia Rudolphe Wethers.
1603 Sept. 19. Bannister Bolesworthe, filius Roberti Bolesworthe
1607. May 17 Robert Bolesworth, fil Bolesworthe
1609 Feb 2. Johan Bolesworth, fil Roberti Bolesworthe
1673. July 9 Henricus, filius Egidii Firth
1675. Aug 8 Juditha, filia „ „
1677. Sept. 19 Hanna, filia „ „
1679. Feb 26 Emer, et Gulielmus, filij Egidij Firth bapt *fuit*.
1703. Feb. 2 John, the s of Paintner.
1709. July 10 Elizabeth, da. of Emer Firth and Catherine his wife
1735. Sept. 2. Richard and Mary, s and da of Rev Owen Gough and Mary his wife
1735 Nov. 9 Charles, s of William Williams, a traveller, of the parish of Antony in the County of Cornwall, and Sarah his wife
1736. Aug. 13. Anna Catherine, da of Rev Mr Samuel Clarke and Elizabeth his wife
1736. Oct 17 Edward, s of Mr Anthony Butterfield and Elizabeth his wife.
1737. Feb 26. Samuel, s. of Mr Francis Foster and Elizabeth his wife
1737. Mar 14 Mary, da of Rev Mr Samuel Clarke and Elizabeth his wife.
1740. Aug. 17 John, s. of Thomas Houtaine [? Hawtayne] and Catherine his wife
1740. Jan. 9 Thomas, s of Rev. Mr Samuel Clarke and Elizabeth his wife, born.
1740. Feb. 7 Barbary, da. of Lieut. George Harvey and Peney his wife.
1741 Dec 12. Jane, da of Rev. Mr Owen Gough and Mary his wife
1742. May 18 Trimnell, the s. of Mr Hillersdon Frank, Esq., and Cathrine his wife, of Heath
1742. June 15. William, s of the Rev. Mr Samuel Clark and Elizabeth his wife
1743. Nov 8. Catherine, da of Mr Hillersdon Frank, Esq., and Cathrine his wife (of Heath).
1744. July 8. Sarah, da of Mr Thomas Theed and Sarah his wife, born June 27.
1745. April 4 Isaac, s. of Mr Hillersdon Franks, Esq., and Catherine his wife Heath.
1745 Sept. 26 Charles John, s of Rev. Mr Owen Gough and Mary his wife
1753. Oct. 1. Abraham, s of Mr Abraham Baskerfield and Catherine his wife.
1755. Dec. 12. Abraham, „ „ „ „

1757 April 20 Catherine, da. of Mr Abraham Baskerfield & Catherine his wife.
1758 May 17 William, s of " " "
1762. Jan 1 Thomas, s of " " "

Marriages

1565. Oct 28 Johannes Hortma' et Jone Duncu'.
1567. Oct. 23 Francis Ockly et Jelia Middleton
1571. Jan 20 Antonius Slaterius, vicarius de Lyghto [Leighton] et Margaret Lughborowe
1582. Oct 4. *Anthonie Bentham et Anna Bolesworthe.
1582. Feb 3 Richard Porter et Ellina Okely
1585 Sept 5. Richard Dier et Elizabeth Spicer
1585 Jan 24 Francis Wells et Margaret Saunders
1586 June 2. Randolph Withers et Margaret Holland
1586. Oct 27 Thomas West et Agneta Okely
1590 Sept 4 Tho Baracle et Jane Okely
1592 May 25 Richard Procter et Ala Bolesworthe
1597 Feb 13 Thomas Putnam et Ursula Jackeman
1599 July 30 †Henry Iremonger et Anna Bolesworthe
1607 Jan 6 Morganne Griffithe et Jane Annes
1610 Aug 27. Stephen Wilkes et Alce Deakon
1611. April 11 John Slatior, cleric, et Jone Smith
1612 Oct 21 George Berrie, gener., et Susan Trenly
1613 Jan 20 Thomas Osmond et Agneta Bolesworth.
1615 April 5 ffrancklyn et Alicia Dyer
1615 June 21 Bennedictus Parson et Agneta Bolsworth.
1655 April 3 Samuel Clarke, Minister of Laighton Beau-desart, son of Samuel Clarke, Clerk of London, was married to Sarah Lancaster, da of Nathaniel Lancaster, Clerk of Torperly in ye County of Chester, by John Bruen, Esq Published June 7, 14, 21, 1651
1655 Jan 7 Giles Duncombe, ye son of Edmund Duncombe of Iving-Aston, was married to Alce Lions, widdow of this town, by Francis Astrey, Esq
1655 Mar 29 Robb Atherton fm co Suffolk, to Mary Bowlsworth, widow
1657. April 3 Daniel Vivian of Farndish in this County was married to Joice Asterly ye daughter of John Asterly of Westminster
1657 Jan 10 Mr George Potter . Minister of . in the County of Bucks, and Mtris Sarah Wells, da of Francis Wells of this towne, were married at Great-Brickhill
1657. Jan. 18. Timothy Brewer, son of Wm Brewer of this towne, and Prudence, da of Richard Page Gentleman of ? Garat in the County of Hereford, were married at London at St Margate's
1660 May 8 Robert Fowler and Temperance Okeley.
1661. Nov 12 Thomas Vere and Sarah King.
1671. Nov 30 Caroly Capon et Anne Vaux
1676 June 3 Thomas Turney, gen , et Jone Leach
1678. Sept 3. ‡Altam Ansley, Esq , et Alicia Leigh generosa
1679 June 5 Gulielmus Wilkes et Winifred Pierson
1679 Sept 2. Johannes Potter et Maria Pymbe
1681. Oct 26 Gulielmus Holden et Hana Potter.
1684. Oct 1 Richardus Salisbury et Joan Jefford

(*To be continued.*)

* For arms of Bolsworth, see Harl MSS B M , 1390, fo 32
† The family of Iremonger formerly held the Manor of Stanbridge
‡ Afterwards Lord Altham She was the d of the Hon Charles Leigh, and died June 4th, 1684, æt 23

No. I.—PEDIGREE OF WITHIE, CO. DEVON.

Communicated by the Rev. Dr. LEE, of All Saints' Vicarage, Lambeth.

ARMS OF WITHIE (granted by William Camden in 1615).—*Per pale ermine and or, a lion salient gules.* CREST.—*Out of a ducal coronet or, a cross calvary between two wings argent.*

John Withie of Berry Norbert, co. Devon. ╤ Elizabeth, da. of Nicholas Berry of Berry Norbert, co. Devon, Esq. [Arms of Berry.—*Or, three bars gules.* Visit. Devon, 1620.]

John Jewell of Bowdon. ╤ Alice, da. of Richard Bellamy.

John Withie, son and heir. ╤ Joane, y^e da. of John Jewell of Bowdon in the Parish of Berry.

Joan, 1 da. = John Dum.

John Jewell, 2 son, Bishop of Salisbury ob. s.p.

John Jewell of Northcott in the Parish of East Downe. 1 son. ╤ Agnes, da. & heir of Richard Curcliffe of Northcott.

Joane. = | Margaret. | Anne. | Ciceley.

Jackett, 2 da. = John Reade of Berry.

Christian, 3 da. = Anthony Withie of Berry.

Ciceley. = Henry Down of Barnstable. [N.B.—Mr. Nicholas Downe was Alderman of Barnstable 8 Sept. 1620.]

Ciprian Withie. 3 son, mar. twice, ob. s.p.

Humfry, 2 son, a Captain, slaine at Ostend, s.p.

Joane, = Roger Griffin.

Annie, ob. s.p.

Jane, 3 da. = Walter Smith.

Alice, 4 da. = Hunf. Keep.

Jane, da. of Richard Nicholas of Calne, co. Wilts, gent. 1 wife. ╤ John Withie of Calne and after of Wootton. ╤ Ann, da. of Wm. Chamberlayne of Wootton, 2nd wife, widow of John Parnicheff, Rector of Wootton. ╤ John Parnicheff, son and heir of John Parnicheff, Alderman of Marlborough.

Jordan Withie, 1st son, obiit about 21. s.p.

William Withie of Calne, 2 son. ╤ Dorothey, da. of William Lewes (clerk).

Jane, 1st da. | Frances, ob. s.p. | Joane, ob. s.p.

Margaret.

Anne. ╤ Miles Hicks of London, Haberdasher.

Nicholas Hicks ╤ | John Hicks.

John Hicks. | Mary Hicks.

Margaret, da. of William Salmons of Wildheath, co. Chester, relict of Samuel Bayley of London, grocer. 2nd wife. ╤ John Withie, citizen and painterstayner of London, 3rd son, ætat. 50, 11 Feb. 1643. The arms above were confirmed to this man by Richard St. George, Clarenceux. = Rose, da. of William Tilcock of Kelborne, co. Middlesex.

Jewell, 4th son, b. 13 Dec. 1632.

John, 2nd son.

George, 3rd son.

Augustine Withy, son and heir, born 26 Aug. 1624, ob. s.p.

Alice, 1st dau. born 7 Oct. 1622, ob. 1637, s.p.

Sarah, 2nd dau., born 14 Dec. 1626, ob. s.p.

A

A

John Parnicheff, living at the Bermudies. | Richard Parnicheff, of London, ob. s.p. | Gabriel Parnicheff = of London.

Richard Parnicheff, D.D., Prebendary of Westminster Chapel and Sub-almoner to King Charles II. 1669. Buried in Westminster Abbey 2 Sept. 1673, ob. s p. Prebendary of St. Paul's, London: Archdeacon of Huntingdon; Rector of St. Mildred, Poultry, and St. Mary, Colechurch. Will dated 26 August, proved 16 Oct. 1673. = da. and heiress of Basset, bur. in Westminster Abbey 15 June, 1671. | John Parnicheff of Wales.

MONUMENTAL INSCRIPTIONS, ETC., IN THE CHURCH OF ST. PETER, AT ST. GEORGE'S, BERMUDA.*

(*Continued from p.* 354.)

In memory of Harriott Annabella, wife of Lieut.-Colonel William Lloyd, Commandant of the Royal Artillery in this garrison, who departed this life on the 26th day of July, 1830, aged 52 years.

Also of the above Lieut.-Colonel William Lloyd, R.A., who departed this life on the 26th day of May, 1831, aged 52 years.

This tablet is erected by Hugh Morris Lang, William Lang, and Jane Montgomerie Lang, Largs, N.B., to the memory of their brother John Lang, a native of Largs, Scotland, who died on board the steamer Merlin, on a voyage from St. Thomas to Bermuda, on the 25th August, 1851. Interred in the vault of Mr. John Barr.

"Blessed are the dead which die in the Lord." Farewell! Sacred to the memory of Mary, wife of Commodore Sir John Poer Beresford, Kt., on whom, during a short but highly exemplary life, Providence bestowed the greatest of its blessings, true benevolence of heart, a lively imagination governed by a sound judgment, correct and pleasing manners, an attractive person, the love of an affectionate husband, and friendship that survives the tomb; she died on the 1st of July, 1813, aged 23, and lies buried near this monument.

To the memory of Margery, the beloved wife of Dr. Joseph Stuart Hunter, and fourth daughter of Major Dunn, of Maskinongé, Canada East, who died of yellow fever at St. George's, on the 27th October, 1853, aged 25 years.

Also of Dr. Oscar Dunn, her brother, who died of pulmonary consumption, on the 15th of December, 1851, aged 28 years. This tablet is erected by a bereaved husband.

Sacred to the memory of Christopher Hyland, late a Lieutenant in H.M. 62nd Regiment of Foot, who departed this life on the 14th of November, 1817, aged 34 years and 4 months, who has left an affectionate wife and infant son to lament his loss.

To the memory of Thomas Burch Tucker, M.D., born June 4th, 1778, died May 5th, 1846. This tablet is erected as a mark of filial affection, by his son-in-law Charles H. Maréchaux, Captain in H.M.'s St. Helena Regiment, and his children Julia Maréchaux and St. George W. Tucker, M.D.

* Communicated by Lieut.-Colonel VIGORS.

To the memory of John Van Norden, Esquire, late Deputy Grand-Master of the Provincial Grand Lodge, of Bermuda, and nineteen years Mayor of the town of St George's, who departed this life, 30th September, 1823, aged 67 years In testimony of their high regard and approbation of his conduct while acting as Master, this tablet is erected by the brethren of St George's Lodge, No 266

In the adjoining churchyard lie the remains of Frederick Arabin, Lieutenant Colonel Royal Artillery, sixth son of Henry Arabin, Esq , of Moyglare, co Meath, Ireland, who while in command of H M Forces in these Islands died August 17th, 1843, in his 57th year

Eliza Arabin died in January of the same year, and is interred in Stonehouse churchyard, Devon, England This monument is erected in loving remembrance by their children " He that believeth in me, though he were dead, yet shall he live, and whosoever believeth in me shall never die" St John xi 25, 26.

Sacred to the memory of James H Scott, first clerk, Ordnance Department, Æ 33, who was drowned by the upsetting of his boat, in a terrific squall, 10th February, 1834 He was universally respected, and his melancholy fate most deeply deplored

---

At the east end near the last is a marble tablet in memory of Martha Bascome, wife of Archibald Shedden, Esq , who departed this life, January 25th, 1839, aged 66 years.

In memory of Fanny Louisa, wife of Captain E F. Hare, and daughter of Colonel W H Eden, 56th Regiment, who died at St George's of yellow fever, on the 15th of September, 1853, aged 20 years

Also of Captain E F Hare, 56th Regiment, son of Major Hare of the Retreat, Plymouth, who died at St George's, of yellow fever, on the 17th September, 1853, aged 30 years, having only survived his beloved wife 48 hours, and to whom he had been united scarcely one year "Lovely and pleasant were they in their lives, and in their death they were not divided " This tablet is erected by their affectionate parents

---

Sacred to the memory of Lieut I M T Borton, of H.M 30th Regiment, who departed this life at Bermuda, April 19th, 1838, leaving an affectionate wife to mourn his loss, and sincerely regretted by his brother officers, one of whom has erected this tablet, in testimony of a friendship which was interrupted only by death.

A handsome white marble monument, thereon the figure of a woman weeping, a plant in a vase at her feet, beside her an urn inscribed W C, and a sword, crown, etc , in her left hand she holds a roll, on which is written, " I shall go to him, but he shall not return to me." J Bacon, sculptor, London, 1798 Sacred to the memory of His Excellency William Campbell, Esquire, Governor of these Islands, and Lieut -Colonel of the 24th Regiment of Foot, who was seized with a fever, and died a few days after his arrival, December 2nd, 1796, in his 46th year Thus by one fatal stroke, the blessings of his public virtues, and the endearments of his private friendship, expired for ever, and his solitary relict, whose happiness was suspended on the tenderness of his heart, endeavours to soothe her sorrow by inscribing this marble with his much loved name

---

Juxta Conduntur Reliquiæ, Adelaidæ Louisæ, Arturi Gulielmi Twiss Conjugis, Unice Dilectæ quæ in spem resurrectionis ad vitam Æternam, obiit Junii Die Vigesimo Sexto, Anno Salutis MDCCCLII, Ætatis xxii.

Died at Bermuda, Nov 17th, 1744, in the 46th year of his age, after nine days illness of a bilious fever, The Good Governor, Alured Popple, Esq, during the course of his administrations, which, to the inconsolable grief of the inhabitants, continued but six years Of the many strangers who resorted thither for their health, the observing easily discovered in him, under the graceful veil of modesty, an understanding and abilities equal to a more important trust The gay and polite were charmed with the unaffected elegance and amiable simplicity of his manners, and all were chear'd by his hospitality and diffusive benevolence, which steadily flowed, and undisturbed, from the heart To praise according to his merit the deceased, would be but too sensible a reproach to the living, and to enumerate the many rare virtues which shone united in the Governor of that little spot, were to tell how many great talents and excellent endowments are wanting in some, whom the capriciousness of fortune exposes in a more elevated and conspicuous station

ARMS —*Quarterly, 1 and 4 Or on a bend gules three eagles displayed of the first 2 and 3 A chevron argent between three heads (?) erased of the second, impaling two coats per fess 1st, ? 2nd, Azure a lion passant gardant gules*

To the memory of Alexander George Woodford, Lieutenant 56th Regiment (third son of Lieutenant-General Sir Alexander, and Lady Woodford), who was cut off in the 29th year of his age, by yellow fever when in the performance of his regimental duties, at St George's, the 12th of September, 1853 This tablet is inscribed by his afflicted widow and parents. His remains are interred in the churchyard

(*To be continued*)

SOME NOTES ON DEVONSHIRE FAMILIES ALLIED TO HARINGTON OF WORDEN IN SHEBBEAR,

VIZ

YEO OF HEANTON AND SHEBBEAR, GAY (PROBABLY THE POET'S KINDRED), SOMERS OF NORTH TAWTON, BRENT OF NEWTON ST PETROCK AND SHEBBEAR

THE FOLLOWING ON YEO IS FROM THE OLD DIARY (see p 334)

"Robt Yeo of Heanton, in Devon Esq, married Alfrida the daughter of Sir Thos Grenvile of Stow, in Cornwall, Kt, and had two sons, viz, Wm the eldest and Robert y[e] youngest Y[e] said Robert Yeo married Juliana [? Elizabeth],* the daughter of Fulke Priddam [Prideaux] of Thuborrow, Devon Esq, and had one son called William Yeo, who married Mary, the daughter of Humphry Battin of Dunsland, in Devon, Esq, by Jane Grenvile, sister to Parson Jo Grenvile, and had one son, viz, Humphry Yeo, who married Agnes, y[e] daughter of Richard Wheeler of Buckland, in Devon, clerk, and Catharine Dennis of Prattcott (the above Richard Wheeler was son to Sir Robt Wheeler, Lord Mayor of London), and had one son Robert Yeo [Humphrey Yeo was born in January, the Saturday before Candlemas Day, 1557, and died Apr 25, 1633, and was buried in y[e] South Isle of Shebbear Church, aged 76, his son Robert Yeo was born in 1595, and died April 26th, 1665, and was buried in y[e] South Isle of Shebbeare Church, aged 70 years] Robert Yeo married Jane, y[e] Daughter of Bartholomew Thorne of Upcott in the Parish of Sheepwash, Devon, Esq, and Mary Hillersdon of Membland, whose son *William Yeo* [William Yeo was born y[e] 7th March, 1640, and died about 1712 aged near 72 years, and was buried in y[e] South Isle of Shebbeare Church] *of Worden* in y[e] Parish of Shebbear, married Margaret y[e] youngest daughter of Mr Wm Marshal of Trevigge in y[e] parish of St Gennis, in Cornwall, and had several children, of whom only two

* She is named in the will of her brother Humph Prideaux of Thewborough, dated 4th July, 1649, pr 10th Jan 1650-1

daughters survived them, Jane and Grace. Y[e] *eldest*, viz, Jane Yeo, married to Wm. Harrington, and left four children, viz, Robert, Sarah, Ann, and Maria Y[e] youngest, viz, Grace Yeo, was married to John Fortescue of St. Budeaux, gent., and left no children."

FAMILY OF YEO

EXTRACTS FROM THE PARISH REGISTER OF SHEBBEAR, CO. DEVON

Baptisms.

1591	Susan, dau'r of Humfry Yeo, gent, and Agnes,			21st July
1593	Mary, dau'r of	,,	,,	13th May
1595.	Robert, son of	,,	,,	27th July
1597.	Zenobia, dau'r of	,,	,,	6th May
1601.	Sarah, dau'r of	,,	,,	24th May
1603.	Agnes, dau'r of	,,	,,	20th May
1605.	Ferdinando, son of	,,	,,	15th Sept.
1607	Joseph, son of	,,	,,	18th Oct
1609.	George, son of	,,	,,	3rd Dec
1611	George, son of	,,	,,	5th July.
$16\frac{13}{14}$	John, son of	,,	,,	16th Jan.
1637	Wm, son of Mr Robert Yeo and Jane,			7th June.
1638	Jane, dau'r of	,,	,,	24th July
1639	Elizabeth, dau'r of	,,	,,	15th Oct.
1641	Wm, son of	,,	,,	25th March.
1642.	Ursula, dau'r of	,,	,,	2d Nov.
1644	Agnes, dau'r of Joseph Yeo and Jane			6th June
1646	Marie, dau'r of	,,	,,	12th Nov.
1651	John, son of	,,	,,	26th Oct.
1653.	Elizabeth, dau'r of	,,	,,	21st Dec
1656.	William, son of	,,	,,	16th Oct
1659.	Jane, dau'r of	,,	,,	15th March
1670	Geo, son of John and Eliza Yeo			26th Dec.
1672	Grace, dau'r of William Yeo, gent, and Margarett,			24th Sept.
1673	Martial or Marshall, } son of	,,	,,	18th Sept.

Burials

1576	Mary,* the wife of William Yeo, gent	14th Nov
$158\frac{6}{7}$	Humfrey Yeo, buried	9th March
1610.	George, son of Humfrey Yeo, gent	28th May.
$16\frac{10}{11}$	William Yeo, gent	19th March
1633.	Humfrey Yeo, gent	26th April.
1642.	Jane, wife of Mr Robert Yeo	2d Nov.
1642.	Elizabeth, dau'r of Mr Robert Yeo	4th Dec
1670	Jane Yeo (wife of Joseph)	5th Oct
1672	George Yeo	27th Dec.
1676	Nobe (*sic* probably for Zenobia)	13th Nov
$167\frac{7}{8}$	Jane Yeo	24th Feb
1682.	ffardinardo (*sic*) Yeo	18th Nov.
1685	Wm. Yeo	1st June
1686	Wm Yeo, buried	26th Dec.
1689	Joseph Yeo, gent	2d Oct.

* On the fly-leaf of Shebbear Parish Register book there is written—"*Mary Yeo* was the dau'r and coh'r of Hump Battin, Esq of Dunsland and Kate his wife dau'r of Jn° Carminowe *Philippo*, the other coheiress, married 1st, Jno Arscott, Esq, to whom she brought Dunsland, and 2ndly, in the private chapel there, privately, William Holland, a younger son of the Hollands of Upcott

1711. Mr. Wm. Yeo, buried 4th Oct.
17$\frac{13}{14}$. Mary Yeo 24th March.
1718. Sarah Yeo 13th Dec.
1721. Jno. Yeo 19th July.
1765. Grace Yeo, buried 14th Nov.
1767. Barnard Yeo 3rd May.

N.B.—A Mem. made in 'The Old Diary,' says—Margarett, the daughter of Robt. Yeo, gent., was buryed at St. Gennys', Aug. 18th, 1708.

Marriages.

1612. Wm. Maynard and Mary, dau'r of Humfrey Yeo, gent., 27th Jan.
1641. Joseph Yeo and Jane Giffard, 23^{d} June.
1648. Mr. John Blight and Mrs. Katharine Yeo, 11th March.
1677. William Yeo and Mary Smale, 1st May.
1682. Jo. Cudmore and Elizabeth Yeo, 16th Nov.
1711. Mr. Jno. Fortescue and Mrs. Grace Yeo, 31st July.
1720. Jno. Yeo of Merton and Mary Short, 12th Feb.
1723. Jno. Andrew and Mary Yeo, widow, 29th May.
1726. Robert Yeo and Elizabeth Branch.

NOTES OF "GAY," (*believed to be of the Poet's kin,*)
SHEBBEAR CHURCH REGISTER, N. DEVON.

Marriages.

1698. James Gawman and Margery Gay, 8th March.
1715. Xtopher Harvy and Agnes Gay, 17th May.

Burials.

1624. Brute, son of Wm. and Margarett Gay, 5th Aug.
164$\frac{0}{1}$. Wm. Gaye, 23 Jan. }
" Margaret Gaye, 30 Jan. }

BRIEF PEDIGREE SHEWING SOMERS OF NORTH TAWTON AND HARINGTON OF WORDEN, CO. DEVON.

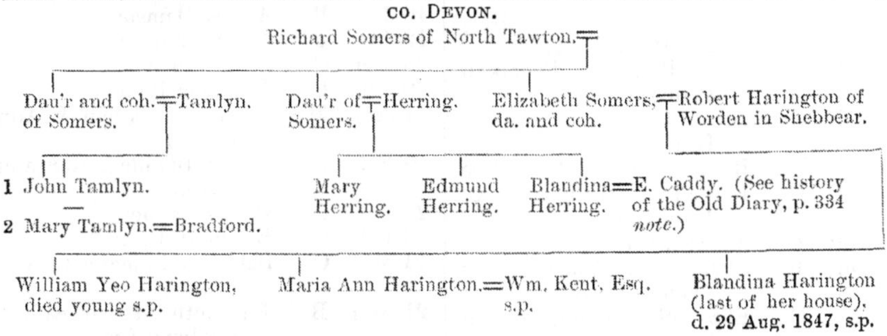

FAMILY OF BRENT.*

EXTRACTS FROM SHEBBEAR REGISTERS.

Baptism.

173$\frac{2}{3}$. William, son of John and Dorothy Brent 14 Feb.

Marriages.

1698. Emanuell Deane (or Dene) and Mary Brynt mar^{d} 9 Nov.
1765. Mr. Wm. Brent and Miss Susanna Harrington, mar. 24 July.
1769. Mr. Hugh Brent of Newton St. Petrock and Miss Ebbet Brent, mar. 29 May.
1800. William Brent and Elizabeth Perkin, mar. 30th March.

* Registers furnished to Rev. F. J. Poynton by the kindness of Rev. J. Ingle Dredge.

The Registers

OF THE

Parish Church of Stock, Essex.

1563

13 Ap	C *	Charles Hedgman s to John Hedgman
8 May	B *	Edwarde Tavernor s to E † Tavernor
15 May	B	Charles Hedgman s to Jo Hedgman
1 June	B	Robt Marwood
7 June	M *	Will'm Whytinge & Elizabeth Luckyn
13 June	C	Thomas Hils s to Henry Hils
20 June	M	Thomas Saveall & Margarett E( )‡
10 July	M.	Roger Boswell & Elizabeth Prints
15 July	C	Joane Hare d to Thomas Hare
18 July	M	Richard Prints & Johan Foe
18 July	C	Benjamyn Damson s to Thomas Damson
23 July	B	Agnes Prints
25 July	B	Christopher Clark s to Thomas Clark
15 Aug	C	Elizabeth Dudley d to Peter Dudley
25 Aug	B	*Margery* (?) Blande s § to Will'm Blande

* From 1563 to 1580 the Baptisms Marriages and Burials are all mixed from 1581 each is entered under its own division C means Christenings, M Marriages and B Burials The name of the Curate who made these entries is written at the bottom of each right-hand page, viz, ' per me JOHAN NEWTON, Curat " His last entry is 30 March 1623

† means that the word is omitted in the Register

‡ ( ) means that the word is illegible

§ "s" is in the Register

5 Sep	B	Elizabeth Dudley
2 Oct	C	John Sweetinge s to John Sweetinge
1 Nov	C	Henry Saveall s to Thomas Saveall
11 Nov	B	Robert Harnes
12 Nov	B	Robt Brett
8 Dec	C	Thomas Bellingham & Ellyn Bellingham
19 Dec	C	Elizabeth Boninge
22 Dec	B	Henry Saveall s to Thomas Saveall
10 Jan	B	Agnes Damson
12 Jan	B	Johan' Stamar
20 Jan	C	John ffynch
20 Jan	C	Dorothie Ram
31 Jan	M	Thomas ffeikman & Anne ( )
6 Feb	M	Will'm Blande & Margarett Taylor
26 Feb	C	Denys Palmer
26 Feb	C	Elizabeth Carr
14 Mar	C	Baldwyn Stamar s to Baldwyn Stamar
21 Mar	B	Elizabeth Stamar wife to Baldwyn Stamar

1564

16 Ap	C	Peter Dale s to Xofer Dale
16 Ap	C	Thomas Parnell s to John Parnell
19 Ap	B	Elizabeth Maybury
2 May	C	Edward Taylor & Barbara Taylor, twins
21 May	C	Loane s to Rich Loane
18 June	C	Margaret Sterlinge d to John Sterlinge

Date		Entry
25 June	C	Baldwyn Crosley s to John Crosley
25 June	M	Thomas Britten & Ellyn Dale
9 July	M	Nicholas *Elie?* & Amye ( )
9 July	M	John Lewes & Alice Chervell
16 July	C	Elizabeth Swalow d to Will'm Swalow
30 July	C	Helyn Osborne d to John Osborne
23 Aug	B	Baldwyn Crosley s to John Crosley
Nov	B	Edward Taylor s to Taylor
19 Nov	C	John & Margarett Amatt, twins
23 Nov	C	Margarett Rawlyn d to Thomas Rawlyn
6 Jan	C	Joane Bondock d of Rich Bondock
7 Jan	C	Thomas Neward s to John Neward
19 Jan	B	Joane Bondock d to Rich Bondock
31 Jan	B	Elizabeth Manninge wife to Robt Manninge
4 Feb	C	John Monks to Robt Monk
8 Feb	B	Joane wife to Rich Loane
5 Mar	B	Helyn Wheatley d to ( ) Wheatley
23 Mar	C	Humfrey Whytinge s to John Whytinge
23 Mar	C	John Botesworth s to John Botesworth

1565

Date		Entry
8 Ap	C	Thomas Bretton s to Thomas Bretton of Bulvan
12 Ap	B	Anne Cherley *alias* Ley the wife to ffrancees Cherley
15 Ap	B	Joane Plome
15 Ap	C	Thomas Lees of Will'm Lee
22 Ap	B	Margaret Saveringe, wydow
24 Ap	B	Ellyn Philip
8 June	B	John Cunsingham
18 July	B	Harman Newman
4 Aug	C	Joane Blande d of Will'm Blande
12 Aug	C	Catharyn Hare d to Thomas Hare
30 Sep	C	Joane Bushe d to Nicholas Bushe
30 Sep	C	Howman d to George Howman
11 Nov	M	William Felix & Johan' Tendrings
23 Nov	B.	Marke Porter s. to John Porter
20 Jan	C	Tomson Younge d to Humfrey Younge
27 Jan	C	Susanna Bonninge d to Robt Bonninge
15 Mar	B	Elizabeth Huppie
15 Mar	B	John Martindale
17 Mar.	C	Margaret Crosley ye d of John Crosley

1566

Date		Entry
31 Mar	C	Will'm Dryver
9 Ap	B	Humfrey Whitinge
14 Ap	B	Joane Reve wife to John Reve
21 Ap	B	Jo'han Blande d to Will'm Blande
28 June	B	William Wheatley s to Thomas Wheatley
30 June	M	Richard Loane & Margaret Humfrey
8 July	B	Joane Lyndsell d to Thomas Linsell
24 Sep	M	Henrie Legatt & Katharyn ffanne
15 July	B	John Kynge
26 Dec	C	Mary Carr d to Robt Carr
19 Jan	C	Johan' Lynsell d to Thomas Lynsell
25 Jan	C	Thomas Bondock s to Richard Bondock
7 Feb	C	Tomazin & Katharyn Wyttenn ds to Will'm Wittenn
11 Feb	B	Joane ffrances wife to Adrian ffrances
1 Mar	B	Katharyn Wyttenn d to Will'm Wyttenn
19 Ap	B	Anne Sterlinge*

1567

Date		Entry
19 Ap	B	Anne Sterlinge*
19 Ap	B	Susana Lone
18 May	C	Raphe Boxer
28 May	B	Tomazin Younge
1 June	C	Margery Beterman
11 June	B	Osmund Hasteler
15 June	C	Thomas Crosley
21 June	C	Joane Osborne
19 Sep	C	Charles Yonge
20 Sep	B	Judith Stile
28 Nov	B	Alice Clark
24 Ap	B	Richard Whalley s to *Philip?* Whaley of London*

* Entered twice in the Register

1568

24 Ap	B.	Richard Whally s to *Philip ?* Whally, londoner
1 May	B	Philip Tyrryll s to Henry Tyrryll, Knight
2 May	C	Roberye Palmer d to Humfrey Palmer
30 May	C	Barbara Sterlinge d to John Sterlinge
29 June	B	Roberye Palmer
27 July	C	Briget Boninge
22 Aug	C	Stephen Muncke
22 Aug	C	Xpofer Hanckyn s to ( ) Hanckyn
27 Aug	B	Thomas Poverley
12 Sep	B	Xpofer Hanckyn
20 Sep	C	Mary Dale
23 Sep	B	Edmunde Saveringe
7 Oct	C	Charles Hatter s to Thomas Hatter
24 Oct	C	Dorothie Hare d to Thomas Hare
Nov	C	Alexander Johnson
14 Dec	C	Anne Taverner d. to Edward Taverner
14 Dec	B	John Damson
15 Dec	C	Osborne s to John Osborne
19 Dec	C	Charles Palmer s to Simon Palmer
19 Dec	C	Margaret Lone d to Rich Lone
4 Jan	B	Humfrey Yonge
15 Jan	B	Will'm Heywood
30 Jan	B	Alice Carr yᵉ wife of Robert Carr
30 Jan	C	Mary Rawlyn yᵉ d of Thomas Rawlyn
7 Mar	C	Mary Bondocke
19 Mar	C	Anne Nuttinge
19 Mar	C	John Stonard s to Will'm Stonard

1569

31 Mar	B	Betterys Twedye, wydow
31 May	B	Edward Radley
7 Aug	C	Agnes Browne d to Robt Browne
4 Sep	C	William Lynsoll s to Thomas Lynsoll
24 Sep	C	George Ram s to Jeffery Ram
2 Oct	B	Alice Ram wife to Jeffery Ram
1 Nov	C	Mary Hally d to John Hally
6 Nov	C.	Elizabeth Hanckyn
26 Nov	M	Robt Carr & Joane Drane
12 Nov	M	Philip Freman & Rachell Crosse

1570

7 May	C	Joane Parnell d to John Parnell
11 June	C	John Palmer s to Humfrey Palmar
11 June	C	Margaret Norham d to Rich Norham
29 June	C	Roberye Freman d to Philip Freman
31 Aug	B	Joan Martindal
	C	Judith Carr d to Robert Carr
30 Sep	B	Margaret Wallehead
1 Oct	C	Joan Dale d to xpofer Dale
20 Oct	B	Agnes Whitehead
29 Oct	C	John Richardson s to John Richardson
29 Oct	C	Will'm Hutt s to William Hutt
8 Nov	B	Thomas Dameson
17 Nov	C	Margaret Stones a begger's child
30 Nov	C	Will'm Lowe s to Richard Lowe (?)
5 Dec	C	Will'm Paine s to Thomas Paine
24 Feb	B	Will'm Wagstaff s. of John Wagstaff
27 Feb	B	Thomas Pale
7 Mar.	B	Robert Canell

1571

31 Mar	B	Richard Barbor
8 Ap	C	Judith Wilson
11 Ap	B	Thomas Glascock
16 Ap	B	John Copland
19 May	B	John Blakemore
16 May	B	Henry Stonard
22 May	B.	Anne Boxer
23 May	B	Symon Palmar
10 June	C	Veyle . to Roger Veall
24 June	M	Robt Oldy & Margaret Moncke
1 July	M	John Woodcocke & Alice Wilson
1 July	B	Richard Tabor
1 July	B	Anne Browne
5 July	B	Roberye Whiskard wife to Charles Wiskard
28 July	B	Margaret Alande
29 July	M.	Tytys Bull & Margaret Tabor

30 Sep. C. Dorothie Boninge
30 Sep. C. Agnes Ram
30 Sep. C. Margaret Fe(r)kman d. to Thomas Ferkman
29 Dec. C. Thomas Hare s. to Thomas Hare
1 Jan. C. Margaret Lowe
4 Jan. B. Thomas Hare
5 Feb. B. Roger Boxwell
15 Mar. C. Judith Carr

1572.

10 Ap. B. Robert Carr
.. May B. Thomas Venter
24 May B. Johan' Amatt, wydow
14 Dec. B. Henrie Savell
14 Dec. C. Humfrey Browne s. to Robert Browne
24 Dec. C. Phinenna James d. to John James
2 Feb. C. George Bush s. to Nicholas Bush
9 Feb. C. Magdalen Dale d. to Xxofer Dale
9 Feb. C. John Osborne s. to John Osborne
15 Feb. B. Richard Heminge
26 Feb. B. John Humfrey

1573.

5 Ap. C. William Bover s. to J. Bover
7 May B. Thomas Hare
12 May B. Dorothie Bright wife to Thomas Bright
1 Nov. C. Alice Wilson d. to Leonard Wilson
1 Nov. C. John Crosley s. to John Crosley
29 Nov. C. Jeffery Boxer s. to Thomas Boxer
27 Dec. C. Christofer Parnell s. to John Parnell
17 Jan. C. William Hanckyn s. to Edward Hanckyn
2 Feb. C. Humfrey Beall s. to Roger Beall
11 Feb. B. Thomas Lyndsoll
12 Feb. C. Susan Ram d. to Jefery Ram
6 Mar. B. John Robiont
12 Mar. B. William Whitinge
13 Mar. B. John Osborne
17 Mar. B. Johan Robiont, wydow

1574.

22 Ap. B. William Glascock
5 May B. Humfrey Browne
6 May C. Elynor Boning d. to Robt. Bonninge
9 May C. Thomas Jennous (?) s. to William Jennous (?)
10 May M. Thomas Rigs & Mary Hare
25 July B. John Greene
7 Aug. C. Thomas Ellyott s. to Henry Ellyott
7 Aug. C. Sterlinge s. to John Sterlinge ye younger
8 Aug. B. Richard Bondock
7 Oct. B. Robert Humfrey
16 Oct. B. Sylvester Walles
16 Oct. B. Agnes Whiskard
1 Nov. C. Elizabeth Kellie
30 Dec. C. Henry Martyn s. of Thomas Martyn
2 Jan. C. Mary Hare d. of Rowland Hare
3 Jan. C. Jane Palmar d. of Robert Palmar
17 Jan. B. Margaret Hare ye wife of Rowland Hare
17 Jan. M. Jeffery (. . . .) & Ellyn Osborne

1575.

30 Mar. C. Mary Rigs d. of Thomas Rigs
24 Ap. C. George Grante s. of George Grante
24 Ap. B. Katharyn Wagstaffe
25 May M. Thomas Perhie & Briget Linsoll
7 June B. Rowland Hare
5 June M. Thomas Wise & Annys Childerley
7 June B. Rowland Hare
30 June M. Jefrey Tabor & Allice ffrances
6 July B. Margarett Loane ye wife of John Loane
4 Sep. M. Abraham Drane & Agnes Taylor
13 July B. John Whitinge
11 Sep. M. John Perryn & Johan' Luckyn
17 Dec. B. Thomas Wise
2 Dec. M. John Cartrell & Catharyn Bondock
1 Jan. C. William Vttinge s. of William Vttinge
1 Jan. C. Will'm Barker s. of Thomas Barker
7 Jan. C. Thomas Hoxton s. of John Hoxton of Buttsbury

Burials

1684. Rebecca Brynt, 23[d] Nov.
16$\frac{89}{90}$ Hugh Brynt, 6th Jan
1773 Mr. John Brent, buried 4 Oct
1780. Susannah Brent, buried 20th Oct.
1801 Mr John Brent, buried 3[d] June
1812. Elizabeth, wife of Hugh Brent, gent, aged 40, 10th Jan

NEWTON ST PETROCK

Marriages.

1720 Hugh Brent and Dorothy Bowman, mar. 24th May
1762 John Brent and Elizabeth Broad „ 11 Sept
179$\frac{2}{3}$. Thos Burnard of Bideford and Mary Judd Brent, by lic, 18 Jan
1800 Bryan Reed of Gt Torrington and Dorothy Brent, „ 17th April

Baptisms

1688. John, s of *John* Brent (of Shebbere) and *Mary*, bapt 22 March
1691. Hugh, s of „ „ „ 30 Dec.
1694. Hugh, s of „ „ „ 31 Oct
1697 Mary, d[r] of „ „ „ 25 Aug.
1721 Mary, d[r] of Hugh and Dorothy Brent 3 May
1724. John, s. of „ „ 13 Dec.
1733 Dorothy, d[r] of „ „ 6 June
1735 Hugh, son of „ „ 20 Aug.
1738. Rebecca, d[r] of John and Dorothy Brent 15 Feb
1741 John, son of Hugh and Dorothy Brent 23 July
1762 John, son of John Brent and Elizabeth 23 Dec.
1764. Dorothy, d[r] of „ „ 13 Nov
1766 Hugh, son of „ „ 21 Nov
„ Dorothy, d[r] of Wm Brent and Susanna (Harington) 18 Nov
1769 Mary, d[r] of „ „ 8 March.
1770 John, s of Hugh Brent and Ebot 26 Feb.
1770 Wm, s of John Brent and Elizabeth, bapt 18 July
1771. Hugh, son of Hugh Brent and Ebot „ 3 July
1773 John, „ „ „ 20 Aug.
1773 Mary, d[r] of John Brent and Elizabeth 16 Sept.
1775. Dorothy, d[r] of Hugh Brent and Ebot 15 Sept.
1778. Rebeckah, d[r] of „ „ 15 Feb
1781 Rebeckah, d[r] of „ „ 15 June.

Burials

1740. John, son of Hugh and Dorothy Brent, buried 24 Dec.
1742 Hugh Brent, „ 25 Aug.
1768 Dorothy Brent, widow „ 13 June
1770 John Brent, son of Hugh Brent and Ebot, buried 31 May.
1778 Rebeckah Brent, an infant „ 4 Oct
1785 John Brent „ 5 Aug.
1797 Elizabeth Brent „ 20 Nov
1799. Wm Brent „ 26 Feb.
1820. Mrs. Ibbot Brent, aged 83 and ten months „ 15 Jan.
1821 Hugh Brent, aged 85 years „ 1 March

LANGTREE, CO DEVON

Marriages

1688. John Brunt* of Shebbear and Mary Heaman of Frithelstocke. 23 May
1722. John Brent of Shebbear and Dorothy Smale, 8th June
1813 Hugh Brent of Shebbear, wid[r] & gent, and Mary Ley of this Parish, by lic. 5 May.

* Brunt in the Register, but the Newton St Petrock baptisms prove that it should be Brent.

Burials

1775 Mrs Dorothy Brent of Shebbear, bur 4 Dec
1782 Dorothy Brent of Shebbear 26 Jan
1788 Rebecca Brent 12 April
1796 Rebecca Brent of Newton 9 Nov.

MONUMENTAL INSCRIPTIONS, NEWTON ST PETROCK

1 Nave, north wall —To the memory of Hugh Brent of Slew in this parish, who died the 26th day of February, 1821, aged 85 y[rs], also of Ebbett his wife, who died the 21st day of Jan[y] 1820, aged 83 years

2 S Aisle, south wall —Sacred to the memory of William Brent of Lane in this Parish, who died 21st Feb 1799, aged 67 y[rs].

3 S Aisle, south wall —To the memory of John Brent of Down in this parish, who died 18th day of February, 1837, aged 63 y[rs], also of Wilmot his wife, who died the 10th day of Feb 1837, aged 57 years

SHEBBEAR.

Nave S wall —"Sacred to the memory of Hugh Brent of Binworthy in this Parish, who died 23rd Dec 1811, aged 73 Also of Elizabeth his wife, who died 7th Jan[y] 1812, aged 40 years Also of Mary his second wife, who died the 19th day of December, 1811, aged 56 years

Burial of Mary Parkins, 5th Feb 169$\frac{2}{3}$ Rich[d] Parkins, 15th March, same year

(*To be continued*)

ABSTRACT OF THE LAST WILL OF LADY DOUGLAS SHEFFIELD, THE REPUDIATED WIFE OF ROBERT DUDLEY, EARL OF LEICESTER *

But few notices are recorded by heralds and historians of the eventful life of the Lady Douglas Sheffield—as she was commonly called—the repudiated wife of Robert Dudley, Earl of Leicester Almost all that we know of her is contained in Camden's 'Annals of the Reign of Elizabeth,' Gervase Holles's 'Memoirs of the Holles Family,' and Dugdale's 'Abstracts (see his '*Warwickshire*' and '*Baronage*') of the Depositions and Judgment in the Court of Star Chamber in a suit commenced in February, 1603-4, by Lettice, widow of the Earl of Leicester, against Sir Robert Dudley, Kt, and Alice his wife, the Lady Douglas Sheffield (then wife of Sir Edward Stafford, Kt), mother of the said Sir Robert Dudley, Sir Thomas Leigh (father of Alice Lady Dudley), and others

After the close of those proceedings in Easter term, 3 Jac 1605 the only further mention of her is made in a News letter of John Chamberlain to Dudley Carleton, under date of 16 December, 1608, wherein he remarks "that the old Lady Sheffield is dead"

The following is a summary of the information derived from these sources —Lady Douglas Sheffield was born about the year 1545, eldest daughter of Lord William Howard, Lord Howard of Effingham, by his second wife, Margaret, second daughter of Sir Thomas Gamage, Kt, of Coity, co Glamorgan She married first, about 1562, when she was seventeen years old, John, second Baron Sheffield, by whom she had a son and daughter, viz, Edmund, third Baron, and Elizabeth, who became the second wife of Thomas Butler, Earl of Ormonde The Earl of Leicester—attracted by Lady Sheffield's youth and beauty—had an intrigue with her in her husband's life-time, and after Lord Sheffield's death,—which occurred in December, 1568, not without suspicion of poison,—she entered into a contract of marriage with the Earl of Leicester, in Cannon Row, Westminster, and two years after they were

* Communicated by B W GREENFIELD, Esq.

married at Esher, Surrey, according to the rite of the Church of England, about the year 1572, the Earl binding her to secrecy for fear of the Queen's displeasure In 1573, she gave birth, at Shene, near Richmond, Surrey, to their only son, afterwards Sir Robert Dudley, Kt Walter Devereux, Earl of Essex,—dying in September, 1576,—the Earl of Leicester, being captivated by the beauty of Lettice, the widowed Countess of Essex, tried to persuade Douglas, his wife, to disclaim her marriage with him, offering to settle £700 per annum upon her if she would do so, and to give her a further sum of £1000 if she would give up the custody of their son The consequence of her refusal was that the Earl of Leicester repudiated his marriage with her, and married the Countess of Essex at Wanstead House, Essex, in September 1578, and so terrified his repudiated wife that she, for protection, and the security of her life, contracted marriage with Sir Edward Stafford Kt, of Chebsey, the Queen's Ambassador at the French Court Of this marriage there does not appear to have been any issue, and she died in December, 1608

To these particulars, I am able to add the following —In ADDITIONAL MS 15,506, in the Brit Museum, are three letters, dated in October, 1594, from Lady Sheffield and her husband, Sir Edward Stafford, addressed to Sir Julius Cæsar, then Judge of the Court of Admiralty, which throw a ray of light on her life No 323, without date, is written from Richmond, (probably from her house at Shene, where her son Robert Dudley was born), by "*Dougless Sheffield*," inviting Dr Cæsar to go down to have an interview with her own brother upon her affairs, and offering the use of her horses for the journey, and that he can obtain them at her house at Westminster.

No 368, dated 16 October, 1594, is in the handwriting of Sir Edward Stafford, and signed by both himself and his wife, "*Dougless Sheffield*" Therein, Sir Edward asks—in the names of "*my wife and I*"—Sir Julius Cæsar to interest himself with his father-in-law, the Lord Mayor (Martin), to shew a favour to a prisoner in Newgate, one "*oolde*" (old) Captain Moffet, that his friends may be allowed to visit and speak with him

No 456, dated from Drury House, 22 October, 1594, is from Sir Edward Stafford, thanking Dr Cæsar for his attention to Sir Edward's and his wife's request, and stating that his wife is at Highgate The dating from Drury House is explained by the fact that his sister Elizabeth Stafford, one of the Ladies o. the Queen's Bed-chamber, was widow of Sir William Drury, Kt, of Hawsted, to whom she was married in the Royal Chapel at Greenwich

Both Sir Edward Stafford and his wife, Lady Sheffield, were buried in the parish church of St Margaret's, Westminster, as is shewn by the following extracts from the Burials Register of that Church —

1604[-5] February 5th ✠ *Sir Edward Stafford, Knight* ✠
1608 December 11th *The Lady Dugleys Sheaffeilde*

Her last Will has never been published in type, and seems, hitherto, to have escaped the notice of genealogists I discovered it among the Wills registered in the Court of the Commissary of the Dean and Chapter of Westminster All its chief points of interest are contained in the following abstract

DOWGLAS LADY SHEFFIELD, in health of body and mind, make this my Will To be buried at Rigate (Reigate, Surrey) with my father and mother, or in the parish Church of Westminster (*sic*), by my sister Dudley,* as shall seem good to my children and my executor To the poor of Kenelworth £5, and to Timothy Delayne the preacher there £4 To my beloved son the right honorable Edmund, Lord Sheffield† (some great chairs of silk needle-

* Mary Howard, married 1st, as third wife, to Edward Sutton, Lord Dudley, who died 1586, and was buried in St Margaret's Westminster, married 2nd, Richard Mompesson Esq She died 21 Aug 1600, and was buried in the same church where a monument was erected to her memory

† Third Lord Sheffield, K G, created Earl of Mulgrave, 7 Feb 1 Car I 1625-6 He died 6 October 1646, aged 80.

work, etc) I give to my honorable and beloved son Sir Robert Dudley, Kt (a black velvet bed, etc). To my daughter-in-law Lady Ursula Sheffield* (a velvet gown with buttons of pearl) To my daughter Lady Elizabeth Swift,† whom I brought up from infancy (chairs, etc). To my daughter Mrs Frances Fairfax,‡ (a great chair, etc) To my daughter Mistress Marie Sheffeild,|| a border of gold pearl and stone of seventeen pieces whereof eight be rubies and diamonds and pearl (etc). To my beloved friend the Lady Waller, my hatband To my friend Mr Crawshawe, preacher of the Temple (a bed, etc) To William Lenthall, my old servant, my silver candlestick To Mrs Salisbury § To Mary Morton my woman I give my body linen to Mrs Savile and Mrs Salisbury and my two maids to be divided into four parts one part to Marie Morton, one part to Mrs Savile, and the other two parts equally between Mrs Salisbury and my two maids To Humfry Browne my servant £20 over his wages, and to my other servants half a year's wages extra To my woman Saule a kirtle To Mary Turner my ancient. Whereas I have certain Jewels mortgaged to Lenthall, my will is that my executors shall redeem the same All Residue to William Crawshawe, preacher, and I make him executor of this my Will, and Edmund Lord Sheffeild my son, and Sir Edward Swift, Kt,¶ overseers of the same. Dated 14 September, 1608 I give to my beloved niece Mrs Diana Drurie** a carknett† | with rubies, diamonds and pearle, which is in Lenthall's hands DOUGLAS SHEFFIELD Register ELSAM, folio 575

N B.—In the Act Book, folio 135, the place for the Probate of this Will is left blank the preceding Probate is dated 1 July, 1609, and that following, 30 June, 1609

WILLIAMS—In Prendergast's 'Cromwellian Settlement of Ireland,' p 433, is given the name of "John Williams, ffeltmaker," recorded as No 919 in the "List of Adventurers' who advanced money towards the War Fund, and were repaid in land John Williams subscribed £50, and received therefor lands in Monaghan Co called—either then or subsequently—"The Groves" This John Williams was from a family in Glamorganshire, Wales. I will be very grateful for any information as to his descent, or other particulars regarding his family in Wales

St Paul, U S.A J. FLETCHER WILLIAMS.

---

* Ursula her eldest son's first wife daughter of Sir Robert Tyrwhitt of Ketilby, co Lincoln

† Her granddaughter Elizabeth Sheffield, married 1st to Sir Edward Swift of Rotherham, co York, and 2nd to Sir John Bourchier, Kt

‡ Her granddaughter Frances Sheffield, married to Sir Philip Fairfax of Steeton, co York, Kt

§ Her granddaughter who married, about 1608, Ferdinando 2nd Lord Fairfax

|| This was Magdalene Salisbury who according to the sentence pronounced in Easter Term, 1605, in the Court of Star Chamber asserted that she was present at Lady Sheffield's marriage with the Earl of Leicester and for which assertion she was fined £100 and condemned to be ever after held suspected touching the marriage and legitimation of Sir Robert Dudley Kt the son of Lady Sheffield by the Earl of Leicester

¶ Husband of her granddaughter Elizabeth Sheffield

** Diana Drury was niece of Lady Sheffield's husband, Sir Edward Stafford, being the third daughter of Sir William Drury, Kt, of Hawsted Suffolk who was slain in a duel by Sir John Borough, Kt in 1589, by his wife Elizabeth Stafford Diana Drury in April, 1615, became, with her two elder sisters Frances, Lady Wray of Glentworth and Elizabeth, wife of William, Lord Burghley (afterwards 2nd Earl of Exeter) one of the three coheirs of the Drury estates by the death without issue of her only brother, Sir Robert Drury, Kt In December 1616, she married Sir Edward Cecil (brother of her sister's husband, Lord Burghley) and brought to her husband a fortune of £10 000 or £12 000 She was his second wife In 1625, he was created Baron Cecil of Putney, and in 1626 Viscount Wimbledon Lady Wimbledon died without issue and was buried at Wimbledon 5 May, 1631

†† Carcanet a necklace or bracelet

EXTRACTS FROM THE PARISH REGISTERS OF TODDINGTON, CO. BEDS

Communicated by F. A BLAYDES, Hockliffe Lodge, Leighton Buzzard

Baptisms

1540	Nov 17	William, sone of Henry Burye *
1544	Oct 10.	Agnis Burye was *buried* ? baptized
1546	June 30	Henrye Burye wasse baptized
1552	Nov 9.	Richard Johnsonn, sone of Richard Johnson.
1561.	June 24	An da to Humphrey† Burye, Gent
1563	July 24.	Joahne, da to Wm Dawson ‡
1564	Mar. 27	Margaret, da to Richd Gill
1565.	. 27	Richard, sone to Humphrie Burie, gent
1566	Feb 3	Jane, da to Richd Johnson, gent
1567	Aug. 6	George, sone to Humphry Burie, gent
1568.	Feb 5.	, sone of Humphrey Burie, gent
1571.	Ju 10	Elizabeth, da to Huphry Burie, gent
1571		Joahne, da to Wm Dawson
1573	Nov 20	Henrie, sone to Wm Sage, minstr
1574	Oct 21	Thomas, sone to Wm Dawson.
1574	Nov 18	Blandina, da to Huphrie Burie, gent
1574.	Feb 19	Phebie Sage, da to Alexandr Sage.
1575	Feb 2	Bridgett, da to Huphrie Burie, gent
1576	June 23	. , da to Wm Sage
1578	Sep 29	Matye, da to Humphrie Burie, gent
1578	Mar 15	Susana, da to Wm Sage.
1579	April 1	John, sone to Wm Dawson
1579	Mar	Audrey, da to Robte Smith, gent
1581	June ? 5.	Marie, da to Humphrie Burie, gent
1581.	Nov 6	Grace, da to Robte Smith, genr
1582	July 23	John, sone to William Sage.
1583	Nov 24	Willm , sone to Willm Sage
1583	Feb 26	Susana, da to Humphrie Burie, gent
1584.	May 22	Thoms , sone to Richd Johnson, gent
1585	April 18	Samwell, sone to Wm Sage, minister
1586	April 10	Peter, sone to Richd Johnson, gent
1587	Sep 13	? *Myles*, sone to Richard Johnson, gent
1588	Nov. 17.	Marie, da to Richard Johnson
1591.	Jan 16	Pheby, daughter to Wm Sage
1593	Jan	Elizabeth, da to Gregory Shawe
1596	Sep. 5	Mary vel dynis Rowley, da to John Rowley
1597.	Oct	Marie, da to John Crofte, esquier.
1598	Dec 20	John, sone to John Crofte, esquier
1599.	Aug . .	Elizabeth Butt, da to Cuthberd B
1602	April 11	Anne, da of Cutbert But
1602	April 29	Alice Collop, da of John Collop,§ gent.
1604.	Feb 17	Jane, da of Cutbert But
1605	Sep. 10	Edward, sonne of William Brett

* A branch of the family of that name of Bury Hall co Lanc

† I should be glad to know which Humphrey this is, and the names of his parents, wife, etc In the 'Visitation of Bedfordshire, 1566,' there are two Humphreys mentioned, but I am unable to identify the Burys in these extracts with the pedigree, as the names of the children of Humphrey Bury of Toddington as set out in the Visitation, do not answer to the names of those of Humphrey Bury above mentioned Can any genealogist kindly assist me?

‡ William Dawson mar Margaret Bury, June 18, 1562.

§ John Collop mar. An Bury, April 22 1589

(*To be continued.*)

STURMY AND STOKES

The following entries are from an octavo Bible printed 1606, now in my possession.—H. ASTLEY WILLIAMS.

Katherin Sturmy eldest daughter of Thomas Sturmy borne 13° Junij 1638 being thursday & chrystened 20° eiusd'm mensis Sr Jo^n Melton godfather Aunte Peacocke & Mother Townley godmothers

Katherin Sturmy second daughter of Thomas Sturmy borne 13° Augusti A^no D^ni 1639 A^no gr Rs Car nunc Anglie &c 15° being tuesday betweene 7 & 8 of the clocke in the evening Chrystened 19° eiusdem mensis Augusti in St Gyles in the fields Mr Wm Hall godfather, Mother Townley & Mrs Partridge godmothers

Thomas Sturmy eldest sonne of Thos Sturmy borne 15° Julij A^no D^ni 1642 A^no gr Rs Car &c 18°, being fryday betweene 11 & 12 of the clocke at night, chrystened 20° eiusdem mensis Julij 1642 Mr Tho ffoster of Iden & M^r ffrauncis Rowdon godfathers & Mrs Mary White godmother In St Clements Danes

ffrauncis my third daughter borne 8° Augusti A^no D^ni 1643 being tuesday att a quarter befor 12 att noone & christened 14° eiusd'm mensis in St Clements Danes Bro ffrancis Townley godfather by Mr Tho Rowdon's deputie M^rs ffrancis Parker & sister Sturmy godmothers

John my second sonne borne 13° Aprilis A^no D^ni 1646 halfe an houre past 10 of the clock att night & christened fryday the first of May in St Clements Danes Bro Nicholas Townley

Wm Sturmy sonne of Thos Sturmy . ½ houre past 8 att night Sunday 21° Martij baptized fryday 2 1647 att St Clements Danes Cosen Jo^n Williams & Mr Wm Lanygan . Mrs Anne Butler

---

Ben Stokes of Haverfordwest scriptaque tertius dies in mensem Februarii anno domini 1717

Nathaniel Stokes ab Haverfordwest scriptaque in tertium diem mensis Februarii anno domini 1717.

Mary Stokes ab Haverfordwest scriptaque

Mary Stokes was born ye 9th of May in ye year 1695
Benjamin Stokes was born ye 28th of October in ye year 1699

CAREY AND YOUNG.—I shall be glad if any of your correspondents can give me any information concerning the family of a maid of honour of Queen Elizabeth of the name of Carey or Cary, who married a merchant of London named Christopher Young, whose eldest son Christopher was possessor of and known as of Etherdacres (Edderacres or Edward's Acres), parish of Easington, co Pal., who married Jane, dau. of Reed, Esq., of Shotton, co Pal., whose son Robert married Jane, dau. of Edward Johnson, merchant of Newcastle (Mr. Robert Young died *circa* 1665) and his son, Christopher Young, a Doctor of Physic at Newcastle, who in 1666 was aged 29. He married Sarah, dau. of Ralph Maddison, merchant of Newcastle. In addition to daughters, he had surviving of a family of fourteen children, five sons—Ralph, Christopher, Thomas, Robert, and Lionel—all christened at the Church of St. Nicholas at Newcastle. What became of his descendants?

L. YOUNG.

No. II.—PEDIGREE OF WITHY OF BERRY NORBERT AND WESTMINSTER.

Communicated by the Rev. F. G. LEE, D.D., F.S.A., Vicar of All Saints', Lambeth.

ARMS OF WITHIE OR WITHY. Devonshire Visitation, A.D. 1620, Harl. MSS. 1080. Pluto, LVI. E., pp. 353, *et seq.*

Anthony Withie of Berry Norbert, Esq., 2nd son of John Withie of Berry, by Elizabeth, dau'r of Nicholas Berry of Berry, co. Devon. = Christina, da. of John Jewell of Bowdon in the parish of Berry, co. Devon, by Alice, da. of Richard Bellamy, and sister of John, sometime Bishop of Sarum.
[Arms of Jewell.—*Or, on a chevron az., between three gilly-flowers gu., stalked and leaved vert, a maiden's head of the field ducally crowned of the third, on a chief sable a hawk's lure double stringed, between two falcons ar., beaked and legged or.*]

Issue:

- 1. John. — 2. Anthony. — 3. Jewell. } Died in infancy.
- 4. Robert Withie or Withy of Berry Norbert, died 1669 (?), bur. at St. Mary's, Westminster. = Mary, dau'r of John Seymour of Berry Pomeroy, and niece of Sir Edward of that House. Mary, a widow, living in 1672.
  [Arms of Seymour.—*Gules, two wings conjoined in lure or.*]
- 1. Christian. = John Courtenay, mar. at Exeter 16 May, 2d year of Charles I. Died in the Low Countries 1659.
  [Arms of Courtenay.—*Or, three torteaux.*]
- 2. Alice, died unmarried *ante* 1672.

Issue of Robert Withie and Mary:

- 1. John, d. unmarried 1669 (?), bur. at St. Mary's, Westminster.
- 2. Robert, of Berry and St. Clement Danes in the City of Westminster, mar. at St. Mary in the Savoy A.D. 1689. = Elizabeth, da. of John Guy, jun., of Stroud, co. Kent, gent.
- 1. Christian, ob. infans.
- 2. Mary, died unmarried: bur. 26 Aug. 1670, at St. Martin's in the Fields.
- 3. Elizabeth. mar. at St. Giles's, Cripplegate, 29 April, 1639. = Thomas Dennis of Berry Pomeroy, gent., descended from the House of Dennis of Holcombe.
  [Arms of Dennis.—*Erm., three bills gu.*]

Issue of Robert and Elizabeth:

- 1. Robert, *ob. infans.*
- 2. Anthony Withy of Berry Norbert and Westminster, b. 25 March, 169½, mar. 1 Dec. 1709, at Kingsdowne, co. Somerset. = Mary, da. of Courtenay Hilborne of Kingsdowne, Esq.
  [Arms granted, A.D. 1708.—*Per saltire gu. and or, two garbs in pale of the last, in fesse as many roses proper.* Crest.—*On a mount vert a sun-flower proper, between two ears of wheat stalks interlaced or.*]
- Elizabeth, ob. infans.

Hilborne Withy of Coleman Street in the City of London, only son, b. 5 January, 1711, mar. 5 January, 1732. = Elizabeth, da. of . . . .

A

A

Elizabeth (2nd wife), da. of James and .... Pemberton of Whitchurch, co. Salop, and widow of Major Anthony Morgan, 7th Royal English Fusileers, mar. 22 Feb. 1783, d. s.p. = Robert Withy, b. 11 Dec. 1732, m. as his third wife, 11 Aug. 1794, Mrs. Mary Lupson of Epsom, co. Surrey, a widow. He died 19 Sept. 1803. Bur. in the Church of Newington. = Mary (1st wife), da. of William and Elizabeth Johnson of Rotherhithe, co. Surrey, b. 22 May, 1734, mar. at St. Bride's Church 16 March, 1758. Died in childbirth 17 January, 1778, æt. 44.

1. William Johnson, b. 3 Jan. 1759, d. 24 Feb. 1764.

2. Elizabeth, born 4 July, 1760, died 19 Jan. 1777.

3. Mary, b. 26 Oct. 1761, d. 26 Feb. 1764.

4. Robert, b. 7 Nov. 1762, d. 31 Jan. 1763.

5. Sarah, b. 29 Oct. 1763, died

6. Robert, b. 31 July, died 20 Aug. 1765.

Mar. 1stly Sarah Busby, stepdaughter of Richard Burton, Esq., at the par. church of Lambeth, 12 Aug. 1788. She died 23 Nov. 1794, aged 24, bur. in Tottenham Court Chapel. M.I. at St. Martin's in the Fields. = 8. Robert Withy, b. 20 June, 1768, of St. Martin's in the Fields, afterwards of Broad Oak, in the par. of Brenchley, co. Kent, bur. at Brenchley. M.I. = Mar. 2ndly on 1 Dec. 1795, Anne, dau'r of Charles and Anne Fourdrinier of Westminster. Bur. at St. Martin's. M.I.

7. Mary, b. 1 Sept. 1766, d. 29 Mar. 1845. Bur. at Hackney. M.I.

9. Harriett, b. 23 May, 1770. Died in May, 1771.

10. Anna Maria, b. 19 May, 1772, died 31 Jan. 1819.

11. Harriett, b. 21 Dec. 1774.

12. Twins, b. 17 Jan. 1778.

1. Robert Burton Withy, b. 22 Nov. 1790, educated at Winchester, died Sept. 1832, bur. at St. Giles' in the Fields. = ...

1. Sarah Withy, eldest da., b. 15 Sept. 1789, mar. 27 April, 1815. = Mortimer, 3rd son of George, 2nd Baron Rodney, by Anne, da. and coheiress of Right Hon. Thomas Harley, and granddau. of Edward, 3rd Earl of Oxford. [Arms of Rodney.—*Or, three eagles displayed purp.*]

2. Augusta, b. 10 Dec. 1791. Died unmar. Bur. at Creech St. Michael, co. Somerset.

3. Mary, b. 9 Aug. 1793. Died unmar. Bur. at Fishponds, co. Gloucester.

4. Harriett, b. 16 Oct. 1794. Died and buried at Bushey, co. Herts. = Alexander, son of Dr. Thomas Monro of Bushey, co. Herts.

Children of Robert Burton Withy:

1. Henry Withy.

2. Arthur Withy, mar. and settled in Australia.

Children of Sarah Withy and Mortimer Rodney:

1. Mortimer.

2. Frederick.

3. Arthur.

1. Sarah.

2. Augusta.

3. Frances. = Baldwin J. Bastard of Kitley, co. Devon, Esq. [Arms of Bastard.—*Or, a chevron azure.*]

B

B

Emily, da. of James Mangles of Woodbridge, co. Surrey, Esq., M.P. for Guildford, mar. August, 1825. Died January, 1828. 1st wife. Buried at Claverton, co. Somerset.
[Arms of Mangles.—*Or, a bend vair between two crosses verdée, voided sable.*]

= Henry Withy,* b. 10 May, 1800, educated at Westminster and Merton Coll., Oxon. M.A. Nov. 4, 1824. Clerk in Holy Orders; sometime Vicar of Holy Trinity, Huddersfield. Deceased 4 Apr. 1837. Bur. at Tunbridge Wells.

= Christian Dottin, b. 12 Feb. 1795, 4th da. of the Hon. Sir John Gay Alleyne of Barbadoes, Bart. 2nd wife. Mar. in 1829. Died at Weston, co. Somerset, 11 Feb. 1873.
[Arms of Alleyne.—*Per chevron gules and ermine, in chief two lions' heads erased or.* Crest.—*Out of a ducal coronet a horse's head ar.*]

2. William Henry Harris Withy, died æt. 7.

3. Emily, 4. Bouverie Galitzen. 5. Emily Mangles. Died young.

1. Henry Alleyne Withy, b. 19 Feb. 1830, d. March 9, 1863, buried at Weston, co. Somerset. = Emma Florence, dau'r of John and Emma Shillinglaw of St. Martin's, Westminster, mar. 7 Aug. 1855.

William Walter Rowley, M.A. Oxon. Vicar of Emmanuel Church, Weston-super-Mare, co. Somerset, and Prebendary of Wells. = 6. Emma Pennant, m. 14 Jan. 1874, at Wittington, co. Hereford.

1. Charles Henry Alleyne Withy, b. 7 Feb. 1861.

1. Mary Florence Alleyne Withy, b. 22 April, 1857; married at St. Mathias's, Kensington, 31 July, 1878. = Samuel Clarke of Cheyne Walk, Chelsea, son of Samuel and Mary Clark of Marylebone.

Winifred Mary Withy, b. 16 Feb. 1880.

2. Ethel Emma Fanny Withy, b. 27 Nov. 1858.

1. Walter Alleyne Moss, b. Dec. 1876. Died an infant.

2. William Lawrence Pemberton, b. 18 May, 1878.

Anne Withy, born 18 Feb. 1797, mar. at St. Martin's in the Fields. Died 21 March, 1870. Bur. at Creech St. Michael. M.I. at Creech.

= Joseph Duncan,† born 17 Oct. 1799, son of Joseph Ostrehan of Barbadoes, Esq., by Elvira, only da. of Haldane Duncan, of Lundie, Esq., and Miss Dunlop, his wife, and niece of Adam, 1st Viscount Duncan. B.A. Worc. Coll., Oxon., Vicar of Creech St. Michael, co. Somerset. Died 11 Sept. 1870. M.I. at Creech.
[Arms of Ostrehan.—*Ar., on a chevron gules, three hunters' horns or between three lions rampant gules.*]

C

* "It is an interesting fact that he sprang from the same stock with that great luminary of the Reformation, Bishop Jewell. Two brothers of the Withy family, which in those days was possessed of considerable property in the county of Devon, married each a sister of that eminent prelate, and from one of these marriages Henry Withy is lineally descended."—Memoir, p. ii., to 'Expository Lectures,' by Rev. Henry Withy, M.A. London. 1839.

† Monumental Inscription, Creech St. Michael, co. Somerset, north side of the Sanctuary. (Arms.—*Ostrehan impaling Withy.*) In memory of Joseph Duncan Ostrehan, B.A., Vicar of this Parish, son of Joseph Ostrehan of St. Michael's, Barbadoes, Esq., who died September 11, 1870, aged 71. Also of Anne, wife of the above, who was the fifth daughter of Robert Withy, of Broad Oak, in the county of Kent, Esq. She died March 21, 1870, aged 72. "The Lord grant unto them that they may find mercy of the Lord in that day."

c

1. Joseph Duncan Ostrehan, b. 3 Dec. 1829. B.A. Worc. Coll., Oxon. Clerk in Holy Orders. Chaplain at Secunderabad, Madras. Died at Cheltenham, 4 Feb. 1880. = Harriett Lucy, 2nd da. of the Rev. John Barnwell, B.A. Oxon., Rect^r of Holdford, co. Somerset, and granddau'r of the Rev. William Goodall of Dinton Hall, co. Bucks.

2. Eliott Seward Ostrehan, born 18 July, 1835. Major in the 25th Bombay Staff Corps. = Isabel Jane Woodward, eldest da. of William Sadleir of Ballinderry and Castletown, co. Tipperary, Esq., J.P. and D.L., m. at Creech St. Michael in 1858. Died 17 Apr. 1871. Bur. at Kensal Green. M.I. [Arms of Sadleir.—*Or, a lion rampant per fesse az. and gu.*]

Issue of Joseph Duncan Ostrehan and Harriett Lucy:

1. John Eliott Duncan, b. at Secunderabad, 28 June, 1856.

2. Arthur Frederick, b. 12 Nov. 1857, of Sidney Sussex Coll., Cambridge.

3. Francis George Rodney, b. 20 Aug. 1859. Lieutenant in the Army.

4. Henry Fortescue, born 26 Jan. 1863.

5. George William, b. 9 Aug. 1868.

6. Edward Alfred, b. May 31, 1872.

Edith Emilia Janette, b. 16 June, 1861.

1. Lucretia Anne.

2. Ellen Josephine.

3. Georgiana Augusta, a nun of the Order of St. Francis.

4. Elvira Louisa, m. at Creech St. Michael, 9 June, 1859. = Frederick George, D.D., Vicar of All Saints', Lambeth, eldest son of Frederick Lee, M.A. of Merton Coll., Oxon. Rector of Easington, and grandson of T. T. Lee, B.A., Vicar of the Prebendal Church of Thame, co. Oxon. [Arms of Lee.—*Ar., a fesse betw. three crescents sable.*]

Issue of Eliott Seward Ostrehan and Isabel Jane Woodward:

1. Annie Serena Isabel, b. 16 Aug. 1859.

2. Agnese Kathleen Mary, born 12 Aug. 1860.

3. Mabel Maude Josephine, born 15 July, 1864.

4. Adrian Harry Mellerish, born 6 Sept. 1867.

Issue of Frederick George Lee and Elvira Louisa:

1. Reginald Frederick Benedict Duncan Lee, b. 2 July, 1861.

2. Gordon Ambrose de Lisle Lee, b. 11 July, 1863.

3. Mary Louisa Gwendoline Lee, b. 25 Sept. 1865.

4. Leonard Miles Henry Lee, b. 24 Feb. 1867.

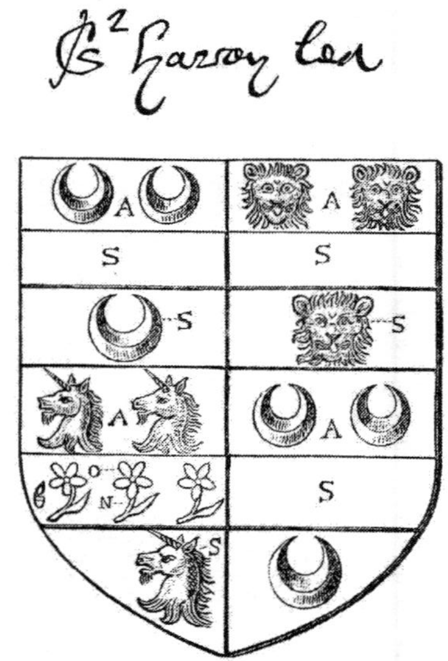

Arms of Sir Henry Lee, co. Bucks and Oxon., from folio 118 of Heraldic MS. No. 570, in the Library of Caius College, Cambridge.

FROM THE WITHY FAMILY BIBLE.

Illustrative of Pedigree No II.

Robert Withy, son of Hilborne and Elizth Withy of Coleman Street, London, born December ye 11th, 1732, and Mary Johnson, daughter of William and Eliz Johnson of Rotherhith, Surry, born May the 22nd, 1734, were married at St Bride's Church, Fleet Street, March ye 16, 1758, and had issue as follows, viz —

1. William Johnson, born Wednesday, January the 3rd, 1759, at ½ hour after seven in the morning, and christened in the Parish of St Michael, Cornhill, on Tuesday, Jan 16th, 1759 Mr. William Johnson, Capt Daniel Grimball, and Mrs Grace Jordan were sponsors Died Feb 24, 1764, of the small pox

2 Elizabeth, born July 14th, 1760, on Wednesday, at ½ an hour past 3 o'clock in the afternoon, and christened in the Parish of St Dionis Back-Church, Fenchurch Street, on Thursday, the 22nd of July, 1760 Mr Hilborne Withy, Mrs Eliz Withy, and Mrs Eliz Johnson were sponsors Died of a consumption Jan 19, 1777.

3 Mary, born October 26, 1761, on Monday, at 2 o'clock in the afternoon, and christened in the Parish of St Michael, Cornhill, on Wednesday, November ye 18, 1761 Mr Saml Sparrow, and Mrs Jackson, and Mrs. Whitewood were sponsors Died Feb 26, 1764, of the small pox.

4 Robert, born Nov 7, 1762, on Sunday, at ½ an hour after one in ye afternoon, and christen'd in ye Parish of St Michael, Cornhill, on Monday, Nov 15, 1762 Mr and Mrs Withy, Senr, and Mrs Richard Whitewood, were sponsors He died on Monday, Jan. 31, 1763, aged 12 weeks

5 Sarah, born on Saturday, October ye 29th, 1763, at ¼ after nine in the morning, and christen'd on Thursday, the 25th November, 1763. Mrs Watlington, Mrs Smith, and Capt Grimball were sponsors in the Parish of St Michael, Cornhill Died

6 Robert 2nd, born July 31, 1765, on Sunday morning about half-past one at noon, and christen'd on Sunday, Aug 9, and died Aug the 20th of the same month and year. N B —Only half-baptized, and no sponsors, in the Parish of St Michael, Cornhill

7 Mary ye 2nd, born Sept 1, 1766, on Monday, in the Parish of All Hallows, Bread Street, about half-past 5 afternoon, and christen'd Sep. 25, 1766 Mrs. Longden, Mrs Withy, Senr and Mr A Williams were sponsors

8 Robert 3rd, born on Monday, June 20, 1768, about six in the afternoon, in the Parish of St Mary, Islington, and christen'd on Monday, the 18th July, 1768, Mrs Russell, Mr Withy, Senr, and Mr Cornelius English were sponsors

9 Harriett, born on Wednesday, ye 23rd May, 1770, in the Parish of St Mary, Islington, and christen'd on June 20th, 1770 Mrs Hooper, Mrs Withy, Senr, and Mr Griffin were sponsors, and died on Friday y^{e} of May, 1771.

10 Anna Maria, born on Tuesday, May 19, 1772, at half-past 5 o'clock in the morning, and christened on Sat. June 20, 1772. Mr Shea, Mrs Jackson, and Mrs. Davies were sponsors [St Mary, Islington, and died Jan 31, 1819 *]

11. Harriet 2nd, born Dec 21, 1774, in the Parish of St Martin in the Field Mr Saml Burchett, in the Parish of St Martin in the Fields, London

12 and 13 Twins, Jan 17, 1778, at 4 o'clock in the morning, which was fatal to them and the mother, who died in convulsions, and thus unhappily for the family ended a life spent in the constant exercise of every conjugal and parental duty, the brightest example of her sex To sum up her character, Her virtues when living were too conspicuous to need recital, and no earthly enjoyments being equal to her merits, Heaven only could compensate for the patient exercise of so many virtues

Reader,
Weep not for her, but for her
surviving family

* In a later hand.

*Died 19th Sept. 1803. Robert Withy, father of the above, aged 70, and buried in the Parish Church, St. Mary, Newington, and left a widow, who was his third wife

Robert Withy was married Feb 22nd, 1783, to Elizabeth Morgan, widow of Anthony Morgan, Esq, Major in the 7th Regt of Royal English Fuzileers, and daughter of James and Pemberton of Whitchurch in Shropshire, watch-maker, and died soon afterwards.

Robert Withy, the youn' son of the before-named Rob[t] and Mary Withy was married to Sarah Busby, his wife, on the 12th of August, 1788, at the Parish of St. Mary, Lambeth, and had issue —

1 Sarah Burton, born Tuesday, 15th Sept 1789, at 10 o'clock in the morning, in the *Parish of St Giles in the Fields* Sponsors, Mr Burton, Mrs Burton, and Mrs Brumfield Had the small-pox, measles, and hooping cough Married Honble. Mortimer Rodney, son of the late Lord Rodney, had issue Sarah, Mortimer Harley, Mortimer, and others

2 Robert Burton, born Monday, 22nd Nov, 1790, at 8 o'clock at night, in the Parish of St Martin in the Fields Sponsors, Mr Withy, Sen[r], Mr Pitter, Jun[r], and Mrs King. Had the small-pox, measles, and hooping cough. Died in Sept 1832, buried at St Giles, leaving a widow and two sons

3 Augusta, born Saturday 10th Dec 1791, at 5 o'clock in the morning, in the Parish of St Martin in the Fields Sponsors, Mr James Maidment, Mrs Pitter, and Mrs Dickenson Had the small-pox, measles, and hooping cough

4. Mary, born Friday, the 9th August, 1793, at one o'clock in the afternoon, in the Parish of St Martin in the Fields Sponsors, Mr William Payter, Mrs Maidment, and Miss Mary Withy Had the small-pox, measles, and hooping cough

5. Harriet, born the 16th October, 1794, in the Parish of St Martin's in the Fields Sponsors, Robert Woolley, Esq, Miss Harriett Withy, and Miss Harriett Dickenson Christened in the above parish on 1795 Had the small-pox, measles, and hooping cough Married Alexander Monro, Esq, youngest son of Thomas Monro, Esq, M D Died leaving Donald her only child

Sarah, wife of the above-named Robert Withy, the younger, and mother to the above five dear children, exchanged this Life for a Happy eternity the 23rd Nov 1794, after a severe Illness In Her were concentrated the most affectionate wife, the tenderest mother, and the True Christian, and an example to all her sex, aged 26 She was buried in the Vault belonging to Richard Burton, Esq, in Tottenham Court Chapel, about two months after the death of her mother

Robert Withy the younger was married to Ann Fourdrinier, daughter of Charles and Ann Fourdrinier, the 1st December, 1795, at the Parish of St Martin's in the Fields, and had issue as follows —

1. Ann, born the 18th Feb 1797 at 7 o'clock in the morning, and christened in the Parish of St Martin in the Fields, the 18th of March following Sponsors, Mr Charles Fourdrinier, Mrs Anne Fourdrinier and Miss Elizabeth Fourdrinier Had the small-pox, measles, and hooping cough Married the Rev Joseph Duncan Ostrehan, and has issue

2 Charles Francis, born the 7th of July, 1798, at 10 o'clock in the evening, and christened in the Parish Church of St Martin in the Fields the 3rd of August following Sponsors, Mr Charles Fourdrinier, Captain Francis William Leigh, and Mrs Ann Fourdrinier Died 7th of April following in cutting teeth, aged 9 months, and buried at St Martin's

3 Henry, born 10th of May, 1800, at 10 minutes before 6 in the morning, and christened in the Parish Church of St Martin's in the Fields the 11th of June following Sponsors, Mr Henry Fourdrinier, Mr John King, and Mrs Hodgson Had the small-pox, measles, and hooping cough Married August, 1825, Emily Mangles, d[r] of James Mangles of Woodbridge, Surrey, Esq, died Jan 7, 1828, leaving one child, who died soon afterwards Married 2ndly, 1829, Dottin Alleyne, youngest daughter of the late Sir John Gay Alleyne, baronet, of Barbadoes.

* In another handwriting, *i e*, Robt Withy, Esq of Buckingham Street Strand

4. Jemima, born at 11 o'clock at night, 1801, Sept. 11th, and christened in the Parish Church of Putney, in Surrey, the 1st Nov. following. Sponsors, Edward David Batson, Esq., Mrs. John Newman, and Miss Mary Withy. Died 6th May, 1802, and buried at Putney, Surrey.

5. John, born 17th April, 1803, at 5 minutes after 10 in the morning in the Parish of St. Martin in the Fields. Half baptized. Died 10th May, 1804, and buried at Putney, Surrey.

6. Elizabeth, born 22nd Dec. 1804, at 8 o'clock in the evening, in the Parish of St. Martin in the Fields. Half baptized. Had the vaccine pox and measles. Died. Buried at Lamberhurst.

7. Clara, born Died

GRANT OF ARMS TO FRANCIS TYSSEN OF LONDON, 1687.*

To all and singular to whom these presents shall come S[r] Thomas S[t] George Knight Garter Principal King of Arms, and S[r] Henry S[t] George Knight Clarenceux King of Arms send Greeting Whereas Francis Tyssen who hath lately fined for Alderman and Sheriff of the City of London hath made application to the Most Noble Prince Henry Duke of Norfolk Earl Marshall of Engl[d] Knight of the most Noble Order of the Garter etc. for a Grant of Arms, the said Earl Marshall did in consideration of the Loyalty and other due qualifications of the said Francis Tyssen, signifie unto Us his consent (by Warrant or Order under his hand and the seal of his Office of Earle Marshall bearing date the 21st day of this inst[t] November) for Our Devysing Granting and Assigning unto the said Francis Tyssen, such Arms and Crest as he and his descendants may lawfully bear. Know ye therefore that we the said Garter and Clarenceux Kings of Arms in pursuance of the said Order, and by virtue of the Letters Patents under the Great Seal of England to Us respectively granted have devysed and do by these presents grant and assign unto the said Francis Tyssen the Arms hereafter mentioned, viz[t] Or on a Cheveron Azure between three French Marigolds slipped proper, two Lions respecting each other of the first; And For the Crest, on a Wreath of his Colours a Demy lion Or, Crowned Gules, supporting a Shield Azure charged with a Starr gold; as in the margin hereof is more plainly depicted. Which Arms he the said Francis Tyssen and the descendents of his body lawfully begotten (with their due and proper differences) shall and may bear and use according to the Laws of Arms without the lett or Interruption of any person or persons whatsoever. In Witness

* Communicated by J. B. Daniel-Tyssen, Esq., F.S.A.

whereof We the said Garter and Clarenceux have hereunto subscribed Our Names, and affixed the Seals of our Offices this 24th day of November 1687 in the third year of the reign of Our Sovereign Lord James the Second, by the Grace of God King of England, Scotland, France, and Ireland, Defender of the Faith, etc^a.

THO. ST. GEORGE Garter Principall King of Arms. HEN. ST. GEORGE Clarenceux King of Arms.

I do hereby Certify that the above is a true copy from the Record thereof in the Register of Grants, vol. iii., p. 332, remaining in the College of Arms, London. Witness my hand at the said College this Fifteenth day of December, 1870.

THOS. WM. KING, York Herald.

TYSSEN PEDIGREE.

FROM THE VISITATION OF LONDON, 1687.

St. Andrew's upper precinct, Billingsgate Ward. Turners' Hall afores^d Satt. 25° Junij, 1687.

ARMS.—*Or, on a chevron azure between three French marigolds, slipped and leaved ppr., two lions passant, respecting each other of the first.*
CREST.—*A demi-lion rampant or, ducally crowned gules, holding in the paws an escutcheon azure, thereon an estoile of the first.*
MOTTO.—*Post mortem virtus virescit.*

Francis Tyssen of Gent in Flanders afterwards of Ulyssing in Zealand

Daniell Tyssen, born at Ulyssing in Zealand, and there dyed about the year 1647, æt. circ. 46. Note that the said Daniel was there born when King James 1st had it in caution. = Appolonia, one of the dau'rs of Baldwin Ridley of Ulyssing, a nephew to Bp. Ridley. She was likewise borne at Ulyssing, when King James the 1st had it in caution.

Francis Tyssen of London, merchant, ætatis 63 ann. 1687, born at Ulyssing, but naturalized by Act of Parliament. = Dorothy, one of the dau'rs of Gerard Collent of London, merchant.

Francis Tyssen, only son, ætatis 34 anno 1687. = Mary, da. of Tho. Western of London, Esq., Merch^t, fined for Alderman.

GLANVILLE ARMS.—At what period, and which Glanville, first assumed *Azure, three saltires or;* and is there any reason given for the discontinuance of the old bearing—*Argent, a chief indented azure?*—W. U. G. R.

MONUMENTAL INSCRIPTIONS, WITH NOTES, FROM THE CHURCH AND CHURCHYARD OF AXBRIDGE, CO SOMERSET *

(*Continued from p.* 313)

In affectionate remembrance of Albert Maurice Jervis, beloved and only child of Henry and Frances Jervis, who died March 9th, 1866, aged 22 years Also of Henry Jervis, who died July 11th, 1872, aged 56 years

---

In memory of Elizabeth, wife of Maurice Jervis of this Town, who died January 21st, 1845, aged 55 years Also the above-named Maurice Jervis, who died November 4th, 1859, aged 67 years

---

In memory of John Foster Read, son of Frederick and Catherine Read, who died May 26th, 1840, aged 2 years and 9 months Also Andrew, died in infancy.

In memory of Lydia Cox, who died February 26th, 1829, aged 83 years. Also Richard Cox, who died January 10th, 1836, aged 79 years

---

In memory of Elizabeth, beloved wife of Robert Allford, of Cheddar, who died March 25th, 1867, aged 80 years Also in memory of Robert Allford, of Cheddar, who died January 6th, 1867, aged 86

In loving memory of William Samuel Thompson, who passed through the valley of the shadow of death September 28th, 1878, aged 45 years

Sacred to the memory of Elizabeth, wife of Joseph Read of this Town, who died December 19th, 1856, aged 55. Also the above-named Joseph Read, who died October 22nd, 1862, aged 67

In memory of Mary Ann, wife of James Durston, of this place, who died May 6th, 1846, aged 46 Also of Phœbe Cillinda, beloved and only child of Henry and Fanny Durston, who died November 17th, 1860, aged 14 years.

In affectionate remembrance of Fanny, the beloved wife of Henry Durston, of Axbridge, who died January 19th, 1875, aged 59 years

---

Here rests the body of Hanna, the wife of John Durston, of this parish, who was interred September 28th, 1759, aged 40 years

---

In memory of George Owen Fursdon, who died May 7th, 1865, aged 6 years and 9 months

---

Also of George Willingale, who died June 6th, 1867, aged 74 years

To the memory of John Rogers, gentleman, who died 4th August, 1780, aged 65 years, and of John, son of John and Sarah Rogers, who died 12th March, 1771, in infancy Also Sarah, wife of the said John Rogers, who was buried 11th Nov., 1782, aged 42

Sacred to the memory of Henry Rawlins, of this town, who died 9th March, 1793, aged 80 years.
Sarah, his wife, died 23rd May, 1785, aged 50 years
Ann, their daughter, died 1st January, 1813, aged 55 years.
Elizabeth Rawlins, daughter of the said Henry and Sarah Rawlins, died 7th February, 1850, aged 82 years, and
Mary Spencer, widow, their daughter, who died 28th June, 1851, aged 76 years

* Communicated by EDWARD FRY WADE, Esq

In memory of Elizabeth Collings, daughter of John and E. Day, who died June 27th, 1856, aged 10 years.

Also to the memory of Charity Collings, daughter of John and E Day, who died June 30th, 1856, aged 4 years and 8 months

In memory of Hannah, wife of John Day, who died April 21st, 1843, aged 32 years

Also Elizabeth, second wife of the said John Day, who died September 20th, 1861, aged 47 years Also John Day, who died May 1st, 1872, aged 59 years

---

In memory of George William, second son of John and Jessalina Walker, who died August 12th, 1819, aged one year and two weeks

Also their sixth son, born August 9th, 1828, buried in Cheddar churchyard August 10th, 1828

Also Arthur, their seventh son, who died December 5th, 1842, aged 9 years 8 months

---

In memory of Fanny Coombs, late of the parish of Compton Bishop, widow, who died January 6th, 1836, aged 67 years

---

Sacred to the memory of Lucy, the beloved wife of Isaac Headford, who died June 30th, 1855, aged 70 years

Also the above-named Isaac Headford, who died May 15th, 1863, aged 82 years

Also Susan Frances, their daughter, who died May 2nd, 1864, aged 38 years

---

Sacred to the memory of Bruges Fry, solicitor, and for 15 years Coroner for the northern division of this County, who died 28th September, 1867, aged 54 years

Also in memory of Anna Maria, wife of the late Bruges Fry, Esq, of Cheddar, who died December 4th, 1869, aged 52 years

---

Near this place are deposited the remains of Ann, wife of Henry Mills, of Cross. She died September 26th, 1812, aged 53 years

Also of two children who died in their infancy

To the memory of Elizabeth, wife of Joseph Phillips, of this parish, who died March 27th, 1873, aged 62 years.

Sacred to the memory of Charles, eldest son of Charles and Martha Fowler, who died March 13th, 1867, aged 16 years Also of Martha, wife of Charles Fowler, and mother of the aforesaid, who died 2nd September, 1870, aged 41 years Also Ada, daughter of the said Charles and Martha Fowler, who died June 11th, 1872, aged 18 years

---

Beneath lie the remains of Henry Symons, Esq[re], many years an active Magistrate of this Town, died March 1st, 1870, aged 80 years Also Jemima, his wife, sixth daughter of William Dyne, Esq[re], of Milton, Kent, died March 20th, 1862, aged 86 years

---

Hellier Garbet Jeune, son of the Rev[d] Francis* and Margaret Jeune, died March 9th, 1848, aged 9 months

---

In memory of George G Smith, who died 3rd March, 1855, aged 1 day.

* Afterwards Bishop of Peterborough Margaret Jeune was a daughter of Henry Symons Solicitor, of Axbridge

In affectionate memory of Bertha Salisbury, only daughter of James and Elizabeth Salisbury, of Axbridge, who died on Sunday, 22nd June, 1873, aged 17 years. Also of Hubert and Herbert, her brothers, who died in infancy Also to the beloved memory of Samuel William Salisbury, who died November 5th, 1877, aged 24 years.

Harriet, daughter of Robert and Maria Parker, 1823.

To the memory of Maria, wife of Robert Parker, of this parish, gentleman, who died August 5th, 1852, aged 65 years. Also in memory of Robert Parker, gentleman, who died April 29th, 1860, aged 72 years

---

EXTRACTS FROM THE PARISH REGISTERS OF TODDINGTON, CO. BEDS *

(*Continued from p* 371)

Baptisms

1606	Feb.	2.	ffrancis, the sonne of Willm. Dier
1607.	May	3	Susanna, da. of Gylbert But
1607	Nov	..	. ., the sonne of Thomas Dier
1608	May	1.	Edmund, ye sonne of William Britt, gentleman
1608.	July	25	Margaret Shawe, the da of Sir John Shawe† (as the mother said)
1609	Jan.	28	John, the sonne of Willm Bret
1610.	May	16.	Dorathy Batt, da of George Bat.
1610	June	1.	Margaret, da of Wm Dier, gentleman
1610.	July	16	John Crumpton, ye sonne of John Crompton, Knight
1611	July	7	Thomas, ye sonne of George Bat
1612	Nov.	15	ffrauncis, ye sonne of Wm Brett, gent.
1612.‡	Jan	1	John, sonne of Sr Henrie Croftes, knight
1612 ‡	Feb	2	Thomas, the sonne of Thomas Lord Wentworth
1612 ‡	Feb	3	Robert Crompton, the sonne of Sr John Crompto', knight
1613	Oct	3	George, ye sonne of George Bat.
1613 §	Feb	3.	Elizabeth, ye da of Sr John Crompton
1613 §	Mar	6.	Marie Wentworth, the da of Thomas, Lord Wentworth
1614	April	25.	Constance, ye da of ffraunces Rollinson.
1614.	Oct	9.	Constance, the da of Henry Johnson.
1614	Nov	2	Henry, the sonne of Thomas Dier
1615	Nov	5	ffraunces, the sonne of George Bat.
1616.	April	28	Dorathy, the da of ffraunces Rallinson
1616	June	16.	Prudence, da of Dawson
1617	Sep	9	Beniamin, the sonne of Willm Bret, gentleman.
1617.	Sep	21.	Mary, the da of George Bat, gent
1617.	July	26	William Wentworth, the sonne of Thomas, Lord Wentworth, was baptized at Todington Manor
1618	April	19	ffrancis, the sonne of ffrancis Rollenson
1618	Jan	6	John & Mildred, the sonne & da of Robt. Smith.
1619	Sep	23	Margery, the da of George Bat, gentlema'
1620	May	22.	Hugh, the sonne of ffraunces Rallinson, cleark.
1621	Aug.	12	John, the sonne of Robert Smith

* Communicated by F. A BLAYDES, Esq , Hockliffe Lodge, Leighton Buzzard

† Of what family was this Sir John Shaw? There was a family of that name for many generations settled at Toddington as yeomen, but I cannot find that he was of that family

‡ The entries marked thus are in a different hand, and have evidently been inserted for some reason at the end of the year 1612, as they are out of place

§ The same remark as the preceding applies to these two entries, which have been inserted out of place at the end of the year 1613

1621.	Dec. 2.	Henry, the sonne of George Batt.
1622	July 28	Marie, da. of ffrancis Rollenson, clerk
1623	July 29	Anne Wentworth, the da. of Thomas, Lord Wentworth, and Dame Anne his wife
1623	Oct 5.	John, the sonne of Hierome Grimwood

Weddings.

1558	July 24	Thomas Hilersden & Joahne Potts *
1560	Oct 9	John ffuller & Anis Dawson
1562	June 18	Willm Dawson and Margarett Burre
1563	Julie 4	Peter Dare and Margerie Gill
1582	Nov 4	Richd Porter and Ellin Okeley.
1589	April 22	John Collupp and An' Burre
1591	Dec 1	Gregorie Shawe and Katherine Whitway
1595	Sep 7	John Rowlie and Jane Sage
1603.	Sep 12	Thomas Dier and Catherin Shaw
1603	Oct 13	Robt Smith and Ellen Clarke
1614.	July 10	. But *was* Margaret Billengsley
1614	Feb 6	Willm. Dey (?) and Margaret ffisher
1616	April 6	ffrances But and Phebe Garret.
1617	Oct 27	*Ralfe* Lord and Mary Longe

Burialls

1583.	May 24	Catherine Cornelius, gentillwo'
1584	May 15.	Robte Smythe
1584	July 22	ffrances Lofborough
1587.	Sep. 3	Henrye, Lorde Cheney †
1594	Oct 28	Winifred Senjohn, wife of Thomas Senjohn, gentle'
1595.	Aug. 4	Luce Johnson, da of Richard Johnson, gent
1595	Mar. 14	Nicho Bruce, gent
1596	Jan 20.	Gregorie Shawe
1597.	Oct. 14	Richd Johnson, gent
1597.	Mar 2.	Margarett Johnson, gent
1598.	Aug. 7.	William Sage, minister
1599	Aug 24.	Margaret Senjohn, wife to Thom Senjohn, gent
1599	Mar. 15	Mathia, da to Richd Burre, gent
1600	April 22	Thomas, sonne to Sir John Crofts,‡ knight
1601.	Aug 21.	Charles Glemham, esquire
1605.	Sep 26	Henry, sonne of Willm Dier
1606.	April 27	George Cragge, gentleman.
1606	Feb 21.	Edward ffenne, gentleman
1607.	April 2.	ffrancis ye sonne of Willm Dier
1607.	May 4	Willm. Dyer
1608	May 29.	Charles, the sonne of Sir John Crofts, Knighte.
1608.	June 13	Nicholas ye sonne of Thomas Dier
1610	July 1	Sisley Okeley, widdow
1610.	Jan 16.	Margaret, the da. of William Dier, gentleman
1612.	July 4	Anne Wainteworth, ye da of Thomas, Lord Waintworth
1613	Nov. 25	Elizabeth, ye wife of Thomas Harris, gent
1614.	April 17	The honorable lady Jane Cheney§

* The family of Potts was seated at Chalgrave in the sixteenth century

† Son and heir of Sir Thomas Cheney of the Isle of Sheppey, by Anne, daughter and one of the heires of Sir John Broughton Through this marriage the Cheneys became possessed of the Toddington estates He lies buried in the south transept of Toddington Church

‡ Sir John Crofts mar Margaret, dau of Thomas Baron Wentworth of Nettlested, and successively widow of John Lord Williams and Sir William Darcy

§ She was the seventh dau of Thomas, Lord Wentworth, of Nettlested Her tomb may also be seen in the south transept of the parish church

(*To be continued*)

Communicated by the Rev. F. G. Lee, D.D., *Vicar of All Saints, Lambeth.*

Henri Fourdrinier, born at Caen, Normandy, *circa* 1575. Sometime Admiral of France, and subsequently created a Viscount.═ . . . .
Arms of Fourdrinier.—*Per bend argent and sable, two anchors, the upper one reversed, counterchanged.*

1. Henri, born at Caen *circa* 1615.═ . . . . — 2. Charles.

Louis Grolleau, of Caen, and subsequently of Gronigen.═ . . . .

1. Henri, born at Caen *circa* 1658. Fled from France with his family to Gronigen in Holland.═ . . . . — 2. John. — 3. Charles.

Louis Grolleau, born in 1662. Naturalized 8th March, 1682.═Mary, born 1660. Died 5 Feb. 1729. — Judith, born 4 Oct. 1689. Died 3 Nov. 1750.

Paul Fourdrinier, born at Gronigen 20 Dec. 1698. Bur. at Wandsworth 3 Feb. 1758.═1. Susanna Grolleau, born 11 July, 1693. Mar. 5 Oct. 1721. Died 15 Nov. 1766, bur. at Wandsworth.

David, son of Captain William Lloyd, born 28 May, 1712.═2. Mary, born 20 Nov. 1712. Mar. 25 Jan. 1738. Died 5 Oct. 1770, bur. at Wandsworth. — 3. Bridget, born 20 Jan. 1717.

1. Henry Fourdrinier (2nd husband). Born 25 Feb. 1730. Died 11 Jan. 1799, buried at St. Mary Woolnoth.* M.I.═Jemima White, born 11 March, 1730. Died 5 Sept. 1781, buried at St. Mary Woolnoth.═Mr. Manning (1st husband).

2. Charles Fourdrinier born 9 August, 1735. Mar. 28 March, 1765.═Anne, born 14 Feb. 1748. Died 5 May, 1802, æt. 55. (Mourning ring in Mrs. Lee's possession.)

1. Elizabeth, born 5 Dec. 1725. — 2. Judith, born 19 Jan. 1727. — 3. Mary, born 21 June, 1728. — 4. Jane, born 1736. Died 8 May, 1752, bur. at Wandsworth.

1. Charles Kenneth, born 20 May, 1766. — 1. Isabella, born 7 Aug. 1767. Died 22 Sept. 1775. — 2. Elizabeth, died æt. 30, 30 Nov. 1803, buried at Putney. (Mourning ring in Mrs. Lee's possession.) — 3. Anne (2nd wife). Mar. at St. Martin's, Westminster, 1 Dec. 1795.═Robert Withy. [See Pedigree of Withy of Devonshire and Westminster, pp. 361-2, and 373-6.]

Anne, 5th daughter, born 18 Feb. 1797.═Joseph Duncan Ostrehan.

Elvira Louisa, 4th daughter, living 1880.═Frederick George Lee.

A

* Church of St. Mary Woolnoth :—"In the Chancel Vault of this Church lie the remains of Henry Fourdrinier, Esquire, who departed this January 11th, 1799, aged 68. In his character were combined the kind Husband, good father, and sincere friend. Also of Jemima his amiable wife, who died September 5th, 1781, aged 51. In grateful remembrance of their virtues this monument is raised by their surviving children. Also the remains of Edward and Randolph, children of the above, who died in their infancy. 'The Earth is the Lord's and the fulness thereof.'"

A

1. Henry, born 11 Feb. 1766. Of Burston Hall, co. Stafford. Died 3 Sept. 1854, bur. at Stone. = Sarah Anne Walker, mar. 6 Dec. 1790. Bur. at Stone.

2. Charles, born 15 March, 1768. Died 7 Feb. 1841. = Mary, daughter of General John Jenkin of Waterford, by Mary Franklin his wife. Mar. 25 May, 1795.

3. John Rawson.

4. Sealey, born 1747. Died 1777. = Harriett, daughter of James Pownall of Winslow and Gawsworth, co. Chester, gent.

Jemima, born 19 Nov. 1772. Mar. at St. Mary's, Lambeth, 29 Oct. 1799. Died 17 May, 1836, buried at Littlemore, co. Oxon. M.I.* = John Newman, only son of John Newman of Lombard Street, London, and Elizabeth Good his wife. ARMS OF NEWMAN, granted 15 Feb. 166¾.—*Or, a fess dancettée between three hearts gules.*

---

1. John Henry Newman, born 21 Feb. 1801. Scholar of Trinity Coll. Oxon; Fellow of Oriel; M.A.; Vicar of St. Mary's, Oxford; subsequently Founder and Superior of the Oratory of St. Philip Neri, at Edgbaston; D.D. of Rome; and created Cardinal Deacon of the Holy Roman Church, with the title of St. George in Velabro, by His Holiness Pope Leo XIII. in 1879.

2. Charles Robert, died young.

3. Francis William, born 27 June, 1805. Commoner of Worcester Coll. Oxon, 1822; B.A. and double first-class man 1826; Fellow of Balliol, which he resigned in 1830. The author of many miscellaneous works. = Maria, 2nd daughter of Sir John Kennaway of Escott, co. Devon, Bart. (by Charlotte, 2nd daughter of James Amyatt, Esq., M.P.). Mar. 22 Dec. 1835. Deceased. ARMS OF KENNAWAY.—*Argent, a fesse azure between two eagles displayed in chief, and in base through an annulet gules a slip of olive and another of palm, in saltire proper.*

1. Harriette-Elizabeth. = Thomas Mozley, M.A., Clerk in Orders, Rural Dean, and Rector of Plymtree, co. Devon.

2. Jemima Charlotte, died 25 Dec. 1879. = John Mozley of Derby.

3. Mary Sophia, born 9 Nov. 1809. Died unmarried 5 Jan. 1828.

---

1. James Sealey, died 1870.

2. Harriett. = M. H. Shuttleworth.

3. Louisa Elizabeth. = John Bathurst Deane, M.A., F.S.A., Rector of St. Helen's, Bishopsgate, with St. Martin Outwich, London.

---

1. Hugh Pollexfen, Major 31st Regt. = Juliet, daughter of Captain Daniell of co. Cornwall.

2. Walter Meredith, Captain of Police, Hong Kong. = Mary, daughter of Edward Taverner, of Deal, co. Kent.

John, Lieut. R.N.

Daughters.

---

1. Henry William, born 7 Jan. 1798. Of Sherborne Lane, London. Died 21 April, 1879. Will dated 4 May, 1877, proved 15 May, 1879. = Anna Maria, 2nd daughter of Charles Coles. Living 1880.

2. John Coles, born 30 April, 1803. Living 1880.

1. Jemima, born 6 May 1799. Mar. 28 Aug. 1828. Died 6 Jan. 1853, buried at Tooting. = Richard Marsh of Canterbury, only brother of Dr. Herbert Marsh, sometime Bishop of Peterborough. Died 1 July, 1847, aged 89. ARMS OF MARSH.—*Sable, a cross argent fretty of the first, between four lions' heads erased of the second.*

2. Anna Maria, born 13 July, 1807. Deceased.

3. Eliza, born 30 May, 1812. Living at Herne Bay, 1880.

B

B

1. Joseph, of Hanley, co. Stafford. Died A.D. 1862, bur. at Nunhead. = Sophia Brooks, died 16 Nov. 1868.

2. Charles John, of Hanley. Died there. = Sarah Elizabeth Keys, died at Weston on Trent Vicarage in 1869, bur. at Stone, co. Staff.

3. George Henry, of Hanley, died 1869. = Jane Harding, mar. in 1826. Died 25 Dec. 1856.

4. Edward Newman, of Hanley, died 4 October, 1858, buried at Norwood. = Anne Moyle, mar. 1834. Died 22 Mar. 1868, bur. at Norwood.

1. Harriett Elizabeth, died unmar. 1879.

2. Mary Anne Sarah, living unmarried 1880.

Children of Joseph and Sophia Brooks:

1. Alexander Robert, died young.

2. Horace Mackinnon, living unmarried 1880.

3. Alfred, living unmar. in Australia.

1. Mary Agnes. = Anthony Cox Fenn, B.A., Clerk in Holy Orders.

2. Sophia Josephine, living unmar. 1880.

Children of Charles John and Sarah Elizabeth Keys:

1. Henry Richard, living at Birmingham unmarried.

2. Charles Edward, died young.

3. Joseph William, living in Australia. = Caroline Elizabeth Webb, mar. in 1863.

1. Fanny Susannah, living unmarried 1880.

2. Emma Georgina, living unmarried 1880.

3. Antoinette Sarah. = Samuel Plant, M.A. B.N. Coll., Oxon 22 April 1847. Prebendary of Lichfield and Vicar of Weston upon Trent, co. Stafford.

Children of George Henry and Jane Harding:

1. Henry John, emigrated to Canada. Twice married. No issue.

2. George, died unmar. 1860.

3. Arthur William, died young.

4. Francis Egerton, emigrated to Canada. Died 1875. = Jane Ellis.

5. Herbert, died young.

6. Samuel Harding, living unmarried 1880.

7. Charles William, emigrated to America. Living unmarried 1880.

8. William Henry, died young.

1. Elizabeth Sarah, mar. 1863. = Septimus Bourne, deceased. One son.

2. Ellen Jane, mar. 1857. = William H. Folker, of Hanley, Surgeon.

3. Emily, mar. 1855. Living 1880. = William James Dixon of Chester, deceased.

4. Marian, mar. 1860. Died 1861. = . C. Brown-Westhead.

5. Agnes, mar. 1872. = Charles Henry Stevenson, 18th Royal Irish Regt.

6. Ada Mary, died an infant.

Children of Edward Newman and Anne Moyle:

1. Frederick Moyle, died 1857.

2. Anna Maria, died young.

3. Edward Henry, died young.

4. Percy, died 1867.

5. Douglas, living unmarried 1880.

The Huguenot Refugee Family of Guillemard.

Communicated by HENRY WAGNER, Esq., F.S.A.

According to family tradition, John Guillemard was brought over to England as a child from the neighbourhood of Caudebec (probably Bolbec) in Normandy, in the care of a grandfather, his father having "shortly before the emigration dropped down dead in the market place." By his will he left £100, "if the Protestant subjects residing in Bollebec, in Upper Normandy, obtain leave to erect and build a church before or by the expiration of 1780," towards that object, and, failing this, to go in equal shares to the French Church in Threadneedle Street and the French Hospital of "La Providence," Old Street Road.*

Directors of the Hospital of "La Providence" for Poor French Protestants and their descendants:—

Elus.		
1754.	3 Avril.	Daniel Pilon.
1769.	12 Avril.	Jean Guillemard.
1785.	12 Juil.	Isaac Guillemard.
1789.	7 Oct.	Jaques Guillemard.
1793.	10 Avril.	Jean Guillemard.
1810.	7 Juil.	Daniel Guillemard.
1795.	8 Avril.	Guillaume Griffin.
1796.	13 Juil.	Jean Griffin.
1845.	5 Avril.	Ashhurst Majendie.

JOHN GUILLEMARD, came to England from (? Bolbec in) Normandy. Described as of the Liberty of the Tower of London in his will dated 14 April, 1779, and proved by his three sons, the ex'ors therein named, John, Isaac, and James, 11 Mar. 1782. = Magdalene, dau. and coheir of Isaac Leplay.

John Guillemard, bapt. in Walloon Church, 5 Nov. 1729. Of Spitalfields and Tottenham High Cross, Silkweaver. Died Feb. 1793. = Frances, dau. of Daniel Pilon by Jane, his wife, dau. of Pierre Bourdon.

Peter Guillemard, of the Old Artillery Ground, bapt. at Walloon Church, 26 May, 1731. *Sponsors*, Louis Guillemard and Marie Leplay. Died unmar. 1764. Admon. granted 11 Apr. 1764, to John Guillemard, the father.

Isaac Guillemard, bapt. at Walloon Church 22 March, 1744; d. 22 Dec. 1816, æt. 73. Of Spitalfields and Waltham Cross, Silkweaver. = Anne, dau. and sole surviving child of Daniel Le Maitre by Magdalen, his wife, dau. of Matthieu Paroissien, born 24 Oct. and bapt. at La Patente 4 Nov. 1746. Sponsors, Jean Le Maitre and Anne Paroissien. Marr. 5 April, 1770, at S. Matthew's, Bethnal Green. Died 26 May, 1784, and bur. at Ch. Ch., Spitalfields.

James Guillemard, b. 1748; d. 1826, unmarried.

John Guillemard, b. 31 Aug. 1764, bapt. at S. Jean, Spitalfields, 4 Sept. 1764. Of S. John's Coll., Oxford. B.A. 1786; M.A. 1789; F.R.S. Died 22 Nov., buried in the Pilon vault at Dagenham, Essex, 30 Nov. 1844, s.p.† = Mary Philippa, dau. of Rev. Edw. Giddy (by Catherine Davies, his wife, coheir of the Barony of Sandys), j.u. of Treadrea, co. Cornwall, and sister of Davies Gilbert, President R. S. Born ... Died Dec. 1850.

Jane Guillemard, bapt. at S. Jean, Spitalfields, Sept. 21, 1765. *Sponsor*, Jeanne Agace, *née* Pilon, mar. . . April, 1786; died . . . . 1795. = John Griffin of Steward Street, Weaver, and of the Goldsmiths' Company, and Bedford Place, London. Born 1757; died 2 May, 1852. He was son of William Griffin of London, weaver (1729-1803), by his wife Elizabeth Bodenham of Ludlow (1728-97), and had a brother William (1759-1808), who married, but has no representatives now living.

A B

* Mr. Samuel Smiles ('The Huguenots,' 1870), alleges John Guillemard, refugee from Champdeniers, where he had been minister, who "abjura le Protestantisme, & fut dépogé au Synode de Charenton en 1613," to have been ancestor of this family. This appears more than doubtful. But probably Marie Guillemard, "femme de Jaques Beuzeville de Bolbec, refugiée en Angleterre, en 1711," by whom she left issue, belonged to it.

† John Guillemard was a remarkable man, and on terms of friendship with Louis Philippe, Talleyrand, Washington, etc. He travelled much in his youth with the Duc de la Rochefoucauld-Liancourt, in whose volumes he is frequently mentioned, especially in America; and was appointed (about 1800) one of the Commissioners for settling disputed points between Great Britain and the United States of America.

A | B

John, b. 12 March, 1787; died young c. 1800.

Frances Griffin, b. 30 May, 1788, m. at St George's, Bloomsbury, 1831; died s.p. 6 Aug. 1868. = Ashurst Majendie, Esq., of Hedingham Castle, co. Essex, F.R.S., F.S.A., etc. Born 1784; died 8 Oct. 1867.

Jane Griffin, born 4 Dec. 1791; mar. 5 Nov. 1828, at Great Stanmore. Died s.p. 18 July, 1875, bur. in Kensal Green Cemetery. = Sir John Franklin (Arctic Explorer), Kt., K.C.H., K.R.G., F.R.S., D.C.L., b. 1786; d. 11 June, 1847. = Eleanor Anne, y^t dau. of William Porden, Esq. 1st wife. Born Mar. 19 Aug. 1823. Died 22 Feb. 1825.

Eleanor Elizabeth, b. 3 June, 1824; d. 30 Aug. 1860. = Rev. John Philip Gell, R. of Buxted, Sussex.

Mary Griffin, b. 30 Aug. 1793; m. 14 April, 1814; died 13 Dec. 1854; bur. in Kensal Green Cemetery. = Sir John Augustus Francis Simpkinson, Student of Ch. Ch., Oxford, B.A. 1802, and M.A. 1804; Q.C., and Bencher of Lincoln's Inn. Knighted 30 Oct. 1845. B. at Geneva . . . Dec. 1780. D. 8 July, 1851, æt. 70, and bur. under the Chapel at Lincoln's Inn. He was only son of Rev. John Simpkinson, R. of Cliffe, Kent, by Renée, dau. and coh. of Abraham De Wesselow.*

Rev. John Nassau Simpkinson, educated at Rugby and Trin. Coll., Cam. Curate of Hurstmonceux, 1840-45; Assist. Master in Harrow Sch. 1845-55; Rector of Brington, Northants, 1855-68; Rector of N. Creake, Norfolk, 1868. Author of 'Life of Rev. George Wagner,' 1858; 'The Washingtons,' a tale of the seventeenth century, 1860; etc., etc. Born 1 Jan. 1817. = Sarah Dorothea, dau. of Rev. E. T. Vaughan of Leicester (and sister of Dr. Vaughan, Head Master of Harrow School, 1844-59, and now Master of the Temple, and Dean of Llandaff), born 30 July, 1823; marr. 6 Dec. 1849, at St. Martin's, Leicester.

Francis Guillemard Simpkinson, late R.N., of Victoria Street, Westminster, & Villa La Cava, Cannes, in France. Born 26 May, 1819. Assumed, 20 Nov. 1869, the additional name of De Wesselow. = Emily, 2nd dau. of George Henry Malcolm Wagner, Esq., somewhile of Hurstmonceux Place, co. Sussex, b. 29 June, 1819; m. at St. Leonards on Sea, 14 Dec. 1858.

1. Francis Vaughan, b. 9 Oct. 1851, at Harrow. Caius Coll. Cam. Died 15 Dec. 1873.

2. Henry Walrond, b. 5 Jan. 1853, at Harrow. Fellow of St. John's, Cam.; Barrister-at-Law, Lincoln's Inn.

3. Ellen Renée, b. 16 Feb. 1854, at Harrow.

4. Charles Hare, b. 11 Mar. 1855, at Harrow. Balliol Coll., Oxford. Ordained Dec. 1878. Curate of St. Mark's, Kennington.

5. John Edgar Guillemard, b. 29 July, 1856, at Brington. Of Canterbury, New Zealand.

6. Frederick George, born 6 Dec. 1857, at Brington.

7. Edward Franklin, born 5 June, 1859, at Brington. Of C.C.C. Oxford.

8. Margaret Dorothea, born 20 Oct. 1860, at Brington.

9. Katharine Louisa, born 3 Oct. 1862, at Brington.

10. Charlotte, born 6 Apr. 1864, at Brington.

11. Theodore, b. 12 Apr. 1866, at Brington.

12. Edwyn Vaughan, b. 26 April, 1869, at North Creake.

C | B

* Abraham Wesselowski, a Russian of noble birth, was somewhile Ambassador of Peter the Great to the Court of Vienna, but fled thence on his summons to St. Petersburgh, after the sentence and supposed violent death, in 1718, of the Czarevitch Alexis, whose personal friend he had been. He proposed to settle in England, where his brother Theodore was Russian Ambassador from 1717 to 1720, and, some years after, obtained an Act of Naturalization, but finally elected to settle at Geneva (when he changed the form of his name to De Wesselow, and), where he married into the family of Fabri, and died, in his 100th year, in 1782. Cf. (a) Articles in the Russian Encyclopædic Lexicon on the three brothers, Abraham, Theodore, and Isaac Wesselowski; (b) Act of Parliament for the Naturalization of Abraham, Anno 1° Georgii 2^di; (c) 'Memoire de M. [Théodore] Wesselowsky à la Reine d'Angleterre,' and (d) 'Memoirs of Princess Daschkoff,' English Translation, London, 1845.

C | B

Louisa, born 24 Jan. 1815; m. at Harrow 2 Oct. 1851; died 22 Oct. 1870; bur. in Hastings Cemetery, co. Sussex. = James Dixon, Esq., F.R.C.S., of Portman Square; Surgeon to Royal London Ophthalmic Hospital; Author of several works on Ophthalmic Surgery; b. 22 Dec. 1813.

Anna Louisa, born 19 April, 1856.

Emma, b. 12 Nov. 1827; died 26 June, 1868; bur. in Hastings Cemetery, co. Sussex.

Marianne Jane, b. 8 Oct. 1825; mar. 31 July, 1858; died 20 May, 1865, and bur. in Church of S. Marcello, Rome. = Marchese Annibale Paulucci dei Calboli-Piazza of the Guardia Nobile of H. H. the Pope. Died 23 Sept. 1865, and bur. in San Marcello, Rome.

Luigi Giuseppe Francesco Maria Pelegrino, b. 23 May, 1859.

Raniero Pio Giuseppe Gaetano Francesco Nicola Maria, b. 15 March, 1861.

Guido Antonio Luigi Giacomo Nicola Maria, b. 25 July, 1862.

Peter Guillemard, b. 4 Jan., & bapt. at S. Jean, Spitalfields, 27 Jan. 1771; died at Reading 13 April, 1828; bur. at Ch. Ch. Spitalfields. = Tamazine, 5th dau. of Henry Venn, Esq., of Payhembury, co. Devon. Born ; mar. 11 Jan. 1802, at Holy Trinity, Exeter; died at Tottenham, 28 Jan. 1818, and bur. in Spitalfields.

Jane, dau. of Robert Hebert of Spitalfields, b. ; mar. 15 Sept. 1796, at St. Botolph's, Bishopsgate; d. 26 May, 1798. First wife. Buried in Spitalfields. = Daniel Guillemard, of St. Botolph's, Bishopsgate, born 7 Feb., and bapt. at S. Jean, 8 March, 1772; died 7 Aug. 1822; buried in Spitalfields Chyd. = Susan, 4th dau. of Henry Venn, Esq. of Payhembury, co. Devon, b. 1774; mar. 27 May, 1806, at Payhembury; died at Eltham, 29 June, 1853, æt. 79, and bur. at Hackney.

Ann, born 1773. — Ann, born 1775. — Isaac, b. 1777. Died infants.

Anne, b. 27 Nov., and bapt. 25 Dec. 1802; mar. Sept. 17, 1839, at Hackney. = William Deane Bath, Esq., of Bridgwater.

Rev. William Henry, Worc. Coll. Oxford. B.A. 1867, M.A. 1869.

Ellen.

Mary Tamazine, b. 6 Mar., and bapt. 3 April, 1804; died 26 May, 1830, unmar., and bur. in Spitalfields. — Jane Louis, b. 1 May, and bapt. 28 May, 1805; died 17 June, 1806.

Jane Sadler, b. 18 Nov. and bapt. 23 Dec. 1806. — Susan, b. 13 Mar., and bapt. 19 Apr. 1808; d. 28 April, 1832, unmar. Buried in Spitalfields.

Peter, b. 29 Nov., and bap. 25 Dec. 1809; d. 4 Feb. 1811.

Rev. Henry Peter Guillemard, Fel. of Trin. Coll., Oxford, and Rector of Barton on the Heath, Glosters. Born 27 Sept., and bap. 26 Dec. 1812. Died April, 1857, s.p., and buried at Barton. = Julia, dau. of Rev. G. Hulme, of Shinfield, n[r] Reading. Mar. at Worcester. Died 1878. Bur. Barton.

Elizabeth Venn, born 8 Feb., and bapt. at Tottenham 23 March, 1815; d. 18 Mar. 1839, unmarried, and buried in Spitalfields.

John Guillemard of born 14 Nov. 1797, and bapt. 13 Dec. in Walloon Church; d. 30 Jan. 1873; buried in Tower Hamlets Cemety. = Amelia, dau. of . . . . Gullick of Guernsey.

Emily. b. 1844.

Harvey Milne, b. 1847. Author of *The Countess and the Painter*, 1875, 16º, etc.

Mary Frances, b. 1852.

Ellen, b. 1856.

(All, except Elizabeth Venn, baptized at Christ Church, Spitalfields.)

D

D

Louisa, dau. of G. Tyser, M.D., b. m. 1839; d. 1840, s.p. = Rev. James Guillemard, b. 14 July, and bapt. 7 Dec. 1807; Fellow of S. John's, Oxford; B.A. 1830; M.A. 1834; Vicar of Kirtlington, 1838; died Jan. 1858; bur. at St. Mary's, Tenby. = Louisa Elizabeth, dau. of Henry Watson, Esq., mar. 1843, at Ryde.

Frances, born 23 June, 1809, bapt. 17 Jan. 1810; mar. 28 May, 1833, at S. Lawrence, Isle of Wight; d. 1877, s.p.; bur. Tenby. = Frederic Daniel Dyster, M.D., F.L.S.

Isaac Guillemard, M.D., of Eltham, b. 25 June, 1811, bapt. 22 Jan. 1812; d. 18 Oct. 1852, bur. at Eltham. = Ann Pierce, eldest dau. of John Upham of London, West India Merchant; b. m. 8 June, 1839.

(All bapt. at St. John's, Hackney.)

Caroline Ann, b. 1 May, and bapt. 9 July, 1840.

Frederic, b. 14 July, 1841; bapt. 29 June, 1843; died 2 June, 1847.

Charles Edward, b. 30 Jan., and bapt. 29 June, 1843.

Arthur George, b. 18 Dec. 1845; bapt. 3 Sept. 1846. Author of 'Over Land and Sea: a log of Travel round the World.' 1875.

William Mountrich, b. 19 Feb., and bapt. 3 Aug. 1848; d. 25 Dec. 1866.

Francis Henry Hill, M.B. Caius College, Cambridge; b. 12 Sept. 1852.

(All baptized at Eltham.)

Rev. William Henry Guillemard, D.D., late Fellow of Pemb. Coll. Camb. Head Master of the Royal Sch., Armagh, 1848-69; Vicar of St. Mary the Less, Camb., 1869. Author of 'Greek Testament,' Hebraistic Ed. 1875. Born 23 Nov. 1815; bapt. 13 Jan. 1816. = Elizabeth Susanna, elder dau. of W. H. Turner, Esq., of Birmingham, born 24 May, 1823; mar. 12 July, 1849, at S. Paul's, Knightsbridge.

George Guillemard, b. 29 Jan., and bapt. 20 May, 1817; d. in Madeira 6 April, 1844, æt. 27, unmar., and bur. at Funchal.

Harriet Louisa, b. 10 Dec. 1820, bapt. 4 Feb. 1821; died 17 Aug. 1842, æt. 21; buried at Hackney.

Elizabeth Susanna, b. 23 May, 1850; d. 7 Nov. 1873; bur. at Cambridge.

Rosamond Harriet, b. 20 Nov. 1853.

Mary Frances, b. 8 June, 1855.

Katharine Stéphanie, b. 26 Dec. 1859.

Laurence Nunns, b. 7 June, 1862.

Lucy Jane, b. 3 March, 1866.

(All bapt. at the Cathedral, Armagh.)

Fanny Marian, b. 1844. = Percy Swan Wilford, mar. Jan. 1879.

Edith Harriet, born ... 1845; m. ... Ap. 1870 (St. Thomas's, Winchester). = Rev. Frederic Dobree Teesdale, Warden of the College, and Canon of St. Andrew's Cath. Inverness, N.B. Author of Poems, 1871.

Kenneth, born 1871.

Walter George Guillemard, New College, Oxford, b. 20 Nov. 1847.

Agnes Elizabeth, b. mar. at St. Thomas's, Winchester, ... Sept. 1873. = Rev. John Henry Wilkinson of Clifton. Magd. Coll. Oxford; B.A. 1870, M.A. 1872.

Arthur Franklin, Keble College, Oxford, b. 14 July, 1851.

Ada Madeleine, b. 1853; marr. at St. Thomas's, Winchester, 10 Aug. 1875. = Rev. John Neal, M.A., Corpus Christi College, Cambridge.

Bernard James Guillemard, M.R.C.S., b. 5 Oct. 1854.

MONUMENTAL INSCRIPTION TO SIR JOHN AUGUSTUS FRANCIS SIMPKINSON, AT LINCOLN'S INN.

Memoriæ Sacrum Johannis Augusti Francisci Simpkinson Equitis Aurati Jurisconsulti regii hujusce Societatis e præfectis Consessoribus qui thesaurarius anno MDCCCXLV creatus reginam Victoriam Aedes Collegii magnificentius exstructas inaugurare dignantem publico hospitio præses excepit annuo qui apud suos est magistratu singulari cum honore functus vii legum peritissimus plurimis literis ornatus benignus fidelis verax summa probitate simulatione virtutum nulla ita ad majora se in Deum officia paratius accessurum credebat si suos pietate bonos omnes observantia inopes misericordia prosequeretur Genevæ natus matre Helvetica prid Kal Dec MDCCLXXX obiit Londini octav Id Jul. M.DCCC Anno Ætat LXXI° subter hoc sacellum sepultus jacet monumentum hoc uxor et filii mœrentes posuerunt

WILL OF FRANCIS TYSSEN, 1690.

(Extracted from the Registry of the Prerogative Court of Canterbury)

In the Name of God Amen. I Francis Tyssen the Elder of the City of London Esqr being in health of Body and of sound and perfect mind and memory (thanks be to God for the same) and considering the certainty of Death and the uncertainty of the time thereof and for preventing of all differences that may arise touching my Estate after my decease do hereby make publish and declare this to be my last Will and Testament and first and principally I commend my Soul into the hands of my Creator who gave it hoping that through the Passion Death and Merits of my dear Lord and Saviour Jesus Christ to have remission of all my Sins and partake of the benefits of a joyfull resurrection and my Body I commit to the Earth to be decently buried at the discretion of my Executors hereinafter named and for my worldly Estate which it hath pleased God to bless me with I will devise and bequeath in manner and form following (that is to say) Imprimis I give devise and bequeath unto my Son Francis Tyssen of Shacklewell in the County of Middlesex Esquire and his Heirs all and every of my Messuages Lands Tenements and hereditaments whatsoever both Freehold and Copyhold situate lying and being in the City of London Counties of Middlesex and Huntingdon and elsewhere within the Kingdom of England To have and to hold the said Messuages Lands Tenements and hereditaments unto my said Son Francis Tyssen his Heirs and Assigns for ever Provided always upon condition and my Will and Mind is and I do hereby will direct and appoint that my said Son Francis Tyssen and his Heirs shall out of the Rents Issues and profits of all my said Lands Tenements and Hereditaments to him before devised well and truly pay or cause to be paid unto my loving Wife Dorothy Tyssen the yearly sum of five hundred pounds of lawfull money of England for and during her natural life by equal quarterly payments the first payment to be made on the next quarter of a year after my decease and I the said Francis Tyssen the elder do hereby charge all my Freehold Messuages Lands Tenements and hereditaments in the said City of London Counties of Middlesex and Huntingdon and elsewhere within the said Kingdom of England with the payment of the said yearly sum of five hundred pounds unto my said Wife Dorothy Tyssen for her natural life aforesaid Item I give devise and bequeath unto my said Son Francis Tyssen and his Heirs all my Lands or Plantations and Stocks upon the said Plantations with the appurtenances in their Majesty's Island of Antigua in America and also all my Messuages Lands Tenements and Hereditaments in the Province of Zealand and elsewhere in parts over the Seas to hold the said Plantations and Stocks thereon and the said Messuages Lands Tenements and Hereditaments in the Province of Zealand and elsewhere in parts over the seas unto my said Son Francis Tyssen his heirs executors administrators and assigns for ever. Item I give and bequeath unto my ssid Son Francis Tyssen my great Silver Bason with my Coat of Arms and Crest on it my Silver Gilt outlandish Flaggon two Silver Plates whereon my Coat of Arms and Crest are engraven a Silver Tangard whereon my Coat of Arms and Crest are also engraven my Gold Ring with my Arms and Crest on it my Silver Tea Pot and my Steel Seals Silver Toockpick Case and Picker within with my Coat of Arms and Crest on them my Coat of Arms painted upon Cloth which hangs in a Wainscott Case in the Dining Room and all that shall be found at my decease in my Cabinet in my Closet except a parcel of Baby's Plate five pounds in Silver three pences and two five pound pieces of Guinea Gold in the said Cabinet which I give and bequeath unto my said Wife Dorothy Tyssen. Item All my Household Goods Linen Plate Gold Silver and Jewels which I shall have in my House in Philpot Lane London at the time of my decease and not hereinbefore bequeathed to my said Son Francis I give and bequeath the same unto my said Wife Dorothy Tyssen. Item I give and bequeath unto my said Wife Dorothy Tyssen the sum of one thousand pounds of lawful money of England to be paid her immediately after my decease. Item I give and bequeath unto the Dutch Church in Austin Friars London the sum of One hundred pounds of lawful English money to be paid unto the Elders of the said Church or any three of them for the use of the said Church. Item I give and bequeath unto the Poor of the said Dutch Church the sum of One hundred pounds of like lawful money to be paid to the Deacons of the said Church or any three of them for the use of the said poor. Item I give and bequeath unto the two Ministers of the said Church at the time of my decease the sum of ten pounds a piece and to the Reader of the said Church at the time of my decease the sum of forty shillings and to the Sexton of the said Church the sum of twenty shillings. Item I give and bequeath unto the Poor of the Parish of St. Andrew's Hubbard London the sum of fifteen pounds of lawful money of England to be paid to the Church Wardens of the said Parish for the use of the said Poor. Item I give and bequeath unto The Reverend Doctor Edward Lake Minister of the Parishe of St. Mary Athill London the sum of five pounds of lawful money and to Joseph Taylor Clarke of the said Church the sum of forty shillings. Item I give and bequeath to the Poor of the Great Church in Flushing in Zealand the sum of twenty pounds of lawful English Money. Item I give and bequeath unto Captain Cornelius Loncke of Flushing in the Province of Zealand aforesaid the sum of Forty pounds of lawful money of England. Item I give and bequeath unto Daniel Loncke son of the said Cornelius the sum of fifty pounds. Item I give and bequeath unto Apolonia Loncke Daughter of the said Cornelius the sum of fifty pounds of like lawful money of England. Item I give and bequeath unto the children of Cornelius Brandt late Master of a Ship at Flushing aforesaid deceased the sum of fifty pounds of good English money to be equally divided amongst the said children share and share alike. Item I give and bequeath unto John Tyssen of Flushing aforesaid the sum of One hundred pounds of lawful money of England. Item I give and bequeath unto my Sister in law Mary Vanderpost the sum of ten pounds of like lawful money of England. Item I give and bequeath unto her Son Adrian Vanderpoest and his Wife the sum of six pounds a piece to buy them mourning and the ten pounds before bequeathed to my said Sister in law Mary Vanderpoest is to buy her mourning. Item I give and bequeath unto Mary Stockden Daughter of the said Mary Vanderpoest the sum of six pounds of good English money to buy her Mourning. Item I give and bequeath unto the said Cornelius Loncke the sum of Six pounds more of like money to buy him mourning. Item I give and bequeath unto the said Daniel Loncke the like sum of Six pounds more to buy him mourning. Item I give and bequeath unto the said Apolonia Loncke the like sum of six pounds more to buy her mourning. Item I give and bequeath unto the said John Tyssen the like sum of six pounds more to buy him mourning. Item I give and bequeath unto William Garrett the sum of twenty shillings. Item I give and bequeath unto my said Son's Servants who shall dwell with him at the time of my decease the sum of three pounds a piece to buy them mourning. Item I give and bequeath unto all my Servants which shall dwell with me at the time of my decease the sum of five pounds a piece to buy them mourning. And lastly all my Leasehold Messuages Lands and Tenements Leases

Mortgages Goods Merchandizes Monies Debts Stocks and all my Estate whatsoever not hereinbefore bequeathed I give and bequeath unto my said Son Francis Tyssen and I the said Francis Tyssen the elder do hereby make nominate and appoint my said Son Francis Tyssen sole Executor of this my last Will and Testament so revoking all former Wills I publish and declare this to be my last Will and Testament In witness whereof I the said Francis Tyssen the Elder to this my last Will and Testament contained in one sheet of paper and part of another sheet have subscribed my name at the bottom of the first sheet and set my seal at the top of the same sheet and at the end of my said Will on the other sheet of Paper have also set my hand and seal this fifth day of May Anno Domini One thousand six hundred ninety and in the second year of the Reign of our Sovereign Lord and Lady William and Mary by the Grace of God King and Queen of England Scotland France and Ireland Defender of the Faith etc —Francis Tyssen

Signed Sealed Published and Declared by the said Francis Tyssen the Elder as and for his last Will and Testament in the presence of us this fifth day of May One thousand six hundred ninety —John King—William Higgs—Wm. Garrett—Mary Stockton

[Probatum fuit apud London tricessimo die mensis Julij Anno Domini millesimo Septengentesimo]

Family of Gresham.*

(*Continued from p.* 338.)

GRANTS OF LAND.

Patent Roll, 37 Henry VIII, part 1, m 11, No 33

Grant in consideration of the sum of £408 18s 10d to Richard Gresham and John Gresham of London knights and William Gresham Citizen and mercer of London of all lands meadows feedings pastures woods underwoods rents services and hereditaments called Rowholte with the appurts now or late in the tenure of the said John Gresham knight scituate lying and being in the parish of Chelsham co Surrey to the late Monastery of Shene now dissolved formerly belonging Also the messuage tenement and farm called Westbarnes with the appurts in all five hundred and seventy-six acres and a half lying and being in the parish of Marten to the late monastery of Marten belonging, also all tithes of sheaves grain and hay, also all those woods there containing 20 acres in the parish of Marten Also all that messuage called Welcombes and Laurence lying in Whatyngdon to the late Monastery of Chertsey belonging And also a croft and half a virgate of land called Stacye's, etc in Whatyngdon formerly belonging to Thos Bassett and to the late Monastery of Chertsey and now parcel of the honor of Hampton Court Also all woods underwoods and trees, etc, on the above premisses growing and belonging also all rents and yearly profits whatsoever reserved etc Also grants that the said Richard John and William have the premisses as freely and fully as the last Prior of Shene, the last Prior of Marton, and the last Abbot of Chertsey respectively held the same The possessions in Chelsham extend to the clear yearly value of 26s 8d, in Westbarnes to £18 10s and in Whatyngdon 50s 1d To have, etc, to them and the heirs and assigns of the said John Gresham for ever to the use and behoof of the said Richard John and William and the heirs and assigns of the said John for ever To hold, etc, Westbarnes Welcombes and Laurences and other the premisses in Marton and Whatyngdon in capite by service of the 40th part of one knight's fee Rendering yearly for Westbarnes, etc, 39s 8d, for Welcombes and Laurences and other the premisses in Whatyngdon 5s 1d, into the Court of Augmentations. [T R Westm 12 September by the King himself]

Patent Roll, 2 Edward VI, part 6, m. 8

Reciting letters patents of 3rd April, 1 Edw VI, ordering Sr John Gresham Knt "*now Maior of oure Cytie of London*" and Andrew Judde, Alderman of the same, to be commissioners for the sale of a certain quantity of Allum and Leade, and now acquitting them of the sum of £669 17s 10d for all manner of accounts, etc, concerning the same [Hatfield, 3rd September]

Patent Roll, 4 Edw VI, part 8, m 26

Grant to John Gresham, Knight and Alderman of London, and others, in consideration of the sum of £1,276 0s 10d of divers premisses in Barbican, Swanne Alley Golden Lane, Bichlane, Redcross St, Whitecross St Grub St, and Moor Lane in the parish of St Giles Cripplegate All which premisses extend to the clear yearly value of £91 2s 11d To hold, etc, in free burgage of the City of London, and not in capite [Leiges, 12th April]

* Communicated by GRANVILLE LEVESON GOWER, F.S A, Esq

Patent Roll, 5 Edw. VI., part 4, m. 10.

Grant to Sir John Gresham, Sir Rowland Hill, and Geo. Barons, Citizen and Alderman of London, and Wm. Blakwell, gent., common clerk of the City, in consideration of the sum of £1,461 2s. 6d., of 5 closes of land, containing 27 acres next Gallowe feld being in Lambeth, co. Surr., to the late Hospital of Thomas Becket in Southwark late belonging; one croft of land and meadow called Jewes meade containing 1 acre in Camberwell, And all lands, etc., lying in Wymbledon and Mitcham; 26 acres in St. George feld, Southwark; an annual rent of 13s. 4d. issuing from a tenement in Blackman St.; an annual rent of 18d. issuing from lands and tenements in Penge to the late Hospital formerly belonging. Also an annual rent of 24s. in Dunsford, co. Surr., an annual rent of 40s. issuing from the manor of Chilworth, co. Surr. Also the Rectory of Great Wakeryng, co. Essex, etc., to the said late Hospital belonging. Also an annual rent of 13s. 4d. issuing from land called Medewocke. Also divers possessions in London and Southwark. [Westminster, 13th August.]

Patent Roll, 33 Henry VIII., part 4, m. 1-48.

Licence to William Rede to alienate the site of the house or late priory of the Carmelite Friars, commonly called the Whyte Fryers of Blakeney, co. Norf., with lands in Blakeney and Wyston, co. Norf. To Richard Gresham, Knt., his heirs and assigns for ever. [T. R. apud Westminster, 20th March.]

Patent Roll, 37 Hen. VIII., part 8, m. 20-26.

Licence in consideration of £20 17s. 4d. to Richard Gressham, Knight, to alienate the manor of Wetherwyke in Holdernes, co York, also the moiety of the manor of Tassborough, co. Norfolk, etc., to John Gressham, knight, and Thomas Gressham, Citizen and Mercer of London. To have and to hold to them and their heirs for ever. [T. R. apud Westminster, 11th July.]

Patent Roll, 7 Edw. VI., part 11. m. 20.

Grant to Thomas Gresham, Esq., in consideration of his services beyond the seas, of the reversion of scite of the late Monastery of Westacre, co. Norf., and of the manors of Westacre and Custhorpe, and the Rectory of Westacre, etc., and other premisses in the said County of Norf., etc. [Westm., 1st of July.]

Redmayne or Redman Family.—How or when did the connection of this Family terminate with Harewood Castle, Yorkshire, and what became of them afterwards?—R. N. R.

Fowler and Holland.—I am desirous of obtaining genealogical or heraldic information respecting the family of Fowler of Coleby, Lincolnshire. Thomas and Mellicent Fowler in the time of James II. had a daughter Elizabeth, heiress of property there and in several adjoining places. Also as to the family of Holland of Featherston, Yorkshire, about 1760.

18 *Oppidans Road,* James Rusby, F.R. Hist. Soc.
Regent's Park.

Sir Anthony Greenway, Knt.—In a deed dated 15 April, 2 Charles I., 1627, Anthony Greenway of Leckhamsted, co. Bucks, Dame Amphillis Millicent his wife, William Wise of Lincoln's Inn, Esq., and Beale Sapperton of Leckhamsted, convey certain lands in Leckhamsted to John Pollard of Wickin, co. Northampton, gent., for £2080. The deed discloses the following Pedigree:—

Sir Anthony Greenway, Knt., deceased.=
|
Richard Greenway, Esq., deceased.=
|
Anthony Greenway, Esq.=Dame Amphillis Millicent.

Can any readers of 'Mis. Gen. et Heraldica' inform me who Sir Anthony Greenway was, and what relationship, if any, existed between William Wise, Beale Sapperton, and the last-mentioned Anthony Greenway of the Pedigree?—T. N.

FITCH PEDIGREE.

FROM THE VISITATION OF WARWICK IN 1683.

KNIGHTLOW HUNDRED. HINCKLEY, 4° Sept. 1682.

These Armes were taken from a Buckram Scocheon produced by Mr Fitch, and he says the Crest is a Leopard's head pierced through with Two Swords, but it does not join to the Essex family, therefore better proof must be made.

James Fitch of Bocking in Essex.=

1. Thomas Fitch of Hinckley in com. Leic., obiit circa an. 1672, ætat. circa 67 an. s.p. = Eliz. da. of Sr Tho. Cæsar of . . . . in Hampshire.

2. Gilbert Fitch of Wolvey in com. Warr. obijt circa ann. 1673, ætat. circa 65 ann. = Mary, da. of Giles Alington of Westley, in com. Cantabrig; she dyed about 1670.

Margaret wife of . . . . Plummer of . . . . in com. Kent.

Children of Gilbert Fitch and Mary:

3. James, dyed an infant.

2. Thomas Fitch, dyed unm. ætat. 24 ann.; d. circa an. 1658.

1. Gilbert Fitch of the Temple, of Woolvey in com. Warr., now living, ætat. circa 48 ann. 1682. = Anne da. of Adrian Allington of Hansyate Hall, in co. Cambridge (or Suff.) She died 1671. = Elizabeth, 5th da. of William Whitehall of Oldbury in com. Warr., and widow of Ezekias Smallbrook of Woolvey aforesaid.

1. Anna, wife of Scaruing Phillips of Woolvey, com. Warr., and after to Edward Phipps of Woolvey aforesaid.

2. Mary, dyed unm.

3. Elizabeth, and

4. Margaret, dyed infants.

4. Margaret, wife of Roger Gale of Taunton in com. Somerset, a twinn with Gilbert.

Children of Gilbert Fitch and Anne:

2. James, dyed young, ætat. 1 year and half.

1. Thomas Fitch of the Temple, of Woolvey in com. Warr., now living ætat. 16 an. 1682. = Sarah, da. and heir of Ezekias Smalbrook of Woolvey Temple, in com. Warr., she is now living æt. 14 ann. 1682.

2. Eliz., dyed young.

2. Eliz., ætat. 12 ann. 1682.

3. Anna, ætat. circa 10 annor.

Children of Gilbert Fitch and Elizabeth:

3. Gilbert, æt. 8 annor, 1682.

4. Mary, æt. 7 annor 1682.

5. Dorothy, ætat. 6 annor, 1682.

*Seal of Sébastien Balicourt.**

Sébastien Balicourt.†=Marie Pierseni, b. 1664; m. 1701; b. 26 May, 1753, æt. 89.

Simon Balicourt, died in Wood Street, London, 1 Dec. 1757; bur. in Churchyard of S. Andrew Undershaft. Will dated 22 Nov. 1757; appoints as Ex'ors his cosen Tobias Kleinert, ffurrier to H.R.H. the Princess Dowager of Wales, and Mr. Henry Haskye of Lombard Street, Apothecary. Proved by them 26 June, 1758. (Hutton, 179.)=Sarah . . . . b. m. d. 10 April, 1752.

Sarah Balicourt, b. Jan. 19 (?), 1738, bapt. at S. Michael, Wood Street, London; m. about 1763; d. Sept. 14, 1811, aged 73, buried in South Cloister, Christ's Hospital.=John Wilkinson Long of Christ's Hospital, London, born 7 Aug. 1737; d. 28 Oct. 1799, æt. 62, buried in South Cloister, Christ's Hospital.

Marie Caroline, born 1745; d. unm. 1784, buried in South Cloister, Christ's Hospital.

1. John Long, b. 2 July, 1767; d. s.p. 5 Aug. 1820, and bur. at Christ Church, Newgate Street. Author of 'Some Account of the Reformed Church of France,' 1819, privately printed. On tablet on south wall of Christ Church, a long Inscription with Pedigree.=1st to Catharine Hearn, d. 5 May, 1811, aged 21. 2nd to Ann Clark, who survived him. No issue.

2. Sarah Long, b. 24 Jan. 1769; m. 22 Oct. 1800; d. 12 Nov. 1848.=Rev. Henry George Watkins, born 5 Feb. 1765; Edm. Hall, Ox.; B.A. 1791; M.A. 1794; Rector of St. Swithin's with St. Mary Bothaw, London, 1805-50; d. 9 Jan. 1850, in his 85th year.

3. Thomas Long, b. 1771; d. 1826, bur. at Bunhill Fields.=Katherine Darling, dau. of James Burgh, d. 1833, aged 64, bur. at Bunhill Fields.

Other issue d. s.p.

Rev. Henry George Watkins, b. 8 June, 1808; Worc. Coll. Ox.; B.A. 1831; M.A. 1833; Vicar of St. John's, Potter's Bar, co. Midd. 1835.=Sarah Lea, dau. of Charles Pritchett Bousfield, Esq., of Adelphi Place, Camberwell, Surrey; b. 29 February, 1820; m. 10 April, 1845.

Seven other children, died in infancy.

Thomas Burt Long, b. 13 Feb. 1801; m. 13 June, 1822; d. 6 Dec. 1848.=Charlotte Jane Anstey. Born Jan. 11, 1800. Died July 4, 1878.

Sophia Bishop, b. 1803; m. 1822. No issue.=James Burgh, b. 1761; d. 1843.

1. Sarah Mary, b. 4 June, 1846; m. 21 Feb. 1871.=Alexander Grubb, R.A., b. 28 April, 1842; Lieut. 1861; Capt. 1874.

2. Elizabeth, b. 7 Sept. 1847; m. 25 July, 1872.=Edmund Symes Thompson, M.D., of Cavendish Square, London, Gresham Professor of Medicine, etc. Author of various contributions to Medical Journals. B. 16 Nov. 1837.

3. Rev. Henry George Watkins, Ch. Ch. Ox.; B.A. 1872; M.A. 1874; Curate of S. Michael's, Chester Square, 1876-78; b. 1 June, 1849.=Marie Heloise De Mailly, dau. of Rev. Charles Beighley, D.D., b. 30 Nov. 1858; m. 4 Nov. 1879.

Sarah Mary Watkins, b. 22 Dec. 1871. | Alexander Henry Watkins, b. 18 April, 1873. | Herbert Watkins, b. 26 Dec. 1875. | Ernest Watkins, b. 8 Feb. 1877. | Walter Bousfield Watkins, b. 1 July, 1879.

Henry Edmund Symes, b. 22 June, 1873. | Francis Symes, b. 2 Feb. 1875. | Arthur Howard Symes, b. 6 Nov. 1876. | Lilian Symes, b. 7 April, 1878.

Thomas Balicourt, b. 24 May, 1823.

Katherine Mary, b. 23 June, 1831; m. 26 April, 1856.=William Dollond, 2nd son of George Dollond of St. Paul's Churchyard (of a Huguenot Refugee Family).

Eight others.

* The original seal is of brass, and around it is inscribed "Sebast. Balicourt, 1684." It is in the possession of the Rev. H. G. Watkins.

† Né à Verdun en 1660, pasteur aux environs de Metz en 1685. L'ordre ayant été donné aux Ministres de Metz de sortir de France, Balicourt y désobéit et il continua à prêcher en prenant toutes fois les précautions nécessaires pour ne point être arrêté; mais il ne put échapper longtemps aux recherches de la police. Traqué de tous côtés & sur le point d'être pris, il se réfugia chez un épicier, prétendu converti, qui le cacha et lui fit passer la frontière dans un tonneau. Balicourt arriva heureusement à Berlin. On lit dans les listes de Dieterici que "M. de Balicourt fut ministre de la colonie de François refugiés à Boucholtz et Pancou en 1698." Il y resta jusqu' en 1707. En 1716, il remplaça Jean de Convenant comme Ministre de la Friedrichstadt, ety mourut le 4 fév. 1731. Il laissa un fils qui, ayant passé en Angleterre, mourut en Londres en 1757 . . . " etc., etc. (Haag's 'La France Protestante,' new Edition of 1877.) His portrait is in the possession of the Rev. H. G Watkins, at Potter's Bar, Middlesex.

HARINGTON OF SOMERSET

(*Continued from p* 318.)

In returning from Devon to the main line of Harington in Somerset, we give

A Brief Memoir and some other Notes of John Harington, Esq., of Kelston.

M.P. for Bath 1646-51-56.

John Harington, Esq., Member of Parliament for Bath, Justice of the Peace for the county of Somerset, son and heir of Sir John Harington, Knt., was born in 1589, and succeeded to the family estates in 1612. By some strange fatality—whether by the teaching of his tutor, as some allege, or by the force of his own inward promptings—he adopted Puritan principles, and to the great surprise of his father's friends and connection at large, remained a strong Parliamentarian through life. His political bias enables us to attribute to him, for distinction among many John Haringtons in succession, the *sobriquet* of "the Parliamentarian," and henceforth we intend to particularize him by that designation, just as we distinguished the John Harington who was father of the Knight by calling him "John of Stepney."*

The future "Parliamentarian" matriculated at Oxford 7 Dec. 1604, from Trinity College (which was also the college of James Harington, the author of the 'Republic of Oceana'), as a Knight's son, at the early age of thirteen. After taking his degree, he became a member of Lincoln's Inn, and spent much of his early life there engaged in literary pursuits. It is said that besides Law and Mathematics, he then took up the study of Hebrew, which special study would seem to point him out as the John Harington whose name is associated with some metrical translations of the Psalms from the original Hebrew.

The tone and character of this Son were in complete contrast with his father. The Knight had been everything by turns,—courtier, soldier, wit, poet, country squire, mechanician, satirist, church restorer,—nay more, it was by no means his own fault that he had not late in his life taken Holy Orders, like his ancestor the Dean of York, Sir James Harington of Brierley, and become *per saltum* Archbishop of Dublin and Governor of Ireland, for which according to his own shewing in his 'Treatise on the State of Ireland,' he was in every way supremely qualified. John Harington, the son, was on the other hand careful, cautious, sober-minded in everything. If he retained the family taste for poetry and music, he took care to apply it to psalms and psalm-tunes. He never wrote such a stave as that from the Black Sanctus of John of Stepney, which we are told used to haunt King Henry, the Defender of the Faith, and move him to whistle or hum it as he reflected on Monks, Religion, and Reform. John the Parliamentarian was the writer of 'Essays and Dialogues in favour of the Presbyterian Doctrine.' We cannot by any stretch of imagination suppose him to have been the author of the fugitive pieces printed in the 'Nugæ,' entitled Polindor and Flostella. Nor do we suppose that he ever wrote sonnets for ladies of the county when engaged at Quarter Sessions, which would have been quite "the thing" for his father to do. Much less could

* To set up a clear distinction between the successive John Haringtons would seem to be the more needful, because some confusion in their biographies has been already created by various writers. For instance the learned authoress of 'The Queens of England' in treating of the reigns of the Queens Mary and Elizabeth and the confidential doings of the Lord High Admiral Seymour, has usually spoken of John Harington the elder (who was in the household of the Lord Admiral) as Sir John Harington, thus leading many to think of the son who was a Knight and courtier during the close of Queen Elizabeth's reign, and for a short time in that of King James. But that the elder Harington was not a Knight is indisputably proved by the wording of the grant of arms made to him in 1568 in which he is expressly described as John Harington, *Esquire*.

we conceive that any index-maker* would give us a reference to *him* as Sir "*Ajax*" Harington There was not a spark in him of such humour as the Ajax contained. The bent of his mind, after pursuit of studies, was sedulously to discharge his public and private duties

Indeed it is said (and the tradition may be true?) that he had a rigid ruler in Dionysia his wife, one of the daughters of James Ley, first Earl of Marlborough Moreover, he became connected by the alliance of his daughter with such families as Pym and Rous He was certainly the only Harington of Kelston with so grave a temperament, but the Puritan was unmistakeable in him [His name may be seen recorded in Prestwich's 'Republic'] There is a story on record about this John Harington, that he once sought an audience with King Charles at Carisbrooke Castle, and the audience having been granted, the King said of him after the interview, that he could "see that man's pride through the hole in a stocking!"

We will only say further that this is the John Harington named in the Herald's note at the end of the County Visit 1613, under "Bath Forum Hundred"—"John Harington Ar will be at London He married the Lord Chief Justice's daughter" [Dionysia Ley] His matrimonial connection is further testified to in State Papers (Domestic), Sept 24, 1626, where the Lord Treasurer Ley desired that his "son-in-law Mr Harington might serve as Deputy and give the Charge at the Sessions held at Bridgewater"

He died, we know, in April, 1654, but we can find no register of his burial, nor any tablet to his memory We are guided to the date of his decease by the probate of his will in July of that year He is supposed to have been buried at Kelston, but the registral entry is wanting, as already stated, and it seems most remarkable that with such county position there should be no tomb nor mural monument erected, either to *his* memory or to that of the witty Knight his father, either at Kelston or in Bath Abbey †

Memoranda left by John Harington, Esq, M P for Bath 1646, as to his Entry in Parliament

March 31st, 1646		I first sate in the House of Commons.
April 6,	,,	I attended Sir John Danvers to the Lords
,, 7th,	,,	A Committee concerning filling of Churches, I one of them
,, 24,	,,	It was last night resolved at the Committee for the North, that Sir John Horner had done illegally, and the election of his son and me was unlawful
June 23,	,,	I took the oaths of a Justice of the Peace
July 21,	,,	I deliver in the return and get a ticket writ for 19s 2d, not less
,, 22d,	,,	I got the ticket on promise to behave myself an honest man, took the Oaths of Supreme Allegiance. Set in Parlt
,, 23d,	,,	A great Committee of Members to suppress insolent Cavaliers, Sir James Harington one of them.
Oct 28th,	,,	I spake in the Debate with approbatn. (I Thank God)

An Enumeration of Lands belonging to John Harington of Kelston, Esq, taken from a MS in his handwriting in the early part of 17th century,—probably made in 1612, when he succeeded his father the Knight

(*Compare with this the estates named in Lady Rogers' Will, 'Mis Gen. et Her,' Vol. III, p 228.*)

* *Cf* Cal State Papers Dom 1599 (Vol 1598-1601), p 306—"Sir *Ajax* Harington"

† The monument attributed to Sir John Harington's memory by Collinson, in his 'History of Somerset,' is extant still at Kelston It is, however, a ledger stone of no *real* antiquity (laid down as a record of their genealogy by some late member of the family?) upon which reference is made to their Cumberland origin, and the name of Sir John Harington, Kt is inscribed (See 'Mis Gen et Her.' Vol III p 31)

In Cornwall. †

Roseglase of Trembletier* in poss'on of Thomas Pierce 7th Sept. 1611.
Bery Close in poss'on of Abel French jure uxoris.
Veule's [? Veale's] Close in poss'on of Thomas White.
Borehill in poss'on of Nicholas Harvey.
Do. „ of Gilbert Mitchell.
All of Bodmin Sept. 12, 1611.
Trevellic in poss'on of Edwd Glanvill of St. Tenedre.
Saint Key in poss'on of Sheperd 13th Sept. 1611.
Killenerry „ „ Piers Tomkins under Tenant to Wales.
(Note that this Killinerry and St. Tenedre and St. Key are parts of the Manor of Redruth.)
Convellet of Trembletier* 20th Sept. 1611.
Trevena (of St. Gennys) in poss'on of . . . . ?
The Barton of St. Gennys in poss'on of . . . . French 20th Sept. 1611
Certain ground and a stamping Mill in poss'on of Stephen Cook.
A close and the Boring House in poss'on of Paul Mitchell.
Another stamping mill in poss'on of Stephen Cooke.
Also all of Redruth.
A Tenement in Maran (? Meadon)‡ in poss'on of Richd Gibbons 20th Septr, 1611.
Other Ground in poss'on of . . . . ?
All of Allercombe and Kilkampton 21 Sep. 1611.

In Somerset.

Maneria Cannington.
„ Radway Fitzpayne.
„ Buckland Sorrorum, & Witcombe [in Martock].
Divers lands, tenements, rents, and services in prædict. Cannington, Radway Fitz-Payne, Powlet, Murlinch, Grinton, Edington, Martock, Ilminster, [Commage now Combwich], Spaxton, Otterhampton, Stockland, and Huntspill
in Comitatu Somerset.
The Manors of West Pennard and Kingsbury
in Com. Somerset.

In Wilts and Dorset.

All my lands purchased of my Cousin Anthony Rogers, Esq.. lying in Bradford, Wilts.
Warell Wood.
All my lands, tenements, houses in Wimborne St. Mary, Dorset.
My lands called Hide and Malexdon in Wilts and Dorset.
Maneria et tre' Colingborne.
Divers lands, Tenements, and Heredit's in prædicta Colingborne tre' Wilcot, Draicot et Chicklade (? Cricklade)
in Comitatu Wiltonens.
The free Chapel of Piddleton and Piddlewaterston and of Divers lands, tenements, rents, services and heredit's in p'dict. Piddletowne and Piddlewaterston in Comitatu Dorsestriæ.

* "Trembletier." Query this the same with Trembelthee of Lady Rogers' will?

† In this enumeration of Cornish estates the absence of Trebarveth is to be noticed. It certainly belonged to John Harington the Parliamentarian (see his will). Perhaps the explanation may be that Trebarveth Manor passed to him direct (1598) from his grandmother; whereas the properties now enumerated came to him at his father's death only (1612). His mother (*née* Mary Rogers) may have been dowered out of them even then, and later, down to 1634, the date of her death.

‡ "Maran." Can this be the Westmeadon of Lady Rogers' will?

CONTENTS IN BRIEF OF THE WILL OF JOHN HARINGTON, ESQ., OF KELSTON (THE PARLIAMENTARIAN).

(Will Aylett 300.) Dated 21st April, 1654.

Confirms the settlement of Kelston on his wife for life. And as to Corston Manor farm and parsonage—my meadow, etc., at Compton—my manor of Trebarveth, co. Cornwall—the Parsonage of Weston—Rents of £20 per An^{m} out of Catherine's [near Bath]—I bequeath these all wholly to my eldest son John, on condition that he provide for my dau'r Phœbe's marriage* portion £1500, and for my son William £1000, and to him I give the lands I purchased according to Parliamentary proposition in co. Waterford, Ireland, for £200. My wife to be Ex^{x}.

Signed in the presence of Griffin Smith (*Minister of the Parish from* 1653 *to* 1681) and John Merewether. Proved 6th July, 1654, by Dionis Harington, relict.

MEMORANDUM IN JOHN HARINGTON'S PRIVATE PAPERS.

"Jany 28th, 1650. Mr John Gostlet married my daughter Mary, he received of me £50. I had paid him £1150 before. I and my son John enter into 3 Bonds to pay £100 on 3^{d} March, £200 25 July, £200 on 29th Sept. next."†

(*To be continued.*)

BRIANT.—I should be very much obliged for any notes or suggestions relating to the pedigree of William and Elizabeth Briant, and also for any advice as to the means of obtaining information about this Swedish family of Nyberg. Is it possible that L. T. Nyberg was related to the great Swedish General Torstenson?

William Briant of New York. [? of Huguenot descent.] = Elizabeth . . . . died aged 44, either at New York or Bethlehem, P^{a}. [Her mother, who died in London, came of a Huguenot family—name unknown—which emigrated from France to London circ. 1700.]

Martha Briant, born at New York 4 Feb. 1725; marr. at Bethlehem, P^{a}, 23 May, 1745; bur. at Fulneck, Yorkshire, 25 June, 1803. = Laurence Torstenson Nyberg, born in Sweden 4 March, 1720; probably graduated at Upsala; went to Lancaster, P^{a}, as a Lutheran minister, but became a Moravian minister at Bethlehem in 1746 or 1748. In the course of his ministry visited London, Herrnhut, Dublin, Bristol, Leominster, and Fulneck. Returned to Sweden in 1774, and again became a Lutheran minister. Died in Sweden 30 May, 1792.

Jeremiah Carter of Hill Top House, Pudsey, great-grandson of Jeremiah Carter, who in 1664, mar. Mary Miller at Elland Church, Yorkshire. = Mary Agnes Nyberg, born at Dublin 13 Oct. 1766; mar. at Parish Church of Calverley Yorkshire, 24 July, 1780.

Hazelwood. WILLIAM F. CARTER.

---

* His eldest daughter, Mary, had been provided for at marriage. See Memorandum.

† She was probably married by civil ceremony, of which marriages there are no records extant at Kelston. The same remark will apply to the marriage of his dau'r Phœbe with Robert Rous of Wotton, co. Cornub.

Armorial Bookplate.

Seal of the Archdeaconry of Carlisle, and Arms of the Venble William Jackson, D D, Archdeacon of that Diocese from 1856 to 1862. The seal is of great antiquity, representing the blessed Virgin and child, with St Peter bearing the keys

Arms.—Arg on a fess between 3 cocks' heads erased sable a greyhound courant between 2 pheons or, all within a bordure azure platée (JACKSON), impaling, Gules, a chevron between 3 quatrefoils or (CRUMP)

Crest.—A cock's head erased sa, combed and wattled gules

Motto —Virtuti Vigila.

The Venble William Jackson, D D, younger son of the Rev. Thomas Jackson, Rector of Grasmere. Westmorland, by Sarah, dau and heiress of Thomas Partridge, Esq, was born at the Rectory, Grasmere, 17th Dec. 1792 In 1811 he took his degree of B A with honours (2nd class lit hum) at Queen's College, Oxford, of which he was a scholar, and subsequently fellow, tutor, and bursar In 1827 he was Whitehall preacher Domestic Chaplain to the Earl of Verulam and the Earl of Lonsdale, he was presented by the latter in 1828 to the living of Lowther, Westmorland, which he held up to the time of his death At various times he also held the livings of Cliburn, St John's, Whitehaven, and Penrith. From 1816–1855 he was Chancellor of the Diocese of Carlisle, Archdeacon from 1856–1862, and Canon of Carlisle 1858–1862, in which year he was elected Provost of Queen's College, Oxford He was also a J P. for the counties of Westmorland and Cumberland

Dr Jackson married 9th May, 1829, Julia Eliza, eldest dau of John Gregory Crump of Allan Bank, Westmoreland, Esq, by his wife Mary, only dau and eventually heiress of John Hamerton, Esq, by whom he had issue four daughters (1) Julia-Marian, (2) Louisa-Lilias both died young, (3) Georgiana-Isabella, and (4) Agnes-Beatrice, married 17 April, 1879, her cousin John Hamerton Crump, 2nd son of the late George Hamerton Crump of Chorlton, Cheshire, Esq, J P for co Salop, by his 2nd wife Harriet-Fanny, dau. and heiress of Lieut-Col Thomas Maddock

The Venble Archdeacon Jackson died 13th Sept 1878, his wife having died 7th March, 1873 Both are buried at Lowther Dr Jackson quartered with his paternal coat the arms of Partridge, Dalton, and Braithwayte

---

EXTRACTS FROM THE PARISH REGISTERS OF PENISTONE, RELATING TO THE FAMILY OF WORDSWORTH, FROM 1644 TO 1805 *

1644.	Dec 21	Martha, f. Ambrosii Wordsworth, bap
„	July 31.	Hellena Wordsworth, sep
„	Oct 17	Nicholaus f. Wordsworth, sep
1645	April 6.	Isaacus f Isaccii Wordsworth, bap
„	July 10	Infans Gulielmi Wordsworth, sep
„	Oct 21.	Sara f. Johannis Wordsworth, sep.
„	Jan 21.	Anna f. Ambrosii Wordsworth, sep
„	March 9.	Robertus f Robert Wordsworth, sep.
1646.	May 18.	Elizabetha f Gulmi Wordsworth, bap
„	May 25.	Gregorius f Ambrosii Wordsworth, bap
„	Oct 5	Gulielmus Wordsworth, sep
„	Feb 13	Anna, uxor Gulmi Wordsworth, sep
„	Feb 26	Vidua Wordsworth, sep

* Communicated by EDWIN JACKSON BEDFORD, Esq

SIGIL GUIL JACKSON S T P ARCHIDIACONI CARLIOLENSIS
VIRTUTI VIGILA

1647	Nov 24	Joh Coldwell et Dionissa Wordworth, nup
1648.	July 27.	Dorethea f Vidua Wordsworth, bap
1649	Nov 4	Anna f Ambrosii Wordsworth, bap
,,	May 31	Joh Micklethwaite et Sara Wordsworth, nup
,,	Oct 4	Anna f Nicholai Wordsworth, sep
1650	Aug. 11	Sara f Isaaci Wordsworth, bap.
,,	Sept 27.	Maria f Johannis Wordsworth, bap
1651	Feb 2	Johannes Wordsworth, sep
1652	May 2	Johannes f Ambrosii Wordsworth, bap
,,	Sept 23.	Johannes f Gul[mi] Wordsworth, bap
,,	Nov. 4	Maria f. Johannis Wordsworth, bap
,,	Jan 20.	Susanna f Gul[mi] Wordsworth, bap
,,	Feb 12	Sara f Johannis Wordsworth, bap
1653	Dec 13	Francis Wordsworth et Elizabetha Healwell, nup
,,	Aug 24	Vidua Wordsworth, sep
,,	Dec. 30.	Margareta f Johannis Wordsworth, sep
1654.	Jan 15	Sara f Gul[mi] Wordsworth, bap
,,	Jan 29	Anna f Johannis Wordsworth, bap
,,	Feb 23	Richard f Gulielmi Wordsworth, generosi, bap
,,	May 16.	Gulielmus f Ambrosii Wordsworth, sep
,,	Feb. 11	Nicholaus Wordsworth, sep
1655	Jan 14	Johannes f Francis Wordsworth, bap
,,	Feb. 2	Johannes f Isaaci Wordsworth, bap.
1657	May 27	Martha f Gul[mi] Wordsworth, bap
,,	Dec 22.	Jane f. Johannis Wordsworth, bap
,,	March 6	Maria f. Gul[mi] Wordsworth, de Snoden Hill, bap
,,	Feb 16	Johannes f Josias Wordsworth, natus et baptizatus fuit Dartonia Feb 8
,,	Nov 19	Nicholaus Wordsworth, Æditnus Ecclesia Penistonensis, sep
,,	Jan 21	Vidua Wordsworth, sep
1658	April 16	Gulielmus Wordsworth generosi de Wraithe House, Sepultus fuit Silkstonea
1659	June 6	Sara f Jonathan Wordsworth, bap
,,	Jan 2	Francis Wordsworth et Elizabetha Riche, nup
,,	June 8	Johannes f Gul[mi] Wordsworth, sep
1660.	March 28.	Maria, f Johannis Wordsworth, bap
,,	Aug 25	Ralph f Francis Wordsworth, bap
,,	Dec 8	Grace f Gul[mi] Wordsworth, bap
1660	Jan 10	Elias f Jonathan Wordsworth, bap
,,	Jan 29	Josias f. Josias Wordsworth, natus et baptizatus fuit Dartonia
,,	June 2.	Gulielmus Wordsworth, sep
,,	Sept 15	Maria f Gul[mi] Wordsworth, sep
,,	Nov. 19.	Elias Wordesworth, Artium Magister Juvenis pius et egregie eruditus, sepultus fuit in Cemeteria Ecclesiæ Penistonensis.
1661.	Jan 7.	Francis Morton et Grace Wordsworth, nup.
,,	April 26	Vidua Wordsworth, sep
1662.	Oct 21	Gulielmus Beever et Maria Wordsworth, nup
1663.	April 11.	Gulielmus f Francis Wordsworth, bap
,,	April 14	Jonathan f Jonathan Wordsworth, bap.
,,	Jan 24	Elias f Josias Wordsworth, bap.
,,	March 19	Gulielmus f Gul[mi] Wordsworth, bap
,,	Feb. 11	Robert Roydes et Jane Wordsworth, nup
,,	Aug 14	Radulphus Wordsworth, generosi, sep
,,	Feb 29	Radulphus f Francis Wordsworth, sep
1664.	May 17	Johannes f Johannis Wordsworth, bap
,,	Jan. 18	Gulielmus Earnshaw et Martha Wordsworth, nup.
1665.	Jan 1.	Georgius f. Francis Wordsworth, bap.

1665	Feb 20.	Sara uxor Johannis Wordsworth, sep
,,	Nov 10	Elizabetha Wordsworth de Water Hall vidua, sep
1666	April 19.	Josias et Martha, gemelli Jonathan Wordsworth de Peniston, bap
,,	Dec. 29.	Anna f Gulielmi Wordsworth, bap.
,,	Dec 29	Anna f Gulielmi Wordsworth, sep
,,	May 8	Josias f Jonn Wordsworth, sep.
,,	Dec 18	Martha f. Jonn Wordsworth, sep
1667.	June 23	Samuel f Josias Wordsworth, bap
,,	Feb 4	Gregory Wordsworth et Priscilla Bamforth, nup
,,	Nov 9	Gulielmus Wordsworth, sep
1668.	March 4	Elizabetha f Jonathan Wordsworth, bap
,,	Aug. 30.	Johannes Marsden et Anna Wordsworth, nup
1669	June 10	Gulielmus f Johannis Wordsworth, bap
,,	Oct 2.	Elizabetha f Gregory Wordsworth, bap
1670	Oct. 3	Johannes f Joh Wordsworth, de Softley, bap.
,,	May 20	Isaacus Wordsworth de Brookhouse, sep
,,	Oct 6	Alicia uxor Johannis Wordsworth, sep
1671	Jan 11	Ambrose f. Gregory Wordsworth, bap
1672	March 31	Maria f Johannis Wordsworth, bap.
,,	Feb 15	Johannes f. Johannis Wordsworth, bap
,,	Feb 27.	Elizabetha f Elizabetha Wordsworth, de Softley, bap.
1673	Dec. 1.	Gulielmus f Johannis Wordsworth, bap.
,,	March 17.	Josias f Johannis Wordsworth, bap.
1674.	May 21.	Johannes f Gregory Wordsworth, bap.
,,	Nov 21	Ricardus f Jonathan Wordsworth, bap.
,,	Jan 1	Gulielmus f Johannis Wordsworth, sep.
,,	Jan 21.	Alicia Wordsworth, vidua, sep
1675	Feb 27	Martha f Joh Wordsworth, de Cubley, bap.
1676	Oct 12	Jonathan f Joh Wordsworth, bap.
,,	March 10	Phemas f. Gregory Wordsworth, bap
,,	Feb 13	Joh Wordsworth et Elizabeth Smith, nup.
,,	March 28.	Maria Wordsworth, de Peniston, sep
1677.	Oct 9	Gulielmus f. Jonathan Wordsworth, bap
,,	Dec 8	Martha f. Martha Wordsworth, bap
1678	Dec. 25.	Gulielmus f Joh Wordsworth, de Cubley, bap.

(*To be continued*)

FENWICK FAMILY, SOUTH CAROLINA

The Genealogy of the Births and Deaths of the Line and Stock of John Fenwicke (a younger son of Robt Fenwicke of the Family of Stanton in Northumberland) who Arriv'd in So Carolina in the Year 1700 in Order to Settle there and the next Year following maryed the eldest Daughter of Major John Boone, who Dyed about 3 months after And on the 20th March 170$\frac{6}{7}$ he Maryed Mrs Elizabeth Gibbes Daughter of Coll Robt Gibbes and had Several Children born by her, viz —

Febry the 25th, 170$\frac{7}{8}$, was born their Eldest Daughter who was Baptized and named Mary after her Grandmother by mother side

Decbr the 8th, 1710, was Born their Eldest Son who was Baptized and named Robert after both Grand Fathers

Feb[ry] the 25th, $171\frac{2}{3}$, was born their second Daughter who was Baptized and named Ann after her Grandmother by Father's side.

June the 21, 1714, was born their third Daughter who was Baptized and named Elizabeth after her mother.

May, 1715, their s[d] Daughter Elizabeth Dyed.

June the 16, 1715, their s[d] Daughter Ann Dyed in Virginia.

Feb[ry] the 17, $171\frac{7}{8}$, was born their fourth Daughter who was Baptized and named Elizabeth also after her Mother.

Jan[ry] 22[d], $172\frac{0}{1}$, was born their second son who was Baptized & named Edward after his only Unkle living by Father side.

May the 7, 1723, was born their 3[d] son who was Baptized & named John after his Father.

Aug[st], 1723, their s[d] son John Dyed.

Feb[ry] 4, 1724, was Born their fifth Daughter who was Baptized and named Ann also after her Grandmother.

Dec. 4, 1724, their s[d] Daughter Ann also Dyed.

June 19, 1726, was born their sixth Daughter named Sarah.

SCOTT FAMILY.*

SIGNATURE OF ELIZABETH SCOTT,

daughter of Richard Scott of Smeeth, Esq., to an Indenture dated 1 July, 1621, between Sir Thomas Derham of West Derham, co. Norfolk, Kt., and Dame Anne his wife of the first part; and Thomas Derham, Esq., sone and heir apparent of the said Sir Thomas Derham, and Hugh Hamersley, Alderman of the City of London, of the second part; and Elizabeth Scott, da. of Richard Scott, late of Smeeth, co. Kent, Esq., deceased, Sir Richard Smyth of Leeds Castle, co. Kent, Kt., and Edward Scott of Scotts Hall in said county of Kent, Esq., of the third part: being settlement on marriage of Thomas Derham with Elizabeth Scott.

To make this extremely interesting instrument thoroughly intelligible, it is merely necessary to append the following genealogical table, which exhibits the relationship and family connection of the principal persons mentioned in the deed.

The family of Derham of West Dereham in the county of Norfolk were some three or four centuries ago people of county consideration, and one would judge from the tenor of the terms of the settlement that the Dame Anne mentioned as the wife of Sir Thomas Derham was either a daughter or sister of Sir Hugh Hammersley, Alderman of London,—doubtless of the same family as the Hammersleys recently, if not now, Bankers in London. The eldest branch of the Smythe family has come to an end, the Viscount Strangford, who died a few years ago, having been the last male heir of that branch. The importance of the family of Smythe of Ostenhanger and Leeds Castles in Kent is indicated below. Ostenhanger Castle, with its 126 rooms and 365 windows, now only exists as an interesting ruin,—the tower in which Rosamond Clifford (Fair Rosamond) is traditionally said to have been some time concealed by her Royal lover being still a portion of the embattled walls;—whilst Leeds Castle remains the most interesting moated and castellated mansion in Kent.

Sir John Scott of Nettlested, uncle of Elizabeth Scott, wife to Thomas Derham, was employed in high situations of trust in the military enterprizes of the unfortunate Earl of Essex, in Flanders, Spain, and Ireland, and was with that unhappy

* Communicated by J. R. SCOTT, Esq., F.S.A.

nobleman confined in the Tower of London, and doomed to death for participation in the quixotic conspiracy of the favourite of Queen Elizabeth. Sir John Scott's life was however spared at the intercession of his first wife (granddaughter of Edward, last Duke of Buckingham of the Stafford line) with the Queen, Elizabeth Stafford being one of the Ladies of the Bedchamber to that monarch. Sir John Scott, as an expiation of his treasonable offence, served the Queen in Flanders for the remainder of that monarch's existence, and then returned to England.

Genealogical Table explanatory of the foregoing.

Sir Thos. Smythe of Ostenhanger Castle (who farmed the Customs of London). Died 1591; buried at Ashford, Kent, where the magnificent monuments of three generations of this family exist to this day. = Alice, da. of Sir Andrew Judde, Lord Mayor of London.

Sir John, eldest son. Sheriff of Kent 42 Eliz. Buried at Ashford. =

Sir Thomas Smythe of Bidborough, Kent (2nd son). Sheriff of London 1601. Ambassador to Russia. Died of the plague at his house in Philpot Lane, London, in 1625. Left many benefactions in Kent, administered by the Skinners' Company of London. = 3rdly Sarah, da. and heir of William Blount. She remarried Thomas Sidney, Earl of Leicester. Witness to the will of Sir John Scott of Nettlested, Kent.

Sir Thomas, created Viscount Strangford of Ireland, *a quo* the late and last Lord Strangford.

Sir John Smythe. = Isabella, da. of the Earl of Warwick.

Sir Richard Smythe, 4th son, of Leeds Castle, Kent. Buried at Ashford. = Elizabeth, da. of Sir Thomas Scott of Scotshall, widow of Richard Knatchbull.

Catherine. = (1st) Sir Rowland Hayward, Knt., Lord Mayor of London. (2nd) Sir John Scott of Nettlested, died s.p. Son of Sir Thos. Scott of Scotshall, Kent.

Sir Thomas of Leeds Castle. =

(1stly) Richard Scott, son of Sir Thomas and brother of Sir John Scott of Nettlested. Killed in battle. = Catherine. = (2ndly) Sir Richard Sondes of Throwley, Kent. He remarried Sarah Montague.

Elizabeth = Thomas, son and heir of Sir Thomas Derham of West Dereham, Norfolk, and heir of Hugh Hammersley, Alderman of London.

Mary.

EXTRACTS FROM THE PARISH REGISTERS OF TODDINGTON, CO. BEDS.*

(*Continued from p.* 384.)

1614. Dec. 2. Thomas St. John, gent:
1614. Oct. 22. Ralfe, ye sonne of Roger Dawson buryed.
1615. July 4. Jane, ye da. of Roger Dawson buried.
1616. Aug. 6. Mr Brogden, seruant to ye lord Clifford.
1616. Sept. 22. Thomas, the sonne of Gregory Shawe.
1618. Aug. 21. ffranncis Wood, gent.
1618. Nov. 25. Willm., ye sonne of Thomas ffleetewood.
1618. Jan. 17. John & Mildred, children of Robt. Smith.
1619. July 28. Margaret, the da. of Willm. Bret, esquier.
1619. Oct. 16. John Potts, gentleman.

* Communicated by F. A. Blaydes, Esq., Hockliffe Lodge, Leighton Buzzard.

1619 Feb. 19 Robt. Smith
1621 April 12 Alecxander Harper of Wakefeelde of the county of York
1621. June 2. Mr Robert Porie [Perry], clerke
1622. July 4 Charles Wentworth, the sonne of Thomas, Lord Wentworth.
1623. May 13 Mr William Wentworth, the sonne of Thomas, Lord Wentworth.
1623. Oct. 5. Lawrence Cockaine.

Baptisms

1624 Oct. 17. Thomas, the sonne of ffrancis Rollenson
1624. Jan 9. Martha, da to Ralph Johnson.
1625. Dec 22 Margaret Christian, da of Jeremie Grimwood.
1625 Feb 2 George Shaw, the sonne of George Shaw
1625. Feb. 5 Matthew, the sonne of George Batt
1627 May 14 Will'm, sone of Robeid Bvtt
1627. April 19 John, sone of John Dovncom
1627 Sept 9 Catherine, da of ffrauses Rollenson
1627. Dec. 26. Anne, da of Ralfe Johnson
1629 Nov 1 Thom Bvtt, the sonne of Rob Bvtt
1630. April 18 Mary, the da of Richard Tier (? Dier)
1632. Oct 7 Richard, the son of Rob Bvtt
1634 Feb 27. John, the sonne of Katherin Neile

Burials

1624. Dec 20 Thomas Dyer
1625 July 18. Joane, the wife of John Duncombe
1626 Sept. 24 Joane, the wife of Richard Johnson.
1626 Mar 1 Richard Johnson
1627. April 30 Widow Birt (? Bret)
1628 Nov 19 Richard Bary (? Burie)
1629 Dec 2 William Prior buried
1630 Aug 18 ffrancis Rawlinson, minister of this towne.
1630 Nov 17 Mathey Bere (? Burie)
1632 Oct 13 Diany Hares, the wife of Roger Hares
1632 Jan 30. The Lady Marye Wentworth, da to the right hon'able Thomas Earl of Cleveland
1633 April 11 ffranses Bvtt
1634. Mar 19 William, the sonne of Robert Smith
1635. Jan 10 ffrancis Johnson.
1636 Oct. 21 Dorathy Pottes
1637. April 25 Thomas Abdn, the sonne of Christopher Abdir Knight and of Dame Mary
1637. June 11. Gilberte Capon.
1637 Jan 7 The Ladie Anne Wentworth, wife to the right Hon'able Lord Thomas Earle of Cleueland (Daughter of Sir John Crofts of Saxham, Suff Knight)

Weddings

1624 April 29 George Shawe and Anne Webb
1625 June 30 Thomas Smith and Jane Rowlie
1625. Aug 15 Wm Isham and Marie Brett
1626 June 15 John Duncombe and Philipp Powell
1628 July 10 Robeid Tier and Mary Barye
1628 Nov 5 Richard Wab and Phillip Doncom, widowe
1630 Sept. 26 Thomas Claver and Mary Pennington
1632 Nov 12 Richard Grissell and Anne Dyer.
1636 July 15 Robert Wincoate (? Wingate) and Anne Fowler.
1637. June 18 Theodor Pottes and Sary Coddon.

1646. Feb. 2. Thomas, sonne of Theodore Potts was borne.
1650. Dec. 30. John, sone of Theodore Potts was borne.
1652. Dec. 30. Joseph, sone of Theodore Potts was borne.
1642. Dec. 1. Lucy, da. of Thomas Pennington* gent. was bapt.

(*To be continued.*)

JACKSON FAMILY.—If any of our readers can kindly help to establish the connection between the Anthony Jackson, aged 14 in 1613, in Pedigree I., and the Anthony Jackson of Yorkshire in Pedigree II.; or, indeed, afford any information regarding the issue of the last-named individual, they will greatly oblige,

14 *Hill's Place, Oxford Circus, W.* W. H. M. JACKSON.

PEDIGREE I.

From Harleian MSS. No. 1487, f. 475-6.

ARMS.—*Gules, two bars dancetes erm. on a chief of the second three suns in splendour.*
Confirmed 16th June, 1613, to Richard Jackson of Killingwold, son of Anthony, son of Richard.

RICHARD ST. GEORGE, *Norroy.*

Richard Jackson of Killingwold Grand, in com. Ebor. = Ann, dau. of Robert Todd of Sawton.

. . . . = Anthony Jackson of Killingwold Grand, Esq., Justice of the Peace and Quorum. = Margaret, dau. of Gregory Furbusher, Esq., of Altoft, in com. Ebor.

John Jackson. — Christopher Jackson. Samuel Jackson. — Julyan Jackson. Richard Jackson of Killingwood. = Ursula, dau. of Richard Hillyard of Routh, Esq. Isabell ux. Christopher Ridley.

Anthony Jackson, æt. 14 aº 1613. Frances. Elizabeth. Jane.

Thomas Jackson. William Jackson. = Martha, dau. of Frances Teringham of Weston. Marmaduke Jackson.

PEDIGREE II.

Oxford Visitation, 1669.
Heralds' College, D. 25-40 B.

Anthony Jackson of Yorkshire. = ...

Gilbert Jackson of Brightwell in com. Oxon. = Anne, dau. of Richard Eldridge of Brightwell, in com. Oxon.

Gilbert Jackson of Cuddesden in com. Oxon, Gent. = Elizabeth dau. of Richard Towersey of Holton, in com. Oxon.

John, sonne and heire, an infant.

---

* These entries of the Pennington family appear to have been collected from various pages of the Registers, and transcribed as above in the second volume.

EXTRACTS FROM THE PARISH REGISTERS OF PENISTONE, RELATING TO THE FAMILY OF WORDSWORTH, FROM 1614 TO 1805 *

(*Continued from p.* 404.)

1678.	Jan 3.	Joshua, f. Joh Wordsworth, de Heeley, bap
,,	Feb 15	Sara f Joh Wordsworth, de Softley, bap.
,,	April 18	Johannes Nettleton de Dewsbury et Elizabetha Wordsworth de Swathe, nup.
,,	Dec 24	Johannes Batty et Martha Wordsworth, nup
,	April 13.	Gulielmus Wordsworth de Softley, sep
,,	July 18	Jonathan Wordsworth, sep.
1679	Nov 29	Johannes f Martha Wordsworth de Cubley, bap
,,	Aug 12	Ricardus, quondam filius Jonathan Wordsworth, sep.
,,	Nov 29.	Elias Wordsworth de Peniston, sep.
,,	Jan. 21.	Francis Wordsworth, sep.
1680.	April 3	Maria f. Gregory Wordsworth, bap.
,,	Feb 9	Ambrose Wordsworth, sep
1681.	March 27	Elizabetha f. Joh. Wordsworth de Cubley, bap
,,	Sept 27	Maria f Mathew Wordsworth, bap
,,	May 25	Elizabetha f. Joh Wordsworth de Hand bank, sep.
,,	Sept. 28	Maria f. Mathew Wordsworth, sep.
1682	June 24.	Jonathan f Joh Wordsworth de Heeley, bap
,,	Oct. 7	Sara f Joh Wordsworth de Hand bank, bap.
,,	Feb 10	Maria f Mathew Wordsworth, bap
,,	Feb 26.	Robertus Wordsworth et Maria Gaunt, nup.
,,	Sept 23	Elizabetha Wordsworth, vidua, de Schole Hill, sep.
,,	Oct. 5.	Jane uxor Joh Wordsworth de Heeley, sep
1683	July 17	Gregory f Gregory Wordsworth, bap
,,	Aug. 14	Hannah f spu. Sara Wordsworth de Snodhill, bap.
,,	Oct 23	Thomas Morton et Sara Wordsworth, nup.
1683	July 17	Priscilla uxor Gregory Wordsworth, sep
,,	Aug 10.	Gregory f Gregory Wordsworth, sep
1684	April 12.	Sara f Jonathan Wordsworth, bap
1685	Oct. 17	Elias f. Jonathan Wordsworth, bap
,,	Feb 4	Johannes Wordsworth de Water Hall et Anna Milner de Grange, Nupti Roystonia
1686	Jan 4	Sara f Johannis Wordsworth de Burton Grange, baptizatus, Feb. 20.
1687	Oct 8	Johannes f Joh Wordsworth de Snodhill, bap
,,	Oct 1	Joseph Hague et Martha Wordsworth, nup
,,	Nov 17	Gulielmus Wordsworth et Martha Hinchliffe, nup
1688	April 26	Maria f Jonathan Wordsworth, bap
,,	Jan 19	Benjamin et Joseph, gemelli Gulielmi Wordsworth, bap
,,	Jan 24	Robertus f Roberti Wordsworth de Thurgoland, bap
,,	March 12	Johannes f Gulielmi Wordsworth, bap
,,	Nov 18	Gregory Wordsworth et Anna Couldwell, vidua, nup
1689	April 27	Jane f Joh Wordsworth de Heeley, bap
,,	Aug 20	Maria f Gregory Wordsworth, bap
,,	Dec 25	Elizabetha f Gregory Wordsworth, sep
1690	April 30	Jonathan f Jonathan Wordsworth, bap
,,	Oct 27	Susanna f Joh Wordsworth de Snodhill, bap
,,	April 7	Johannes Wordsworth de Swathe Cubley (?), sep
,,	June 4	Maria uxor Gul Wordsworth de Snodhill, sep

* Communicated by EDWIN JACKSON BEDFORD, Esq.

1691	Oct 22	Hannah f Gul Wordsworth de Rough Birchworth, bap
,,	Jan 7	Elias f Gregory Wordsworth, bap
,,	April 30	Josias f Joh Wordsworth de Burton Grange, bap
,,	Feb 16	Sara uxor Josias Wordsworth, sep
1692.	Oct 20	Ricardus f Jonathan Wordsworth, bap
,,	Dec 30	Robertus f Guliel Wordsworth de Oxspring, bap
,,	Feb 27	Elizabetha f Joh Wordsworth de Snodhill, bap
1693	March 1	Gregory f Gregory Wordsworth, bap
,,	June 21	Gulielmus Wordsworth de Oxspring, sep
,,	Sept 12	Jane uxor Mathew Wordsworth, sep
1694	April 27	Elizabetha f Joh Wordsworth de Burton Grange, bap
,,	May 27	Gulielmus Wordsworth de Snod Hill, sep
1695	Dec 7	Gulielmus f Joh Wordsworth de Snod Hill, bap
,,	Dec 14	Mathew Wordsworth et Martha Marshland, nup
,,	April 20	Maria Wordsworth de Brook House, sep
,,	Nov 23	Maria f Jonathan Wordsworth, sep
1696	Nov 21	Anna f Gregory Wordsworth, bap
,,	May 8	Gulielmus f Joh Wordsworth de Snodhill, sep
1697	April 22	Jonathan f Joh Wordsworth de Snodhill, bap
,,	Jan 6	Lydia f Gul Wordsworth de Softley, bap
1698	Oct 6	Johannes Wordsworth et Diana Gelsthorp nup
1699	Dec 4	Richard Gillott et Sara Wordsworth de Softley, nup
,,	Jan 10	Elizabeth Wordsworth, vidua, de Hunshelf, sep
,,	Feb 10	Isaac f Isaac Wordsworth, sep
1700	April 20	Sara f Joh Wordsworth de Schole Hill, bap
,,	Sept 5	Gulielmus f Joh Wordsworth de Snodhill, bap
,,	Oct 14	Anna f Gul Wordsworth de Softley, bap
1701	Aug 16	Gulielmus f Joh Wordsworth de Softley, bap
,,	Jan 17	Maria f Joh Wordsworth de Schole Hill, bap
,,	Aug 12	Johannes Wordsworth de Softley sep
,,	Aug 13	Maria uxor Rob't Wordsworth de Thurgoland, sep
,,	Jan 24	Jonathan Wordsworth de Peniston, sep
1702	Aug 20	Sara f Josias Wordsworth de Peniston, bap
,,	July 20	Hannah f Isaac Wordsworth de Langsett, bap
,,	Nov 11	Lydia f Joh Wordsworth de Cathill, bap
1703	March 29	Thomas f Joh Wordsworth de Hunshell, bap
,,	April 2	John f William Wordsworth de Softley, bap
,,	Dec 26	John f John Wordsworth de Peniston, bap
,,	Jan 31	John Parkin de Bradfield et Sarah Wordsworth de Peniston, nup
1704	July 23	Thomas Ibotson et Hannah Wordsworth de Peniston, nup
1705	Nov 12.	Mary f William Wordsworth de Thurlstone, bap
,,	Feb 6	Priscilla f John Wordsworth de Peniston, bap
,,	Nov 24	Elias Micklethwaite de Denby Hall et Mary Wordsworth, nup
,,	April 7	Elias Wordsworth de Peniston, sep
1706	Feb 1	Ann f Jonathan Wordsworth de Thurlstone, bap
1707	July 29	Josias Wordsworth de Proct Silkstone, sep
,,	Jan 31.	Sarah Wordsworth vidua de Softley, sep
1708	July 28	Gregory f John Wordsworth de Scole Hill, bap
,,	April 27	William Wordsworth de Softley, sep
1709	April 3	Jane f Joseph Wordsworth de Thurlstone Mill, bap
,,	Feb 13	Sarah f Jonathan Wordsworth de Softley, bap
,,	March 1	Phineas f John Wordsworth de Shepherd's Castle, bap
,,	Aug 27	Thomas Passley et Sarah Wordsworth, nup
,,	Aug 28	John Newton et Mary Wordsworth, nup
,,	May 30	Gregory f John Wordsworth, Shepherd's Castle, sep
,,	Sept 20	William f Matthew Wordsworth de Peniston, sep

1709	Oct 22	Susan f John Wordsworth de Oxspring, sep
1710	Feb 4	. (qy) f. John Wordsworth de Oxspring, sep
1711	Nov 3	Sarah f Jonathan Wordsworth, mercer, Peniston, bap
,,	Jan 22	William Wordsworth et Elizabeth Passley, nup
,,	March 2	Jonathan f John Wordsworth, sep.
,,	Oct 1	Mary f Isaac Wordsworth, sep
,,	March 1	Anne Wordsworth widow, sep
1712	April 11	John f William Wordsworth, Bl M (Black Moor), bap
,,	Nov 1	Mary f Jonathan Wordsworth, Softley, bap
,,	Nov 24	Margaret f John Wordsworth, Schole Hill, bap
1713	Aug 5	Mary f Jonathan Wordsworth, mercer, Peniston, bap
,,	March 30	Priscilla f John Wordsworth, Schole Hill, yeoman, sep
1714	Dec. 29	Ambrose f John Wordsworth, Schole Hill, yeoman, bap
,,	Sept 23	Sarah Wordsworth Mur Oxspring, sep
,,	Jan 3	Ambrose f John Wordsworth, Schole Hill, sep
,,	Jan 18	Martha wife of Matthew Wordsworth, Peniston, sep
1715	Aug 7	Jonathan s of Isaac Wordsworth, Oxspring, bap
,,	Aug 28	Rebecca dau of Jonathan Wordsworth, Ingbirchworth, bap.
,,	Feb 25	Jonathan s of John Wordsworth, Schole Hill, bap.
1716	May 2	Martha wife of William Wordsworth, bur
1717	Jan 15	Gregory Wordsworth, Peniston, yeoman, bur.
1718	June 17.	Ann dau of Elias Wordsworth, agrn, bap
,,	Oct 17	Mary dau of Robert Wordsworth, bap
,,	July 1	Rebecca of Jonathan Wordsworth, bur.
,,	Oct 5	Margaret dau of John Wordsworth, bur
1720	April 29	Elizabeth dau of Elias Wordsworth, bap
,,	March 11	Martha dau of John Wordsworth, bap (Schole Hill)
1721	Aug 13	John son of Robert Wordsworth, bap
,,	Jan 5	Mr Gregory Gibson and Miss Sarah Wordsworth, mar
1723	June 8	John Wordsworth and Martha Crossley, mar
,,	June 22	John son of Thomas Wordsworth, bur
1724.	April 24	Sarah dau of John Wordsworth, bap
,,	Sep 26	Rebecca Wordsworth, bur
1725	May 8	Elias son of Elias Wordsworth, bap
,,	June 6	John son of John Wordsworth, bap
,,	Oct 5	Widow Wordsworth, bur
1726	June 24	Ann dau of John Wordsworth, bap
,,	Jan 17	Mary dau of John Wordsworth, bap
,,	May 19	Joseph Beaumont and Sarah Wordsworth, mar
,,	Oct 26	Hannah d of Elias Wordsworth, bur
,,	Jan 9	Esther wife of John Wordsworth, bur
,,	Feb 22	Richard son of Richard Wordsworth, bur
,,	March 15	Ambrose son of John Wordsworth, bur
1727	Dec 3	Elias son of Elias Wordsworth, Gravels, bap
,,	March 5	Ann dau of Thomas Wordsworth, bap
,,	May 27	Lydia Wordsworth, bur
1728	Sept 21	Lydia dau of John Wordsworth, yeo, Softley, bap
,,	Oct 12	Martha dau of John Wordsworth Langsett, bap.
,,	July 10	Ralph son of Jonathan Wordsworth, bur
,,	Dec 27	Martha dau of John Wordsworth, bur
1729	July 13	Robert son of Robert Wordsworth, Bower Hill, bap
,,	Aug 24	John son of William Wordsworth, bap
,,	Nov 23	Joseph Parkinson, Apothecary, and Mary Wordsworth, mar by licence
,,	Nov 27	Mathew Wordsworth, tailor, bur
1730.	April 16	Barbara dau of John Wordsworth, bap
,,	May 24	Gregory son of Elias Wordsworth, bap

1730.	Jan 5	William son of John Wordsworth, yeo, Softley, bap.
„	Feb 14	William son of William Wordsworth, Welly House, bap.
„	July 25.	Jonathan Wordsworth and Elizabeth Shaw, mar
„	July 26	John Wordsworth and Ann Burgh, mar
„	April 5	John son of William Wordsworth, bur
„	July 5	Martha wife of Ambrose Wordsworth, bur
„	Nov 23	Gregory son of Elias Wordsworth, yeo, bur
1731	July 17.	William son of Jonathan Wordsworth, innkeeper, bap
„	Oct 29	John son of John Wordsworth, mercer, bap
„	June 23	Mary wife of Joseph Wordsworth, bur
„	Jan. 14	Eliza dau of Joseph Wordsworth, bur
1732	June 29	Gregory son of Elias Wordsworth, bap
„	Nov 29	William son of William Wordsworth, bap.
„	March 7	John son of John Wordsworth, Softley, bap
„	July 2	William Wordsworth of Bradfield and Ann Copley of Peniston, mar.
„	May 5	John Wordsworth, Schole Hill, bur
„	June 23.	Isaac Wordsworth, Brookhouse, bur.
1733	June 9	John son of John Wordsworth, Cott, bap
1734	Dec 14	John son of Elias Wordsworth, bap
„	June 24.	John Marton and Sarah Wordsworth, mar

(To be continued)

THE PENN FAMILY, OF HARBOROUGH, CO. WORCESTER.*

THE WILL OF JOHN PENNE, 1651

In the name of God, Amen Upon the two and twentieth day of Aprill in the yeare of our Lord God One thousande sixe hundred fyftie and one, I John Penne, sonne of William Penne, of Harberrow, in the parishe of Hagley, and countye of Worcester, sicke in body but of a good and perfect memory, doe make and ordeine this my last will and testament in manner and forme followeinge First I comende my soule into the handes of Almighty God, my maker and creator, and my body to the earth from whence it came Item I give and bequeath unto my brother Richard Penne and to his executors and assignes all my right, title, and interest to a lease of One thousand yeares made by Thomas Blount and George Tokey, Esq'rs, to my grandfather Thomas Cookes and his brother William Cookes deceased, beareing date the first day of May in the fowerth and fifte yeares of the raigne of our late soveraigne Lord and Lady Kinge Phillip and Queene Mary, lately given unto me by the last will and testament of my uncle William Cookes and alsoe all that my messuage or tenement with th'appurten'ces in Romsley in the parishe of Halesowen and county of Salop, com'only called and knowne by the name of Smythes Grounde, with all meadowes, leasowes, and pastures thereunto belongeinge, and thirtye acres of lande lyeinge in the com'on feildes of Romsley aforesaid, with there and ev'rie of there appurten'ces, for all the rest and residue of the said terme of One thousand yeares which shall be to come and unexpired at the tyme of my decease which said messuage and landes with theire appurten'ces are nowe in the tenure of Fortune Powell or of her assignes Item I give and bequeath unto my brother Gervase Penne the so'me of five poundes to be paid to him by my execut'rs within the space of one yeare after my decease Item I give and bequeath unto William Penne, sonne of my brother William Penne, and to Anne Penne, and Mary Penne, daughters of my brother Thomas Penne, and to Thomas Dickens and Mary Dickens, sonne and daughter of my brother in lawe Thomas Dickens and my sister Mary his wife, the som'e of fortye shillings a peece, to be paid to them by

* Communicated by H SYDNEY GRAZEBROOK, Esq

my Executor within the space of five yeares after my decease And I make and ordaine my said brother Richard Penne the sole Executor of this my last will and testament In witness whereof I have to this my last will and testament subscribed and sett my hande and seale the two and twentieth day of Aprill aforesaid, Anno Dm. 1651 by me—JOHN PENNE

Sealed and subscribed in the p'sence of William Penne, Edmund Kettle, Thomas Penne.

[Proved in common form May 13, 1653]

THE WILL OF WILLIAM PENNE, OF HARBOROUGH, 1664 *

In the name of God, Amen. The thirteenth day of Aprill, 1664, and in the 16th yeare of the raigne of our sou'raine Lord Charles the Second, by the grace of God King of England, Scotland, France, and Ireland, Defender of the Faith, etc I William Penne, of Harborough, in the p'ish of Hagley, in the county of Worcester, gent, being weake in bodye but of sound and perfect memory, prayse be given to God for the same, and knowing the uncertainty of this life on earth, and being desirous to settle things in order, doe make this my last will and testam't in manner and forme following, that is to say First and principally I commend my soule to Almighty God my creator, assuredly believing that I shall receive full pardon and free remission of my sins, and be saved by the precious death and meritts of my blessed Saviour and Redeemer Christ Jesus, and my body to the earth from whence it was taken to be buried in such decent and Christian manner as to my Executor hereafter named shall be thought meet and convenient And as touching such worldly estate as the Lord in mercie hath lent me, my will and meaning is the same shalbe imployed and bestowed as hereafter by this my will is expressed. And first I doe revoke, renounce, frustrate, and make void all wills by me formerly made, and declare and appoint this my last will and testam't Item I give and bequeath unto my grandchild William Penne, son of my son Thomas Penne, one great brass pot and one two-yeared postnett, and my meaning is that they shall remaine as chieves to the house so long as there is an heire male of my name to make use of them Item I give and bequeath to my son Gervase Penne the bed in the porch chamber and all its furniture w'tsoever, two coffers which now he maketh use of, one other bed in the buttery chamber and all its furniture whatsoever, one trunke in the said chamber now standing, and all my cattell after my heriots are discharged Item I give and bequeath unto my beloved sonne Thomas Penne the bed in the great chamber and all furniture thereunto belonging, the bed over the parlour and all furniture thereunto belonging, the coffer at my son Gervase his bed's feet wherein my writings are, and all my sheep All the rest of my goods, chattells, and debts undisposed of I doe give and bequeath unto my said son Thomas Penne, and I doe make him the said Thomas Penne my sole Execut'r to see this my last will and testament truly executed and performed In witness whereof I have hereunto put my hand and seale the day and yeare first above written in the p'sence of Richard Amphlett, Thomas Nash —WILLIAM PENN.

THE WILL OF WILLIAM PENN, 1729.

In the name of God, Amen I William Penn the elder, of Harborow in the p'ish of Hagley and county of Worcester, being of sound and perfect mind and memory, thanks be to God therefore, and calling to mind the uncertainty of this mortal life, do make and ordain this my last will and testament in manner and form following, viz Impr'is I give and bequeath my soul into the hands of Almighty God my Creator, and my body to be buried in a decent and Christian manner, hoping through the merits of Jesus Christ my blessed Saviour and Redeemer for a happy resurrection to eternal life And as for that worldly estate with which it

* This is the *original* will It is on parchment in the form of a deed —H S G

has pleased God to bless me, my will is as followeth. Item I give and bequeath unto my only son William Penn, his exec'rs or assigns, all those my lands, tenem'ts, and p'misses with their appurtenances now in the possession of William Hornblower and the Widow Powell or their underten'ts, situate and being in Romsley, in the parish of Halesowen and county of Salop, granted by lease for the term of a thousand years save one to Thomas Cookes and William Cookes his brother jointly from Thomas Blount and George Tuckey, Esq'rs, Comm'rs appointed for that purpose, and also all assignm'ts thereof made and executed, and all the term of years which shall be to come and unexpired at my decease, and also all that message house called Adam's Hill now in the possession of William Hall or his underten'ts together with the barn, stables, buildings, gardens, orchards, and backsides thereunto belonging, situate and being in the parish of Clent and county of Stafford, granted by lease for the term of ninety and nine years from Richard Amphlett Esq to Thomas Penn my father deceased, both which aforesaid leases and all the lands, tenem'ts, and p'misses therein demised, with all and singular their appurten'ces, and all my right, title, or interest in the same or in any part thereof, I do freely give unto my said son William Penn, his exec'rs and assigns, on condition that he my said son shall pay all my debts, discharge all my legacies, and fulfill and perform faithfully all this my last will and testament as it is hereinafter specifyed and declared Item my said son shall pay unto my sister Esther Penn the sum'e of one hundred pounds which I owe her upon bond. Item my said son shall pay unto my son-in-law Mr Thomas Dolman* the sum'e of one hundred pounds at such time as I have engaged it shall be paid in the marriage articles of the said Mr Thomas Dolman Item I give unto my eldest daughter Ann Shenston† the sum'e of one hundred pounds . on the day of the marriage of my said son William Penn, if he my said son shall happen to be unmarried at the time of my decease Item I give unto my second daughter Mary Dolman that feather bed, blanketts, and all things belonging to it that stands in the buttery chamber Item I give to my youngest daughter Sarah Penn the sum'e of three hundred and fifty pounds. Item I give to my said youngest daughter Sarah Penn, her exec'rs or assigns, all my right, title, and interest in certain lands, tenem'ts, and p'misses situate in the parish of Pedmore and county of Worcester now in the possession of Richard Lowe or his underten'ts held by a lease of one hundred ninety and nine years from the feoffees of the hospital of Thomas Foley Esq deceased Item I give unto my said youngest daughter Sarah one half of my household goods All the rest of my goods, chattells, and credits whatsoever I give and bequeath unto my said son William Penn, whom I make and ordain sole executor of this my last will and testam't revoking all other wills by me heretofore made In witness whereof I have hereunto put my hand and seal this 28th day of August Anno Dom 1729 — WILLIAM PENN

Sealed and delivered and declared by the testator to be his last will and testam't in the p'sence of Thomas Dolman, Edward Oldnall

[Administration with will annexed granted at Worcester on the eighth day of March, 1731, to Anne Shenston, Mary Dolman, and Sarah Penn, the natural and lawful daughters and legatees named in the said will, William Penn, the Executor therein named, having died in the lifetime of the said testator ‡]

* "1725, Feb 17 The Rev Mr Thomas Dolman, rector of Broom and Mrs Mary Penn were married" (*Churchill Registers*)

† Mother of William Shenstone, the poet, and wife of Thomas Shenston of "The Leasowes," Halesowen

‡ "On the south wall [of Hagley Church]," says Nash ('Worcestershire,' i 506), "is a handsome monument of black and white marble for the Penns of Harborow in this parish a family of great repute who flourished here above four centuries but were extinguished in my time" The inscription is in Latin to the memory of William Penn of Harborow, gent, who died Jan 26, 1731-2, aged 71, Mary his wife dau of William Tristram of Oldswinford, gent died July 21, 1729, aged 51, William Penn, their only son, died Dec 31, 1731, aged 29, and Sarah Penn their dau who died Jan 9 1733, aged 35

(*To be continued*)

EXTRACTS FROM THE PARISH REGISTERS OF TODDINGTON, CO. BEDS.*

(*Concluded from p 408*)

1644 April 24 Thomas, sone of Thomas Pennington gent. was bapt
1646 Aug. 1. Ann, da of Mr Thomas Pennington gent was bapt
1648 Jan 9. Wentworth, sone of Mr Thomas Pennington gent was bapt
1651. May 22. Mary, da of Mr Thomas Pennington was bapt
1654 Mar. 27. Jane, da of Tho Pennington gent was bapt
1657. April 1. Cecely, da of Tho Pennington gent was borne on Wednesday the first of Aprill in the yeare of our Lord God 1657 about eight of the clock at night.
1655 Nov 2 Sarah, the da of Theodor Potts was borne.
1657 Feb. 24 Mary, da to Theodor Pottes borne
1654. Sept 9. Thomas Claver (Clerke, Rector of Toddington, but unjustly sequestered) buried
1655. June 8 Widdow Dier was buried
1656. Nov. 27 Mrs Barbara, the wife of Thomas Reston was buried
1656. Jan 18 Raphe Johnson buried
1657. Dec 7. Mr John Chinckett buried
1658. Sept 10 Mrs Sara Prior, wife to Mr William Prior buried
1658. Nov 14. Thomas Matthew, died the 12th day of November and was buried the 14th day of November 1658 in his garden Late Taken out of his orchard
1659. April 5. Mrs. Impie, wife to Mr Thomas Impie buried
1659 May 14 Mr francis Astrey† buried
1659. April 6. Mr Thomas Pottes buried
1660 April 10 Mr John Win buried.
1660 Dec. 20. Charles Win buried
1663 June 26 Lettice ye da of Tho Pennington & Ann his wife bapt
1663 July 28. Lettice Pennington, da of Tho & Anne his wife buried.
1663 Oct 8 Anne White widow buried in the quakers burying place by Edmund White ye Anabaptist contrary to law
1663 Sept 12 Anne lyons was buried by White ye Anabaptist (during my absence in Lancashire) in the church yard
1663 Sept 16 Thomas Pennington,‡ gentleman, was buried
1663 Jan 30 Jacobus Matthew, vir probus sepultus erat ætat. 7.
1663 Mar 13 Gulielmus Shakespeare de Fancat sepultus erat
1664 Mar 7 Honoratissimus D D Thomas, Baro Wentworth prænobilis viri Thomæ clemæ clerice filius solemniter sepultus erat (in crypta) p R Kearsley Cubicularius erat et consiliarius serenissimo regi Carolo secundo
1667 April 4 Honoratissimus D D Thomas Wentworth Comes clmæ fidelissimus regis subditus patronus meus multis nominibus colendo sepultus erat in crypta circiter hor 9 nocte April 4° (æt 76)
1668. June 30 Ignotus quidam (in submersus)
1668 July 23 Richardus Kearsleius ὁ μακαρίτης hujus ecclesiæ Rector venerabilis sepultus erat
1668 Oct 3 Ann Shackspere, da to Will Shackspear, buried
1670 Jan 30. Thomas, ye sonne of Isaac Bringhurst & Ann his wife, borne
1671. Oct 30 John, sonne to John Baile gent baptized.

* Communicated by F A BLAYDES Esq, Hockliffe Lodge, Leighton Buzzard

† A family of the name of Astrey was seated at Woodend, a manor in the parish of Toddington

‡ There is a small brass to his memory under the altar

1669 Dec 13 Mrs Pryor wido buried.
1670 Sept 20 Joseph, sonne to Theoder Pots buried.
1670 Sept 23. Mr Thomas Roystern buried
1671 Mar 1. Mrs Cleaver (? Claver) buryed.
1672 June 11. Mistris Win buried
1674 Aug. 24 Mr Thomas Goldsmith, buried
1674. Oct. 20 Elizeus, sonne to John Beale, bapt
1675 May 3 Mr William Hazell was buried
1675 Dec 4 Mr Robert ? Cranwa buried
1672. July 28 Dorothea bringhust, da to Mr Isack bringhouse & Ann his wife was baptized
1675. . . . Isaac, ye sonn of Isaac Bringhurst borne ye 12 of May, and baptized Thursday in Whitsuntide following
1676 Aug 20 Mary, da of Mr John Beale, bapt.
1677 Dec 8 Jane, wife to Robert Cranwa buried
1678 Aug. 3 Mary, da to Mr Joseph Cloudley, bapt.
1680 April 22 John, sonn to Mr Isack Bringhurst & Ann his wife, bapt.
1680 Oct 2 Edward, sonn of Mr Lenton, bapt.
1681 Mar 31 Elizeus, son to Mr John Beale, was bapt.
1681 Mar. 31 Mrs Beale, wife of Mr John Beale, buried
1683 Aug 5. Mrs Laine, the wife of Master Laine, buried
1680 Nov 13 Sara, the dahter of Muster Whitway, bapt
1685 May 2 Mistris Goldsmith was buried
1686 April 30. The Lady Henrietta Maria Wentworth* was buried
1686 Jan 31. Sari, the da of Muster Whildman, buried
1689 May 5. Alles, the wife of Henry Dier, was buried
1691 Jan 26 Muster Jhon belle gentleman, buried, ? Beale.
1691 Jan 29 ffrances, da of Muster Hy Whiteway, buried
1678 Jan 15 Peter the sonn of Muster Whiteway, bapt
1689 Mar 17 ffrances, da of Muster Whiteway, bapt
1694 Feb 20. Sara da of Muster Whiteway, bapt
1696 Feb 1 hue, the sonn of Muster Mathew Goldsmith, bapt
1696 May 9 The Right Honble Philadelphia Lady Wentworth was Buryed
1696. June 20 Henery, the sonn of Muster hennery bele, buried
1696. Jan 9. Master Richard Burbibys, buried
1697 Oct 12 The Reverend Doctor Isaac Bringhurst, being Rector of Toddington, was buried
1699 Mar 7. Henry Dyer Buried
1699 July 22 Zachariah Wildman Clerk, buried
1700. Dec 23 John, s of Dorothy Symons, bapt
1701 Sep 18. Rebecca, ye da of George Gurney gentellman, bapt
1703 Jan 12 Jane, the wife of Mr Ranstord, buried
1703 April 14 Joseph, the son of John Loande was boarn
1703 Aug 13. Helinea, the dahter of Mr Thomas Gregory, Recter of Toddington, bapt
1707. Mar 22 John Wentworth Nazianzen Gregory, son of Mr Thomas Gregory, Rector of Toddington, was born March the 18th 170$\frac{7}{8}$ and baptized the 22cond 170$\frac{7}{8}$
1710 Feb 2 Mrs Ann Pennington, buried
1711 Aug 4 Mr Stephen Clay, buried
1714 Feb 2. George Reeves, gent, buried
1715 Oct 18 Thomas Goldsmith gent, buryed
1716 July 8 William Chichley of Barton and Rebecca Digby of Stratley marryed p L

* Celebrated for her attachment to the unfortunate Duke of Monmouth Cf Macaulay's 'History of England' vol i pp 531-2 In the north transept of the parish church are the dilapidated remains of the monument erected to her memory, which cost £2000.

1716 Dec. 30 John Hawks of London, Brewer, Buryed

1719 Oct 14 Sir Henry Johnson,* Knight, buryed

1722. Dec 9. Captn John Symmonds, buryed.

1723. July 18 Elizabeth Clay of London, widd, buryed

1723. July 26. Thomas Goldsmith, Gent, buryed

1726 July 15 Elizabeth Fairy, gent, buryed

1727. Nov. 1. George Isaacson, gent, buryed

1727. Jan 31 The Reverend Mr John Lord A M Rector of Dunstable in this County & Vicar of Kensworth in ye County of Hertford, dyed at ye Parsonage house in this parish on Fryday January 26 about a quarter of an hour before eight in ye morning and was Buryed near ye North-Wall in ye Vestry of this Parish Church on Wednesday January 31 in ye 81 yeare of his age He was instituted into ye Vicarage of Kensworth Jan 27, 1680, and into ye Rectory of Dunstable February 11, 1683

1730 May 5 John Potts & Ann Symmonds, marryed p L Archiepisc

1731. June 5 Patience Lord, widdow, in ye 86 year of her age She was ye Relict of ye late Reverend Mr John Lord & was buryed in ye same grave on Saturday June 5 being Whitsun-Eve

1733. Nov 22 Mary Lord, Spinster, she was sister to ye late Revd Mr John Lord, and was buryed in ye same grave on Thursday Nov. 22 in 77 year of her age

1736 Feb. 18. Mary, wife of John Lawson Esq of Barton bury'd

1736. Mar 3. John Lord my grandson aged 9 weeks & 6 days was Buryed just within ye vestry Door

1738 May 14 John Potts, yeoman, buried.

1738 Aug 31. John Tidcombe, officer in ye excise at Tring in ye County of Hertford, and Catherine Parker of ys Parish Gent by vertue of a License granted by Tho Reynolds Esq M A & Commissary & sign'd by W Capell Surrogate were married

1738 Oct 19 Frances, Dater of Nehemiah & Frances Brandreth gent bapt

1738 Mar 23. Ann Symmonds, Widow & Relict of Captn John Symmonds, Bury'd

1739 Oct. 16 Nehemiah, Son of Nehemiah & Frances Brandreth† gent bapt

1739 Dec 2 The Rt Hon Thomas Earl of Strafford, Buryed

1740 Nov 20 Elizabeth, Dater of Nehemiah & Frances Brandreth gent bapt

1741 Jan 6 William Alston, son of Nehemiah & Frances Brandreth gent bapt

1742 Jan 10 John, son of Nehemiah & ffrances Brandreth gent privately baptis'd

1748 Dec 10 Elizabeth, Dather of the Reverend Mr William Jeffreys, Curate of Toddington and Judith his wife, bapt

1748 Dec 27 Elizabeth Jeffreys, the infant above written, buried

1749 Feb 2. Elizabeth, da of the Reverend Mr William Jeffreys & Judith his wife was baptized

1752 Jan 13 William, s of the Rev Mr William Jeffreys and Judith his wife, bapt

1754 Aug 25. Elizabeth Jeffreys, above written, buried

1756 Nov 8 Thomas, s of the Rev Mr William Jeffreys and Judith his wife, bapt.

1756 Dec 27 Thomas Jeffreys, above written, buried

* An eminent ship builder of Poplar He m. (1) Anne dau of Sir Hugh Smithson of Stanwick, co Yorkshire and (2) Martha only dau of John, Lord Lovelace by Martha dau and heir of Sir Edmund Pye, Bart of Bradenham, and granddaughter maternally of Thomas, Earl of Cleveland

† These Brandreths are of the family of Houghton Hall, near Dunstable

1758	July 19	Thomas, s of William & Judith Jeffreys, bapt
1758	July 22.	Thomas Jeffreys, above-written, buried
1759	July 9	James Simmonds, gentleman bur.
1759.	Sept. 21.	Mary, da of the Rev[d] M[r] William Jeffreys and Judith his wife, bapt.
1759.	Nov 7	Mary Jeffreys, above-written, buried
1761	April 26	Richard, s of the Rev[d] William Jeffreys and Judith his wife, bapt
1761	June 2	Richard Jeffreys, above-written, buried
1761.	Dec 11	Thomas Cooke silversmith (*Goldsmith*) of St Leonards Parish in Foster Lane, London, buried.
1762	June 29	Richard Hillersden, a child, bur
1766	June 7.	Isabella Louisa Grimaldi, an infant, bapt
1767	July 27	Richard Gurney (*Mr., Citizen, and Goldsmith of London*), bur.
1768	Sept 7	Judith Jeffreys buried

GLANVILLE OF HALWELL

Extracts from the Registers of Whitchurch, co Devon *

Baptisms

Elizabeth, the daughter of Thomas Glanvill, was baptized the 10th daye of August, 1572

Dennis, the daughter of Thomas Glanvill, was baptized the 30th of January, 1571.

Marjory, the daughter of Thomas Glanvill, was baptized the 4th day of September, 1575

Jane, the daughter of Thomas Glanvill, was baptized the 2nd day of February, 1578

Pastis, the daughter of Thomas Glanvill, was baptized the 5th day of June, 1580.

Dorothy, the daughter of Thomas Glanvill, was baptized the 15th of April, 1582

Agnes, the daughter of Thomas Glanvill, was baptized the 28th of May, 1584

Thomas, the son of Thomas Glanvill, was baptized 21st February, 1586

Alice, the daughter of Thomas Glanvill, was baptized the 27th of August, 1587

Grace, the daughter of Thomas Glanvill, was baptized the 2nd of January, 1600

Nicholas, the son of Thomas Glanvill, was baptized the 15th of April, 1611

Dorothy, the daughter of Thomas Glanvill and Ursula his wife, was baptized the 18th July, 1613.

Francis Glanvill, the son of Thomas Glanvill and Ursula his wife, was baptized the 16th day of January, 1615

John, the son of Thomas Glanvill the younger, was baptized the 27th day of January, 1633

Dorothy, the daughter of Nicholas Glanvill, was baptized the 21st day of October, 1638

Matthew, the son of Thomas Glanvill of Holwell, the younger, was baptized 21st day of October, 1638

Jane, the daughter of Nicholas Glanvill, was baptized the 5th day of December, 1638

Dorothy, the daughter of Thomas Glanvill was baptized the 20th of April, 1641

Elizabeth, the daughter of Nicholas Glanvill, was baptized the 26th of April, 1641

John, the son of Nicholas Glanvill was baptized the 16th of March, 1643

Nicholas, the son of Nicholas Glanvill, was baptized the 29th of Julie, 1645

John, the son of John Glanville the younger, was baptized 9th May, 1645

Winifred, the daughter of John Glanvill, was baptized the 22nd day of July, 1648

Francis, sonne of John Glanvill the younger, was baptized the 12th day of November, 1650

* Communicated by W Glanvill Richards, Esq

John, the son of John Glanvill, was born the 21st day of June, 1655
Dorothy, the daughter of John Glanvill, was born the 8th day of October, 1657.
Margaret, the daughter of John Glanvill, was born the 24th of September, 1659
Oliver, the son of Francis Glanvill, was baptized the 29th of Januarie, 1660
Ellinor, daughter of Matthew Glanvill, was baptized the 2nd of November, 1661.
Thomazine, daughter of Matthew Glanvill, was baptized 27th May, 1663
Honour, daughter of Matthew Glanvill was baptized 21st of December, 1664
Abagail, daughter of John Glanvill, was baptized 4th of June, 1665
Thomas, son of Matthew Glanvill, was baptized 25th of May, 1667
Francis, sonne of John Glanvill, was baptized the 3rd day of May, 1668
Nicholas, sonne of Matthew Glanvill, was baptized 20th of September, 1669
John, sonne of Matthew Glanvill, was baptized 19th of May, 1672
Dewence, daughter of John Glanvill, was baptized 6th of July, 1672
George, sonne of Nicholas Glanvill, was baptized 9th of January, 1676
Grace, daughter of Matthew Glanvill, was baptized 27th day of December, 1677
John, son of John Glanvill (the younger), was baptized 4th day of June, 1678
Richard, son of John Glanvill, junior, was baptized 22 August, 1680
George, the son of Ollever Glanvill, baptized the 8th of January, 1688
Henery, the son of Ollever Glanvill, baptized the 9th day August, 1691
Susana, the daughter of Ollever Glanvill, was baptized 13th of May, 1693
Nicholas, the son of John Glanvill, was baptized the 7th of October, 1695
John, the son of Thomas Glanvill, was baptized 5th of November, 1695
William, the son of Ollever Glanville, was baptized the 17th of June, 1697
September 24th, 1700 Olliver Glanvill had a son, born by Sarah his wife
Thomas, son of Olliver Glanvill, was born October 6th and baptized 20th, 1703
John, son of John and Sarah Glanvill, was born the 22nd day of September, 1716
Dorothy, daughter of John Glanvill of Holwell, was born the 8th of June, 1718
William, son of William Glanvill, was baptized 22nd day of June, 1721
Nicholas, son of John Glanvill, was born 1st of January, 1721
Mary, the daughter of John Glanvill of Holwell, was born the 18th day of March, 1722
Sarah, daughter of William Glanvill, was baptized 3rd of January, 1725
Mary, daughter of William Glanvill, was baptized April 4th, 1728
Thomas, son of William and Rose Glanvill, was baptized May the 7th, 1730
Elizabeth, the daughter of William and Rose Glanvill, was baptized August 14th, 1736
Richard, son of William Glanvill, was baptized November 3rd, 1739
John, son of John Glanvill, junior, was baptized February 8th, 1742
Elizabeth, daughter of Mr John Glanvill, junior, was baptized May 13th, 1745
Sarah, daughter of Mr John Glanvill, was baptized January 4th, 1747
John, son of John Glanvill was baptized August 15th, 1750
Jinny, daughter of Mr John Glanvill, was baptized December, 1751
Julius, son of John Glanvill of Holwell, was baptized June 1st, 1751
Mary, daughter of Mr John Glanvill, was baptized November, 1756
Joan, the daughter of John Glanvill, was baptized March 17th, 1759
Mary, daughter of Nicholas Glanvill, was baptized March 6th, 1760
Mary, daughter of John Glanvill, was baptized May 26, 1761
John, son of Nicholas Glanvill, was baptized June 9th, 1762
Nicholas, son of Nicholas Glanvill, was baptized April 3rd, 1764
Jinny, daughter of John Glanvill was baptized June 30th, 1764
John, son of John Glanvill, was baptized November 26th, 1766
Richard, son of Nicholas Glanvill, was baptized August 1st, 1769
Walter, son of Nicholas Glanvill, was baptized April 21st, 1772
Thomas, son of Mary Glanvill, was baptized Dec 9th, 1778
Susannah, daughter of John and Joan Glanville, was baptized December 22nd, 1788
Mary Ann, daughter of Walter and Ann Glanville, was baptized January 25th, 1801.
John, son of Walter and Anne Glanville, was baptized March 13th, 1803.

(*To be continued*)

VARIAN.—I should be pleased if any of your readers could furnish me with information concerning the place of origin of this family, a branch of which (Thomas Varian) was settled at Cork, Ireland, about 100 years since.

Cleveland, Ohio, U.S.A. SAM. BRIGGS.

FINISTON FAMILY.—Since inserting my query in the 'Misc. Gen. et Heraldica,' I have ascertained the following particulars respecting this family, and shall be much obliged to any correspondent who can give me any further information, especially with regard to the parentage of Dorothea, wife of the Rev. Joseph Finiston. The names of Finiston and Mackay seem in a list of families connected with the O'Neills of Clannaboy. The "Revd Skeffington Bristow, Clerk," and "James Stewart, Esq., Counsellor at Law," were trustees of the will of the Rev. Joseph Finiston.

John Finiston of the City of Dublin.=. . . .

Rev. Joseph Finiston, Vicar of Antrim, B.A. Trin. Coll., Dublin, 1701; M.A. 1714. Will dated 4 Dec. 1754. Born about 1676-7; died about 1754-5.=Dorothea, dau. of . . . . ?

James Finiston, Esq., of Antrim. His name appears in a list of Magistrates for the co. Antrim in 1773.	Catherine.	Frances, m. the Rev. William Williamson. — Christian, mar. Joseph Macay.	Rachael, m. Robert Clarke. Query of Ballycastle, co. Antrim.	Helena. — Josepha.	Charlotte, m. William Shaw, Esq., of Ballytweedy, co. Antrim. =	Dorothea, m. . . . . Wilson.

Broomfield, near Huddersfield, Yorkshire. WALTON GRAHAM BERRY.

PRICE AND BROWN.—A marriage settlement dated 16 January, 1626, discloses the following pedigree :—

John Price the elder of Kingston-upon-Thames, gent.=

Sir Anthony Brown of Kingston-upon-Thames, Knight.=

John Price the younger of Kingston-upon-Thames, son and heir.=Mary, about to be married to John Price.

The above-mentioned John Price, father and son, convey lands, etc., in Kingston-upon-Thames, to Sir Anthony Brown and Thomas Haward the elder, also of Kingston, gent., to secure a jointure of £100 per an. to Mary, the da. of Sir Anthony Brown. The seal affixed by John Price the elder is indistinct, but the arms appear to be,—Quarterly, 1. A lion rampant regardant, a canton . . . . 2. A lion rampant. 3. Indistinct (3 roses, and on a canton a fleur de lys ?). 4. A lion rampant issuing from a mural crown (holding 3 roses ?). On the seal of John Price the younger is a lion rampant issuing out of a mural crown, holding in the paw three roses. Manning and Bray mention a Sir Anthony Brown at this period who was comptroller to Kings James and Charles. From what families did this Sir Anthony and the Prices descend ? The witnesses to the deed were Edw. Hurst, Brian Blomely, and Joane Ward.—T. N.

Pedigree of Percy Bysshe Shelley.*

JOHN MIDDLETON of Horsham, co. Sussex. = FRANCES, dau'r of Nicholas Fowle of Rotherfield, co. Sussex.

FRISWIDE, dau'r of Sir Thomas Walsingham of Scadbury, co. Kent, Knight, died without issue. 1st wife. = HENRY SHELLEY of Worminghurst, co. Sussex, Esquire. Died in December, 1623, buried there 9th same month. = BARBARA, eldest dau'r of William Cromer of Tunstall, co. Kent, Esq. Buried at Worminghurst 3 Nov. 1612. 2nd wife.

Richard Middleton of Horsham in the county of Sussex, gent., 4 son. Buried there 4 May, 1604. = Elizabeth, dau'r and heir of Robert Eversfield of Horsham aforesaid, gent.

Thomas Middleton of Horsham, Esquire, son and heir. = Barbara Shelley, eldest dau'r, bapt. 11 Feb. 1588, and marr. at Worminghurst 29th May, 1610.

Thomas Shelley of Worminghurst aforesaid, Esq., eldest son and heir. = Mary, eldest dau'r of Edward Goring of Okehurst, co. Sussex, Esq. Marr. at Worminghurst 26 June, 1600.

Henry Shelley, Esq., 2nd son, bapt. at Worminghurst 2 Sept. 1582, and bur. there 3rd Mar. 1644.

Edward Mitchell of Stamerham in the said county of Sussex, Esq., died 18th April, , buried at Horsham. M.I. = Mary Middleton, 3rd dau'r as named in the will of her grandfather Eversfield 10th Aug. 1629. Marr. at Horsham 23rd Sept. 1641.

John Middleton and other issue.

Barbara Shelley, eldest dau'r, bapt. at Worminghurst 7 June, 1601.

Henry Shelley of Worminghurst, Esq., eldest son and heir, bapt. there 1st Aug. 1602; died s.p. in June, 1687, bur. there 11th same month.

Thomas Shelley, gent., 2 son.

John Shelley.

Edward, bapt. 12 July, 1606.

William Shelley, 4th son, bapt. at Worminghurst 3rd June, 1612.

Dorothy Shelley, 2nd dau'r, bapt. at Worminghurst 19th Oct. 1603.

George Shelley of Hindon, co. Sussex, gent., 5th son, bapt. at Worminghurst 9th July, 1611; buried at Finden 3 Dec. 1661.

Mary Shelley, 3rd dau'r, bapt. at Worminghurst 5th Oct. 1613, and bur. there 22nd Jan. 1615.

Frances, bapt. at Finden 19 Oct. 1615.

Mary, bapt. at Washington 10 May, 1618.

Mary, dau'r of .... White, gent. Married at Horsham 18 August, 1675. 1st wife. (A) = Robert Michell of Petersfield, co. Hants, Esq., 3rd son. Bapt. at Horsham 24 April, 1653; died in August, 1729, buried 10th of same month at Horsham. Will dated 10th April, 1724, proved at London 3rd Sept. 1729. (252 Abbot.) (B) = Theodosia, dau'r of George Montagu of Horton, co. Northampton, Esq., son of Henry, Earl of Manchester. Sister of Charles, Earl of Halifax. Buried at Horsham 4th Dec. 1718. (16 Leeds.) 2nd wife.

Walsingham Michell, of Horsham aforesaid, gent. Bapt. there 4 Nov. 1658. Will dated 13th May, 1704, proved at London 7 Jan. 1713. (10 Aston.) (C) = Margaret, dau'r of .... Living a widow, and ex'trix to her husband's will, 7 Jan. 1713.

Katherine. *See page* 423. (D)

* Communicated by H. BUXTON FORMAN, Esq. Monumental inscriptions and other evidences relating to the Shelley family have, in addition to this pedigree, been published in the recent edition of Shelley's Prose Works, edited by him, and published by Messrs. Reeves and Turner.

A | B | C | D

Edward Michell, eldest son and heir, bapt. at Horsham 15 June, 1676. Living 10 April, 1724.

. . . . Michell, 2nd son, bapt. at Horsham 31 July, 1677.

Catherine Michell, only child of her mother, bapt. at Petersfield 1695. Unmarr. and ex'trix to her father's will 3rd Sept. 1729. Married before 30 July, 1731, to John Jolliffe, of Petersfield, Esq. Died s.p. 26 June, 1731, buried at Horsham.

Robert Michell, 2nd son, under age 1704. Living 13 Mar. 1737.

Katherine Michell, 2nd dau'r, unmarr. and under age 1704.

Edward Michell, 3rd son, bapt. at Horsham 5 Feb. 1683.

John Michell, youngest son, bapt. at Horsham 3 Feb. 1685. Living 1704.

John Pilfold of Baylings in Warnham, co. Sussex, gent, living 13 March, 1737. = Mary Michell, eldest dau'r, living unmarried 13th May, 1704. Married at Horsham 8 May, 1716. Living 13 March, 1737.

Rev. Theobald Michell of Horsham, Clerk, eldest son and heir. Married at Ifield, co. Sussex, 3rd July, 1733; buried at Horsham 23rd March, 1737. Will dated 13 March, 1737, proved at London 12th May, 1738. = Mary, dau'r of . . . . Treadcroft of Horsham, gent., sister of Edward Treadcroft, Esq. Living a widow and ex'trix to her husband's will 12 May, 1738.

Charles Pilfold of Effingham in the county of Surrey, gent. = Bethia, daughter of William White of Horsham, gent.

Mary Catherine Michell, only child and heir, bapt. at Horsham 14th March, 1734; marr. at Keith's Chapel, May Fair, in the parish of St. George's, Hanover Square, 1752; died in November, 1760, aged 26, buried 15th same month at Horsham. = Bysshe Shelley, of Castle Goring. *See page* 4.

Elizabeth, mar. to Timothy Shelley of Field Place. *See page* 424.

William Holland of Chichester and of West Burton, co. Sussex, gent. Marr. at Worminghurst 17 Aug. 1614. 1st Husb. = Francis Shelley, 2nd dau'r, bapt. at Worminghurst 21st Nov. 1592. Marr. to her 2nd husband, Richard, Lord Viscount Lumley, of whom the present Earl of Scarborough is descended.

Richard Shelley, gent., 3rd son, bapt. at Worminghurst 17th Nov. 1583. = Joan, dau'r and heir of John Fuste.

William Shelley, 4th son, bapt. at Worminghurst 1st Jan. 1585. Died young.

Mary Shelley, 3rd dau'r, bapt. at Worminghurst 30 June, 1594. Unmarr. 1615, afterwards 2nd wife of Thomas Warneford of Sevenhamton, co. Wilts.

Frances Holland, only dau'r and heir of her father, wife of John Ashburnham of Ashburnham, co. Sussex, Esquire.

Joan Shelley, 2nd dau'r, married at Horsham to Richard Wheatley 25 June, 1640.

E

John Shelley of Ichingfield, afterwards of Thakeham, co. Sussex, Esquire, eldest son and heir, died 3rd July, 1673, buried at Thakeham 6th of same month. Will dated 9th June, 1673, proved at Chichester 24 Dec. following. (M.I.) = Bridget, 3rd dau'r of Sir Thomas Eversfield of Denn, co. Sussex, Knight, bapt. at Worth 19 April, 1602; died in Nov. 1671, bur. at Thakeham 23rd same month. Adm'on 22nd May, 1682, to Christian Ellis, her daughter.

F

Edward Shelley of Horsham, gent., 2nd son, living 1615. Died unmarr., bur. at Thakeham 1st April, 1686. Will dated 21 Feb. 1678, proved at Chichester 1686.

Richard Shelley, 3rd son, living 1615.

Barbara Shelley, eldest dau'r, marr. to Michael Merryam. Died before 16 July, 1689.

Theobald Shelley of Steyning, co. Sussex, gent., 4 son. Died without issue. Will dated 16 July, 1689, proved at London 22nd Dec. 1692. (142 Fane.) = Mary, dau'r of . . . . Davis. Living a widow and sole ex'trix to the will of her husband 22nd Dec. 1692.

G

E — F — G

Katherine Michell, dau'r of Edward Michell, Esq. Married at Horsham 22nd Dec. 1664. = Timothy Shelley of Champneys in the parish of Thakeham aforesaid, gent., 2nd son and heir. Buried at Thakeham 3rd July, 1671. Will dated 18 May, 1671, proved at Chichester 21st Oct. following. = Mary, dau'r of .... Cheale, and sister of John Cheale of Finden, co. Sussex, Esq. Marr. settlement dated 11 Oct. 21st Car. II. Marr. at Finden 12th Oct. 1669; died in June, 1731, aged 89, buried at Warnham. M.I. = John Michell of Field Place, co. Sussex, gent., 2nd husband of Mary Cheale. Married at Thakeham 23rd June, 1687. = Johanna Wheatley, sole heir of her uncle John Wheatley. M.I.

William Shelley of Sullington, co. Sussex, gent. eldest son and heir apparent, died s.p. Will dated 27 June, 1658, codicil 28 August, and proved at London 9 Nov. following. (600 Wootton.) = Adria, dau'r of Henry Bridger of Worminghurst, and sister of Richard Bridger of Ashurst, co. Sussex, Esq.

John Shelley, bur. at Thakeham 7 Nov. 1668.

Richard Shelley, 5th son, citizen and Merchant Taylor of London. Marr. Mary, dau'r of .... and died s.p. Will dated 27 Feb. 1672, proved at London 26 Mar. 1673. (39 Pye.)

Elizabeth Shelley, eldest dau'r. Marr. at Horsham 21st Nov. 1652 to Humphry Covert of Shepley, co. Sussex. Living 9 June, 1673.

Christiana Shelley, 2nd and youngest dau'r. Adm'ix to her mother 22nd May, 1682. Afterwards remarr. to .... Paulkhurst of .... = Thomas Ellis of Steyning, co. Sussex. Marr. at Thakeham 26 May, 1670. 1st husband.

Mary Shelley, only dau'r, born at Horsham 21st Dec. 1665, bapt. there 4 Jan. following.

John Shelley of Fen Place (jure uxoris), co. Sussex, Esq., eldest son and heir, born at Wolfshill in West Chiltington in said county 27 Jan. 1666. Adopted heir to his great uncle, Theobald Shelley, by will dated 16 July, 1689. Died 4th Feb. 1739, buried in the chancel of the Church of Worth (M.I.). Will dated 24 July, 1738; codicil 15 Oct. 1739; proved 18th March following. (91 Browne.) = Hellen, younger of the two daughters and coheirs of Roger Bysshe of Fen Place, aforesaid, Esquire. Born 16 April, 1667; marr. settlement dated 4 Sept. 1692; died 10 Feb. 1742, bur. at Worth (M.I.).

Edward Shelley of Field Place, co. Sussex, Esq., Barrister at Law, bapt. at Thakeham 3 Nov. 1670; died in March, 1747–8, buried at Warnham 12th same month. By his will, dated 4 August, 1746, proved at London 2nd June, 1748, he recites that (*inter alia*) he had purchased Field Place of the family of Michells, which he thereby settled, etc. etc.

Wheatley Michell.

John Michell.

Richard Michell, bapt. at Warnham 20 Oct. 1680.

John Ellis of Steyning, Esq., living 16 June, 1689. = ...

Mary Ellis, named in the will of her great uncle. Theobald Shelley, 16 June, 1689.

Hellen Shelley, eldest dau'r, bapt. at Worth 22nd Nov. 1693; marr. to John Holman of the parish of Worth before 4 August, 1746. Living a widow 26 July, 1762.

Bysshe Shelley, Esq., eldest son and heir apparent, bapt. at Worth 5 Feb. 1695. Died unmarr. 2nd Jan. 1733, bur. at Worth 4th same month. W.R. (M.I.)

John Shelley of Fen Place aforesaid, Esq., 2nd son, a lunatic. Bapt. at Worth 1st Sept. 1696; died unmarr. at Uckfield 7 Oct. 1772, bur. at Worth 13th same month. W. R. (M.I.)

Margaret Shelley, 2nd dau'r, bapt. at Worth 9 Sept. 1698. Marr. to her first husband .... Living a widow to her 2nd husband 26 July, 1762. = ... Payne of Ligg's Heath, co. Sussex, Esq., sometime High Sheriff of the said county, 2nd husband, by whom an only child named Margaret, who died young.

H I

H | I

Timothy Shelley of Fen Place aforesaid, Esq., 3rd son and heir, bapt. at Worth 19 April, 1700; died 11 Mar. 1770, aged 70, bur. in the chancel of the Church of Warnham. ═ Johanna, dau'r of . . . . widow of . . . . Plum of New York in America.

Catherine Shelley, unmarr. in July, 1738. Married to John Thornton of Apthorp Common, co. Sussex, before 4 August, 1746. Both living 26 July, 1762.

Percy Shelley of Bookham, co. Surrey, gent., 4 son, living 26 July, 1762. Will dated 11 Dec. 1771. Proved 16 Jan. 1772. ═ Mary, dau'r of . . . . Living a widow and ex'trix to her husband's will 16 Jan. 1772.

Richard Shelley, 5th and youngest son, died unmarr.

Anne Shelley, bapt. at Worth 6th Dec. 1701. Married to her 2nd husband, John Parr of Warnham, gent. He was buried at Warnham 14 Sept. 1754. She was buried there 4 July, 1771. ═ John Michell of Warnham aforesaid, gent., first husband. Died 20 Oct. 1740, aged 32 years, buried at Warnham. Adm'on granted 9 March, 1741, to Anne, his widow and relict. (M.I.)

Anne Shelley, one of the two surviving dau'rs and coheirs of her father. Unmarried December 1771.

Two other dau'rs, died unmarried in the lifetime of their father.

Catherine Shelley, one of the two surviving dau'rs and coheirs of her father. Wife of John Bayley of Bookham aforesaid in Dec. 1771.

Anne Michell, eldest dau'r and coheir, bapt. at Warnham 16 Dec. 1735. Named in the will of her great uncle, Edward Shelley, 4 Aug. 1746. Marr. at Warnham 8 Oct. 1753, to Rev. Samuel Shuckford, Rector of Warnham. He was living 13 December, 1783.

Hellen Catherine Michell, 2nd dau'r and coheir. Living unmarr. 4 Aug. 1746, afterwards wife of . . . . Millar of Dorking, co. Surrey,

Henrietta Michell, youngest of the three dau'rs and coheirs. Living 4 August, 1746; died unmarried.

Mary Catherine Michell, 1st wife. *See page* 422. ═ Bysshe Shelley of Castle Goring, co. Sussex, Esquire, 2nd and youngest son. Born 21 June, 1731, and bapt. 1st August following in the parish of Christ Church, Newark, America; died 6 January, 1815, buried in the Church of Horsham. ═ Elizabeth Jane Sidney, only surviving dau'r and heir of William Perry of Penshurst, co. Kent, Esq., by Elizabeth Sidney his wife. Born 22nd Dec. 1741; marr. at St. James, Westminster, 1769; died at Turville Park, in May, and bur. 17th same month, 1781, at Penshurst.

John Shelley of Field Place aforesaid, Esq., eldest son and heir. Born 10th Dec. 1729, baptized at Newark in America 11 Jan. following; died s.p. 4 Oct. 1790, buried at Warnham. ═ Mary, dau'r of William White, of Horsham, gent. Marr. there 22nd December, 1752; died 4 Jan. 1759, aged 27, buried at Warnham. H.R. (M.I.)

Hellen Shelley, eldest dau'r, born in Red Lion Square. Now wife of Robert Parker of Maidstone, co. Kent, gent. Living s.p. 1806.

Timothy Shelley of Field Place aforesaid, Esq., eldest son and heir apparent, born in Red Lion Square, co. Middx., Sept. 1753; bapt. at St. Geo. Martyr 20th same month. Now M.P. for New Shoreham, co. Sussex, 1806. ═ Elizabeth, dau'r of Charles Pilfold of Effingham, co. Surrey, gent. Married at West Grinstead, co. Sussex, October, 1791. *See page* 422.

J

Mary Catherine Shelley, 2nd dau'r, born at Steyning aforesaid; bapt. there 24 Dec. 1760; died unmarr. in July, 1784, bur. 26th same month at Horsham.

K | L

J | K | L

Percy Bysshe Shelley, eldest son and heir apparent, born at Field Place 4th August, 1792, baptized at Warnham 7 September following.

Elizabeth Shelley, eldest dau'r, born 10th May, 1794, bapt. at Warnham 2nd July following.

Hellen Shelley, 2nd dau'r, born 29th Jan. 1796, bapt. 27th Feb. following; died an infant, bur. at Warnham 25th May, 1796.

Mary Shelley, 3rd dau'r, born 9 June, 1797, bapt. at Warnham 17 July following.

Hellen Shelley, 4th dau'r, born 26th Sept. 1799, bapt. at Warnham 6th Oct. following.

Margaret Shelley, 5th dau'r, born 20th Jan. 1801, bapt. at Warnham 12 March following.

John Shelley, 2nd son, born 15 March, 1806, bapt. at Warnham 14 Aug. following.

Arriana Shelley, eldest dau'r of her mother, born at Penshurst; bapt. there 30th Dec. 1770. Now wife of Francis Aicken, Esq., Capt. in the 5th Regt. of Dragoon Guards. Living s.p. 1806.

John Shelley Sidney of Penshurst aforesaid, Esq., eldest son and heir of his mother, born at Hambledon, co. Hants, 10th Nov., and there bapt. 18 December, 1771. Took the surname of Sidney in addition to Shelley by Royal Sign Manual dated 6 March, 1793, and the Arms of Sidney by Patent 16th same month. =Henrietta Frances, 7th dau'r of Sir Henry Hunloke of Wingerworth, co. Derby, Baronet; marr. at Wingerworth 29 April, 1799; died 5 Feb. 1811, bur. at Penshurst.

Elizabeth Jane Caroline, 2nd and youngest dau'r of her mother, born at Turville Park; bapt. there 2nd Jan. 1776; married at St. George's, Hanover Square, to the Rev. Joseph Harris of Turville, co. Bucks, Clerk. =

Emily Elizabeth Sidney, only dau'r, born 10th February, 1801, bapt. at Penshurst 8th March following.

Philip Charles Sidney, only son and heir apparent, born 11 March, 1800, bapt. 9th April, and publicly received 29 May following in the parish of St. James, Westminster.

Phillip Shelley, Esq., 3rd son of his mother, born at Turville Park; bapt. there 20th Feb. 1778. Sometime Captain in the 4th Regt. Foot. Took the surname and arms of Sidney only by Royal Sign Manual dated 10th April, 1799. Died unmarr. in August following, buried 31st same month at Penshurst.

Percy John Borlase Shelley, 2nd son of his mother, born at Hambleton, co. Hants; bapt. there 23rd July, 1773; died at Turville Park, co. Bucks, and buried there 27 Nov. 1782.

Robert Shelley, Esq., 4th son of his mother, born at Turville Park, bapt. there 4 Jan. 1780. Now a Captain in the West Kent Militia. Unmarried 1806.

Algernon Bysshe Shelley, youngest son, born at Turville Park, bapt. there 12th May, 1781; died an infant, and buried there 13th Oct. following.

Walter Shelley, gent., 5th son, bapt. at Worminghurst 4 Oct. 1587. Living unmarr. 1615.

Anthony Shelley, bapt. 30 Mar. 1591; died young, bur. at Worminghurst 13th June, 1597.

Ambrose Shelley of Horsham, aforesaid, gent., 7th son. Will dated 4 Nov. 1647, proved at London 13th Nov. 1649. (154 Fairfax.) =Grace, dau'r of .... Staker. Died 28th April, , in the lifetime of her husband, buried at Horsham.

M

James Shelley, gent., 8th and youngest son, bapt. at Worminghurst 3rd June, 1599. Living unmarr. 1615.

Elizabeth Shelley, 4th and youngest dau'r, bapt. at Worminghurst 19 Aug. 1604. Unmarr. 1615, afterwards wife of William Keete of Little Hinton, co. Wilts.

M

Henry Shelley of Horsham, gent., only son and heir, under 21, 1649. In 1689 was made heir in remainder on failure of issue of John, son of Timothy Shelley, to estates of Theobald Shelley. Will dated 13 Jan. 1693, proved at Chichester 28 May following. = Mary, dau'r of .... Will dated 15 Dec. 1696, pr. at London 26 March, 1698. (206 Lort.)

Grace Shelley, living under 12 years of age 4th Nov. 1647.

Frances Shelley, 2nd dau'r, bapt. at Horsham 12 April, 1647. Living 4 Nov. following.

Issue of Henry and Mary:

Edward Shelley, eldest son and heir, bapt. at Horsham 16 Feb. 1676. One of the ex'ors to his mother's will, which he proved 26 Mar. 1698.

Mary Shelley, eldest dau'r, bapt. at Horsham 29th Dec. 1671. Marr. before 15 Feb. 1696 to Benjamin Knight. Both then living.

Barbara Shelley, 2nd dau'r, bapt. at Horsham 14 April, 1676. Living unmarr. 1696.

Grace Shelley, 3rd dau'r, living unmarr. 29 Feb. 1696.

Jane Shelley, died young, 1678, bur. at Horsham.

Elizabeth, died young, 1681, bur. at Horsham.

Henry Shelley, 2nd son, bapt. at Horsham 27 April, 1682. Living 1696.

Theobald Shelley, 3rd and youngest son bapt. at Horsham 14 Oct, 1686.

The above Pedigree is true to the best of my knowledge and belief.

Witness my hand this twentieth day of May, 1816.

The above Pedigree of my Family is true to the best of my knowledge and belief.

Witness my hand this sixth day of March, 1816.

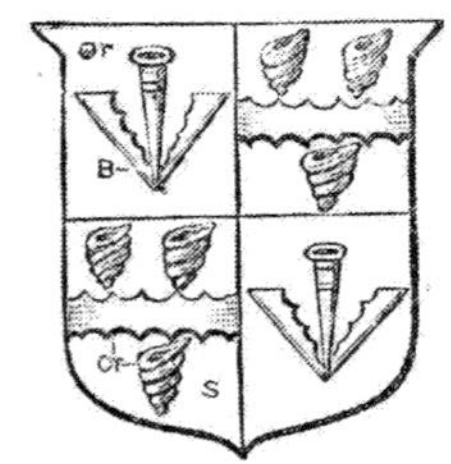

I certify this to be a true copy of the original record now remaining in the Heralds' College, London.

STEPHEN TUCKER, Somerset Herald.

John Clare Ridgway, mdccclxxi.

Pedigree of Onslow.

Henry Onslow, 3rd son of Sir Richard Onslow (see Earl of Onslow), bapt. 4 Oct. 1621. Of Warnham and Drungwick, in Wisborough Green, co. Sussex. Knighted 18 May, 1664. Admon. 23 Nov. 1667, to Jane, the widow, and further grant 21 Jan. 1688-9, to Richard Onslow, the son. (See Le Neve's 'Knights,' published in 1873 by the Harleian Society.) ╤ Jane, dau. of Sir Francis Stydolph, Knight, of Mickleham, Surrey (by his wife Mary, dau. of Sir James Altham, Baron of the Exchequer), widow of Henry Yates of Warnham, Sussex. Mar. 3rd, John Amhurst (Marriage Licence.—Vicar-General John Amhurst of Gray's Inn, Widower, and Dame Jane Onslow of Warnham, Sussex, Widow, 7 Nov. 1668, and mar. at Horsham, Sussex, 10 Nov. 1668). Monument formerly at Mickleham, Surrey. Will dated 9 May, 1684, and then of St. Andrew's, Holborn, proved 4 Nov. 1684. P.C.C., Hare 151.

Richard Onslow, of Drungwick. Of Little Chelsea in will dated 11 June, 1711; pr. 10 April, 1712. P.C.C. Barnes 74. ╤ Sarah, dau. of Thomas Calvert of Red Cross (? White Cross) Street, London, Brewer and M.P. for Reading, by his wife Ann, da. of Wm. Ambrose of Reading. Marriage settlement dat. 23 April, 1689; died 1750, aged 80. See Berry's 'Hertfordshire Genealogies.'

Threele Onslow, bapt. 25 Aug. 1661, at Warnham, Sussex.

Edward Manning of Kevington, St. Mary Cray, Kent (query bap. 26 Apr. 1655, at St. Mary Cray), son of Edward Manning of Kevington, by Elizabeth Masters, whom he mar. 7 July, 1654, at Chislehurst, Kent. Died 23 Dec. 1703, and bur. at St. Mary Cray, aged 49. 1st husband. ╤ Anne, mar. 2ndly, 30 Mar. 1707, at St. Mary Cray, Kent, Stephen Parker, 2nd husb.

Richard Manning, succeeded his father, & resided at Kevington, bapt. 9 Apr. 1697, at St. Mary Cray; died 24 April, 1753; bur. at St. Mary Cray, s.p. Devised Kevington to his cousin, Denzil Onslow. Will dat. 21 May, 1751; pr. 7 May, 1753. P.C.C., Searle 146.

Mary, *query* bapt. 18 Nov. 1695, at St. Mary Cray, & there bur. 27 Feb. 1729-30. = Denzil Onslow of Drungwick. *Query* this marriage. See Hasted's 'Kent.'

13 other children.

[St. Mary Cray Church, Kent.—Arms on ledger stone: MANNING impaling ONSLOW.]

Denzil Onslow of Drungwick and of Kevington, St. Mary Cray, a Commissioner of Salt Office, J.P. of co. Surrey, died 16 Nov. 1765, aged 67. Tablet at Mitcham, Surrey. Will dat. 18 Feb. 1762, and pr. 27 Nov. 1765. P.C.C., Rushworth 422. ╤ Anne, dau. and coheiress of Thomas Middleton of Stanstead Mountfitchet, Essex, M.P. for that County, by Anne dau. of Sir Richard Onslow, who was nephew of the above Sir Henry Onslow. Married 25 April, 1730, by licence of 22 April, 1730 (Faculty); died 6 Jan. 1772. See Le Neve's 'Knights.'

A

Thomas Onslow, bur. 7 Sept. 1705, at Warnham.

. . . . = Sarah. Stone.

Jane. ╤ Galen, 3rd son of Sir John Cope, Bart., Capt. in the Army, and then took Orders, and became Rector of Eversley, Hants.

B

Anne.

Mary, of St. James', Clerkenwell. Will dated 21 Oct. 1748, and pr. 6 Dec. 1748. P.C.C., Strahan 373.

A

Middleton Onslow of Drungwick, and at one time of Kevington, St. Mary Cray, which he sold to the family of Berens. J.P. for Surrey, 1760. Died 29 Oct. 1801, bur. at Shoreham. ═ Anne, only dau. of Trevor Borrett of Shoreham Place, Kent, widow of Arthur Reid. Mar. 2ndly, 24 Aug. 1769. See Hasted's 'Kent.'

Richard Onslow (Captain), bapt. 31 Dec. 1734, at Mitcham, Surrey. Named in his father's will.

B

Richard Cope, Rector of Eversley, Prebendary of Durham, 9th Bart. Married, but died 26 Nov. 1806, s.p.

William Cope of Bridgen Place, Kent. ═ Anne, dau. and heir of Captain Benjamin Greenwood, of St. Mary Cray, Kent, bapt. 8 Oct. 1733, at St. Mary Cray.

Denzil Cope, 10th Bart. Died s.p. 30 Dec. 1812. 1st husband. ═ Elizabeth Dorothea Francis (who married 2ndly Henry Rush), died 16 Feb. 1840.

John Cope, 11th Bart. Died s.p. 18 Nov. 1851.

Honble. Anne Catherine, only dau. of Robert Edward, 9th Lord Petre, b. 8 March, 1769; mar. 7 Aug. 1796; died 23 Sept. 1798, s.p. 1st wife. ═ Denzil Onslow of Staughton, co. Hunts, General in H.M.'s Army, J.P. High Sheriff co. Hunts, 1833; d. 20 Aug. 1838, bur. in Great Staughton Church. ═ Sophia, 3rd dau. of Sir Stephen Lushington, Bart., of Southill Park, Berks, mar. 20 Sep. 1800, at Wimbledon by special licence; d. 17 March, 1860, in Regent's Park. 2nd wife. Bur. at Kensal Green.

Middleton Onslow, B.A. King's Coll., Camb., Rector of Bradford Peverell, co. Dorset, died 26 Jan. 1837; bur. at Weald, Kent. ═ Matilda, 7th dau. of Thomas Boddington of Hackney, co. Middlesex, by Maria Catherina his wife, born 29 June, 1776; mar. 16 July, 1802, at S. John's Church, Hackney; d. 30 June, 1824; buried at Clifton, near Bristol. See 'Misc. Gen. et Her.,' Monthly Series, Vol. I., p. 348, and Vol. II., p. 244.

William Onslow, Colonel of 18th Hussars. Buried at Pisa. ═ Mildred, dau. of Col. Jones of East Wickham, Kent, buried at Pisa.

Philip Onslow. ═ . . . .

Emma, bur. at Pisa.

Middleton Onslow, M.A. Queen's College, Camb., Vicar of East Peckham, co. Kent, lately Rural Dean, born 29 Nov. 1805.

Thomas Onslow, b. 20 Feb. 1809; d. 6 July, 1862; bur. at Clifton. ═ Lucy Anne Katherine, dau. of Rev. John Cutts Lockwood, born 4 Aug. 1802; mar. 7 Dec. 1836, at Melcombe Regis, co. Dorset, she being his first cousin; died 10 July, 1859; bur. at Torquay.

Charles Onslow, M.A. Trin. Coll. Camb., Vicar of Holt, co. Dorset, and Prebendary of Salisbury, born 18 April, 1810. ═ Elizabeth, dau. of John Bond of Grange, Isle of Purbeck (see Burke's 'Landed Gentry'). Born 13 March, 1804; mar. 24 Oct. 1840, at Steeple Church, Isle of Purbeck; died 21 Aug. 1876, at Holt.

Lucy Lockwood, born 10 June, 1839; mar. 9 Feb. 1865, at East Peckham. ═ Anthony Powell, son of Morgan Popkin Traherne, born 4 Jan. 1834. J.P. for Co. Glamorgan, etc. See Burke's 'Landed Gentry.'

Onslow Powell Traherne, born 12 March, 1866.

Elizabeth.

Sophy, died 21 Oct. 1871, aged 28, bur. in Cemetery, Wimborne, Dorset.

Charles Middleton Onslow, born 17 July, 1844; died 24 Nov. 1862; buried in Cemetery, Wimborne.

C

D

William Onslow, b. 8 June, 1812; died Feb. 1837; buried at Weald, co. Kent.

Edward Onslow, b. 1815; died 1815; bur. at Bradford Peverell.

Matilda, born 24 Sept. 1804; died 23 Dec. 1875, at East Peckham, Kent; bur. at Weald.

Maria, born 9 June, 1807; died 26 March, 1876, at her brother-in-law's, George Churchill, Alderholt Park, and bur. at Alderholt.

Frances, born 23 Dec. 1813; mar. 14 May, 1835, at Bradford Peverell; died 30 Oct. 1879, at Weymouth. = George Churchill of Alderholt Park, co. Hants, born 10 March, 1811. See Burke's 'Landed Gentry.'

Harriet, born 18 May, 1817; died 18 Jan. 1839; bur. at Weald.

Matilda Louisa.

George Onslow Churchill, born 1 Nov. 1838, late Lieut. 15th Foot, & Major 7th Royal Lancashire Rifle Militia; J.P. for co. Dorset.

Harriet.

Charles Morant Churchill, born 19 May, 1842. Capt. 50th Foot. = Ellen Harriette Augusta, only dau. of Edmund Waldo Meade Waldo of Hever Castle, and Stonewall Park, Kent. See Burke's 'Landed Gentry.'

Emma Isabella, died 5 March, 1845; buried at Buckland Ripers, co. Dorset.

Lucy Sophia.

Emma.

Arthur Hallet Churchill, born 9 and died 10 Feb. 1849; bur. at Buckland Ripers.

---

1. Denzil Onslow, b. 27 July, 1802; died 10 Feb. 1879; bur. in Great Staughton Church.

2. Henry Cope Onslow, born died 23 April, 1870; buried in Great Staughton Church.

3. William Onslow, born died April, 1847.

4. Frederick Onslow, born died 29 March, 1810.

Emma Gayford, died 9 Jan. 1861, at Bournemouth; bur. at Kensal Green. 1st wife. = 5. Arthur Robert Onslow, born died 1 Feb. 1877, aged 54, at St. Leonards-on-Sea; bur. at Kensal Green. = ... 2 wife.

Neville Day of St. Neots, co. Hunts, died 25 Aug. 1839. 1st husband. = 1. Sophia, died 22 Nov. 1878, aged 78; buried at Kensal Green. = ... Wilkinson. 2nd husband.

2. Emma, died 25 March, 1879, aged 75; bur. at Tunbridge Wells. = Wade Meara, in Holy Orders.

3. Louisa, died 7 July, 1879, aged 74; bur. in Cemetery, Great Staughton.

George Newton of Croxton Park, co. Cambridge, died 1837. 1st husb. See Burke's 'Landed Gentry.' = 4. Charlotte, mar. 1stly 1829; 2ndly, 1845. = Honble. Craven Fitzhardinge Berkeley, M.P., born 1805; d. 1 July, 1855. 2nd husb.

George Onslow Newton of Croxton Park, co. Camb. J.P. and D.L. Born 22 Feb. 1830. = Mary, dau. of Wyndham Berkeley Portman of Hare Park, Newmarket, mar. 7 June, 1852; died 1855. 1st wife. = Cecilia Florence, dau. of Edwyn Burnaby of Baggrave Hall, co. Leicester. See Burke's 'Landed Gentry.' Mar. 24 June, 1858; died 1869. 2nd wife. = Lady Alice Laura Sophia Cochrane, 2nd dau. of 11th Earl of Dundonald, mar 27 July, 1878. 3rd wife.

Emily Charlotte, mar. 24 Mar. 1854. = Wyndham Berkeley Portman, born 1831.

Arthur Fitzhardinge Berkeley Portman.

Etheldreda Julia, mar. 7 Nov. 1855. = Astley Paston, eldest son of Sir Astley Cooper, Bart., born 23 Feb. 1824; succeeded as 3rd Bart. Formerly of the Rifle Brigade.

---

5. Amelia, mar. 6 Sept. 1830. = Thomas Chamberlayne of Cranbury Park, co. Hants, J.P. and D.L. Born 12 April, 1805; died 21 Oct. 1876. See Burke's 'Landed Gentry.'

E

6. Maria.

7. Julia, mar. 27 Oct. 1847. = Robert Alexander, eldest son of Capt. Archibald Cochrane, R.N., and grandson of the 9th Earl of Dundonald, born 18 March, 1816.

8. Rosa Anne, mar. 28 Apr. 1838. = Guildford James Hillier Mainwaring Ellerker Onslow, born 29 March, 1814, M.P. for Guildford (late of the Scots Fusilier Guards). Of Risby Park, co. York. See Earl of Onslow.

Rosina Augusta, born 6 June, 1839; d. 2 July, 1840.

9. Selina, mar. 22 Oct. 1842, at Great Staughton. = Thos. Bourke of Holywell House, co. Hants. See Burke's Peerage, Earl of Mayo. Born 24 Aug. 1820. Died 5 May, 1856, at Milan, and there buried.

F

10. Anne, died 1817, unmar.

E | F

Edmund George Bourke, Commander R.N., born 6 Dec. 1843.

Augusta, mar. 24 Aug. 1871, at Marylebone Church; died 1 July, 1872; bur. at Spa. = Edouard Speder of Spa, Belgium.

- Edward Augustus Charles Speder, born 7 June, 1872.

Frances Selina, mar. twice as given under issue of Thos. Chamberlayne by Amelia (Onslow) his wife.

Amelia Rosa, mar. 31 Oct. 1871, at St. Matthias, Oakley Sq. = Charles George Hean.

Clara, mar. 29 July, 1873, at St. George's, Hanover Square. = Alfred James Paterson, Capt. 19th Foot.

- Clara Frances, b. 14 May, 1874.
- Edmund Onslow Paterson, born 6 May, 1875.
- Rosa Mary, born 13 March, 1879.

Denzil Thos. Chamberlayne, born 9 May, 1833, Capt. in the 13th Light Dragoons; died 16 April, 1873; buried at Dartmouth, co. Devon. = Frances Selina, 2nd dau. of the late Thos. Bourke of Holywell House, Hants. Mar. 1st, Feb. 26, 1867, at St. George's, Hanover Sq.; and 2ndly. 19 July, 1877, at St. Michael, Chester Sq. = Henry Spencer, eldest son of the Rev. Canon Thos. Walpole. See Earl of Orford.

- Frances Rose Caroline, b. 9 May, 1868; died 4 Sept. 1868; bur. at Dartmouth, co. Devon.
- Elizabeth Amelia, b. 7 Nov. 1869.
- Thos. Henry Bourke Walpole, born 2 Sept. 1879.

Tankerville Chamberlayne, born 6 Aug. 1840. Of Thames Bank, Pangbourne, and Cranbury Park, co. Hants.

Amy Sophia, mar. at Otterbourne Church, co. Hants, 10th Sept. 1862. = Captain John Croft, "Prince Consort's Own" Rifle Brigade, son of Rev. George Bridges Moore, Rector of Tunstall, Kent.

Francesca Maria, mar. 23 March, 1876, at Christ Church, Down St., Piccadilly; died 3 Dec. 1877. = Honble. Cecil Ralph Howard, only brother of 5th Earl of Wicklow, late Capt. 60th Rifles.

Rosalie Amelia, mar. 9 Feb. 1865. = Sir Alexander Palmer Bruce Chichester, Bart.

Agnes Caroline, mar. 29 June, 1875. = George Charles Keppel, 2nd son of the late Sir George Frederick Johnstone, Bart., Col. Grenadier Guards.

Dame Jane Onslow, widow of Sir Henry Onslow, and wife of John Amherst, named in will of her brother, Sir Richard Stydolph, dat. 20 April, 1676. P.C.C. Hall 41.

Wisborough Green.—On a gravestone of black marble in the chancel: Gulielmus Threele de Drungewick Armiger Incujus Memoriam Domina Jane Onslow uxor Johannis Amherst Armigeri hoc posuit Monumentum. Inhumatus fuit 20 Novembris Anno Domini 1667.

Burial Register, Wisborough Green.

1667. Nov. 20. William Threele of Drungwick, Esq.

Burial Register, Warnham.

1658. Dec. 11. Henry Yates, Esq.
1716. May 10. Henry Yates, Esq.

Stone at Warnham.

Under this marble lyeth the bodys of John Richard and Charles Amherst, sons of Jeffrey Amherst, Esq., by Elizabeth his wife, who was daughter of Henry Yates, Esq., late of this Parish, by Jane his wife, who was one of the daughters of Sir Francis Stydolph of Mickleham in Surrey, John being their eldest son, dyed ye 10th of March, 1676, being near 5 years of age; Richard, being their 5th son, dyed ye 11th March, 1681, being near 3 years of age; Charles, being their 6th son, dyed 11th August, 1682, being near 7 months old.

Faculty Office, 22 April, 1730. Denzil Onslow, Esq., of Wisborough Green, co. Sussex, Bachelor, aged above 22 years, and Anne Middleton of the parish of St. James's, Westminster, co. Middlesex, spinster, aged above 21 years. To marry at St. George's, Hanover Square, or in the Chapel in Conduit Street in said co. of Middlesex.

GLANVILLE OF HALWELL

EXTRACTS FROM THE REGISTERS OF WHITCHURCH, CO DEVON *

(*Concluded from p.* 419.)

Marriages from 1568 *to* 1800

Thomas Glanvill and Dorothy Willye were married the 5th of May, 1568
John Hoodje & Samson Glanvill were married the 3rd of May, 1585
John Drake and Jane Glanvill were married the 26th of January, 1596
Thomas Glanvill and Ursula Holls were married the 24th of July, 1604
Christopher Palmer and Agnes Glanvill were married 9th day of June, 1607
Hew (Hugh) Holname was married to Grace Glanville the 8th of August, 1610.
Thomas Glanville was married to Grace Brownson the 27th of November, 1628.
John Brownson was married unto Dorothy Glanville the 27th day of November, 1628.
William Cawse was married to Anne Glanvill the 7th day of June, 1635
Nicholas Glanvill was married to Jane Bickford, widow, the 26th January, 1635.
John Glanvill was married to Marione Mattacott the 17th of May, 1652.
John Drake and Elizabeth Glanvill were married the 3rd of February, 1661
Nicholas Glanvill of this parish and Grace Clarke of the parish of Beerferris were married the 12th of October, 1672
John Glanvill of this parish and Dorothy Short of the parish of Stoke Climsland, in the countie of Cornwall, were married the 31st of Oct 1676
Nicholas Ash and Dorothy Glanvill, both of this parish, were married the eleventh day of February, 1681
Olleverr Glanvill and Sarah Hamberry were married the 3rd day of November, 1687
Willum Stepsen and Grace Glanvill (widow) were married February 26th, 1692
John Glanvill and Margaret Jope, both of this parish, were married the 2nd day of October, 1693
Thomas Glanvill of Whitchurch and Marjory Knight of the parish of Tavistock were married the 25th day of December, 1693
John Lobes of Tavistock and Abbeygalle (Abigail) Glanvill of Whitchurch were married the 13th day of April, 1699
John Foot and Grace, da of Matthew Glanvill, were married October 21st, 1703.
Francis Spry and Honor Glanvill were married April 10th, 1710
John Glanvill and Mellin Wilcocks were married May 11th, 1742
Nicholas Michell and Dorothy Glanvill were married March 26th, 1744
Hugh Hunsden Smart and Mary Glanvill were married June 19th, 1748.
Nicholas Glanvill and Susanna Gribble were married June 28th, 1752
David Walters and Elizabeth Glanvill married May 10th, 1768.
John Bone and Sarah Glanvill were married June 6th, 1769
William Ware and Mary Glanvill were married May 21st, 1782
Andrew Harris of Tavistock and Anis Glanvill were married June 25th, 1784
Robert Strong of Tavistock and Mary Glanvill were married July 11th, 1787.
John Glanvill and Joan Knight were married April 1st, 1788
Henry Knight and Jenny Glanvill were married May 3rd, 1796.
Walter Glanvill and Anne Windeatt were married March 27th, 1800

Deaths from 1599 *to* 1799

Thomas Glanvill was buried the 17th January, 1599.
Elizabeth, daughter of Thomas Glanvill, was buried the 15th of July, 1630.
Dorothy, the daughter of Thomas Glanvill, was buried the 13th of October, 1641.
Ursula, the wife of Thomas Glanvill, was buried 10th of Julie, 1644.
John, son of John Glanvill of Peterstvie, was buried 22nd of Februarie, 1649
Thomas Glanvill the elder was buryed 20th day of Januarie, 1650
Thomas Glanvill was buried the 8th day of June, 1659.
A daughter of John Glanvill dead borne, was buried 12th of October, 1661.

* Communicated by W. GLANVILL-RICHARDS, Esq

A sonn of John Glanvill dead borne, buried 20th of October, 1662.
Nicholas Glanvill was buried 14th of Januarie, 1662
Francis, son of John Glanvill of Peterstavie, was buried the 25th of May, 1663.
A son of John Glanvill was buried the 15th day of Januarie, 1663.
Joane Glanvill was buried 15th of Januarie, 1663
Joane Glanvill, widow, of the parish of Peterstavy, was buried 11th November, 1664
George Glanvill was buried 25th of Februarie, 1665
A daughter of John Glanvill buried 15th of Februarie, 1667.
Ellinor, daughter of Matthew Glanvill, was buried the 31st of October, 1668.
Grace Glanvill, widow, was buried 26th of Sept^r, 1671
Susanna, wife of Francis, was buried 22nd day of Februarie, 1675.
Nicholas Glanvill buried 18th day of Aprill, 1678
Nicholas, son of Matthew Glanvill, was buried 29th of Sept^r, 1679
Nicholas Glanvill was buried the 10th day of March, 1688
Thomasene Glanvill was buried the 16th of March, 1691
Marjory Glanvill was buried 9th day of June, 1692
John Glanvill, gentleman, was buried 11th day of December, 1693.
Elizabeth Glanvill was buried 18th day of May, 1693
Joane Glanvill, widow, was buried 3rd day of May, 1696
John Glanvill, of Headwell, was buried November 19th, 1699
John Glanvill, 7th sonne of John Glanvill, jun^r, of Headwell, was buried January 17th, 1699
Hannah, d^a of Tristram Glanvill of Milton Abbot, was buried April 30th, 1705
Sarah, wife of Olliver Glanvill, was buried 25th of June, 1712
Marjory, wife of John Glanvill, was buried November 12th, 1701
Oliver Glanvill was buried August 29th, 1715
John Glanvill, son of John Glanvill, was buried 14th of May, 1716
John Glanvill of Holwell, aged above 80, was buried the 15th of January, 1717
Margaret, widow of John Glanvill, was buried April 5th, 1722.
Olliver Glanvill was buried April 15th, 1723
Dorothy Glanvill, widow, was buried February 12th, 1723
Mary Glanvill, widow, was buried December 6th, 1730.
Richard, son of William Glanvill, was buried Sepr 20th, 1735.
Thomas, son of Wm Glanvill, was buried Septr 15th, 1741
John, son of John Glanvill, jun^r, buried February 10th, 1742
Mr. John Glanvill of Holwell was buried February 8th, 1747.
Marjory Glanvill was buried July 27th, 1748.
Mr. Richard Glanvill was buried March 28th, 1749
John, son of John Glanvill, was buried October 30th, 1750
Jenny, daughter of Mr John Glanvill, was buried Jan^ry 2nd, 1758
Mary, daughter of Mr John Glanvill, was buried January 28th, 1758.
Jenny, daughter of Mr John Glanvill, was buried November 19th, 1761
Sarah, wife of Mr John Glanvill, was buried June 3rd, 1764
John Glanvill was buried January 4th, 1790
John Glanvill was buried July 24th, 1795
John Glanvill was buried July 27th, 1799.

GIDLEY.—Wanted to find record of the marriage and burial of John Gidley, "of London, Chirurgeon" whose eldest son was born in 1669. By his will dated 21st September, 1712, proved in London 24th April, 1713, John Gidley (who therein describes himself as 'of Winckley in co Devon gentleman") gives unto his wife "the use of all my goods I left in my house in London when I last came from thence for the term of her natural life and after her decease unto my son John Gidley and daughter Rebecca Graham for ever that is to say All my Silver Plate then there All my Tapestry & other hangings in eleaven rooms and eight closetts there All my Bedding Bed and Table linnen then there, and all my pewter and brass there, and all other my implements of household and household goods then there but not elsewhere." There is no record of his burial at Winkleigh, and it is probable that after making his will he returned to his house in London, and there he died. The name of his wife is not mentioned in the will.—B. G.

Armorial Bookplate.

JAMES ELWIN MILLARD, D.D.

ARMS.—*Azure four mascles Or.*
MOTTO.—QUIS IDONEUS.

James Elwin Millard, born at Norwich, 18 May, 1823, was baptized at St. George's Tombland, Norwich. He was elected Demy of Magdalen College, Oxford, July, 1842, and Fellow of the same College in July, 1853. Head Master of Magdalen College School from 1846 to 1864, and became Vicar of Basingstoke, Hants, in the latter year. He was appointed Rural Dean of Basingstoke (S.W. Division), by Bishop Wilberforce, in 1873. He married, at Upton Grey, Hants, on 5 April, 1866, Dora Frances, da. of William Lutley Sclater, of Hoddington House, Hampshire, sister of the Right Hon[ble] George Sclater-Booth, M.P. for North Hants, and has issue :—

1. Magdalen, born March 5, 1867.
2. George Michael, born July 16, 1868.
3. Theodora Elwin, ob. infans.
4. Philippa Sibyl, born May 30, 1871.
5. Christopher Sclater, born Nov. 7, 1872.
6. James Laurence, born July 1, 1875 ; died Sept. 24, 1876.
7. Dorothy Virtue, born Nov. 23, 1878.
8. Paul Elwin, born, Sept. 8, 1876.

The Rev[d] Charles Millard, M.A., formerly of Magdalen College, Oxford, Chancellor of the Diocese of Norwich, and Domestic Chaplain to Bishop Horne, whom he attended in his last hours, was born in 1748, and died in 1814. He married . . . . Elizabeth, da. of the Reverend Samuel Salter, D.D. (Master of the Charterhouse), and had issue :—

1. Charles Freeman Salter Millard, B A., Minor Canon of Norwich, Vicar of Hickling, and of St Giles and St Martin's, Norwich, died in 1849, and was buried in the Cathedral Cloisters. He married Mary Ann, da. of Sir Edward Berry, K C B, R N, and had issue —1. Edward, who died Oct. 1844. 2 Charles, married Jane, da of T Amyot, Esq, F.R S 3 Frances, died unmarried
2. Anna Maria, eldest da, married in 1787, the Rev. George Wilson, brother of Lord Berners, and had issue .—1 George Knyvett, Admiral R N 2 Edward, Rector of Topcroft, Norfolk 3 William, R N., died unm. 4. Charles H E I C S. 5. Archdale (Major-Gen Sir Archdale Wilson, of Delhi, Bart., K C B) 6 Philip. 7 George, Lieut-Col H E I.C.S 8 Roland, Chaplain, R.N 9 Charlotte, marr Henry Amsinck. 10 James. 11 Frederick 12 Arthur. 13. John Coombe. 14 Herbert, Rector of Fritton, Norfolk.
3 Jane, married to Rev. W. Bushell, Rector of Tibberton, Gloucestershire.
4. Eliza (d unmarrd)
5 Wm Salter
6. Philip, ob s p
7 Philip, married Virtue, dau of Robert Elwin, and had issue —1 Elizabeth Salter Virtue. 2 Maria Jane 3 Lucy Elwin 4 Philippa. 5 Mary Whittingham 6. Arthur Wilson. 7 Augusta Schutz.
8. James, d infant, 1789

William Salter Millard, born June 26, 1783 He served in the R N as Midshipman on board the "Monarch," and was wounded at the Battle of Copenhagen, in 1801 He died July 2, 1862, and was buried at Catton, Norfolk. He married Philippa Frances, da of Robert Elwin, of Booton, co Norfolk, by whom he had issue —

1. Charles William, born Dec 4, 1813, marr 1842, Catherine, da of G. Barker.
2. Frances Maria, born April 1, 1815, died Sept 15, 1876
3 Philip Salter, born Feb 10, 1817, died 1868 Married Eliza, da. of. Lionel Gowing, and had issue —Lionel Gowing and Alice, who died inf
4. Caroline, born May 13, 1819; died April 22, 1875.
5 Henry James, born Oct 4, 1821, died 1822.
6 James Elwin, D.D, born May 18, 1823

He married, secondly, in 1828, Isabel, da. of Samuel Shaw, of Aylsham, co. Norfolk, by whom he had issue —

1 Charlotte Mary, born Aug 11, 1829
2. Rev Jeffery Watson, M.A., Rector of Shimpling, Norfolk, born Sept 23, 1830, married, 29 Oct 1868, Sara Elizabeth, 2nd da. of Charles Shaw, Commander R N, and has issue —1 Isabel Maud, born 16 Dec. 1869. 2 Beatrice Annie, born 3 March, 1871 3 Mary Shaw, born 9 March, 1872; died 11 Sept 1880 4 Charles William Salter, born 15 June, 1874 5 Margaret Alice, born 3 Aug 1875 6 Frederick Thornton Sutton, born 6 Dec 1877
3 Rev Henry Shaw, M.A, born Dec 14, 1831 Head Master of St John's Collegiate School, Newcastle, N.S Wales Marr April 13, 1858, Eliza, da. of Peter Hazeon, has issue —1 Isabel, b Sept 14 1859. 2 Fanny, b Dec 22, 1860. 3 Godfrey William, b Sept 27, 1862 4. Alfred Charles, b Feb 10, 1865 5 Reginald Jeffery, b May 1868 6 Valentine Henry, b Feb 14, 1870 7 Bertram George, b Aug. 1871. Flora, b Sep 27, 1872 9. May Rachel, b May 1875.
4 Barbara Isabel, born May 15, 1833
5 Rev Charles Sutton, B A, Rector of Costock, Notts, born July 30, 1834, m July 23, Mary Harriet, da of Henry Killick, of Walton Hall, Stafford, had issue.—1 Fred Sutton, b. Jan, 31, 1865, d. Nov. 17, 1877.

Brass: South Transept Christ Church Cathedral.

DUBLIN.

FROM A DRAWING BY J. F. FULLER ESQ. F.S.A.

2. Marg[t] Anne, b. Aug. 6, 1866. 3. Mary, b. Nov. 12, 1867. 4. Arthur Henry, b. March 1869. 5. Charles Killick, b. Aug. 1870. 6. Edwin, b. 1873. 7. Laura, b. April 1875. 8. Philip Ernest, b. Jan. 1876. 9. Alfred, b. Dec. 1878.

6. Rev. Frederick Maule, M.A., Rector of Otham, Kent, and late Fellow of Magd. Coll., Oxford, born Nov. 7, 1835; married April 13, 1871, Mary, da. of Ed. Hoar, Maidstone.
7. George, born Oct. 17, 1837; married 1874, Anna Maria, 2nd da. of George Wilson, Lt.-Col. H.E.I.C.S. Issue:—1. Jessie Isabel Ellen, b. July 7, 1874. 2. Cicely Rosamond, b. Jan. 31, 1876. 3. Elsie Muriel, b. Oct. 17, 1877. 4. George Knyvett Wilson, b. Sept. 1879.
8. Agnes Jane, born Aug. 7, 1839.
9. Augusta Sarah Bushell, born May 23, 1841; died June 20, 1865.
10. Jane Bushell, born Sept. 27, 1842; died Jan. 4, 1844.

GRANT OF ARMS TO JOSEPH MAWBEY OF KENNINGTON, 1757.

To all and singular to whom these Presents shall come Stephen Martin Leake Esquire Garter Principal King of Arms and Charles Townley Esquire Clarenceux King of Arms of the South East and West Parts of England from the River Trent Southwards send greeting—Whereas these ancient Badges or Ensigns of Gentility commonly called or known by the name of Arms have heretofore been and still are continued to be conferred upon deserving Persons to distinguish them from the common sort of People who neither can or may pretend to use them without lawful authority and Whereas Joseph Mawbey of Kennington in the Parish of Lambeth in the County of Surrey Esq[r] High Sheriff of the said County for the present year hath represented unto the Right Honourable Thomas Earl of Effingham Deputy with the Royal approbation, to the most noble Edward Duke of Norfolk Earl Marshal and Hereditary Marshal of England that he is desirous of having the Arms himself and his Family have usually Born (concerning which he has some doubt) confirmed viz. Or a cross Gules fretty of the field between 4 Eagles displayed Azure and a like Eagle for the Crest, hath therefore prayed his Lordship's Warrant for our assigning granting and confirming the above arms properly varied to be for ever hereafter borne by him and his descendants and the descendants of his late Father John Mawby of Ravenston in the County of Leicester Gentleman, and Forasmuch as his Lordship duly considering the Premises did by Warrant under his hand and seal bearing date the 3[d] day of Sept[r] Instant order and direct us to Grant and assign to the said Joseph Mawbey and his descendants and to the descendants of his said Father such arms and crest accordingly Know y[e] therefore that We the said Garter and Clarenceux in Pursuance of the consent of the said Earl of Effingham and by virtue of the Letters Patent of our sev'ral offices to each of us respectively Granted under the Great Seal of Great Britain have assigned and do by these presents give grant ratifie and confirm to the said Joseph Mawby the Arms following viz.—Or a cross Gules Fretty of the Field between 4 Eagles displayed Azure each charged on the Breast with a Bezant and for the Crest on a Wreath of the colours an Eagle displayed Azure charged on the Breast with a Bezant together with this motto—Auriga Virtutem Prudentia as the same are in the margin hereof more plainly depicted to be borne and used for ever hereafter by him the said Joseph Mawbey and his descendants and by the descendants of his late Father John Mawbey aforesaid with their due and proper differences according to the ancient Practise and Custom of Arms without the let or interruption of any Person or Persons whatsoever. In witness whereof We the said Garter and Clarenceux Kings of Arms have to these Presents subscribed our names and affixed the seals of our several offices the 15 day of Sept[r] in the 31 year of y[e] Reign of our Sovereign Lord George y[e] 2[d] by y[e] Grace of God King of Great Britain France & Ireland Defender of the Faith and in y[e] year of our Lord 1757.

M. LEAKE, Garter. CHARLES TOWNLEY, Clarenceux.

CAGE OF SUFFOLK.*

Edward Cage baptizat. fuit xxiiij° die Septembris Anno D'ni 1618.
Will'm Cage baptizat. fuit viij° die Augusti 1621.
Anna Cage baptizat. fuit ij° die July 1622.
Bridgitt Cage baptizat. xxx° die Aprill 1626.

Edward Cage fuit apprentic' cu' Thomee Cosen de Colchester Tallow Chandler secondo die Maij Anno R[s] Caroli nunc Angl &c decimo Annoque D'ni 1634. I doe suppose that Edward Cage when his tyme cometh yt will come vnto xxviij[li] x[s] and that is vse vpon vse.

At the Roules Mr Justice Vernone Sr Robt Ritch Sr John Michell	Martis xxij[to] die Novembris Anno R[s] Caroli nono inter Will'm Cage & Thomam Bull Gardian' Edwardi Cage Will'mi Cage et Anne Cage Querent' et Johem Montford Sacræ Theolog doctor defet.

By Mr Lanie beinge of the p'ts councell in the presence of Mr. Bullock being of the def't his councell that Forasmuch as this court was this daie informed that Margaret Cage deceased naturall sister of the said Will'm Cage did by her last will & testam[t] in writinge give and bequeath vnto the said Edward William and Ann Cage the children of the said William Cage Twentie pounds a peace to be paid into the hands of her brother Anthonie Cage late Doctor of Divinitie deceased to be imployed usered & bestowed for their benefitt & preferm[t] accordinge to his discretion: and did name and appoint Martha Cage her sister to be her onelie executrix and died: that the said Martha Cage p'ved the will, and did paie & deliver into the hands of the said Anthonie Cage threescoare pounds in monie to the use of the said children who received the same and did imploye it to and for the benefitt of the said children accordinge to the trust reposed in him; and raised the said some of Threescoare pounds to Fower scoare & Fower pounds: that the said Anthonie Cage made his last will & testam[t] and did thereby nominate the def't his sole executor and died possessed of a good p'sonall estate, who p'ved the said will and tooke upon him the execution of the same. But forasmuch as the said def't was unwillinge to be charged with the said severall porcions. or to ymploye the same for the benefitt & use of the said children as his said Testator had formerlie done Thereupon the said Will'm Cage the Father and the said Thomas Bull the uncle to them on the mothers side did exhibit their bill into this court that the said def't might paie the said Fourscoare & fower pounds to them or one of them vpon sufficient securitie to paie the same to the said Children & to ymploye the same Fowerscoare & Fower pounds for the benefitt & encrease of their said porc'ons as this Court should think fitt, unto which Bill the said deft hath annswered & confesseth the effect & substance of the pl'ts informac'on and saith that he is willinge to paye in the said Fowerscoare & Fower pounds into this honorable court or to such p'sone & p'sons as will give good and sufficient securitie to this honorable court, and that maie discharge the said deft and the said Martha their executors & administrators against the said children, and that the said some of monie maye be ymployed for the encrease thereof to their best benefitt and be paied to the said children accordinge to the true intent & meaninge of the last will & testam[t] of the said Margaret. It is therefore this present daie ordered that the said def't shall forthw[th] satisfie & paie unto y[e] said Thomas Bull one of the said Compl[ts] who is esteemed an able & sufficient man to answere the same to the said children the said some of Fowerscoare & Fower pounds & upon paiem't of the same yt is ordered that the said def't and the said Martha Cage shall from thenceforth be absolutelie acquitted and discharged of the said several porc'ons and the encrease of them against the said children & the said compl[t] Thom. Bull vpon the receipt of the said Fowerscoare & Fower pounds from the said def't shall presentlie enter into a Recognizance of two hundred pounds, to this Court for the paiement of the said and Fowerscoare Fower pounds to the said children parte & parte like, and for the vse

* Communicated by GEO. A. CARTHEW, F.S.A.

BRASS IN SOUTH TRANSEPT OF CHRIST CHURCH CATHEDRAL, DUBLIN.

The accompanying facsimile of a Brass Plate in Dublin Cathedral has been presented by Sir Philip Grey Egerton, Bart, M.P A Paper on this Brass was communicated by Sir Philip to the Journal of the Archæological Institute, and will be found at page 213, No 143, vol XXXVI.

THE PENN FAMILY OF HARBOROUGH, CO WORCESTER.*

(*Concluded from page* 444)

EXTRACTS FROM THE REGISTERS OF CLENT, CO WORCESTER.

1568	Oct 31	Roger Dugar and Benet Penn, married
1572.	Oct 26	Simon Skinner and Elizabeth Pen, married.
1574	Nov 1	Johane, wife of Richard Pen, buried
„	Feb 22	Mathew, daughter of Humfrey Pen, gent, and Alice his wife, bapt
1581.	May 22	George, son of Richard Harris of St Kellam's, and Jane, daughter of Humfrey Pen, gent, married
„	Nov 18	John Penn and Joyce Can, married
1582	March 12	Elizabeth, daughter of John and Joyce Pen, bapt.
1587	Oct 2	Margerye, wife of John Penn, buried
1593	May 12	John Pen, father of Richard Pen and Benet Pen, buried
1594	Sept 10	William Pearson, gent, and Mathew, daughter of Humfrey Pen, gent, married
1596.	Dec 9	Roger, son of Henry Pen, bapt
1597	May 23	William Pagett and Benet Pen, married
1598	May 6	Humfrey, son of Henry Pen, gent, bapt
1605	Oct 6	John Cocks and Elizabeth Pen, married
1611	Jan .	Richard Pen was baptised
1612	Dec 10	Joice Penn, widow, buried
1615	March 5	Ales, wife of Humfrey Pen, gent, buried
1616	April 20	Humfrey Pen, gent, buried.

Register illegible from 1626 *to* 1636

1655.	March 5.	Hester, daughter of Thomas and Joane Pen, was borne
1658	Sept 29	William, son of Thomas and Joane Pen, was borne.
1661	March 25.	Joane, daughter of Thomas and Joane Pen, bapt
1668	May 28	Jonas, bastard of Ann Penn, bapt
1703	.	William Penn of the parish of Kingswinford, and Sara Pearman of this parish, were married Feb 28 at St Kenelm's Chapel
1704	May 25	Sara, wife of William Penn of Swinford Regis, buried.
1726.	May 31	Anne, daughter of Samuel and Eleanor Penn, bapt
„	June 4	Anne, daughter of Samuel Penn, buried
1728	March 19	William, son of Samuel and Eleanor Penn, bapt
1731	Jan 25	Mary, daughter of Samuel and Eleanor Penn, bapt
1735	April 8	James Thomas and Mary Penn, married

* Communicated by H. SYDNEY GRAZEBROOK, Esq

1740	Feb 7.	John Osborn and Hannah Penn, married
1750	Aug 5	Elianor, wife of Samuel Penn, buried
1751	May 3	Samuel Penn, buried with affidavit
1753	Nov 13	William Penn of this parish, and Mary Jones of Frankley, married

(*Searched to* 1780)*

EXTRACTS FROM THE REGISTERS OF OLDSWINFORD, CO. WORCESTER

(*Commence* 1602.)

1606	Sept. 21.	Henry Hart and Elizabeth Penn, married
1611	Oct 6	William Penne and Mathew Willetts, married.
1612	June 13	Thomas, son of William Pen, bapt.
1669	May 13.	John Penn, buried
1673	April 1	Morrice Penn and Mary Parkes, married
1676	July 13	Mary, dau of Morris Penn, buried
1677-8	Jan 8	Edward Raby and Ann Penn, married
1679	April 22.	Elizabeth, dau of Morice Penn, bapt.
1680	Oct. 30	John, son of John Penn, bapt
,,	June 10	Elizabeth, dau of Morris Penn, buried
1681.	Oct 8	Samuel Barnet and Sarah Penn, married
,,	June 5	Ann, dau of Morris Penn, bapt
1684	June 23	John, son of Morriss Penn, buried
1685.	April 20.	Mary, dau of John Penn, bapt
1685-6	March 11	Mary, dau of John Penn, buried.
1687-8.	March 10.	John, son of Morris Penn, bapt
1688	Oct 14	Caleb Coley and Margrett Pen, married
1689	Oct 5	William, son of John Pen, bapt
1691	Aug 10.	Joseph and Mary, children of Moris Pen, bapt
,,	July 28	John, son of Morris Penn, buried
,,	Sept 23.	Joseph, son of Morris Penn, buried
1692	April 3	Edward, son of John Penn, bapt
,,	Sept. 27.	Elizabeth, dau of John Penn, buried
,,	Nov 23	Sarah, dau of John Penn, buried
1694	Sept. 16.	Infant, of John Penn, buried
1696.	. .	John, son of John Penn, born Aug 12, bapt Aug 22.
1697		Joseph, son of John Penn, born July 15, bapt July 18.
1699.	April 12	John Pen, buried
1702	May 4	Morris Penn, buried

Examined to 1702 ; *the name of Penn occurs frequently after that date, but its bearers do not appear to be nearly, if at all, related to the Harborough family.*

WIGHTWICK —Can any of your readers give me any information concerning the ancestry of Humphrey Wightwick of Kingsnorth and Tenterden, gent, who, with his son Edward, purchased the Manor of Mumfords in Kingsnorth, co Kent, temp Ch I., from John Taylor of Winchelsea, gent ? Hasted says that the family came originally from Staffordshire

---

* For these Register extracts (Hagley, Churchill, and Clent), I am indebted to John Amphlett of Clent, Esq —H. S. G

ALPORT *

(Vol. III, pp 288, 325)

14 January, 1578-9. Settlement on the marriage of Barnaby Ensor of Wilnecote, and Agnes, dau and coheiress of John Alport of Hatherton Trustees Raphaell Yardeley, gent, William Fynney of Cannok, William Ensore of Wilnecote, and Rauff Alport of Cannok

Barnaby Ensor's Will was proved at Lichfield, 23 February, 1598-9. Executors William Colmore of Birmingham, and John Alport of Longdon waye

William Colmore, by his wife Anne, dau of William Finney of Cannock, had a dau Dorothy, who was bapt. at St. Martin's, Birmingham, 29 May, 1575, and married William Alport of Cannock See Pedigree of Colmore in Vis Warwick, 1619, and monument to Wm. Colmore and Anne his wife in St. Martin's, Birmingham

For the whole of the above I am indebted to H Sydney Grazebrook, Esq.

Isabel Alport was a witness to the Will of Thomas Fletcher of Cannock, dated 14 July, 1710, and proved at Lichfield. (D and C)

Depositions by Commission —Exchequer

35 & 36 Eliz. Mich. 19	William Alport and others, plts, re Bentley Hay, Cannock, etc.
36 & 37 Eliz Mich 28	William Alport, jun, and others, plts, re Bentley Hay and Cannock
9 Car I. East 2, & Mich 10	Rowland Frith and Peter Alport, defts, re Moss House Manor.
9 & 10 Car I Hil 31	ditto ditto
10 Car I East 47	ditto ditto

License to John Alporte to pass from England to Flanders, 1654

(Rawlinson MS, A 328, fo 93)

Oliver P.

John Alport. These are to will, and require you to permit and suffer the Bearer hereof, John Alporte, with his necessaries, to passe from England to Flanders, and to returne without any your Lets, hindrances, or molestatc'ons, Given at Whitehall this 4th day of July 1654

To the Governo^rs &c

Extracts from the Registers of Shareshill, co. Stafford.

(Commence 1565.)

1594. August 8th bur Margery Alport.
1623 Feby 18th bur John Alport.
1749. Jany 30th mar. John Alport and Mary Mount.
1750. Feby 24 bap Mary d of John Allport of Great Sardin
1787. June 3rd bap. John son of John Alport.
1789 Augt 16 bap Thomas son of John Allport, Hilton.

Rev William Alport of Stewkley, co. Bucks.

Lipscomb's Bucks, iii, 474, tells us, under "*Stewkley,*" that "*William Alport* was presented by Crew, Bishop of Oxford, being of Lincoln College, instituted 13 March, 1673 He died in 1722, having been Vicar above fifty years, and was buried among his relations in Staffordshire"

---

* Communicated by the Rev. W G. DIMOCK FLETCHER, B.A, Oxford.

GOSTLETT OF MARSHFIELD, ALLIED TO HARINGTON OF KELSTON.

EVIDENCES IN SUPPORT OF THE GOSTLETT PEDIGREE

(*Continued from p.* 438)

SUMMARY OF THE WILL OF MARY GOSTLETT OF MARSHFIELD, CO GLO, WIDOW OF JOHN GOSTLETT, FEB. 14, 1695-6.

(Lort, 232.)

The children of my niece Elizabeth, wife of Henry Gibbs of Bristol, merchant, £10 each.

My cousin Ann Harington, widow of Edward Harington,* late of North Petherton, Devon (? Petherwyn, near Launceston), my niece Rebecca Harington, £20; my cousin Jane Watts; Martha Lilburne, my late husband's half-sister's daughter, £10, my cousin Phœbe Harington, daughter of my brother William To the poor of Kelston, £10; of Marshfield, £20 Mourning to my brothers John and William Harington, their wives and children To John Harington, son of Benjamin Harington, my niece Virtue Higginson £300 when her husband Mr. Joshua Higginson shall settle lands, etc, for her jointure, my cousins Henry and William Harington, Virtue Higginson, Amy Harington, and Alice Chetwynd, widow, £20 each.

£300 to be spent on my fur al

My nephews Benjamin Harington, son of my brother John Harington, and Anthony, son of my sister Rous, to be executors

Proved by them Nov 18, 1698

HELENA HARINGTON [*née* GOSTLETT] OF KELSTON, SOMERSET, WIDOW

(Browning, 236)

March 25, 1718 To my son John Harington, my silver standish and 20s; my daughter Dorothy, his wife, my son Henry Harington and Mary his wife, my son William nd Sarah his wife, my son Robert and Susanna his wife; to Rev Mr Hudlest e 20s for a ring, to my daughter Hudlestone 20s, and my son John Harington's picture set in gold, to my son Edward Harington an annuity of £12 from the Exchequer for the life of my son Henry, to my daughter Isabella 20s and her father's picture set in gold, to my grandchildren, Lawson and John Hudlestone, a broad piece of gold, to be buried near my husband in the chancel, etc Residue to my son Edward Harington, and my daughter Isabella, executors.

Proved by them Dec 24, 1719

REGISTERS OF GOSTLETT AT KELSTON

Marriages

1678 Aug 6 John Harington Esq, and Miss Helena Gostlett

1684. April 1. Mr. Geo. Adams of Weston, and Miss Mary Gostlett of Kelston were married

Burial

1702-3 March 2 Mrs Elizabeth Gostlett, widow of Benjamin Gostlett, gent, was buried.

REGISTERS OF ADAMS AT KELSTON

Baptisms

1685. April 9. Benjamin, son of Mr. Geo Adams and Mary his wife

1687 Sept 21 Elizabeth, dau of Mr. Geo. Adams.

* Cf Harington of Worden Ped. North Petherton is in Somerset, not Devon.

GOSTLETT OF MARSHFIELD, ALLIED TO HARINGTON OF KELSTON.

EVIDENCES IN SUPPORT OF THE GOSTLETT PEDIGREE

(*Continued from p.* 438.)

SUMMARY OF THE WILL OF MARY GOSTLETT OF MARSHFIELD, CO. GLO, WIDOW OF JOHN GOSTLETT, FEB 14, 1695-6.

(Lort, 232)

The children of my niece Elizabeth, wife of Henry Gibbs of Bristol, merchant, £10 each.

My cousin Ann Harington, widow of Edward Harington,* late of North Pether*ton*, Devon (? Petherwyn, near Launceston); my niece Rebecca Harington, £20; my cousin Jane Watts, Martha Lilburne, my late husband's half-sister's daughter, £10, my cousin Phœbe Harington, daughter of my brother William To the poor of Kelston, £10, of Marshfield, £20 Mourning to my brothers John and William Harington, their wives and children To John Harington, son of Benjamin Harington, my niece Virtue Higginson £300 when her husband Mr Joshua Higginson shall settle lands, etc, for her jointure, my cousins Henry and William Harington, Virtue Higginson, Amy Harington, and Alice Chetwynd, widow, £20 each.

£300 to be spent on my fur[illegible]l

My nephews Benjamin Harington, son of my brother John Harington, and Anthony, son of my sister Rous, to be executors

Proved by them Nov 18, 1698

HELENA HARINGTON [*née* GOSTLETT] OF KELSTON, SOMERSET, WIDOW.

(Browning, 236.)

March 25, 1718 To my son John Harington, my silver standish and 20s; my daughter Dorothy, his wife, my son Henry Harington and Mary his wife, my son William [a]nd Sarah his wife, my son Robert and Susanna his wife; to Rev Mr Hudlest[o]ne 20s for a ring, to my daughter Hudlestone 20s, and my son John Harington's picture set in gold, to my son Edward Harington an annuity of £12 from the Exchequer for the life of my son Henry, to my daughter Isabella 20s and her father's picture set in gold, to my grandchildren, Lawson and John Hudlestone, a broad piece of gold, to be buried near my husband in the chancel, etc Residue to my son Edward Harington, and my daughter Isabella, executors

Proved by them Dec 24, 1719

REGISTERS OF GOSTLETT AT KELSTON

Marriages

1678. Aug 6 John Harington [E]sq, and Miss Helena Gostlett
1684. April 1. Mr. Geo. Adams of Weston, and Miss Mary Gostlett of Kelston were married

Burial

1702-3 March 2 Mrs Elizabeth Gostlett, widow of Benjamin Gostlett, gent, was buried.

REGISTERS OF ADAMS AT KELSTON.

Baptisms

1685. April 9. Benjamin, son of Mr. Geo Adams and Mary his wife
1687. Sept 21 Elizabeth, dau of Mr Geo. Adams.

* Cf Harington of Worden Ped. North Petherton is in Somerset, not Devon.

Pedigree of the Longs of Semington,

ROOD ASHTON AND PRESHAW BRANCHES.

(CURANTE GULIELMO LONG, A.M., A.D. 1878.)

1688. Oct. 16 John, son of Mr. George Adams and Mary his wife.
169½ Jan. 21 Mary, dau of Mr Geo. Adams and Mary his wife
1694 Dec 31 Keturah, dau. of Mr. Geo Adams and Mrs Mary his wife
1697 Sept 24 Helena, dau of Mr Geo Adams and Mary his wife
1700 May 13 George, son of Mr Geo Adams and Mary his wife
1702 Feb 23. Elizabeth, dau of George Adams and Mary his wife bapt

Marriage

1684 April 1 Mr. George Adams of Weston and Mrs. Mary Gostlett of Kelston were married.

Burials.

1687 Sept. 21 Elizabeth Adams was buried
1704 Sept 17. Mary Adams was buried
1708 Sept 17. John Adams
1730 June 27. Mr Geo Adams.
1733. March 15. Mr Benjamin Adams
1766 March 21 Mrs Keturah Adams of Keynsham
1766. July 2. Mrs Betty Adams of Keynsham

REGISTERS OF BROAD OF KELSTON

A FAMILY CONNECTED BY MARRIAGE WITH THE GOSTLETTS AND HUDLESTONS, AND PROBABLY WITH THE HARINGTONS ALSO

Marriages

1617 Nov. 20 Giles Broad and Agnes Brittaine.
1634 Nov. 6 John Broad and Margaret Billbee

Baptisms

1618 Oct 3. John, the sonne of Giles Broad.
1691. June 24 Betty, dau. of Mr John Broad and Elizabeth his wife *
1700 Nov. 9 John, son of John Broad and Elizabeth his wife

Burials

1703 (No month) Elizabeth Broad was buried
1712. Jan 2 John Broad
1726 Feb 26 John Broad

REGISTERS OF CROOM OF KELSTON

A FAMILY CONNECTED BY MARRIAGE WITH BROAD, BRITTAINE & HUDLESTON ABOUT THE SAME TIME THE HARINGTONS WERE CONNECTED WITH THESE FAMILIES

Christenings

1713 Sept 14. James, the son of Hiern Croom
1715 Jan. 3. Hiern, the son of Hiern Croom
1716. Dec 11 Elizabeth, ye daughter of Hiern Croom
1721 Nov. 19 Ann . .
1727. Aug 9 Dionesse . . . .
1740 Nov 29 William, son of Hiern Croom, Junr.
1744 June 4 Elizabeth or Betty, the daughter of Hiern and Mary Croom
1751. April 21 Eleanor, daughter of Mr John & Elizabeth Croom

(*To be continued.*)

* This was Elizabeth, the dau of Benjamin Gostlett, Esq, of Marshfield, by Elizabeth his wife

PENKETT DESCENT.

David Williams of Bunbury.

Philip Williams of Chester, born 1643. = Bridget Pownall.

Thomas Penkett of Great Neston, co. Chester.

1st wife. Mary Williams, born 1680; mar. 1699; died 1711. = Richard Penkett, born 1675. = 2nd wife. Elizabeth Corbett, dau. of William Corbett of Dovaston, co. Salop, mar. 1712.

1. Ann Shaw, dau. of Thomas Shaw of Ditton Hall, co. Lancaster. = William Penkett, born 1719.

2. John Penkett, ob. 1758, unmarried.

Hannah Maddock, 5th dau. of the Rev. Thos. Maddock, Rector of Liverpool, by his wife Rachel, dau. and coheiress of Peter Rainford, Esq., born 27 Nov. 1750; died 29 Feb. 1828; bur. in the family vault under St. George's Church, Liverpool. = John Penkett, only son, born 26 June, 1752; mar. 18 May, 1790; died 8 April, 1838. Lord of the Manor of Liscard, co. Chester. Bur. under St. George's Church, Liverpool.

1. Elizabeth. — Alice. 2. 3. Ann. — Mary. All died unmar.

1. William Penkett, only son, born 12 July, 1792; died unmar. 4 Sept. 1841.

2. Elizabeth Penkett, born 1 June, 1791; died unm. Dec. 1820.

John Dennil Maddock, younger son of Edward Maddock, Esq., 6th son of the Rev. Thos. Maddock, Rector of Liverpool; born 7 May, 1790; died 28 July, 1854; J. P. and D. L. for co. Chester, and j. u. Lord of the Manor of Liscard. Bur. under St. George's Church, Liverpool. = 3. Mary Ann Penkett, 2nd dau. and eventually sole heiress, born 28 May, 1797; mar. 12 Oct. 1820; living in 1880. Lady of the Manor of Liscard, co. Chester.

The above short Pedigree is copied from a MS. in the handwriting of the late Robert Maddock of Chester, a son of the Rev. Thos. Maddock, M.A., Prebendary of Chester, and Rector of Northenden, and grandson of the Rev. Thos. Maddock, Rector of Liverpool, above-mentioned, and a zealous antiquary and genealogist, the later dates being filled in on the information of Mrs. J. D. Maddock of Liscard Manor.

The compiler of the above also writes:—"Dovaston is in the parish of Kinnerley, seven and a half miles S.E. of Oswestry. Peter Corbet, Baron 1295, died seized of the manor of Dinoreweston, a member of the Barony of Caus, 28th Edward I., A.D. 1300. Robert Corbet, Lord of Caus, etc., ob. 1221; his son and heir Thos. Corbet, ob. 1273; his son and heir Peter Corbet, ob. 1300; his son and heir Peter Corbet, ob. 1322, and his brother John ob. s.p."

Several pieces of plate bearing the Corbet Crest—the elephant and castle—were recently in possession of the descendants of Richard Penkett.

This family is supposed to be descended from the Penkeths, Lords of Penketh, co. Lancaster, and bears the same Arms:—"Argent, 3 Kingfishers ppr." "The Lord of Penketh, says the ancient Duchy Feodary, holds of Sir Wm Boteler, the 5th part of a Knight's fee in Penketh, which Roger Penketh formerly held." This Lord was probably Jordan de Penket, who, in 1363, gave to his son Robert all his lands in Penket. Among the witnesses is Richard de Ashton.

Lucas says: "The Lordship of that name in the parish of Prescot was held by them till Margaret, dau. and heir of Richard Penketh of Penketh, mar. Richard Ashton, and became seized thereof."

In King's 'Vale Royal' (Ormerod, vol. i., 38), we find in the list of "Cheshire Knights and gentlemen who compounded with parliament for their Estates" the name of "Thomas Penkett of Sutton £66 : 5 : 0." Is not this the Thomas Penkett of Great Neston at the head of the above Pedigree, or his father?

Any information regarding the families above mentioned will be very acceptable to me.

30 *Albemarle Street, W.* JOHN HAMERTON CRUMP.

END OF VOLUME III.

Attention Scanner:
Foldout in Book!

CPSIA information can be obtained
at www.ICGtesting.com
Printed in the USA
BVHW012155291021
620345BV00002B/5

9 781371 236748